The Denver Snuffer Podcast

Answering Questions About What God is Doing Today

VOLUME 3
EPISODES 100-150

Denver C. Snuffer, Jr.

Hard Cover ISBN 978-1-951168-81-0
Soft Cover ISBN 978-1-951168-80-3

Cover art by David Christenson

Published in the United States by
Restoration Archive LLC

The Restoration Archive website address:
www.restorationarchives.com

Table of Contents

Introduction

Welcome to the Denver Snuffer Podcast! When Denver began teaching about what God is doing today in continuing the Restoration of the Gospel that commenced in the days of Joseph Smith, it became obvious that sincere learners had many questions—and the same questions were often asked over and over. This podcast began early in 2018 as a simple way to provide answers to those common questions.

This volume includes transcripts of episodes 100-150. Episode 100 was released at the very end of 2019 as the first part of a series that continued into 2020. As such, it is included in this volume, together with all other episodes released during 2020 and 2021.

Each episode consists of one or more of the following kinds of recordings:

- Remarks made by Denver during various lectures, meetings, or Q&A sessions that had previously been recorded and released;
- Remarks by Denver that had previously been recorded but not released;
- Previously-published written material that Denver subsequently recorded for the podcast; and
- Recordings of new material for the podcast.

(Please see "Appendix 1: Episodes Containing New Material" for a list of those episodes that include previously unreleased, unrecorded, or new material.)

Readers with a keen eye will also note that, in some cases, Denver used an audio transcript as the basis for preparing an "expanded transcript" or paper, with clarifying comments or additional material added in that was not part of the original audio recording. This was particularly the case in lectures 5-10 of the "40 Years in Mormonism" lecture series where the original audio transcripts were greatly expanded into papers and, ultimately, into a book titled *Preserving the Restoration*, published by Mill Creek Press in 2015. In some cases, a podcast transcript may include these written additions even though they were not present in the audio version of the podcast. They provide additional depth and detail to the subject matter and may be of value to the reader.

Although these podcast episodes contain much information about the topics addressed, the reader should not assume they include everything there is to know or learn about these topics. The podcasts should rightly be considered as starting points or brief introductions that can *excite...inquiry and diligent search* and *[arouse your] minds to inquire after the knowledge of God* (Lectures on Faith 2:56). Readers are always encouraged to study the Scriptures with great care and use them as they were intended to be used: as a Urim and Thummim capable of revealing knowledge about the character and glory of God and to help one *obtain faith in God and power...to behold him face to face* (Lectures on Faith 2:55):

> The extent of any man's knowledge concerning the character and glory of God depends upon the diligence and the faithfulness of the individual until, *like Enoch, the brother of Jared, and Moses, they shall obtain faith in God, and power with him to behold him face to face. We have now clearly set forth how it is, and how it was, that God became an object of faith for rational beings; and also, upon what foundation the testimony was based which excited the inquiry and diligent search of the ancient saints to seek after and obtain a knowledge of the glory of God; and we have seen that it was human testimony, and human testimony only, that excited this inquiry, in the first instance, in their minds. It was the credence they gave to the testimony of their fathers, this testimony having aroused their minds to inquire after the knowledge of God; the inquiry frequently terminated, indeed always terminated when rightly pursued, in the most glorious discoveries and eternal certainty* (Lectures on Faith 2:55-56).
>
> And what is "the most glorious discovery"? It is the person of God. And what is the "eternal certainty" that you want? It is your own salvation. Because no man can give that to you—but God can. (Denver Snuffer Podcast, Episode 17: Prayer, Part 1)

We remain grateful for the opportunity to assist in some small way in the furtherance of God's great work. We hope that our efforts in this endeavor will be acceptable to our Lord, to whom all glory, praise, and honor rightly belong.

The Denver Snuffer Podcast Team
December, 2021

100. Love, Part 1

This is the first part of a special series on Love, where Denver teaches us how we can live according to the two great commandments: Love God, and Love One Another.

DENVER: King Benjamin had something to say about the character of a child, and he gives this in his big talk, beginning in Mosiah where they're all together for his farewell address. This is Mosiah chapter 3, verse 19:

> *The natural man is an enemy to God, and has been from the fall of Adam, and will be, forever and ever, unless he yields to the enticings of the Holy Spirit, and putteth off the natural man and becometh a saint through the atonement of Christ the Lord, and becometh as a child* (see also Mosiah 1:16 RE).

Then he elaborates what it is about the child that is so useful in yielding to the enticings of the holy spirit, putting off the natural man, becoming a saint through the atonement of Christ—all of those are driven by these kinds of characteristics, which are childlike: *submissive, meek, humble, patient, full of love, willing to submit to all things which the Lord seeth fit to inflict upon him, even as a child doth submit to his father* (ibid). Those are the characteristics of a child that manages to change their mind or to facilitate their development.

Full of love. By the way, "patience of the child" is the relentless openness that a child has to instruction—to receiving more—the perpetual walking about with the empty cup. "I would like my cup to be filled." It is always... The child is always standing with the cupped hand, asking for you to fill it. And *we* go about saying: "I'm gonna offer a prayer now—what's that formula? Oh, we thank thee; we ask thee." We close ourselves off, when the child would open themselves up and extend a hand in a petition, asking for God to give them something. And it doesn't matter how many different ways the Lord goes about trying to teach us that, either with scriptures, or symbols, or signs —it doesn't matter. We, nevertheless, remain committed to closing ourselves off from—and refusing to open up and receive—what things the Lord would offer if we simply would be patient, humble, submissive, and come to Him with an open recognition that we lack.

Full of love. Full of love is one of those things which— It's really a reflection of how close you've drawn to the center point. John, who we call Beloved, seems to have had his eyes opened as to the Savior, because at one point he defines the Lord as love. God *is* love. You draw nearer to that—and it's not a process of drawing nearer without difficulties. When you read, in particular, the strugglings that Enos had in the Book of Mormon, the closer you draw to the center point; the closer it is you reach to the point of love. And you begin to realize that there are people you don't love; indeed, there are people you despise. But the nearer you approach to God, the more you realize that—despite the fact that you have legitimate reasons for harboring resentments or grudges or attitudes about others—it is, nevertheless, the case that if you love, you can't hold onto those things. I could say "I hate it, I just hate this love that I have to show to other people, but I can't resist it. You know, that guy, he deserves to get what's coming to him; and here, I have no more disposition to give it to him. I can actually look upon him with compassion." And yet in my rational mind, "I sure hope the Lord doesn't, because he deserves to get stomped on at some point. I'm not going to do it. You know, live and let live; let him go. I bring no accusation against him."

When you run into a phrase in which you find agreement between John and Paul and Moroni, and they use virtually identical language in what they're saying, then that sort of leaps out, because these divergent personalities converge on a thought, and the thought suggests something, I think, profound. I'm going to take the one that John wrote, which is in 1st John chapter 4, verse 18, and since this is not a sacrament meeting you won't offend me if you get your scriptures out and you choose to turn to 1st John 4:18. The statement that all three of them make is: *there is no fear in love; but perfect love casteth out fear: because fear hath torment.* [Well], *He that feareth is not made perfect in love* (see also 1 John 1:20 RE).

When it comes to the gospel of Jesus Christ, which according to Joseph Smith comprehended all truth, it is our own fear that limits our capacity to gain from what's being offered. And it's a measure of our ingratitude, when declining the invitation that Joseph extended to search deeper and deeper into the mysteries of God, we elect to withdraw fearfully and conclude that we're just not interested in what might have been had.

It's actually a trick of the devil to get people to close their minds and close their hearts, because they fear what they may be learning will do damage to them. You see, when Adam and Eve partook of the fruit and then Satan called to their attention the fact that they were naked—and that's the beginning of the mischief that gets visited on humanity by the adversary who seeks to bind, and control, and to limit the freedom of all mankind, to imprison them—He pointed out to them that they ought to be ashamed. And when, therefore, they heard the voice of God speaking, they withdrew—not because of shame, but because the shame triggered within them fear. They were afraid to come into the presence of that being whom they knew to be just and holy, because now they were in a state in which, fearfully, they were naked. And their "nakedness" came to them as a consequence of understanding the difference between what they were and what they are, and that knowledge came to them by partaking, out of season, of the fruit that they weren't scheduled to receive a command to partake of, until after a day of rest had been observed. So now, not only are they naked before God, they're also violating the Sabbath and beginning the labor of the mortal existence out of time, out of sequence, out of season; and that's the way a great number of errors are made in humanity.

You see, we're commanded *not* to partake of some things out of season, and then we are commanded *to* partake within season; and when we get the timing wrong, we wind up with difficulties and problems that ought not to have been visited. Well, the other references on that same statement, about the opposite of love is fear, is 2nd Timothy chapter 1, verse 7; and Moroni 8, verse 16 (see also 2 Timothy 1:2 RE, and Moroni 8:4 RE).

It is a terrible thing for anyone to presume that they can proscribe and limit the scope of truth into which any of you can inquire and get an answer for yourselves. It is a terrible responsibility. I would suggest that anyone who tries to keep you from inquiring of your Father to know the truth of all things is, like Satan, trying to use fear in order to eliminate your approach to that Being who loves you more than life itself. Who would gather you as a hen gathers her chicks. Who would have done that and brought again Zion time after time after time, but WE would not.

You know, no one should be allowed in the Missionary Department of the Church of Jesus Christ of Latter-day Saints who isn't a convert—better still, an adult convert to the Church; because no one joins because of some silly program. You join because of doctrine. And when you choke away the doctrine, there's no reason to stay.

And so, in gratitude for the principles which brought me aboard the Restoration, we're going to spend this next year looking at the doctrine that compels belief. That doctrine which doesn't abuse, control, compel; but invites and entices, that is delicious, that makes you hunger for more. The principles of the gospel that not only edify but enlighten and enliven. The kinds of things which, despite everything else that separates you, you find you can come together in love and appreciation. That's the gospel. That's the Restoration.

What do you suppose it means: "*having a form of godliness… deny[ing] the power?*" (2 Timothy 3:5; see also 2 Timothy 1:8 RE) How do you deny the power of godliness? How do you obtain the power of godliness? What does it mean to have possession of the power of godliness?

Let's go back to that section 76 again; it's got some nice stuff in it. I want to go to the very end because we're gonna run into the same notion in the First Vision and in section 76. And 76 is a transcript that is given to Joseph that was dictated, transcribed, read back, approved, then the dictation continued until I reach the end. But look at, beginning at verse 113:

This is the end of the vision which we saw, which we were commanded to write while we were yet in the Spirit. But great and marvelous are the works of the Lord, and the mysteries of his kingdom which he showed unto us, which surpass all understanding in glory, and in might, and in dominion; Which he commanded us we should not write while we were yet in the Spirit, and are not lawful for man to utter; Neither is man capable to make them known, for they are only to be seen and understood by the power of the Holy [Ghost], which God bestows on those who love him, and purify themselves before him; To whom he grants this privilege of seeing and knowing for themselves; That through the power and manifestation of the Spirit, **while in the flesh**, they may be able to bear his presence in the world of glory (D&C 76:113-118; see also T&C 69:28-29 RE, emphasis added).

Is this related to *not denying the power of godliness*? I mean, to have the ability to *bear his presence in the world of glory*, as we get farther along in our discussion about the topic of Zion, it becomes critical that you become able to bear His presence. For those who are unable to bear His presence will be destroyed at His coming. Therefore, whatever this power of godliness is, I think we need to get some.

If you turn in Joseph Smith History to the next verse—verse 20, he says: *He again forbade me to join with any of them; and many other things did he say unto me, which I cannot write at this time* (see also Joseph Smith History 2:5 RE). That is always the case. Those the Lord ministers to invariably know more than they say. There are reasons for that. There are laws that involve that. And section 76 suggested that man is not even capable of making some things known. It's really hard to convey into this linear world things that don't relate well here.

Turn back to Mormon—in the Book of Mormon, Mormon chapter 9. I wanna begin in verse 2 of chapter 9. And this stuff really sounds ominous, so

I'm gonna read it with an ominous voice, because I just… I just want to make you feel... *Behold...* You know, this is Mormon; and this is late in the gig. He's lived an NC-17 life. Between the rape, followed by the cannibalism of the women that had been raped, and the murder and the mayhem and the torture, and the...I mean, this is the guy who abridged the Book of Mormon, ...K? That's the life that he was subjected to. So look at these words:

> *Behold, will ye believe in the day of your visitation—behold, when the Lord shall come, yea, even that great day when the earth shall be rolled together as a scroll, and the elements shall melt with fervent heat, yea, in that great day when ye shall be brought to stand before the Lamb of God—then will ye say that there is no God? Then will ye longer deny the Christ, or can ye behold the Lamb of God? Do ye suppose...ye shall dwell with him under a consciousness of your [own] guilt? Do ye suppose that ye could be happy to dwell with that holy Being, when your souls are racked with a consciousness of guilt that ye have ever abused his laws? Behold, I say unto you...ye would be more miserable to dwell with a holy and just God, under a consciousness of your filthiness before him, than ye would to dwell with the damned souls in hell. For behold, when ye shall be brought to see your nakedness before God, and...the glory of God, and the holiness of Jesus Christ, it will kindle a flame of unquenchable fire upon you.* (Mormon 9:2-5; see also Mormon 4:6 RE)

Now I want you to read those verses and ask yourself, "Exactly what is it that God is doing?" The only thing that God is doing is *being*. He simply exists. This is you. God is. And He's simply revealing Himself to you. And this is your reaction. And why is this your reaction? Because you don't have the power of godliness. And why don't you have that? Because you need to repent. And what is it that you must repent of? The absence of knowledge about God. You don't know enough yet to be saved.

The plan of salvation is the plan of education—the plan of knowledge about God and the principles of godliness and the basis upon which all of you can live together and be of one heart and one mind. And it doesn't matter that some of you have strange political beliefs. And it doesn't matter that some of you would like to see every gun in the universe recalled and melted down, so we could all, I don't know, attack one another with the remaining butts of the guns that weren't melted down, 'cause they're wood? I don't know; I mean— And others of you would like every child issued their own concealed-carry permit and to be armed in kindergarten. None of that stuff separates you from being able to love one another and be one. Because much of what you think matters, doesn't matter one whit to the Lord. And you know what? When you're anxiously engaged in the right cause, you'd be surprised how much of our deepest concerns are merely trivial. The things of the heart are what matters. The things upon which we are capable of becoming one, in love toward one another, are infinitely greater.

That's why we really need to keep you distracted in this Telestial kingdom about all the crap that goes on down here. You're worried about the Kardashians—it doesn't matter. (I suppose at a certain level, it's possible that the Red Sox don't even matter. But we're eight and a half games ahead in the A. L. [American League] East right now; and I'm telling ya, it's lookin' good.)

In any event, you take… you mark that page—484 in your Book of Mormon —and you go back and you re-read that, and you ask yourself, "What is God doing, other than merely being?" The only thing He does is "be." And then you react, because *you* are running around hysterically, doing a "pee-pee dance," because you're all concerned that your presence is unacceptable; you're unclean; you're unworthy. That's what He came to fix. And when He fixes it, part of the fix consists of telling you: "Set it aside. Set it aside; be my child. Accept love." And then, in turn, you love. Because what "fixes" is love.

You're supposed to be asking and getting answers from God. And the answers from God are going to tell you what you need to do. And the sacrifices that He will require of you are unique to you, because the contribution that you can make for the salvation of yourself and others is unique to you. There are things that you and only you can do. And if you will sign up with God, He will have you do them. And you may find yourself doing things you would rather prefer not doing. It doesn't matter. If you have faith in Him and you do what He asks, you'll *know* that the course you are pursuing is according to His will. And doing things He asks of you, according to *His* will, invariably produce faith. And they produce faith unto salvation. Because it always grows. Light grows or dims; it never stays static. Therefore, when you set on this course, you never turn back. If you turn back, you lose everything that you've gained up to that point. Look at verse 5 (this is third):

> *An actual knowledge that the course of life which he is pursuing is according to his will. For without an acquaintance with these three important facts, the faith of every rational being must be imperfect and unproductive; but* ***with*** *this understanding it can become perfect and fruitful, abounding in righteousness, unto the praise and glory of God the Father and the Lord Jesus Christ.* (Lectures on Faith 3:5, emphasis added)

Therefore, these three things you need to know. God exists. You need to study until you have a correct understanding of His character, perfections, and attributes. And then you have to live your life so that you actually know that the course you're leading in your life conforms to what He would have. Turn to verse 23:

> *But it is also necessary that men should have an idea that he is no respecter of persons, for with the idea of all the other excellencies in his character, and this one wanting, men could not exercise faith in him; because if he were a respecter of persons, they could not tell what their privileges were, nor how far they were authorized to exercise faith in him, or whether they were authorized to do it at all; but all must be confusion. But no sooner are the minds of men made acquainted with the truth on this point—that he is no respecter of persons—than they see that they have authority by faith to lay hold on eternal life, the richest boon of heaven, because God is no respecter of persons and that every man in every nation has an equal privilege.* (ibid, vs. 23)

That's you, *that's you.* God has done nothing for Joseph Smith He will not do for you. I understand all of the doctrinal arguments. I can make them all. I *have* made them all. And I've made them to the Lord. I've argued with Him on every point of doctrine that any of you— I've quoted to Him every scripture that any of you have advanced, and many more besides. And the Lord has always borne testimony back, consistently. This stuff is true. You're hedging up the way of your own salvation and of the salvation of others when you say, No one has the privilege in our day, yet, to lay hold on salvation. You're hedging up the way, you are damning yourself, and you are damning those that will listen to you when you say people in our time are not yet authorized to exercise faith in God unto salvation, because you *are* authorized.

I have done so. I have spoken with Him as a man speaks to another. He speaks in plain humility, reasoning as one man does with another. He will reason with you. The first night I got a testimony, I was in the middle of an argument with God—I thought with myself—until when I got down to the final question in my mind, which was, "How do I even know there is a God?" To which the response came, "Who do you think you've been talking to the last two hours?" I didn't realize that that still small voice, which will talk with any and all of you, was God. When you exercise the required faith to permit Him to step out from behind the veil, like the brother of Jared, He'll do that, too. He's no respecter of persons. You should not question what your privileges are, nor how far you are authorized to exercise faith in Him, or whether you're authorized to do it at all. Don't have doubts about your privileges.

And then verse 24, twice: *He is love...he is love.* He *is* love.

In verse 3 it talks about:

> *Having the assurance that they were pursuing a course which was agreeable to the will of God, they were enabled to take not only the spoiling of their goods and the wasting of their substance joyfully, but also to suffer death in its most horrid forms, knowing (not merely believing) that when this earthly house of their tabernacle was dissolved, they had a building of God, a house not made with hands, eternal in the Heavens.* (Lectures on Faith 6:3)

That's why Joseph could say, as he did, that he left with a conscience void of offense against God or any man—going as a sheep to the slaughter (see TPJS, p. 379). But he was okay with it. He was okay with it: Such was, and always will be, the situation of the saints of God, that unless they have an actual knowledge that the course they are pursuing is according to the will of God, they will grow weary in their minds, and faint (Lectures on Faith 6:4).

That's the problem with many of us. We grow weary in our minds and faint because we don't know that the course we're pursuing is according to God. Don't grow weary. Stay on that course. I have the absolute conviction that much of the stuff that we plague ourselves with, and think is such a heavy burden of sin, is because our minds are occupied with the wrong stuff. Study the things of God and fill yourself with light—and how quickly it is that all the rest of that stuff will simply dissolve away and evaporate. President Boyd Packer said you can fix behavior a lot more quickly by studying doctrine than you can by studying behavior (see 'Little Children,' Ensign, Nov. 1986, 17).

You know, I have this—well, it's that, ...It's really that first parable where the busy young man who was on his way winds up braiding rope and doing that for years on end; braiding rope, occupying his hands. And then tying the net with the Master. And during the course of that apprenticeship, he came to know who the Master was. So that when, finally, the Master asks him if he knows who He is—and he did—and the Master asks him, "What would you want of Me?" The response comes, "Well, there was a time when I would've asked a lot. But now, I'm just content." Because it's enough. Well, it's enough and to spare (see *Ten Parables*, Denver C. Snuffer, Jr.). Having an actual knowledge that the course that you are pursuing is according to the will of God *is* enough and to spare.

[Paragraph] 4 (towards the bottom of that):

> *...nothing short of an actual knowledge of their being the favorites of Heaven, and of their having embraced [the] order of things which God has established for the redemption of man, will enable them to exercise that confidence in him necessary for them to overcome the world and obtain that crown of glory which is laid up for them that fear God.* (Lectures on Faith 6:4)

Because we ought to fear God more than we fear man. We ought to fear God more than we fear the loss of *anything* that is down here. We ought to fear God more than we fear the approval or disapproval, the criticism, the ostracism. We ought to love God and fear Him because it's our relationship to Him, and Him alone, that matters. This requires more than mere belief or supposition that he's doing the will of God, but actual knowledge. Realizing that when these sufferings are ended, he will enter into eternal rest and be a partaker of the glory of God. It does require more than mere belief or supposition. But it's obtained in accordance with this set of principles. And it is purchased by the same price, paid by each of us in turn, on the same conditions. And no one gets it on any other condition.

I genuinely believe that almost every person in this room—I say almost because I know there's a Marine here—almost every person in this room has lived a life that has been better, more pure, more decent, more honorable, more noble than my own. I am unworthy of anything other than your pity. But I can bear testimony of Someone who *is* pure, who *is* true, who *can* save you. My belief is that every one of you, with a couple of exceptions, every one of you have lived lives so much more worthy of the Lord's recognition than my own. That for the life of me, I can't understand why you don't have the faith and confidence to realize that He loves *you*. And *you* are more lovable than am I. He probably finds it a lot easier to love you than me. I feel like I'm the idiot that's writing graffiti on the walls of heaven, and they really wish the guy would leave, and wonder what *he's* doing here. I mean, I get that you're into forgiving the sinners, but you've got to be kidding me. I think if *you* were to arrive there, there would be a lot more propriety to that. Have faith. Be believing. Trust in Him.

Verse 10:

> *Those, then, who make the sacrifice will have the testimony that their course is pleasing in the sight of God, and those who have this testimony will have faith to lay hold on eternal life and will be enabled, through faith, to endure unto the end and receive the crown that is laid up for them that love the appearing of our Lord Jesus Christ.* (ibid, vs. 10)

Them that love the appearing of our Lord Jesus Christ is talking about not just the Second Coming, that is talking about the coming of the Lord Jesus Christ —whenever He should come, to whomever He should choose to come to, when He chooses to do that. And it is supposed to be an ongoing event.

The foregoing excerpts are taken from:

- Denver's talk given at the Chiasmus Conference in American Fork, Utah on September 18, 2010
- His talk titled "The Mission of Elijah Reconsidered", given in Spanish Fork, UT on October 14th, 2011
- Denver's *40 Years in Mormonism Series,* Talk #1 titled "Be of Good Cheer" given in Boise, ID on September 10th, 2013
- Denver's *40 Years in Mormonism Series,* Talk #2 titled "Faith" given in Idaho Falls, ID on September 28th, 2013

101. Love, Part 2

This is the second part of a special series on Love, where Denver teaches us how we can live according to the two great commandments: Love God, and Love One Another.

DENVER: Doctrine and Covenants section 93, verse 1, says: VERILY, thus saith the Lord: It shall come to pass that every soul who forsaketh his sins and cometh unto me, and calleth on my name, and obeyeth my voice, and keepeth my commandments, shall see my face and know that I am (D&C 93:1; see also T&C 93:1 RE).

Every soul who forsaketh his sins—you're not gonna get past your sins until God forgives you, but you need to awaken to the fact that you possess them, and turn from them; because turning from them is repentance—turning to face Him. You can still have a load that needs to be dropped because we are all heavy laden with sin. But forsaking your sins means that you would prefer Him over everything else there is. So turn and face Him.

Cometh unto me—well, the only way you can leave that load behind is to get down in prayer, seeking Him, and asking Him to free you from the load, and to allow you—as Alma recounts in his 36th chapter of the book of Alma: the terrible agony that he felt, and calling upon God to be redeemed, and then, when God answered, he could remember—the pain, the distress that he had, was equaled by the joy and the exhilaration he felt on the other side of that—being cleansed.

Calleth on my name—you have to do that.

And obeyeth my voice—that would include not merely the things that were given to us by Joseph Smith that you may be neglecting, but obeying His voice in what He tells you here and now. Because your agenda is different from mine. Your needs are different from mine. Your responsibilities are different from mine. You have your own family; you have your own ward; you have your own neighbors; you have your own issues. Fathers and sons, mothers and daughters—you're part of a community somewhere, and inside of that, all of you need to listen to the voice of God, because He loves everyone. He loves that eccentric aunt that you just dread having come around, and you can't for the life of you understand why she thinks cloves should be poked into a turkey on Thanksgiving. And you wonder if maybe there shouldn't be a procedure that more easily confines her to someplace where they administer psychotropic drugs. God loves her as much as He loves you. God loves all of us. And the agenda that you have, and the people you can affect, and the relief that you can administer, and the needs that go in front of your eyes day by day are uniquely yours. And the relief that you can grant to those around you—that's yours. It was given to you by God as a gift. Don't harden your heart.

I was reading about the problems that the early saints experienced in that 1857/1856/ 1858 timeframe—from the diaries; not the official history, not from the stuff that is made public; these are the private diaries and journals—I was reading from that in Sacrament (we went home, and I attended my church meetings this morning), and I literally cried as I read what they were called upon to go through. I am very disinclined to be critical and non-appreciative of the fact that those who went before us suffered as they suffered, in order to preserve and make possible for us today the programs, the scriptures—the fact that they would not allow the Restoration through Joseph to lapse into silence and neglect. It doesn't matter that they made mistakes. We make mistakes, too—every one of us. If you'd lived a perfect life, you wouldn't be here. The fact is, we **all** are broken, and we are **all** in need of repair.

Come to Him, because the only repairman that exists in the universe—inside of **this** matrix—is Christ, whose assignment it is to repair and redeem and to heal us. Obey His voice, no matter how much it may disagree with the flow of that that goes on all around you. People thought I was a madman (teaching gospel doctrine) when we got to the King Benjamin talk about not allowing beggars to go by and neglecting them. And I got push- back every four years when we got through that material because I'm saying, "You don't judge the beggars." You really don't have any right to do that. And then you have Paul's statement about being careful to entertain strangers because angels sometimes come among you unawares.

Let's assume, for argument's sake, that John lingers still. And let's assume, for argument's sake, that John would like to know your heart. How might he do that best? I would suggest, coming to you as a beggar, smelling foul and in need, asking you for relief is the perfect way to find out if that same spirit animates you as animated King Benjamin, when King Benjamin said, 'Don't suffer the beggar to put up their petition to you in vain because are we not all beggars?' And of course, that's not merely a rhetorical question. Are we not all beggars? Well, it's self-evident—yeah.

Obeyeth my voice and keepeth my commandments—my commandments—given to the Prophet Joseph Smith, entrusted to you, should be respected by you; given by the voice of the Spirit to you, asking you to help those around you, because the relief that people need sometimes can only come from one source, and that is you; under the inspiration of the Spirit, relieving the burdens of those around you. Why do you think God cares about the widows, and the orphans, and the poor, and the infirm? And who at Bountiful appreciated His coming the most? Was it those that were called to preside, whose names are given to us because they were recorded in the record? Or was it those that He said—the nameless group—'Bring them up here, and let me heal them?' And all of those in need of healing were brought forward and healed. We read the record and say, 'I got a name here; I got a Timothy. I got a name here; I got a Nephi. I got a name here, and this must be someone big and great and important.' But unto whom did the Lord minister more? And who was it in Bountiful who appreciated more what the Lord had come to do?

Be like your Master. Do what you can for those around you who are infirm. They are here in abundance—the brokenhearted, the families that are in need. If you want to be saved, help the Lord save others—not by preaching and clamoring and demanding that they view the world like you do, but by giving them a hand. Your most powerful sermon can be in the effort that you make and the time that you take to let people know that you care about them. If you would like to repent of your sins, take a look around at those in need and do what you can for them, because you've begun the first step. When your heart is like Him, then you open up so that He can enter in. And when your heart is unlike Him, well, there's no room except if He break it, which He will do. You do these things, *you shall see my face and know that I am*—**know**; not believe, but know.

This is still that paragraph nine of the Lectures on Faith, 7th lecture about—I don't know; it looks like it's only a third of the way down; it's a long paragraph. (By the way, in that 1835 edition of the Doctrine and Covenants, section 76, which in our current edition is like 118 verses, I think it's eight verses there. So, if you're gonna memorize a verse in those days, dude, you're like Gettysburg-Address-worthy. I mean, it's *form*idable. For*mid*able, depending on what part of the country you reckon from.) Okay, so about a third of the way down, it says—it poses the question:

> *Where shall we find a saved being? For if we can find a saved being, we may ascertain without much difficulty what all others must be in order to be saved. We think that it will not be a matter of dispute, that two beings who are unlike each other cannot both be saved; for whatever constitutes the*

> *salvation of one will constitute the salvation of every creature which will be saved; and if we find one saved being in all existence, we may see what all others must be, or else not be saved. We ask, then, where is the prototype? Or, where is the saved being? We conclude, as to the answer of this question, there will be no dispute among those who believe the Bible, that it is Christ: all will agree in this,* ***he*** *is the prototype or standard of salvation; or, in other words,* ***he*** *is a saved being. [Skipping down a couple of lines:] If he were anything different from what he is, he would not be saved; for his salvation depends on his being precisely what he is and nothing else.* (Lectures on Faith 7:9)

So according to the Lectures on Faith, if you would be saved, you have to be **exactly**, **precisely** what Christ is **and nothing else**. Now, you've been told all your life that's an impossibility. Well, it's an impossibility in one sense, and it's a mandatory requirement in another sense. It's an impossibility because, as it turns out, we all err. All of us err; we always have. And that's what the atonement was designed to fix—because He picks that burden up, and He carries it for us.

But the fact that He will carry **that burden** for us doesn't relieve **us**—from the moment that He's taken that away—from then going forward to do good. You **can** be Christ-like. You **can** administer relief to those around you. You **can**, as He said, clothe the naked, feed the hungry, visit those who are in prison. Some of the most profound, deepest, spiritual experiences that I have had recounted to me by people I know, came from people who go out to the prison in Bluffdale and hold family home evenings with prison inmates. That ministration, that service, elevates the servant. Their heart gets moved with compassion. Your heart needs to be like Christ's—moved with compassion for others.

And the way you do that is imitative at first, and then it is informed by the experience later. What begins as imitation, and merely that, finds room within to have genuine compassion for the needs of others. Christ is the prototype, but you can be like Him. There are godly people walking around; many of them are elderly. Many of them have long since forgotten their own needs, and they spend their lives in service of others. You can find that even within the church with Relief Society presidents. You can find that within the church with people who do legitimate-needs home teaching. You don't have to go find another church in which to serve. You don't have to find new neighbors, and you don't have to have a new family. That eccentric group of people, that tribe into which you were born—you belong there. You belong there as an example—as an example of love and compassion.

And you know, the reason why in the sermon on the mount He says they're going to speak *all manner of evil against you falsely, for my name's sake* (Matthew 5:11; see also Matthew 3:14 RE) is not because of anything you've done. It's because down here, no one believes. No one believes the genuine thing exists. Everyone's heart has been broken; everyone has been disappointed. Everyone says, "The man I thought was going to be so great has turned out, instead, to be just another broken ship-wreck." Their skepticism of you has been earned in this environment by everyone they've ever met. Therefore, you've got to be different. And you've got to expect their broken heart is going to be taken out on you, until you at last—and it may require your life to do it—until you at last show that faith can yet exist here.

Let it exist here in you. Let it live and breathe in you. You needn't look for another life, another opportunity, somewhere else far away to go. It's right here; it's in your lap; it's in your family; it's in your home; it's in your community; it's among all those egotistical, hard-headed, stubborn Gentiles—that we parade around, lauding one another, and talking about what great things we are. Serve them. Submit to their rule. Do it in a way that will touch their hearts and be the real thing. Be the real thing, and finally, at last, there will be those who are worthy to lead.

You need to be like Christ. It is precise. It is exact.

Some things get asked of you that require you to lay *even the things you love most* on the altar, and you have to choose. Each of you must choose for yourself the things that you would prefer. But if you don't give primacy to the voice of God speaking to you, you'll never lay hold upon any key, any blessing, any right, any priesthood, if all you do is what some man tells you to do.

Until you listen to God and do what God tells you to do, you will never lay hold upon anything that gives you the ability to declare your own rights, keys, honor, majesty, glory, and power of your own priesthood.

The atonement isn't like Tinkerbell spreading some magic dust that will make you rise up. The atonement will erase your sins and mistakes, but **you** must rise up. **You** must acquire those virtues. The glory of God **is** intelligence. And repentance requires you to acquire that intelligence—that glory of God. And you acquire it by the things that you do in His name and for His sake. And those that are here with you, in need, they represent Him. And when you do it to even the least of them, He will credit that as having been done for Him. And no good deed will be gone unnoticed with Him. He even notices when the sparrows fall. So is He not going to notice when your knee bends with compassion, praying for His mercy for someone that has offended you? And when you pray for those who have offended you, do you think for one moment that that doesn't change your own heart?

The reason to rejoice and be exceedingly glad when they *say all manner of evil against you falsely* is because it affords you the opportunity, with compassion —like our Lord, who forgave even those who were in the act of killing Him —not their brutality, but their ignorance; because when the day arrives that they see things aright finally, and they realize what offense they gave out— they had no intention of offending their Redeemer; they were carrying out the execution of a criminal—and so, He had compassion on them for their ignorance.

You have compassion for all those around you who are ignorant. If you think you know a little more than them, then use gentleness and meekness to persuade them. Sometimes what you try to persuade them of is going to offend them; couple it with your own testimony of the truth. Don't let them simply go away offended. Let them know that when you give offense, and you surely will give offense, let them know that you did it because of your love for them, your love of God, and your faith in the things that God is doing. When you offend, do it kindly and while bearing testimony of the truth and with the compassion that should hail from a position of greater light and truth, or intelligence. They don't know what they're doing. They don't understand it yet. So help them.

All priesthood is perishable. We saw that in Doctrine and Covenants section 121, verse 37.

That they [it] may be conferred upon us, it is true; but when we undertake to cover our sins, or to gratify our pride, our vain ambition, to exercise control or dominion or compulsion upon the souls of the children of men, in any degree of unrighteousness…[And let me couple that with, what is the tool? How do I get to use the Priesthood? How is it that I do get to exercise some influence?] No power or influence can or ought to be maintained by virtue of the priesthood, only by persuasion, by long-suffering, by gentleness and meekness, and by love unfeigned. (D&C 121:37, 41; see also T&C 139:5-6)

I thank God that I do not preside over any of you! I thank God I have no responsibility for any of you, my family aside. Let me tell you that even within my own family, I don't feel it is my prerogative to do anything other than to use persuasion, to use long-suffering, to use gentleness and meekness, and love unfeigned. And to try kindly to use pure knowledge to lay the matter out. But it is ever so much better to lay that out when the question is asked, rather than it is to lay out the answer and force-feed it to someone who doesn't even have the idea occur to them that there is an issue to be discussed.

Turn to Doctrine and Covenants section 63, beginning—this is talking about Zion, beginning at verse 20 of section 63:

> *Nevertheless, he that endureth in faith and doeth my will, the same shall overcome, and shall receive an inheritance upon the earth when the day of transfiguration shall come; When the earth shall be transfigured, even according to the pattern which was shown unto mine apostles upon the mount; of which account the fulness ye have not yet received.* (See also T&C 50:5)

He promised them that they would get to see the latter-day triumph. He took three of them up on the mountain, and He showed them the latter-day triumph. Therefore, there were those that were standing in that generation who did not die until they had seen the latter-day triumph of the Kingdom of God. He fulfilled His own word. And it was put into the gospel in that fashion for that reason.

It will happen! But it requires an awakening, and it requires an arising. It does not require a leader—a servant, maybe; not a leader. It does not require a president. It requires your common consent, by your deeds—not only to say, but to do. It will not be achieved by control. It will not be achieved by coercion. It will not be achieved by force. It will not be achieved because there's some big, strongman among you. It will only happen if each of you are strengthened in your faith and **know the Lord**. It **will** be achieved by humility. It **will** be achieved through meekness. It **will** be achieved by love which is unfeigned—the real thing.

Today, we manufacture leaders. Today, we produce them as a result of a skill set. And they will mimic it, and they will appear as though they are something that they are not. So when I say *love unfeigned*, it cannot be feigned. There cannot be anything about the establishment of Zion that is inauthentic, illegitimate, or insincere. You have to be your own judge about who you are and what you're about. But to the extent that you think you can behave and imitate and get in, all you would do is jeopardize your life. You have to **be** it; you can't feign it. Because if it is feigned, it will not satisfy you.

If you decide to experiment upon the words we have found in scripture today, and **if** you decide that you're going to try and, together, collect your own tithes and administer to your own poor among you, I would suggest that not only should women have an equal voice, but that Joseph Smith was really on to something. Long before the notion of a bishop controlling a storehouse, and even after the existence of a storehouse, the Relief Society was a lively partner in the process. I would suggest when you are 'one,' and when there is relief that is needed, and when, as a result of what the Lord needs to have happen is for people to gather with *love unfeigned*, forget the nonsense about who is greater and who is less. Look among whatever group you participate in and ask yourself, 'Who's more compassionate, and who loves more?' And listen to **her** [laughter], and listen to all of the **hers,** because when it comes to the home and the hearth and the needs of children, there is a competency among the women that is innate. And love can be feigned by the presiding authorities. But women generally have a difficult time pulling that kind of nonsense off. Men can pretend to many things.

Read the chapter on "Gethsemane" in *Come, Let Us Adore Him*, and you'll read an eyewitness account of how our Lord was smitten and afflicted, even beyond what man can endure. And each time, He was able to find peace and reconciliation and love, despite what He was put through.

This is the One about whom the scriptures are speaking. This is the Lord who's asking you to come to Him. He's not aloof, and He's not distant. If He'll speak to someone in a military barracks, He'll speak to you, every one of you. And what He has to say to you is far more important than anything I can say. But I can bear testimony of Him. And I can assure you that He will not leave your petitions unanswered. And I can also assure you that today is once again *a day of salvation*. And He has set His hand again. No matter how unlikely it may appear. No matter how much reason there is to be skeptical. No matter how many more signs you think may need to be fulfilled. I'm telling you, He has set His hand again. The Heavens are open for business, and the question is whether you're interested in becoming a customer or not.

A while ago we read a quote from Joseph in Orem about where the Kingdom of God is. And Joseph said [paraphrasing], "If you can find anyone sent by God, there **is** the Kingdom of God" (*History of the Church*, 5:259; emphasis added). It was good doctrine when Joseph declared it. It was good doctrine when Mosiah declared it. It's good doctrine when I declare it. Because any of you who will hear, and then who will hearken unto their words, you become His seed. You have to hear it. You have to hear it from someone who has been sent. But it does you no good at all if you will not hearken to it, because it is in the hearkening that *you* will meet God; *you* will find redemption. *You* will hear His voice and *you* will become a holy vessel, because His word will be animated in you. And you will have no doubts about your salvation, because *you* will hear Him declare it in His own voice. And you will know that He's no respecter of persons. And you'll know that you, like any other person, can come unto Him; and look to Him and Him alone for your salvation, and not be dependent upon any other person or system. And you too can join in singing a *song of redeeming love* (Alma 5:26; see also Alma 3:5 RE).

Listen. **Religion is, or ought to be, deeply personal.** Religion is not something that at its most intimate level—it's not even something that can be shared.

Go to Doctrine and Covenants section 76. There's some closing verses in the vision in 76, beginning at verse 114:

> *Great and marvelous are the works of the Lord, and the mysteries of his kingdom which he showed unto us, which surpass all understanding in glory, and in might, and in dominion; Which he commanded us we should not write while we were yet in the Spirit, and are not lawful for man to utter; Neither is man capable to make them known, for they are only to be seen and understood by the power of the Holy Spirit, which God bestows on those who love him, and purify themselves before him;* ***To whom he grants this privilege of seeing and knowing for themselves****; That through the power and manifestation of the Spirit,* ***while in the flesh****, they may be able to bear his presence in the world of glory.* (emphasis added; D&C 76:114; see also T&C 69:29)

I have been in that world of glory. I have abided in His presence. I know things not lawful to be uttered. But everything I've uttered today is lawful to be said, is contained in scripture, is the Lord's invitation to you, and you need to realize that this language is your invitation. Because God did not say, "There's some folks I don't love." He says He bestows it on any who love Him. The question isn't His love of us; that is a given. Those few of you who are sitting in this room with a hard heart, rejecting what I have to say, He loves every bit as much as those of you whose hearts are soft, and are open, and are willing. It is not that God loves one more than another; it is that some of you love Him, and others do not. And by this He knows whether you love Him: It's whether your heart is soft and willing to receive, or you deliberately choose to be blinded by the false traditions that you've studied through and hold fast to because you have not faith.

He came. He suffered. He lived. He died. He did what He did in order to lift all of Creation, and you are inextricably connected to Him. Therefore, trust that. Receive Him. It may start very slow, very small, very distant. Act on that! Hearken to that! It gets louder. You will never wind up in the company of Gods and angels if you're not willing to have faith in those preliminary things that you receive that ask you to go and to do.

When I first got an answer to prayer sitting in a barracks in New Hampshire, if I hadn't acted on that, if I hadn't have gone and done, I would never have beheld the Lord, much less been taught by Him. But I did, and I do. And whatever He asks of me, that's what I do now. And it doesn't matter how unpleasant I may find it, or how reluctant in my heart I may be to go and do; I go, and I do.

You need to do that. May not even make much sense to you when you're going and you're doing. You may think you're giving offenses where you absolutely do not intend to do so. You may find the people that you love rejecting you, finding a new family, and having that family reject you again. I've laid it all on the line for the Lord, and I've done it twice now in a single lifetime. I can't tell you what sacrifices He may ask of you. But whatever He asks of you, that do you.

The foregoing excerpts are taken from:

- Denver's *40 Years in Mormonism Series*, Talk #3 titled "Repentance" given in Logan, UT on September 29th, 2013
- Denver's *40 Years in Mormonism Series*, Talk #5 titled "Priesthood" given in Orem, UT on November 2nd, 2013
- Denver's *40 Years in Mormonism Series*, Talk #6 titled "Zion" given in Grand Junction, CO on April 12th, 2014
- Denver's *40 Years in Mormonism Series*, Talk #7 titled "Christ, Prototype of the Saved Man" given in Ephraim, UT on June 28, 2014

102. Love, Part 3

This is the third part of a special series on Love, where Denver teaches us how we can live according to the two great commandments: Love God, and Love One Another.

DENVER: Think about what it means to have the power of God. Think about what it means for God to be able to do all things, including sustaining you from moment to moment by lending you breath. And then for God to say, *you* are free to choose to do—with what He's lending to you—whatever it is that *you* choose to do. Think of the patience of our God. Think of the meekness of our God. And think about the test that you are presently taking to prove who and what you are, and whether or not, in the circumstances of this test, you are proving that you can be trusted to have the meekness, to have the patience, to endure in humility what will be done; to endure the abuses that God allows to take place in order to permit His children to gain experience so that, in the long run, they can ultimately know the difference between good and evil and, on their own, choose to love the good and to stay away from the evil.

Think about that. And think about this record, and think about the test that is currently underway. And think about what it is that you, in your life, should be choosing and doing, desiring and holding to your breast.

Your kids are going to make mistakes. It's not your job to force them to not make the mistake. It's your job to counsel them, and to let them have the experience by which your counsel makes sense, and is vindicated. You hope the mistakes that they make are not too serious, but even if they're serious and they involve lifelong struggles, it's their right to choose. And it's your obligation to teach and to persuade, and then to rejoice when they return after they're tired of filling their bellies with the husks that the pigs are fed. It's your job to go and greet them and put a robe on their shoulder and put a ring on their hand and to the kill the fatted calf. It's not your job to beat them and to chain them to the farm so they can't go away and behave foolishly. They need to know that your bonds of love towards them are stronger than death itself. They need to know that they will endure in your heart into eternity. And not only your children, but one another, because we all make mistakes. Do not exercise dominion, do not exercise compulsion; exercise long-suffering, gentleness, meekness, and kindness. Some of the biggest disasters come when you do not give people the right to choose freely, and you attempt to coerce them. Be wise, be prudent, be someone that they would respect and they would listen to.

God doesn't judge righteousness the way we do. If you've read the 10th parable, what was it that attracted the attention of the angels? They looked at the marriage, and they said, "This! This looks like what we come from! This, This relationship, this marriage, the man and the woman, this is what heaven itself consists of. And look! Look! It's on the earth!" And the angels go and they bring the Lord. And they say, "Behold the man and the woman!" And the Lord sets in motion everything that was needed.

What more do you need to see from the theme of the Book of Mormon than *this* passage, in order to realize that when it comes to the relationship of marriage, *this* is the image of God. *This* is what God would like to preserve into eternity. It is so much easier to take people, who have this kind of a marriage, and to preserve them into eternity, than it is to take someone, who may know all mysteries but whose marriage is a tattered ruin, and attempt to preserve them.

Look at the example of your first parents. Moses 3, the last two verses: 23 and 24. Excuse me, the next... There's one other verse after that. And Adam said: This I know now is bone of my bones, and flesh of my flesh; she shall be called Woman, because she was taken out of man. Therefore shall a man leave his father and his mother, and shall cleave unto his wife; and they shall be one flesh. (Moses 3:23-24; see also Genesis 2:14 RE)

You may have a spouse who is Catholic, Lutheran, Presbyterian, or Mormon. You may have a spouse who is Community of Christ Mormon. You may have a spouse who believes in dancing naked at Wiccan ceremonies while high on peyote. You and your spouse need to love one another. You and your spouse have something far, far greater, potentially, between you and your children, than all of the distractions of this world. You and your spouse face the challenge of becoming one. And if you are one... The Lamanites were condemned, consistently, in the Book of Mormon. It came to blows. But they were praised because of their marriages, because of the love of the spouses.

Now, if you claim that you have enough love for two or more women, then I'd ask you, can you not love your one wife enough to give her your full attention?

Every day my wife and I get up. We have a 4 mile hike that we do every morning before we come back and get ready for work and the day. We spend about an hour doing that—that is filled with conversation—every day; about what's going on in my life, what's going on in her life, what's going on in this big problem, or what's going on with our children. Every day.

I come home for lunch very frequently and we spend the noon hour talking. We probably call each other, I don't know, four or five times during the day. I drive down to Utah County a couple of times. Driving down I'm on the phone talking to my wife. Driving back I'm on the phone talking with my wife. We have a lot to talk about.

I do think that marriage can be something that is godlike, and two people can, in fact, become one.

There's so much left to be done! Right now the only thing that can be done is to remind you of the Restoration, and that is available to all. Everyone's invited. Everyone. But don't expect the Lord to give us anything further, or permit us to move one inch further, until we first remember what we've been given. And even if you are in a fallen world, among a fallen people, who are proud, and who are arrogant, and who think themselves more than they really are; if *you* will love your wife, and if your wife will love you, *you* are in the image of God and that will be preserved unto all eternity. No matter what else you may have to go through between now and then, that's what He's trying to preserve. That is the image of God.

DENVER: You know! The fact of the matter is that the freedom…

AUDIENCE: What was the question?

DENVER: The question was a comment on how disjointed or octopoid that is having eight separate folks vying for primacy at how disjointed the fellowships can be. That is not a bad thing. That is a normal thing. Try to envision yourselves as a temporary family. A temporary gathering together of members of a family. If you don't have some wonky aunts and some curious uncles, in fact, maybe an uncle or two that you want to keep the kids away from, I mean, every family has some strange folks in it. Consider the fellowships nothing more than an extension of that and try and love one another. The fact is that there are going to be those who, through their behavior in fellowships, are going to disqualify themselves from being able to be gathered because they're just not the kind of people that can live in peace one with another. That also is a good thing. And then there are others who come to the fellowships and their primary interest is in what they can take; what they can get. And there are others who come with the only idea in their heart being what can I give, how can I serve. And even though they may not be able to give or serve much, that's what's in their heart. And you all recognize that, you can all see that in people. And those are the kinds of people from which the Lord is going to gather and build Zion.

No one in Zion is going to be a threat to someone else. Can't be. It defeats the purpose of it all. To be able to live in peace with one another means that you literally are harmless to one another. And the diversity in which you find yourselves, and the ability to bump the corners off one another in fellowships, those are healthy, good, normal things. And hopefully, they run their course and eventually result in people becoming smoother and becoming easier with one another. There are some people I admire immensely, and they're tough personalities, and they're difficult to deal with. And there are other people who are hard to deal with because they are too easy going and they really need to speak up more. They have more to add but they won't do it until you coax it patiently out of them. If you don't figure out that you have to coax it patiently out of them, you're missing the treasure that this person represents. In your fellowships think of one another as members of a family and then work out your issues, cause that's how you grow into being a community. You may really prize the more difficult members if you take that approach.

So far as I can tell, Joseph Smith greatly respected women, in what he said, and what he taught, and how he taught it. And I know all the arguments. I've read all the histories. I've read what the people say. I've read what the accusations are. The fact of the matter is that they are not accurate. And the histories that they're based upon, and much of the information was ginned up in consequence of litigation, in which Joseph F. Smith went around gathering affidavits, in the two affidavit books, from which we draw most of the information to redefine what Joseph Smith was doing in Nauvoo, and earlier with plural marriage.

Plural marriage was denounced by him as an abomination. And he got up and said before a crowd, "I hear all the time that I have wives, I've got seven wives. I'm looking out in the audience and can only see one" —meaning Emma. If you read the letters that Joseph sent to Emma and you read the letters that Emma sent back to Joseph, (and they are preserved in the correspondence and the documents of the Joseph Smith History,) you realize that those two, whatever else was going on around them, those two were in love with one another. And Joseph relied on her, respected her, and she loved him. They had a fabulous relationship between the two of them. And I don't care what *In Sacred Loneliness* wants to portray otherwise. A fair reading of Joseph's life was that he was a man who was faithful to his wife.

God's hand is moving again. This is going somewhere. It will eventually culminate in the fulfillment of the prophecies. The trouble is whether we do it, or whether it is left for another generation, depends upon what we do. And I don't think religious enthusiasm or religious fanaticism produces it. It's kindness to one another. It's taking seriously the things that God asked us to do, and then in a meaningful way being self sacrificing, and trying to help and lift other people. Because at the end of the day, Christ summarized all the law and all the prophets in loving God and loving your fellow man—which goes back to the question that Louis asked, about all you quirky people liking one another. Well, that's the challenge. If you want to see Zion get a little closer, then love one another.

I mentioned the idea of "kingship" in Moab. Remember the great King, Christ, came not to be served, but to serve. He did not *lord it over* others, but *He* knelt to elevate them. He came as a meek and lowly servant, and went about doing good. He died to save the lives of others. When He arose from the dead, He went to the Father and advocated forgiveness for those who despised and abused Him.

What kind of king would God send? Even if his bowels are a fountain of light and truth, and even if he were to hold *the scepter of power in his hand* (T&C 83:4 RE), I doubt a king sent by the Lord would be markedly different than our *true* King. He would endure the abuse of misunderstanding, criticism, and mockery from those who refuse to understand. He would serve patiently, never asserting any claim to greatness. Joseph said, in this world "the more a man is exalted, the more humble he will be, if actuated by the Spirit of the Lord" (*JS Papers, Documents,* Vol. 4, p. 198).

When such a king dies, and returns to God to report, he will have only kindness for those who opposed him as he served God. *We* should *all* be like that. We should all be like our Lord.

Christ's greatest commandments were simple, and given to every one of us:

> *Thou shalt love the Lord thy God with all thy heart, and with all thy soul, and with all thy mind. Thou shalt love thy neighbour as thyself. Therefore all things whatsoever ye would that men should do to you, do ye even so to them: for this is the law and the prophets.* (see Matt. 22:37, 39; 7:12; see also: T&C Matt.10:23; 3:44 RE)

If we do these things, there is no time to proclaim our greatness, to assert the right to be a leader, or to command others. Servants do not strut, but behave meekly. They only take such acts as the *true* Master commands.

Take courage! Life was meant to be a living sacrifice, to be lost in the service to God. Only by losing your life will you find it. Saving faith is so rare precisely because it requires courage to engage the opposition in this world, and to cheerfully endure the abuse, lies, threats and fiery darts sent by those who fear your faith above everything. Faith in God will save you through his grace. It can render every weapon of this world and hell powerless, but it takes courage. When friends betray you, and fear overtakes your associates, and causes the knees to buckle under the weight of the burdens God allows to be imposed upon you; remember the Lord descended below it all. And when He cried out asking for the bitter cup to be removed, there was no relief. He is the prototype of the saved man and the Father loved him for his sacrifice. It was the Lord's sacrifice for us that perfected His love for us. He values us because of the great price He paid for each one of us. If you love God, you will be given the opportunity to prove your love. You will be proven by the things you endure for His name's sake. Do not fail.

> *I, the Lord say to you: You have asked of me concerning the scriptures prepared on behalf of all those who seek to become my covenant people, ...therefore I answer you on behalf of all the people, and not as to any individual. For there are those who are humble, patient, and easily persuaded. Nevertheless, people who are quarrelsome and proud are also among you, and since you seek to unite to become one people, I answer you as one.*
>
> *I covenanted with Adam at the beginning, which covenant was broken by mankind. Since the days of Adam I have always sought to reestablish people of covenant among the living, and therefore have desired that man should love one another, not begrudgingly, but as brothers and sisters indeed, that I may establish my covenant and provide them with light and truth.*
>
> *For you to unite I must admonish and instruct you, for my will is to have you love one another. As people, you lack the ability to respectfully disagree among one another. You are as Paul and Peter, whose disagreements resulted in jarring and sharp contentions. Nevertheless, they both loved me and I loved them. You must do better.*
>
> *I commend your diligent labor, and your desire to repent and recover the scriptures containing the covenant I offer for the last days. For this purpose I*

caused the Book of Mormon to come forth. I commend those who have participated, as well as those who have offered words of caution, for I weigh the hearts of men and many have intended well, although they have spoken poorly. Wisdom counsels mankind to align their words with their hearts, but mankind refuses to take counsel from Wisdom.

Nevertheless, there have been sharp disputes between you that should have been avoided. I speak these words to reprove you that you may learn, not to upbraid you so that you mourn. I want my people to have understanding.

There is great reason to rejoice because of the work that has been done. There is little reason for any to be angry or to harshly criticize the labor to recover the scriptures, and so my answer to you concerning the scriptures is to guide you in other work to be done hereafter; for recovering the scriptures does not conclude the work to be accomplished by those who will be my people: it is but a beginning.

In your language you use the name Lucifer for an angel who was in authority before God, who rebelled, fought against the work of the Father and was cast down to the earth. His name means holder of light, or light bearer, for he...gathered light by his heed and diligence before he rebelled. He has become a vessel containing only wrath and seeks to destroy all who will hearken to him. He is now enslaved to his own hatred.

Satan is a title and means accuser, opponent, and adversary; hence once he fell, Lucifer became, or in other words was called, Satan, because he accuses others and opposes the Father. I rebuked Peter and called him Satan because he was wrong in opposing the Father's will for me, and Peter understood and repented.

In the work you have performed there are those who have been Satan, accusing one another, wounding hearts, and causing jarring, contention, and strife by their accusations. Rather than loving one another, even among you who desire a good thing, some have dealt unkindly as if they were...opponents, accusers, and adversaries. In this they were wrong.

You have sought to recover the scriptures because you hope to obtain the covenant for my protective hand to be over you, but you cannot be Satan and be mine. If you take upon you my covenant, you must abide it as a people to gain what I promise. You think Satan will be bound a thousand years, and it will be so, but do not understand your own duty to bind that spirit within you so that you give no heed to accuse others. It is not enough to say you love

God; you must also love your fellow man. Nor is it enough to say you love your fellow man while you, as Satan, divide, contend, and dispute against any person who labors on an errand seeking to do my will. How you proceed must be as noble as the cause you seek. [You've] become your own adversaries, and you cannot be Satan and also be mine. Repent, therefore, like Peter and end your unkind and untrue accusations against one another, and make peace. How shall there ever come a thousand years of peace if the people who are mine do not love one another? How shall Satan be bound if there are no people of one heart and one mind? (T&C 157:1-10 RE)

It is not enough to receive my covenant, but you must also abide it. And all who abide it, whether on this land or any other land, will be mine, and I will watch over them and protect them in the day of harvest, and gather them in as a hen gathers her chicks under her wings. I will number you among the remnant of Jacob, no longer outcasts, and you will inherit the promises of Israel. You shall be my people and I will be your God, and the sword will not devour you. And unto those who will receive will more be given, until they know the mysteries of God in full.

But remember that without the fruit of repentance, and a broken heart and a contrite spirit, you cannot keep my covenant; for I, your Lord, am meek and lowly of heart. Be like me. You have all been wounded, your hearts pierced through with sorrows because of how the world has treated you. But you have also scarred one another by your unkind treatment of each other, and you do not notice your misconduct toward others because you think yourself justified in this. You bear the scars on your countenances, from the soles of your feet to the head, and every heart is faint. Your visages have been so marred that your hardness, mistrust, suspicions, resentments, fear, jealousies, and anger toward your fellow man bear outward witness of your inner self; you cannot hide it. When I appear to you, instead of confidence, you feel shame. You fear and withdraw from me because you bear the blood and sins of your treatment of brothers and sisters. Come to me and I will make sins as scarlet become white as snow, and I will make you stand boldly before me, confident of my love.

I descended below it all, and know the sorrows of you all, and have borne the grief of it all, and I say to you, Forgive one another. Be tender with one another, pursue judgment, bless the oppressed, care for the orphan, and uplift the widow in her need, for I have redeemed you from being orphaned and taken you that you are no longer a widowed people. Rejoice in me, and rejoice with your brethren and sisters who are mine also. Be one.

You pray each time you partake of the sacrament to always have my Spirit to be with you. And what is my Spirit? It is to love one another as I have loved you. Do my works and you will know my doctrine, for you will uncover hidden mysteries by obedience to these things that can be uncovered in no other way. This is the way I will restore knowledge to my people. If you return good for evil, you will cleanse yourself and know the joy of your Master. You call me Lord, and do well to regard me so, but to know your Lord is to love one another. Flee from the cares and longings that belong to Babylon, obtain a new heart, for you have all been wounded. In me you will find peace, and through me will come Zion, a place of peace and safety.

There are only two ways: the way I lead [which] goes upward in light and truth unto Eternal lives — and if you turn from it, you follow the way of darkness and the deaths. Those who want to come where I am must be able to abide the conditions established for my Father's Kingdom. I have given to you the means to understand the conditions you must abide. I came and lived in the world to be the light of the world. I have sent others who have testified...me and taught you. I have sent my light into the world. Let not your hearts remain divided from one another and divided from me.

Be of one heart, and regard one another with charity. Measure your words before giving voice to them, and consider the hearts of others. Although a man may err in understanding concerning many things, yet he can view his brother with charity and come unto me, and through me he can with patience overcome the world. I can bring him to understanding and knowledge. Therefore, if you regard one another with charity, then your brother's error in understanding will not divide you. I lead to all truth. I will lead all who come to me to the truth of all things. The fullness is to receive the truth of all things, and this too from me, in power, by my word, and in very deed. For I will come unto you if you will come unto me.

Study to learn how to respect your brothers and sisters and to come together by precept, reason, and persuasion, rather than sharply disputing and wrongly condemning each other, causing anger. Take care how you invoke my name. Mankind has been controlled by the adversary through anger and jealousy, which has led to bloodshed and the misery of many souls. Even strong disagreements should not provoke anger, nor to invoke my name in vain as if I had part in your every dispute. Pray together in humility and together meekly present your dispute to me, and if you are contrite before me, I will tell you my part. (T&C 157:48-54 RE)

Now, hear the words of the Lord to those who receive this covenant this day:

All you who have turned from your wicked ways and repented of your evil doings, of lying and deceiving, and of all whoredoms, and of secret abominations, idolatries, murders, priestcrafts, envying, and strife, and from all wickedness and abominations, and have come unto me, and been baptized in my name, and have received a remission of your sins, and received the holy ghost, are now numbered with my people who are of the house of Israel. I say to you:

Teach your children to honor me. Seek to recover the lost sheep remnant of this land and of Israel and no longer forsake them. Bring them unto me and teach them of my ways, to walk in them.

And I, the Lord your God, will be with you and will never forsake you, and I will lead you in the path which will bring peace to you in the troubling season now fast approaching.

I will raise you up and protect you, abide with you, and gather you in due time, and this shall be a land of promise to you as your inheritance from me.

The Earth will yield her increase, and you will flourish upon the mountains and upon the hills, and the wicked will not come against you because of the fear of the Lord will be with you.

I will visit my house, which the remnant of my people shall build, and I will dwell therein, to be among you, and no one need say, Know ye the Lord, for you [shall all] know me, from the least to the greatest.

I will teach you things that have been hidden from the foundation of the world and your understanding will reach unto Heaven.

And you shall be called the children of the Most High God, and I will preserve you against the harvest.

And the angels sent to harvest the world will gather the wicked into bundles to be burned, but will pass over you as my peculiar treasure.

But if you do not honor me, nor seek to recover my people Israel, nor teach your children to honor me, nor care for the poor among you, nor help lighten one another's burdens, then you have no promise from me and I will raise up other people who will honor and serve me, and give unto them this land, and if they repent, I will abide with them.

The time is now far spent, therefore labor with me and do not forsake my covenant to perform it; study my words and let them be the standard for your faith, and I will add thereto many treasures. Love one another and you will be mine, and I will preserve you, and raise you up, and abide with you for ever [and ever]. AMEN. (T&C 158:9-20 RE)

The foregoing excerpts are taken from:

- Denver's *40 Years in Mormonism Series,* Talk #8 titled "A Broken Heart," given in Las Vegas, NV on July 25th, 2014;
- Denver's *40 Years in Mormonism Series,* Talk #9 titled "Marriage and Family," given in St. George, UT on July 26th, 2014
- Denver's *40 Years in Mormonism Series,* Talk #10 titled "Preserving the Restoration," given in Mesa, AZ on September 9th, 2014
- A regional conference Q&A session held at Big Cottonwood Canyon, UT on September 20, 2015
- His conference talk titled "The Doctrine of Christ," given in Boise, ID on September 11th, 2016
- His Opening Remarks given at the Covenant of Christ Conference in Boise, Idaho on September 3rd, 2017
- The presentation of "Answer and Covenant," given at the Covenant of Christ Conference in Boise, ID on September 3rd, 2017

103. Love, Part 4

This is the fourth part of a special series on love, where Denver teaches us how we can live according to the two great commandments: Love God, and Love One Another.

DENVER: Today—and I say these words advisedly and I want you to take them seriously—today, *all* Christian churches have become corrupt. They love money more, and acquiring financial security and church buildings more, than caring for the poor and the needy, the sick and the afflicted. The institutions claiming to be the Church of God are all polluted by the cares of the world. I want you to understand what I mean by that. During the apostolic era, there was no such thing as a Christian church building. Christians met in homes. They did not collect and compensate ministers. They gathered money and they used it to help the poor and the needy among them.

As soon as you get a church building, I regret to inform you, you'll have to hire a lawyer. In what name are you going to take title to your building? How are you going to hide title, or hold title, and deal with succession? What form will the organization take? Do you intend to qualify for tax deductibility? If so, do you intend to file as a charitable institution—as an eleemosynary institution? As an educational institution? Those are all words that you find in 501(c) of the Internal Revenue Code. And what do you do if you want to hire and fire a minister? And you want to dispossess the one you fired and put into possession the successor in the building? What rights, and who's on the board, and who possesses the right to deal with that? As soon as you own property, the *cares of this world invade*. It's unavoidable.

If you meet in homes as the early Christians did, and if you gather your tithing—one tenth of your surplus after you've taken care of all your responsibilities, all your needs, whatever's left over, one tenth of that is your tithe. After you gather your tithes, then you ought to look at your brothers and your sisters who are there in your meeting, and you ought to help those who have needs—who have health needs, who have education needs, who have transportation needs, who have food needs, who have children that need care. Christians should take care of the poor among them.

And *no one* should be looking at the flock and saying, "I need your money to support myself." Christian charity should be used to take care of the poor among you, and *not* to engage in acquiring the cares of this world. This is why *all* Christian churches have become corrupt. They love money, and acquiring financial security and church buildings, more than caring for the poor and the needy, the sick and the afflicted.

The idea of the love of Christ was preserved in Johanian Christianity. Spirit, knowledge, and ritual were designed to preserve knowledge of Christ. Although lost to western Christianity, John taught that man would become divinitized, or ascend in stages of progression to become *just like God.* His teachings have been lost, but two passages in the New Testament writings of John preserve that teaching still—1 John 3, beginning in verse 1:

> *Behold, what manner of love the Father hath bestowed upon us, that we should be called the sons of God: therefore the world knoweth us not, because it knew him not. Beloved, now are we the sons of God, and it doth not yet appear what we shall be: but we know that, when he shall appear, we shall be like him; for we shall see him as he is. And every man that hath this hope...purifieth himself, even as he is pure.* ([emphasis added] 1 John 3:1-3; see also 1 John 1:13 RE)

And then in Revelation chapter 3, beginning at verse 20, it is Christ who is speaking:

> *Behold, I stand at the door, and knock: if any man hear my voice, and open the door, I will come in to him, and will sup with him, and he with me. To him that overcometh will I grant to sit with me in my throne, even as I also overcame, and am set down with my Father in his throne. He that hath an ear, let him hear what the Spirit saith unto the churches.* ([emphasis added] Revelation 3:20-22; see also Revelation 1:20 RE)

Christ came as the least, as a servant kneeling to wash feet, as a teacher of righteousness. He invited, persuaded, and taught. He did *not* demand respect for His authority. He submitted to abuse, rejection, and ultimately to being slain. He loved mankind. Those who demand their authority be respected are anti-Christ because they oppose the core of Christ's example. We are most Christian when we are most *like Christ.*

Religion should not divide us as it does. It's tragic that anyone's search to find truth and to connect with God should divide them from their fellow man. Christ said the greatest commandment was to love God, but immediately added that the second greatest commandment was *like unto it,* and that commandment was to love our neighbor as ourself (See Matthew 22:35-40; see also Matthew 10:23 RE).

Christ never taught us 'love only those who love us in return'. He taught:

> *Ye have heard that it hath been said, Thou shalt love thy neighbour, and hate thine enemy. But I say unto you, Love your enemies, bless them that curse you, do good to them that hate you, and pray for them which despitefully use you, and persecute you; That ye may be the children of your Father which is in heaven: for he maketh his sun to rise on the evil and on the good, and sendeth rain on the just and on the unjust. For if [you] love them which love you, what reward have [you]? do not even the publicans [do] the same? And if ye salute your brethren only, what do ye more than others? do not even the publicans so? Be ye therefore perfect, even as your Father which is in heaven is perfect.* ([emphasis added] Matthew 5:43-48; see also Matthew 3:26 RE)

Let us make our search for truth one that brings us closer together rather than something to divide us apart. We share more than we disagree. I want you to consider the meaning for us all in the account of Adam and Eve. We all have one set of original parents in common. All of the genetic potential for the entire human race comes from these two original parents. No man or woman possesses any genetic feature that did not first come from them. They set the limits on their descendants' height. They set the limit on how high their descendants could jump, how fast we could run, how intelligent we could become, how strong we could become. Every facet of us, their diverse descendants in the world at this moment, were determined by the genetic makeup of Adam and Eve. When we despise the differences we see in one another, we despise our first parents. Christ taught:

> *A new commandment I give unto you, That ye love one another; as I have loved you, that ye [should] also love one another. By this shall all men know that ye are my disciples, if ye have love one to another.* (John 13:34-35; see also John 9:5 RE; see also T&C 171, The Testimony of St. John 10:7 RE)

Menno Simons, who was one of the Reformation fathers after whom the Mennonites are named, said, "True evangelical faith cannot lie dormant, it clothes the naked, it feeds the hungry, it comforts the sorrowful, it shelters the destitute, it serves those that harm it, it binds up that which is wounded, it has become all things to all creatures" (*Why I Do Not Cease Teaching and Writing*, by Menno Simons, 1539).

Everything Christ taught is tended to change our inner self. He did not want me judging and condemning *you*. If you decide to abuse me, Christ teaches I should forgive you. If you offend me seventy times seven, Christ taught me to forgive (See Matthew 18:21-22; see also Matthew 9:15 RE).

If we believed in Christ enough to live as He taught, our families would heal, our communities would heal, our nations would heal, and the world would heal. Christ was an idealist, but He showed by His life that it is possible to live the ideal. As a Christian I should commit to that ideal, and at every missed step, resolve to do better. Each of us control only our own life, but your example is enough to change the lives of many others.

> *All the Lord had previously done in His mortal ministry by healing the sick, raising the dead, giving sight to the blind, restoring hearing to the deaf, curing the leper, and ministering relief to others as he taught was but a prelude to what the Lord was now to do on this dark, oppressive night.*
>
> *As the Lord knelt in prayer, His vicarious suffering began. He was overcome by pain and anguish. He felt within Him, not just the pains of sin, but also the illnesses men suffer as a result of the Fall and their foolish and evil choices. The suffering was long and the challenge difficult. The Lord suffered the afflictions. He was healed from the sickness. He overcame the pains, and patiently bore the infirmities until, finally, he returned to peace of mind and strength of body. It took an act of will and hope for Him to overcome the affliction which had been poured upon Him. He overcame the separation caused by these afflictions and reconciled with His Father. He was at peace with all mankind.*
>
> *He thought His sufferings were over, but to His astonishment another wave overcame Him. This one was much greater than the first. The Lord, who had been kneeling, fell forward onto His hands at the impact of the pain that was part of a greater, second wave.*
>
> *This second wave was so much greater than the first that it seemed to entirely overcome the Lord. The Lord was now stricken with physical injuries as well as spiritual affliction. As He suffered anew, His flesh was torn which He healed using the power of the charity within Him. The Lord had such life within Him, such power and virtue within Him, that although He suffered in His flesh, these injuries healed and His flesh restored. His suffering was both body and spirit, and there was anguish of thought, feeling, and soul.*

The Lord overcame this second wave of suffering, and again found peace of mind and strength of body; and His heart filled with love despite what He had suffered. Indeed, it was charity or love that allowed Him to overcome. He was at peace with His Father, and with all mankind, but it required another, still greater act of will and charity than the first for Him to do so.

Again, the Lord thought His suffering was over. He stayed on His hands and knees for a moment to collect Himself when another wave of torment burst upon Him. This wave struck Him with such force He fell forward upon His face. He was afflicted by this greater wave. He was then healed, only to then be afflicted again as the waves of torment overflowed. Wave after wave poured out upon Him, with only moments between them. The Lord's suffering progressed from a lesser to a greater portion of affliction; for as one would be overcome by Him, the next, greater affliction would then be poured out. Each wave of suffering was only preparation for the next, greater wave.

The pains of mortality, disease, injury, and infirmity, together with the sufferings of sin, transgressions, guilt of mind, and unease of soul, the horrors of recognition of the evils men had inflicted upon others, were all poured out upon Him, with confusion and perplexity multiplied upon Him.

He longed for it to be over, and thought it would end long before it finally ended. With each wave he thought it would be the last, but then another came upon Him, and then yet another.

But the Lord was determined to suffer the Father's will and not His own. Therefore, a final wave came upon Him with such violence as to cut Him at every pore. It seemed for a moment that He was torn apart, and that blood came out of every pore. The Lord writhed in pain upon the ground as this...final torment was poured upon Him.

All virtue was taken from Him. All the great life force in Him was stricken and afflicted. All the light turned to darkness. He was humbled, drained, and left with nothing. It is not possible for a man to bear such pains and live, but with nothing more than will, hope in His Father, and charity [towards] all men, He emerged from the final wave of torment, knowing He had suffered all this for His Father and His brethren. By His hope and great charity, trusting in the Father, the Lord returned from this dark abyss and found grace again, His heart being filled with love toward the Father and all men.

The waves of torment suffered by the Lord came in pairs which mirrored each other. The first of each wave poured upon the Lord those feelings, regrets, recriminations, and pains felt by those who injured their fellow man. Then followed a second wave, which mirrored the first, but imposed the pains suffered by the victims of the acts committed by those in the first wave. Instead of the pains of those who inflict hurt or harm, it was now the anger, bitterness, and resentments felt by those who suffered these wrongs.

From each wave of suffering, whether as the one afflicting or as the victim of those wrongs, the Lord would overcome the evil feelings associated with these wrongs, and find His heart again filled with peace. This was why, in the vision of the suffering of the Lord, it was in the second waves that there appeared oftentimes to be injuries to His body.

The greater difficulty in these paired waves of torment was always overcoming the suffering of the victim. With these waves the Lord learned to overcome the victims' resentments, to forgive, and to heal both body and spirit. This was more difficult than overcoming the struggles arising from the one who committed the evil. This is because the one doing evil knows he has done wrong and feels a natural regret when he sees himself aright. The victim, however, always feels it is their right to hold resentment, to judge their persecutor, and to withhold peace and love [from] their fellow men. The Lord was required to overcome both so that He could succor both.

In the pairing of the waves, the first torment was of the mind and spirit, and the second was torment of mind, spirit, and body.

The Lord experienced all the horror and regret wicked men feel for their crimes when they finally see the truth. He experienced the suffering of their victims whose righteous anger and natural resentment and disappointment must also be shed, and forgiveness given, in order for them to find peace. He overcame them all. He descended below them all. He comprehends it all. And He knows how to bring peace to them all. He knows how to love others whether they are the one who has given offense or the one who is a victim of the offense.

In the final wave, the most brutal, most evil, most heinous sins men inflict upon one another were felt by Him as a victim of the worst men can do. He knew how it felt to wrongly suffer death. He knew what it was like to be a mother holding a child in her arms as they are both killed by those who delight in their suffering. He knew how it was for ambitious men to rid themselves of a rival by conspiracy and murder. He knew what it was to have virtue robbed from the innocent. He knew betrayal, treachery, and abuse in

> *all its worst degrading horror. There was no cruelty, no offense, no evil that mankind has suffered or will suffer that was not put upon Him.*
>
> *He knew what it is like for men to satisfy their ambition by clothing their hypocrisy in religious garb. He also felt what it was like to be the victim of religious oppression by those who pretend to practice virtue while oppressing others. He knew the hearts of those who would kill Him. Before confronting their condemnation of Him in the flesh, He suffered their torment of mind when they recognized He was the Lord, and then found peace for what they would do by rejecting Him. In this extremity there was madness itself as He mirrored the evil which would destroy Him, and learned how to come to peace with the Father after killing the Son of God, and to love all those involved without restraint and without pretense even before they did these terrible deeds. His suffering, therefore, encompassed all that has happened, all that did happen, and all that would happen in the future.*
>
> *As a result of what the Lord suffered, there is no condition — physical, spiritual, or mental — that He does not fully understand. He knows how to teach, comfort, succor, and direct any who [will] come to Him seeking forgiveness and peace. This is why the prophet wrote: by his knowledge shall my righteous servant justify many; for he shall bear their iniquities. [Isa. 19:2] And again: Surely he hath borne our griefs, and carried our sorrows; yet we did esteem him stricken, smitten of God, and afflicted. But he was wounded for our transgressions, he was bruised for our iniquities; the chastisement of our peace was upon him; and with his stripes we are healed. [Isa. 19:2] He obtained this knowledge by the things He suffered. He suffered that we might avoid sin by being obedient to His commandments. None of us need harm another, if we will follow Him. He knows fully the consequences of sin. He teaches His followers...to avoid sin.* (T&C 161:2-9,11-12,17-24 RE)

The prophet Alma taught and understood our Lord's suffering as he wrote:

> *And he shall go forth, suffering pains and afflictions and temptations of every kind; and this that the word might be fulfilled which saith he will take upon him the pains and the sicknesses of his people. And he will take upon him death, that he may loose the bands of death which bind his people; and he will take upon him their infirmities, that his bowels may be filled with mercy, according to the flesh, that he may know according to the flesh how to succor his people according to their infirmities.* (Alma 7:11-12; see also Alma 5:3 RE)

He can bring peace to any soul. He can help those who will come to Him love their fellow man. He alone is the Perfect Teacher because He alone has the knowledge each of us lack to return to being whole and at peace with God, the Father of us all, after all our transgression of His will. Christ is wise to what is required for each man's salvation.

I believe that there is tension, if not outright hostility, between charity as a priority (on one hand) and knowledge as priority (on the other hand); and that as between the two, it is more important to acquire the capacity for charity, or love of your fellow man, than it is to gain understanding. It's like what Paul said, "If I have all gifts and know all mysteries, but have not charity, I am nothing" (See 1 Corinthians 13:1-2; see also 1 Corinthians 1:51 RE).

Charity or the love of your fellow man is the greater challenge and the more relevant one, and when you've acquired that, you can add to it knowledge. But knowledge has the ability to render the possessor arrogant and haughty, whereas charity renders the possessor humble. If you want the greatest challenge in life, try loving your fellow man unconditionally and viewing them as God would view them, and then behaving according to that view. And out of that you will learn a great deal more about Christ than you can simply by studying. Walking in His path is a greater revelation of who He is than anything else that's provided.

Joseph Smith once remarked that if you could gaze into Heaven for five minutes, you would know more about it than if you read every book that has ever been written on the subject (See *Teachings of the Prophet Joseph Smith,* p. 324; see also *History of the Church,* 6:50). Likewise, if you live charitably for five minutes in the presence of what you would normally condemn, what you would normally find repugnant— If you can deal with that charitably, you will understand Christ better than if you spend a lifetime reading books written about Him.

The foregoing excerpts are taken from:

- Denver's *Christian Reformation Lecture Series,* Talk #1, given in Cerritos, California, on September 21, 2017,
- Denver's *Christian Reformation Lecture Series,* Talk #2, given in Dallas, Texas, on October 19, 2017, and

- Denver's *Christian Reformation Lecture Series*, Talk #3, given in Atlanta, Georgia, on November 16, 2017.

104. Love, Part 5

This is the fifth part of a special series on love, where Denver teaches us how we can live according to the two great commandments: Love God, and Love One Another.

DENVER: Wisdom and prudence go together as companions. *Prudence* means good judgment or common sense. It is the quality of assessing things correctly and making a sound decision in light of the circumstances and persons involved. Prudent judgment is not hasty or unfair. Arrogance is destroyed and pride overtaken by *fear of the Lord*—meaning that we do not want to disappoint our Lord by our low, vulgar, and mean conduct.

She mentions, a second time, Her opposition to the froward. This time She declares She hates the froward mouth. We repel Her by being argumentative and contrary with one another.

Continuing:

> *Counsel is mine, and sound wisdom: I am understanding; I have strength.* (Proverbs 8:14; see also Proverbs 1:36 RE)

The Mother must possess great strength because She hates the froward—the contentious. She does not welcome that spirit in Herself or any of Her offspring. But yet, She loves us.

Christ taught this idea to the Nephites, which seems to be clearly taken from the Mother's wisdom:

> *And there shall be no disputations among you, as there hath hitherto been, neither shall there be disputations among you concerning the points of my doctrine, as there hath hitherto been. For verily, verily I say unto you, he that hath the spirit of contention is not of me, but is of the Devil, who is the father of contention; and he stirreth up the hearts of men to contend with anger, one with another. Behold, this is not my doctrine, to stir up the hearts of men with anger [against one] another, but this is my doctrine, that such things should be done away.* (3 Nephi 5:8 RE)

It requires strength to refrain from contention and disputes with froward and arrogant people. When we feel strongly that we're right or are firmly convinced someone else is wrong, it's difficult to bridle our tongue and meekly persuade without contention. But the Heavenly Mother possesses the strength required to look with compassion on our failings. She deals with Her offspring using good judgment and common sense. She's opposed to arrogance, and when we're arrogant, we offend Her.

How many religious arguments, even religious wars, have been caused because mankind is too weak to patiently reason together? The history of this world is a bold testimony of what weak and deceived men do when they reject wisdom.

Mankind cannot have Zion without wisdom to guide us. Zion must be a community. Developing wisdom requires us to patiently interact with one another. This counsel from the Heavenly Mother is a gift to help us understand what we lack.

When first created, man and woman were joined together by God. This union happened before death entered into the world. Therefore, their companionship was eternal when first established and, when rescued from death, would return. As Christ put it:

> *Have you not read that he who made man at the beginning made him male and female, and said, For this cause shall a man leave father and mother, and shall cleave [unto] to his wife, and they* ***two*** *shall be* ***one*** *flesh? Wherefore, they are no more two, but* ***one*** *flesh. What therefore God has joined together, let not man put asunder.* (Matthew 9:19 RE, emphasis added)

This union of Adam and Eve and this plan of God for all who would thereafter be married was to make the man and the woman *one flesh.* What God has joined together and made into one, no one should *put asunder* by rejecting the eternal nature of marriage. It was always intended to last through the resurrection.

Continuing with the Heavenly Mother's declarations in Proverbs 8:

> *I love them that love me, and those that seek me early shall find me. Riches and honor are with me—yea, durable riches and righteousness. My fruit is better than gold, yea, than fine gold, and my revenue than choice silver.* (Proverbs 1:36 RE)

Of all our Mother's *fruit,* the most valuable to fallen man is, without doubt, the Redeemer, Jesus Christ. The account of how Jesus Christ came into the world begins with a virgin and an angel. There is more to this than Christians have noticed. The prophecy relied on to identify the birthplace of Christ in

Bethlehem continues with a description of His Mother. It was prophesied that only when *she which travaileth hath brought forth: then the remnant of his brethren shall return unto the children of Israel* (Micah 5:3; see also Micah 1:11 RE). Because of the labor and travail of His Mother, the prophecy of Israel returning to God was fulfilled. She made His entry into this world possible. The redemption of the remnant is as much the consequence of Her as of Her Son.

What was Mary's role? Who was She? Is it possible She was the Mother of God before She came into mortality? These are important questions that ought to be asked. If we can learn the answers, they would indeed be glorious.

The Book of Mormon gives an extended description of Mary, the Mother of God. In the original translation text, the words *mother of God* were used, but that was changed by Joseph Smith in 1837 to *mother of the Son of God.* Here is how it reads following that change:

> *And it came to pass that I looked and beheld the great city of Jerusalem, and also other cities. And I beheld the city of Nazareth; and in the city of Nazareth I beheld a virgin, and she was exceedingly fair and white. And it came to pass that I saw the heavens open; and an angel came down and stood before me; and he said unto me: Nephi, what beholdest thou? And I said unto him: A virgin, most beautiful and fair above all other virgins. And he said unto me: Knowest thou the condescension of God? And I said unto him: I know that he loveth his children; nevertheless, I do not know the meaning of all things. And he said unto me: Behold, the virgin whom thou seest is the* ***Mother of the Son of God****, after the manner of [the] flesh. And it came to pass that I beheld that she was carried away in the Spirit; and after she had been carried away in the Spirit for [a] space of [a] time the angel [said] unto me...Look! And I looked and beheld the virgin again, bearing a child in her arms. And the angel said unto me: Behold the Lamb of God, yea, even the Son of the Eternal Father! Knowest thou the meaning of the tree which thy father saw? And I answered him, saying: Yea, it is the love of God, which sheddeth itself abroad in the hearts of the children of men; wherefore, it is the most desirable above all things. And he spake unto me, saying: Yea, and the most joyous to the soul.* (1 Nephi 11:13-23; see also 1 Nephi 3:8-9 RE, emphasis added)

Most who read this passage interpret the *condescension* reference **solely** as Christ's. They view it as Christ alone who descended by being born of Mary here in mortality. However, when leading up to the angel's question (*Knowest thou the condescension of God?*), the text focuses exclusively on Mary. When the angel clarified the condescension, he again focused primarily on Mary and secondarily on Her Son. The angel explained:

> *Behold,* ***the virgin*** *whom thou seest is* ***the mother of the Son of God****, after the manner of the flesh. And it came to pass that I beheld that* ***she*** *was carried away in the Spirit; and after* ***she*** *had been carried away in the Spirit for the space of time the angel spake unto me, saying: Look! And I looked and* ***beheld the virgin*** *again, bearing a child in* ***her arms****. And the angel said unto me: Behold the Lamb of God.* (1 Nephi 11:18-21; see also 1 Nephi 3:8-9 RE, emphasis added)

Who would you reasonably expect to be the woman chosen before the world was organized to become the mortal Mother of the Lord? Who would you expect Heavenly Father would want to bear His child if not His Spouse? Together, God the Father and Mary can be acknowledged as the Parents of Christ. The scriptures shift the focus of the condescension from Christ to His Mother and then back to Her Son, the seed of the woman.

Lectures on Faith describe Christ as *the prototype of the saved man.* Lecture seven focuses attention on Christ as the Savior and Redeemer. But the lecture extends the requirement met by Jesus Christ to also apply for every saved man. In other words, for any man to be saved, they must attain to the resurrection—like Christ. Shifting attention for a moment from Jesus Christ as our Redeemer and Savior to His Mother, we could acknowledge Her as *the prototype of the saved woman.* In other words, we could consider what She did, a Divine pattern to be followed by women.

Returning to the words of the Divine Mother in Proverbs 8:

> *I lead in the way of righteousness, in the midst of the paths of judgment: That I may cause those that love me to inherit substance; and I will fill their treasures.* (Proverbs 8:20-21; see also Proverbs 1:36 RE)

These treasures are not earthly but *durable* and incapable of depreciation. What the Mother offers cannot be harmed by moth or rust nor lost to thieves. They are in Heaven. But obtaining them requires us to walk as She guides *in the way of righteousness, in the midst of the paths of judgment* (ibid, vs. 20; see also vs. 36 RE). The great white throne is not occupied by the Father alone. Nor will that great judgment be made without the Mother's involvement, for She lives in *the paths of judgment* and wisely counsels Her children to obtain durable *riches and honor.*

The Mother explains how She was present from the beginning as part of the God we call Father or, in Hebrew, the Elohim:

> *The Lord possessed me in the beginning of his way, before his works of old. I was set up from everlasting, from the beginning, or ever the earth was. When there were no depths, I was brought forth; when there were no fountains abounding with water. Before the mountains were settled, before the hills was I brought forth: While as yet he had not made the earth, nor the fields, nor the highest part of the dust of the world. When he prepared the heavens,* ***I was there****: when he set a compass upon the face of the depth: When he established the clouds above: when he strengthened the fountains of the deep: When he gave to the sea his decree, that the waters should not pass his commandment: when he appointed the foundations of the earth: Then* ***I*** *was by him, as one brought up with him: and I was daily his delight, rejoicing always before him; rejoicing in the habitable part of his earth; and my delights were with the sons of men.* (Proverbs 8:22-31; see also Proverbs 1:37 RE, emphasis added)

Before this creation, the Mother in Heaven was with the Father. She was beside Him when His work began. She was there when the plan was laid, the boundaries established, and the compass applied to establish order for the creation. All the Father knows, the Mother knows. All the Father established and ordered, the Mother established and ordered. They are one. She is the Father's *delight.* And the potential of Her sons to be like Her Husband, brings Her *delight.*

To be like their Father, Her sons must become one with Her daughters, for it is not good for man to be alone. The Father and Mother are one, and Her sons and daughters must likewise become one. Only when the man and woman were together was the creation *good.* When men rebel, disobey, act cruelly, or mistreat Her daughters, we are anything but a delight to the Heavenly Mother. When we offend Her, we also offend Her Husband.

Before any of us will plan, measure, set a compass, and apportion the foundations of another earth; we must grow together and become like Them. Their work is glorious. They possess love—the power that creates and organizes. Love is the power behind all that They do. We cannot be like them without a loving relationship that mirrors Theirs.

The presence of the female counterpart to God the Father does not include a scriptural command or permission to single Her out and worship Her apart from the Father. Indeed, the psalm of Mary in the book of Luke and the words of the Mother in Proverbs direct our attention to the Father. She may be part of a Divine Couple, but it is clear She wants honor and worship to be on Her Husband and Her Son.

Their character, perfections, and attributes are: mercy, righteousness, love, compassion, and truthfulness. They are without partiality, no respecter of persons, regarding all alike. They make the sun to shine and the rain to fall on both the righteous and the wicked. They regard wickedness as an abomination. They prize truth, meekness, and peacemakers. They *abhor* the froward, prideful, evil, and arrogant. They're full of grace and truth and are more intelligent than us all. They are the Creators and will be the final Judges of this cycle of existence, and no one will be permitted to progress further without Their permission. There is nothing vile or perverse about Them. They are repelled by contention and seek for us all to associate with one another equally, as brothers and sisters. They are *perfect* in the sense of having completed the journey to the end of the path and entered into eternal lives and exaltation. They now seek to guide Their children along the same path.

The law of consecration is almost in and of itself an oxymoron. How might I make your heart and my heart one by a law? Even if with a deed we all have all things in common. Give me the law that will make your heart and my heart one. Give me the law that will make your mind and my mind one. Because against such there is no law. The only way I know to become united in a way in which I care for you and you care for me, in a way that we could successfully consecrate our lives together, is if both of us have for the other love unfeigned. It's easy to feign love. It's very difficult to have unfeigned love– authentic, I would lay my life down for you love. Which doesn't mean you always get along and agree. You can fight and yet love one another. You can disagree and yet love one another. If you love your children, there are times you're going to correct them. There are some times you may reprove them with sharpness, and then reluctantly show forth afterwards an increase of love [*laughs*]. That's just life.

There are two great competing forces in the whole of creation: Love and fear. I think God's love for us is exemplified in Him speaking to Joseph Smith. And I'm grateful for how that has enriched my life.

All truth must come from God. The precepts of men are not only unreliable but they're corrupted by their source. God's truths do not end. This thought, like the one before, reminds us that we must seek the constant nourishment of our minds and souls to be in God's path. When God is silent, then you're cut off from the truth. Those God can save are those who will listen for His voice no matter how unlikely the source from which God's voice comes. If it is God's word, it's to be prized, even when it comes from the Joseph Smith your mother warned you about.

The hallmark reaction from those disinterested in what God is saying is their angry rejection and refusal to acknowledge more. When you are content, you perish. When you hunger and thirst, you live. Living organisms require constant additional nourishment; that's how you know they're alive.

There's another profound declaration along the same line:

> *And because I've spoken one word, ye need not suppose that I cannot speak another, for my work is not yet finished, neither shall it be until the end of man, neither from that time henceforth and forever. Wherefore, because ye have a bible ye need not suppose that it contains all my words, neither need ye suppose I have not caused more to be written.* (2 Nephi 29:9-10; see also 2 Nephi 12:10 RE)

Last year I delivered a talk at the Sunstone Symposium titled *Other Sheep Indeed.* In it I invited others with sacred writings to come and bring them. That invitation was first offered by Joseph Smith in 1840. He anticipated a temple to be built in Nauvoo to which records would be brought from all over the world. "Bring every thing you can bring and build a house of God and we will have a tremendous City which shall reverberate afar…then comes all the ancient records dig them up…where the Saints g[ather] is Zion." Not all of God's words are in the Bible. God has spoken to every nation (meaning every religious division of people). Truth is everywhere, among all people. If we love God and truth we will want to search for it. We will not be content to leave it unexplored and undiscovered. Blessed are those who hunger and thirst after more righteousness. Blessed are those who are followers of righteousness, desiring to possess great knowledge, and to be a greater follower of righteousness and to possess greater knowledge. And blessed are those who do not suppose the scriptures contain all God's words and They (the Gods) have not provided more.

Alma taught a lesson that we accepted by covenant as a statement of our faith:

> *And now my beloved brethren, I have said these things unto you that I might awaken you to a sense of your duty to God, that ye may walk blameless before him, that ye may walk after the holy order of God after which ye have been received. And now I would that ye should* ***be humble and be submissive and gentle, easy to be entreated,*** *full of patience and longsuffering, being*

> *temperate in all things, being diligent in keeping the commandments of God at all times, asking for whatsoever things ye stand in need, both spiritual and temporal, always returning thanks unto God for whatsoever things ye do receive.* (Alma 7:22; see also Alma 5:6 RE, emphasis added)

The greatness of a soul is defined by how easily they are entreated to follow the truth. The greatest of those who have ever lived have been submissive and gentle souls. In a day when Satan accuses and rages in the hearts of men, it requires extraordinary will and steely determination to remain easily entreated by truth.

I have pondered how much more ought to have been accomplished during Joseph Smith's lifetime. Joseph was only able to accomplish a fraction of what needs to be restored. Joseph faced continuing troubles because of the ambition of the believers. Too many of the saints aspired to lead. They wanted control over others. It hindered the work. Joseph was not able to finish the Restoration. Our hearts must turn to the Fathers in Heaven, and we cannot ignore that duty because of any other vain ambition here and now. We should be less astonished by the earlier failure and far more astonished at how little we have learned from their failure.

In a letter written in July 1840 Joseph explained:

> In order to conduct the affairs of the kingdom in righteousness it is all important, that the most perfect harmony, kind feeling, good understanding and confidence should exist in the hearts of all the brethren. And that true Charity—love one towards one another, should characterize all their proceedings. If there are any uncharitable feelings, any lack of confidence, then pride and arrogancy and envy will soon be manifested and confusion must inevitably prevail… (*Joseph Smith Papers, Documents, Volume 7*, p. 362, as in original)

In that same letter Joseph said he wished the people would progress, but did not see that possible until a different spirit led them:

> It would be gratifying to my mind to see the saints in Kirtland flourish, but think the time has not yet come and I assure you that it never will until a different order of things be established and a different spirit be manifested. (*Joseph Smith Papers, Documents, Volume 7*, p. 363)

It is in consequence of aspiring men that Kirtland has been forsaken. (*Joseph Smith Papers, Documents, Volume 7*, p. 364)

After nearly a half-year of imprisonment, Joseph described the importance of a calm mind in order to hear the still small voice of God. His mind was afire with all the distractions of being in prison, and his family and friends expelled from Missouri at gunpoint. Friends had been killed. Church members had betrayed him. God spoke to Joseph when he freed his mind of these concerns and quietly pondered, opening himself up to inspiration.

Learn from these words Joseph wrote while in Liberty Jail about how to set aside all that distracts us to hear God's voice:

> *We received some letters last evening: one from Emma, one from Don C[arlos] Smith, [and] one from bishop Partridge, all breathing a kind and consoling spirit. We were much gratified with their contents. We had been a long time without information, and when we read those letters, they were to our souls as the gentle air is refreshing. But our joy was mingled with grief because of the suffering of the poor and much injured saints, and we need not say to you that the floodgates of our hearts were hoisted, and our eyes were a fountain of tears. But those who have not been enclosed in the walls of a prison without cause or provocation can have but [a] little idea how sweet the voice of a friend is. One token of friendship from any source whatever awakens and calls into action every sympathetic feeling. It brings up in an instant everything that is passed. It seizes the present with a vivacity of lightning. It grasps after the future with the fierceness of a tiger. It retrogrades from one thing to another, until finally all enmity, malice, and hatred, and past differences, misunderstandings, and mismanagements, lie slain victims at the feet of hope. And when the heart is sufficiently contrite, then the Voice of inspiration steals along and whispers, My son, peace be unto your soul, your adversity and your afflictions shall be but a small moment, and then, if you endure it well, God shall exalt you on high[.]* (T&C 138:11)

This world is a place of trial and testing. Before creation it was planned that when we came here we would be **proven** by what we experience. **That happens now.** Prove yourself by listening to God, hearing His voice, and obeying. Sometimes we are like Alma and want to do greater things to help God's work. But the greatest work of all is to respond to God's voice and prove you're willing to listen and obey Him.

The foregoing excerpts are taken from:

- Denver's conference talk titled "Our Divine Parents" given in Gilbert, AZ on March 25th, 2018
- His remarks given at the Joseph Smith Restoration Conference in Boise, ID on June 24, 2018
- The presentation of Denver's paper titled "The Restoration's Shattered Promises and Great Hope", given at the Sunstone Symposium in Salt Lake City, UT on July 28, 2018
- Denver's remarks titled "Keep the Covenant: Do the Work" given at the Remembering the Covenants Conference in Layton, UT on August 4, 2018

105. Love, Part 6

This is the sixth part of a special series on Love, where Denver teaches us how we can live according to the two great commandments: Love God, and Love One Another.

DENVER: In this creation, there are two opposing forces that cause everything there is to be and to exist. Those two opposing forces are not good and evil, although we tend to call them 'good' and call them 'evil.' The two opposing forces are, in fact, love and fear. Everything that is generative or creative comes about as a consequence of love. If you think about all the problems that people have with one another and what would solve them, the one thing that could solve *every* problem is love—if we loved one another enough. And all of those vices—all of the suffering, the anger, the pride, the envy, the impatience, the greed—have their root in fear. "I fear I will not have enough and therefore I envy. I fear for my own inability, and therefore I resent your ability." Everything that produces negativity comes about as a consequence of fear.

Nature testifies over and over again. It doesn't matter when the sun goes down, there's going to be another dawn. It doesn't matter when all the leaves fall off the deciduous trees in the fall, there's going to come a spring. There's going to be a renewal of life. There are all kinds of animals in nature that go through this really loathsome, disgusting, wretched existence, and then they transform. And where they were a pest before, *now* they're bright, and they're colorful, and they fly, and they pollinate. Butterflies help produce the very kinds of things that their larval stage destroyed. These are signs. These are testimonies. Just like the transformation of the caterpillar into the butterfly, the pest into the thing of beauty, the thing that ate the vegetables that you were trying to grow into the thing that helps pollinate the things that you want to grow—that's the plan for all of us.

So when you study the scriptures, the objective should not be, "Can I trust the text? Can I evaluate the text? Can I use a form of criticism against the text in order to weigh, dismiss, belittle, judge?" Take all that you know about nature, take all that you know about this world and the majesty of it all, take all that you know that informs you that there is hope, there is joy, there is love. Why do you love your children? Why do your children love you? These kinds of things exist. They're real, they're tangible, and they're important; and they're part of what God did when He created this world. Keep *that* in mind when you're studying, and search the scriptures to try and help inform you how you can better appreciate, how you can better enjoy, how you can better love, how you can better have hope. What do they have to say that can bring you closer to God, not, "Can I find a way to dismiss something that Joseph said or did?"

As soon as Joseph was gone off the scene, people that envied the position that he occupied took over custody of everything, including the documents. And what we got as a consequence of that is a legacy that allowed a trillion-dollar empire to be constructed. Religion should require our sacrifice; it should not be here to benefit us. We should have to give, not get. And in the giving of ourselves, what we get is in the interior—it's in the heart. It's the things of enduring beauty and value. If your study takes you away from an appreciation of the love, the charity, the things that matter most, reorient your study.

God really is up to a work—right now. And the work that is underway *can* culminate in Zion. Covenants were made; promises were given. God has an obligation to the covenant fathers that He *will* vindicate. God's words *will* be fulfilled, all of them. None of them are going to fall to the ground unfulfilled. The question is not, "Will God bring about the culmination of all His purposes?" The question is, "Are we willing to cooperate with Him to bring those purposes to pass in our day?" It could— The offer that God makes— This appears in scripture nearly as often as the promise in Malachi. God says,

> *How oft would I have gathered you as a hen [gathers] her [chicks] under her wings....and ye would not!* (Matthew 23:37 and 3 Nephi 10:5; see also Matthew 10:36 RE and 3 Nephi 4:9 RE).

Could God have brought about His purposes and vindicated His promises in the days of Moses? Could He have done what He had promised to do when Christ was here on the earth? Could He have done it in the days of Peter? Could He have done it in the days of Joseph Smith? The question is never whether God *will* vindicate His promises. The question is, "Will there ever come a people who will respond to the Lord's willingness to gather them as a hen gathers her chicks under her wings, and be gathered, and be content with being gathered and being at peace with one another?" We have that opportunity, but so many generations before us have had the same opportunity *and they would not.*

The question isn't whether God is going to do it, or whether God is willing to do it now. The question is, "Are we willing to cooperate with Him in that process, to do our part?" We get really petty with one another, and we shouldn't be. We ought to value one another so highly that we'll do anything we can to support one another and to assist in bringing about the purposes of God. At the end of the day, obedience to God is simply blessing one another by the way we conduct ourselves. I like the Lamanite king's prayer: *I will give away all my sins to know [you]* (Alma 22:18; see also Alma 13:10 RE). We tend not to be willing to give away our sins. We want to harbor them, and cultivate them, and celebrate them. We ought to be more— We ought to love God more and our sins less. God *can* fulfill His promises in our day, before *we* leave this stage of the action. It can happen. Whether it happens or not is up to us and how interested we are in doing as He bids us.

Salvation *is* individual. There is *only* individual salvation and no such thing as collective salvation. While I accept this is true, there is something else that is equally true: God wants people to *collectively* be His. In the revelations of July 14, 2017, and Oct 4, 2018, received from God—those are in the Teachings and Commandments as sections 157 and 176—the emphasis has been on people. Both responses by the Lord have gone beyond individual salvation to focus on people, Zion, and the New Jerusalem. Consider these words from the Answer to the Prayer for Covenant, addressing the importance of God's people:

> *I, the Lord, say to you: You have asked of me concerning the scriptures prepared on [your] behalf of all those who seek to become* ***my covenant people****, and therefore I answer you on behalf of* ***all the people****, and not as to any individual. For there are those who are humble, patient, and easily persuaded. Nevertheless, people who are quarrelsome and proud are also among you, and since you seek to* ***unite*** *to become* ***one people****, I answer you as one.*
>
> *I covenanted with Adam at the beginning, which covenant was broken by mankind. Since the days of Adam I have always sought to reestablish* ***people of covenant*** *among the living, and therefore have desired that man should love one another, not begrudgingly, but as brothers and sisters indeed, that I may establish my covenant and provide* ***them*** *with light and truth.*
>
> *For the sake of the promises to the fathers [I will] labor with you as a* ***people****, and not because of you, for you have not yet become what you must be to* ***live together*** *in peace. If you will hearken [unto] my words, I will make you* ***my people*** *and my words will give you peace. Even a single soul who stirs up the hearts of others to anger can destroy the peace of all my people. Each of you must equally walk truly in my path, not only to profess, but to do as you profess.*

There are many things yet to be restored unto my people. It is ordained that some things are only to be given to ***people*** *who are mine and cannot otherwise be given to mankind on earth. You do not yet understand the glory to be revealed* ***unto my covenant people****.*

It is not enough to receive my covenant, but you must also abide it. And all who abide it, whether on this land or any other land, will be mine...I will watch over ***them*** *and protect* ***them*** *in the day of harvest, and gather* ***them****...as a hen gathers her chicks under her wings. I will number you among the remnant of Jacob, no longer outcasts, and you will inherit the promises of Israel. You shall be* ***my people*** *and I will be your God, and the sword will not devour you. And unto* ***those*** *who will receive will more be given, until* ***they*** *know the mysteries of God in full.*

You pray each time you partake of the sacrament to always have my spirit to be with you. And what is my spirit? It is to love one another as I have loved you. Do my works and you will know my doctrine, for you will uncover hidden mysteries by obedience to these things that can be uncovered in no other way. This is the way I will restore knowledge to ***my people****. If you return good for evil, you will cleanse yourself and know the joy of your Master. You call me Lord, and do well to regard me so, but to know your Lord is to love one another. Flee from the cares and longings that belong to Babylon, obtain a new heart, for you have all been wounded. In me you will find peace, and through me will come Zion, a place of peace and safety.*

Be of one heart, and regard one another with charity. Measure your words before giving voice to them, and consider the hearts of others. Although a man may err in understanding concerning many things, yet he can view his brother with charity and come unto me, and through me he can with patience overcome the world. I can bring him to understanding and knowledge. Therefore, if you regard one another with charity, then your brother's error in understanding will not divide you. I lead to all truth. I will lead ***all*** *who come to me to the truth of all things. The fullness is to receive the truth of all things, and this too from me, in power, by my word, and in very deed. For I will come unto you if you will come unto me.*

Study to learn how to respect ***your brothers and sisters*** *and to come together by precept, reason, and persuasion, rather than sharply disputing and wrongly condemning each other, causing anger. Take care how you invoke my name. Mankind has been controlled by the adversary through anger and jealousy, which has led to bloodshed and the misery of many souls. Even strong disagreements should not provoke anger, nor to invoke my name in vain as if*

> *I had part in your every dispute. Pray together in humility and together meekly present your dispute to me, and if you are contrite before me, I will tell you my part.* ([Emphasis added.] T&C 157:1-2,19,44,48,51,53-54 RE)

These are God's words in the Answer to the Prayer for Covenant. The focus is on the community and not on the individual. It's taken me years to notice that. This focus is different for a reason. Our traditions have not and cannot bring Zion. That will require viewing God's work *in a new way*. Individuals may be saved individually, and have been throughout history, but Zion is not about individual salvation. Zion is about covenant people of God—individually saved as a prerequisite, then gathered together to live in peace. As part of the same revelation, there is a covenant that contains language that also moves the focus to community instead of individual:

> *Do you covenant with [the Lord] to cease to do evil and to seek to continually do good? Second: Do you have faith in these things and receive the scriptures approved by the Lord as a standard to govern you in your daily walk in life, to accept the obligations established by the Book of Mormon as a covenant, and to use the scriptures to correct yourselves and to guide your words, thoughts, and deeds?*
>
> *Third: Do you agree to assist* ***all others*** *— who covenant to [do] likewise accept this standard to govern* ***their*** *lives — to keep the Lord's will, to succor* ***those*** *who stand in need, to lighten the burdens of* ***your brothers and sisters*** *whenever you are able, and to care for the poor among you?*
>
> *Fourth: ...do you covenant to seek to become of* ***one heart*** *with those who seek the Lord to establish His righteousness?* ([Emphasis added.] T&C 158:2-5 RE)

After those questions are answered:

> *Now, hear the words of the Lord to those who receive this covenant this day:*
>
> ***All*** *you who have turned from your wicked ways and repented of your evil doings, of lying and deceiving, and of all whoredoms, and of secret abominations, idolatries, murders, priestcrafts, envying, and strife, and from all wickedness and abominations, and have come unto me, and been baptized in my name, and have received a remission of your sins, and received the holy ghost, are now numbered with* ***my people*** *who are of the house of Israel. I say to you:*

> *Teach your children to honor me. Seek to recover the lost sheep remnant of this land and of Israel and no longer forsake them. Bring them unto me and teach them of my ways, to walk in them.*
>
> *And I, the Lord your God, will be with you and will never forsake you, and I will lead you in the path which will bring peace to you in the troubling season now fast approaching.*
>
> *I will raise you up and protect you, abide with you, and gather you in due time, and this shall be a land of promise to you as your inheritance from me.*
>
> *The earth will yield its increase, and you will flourish upon the mountains and upon the hills, and the wicked will not come against you because the fear of the Lord will be with you.*
>
> *I will visit my house, which the remnant of my people shall build, and I will dwell therein, to be* ***among you****, and no one will need...say, Know ye the Lord, for you all shall know me, from the least to the greatest.*
>
> *I will teach you things that have been hidden from the foundation of the world and your understanding will reach unto Heaven.*
>
> *And you shall be called the children of the Most High God, and I will preserve you against the harvest.*
>
> *And the angels sent to harvest the world will gather the wicked into bundles to be burned, but will* ***pass over you as my peculiar treasure****.*
>
> *But if you do not honor me, nor seek to recover my people Israel, nor teach your children to honor me, nor care for the poor among you, nor help lighten one another's burdens, then you have no promise from me and I will raise up other* ***people*** *who will honor and serve me, and give unto them this land, and if* ***they*** *repent, I will abide with* ***them****.* ([Emphasis added.] T&C 158:9-19 RE)

People claim they have kept the covenant, but such claims cannot possibly be true. God's covenant is for and about people—His people. It is not possible for an individual to keep the covenant. Everybody rises together or everybody falls together. The covenant can only be kept as a community. Individuals acting alone can never accomplish what is required of the group. The October 4, 2018, revelation—T&C 176—also focuses on community. It begins by addressing people, and not the individual. The Lord's voice to people begins and ends with two questions. After asking the questions a second time, He gives an answer to what ought to have been learned. Hear the Lord's words to the people:

> *You ask on behalf of my people, and therefore I answer my people. Hear, therefore, my words:*
>
> *What have you learned? What ought you to have learned?*
>
> *[And then at the end:] I ask again, What have you learned? What ought you to have learned?*
>
> *I say to you that there is need for but one house, and I accept the statement you have adopted, and approve it as your statement to be added. But I say again, there was honor in the labor of others. Whereas I look upon the heart and see faithful service, many among you do not look at, nor see, nor value what I, the Lord, love in the hearts of my people. As I have said before, I say again: Love one another, labor willingly alongside each other. Learn what you ought, and when I ask you to labor, do so wisely, even if you know not beforehand what you will find. I do not ask what you cannot do. Trust my words and proceed always in faith, believing that with me all things are possible.* ***All who have been faithful are mine****.* ([Emphasis added.] T&C 176:1-2, 12-13 RE)

Just as an aside, when the sacrament was passed and the group of brethren who came up here to perform that came up on stage in flannel, and shorts, and motley colored shirts—to look upon that, to me, was a delight. It was a statement of the fact that righteousness holds no costume up, to pretend to be something it isn't. Righteousness comes in divergent forms and manifests itself in unexpected ways. Had any one of those individuals come up to pass the sacrament among *some* congregations, dressed as they were today, they would have excited the judgment, the censure, the horror of someone observing them in that garb. But to us it's accepted and it's acceptable. I would hope that if one among us chose to wear a white shirt and a tie to come up to pass the sacrament, while standing among them that none of us would look upon that judgmentally and with disfavor, but that everyone would be welcomed, everyone would be accepted. And that we would be just as tolerant of others and their idiosyncrasies as we are of what we expect to be among us.

God mentions 'His people' in order to get our attention. The prophecies of God's last-days work and the fulfillment of God's covenants with the fathers are not merely for individual salvation. The covenants are about people, or a divinely-organized community. Righteous individuals, isolated and scattered throughout the world, are incapable of vindicating the promises made to the fathers. There *must* be people gathered together and living the correct pattern *before* the Lord returns.

There have been only two societies in recorded history that became Zion. Because of the age of the world at the time, both were taken up into heaven. We have very little to help us understand *why* these two succeeded. Apart from describing them as *of one heart, one mind...and...no poor among them,* we know little else. (See Moses 7:18; see also Genesis 4:14 RE and T&C 175:39 RE.) But perhaps that is one of the most important things we *can* know about them. Maybe the point is that *nothing,* and *no one,* stood out as remarkable or different within the community. There were no heroes and no villains, no rich and no poor, no Shakespearean plot lines of betrayal, intrigue, ambition, conflict, and envy. There was no adultery, theft, robbery, murder, immorality, and drunkenness—in other words, nothing to entertain us—because *all our* stories, movies, music, novels, television plots, and social media are based upon and captivated by everything that is *missing* from these societies.

The centuries-long period of peace described in the Book of Mormon occupies only a few short pages in 4 Nephi. Their society was marked by the presence of peace, the absence of conflict, and abiding stability. This is what they attained:

> *There were no contentions and disputations among them, and every man did deal justly one with another. And they had all things common among them; therefore there were not rich and poor, bond and free, but they were all made free and partakers of the heavenly gift.* (4 Nephi 1:2-3; see also 4 Nephi 1:1 RE)

Because there was no future ministry for them to perform, their Zion society was not taken up to heaven. Because the world was not yet ready for the Lord to return in judgment, neither Enoch nor Melchizedek returned with their people to fall on *their* necks and kiss *them.* These people were most remarkable for what they *lacked.* How they grew to lack these divisions, contentions, and disputes is described in very few, simple words:

> *They did walk after the commandments which they had received from the Lord...their God, continuing in fasting and prayer, and in meeting together oft both to pray and to hear the word of the Lord. And it came to pass...there was no contention among all the people, in all the land.* (4 Nephi 1:12-13; see also 4 Nephi 1:2 RE)

What were the names of their leaders? We don't know because, apparently, there were none. Who were their great teachers? Again, we don't know because they were not identified. Who governed? Apparently no one. They had things in common, obeyed God's commandments, and spent time praying and hearing the word of the Lord. They were *so very unlike us*. To make the point clear for us, the record of these people explains:

> *There was no contention in the land because of the love of God which did dwell in the hearts of the people. And there were no envyings, nor strifes, nor tumults, nor whoredoms, nor lyings, nor murders, nor any manner of lasciviousness.* (4 Nephi 1:15-16; see also 4 Nephi 1:3 RE)

All the negatives were missing because the love of God dwelt in their hearts. Something else describes them:

> *And surely there could not be a happier people among all the people who had been created by the hand of God.* (4 Nephi 1:16; see also 4 Nephi 1:3 RE)

Consider those words carefully. You cannot be happier than by allowing the love of God to dwell in you. The happiest people who have ever lived did so by the profound peace they displayed, equality they shared, fairness they showed one another, and love of God in their hearts. This is a description of our social opposites. Reviewing the Answer to the Prayer for Covenant, the Covenant, and the recent Parable of the Master's House shows that the Lord is pleading for *us* to become *this*. It's not easy. It will require civilizing the uncivilized. However, it is necessary to become the wise virgins and the invited guests wearing the wedding garment.

Five of the virtuous virgins who were *expecting the wedding party to arrive* were, nevertheless, excluded. They were virgins like the others, but the others were allowed to enter and they were not. They did not lack virginity. They did not lack notice. They were not surprised by an unexpected wedding party arriving. But they lacked *oil*, which is a symbol of the Holy Ghost. They failed to acquire the necessary spirit with which to avoid conflict, envy, strife, tumult, and contention. To grow into the kind of people God will want to welcome into His dwelling requires practice, experience, and effort. People have not done it. Devout, religious people are *not prepared* to live in peace, with all things in common, with no poor among them. God is trying to create a civilization that does not yet exist.

It is a *privilege* for God to give guidance to help prepare His people. There has always been a promise from the Lord that those who inherit Zion will be given commandments from Him to follow. He declared:

Yea, blessed are they whose feet stand upon the land of Zion, who have obeyed my gospel; for **they** shall receive for **their** reward the good things of the earth, and it shall bring forth...its strength. And they shall also be crowned with blessings from above, yea...with commandments not a few, and with revelations in their time—[that] they...are faithful and [diligently] before me. ([Emphasis added.] D&C 59:3-4; see also T&C 46:1 RE)

Those who mock or criticize efforts to complete the Restoration are defining themselves as unworthy by their own words. *No matter how good they may otherwise be*, when they embrace conflict, envy, strife, tumult, and contention, they cannot be invited to the wedding of the Lamb.

We need more commandments from God to prepare for what is coming. The example in 4 Nephi commends those people who walk after the commandments received from our Lord and God. There should be fasting and prayer. People should meet together, pray, and review the words of the Lord. Every step taken will make us more like those virgins who have oil in their lamps and less like the foolish virgins who took no effort to make the required preparation.

It's not enough to avoid outright evil—we have to be good. Being 'good' means to be separate from the world, united in charity towards each other, and to have united hearts. If we are ready when the wedding party arrives, we must follow the Lord's *commandments to us*. They are for our good. He wants us to awaken and arise from an awful slumber.

The third such society will not be taken into heaven; instead it will welcome the return of the first two to the earth. Why would ancient, righteous societies caught up to heaven want to leave there to come and meet with a city of people on earth? Why would they fall on their necks and kiss *that* gathered body of believers? And above all else, why would Christ want to occupy a tabernacle and dwell with such a community? Obviously, because there will be people living on earth whose civilization is like the society in heaven.

The Ten Commandments outlines basic social norms needed for peace and stability. Christ's Sermon on the Mount was His exposition on the Ten Commandments. He expounded on the need to align the intent of the heart with God's standard to love your fellow man, do good to those who abuse you, and hold no anger—He took us deeper. Where the Ten Commandments allowed reluctant, resentful, and hard-hearted conformity, the Sermon on the Mount requires a willing readiness to obey. Christ wants us to act with alacrity to follow Him. He taught us to treat others as you would want to be treated.

The answer to these questions is easy to conceptualize and easy to verbalize, but living the answer is beyond mankind's ability to endure. We do not want to lay down our pride, ambition, jealousy, envy, strife, and lusts to become *that* community. Everybody will have to make changes. The most important changes have been provided in a blueprint revealed in the Answer to Prayer for Covenant, including the terms of the covenant. We are expected to remember and obey these words:

> *My will is to have you love one another. As people, you lack the ability to respectfully disagree among one another.*
>
> *Wisdom counsels mankind to align their words with their hearts, but mankind refuses to take counsel from Wisdom.*
>
> *There have been sharp disputes between you that should have been avoided. I speak these words to reprove you that you may learn, not to upbraid you so that you mourn. I want my people to have understanding.*
>
> *Satan is a title and means accuser, opponent, and adversary; hence once he fell, Lucifer became, or in other words was called, Satan, because he accuses others and opposes the Father. I rebuked Peter and called him Satan because he was wrong in opposing the Father's will for me, and Peter understood and repented.*
>
> *In the work you have performed there are those who have been Satan, accusing one another, wounding hearts, and causing jarring, contention, and strife by their accusations. Rather than loving one another, even among you who desire a good thing, some have dealt unkindly as if they were...opponents, accusers, and adversaries. In this they were wrong.*
>
> *For you are like a man who seeks for good fruit from a neglected vineyard — unwatered, undunged, unpruned, and unattended. How shall it produce good fruit if you fail to tend it? What reward does the unfaithful husbandman obtain from his neglected vineyard? How can saying you are a faithful husbandman ever produce good fruit in the vineyard without doing the work of the husbandman? For you seek my words to recover them even as*

you forsake to do them. You have heretofore produced wild fruit, bitter and ill-formed, because you neglect to do my words.

You have not yet become what you must be to live together in peace. If you will hearken to my words, I will make you my people and my words will give you peace. Even a single soul who stirs up the hearts of others to anger can destroy the peace of all my people. Each of you must equally walk truly in my path, not only to profess, but to do as you profess.

The Book of Mormon was given as my covenant for this day and contains my gospel, which came forth to allow people to understand my work and [to] obtain my salvation. Yet many of you are like those who reject the Book of Mormon, because you say, but you do not do. As a people you honor with your lips, but your hearts are corrupt, filled with envy and malice, returning evil for good, sparing none — even those with pure hearts among you — from your unjustified accusations and unkind backbiting. You have not obtained the fullness of my salvation because you do not draw near to me.

Hear therefore my words: Repent and bring forth fruit showing repentance, and I will establish my covenant with you and claim you as mine.

[It's] not enough to receive my covenant, but you must also abide it. And all who abide it, whether on this land or any other land, will be mine, and I will watch over them and protect them in the day of harvest, and gather them...as a hen gathers her chicks under her wings. I will number you among the remnant of Jacob, no longer outcasts, and you will inherit the promises of Israel. You shall be my people and I will be your God, and the sword will not devour you. And unto those who will receive will more be given, until they know the mysteries of God in full.

You pray each time you partake of the sacrament to always have my spirit to be with you. And what is my spirit? It is to love one another as [I've] loved you. Do my works and you will know my doctrine, for you will uncover hidden mysteries by obedience to these things that can be uncovered in no other way. This is the way I will restore knowledge to my people. If you return good for evil, you will cleanse yourself and know the joy of your Master. You call me Lord, and do well to regard me so, but to know your Lord is to love one another. Flee from the cares and longings that belong to Babylon, obtain a new heart, for you have all been wounded. In me you will find peace, and through me will come Zion, a place of peace and safety.

> *Be of one heart...regard one another with charity. Measure your words before giving voice to them.*
>
> *There remains [a] great work yet to be done. Receive my covenant and abide in it, not as in the former time when jarring, jealousy, contention, and backbiting caused anger, broke hearts, and hardened the souls of those claiming to be my saints. But receive it in spirit, in meekness, and in truth. I have given you a former commandment that I, the Lord, will forgive whom I will forgive, but of you it is required to forgive all men. And again, I have taught [you] that if you forgive men their trespasses, your Heavenly Father will also forgive you; but if you forgive not men their trespasses, neither will your Heavenly Father forgive your trespasses. How do I act toward mankind? If men intend no offense, I take no offense, but if they are taught and should have obeyed, then I reprove and correct, and forgive and forget. You cannot be at peace with one another if you take offense when none is intended. But again I say, Judge not others except by the rule you want used to weigh yourself.* (T&C 157:3,4,5,8,9,17,19,20,23,48,51,53,58 RE)

One of the questions that someone asked is, "Why are we admonished to pursue judgment?" The answer are those words I just read to you: "*I say, Judge not others except by the rule you want used to weigh yourself.*" Pursue judgment whenever the opportunity presents itself. Use judgment to evaluate based upon the standard you want applied to yourself, and pursue judgment.

> *The earth groans under the wickedness of mankind upon her face, and she longs for peace to come. She withholds the abundance of her bounty because of the offenses of men against me, against one another, and against her. But if righteousness returns and my people prove by their actions, words, and thoughts to yield to my spirit and hearken to my commandments, then will the earth rejoice, for the feet of those who cry peace upon her mountains are beautiful indeed, and I, the Lord, will bring again Zion, and the earth will rejoice.*
>
> *In the world, tares are ripening. And so I ask you, What of the wheat?*
>
> *Cry peace. Proclaim my words. Invite those who will repent to be baptized and forgiven, and they shall obtain my spirit to guide them.* (T&C 157:63, 64, 65 RE)

That excerpt contains nearly 2,000 words of instruction. There is no basis to claim ignorance. Is it possible for people to change their civilization and go from strident, quarrelsome, and pugnaciousness, to loving one another?

Perhaps the Book of Mormon contains one account to give *us* hope. Following conversion, one group of Lamanites were led by a king who encouraged them to lay down their unbloodied weapons rather than *ever* shed blood again. This meant they could not defend themselves. After their king finished his proposal, this took place:

> *And now it came to pass that when the king had made an end of these sayings, and all the people were assembled together, they took their swords and all [their] weapons which were used for the shedding of man's blood, and they did bury them up deep in the earth.*
>
> *And this they did, it being in their view a testimony to God, and also to men, that they never would use weapons again for the shedding of man's blood; and this they did vouching and covenanting with God, that rather than shed the blood of their brethren they would give up their own lives; and rather than take away from a brother they would give unto him; and rather than spend their days in idleness they would labor abundantly with their hands.*
>
> *And thus we see that, when these Lamanites were brought to believe and to know the truth, [that] they were firm, and would suffer even unto death rather than commit sin; and thus we see that they buried the weapons of peace, or they buried [their] weapons of war, for peace.* (Alma 24:17-19; see also Alma 14:9 RE)

When their resolve was tested, they passed. Rather than take up arms they laid down their lives:

> *Now when the people saw that they were coming against them they went out to meet them and prostrated themselves before them to the earth, and began to call on the name of the Lord; and thus they were in [the] attitude when the Lamanites began to fall upon them, and began to slay them with the sword.*
>
> *...Thus without meeting any resistance, they did slay a thousand and five of them; and we know that they are blessed, for they have gone to dwell with their God.*
>
> *Now when the Lamanites saw that their brethren would not flee from the sword, neither would they turn aside to the right...or...the left, but that they would lie down and perish, and praised God even in the very act of perishing under the sword—*
>
> *Now when the Lamanites saw this they did forbear from slaying them; and there were many whose hearts had swollen in them for those of their brethren*

> *who had fallen under the sword, for they repented of the [thing] which they had done.*
>
> *And it came to pass that* ***they*** *threw down* ***their*** *weapons of war, and they would not take them again, for they were* ***stung*** *for the murders which they'd committed; and they came down even as their brethren, relying upon the mercies of those whose arms were lifted [up] to slay them.*
>
> *And it came to pass that the people of God were joined that day by more than the number who had been slain.* ([Emphasis added.] Alma 24:21-26; see also Alma 14:10-12 RE)

This event is astonishing, and many have been shocked by the extreme behavior of these believers. *We* are not being asked to lay down our weapons and be killed. *We* are only being asked to lay down our hostility, slander, and abuse of one another—to become peaceful and loving. This is a good thing that benefits everybody. Despite this, we keep our pride, ambition, jealousy, envy, strife, and lusts. These destructive desires are *preferred* over forgiving offenses in meekness, love, and kindness.

None of us are asked to die for a covenant, but are only asked to be more like Christ, and forgive and love one another. This seems so difficult a challenge that we quarrel and dispute among ourselves. We remain haughty and self-righteous, and fail to realize self-righteousness is a lie, a mirage, utterly untrue. We must trade our pride for humility or we will never be able to keep the covenant. Remember, it is a group who must keep the covenant, not individuals. Together we must act consistent with the obligation *we agreed* to perform before God.

As aggravating and trying as people are on one another, we need to go through this. There is no magic path to loving one another. Some people refuse and must be left outside. When it comes to loving others, some things must be abandoned, some things must be added, some things must be forgotten, and some things must be ignored. But learning what to abandon, add, forget, or ignore is only through the *doing*. We chip away at ourselves and others by interacting and sharing.

We will learn things about one another that will distress us, and we may well wish we didn't know some things about others. How will the socially offensive become socially acceptable without help from a loving society? And how can a society become loving if people are not broad-minded enough to figure out that some things just don't matter? Few things really are important. If a man is honest, just, virtuous, and true, should you care if he swears? If a man has a heart of gold and would give you assistance if he thought it was needed, should you care if he is rough and uncouth?

The adulterous and predatory will rarely reform, and must often be excluded. They will victimize and destroy. We are commanded to cast out those who steal, love and make a lie, commit adultery, and refuse to repent. The instructions we have been given state:

> *You shall not kill; he that kills shall die. You shall not steal...he that steals and will not repent shall be cast out. You shall not lie; he that lies and will not repent shall be cast out. You shall love your wife with all your heart, and shall cleave unto her and none else...he that looks upon a woman to lust after her shall deny the faith, and shall not have the spirit, and if he repent not...shall be cast out. You shall not commit adultery, and he that commits adultery and repents not shall be cast out; and he that commits adultery and repents with all his heart, and forsakes [it] and does it no more, you shall forgive him; but if he does it again, he shall not be forgiven, [and] shall be cast out. You shall not speak evil of your neighbor [nor] or do him any harm. You know my laws, they are given in my scriptures. He that sins and repents not shall be cast out. If you love me, you shall serve me and keep all my commandments.* (T&C 26:6 RE; see also D&C 42:19-29)

This teaching is still binding. If your fellowship includes those who *ought to be cast out*, you have the obligation to do so rather than encouraging evil. Be patient, but be firm. If a person refuses to repent and forsake sins, you may end fellowship with them, and include those who are interested in practicing obedience and love.

There is work to be done; almost all of it is internal to us. The five prepared virgins and the strangers who brought a wedding garment will be those who keep the covenant. It is designed to give birth to a new society, new culture, and permit a new civilization to be founded.

STEPHANIE: So, in Mark chapter five, verses 44 and ~~43~~ [45] (And you have to excuse me. I have had a terrible cold, and so forgive whatever comes out):

> *And one of the scribes came, and having heard them reasoning together, and perceiving that he had answered them well, asked him, Which is the first commandment...? And Jesus answered him, The first of all the commandments is: Listen, and hear, O Israel, the Lord our God is one Lord. And you shall love the Lord your God with all your heart, and with all your*

> *soul, and with all your mind, and with all your strength. This is the first commandment. And the second is like [unto] this: You shall love your neighbor* ***as yourself****. There is no other commandment greater than these. And the scribe said unto Him, Well, Master, you have said the truth; for there is one God, and there is none other but him. And to love him with all the heart, and with all the understanding, and with all the soul, and with all the strength, and to love his neighbor* ***as himself****, is more than all whole burnt offerings and sacrifices.* ([Emphasis added.] Mark 5:44-45 RE; see also Mark 12:28-33)

So, the question is, "What is this thing about loving yourself?" 'Kay? I'm not sure, but let's take a look at it. So, I'm wondering if God gives "*love your neighbor as yourself*" as the second great commandment because He thinks we're all egomaniacal narcissists, and the only possible way we're able to love *other people* is if we love them as much as we love ourselves? Yes? No, I don't think so. Because there are plenty of examples of people who are literally selfless people, and who give up their lives and everything they have for other people. So, that can't be it.

So, let's start with Romans 1:65:

> *Therefore, owe no man anything but to love one another, for he that loves another has fulfilled the law for this: You shall not commit adultery, You shall not kill, You shall not steal, You shall not bear false witness, You shall not covet; and if there is any other commandment, it is briefly comprehended in this saying — namely, You shall love your neighbor as yourself (love works no ill to his neighbor; therefore, love is the fulfilling of the law) and that, knowing the time — that now...is high time to awake out of sleep, for now is our salvation nearer than when we believed.* (Romans 1:65 RE; see also Romans 13:8-11)

Did you all catch that? If there is any other commandment, it is briefly comprehended in the command to "*love your neighbor as yourself.*" If you love God and your neighbor, the other eight commandments take care of themselves because people who love each other work no ill to their neighbor. Therefore, love is the fulfilling of the law, and our salvation is nearer than when we believed. So it is, quite literally, time to wake up.

The foregoing excerpts are taken from:

- Denver's *Christian Reformation Lecture Series*, Talk #7, given in Boise, Idaho, on November 3, 2018,
- Denver's remarks titled "Book of Mormon as Covenant," given at the Book of Mormon Covenant Conference in Columbia, South Carolina, on January 13, 2019,
- Denver's conference talk titled "Civilization," given in Grand Junction, Colorado, on April 21, 2019, and
- Stephanie Snuffer's remarks titled "Love Others As Yourself," given at a regional conference in Sandy, Utah, on July 14, 2019.

106. Forgiving Others

Today, Denver and Stephanie discuss the mandatory condition that we forgive others in order to obtain forgiveness ourselves.

STEPHANIE: When I read an article or hear a news story about some tremendous act of forgiveness, on the part of someone who has given absolution to another person for some grievous offense, I think, "So *what*?!" The dad who forgives the drunk driver who killed his entire family; the woman who forgives the man who raped her; the elderly man who doesn't hold a grudge against the businessman who conned him and stole all his money—so what?!

We treat these instances as though they are great acts of emotional heroism. We heap praise and adulation upon the people who are so magnanimous that they forgave the horrible bastard who grieved or assaulted or offended them. It's ridiculous! We *lie* to ourselves when and if we think we are *ever* justified in resentment, grudges, judgments, or accusations. *We are not—ever.*

The Lord's standard is pretty clear, and there's not much wiggle room. You want Heavenly Father to forgive *you*? You forgive each other. That sounds like a really good way of *loving yourself*. Forgiveness is a requirement—it is a condition—and the Lord has this to say about it—3 Nephi 5:34:

> *And forgive us our debts as we forgive our debtors....For if ye forgive men their trespasses, your Heavenly Father will also forgive you, but if [you] forgive not men their trespasses, neither will your Father forgive your trespasses.* (3 Nephi 5:34 RE; see also 3 Nephi 13:11, 14-15)

Colossians 1:13:

> *Put on therefore as the elect of God, holy and beloved, hearts of mercies, kindness, humility of mind, meekness, long-suffering, bearing with one another and forgiving one another. If any man have a quarrel against any, even as Christ forgave you, so also do you; and above all these things put on charity, which is the bond of perfectness...Let the word of Christ dwell in you richly, in all wisdom, teaching and admonishing one another in psalms, and hymns, and spiritual songs, singing with grace in your hearts to the Lord. And whatever you do in word or deed, do all in the name of the Lord Jesus, giving thanks to God and the Father by him.* (Colossians 1:13 RE; see also Colossians 3:12-14, 16-17)

This sounds like loving yourself. Teachings and Commandments section 157:58:

> *I have given you a former commandment that I, the Lord, will forgive whom I will forgive, but of you it is required to forgive all men. And again, I have taught that if you forgive men their trespasses, your Heavenly Father will also forgive you; but if you forgive not men their trespasses, neither will your Heavenly Father forgive your trespasses....If men intend no offense, I take no offense, but if they are taught and should have obeyed, then I reprove and correct, and forgive and forget.* (T&C 157:58 RE)

Just as a side note, I'm pretty sure Nephi did not love his brothers, 'kay? I just don't think he did. They were abusive; they were violent; and they were fratricidal, okay? But, this is what he does—Nephi 2:4:

> *And it came to pass that when I, Nephi, had spoken these words unto my brethren, they were angry with me. [Yes, so what's new? They were always angry with him.] But it came to pass that I prayed unto the Lord, saying, O Lord, according to **my** faith which is in thee, wilt thou deliver me from the hands of my brethren?...And it came to pass that when I said these words, behold, the bands were loosed from off my hands and feet, and I stood before my brethren and I spake unto them again...And it came to pass that I did frankly forgive them all that they had done, and I did exhort them that they would pray unto the Lord their God for forgiveness...And after they had done praying unto the Lord, we did again travel on our journey towards the tent of our father.* ([Emphasis added.] 1 Nephi 2:4 RE; see also 1 Nephi 7:16-18, 21)

Genesis 11:4-9— Again, another story of fratricide, 'kay? Pretty sure Joseph didn't love his brothers, and his brothers certainly didn't love him, because—Genesis 11:4-9:

> *And a certain man found him, and behold, he was wandering in the field. And the man asked him, saying, What do you seek? And he said, I seek my [brothers]; tell me, I pray you, where they feed their flocks. And the man said, They are departed from here, for I heard them say, Let us go to Dothan. And Joseph went after his brethren and found them...*
>
> [And when he comes, they see him]...*and they [conspire] against to slay him. And they said one to another, Behold, this **dreamer** comes.* [They don't even call him by name, okay? They have so much contempt for Joseph that they just call him "the dreamer."] *Come now therefore and let us slay*

> *him and cast him into [the] pit, and we will say some evil beast has devoured him, and we shall see what will become of his dreams.*
>
> *And Reuben heard it, and he delivered him out of their hands and said, [Let's] not kill him. And Reuben said...Shed no blood, but cast him into this pit...*[That's great—we'll just cast him in this pit. Verse 7:]
>
> *And it came to pass when Joseph had come unto his brethren...they stripped Joseph out of his coat, his coat of many colors that was on him...they took him and cast him into a pit. And the pit was empty,* [and] *there was no water...*
>
> *And they sat down to eat... [And lo and behold, they see] a company of Ishmaelites [coming] from Gilead with their camels bearing spicery, and balm, and myrrh, going to carry it down to Egypt. And Judah said...[Hey,] What profit [it is] if we slay...and conceal his blood? Come...let us sell him to the Ishmaelites, and let not our hand be upon him, for he is our brother and our flesh.* [Well, that's nice. We don't hate him enough to kill him, but we just sell him to this band of Ishmaelites.] *And his brethren were content.*
>
> [So, they sell him for 20 pieces of silver. Reuben went back to the pit; Joseph wasn't in it. He rent his clothes.] *And he returned to his brethren and said, The child is not; and I, where shall I go? And they took Joseph's coat...killed a...[goat]...dipped the coat in blood. And they sent the coat of many colors, and they brought it to their father and they said,* ["Oh, oh, oh, it's so terrible!"] ([Emphasis added.] Genesis 11:4-9 RE; see also Genesis 37:15-32)

Okay, so you know the story. Lots of stuff happens, and then this—Genesis 11:39 and 40:

> *Then Joseph could not refrain himself before all them that stood by him, and he cried, Cause every man to go out from me! And there stood no man with him while Joseph made himself known unto his brethren. And he wept aloud, and the Egyptians and the house of Pharaoh heard. And Joseph said unto his brethren, I am Joseph. Does my father yet live? And his brethren could not answer him, for they were troubled at his presence. [Because, yeah, "What happened to you?"] And Joseph said unto his brethren, Come near to me, I pray you. And they came near. And he said, I am Joseph, your brother whom you sold into Egypt. Now therefore be not grieved nor angry with yourselves that you sold me here, for God did send me before you to preserve life. For these two years has the famine been in the land, and yet there are five years in which there shall neither be plowing nor harvest. And God sent me before you*

> *to preserve [your] posterity [and] the earth and to save your lives by a great deliverance. So now it was not you that sent me here, but God. And he has made me a father to Pharaoh, and [a] lord of all his house, and a ruler throughout all the [lands] of Egypt.* [And more happens, and more happens.]
>
> *And he fell upon his brother Benjamin's neck and wept. And Benjamin wept upon his neck. And he kissed all his brethren and [he] wept upon them. And after that, his brethren talked with him.* [Wow!] (Genesis 11:39-40 RE; see also Genesis 45:1-15)

The foregoing scriptures illustrate that forgiveness, intercession, and relationships *do not* have to be based on love, as we culturally define it here.

DENVER: Everything Christ taught is tended to change our inner self. He did not want me judging and condemning you. If you decide to abuse me, Christ teaches I should forgive you. If you offend me seventy times seven, Christ taught me to forgive. If we believed in Christ enough to live as He taught, our families would heal, our communities would heal, our nations would heal, and the world would heal. Christ was an idealist, but He showed by His life that it is possible to live the ideal. As a Christian I should commit to that ideal, and at every missed step resolve to do better. Each of us control only our own life, but your example is enough to change the lives of many others.

In His kindness and mercy, Christ revealed yet more of His suffering in His atoning sacrifice in February of 2005, and December of 2007. Again, He provided us with a description of what happened in Gethsemane:

> *The* ***greater difficulty*** *in these paired waves of torment was* ***always*** *overcoming the suffering of the* ***victim****. With these waves the Lord learned to overcome the* ***victims'*** *resentments, to forgive, and to heal both body and spirit. This was* ***more*** *difficult than overcoming the struggles arising from the one who* ***committed*** *the evil. This is because the one doing evil knows he has done wrong and feels a natural regret when he sees himself aright. The victim, however, always feels it is their right to hold resentment, to judge their persecutor, and to withhold peace and love from their fellow man. The Lord was required to overcome* ***both*** *so that He could succor both.*
>
> *In the pairing of the waves, the first torment was of the mind and spirit, and the second was torment of mind, spirit, and body.*

> *The Lord experienced all the horror and regret wicked men feel for their crimes when they finally see the truth. He experienced the suffering of their* ***victims*** *whose righteous anger and natural resentment and disappointment* ***must also be shed****, and forgiveness given, in order for them to find peace. He overcame them all. He descended below them all. He comprehends it all.* ([Emphasis added.] T&C 161:19-21)

D&C 1, verse 31. Oh, here the Lord says it right to us, again, right now, in this dispensation. D&C section 1, verse 31: *For I the Lord cannot look upon sin with the least degree of allowance* (D&C 1:31; see also T&C 54:5 RE). So, contrast that with, "I cannot look at myself without the *enormous* latitude of allowance because I'm very forgiving of myself." You would be better off saying, "I will recognize, I will admit, and I will hold myself to *every failing* that I am prone to make. But as for all the rest of you, I don't see anything wrong with any of you. I can't detect a flaw in the least, because I'm going to judge you by the standard with which I would like to be measured; which is, I take no offense, I freely forgive."

There's an expression— It's found in places some of you would find dubious, but there's an expression about how some people do not "taste death." The statement that they do not taste death doesn't mean they don't die. It just means that their death is sweet because they die in companionship with those on the other side who bring them through that veil of death in a joyful experience.

There are a handful of people who have reported that, as they were dying, angels came and ministered to them. I think *all* authentic Christians, in *any* age, belonging to *any* denomination—I don't care what the denomination is —I think *all authentic Christians* who depart this world find that death is sweet to them and that they are in the company of angels as they leave this world. And I don't think it matters that the *brand* that you swore allegiance to —and you contributed your resources to support— matter anywhere near as much as whether you believe in Christ, whether you accept the notions that He advances about the Sermon on the Mount, and whether you try to incorporate and live them in your life.

Jesus took the Law of Moses as 'the standard.' What the Sermon on the Mount does is say, "Here is the standard, but your conduct should not be merely *this*." 'Thou shalt not kill' is not enough—you must avoid being angry with your brother; you must forgive those who offend you; you must pray for those who despitefully use you. Just refraining from murdering one another, with a reluctant heart, bearing malice at them—"Well, I didn't kill the guy, but I got even!"—that's not enough! That's *not* the standard that Christ is advancing. 'Thou shalt not commit adultery' is not good enough—don't look upon a woman to lust after her in your heart.

Jesus is saying, "Here's the law—and you can do all of those things and be malevolent; you can be angry; you can be bitter; you can be contemptible; you can hold each other out as objects of ridicule—its purpose is to make you something more lovely, more wonderful, more kindly, more Christian." Christ says to be like Him. The Sermon on the Mount is an explanation of what it's like to be like Him.

Perhaps the Book of Mormon contains one account to give *us* hope. Following conversion, one group of Lamanites were led by a king who encouraged them to lay down their unbloodied weapons rather than *ever* shed blood again. This meant they could not defend themselves. After their king finished his proposal, this took place:

> *And now it came to pass that when the king had made an end of these sayings...all the people were assembled together, they took their swords, and all the weapons which were used for the shedding of man's blood, and they did bury them up deep in the earth.*
>
> *And this they did, it being in their view a testimony to God, and also to men, that they never would use weapons again for the shedding of man's blood; and this they did vouching and covenanting with God, that rather than shed the blood of their brethren they would give up their own lives; and rather than take away from a brother they would give unto him; and rather than spend their days in idleness they would labor abundantly with their hands.*
>
> *And thus we see that, when these Lamanites were brought to believe and to know the truth, [that] they were firm, and would suffer even unto death rather than commit sin; and thus we see that they buried the weapons of peace, or they buried [their] weapons of war, for peace.* (Alma 24:17-19; see also Alma 14:9 RE)

When their resolve was tested, they passed. Rather than take up arms they laid down their lives:

> *Now when the people saw that they were coming against them they went out to meet them, and prostrated themselves before them to the earth, and began to call on the name of the Lord; and thus they were in [the] attitude when the Lamanites began to fall upon them, and began to slay them with the sword.*

> *...Thus without meeting any resistance, they did slay a thousand and five of them; and we know that they are blessed, for they have gone to dwell with their God.*
>
> *Now when the Lamanites saw that their brethren would not flee from the sword, neither would they turn aside to the right...or...the left, but that they would lie down and perish, and praised God even in the very act of perishing under the sword—*
>
> *Now when the Lamanites saw this they did forbear from slaying them; and there were many whose hearts had swollen in them for those of their brethren who had fallen under the sword, for they repented of the thing which they had done.*
>
> *And it came to pass that* ***they*** *threw down* ***their*** *weapons of war, and they would not take them again, for they were* ***stung*** *for the murders which they had committed; and they came down even as their brethren, relying upon the mercies of those whose arms were lifted [up] to slay them.*
>
> *And it came to pass that the people of God were joined* ***that*** *day by* ***more*** *than the number who had been slain.* ([Emphasis added.] Alma 24:21-26; see also Alma 14:10-12 RE)

This event is astonishing, and many have been shocked by the extreme behavior of these believers. *We* are not being asked to lay down our weapons and be killed. *We* are only being asked to lay down our hostility, slander, and abuse of one another to become peaceful and loving. This is a good thing that benefits everybody. Despite this, we keep our pride, ambition, jealousy, envy, strife, and lusts. These destructive desires are *preferred* over forgiving offenses in meekness, love, and kindness.

None of us are asked to die for a covenant, but are only asked to be more like Christ and forgive and love one another. This seems so difficult a challenge that we quarrel and dispute among ourselves. We remain haughty and self-righteous, and fail to realize self-righteousness is a lie, a mirage, utterly untrue. We must trade our pride for humility, or we will never be able to keep the covenant. Remember, it is a group who must keep the covenant, not individuals. Together we must act consistent with the obligation *we agreed* to perform before God.

Once you begin to repent, the real work commences. God forgives; but retaining forgiveness requires that we follow Him. We're not going to develop into His children until we have become acquainted with His way. He tells us what we must do to learn of Him. We must do His work—join in His labor —to save souls:

> *And as ye would that men should do to you, do ye also to them likewise.*
>
> *For if ye love them which love you, what thank have ye? for sinners also love those that love them.*
>
> *And if ye do good to them which do good to you, what thank have ye? for sinners also do even the same.*
>
> *And if ye lend to them…whom ye hope to receive, what thank have ye? for sinners also lend to sinners, to receive as much again.*
>
> *But love ye your enemies, and do good, and lend, hoping for nothing again; and your reward shall be great, and ye shall be the children of the Highest: for he is kind unto the [un]thankful and [unto] the evil.*
>
> *Be ye therefore merciful, as your Father also is merciful.*
>
> *Judge not, and ye shall not be judged: condemn not, and ye shall not be condemned: forgive, and ye shall be forgiven:*
>
> *Give, and it shall be given unto you; good measure, pressed down, and shaken together, and running over, shall men give [unto] your bosom. For with the same measure that ye mete withal it shall be measured to you again.* (Luke 6:31-38; see also Luke 5:11 RE)

Once again, we forgive. We take on ourselves the role of the intercessor by accepting the shame and abuse of this world, and both forgive and pray for those who give offenses. Through this, we come to *understand* our Lord because we are like Him.

This is what we see in Lehi. After learning of God's impending judgments against Jerusalem, he prayed on behalf of *"his people"* (those who were condemned) *"with all his heart"* (See 1 Nephi 1:5; see also 1 Nephi 1:3 RE). His example can be found mirrored in all who repent. They display His grace by what they suffer for His cause.

Christ taught who He was, then lived the example of what a redeemed life would look like. He sacrificed Himself. Similarly, His followers sacrifice themselves. Perhaps not by dying as He did, and as Joseph did, and as Steven did, and Paul, and Peter, and Abinadi, and Hyrum, but by the *way they live*—

taking offenses and forgiving. This is how we obtain broken hearts and contrite spirits, because this world is always at war with the Saints of God. Here the Children of God are strangers and sojourners—unwelcomed, unappreciated, often the source of contempt, ridicule, and judgment. Let them judge, but don't judge them in return. Return kindness for evil.

For if ye forgive men their trespasses, your heavenly Father will also forgive you: But if ye forgive not men their trespasses, neither will your Father forgive your trespasses (Matthew 6:14-15; see also Matthew 3:30 RE). This is an absolute condition. It is mandatory. If you *forgive not* men their trespasses, neither will your Father forgive you *your* trespass. You *can't* be forgiven by the Father if you do not forgive others. It can't be done. That grudge you harbor prevents the Father from forgiving you. Those resentments you think are justified are keeping you from being forgiven by the Father. Those injustices imposed upon you by others, who are unthinking or cruel, *must be surrendered.*

The early Saints were victimized by mobs in Missouri and Illinois. They wanted revenge. Brigham Young implemented a covenant to seek vengeance upon the murderers of Joseph Smith until the third and fourth generation. *They* did not build Zion. They wanted vengeance more than they wanted anything else.

The opposite of this is forgiveness. If you forgive, your Heavenly Father WILL forgive you. Offenses are opportunities for you to gain forgiveness. All you need do is forgive them. It is a simple, direct, cause and effect. It was ordained before the world was founded, and applies universally in all ages and among all people. *It lightens the burden.* This is why Christ said His yoke was easy and His burden is light. Because when you lay down all of the offenses that have aggregated over your lifetime against you, you find yourself free indeed.

The world is in Satan's grip, largely because the world seeks vengeance and refuses to forgive. Zion, on the other hand, will be filled with those who forgive. Of course that puts an absolute limit on those who can dwell there, and therefore, will include very few indeed.

The foregoing excerpts are taken from:

- Stephanie Snuffer's remarks titled "Love Others As Yourself," given at a regional conference in Sandy, Utah, on July 14, 2019;

- Denver's *Christian Reformation Lecture Series,* Talk #3, given in Atlanta, Georgia, on November 16, 2017;
- Denver's *40 Years in Mormonism Series,* Talk #6, titled "Zion," given in Grand Junction, Colorado, on April 12th, 2014;
- Denver's *Christian Reformation Lecture Series,* Talk #8, given in Montgomery, Alabama, on May 18, 2019;
- Denver's conference talk titled "Civilization," given in Grand Junction, Colorado, on April 21, 2019;
- Denver's blog entry titled Forgiving to be Forgiven, posted August 3, 2012, and subsequently recorded with additional commentary on February 22, 2020; and
- Denver's blog entry titled 3 Nephi 13:14-15, posted October 21, 2010, and subsequently recorded with additional commentary on February 22, 2020.

107. Renewal, Part 1

This is Part 1 of a special series on Renewal, where Denver discusses the pattern and concept, how it appears in nature, how it appears in our lives, and how it is evident in the Restoration.

DENVER: The fact that Easter is in the springtime, I don't think is any accident. I think it's intended to align with the testimony of nature about the promise of eternal life, the promise of the renewal that comes every spring, and I think the Lord intended that His death and His resurrection should associate with spring. And I think it's appropriate that that be the subject that we look at today.

Look at verse 12, and it's been a discussion of what went on at the beginning —man in the Garden of Eden, God talking to him. Verse 12:

> *From the foregoing we learn man's situation at his first creation: the knowledge [of] which he was endowed, and the high and exalted station in which he was placed—lord or governor of all things on [the] earth, and at the same time enjoying communion and intercourse with his Maker without a veil to separate between.* (T&C 110, Lectures on Faith 2:12 RE)

That's where man began, and that's why knowledge of God existed in the first place. Because in the beginning, God talked to man. *And* if you think, "Well, yeah, that was then, what about now?"—we'll get to now. Verse 18, about halfway down:

> *God conversed with him face to face: in his presence he was permitted to stand, and from his own mouth he was permitted to receive instruction — he heard his voice, walked before him...gazed upon his glory, while intelligence burst upon his understanding, and enabled him to give names to the vast assemblage of his Maker's works.* (T&C 110, Lectures on Faith 2:18 RE)

This was man's original condition—a condition to which the gospel is designed to return man. And in fact, at the Second Coming all who remain will be in that condition once again. The earth is going to be renewed and receive its paradisiacal glory, and it's going to do so because God will come and dwell here again. And man will be able to converse [with] Him.

Beginning at verse 33, of Section 84 of the Doctrine and Covenants:

> *For whoso is faithful unto the obtaining [of] these two priesthoods of which I have spoken, and the magnifying their calling, are sanctified by the Spirit unto the renewing of their bodies. They become the sons of Moses and of Aaron and the seed of Abraham, and the church and kingdom, and the elect of God.* (D&C 84:33; see also T&C 82:16 RE)

"Sons"..."seed"—and it's necessary that you become that in order that you become "*the church and kingdom...the elect of God.*" Because as we saw in the statements made to Joseph Smith, the hearts have to be turned to the fathers because this is going to be reconstructing a Holy Family at some point.

And also all they who receive this priesthood receive me, saith the Lord (D&C 84:35; see also T&C 82:17). Now, many of you read that verse 35 and you think that what that means is if you fetch this priesthood by ordination, *ipso facto*, you have fetched Jesus. "PRAISE JESUS!" (Said in the voice of Joel Osteen.) And by the way, Joel Olsteen is coming to the E Center—you're not going to want to miss that. "It's a mega church! It's a mega church in transit! It's going to come to the E Center! SUNDAY, SUNDAY, SUNDAY!" (Again said in the voice of Joel Olsteen.) I'm sorry. I get worked up when the evangelicals show up on the horizon. He had some nice things to say about Mormons, though. So Joel Olsteen has kind of creeped a little more on the positive column for me of late.

I want to suggest that verse 35 can also be read exactly as D&C section 93, verse 1 (that we were reading a moment ago) is read. And that is to say if you're going to receive this priesthood, you're going to get it from Him. That is, you enter into His presence—you receive *Him*. *If* you have it, then *when* you have it—as a consequence *of* having it—you receive Him.

Oh— *For he that receiveth my servants receiveth me* (D&C 84:36; see also T&C 82:17 RE). I want to suggest that throughout scripture, almost invariably, the word 'servants' is referring to angelic ministrants. And so, angels minister—that would be Aaronic. And then Christ ministers—that would be sons of Moses.

And he that receiveth me receiveth my Father [because it is the purpose of the Son to bear record of the Father. It is the purpose of the Son to bring others to the Father so that there might be many sons of God]. *And he that receiveth my Father receiveth my Father's kingdom* ['cause you can't go where the Father is without entering into and receiving an inheritance] (D&C 84:37-38; see also T&C 82:17 RE).

You know, one of the things that we tend to think is that if you get something (this is based upon statements made in [section] 132)— But if you get something here, and you get it by a covenant, that you are automatically entitled to take it into the *next* world. But what if the covenant that you are to receive, in order to obtain that inheritance in the next world, doesn't reckon merely from something handled by ordinance, but that the ordinance is pointing you to something higher and more holy? What if the thing that secures for you the inheritance in the next life is not the ordinance, but what the ordinance testifies to—that is, embracing the Lord through the veil? And then having conversed with Him, entering into His presence? And then having entered into His presence, being ministered to and taught? What if it means all that?

> *This is according to the oath and covenant which belongeth to the priesthood. Therefore, all those who receive the priesthood, receive this oath and covenant of my Father, which he cannot break, neither can it be moved. But whoso breaketh this covenant after he hath received it, and altogether turneth therefrom, shall not have forgiveness of sins in this world nor in the world to come. [Oh—] And wo unto all those who come not unto this priesthood which ye...received, which I now confirm upon you who are present this day, by mine own voice* ***out of the heavens****; and even I have given the heavenly hosts and mine angels charge concerning you.* ([Emphasis added.] D&C 84:39-42; see also T&C 82:17 RE)

You know, that verse 42 of the oath and covenant of the priesthood— You ought to take a look at Joseph Smith Translation of Genesis chapter 14, verse 29, talking about the priesthood that was given after the Order of the Son of God. It says: *It was delivered unto men by the calling of His own voice, according to His own will, unto as many as believed on His name* (JST Genesis 14:29; see also Genesis 7:18 RE). And so, we have in section ~~76~~ (84) a testimony given, and justification for the translation Joseph rendered of Genesis chapter 14, dealing with the priesthood and qualifying it as coming from the voice of God.

Take a look at Doctrine and Covenants section 93, verse 36: *The glory of God is intelligence, or, in other words, light and truth. Light and truth forsake that evil one* (D&C 93:36; see also T&C 93:11 RE). What if, instead of repentance being related to your misdeeds—which are so plentiful, and persistent, and will continue—what if, instead, it is related to the acquisition of light and truth—that is, intelligence? What if repentance requires you to take whatever it is that you have that is a foolish error, a vain tradition, a false notion, and replace it with the truth?

My suspicion is that whatever it is that is troubling you, it will trouble you considerably less if you begin to fill yourself with light and truth. Until, at last, you arrive at a point where you look back upon your sins and you say, "I have no more disposition for *that* because I frankly know enough not to do that anymore, and because I prefer the light, and because I prefer God's intelligence and glory over that which I used to trade to substitute for it." You see, repentance may have a whole lot more to do with your own *feeble education* in the things of God than it does have to do with the time you spend, wasted, looking at some vile picture or other.

You know, we have this Victorian sexual mores that everyone in Wall Street tacks against— like when you're in a sailboat and there's a headwind, you "tack" against it. Quite frankly, I find most of that stuff boring, and not titillating. Some of it's medical, but it's not enticing. And from a certain perspective, if you will acquire enough light and truth, you're not going to be contaminated by exposure to the things that are degrading.

The Book of Mormon was abridged by a man who lived inside an environment that was *filled* with sex and violence. And he was untouched by it—a man of righteousness. And why is it that he could preserve himself? Because what was in him was light and truth. He had educated himself; he had learned about the things that are true. So that when you minister to someone who is suffering, their sins ought not shock you. They ought to cause compassion to well up *in* you. People struggle with some very difficult, very challenging things. You need to try and overcome that by the light within you. The glory of God is intelligence. Be intelligent!

At one point Christ, talking to Abraham, says He is more intelligent than them all. One will be more intelligent than another: *These two [things]...exist, [if there be two beings], one [will be] more intelligent than the other…I am more intelligent than [them] all* (Abraham 3:19; see also T&C Abraham 5:4 RE). That's what Christ said.

And Joseph Smith, talking about the Holy Ghost, says, "I... know more than all the world... [or] the Holy Ghost does, anyhow, and...[it's in] me" (*Teachings of the Prophet Joseph Smith,* p. 350). The fact of the matter is that you *can* fill yourself *with the mind of God.* And if you fill yourself with the mind of God, you're going to find yourself in a position where you, like the scriptures recite, have no more disposition to do evil but to only do good continually. *That* repentance is as a consequence of the things that you know. *That* repentance comes as a consequence of the light and truth within you.

> *Whoso is faithful unto the obtaining [of] these two priesthoods of which I have spoken, and the magnifying their calling* [see, priesthood is not simply yada, yada, yada; ipso facto; canorus mundorum; there you are! It requires— See you get it, but then "faithful to obtain," and then "faithful to magnify," and "faithful to magnify it as a calling" ('calling' being an operative word there that means service)], *are sanctified by the Spirit unto the renewing of their bodies* ["sanctified by the Spirit," "renewing their body"—these things have meaning. Perhaps we'll get to that at some point]. *They become the sons of Moses and of Aaron and the seed of Abraham, and the church and kingdom, and the elect of God.* (D&C 84:33-34; see also T&C 82:16 RE)

See, they *become*—but they *become* as a consequence of having been sanctified. They become sanctified because they magnified their calling. They had to first obtain the priesthood, and the obtaining of the priesthood requires something that is *faithful.* And you ought to ask yourself, "Faithful to what?" And *always* it is faithful to *Him,* to our Lord, the One who redeems.

All of these things flow together as one continuum. It's not just, "I got ordained." It doesn't matter that you got ordained. There's a process that's involved after ordination in which you follow these steps. We read it as one sentence and say, "There it is! He was faithful—I mean, he passed the bishop's interview; he obtained it." That is, he sat down there, and they got a certificate, I mean— When I was on the high council, I was the one responsible for fetching the Melchizedek priesthood certificates and delivering it to them. And that was a definite point in time at which we could point and say, "On *this* day, *this* person gave *this* authority to *this* guy on *this* occasion. *And,* when that happened, he also got a line of authority."

When I got ordained to be a high priest, the stake president handed me a line of authority which, when I looked at, I found mistakes in. And I went back and I did the research, and I corrected the line of authority. Then I went back to my stake president and I said, "Uh, you gave me your line of authority, but it was wrong. Here's the right one." And then he had to go find all of the people that he had ordained and correct that. Some fellow in the line had thought it would be more commendable to have been ordained by Marion G. Romney *after* he was an apostle rather than as he *was*—when Marion G. Romney was called to be the bishop and he called *this fellow* to be his counselor. And so, Marion G. Romney was ordained to be a high priest, to be the bishop, and he ordained this other fellow to be a high priest and his counselor. And then subsequently, when Marion G. Romney got to be an apostle, this guy hailed his priesthood line from the date on which Marion G.

Romney became an apostle, which screwed the whole line up. And therefore, I had to fix that, and President Pugh was grateful. But it imposed upon him the obligation then to go back and straighten out all those whom *he* had ordained. Well, that's neither here nor there.

"They become the sons of Moses and of Aaron and the seed of Abraham, and the church and kingdom, and the elect of God." I spoke in Centerville about what it meant to be the seed of Abraham. You ought to listen to that talk—we don't have time. We have to accumulate; we have to aggregate information. And we've got to assume that you've *got* what we've talked about before so that we can press on.

Once you have done those: *Also all they who receive this priesthood [now* it's in the singular; *now* it has been reduced back to the unitary. *Now* we're talking about that which *is* the fullness. We're now talking about something other than the different portions; we're talking about *this* priesthood] *receive me, saith the Lord* (D&C 84:35; see also T&C 82:17 RE).

We take that to mean that '*not actually the Lord,* for goodness sake'—but to mean rather instead, that if you have this priesthood, somehow the Lord has received you. Somehow, if you've got this, you belong to Him in some metaphysical sort of fashion, in which, "On account of having priesthood, I am received of Jesus." Take the words literally and say to yourself: if you've got *this*, if *this* is what you have managed to accumulate, *then* one of the evidences of having accumulated it will be receiving the Lord.

For he that receiveth my servants receiveth me (D&C 84:36; see also T&C 82:17 RE). I suggested in Centerville that the word 'servants,' in this context, meant angels. An angel— The word is derived from a Greek word that simply means 'messenger,' and the messenger can't be on their own errand. They have to have a message that is being brought *from* another—the other being the Lord. Therefore, if the message originates *with the Lord* and the message is delivered by a messenger, it does not matter if the one delivering the message is a mortal, as we find in the Book of Mormon where someone says, "Last night"— King Benjamin, I believe, said, "Last night the Lord told me this," or, "Last night the angel taught me this, and so today I'm going to teach *you* this" (See Mosiah 3:2-23; see also Mosiah 1:13-18 RE). In that context, King Benjamin *was* the angel. And therefore, as long as they bear a message from the Lord, they fit the definition.

"He that receiveth my servants receiveth me." That is, if it's the voice of God and it's coming to you from Him, and it's authentically His message, and you

receive it as if it were from His own mouth, then you've received from Him at least His voice. But, it doesn't end there: *He that receiveth me receiveth my Father* (D&C 84:37; see also T&C 82:17 RE).

In this context, what he's talking about is the same thing that you find in the 14th chapter of the book of John, in which Christ says that He will not leave you comfortless, but He will come to comfort you. And then He and His Father will take up Their abode with you (See John 14:23; see also John 9:8 RE and T&C 171 Testimony of St. John 10:13 RE). This is not an abstraction. The idea that this is something that happens in your heart (you can read in the Doctrine and Covenants) *is an old sectarian notion, and is false* (D&C 130:3). It means a literal appearance of these Holy Beings to minister, to comfort, and ultimately to take up their abode.

> *He that receiveth my Father* [and I would add, "while yet in the flesh"] *receiveth my Father's kingdom; therefore all that my Father hath shall be given unto him. And this is according to the oath and covenant which belongeth to the priesthood.* (D&C 84:38-39; see also T&C 82:17 RE)

And what is that oath and that covenant? It is *the Father's word*, which cannot be broken. It's not something you aspire to, but it's something that you accept by the conditions that are set out in Doctrine and Covenants section 84. It is something which [is] received by an oath and a covenant given by the One who *can* give covenants. Just as we talked about in Centerville, it's a covenant which originates from God. It is His word, which cannot be broken (See Ether 3:12; see also Ether 1:12 RE). Therefore, when the Father covenants that you're going to inherit, it is a covenant that *will* surely come to pass.

Therefore, all...who receive the priesthood [singular; implying it in its fullest manifestation], *receive this oath and covenant **of my Father*** [this is not talking about abstractions, quorums, churches, organizations, orders, choruses. This is talking about a direct, covenantal relationship established by *the Father* with *this—this priesthood*—the one about which today I would like to speak: *this* priesthood], *...which [He, the Father] he cannot break* [because if He were to break this once He has made this covenant with someone, He would cease to be God, and He *cannot* do that. Therefore, *this* covenant cannot be broken by Him], *neither can it be moved* ([Emphasis added.] D&C 84:40; see also T&C 82:17 RE). That is, once the Father has made that covenant, earth and hell cannot make it otherwise.

You do not need to leave anything behind that is good or noble or virtuous. And you, and we, do not need to establish another entity. You can serve wherever you are. *However*, to preserve the Restoration itself, starting now, we need to more closely follow the pattern of scripture.

The baptism prayer was given by Christ. This is in 3 Nephi chapter 11, beginning at verse 19:

> *And Nephi arose and went forth, and bowed himself before the Lord and did kiss his feet. And the Lord commanded him that he should arise. And he arose and stood before him. And the Lord* ***said*** *unto him: I give unto you power that ye shall baptize this people when I am again ascended into heaven. And again the Lord called others, and* ***said*** *unto them likewise; and he gave unto them power to baptize.* ([Emphasis added.] 3 Nephi 11:19-22; see also 3 Nephi 5:7-8 RE)

I'm not going to take the time to do it, but if you want to check this out, you can check this out on your own. *Christ did not touch them.* He said to them, "I give you power to baptize." When Christ touches them (which will be later still in the narrative), the fact that He touches them is so remarkable in the narrative that the verse talking about it repeats three times that the Lord touched them. The presence of God touching them, being so significant that it's mentioned three times in the narrative when it happens, drives home the point that it's missing *here*.

How then does the authority to baptize come? Well, once John the Baptist came and laid his hands on Joseph— We've had a practice of continuing that and we ought to continue that. But before any of you baptize any other of you, do this! Do this! It's the same thing that Alma did in Mosiah chapter 18. If you go back to Mosiah chapter 18, before he baptized,

> *Alma took Helam* [this is Mosiah 18:12]*...stood forth in the water, and cried, saying: O Lord, pour out thy Spirit upon thy servant, that he may do this work with holiness of heart. And when he...said these words, the Spirit of the Lord was upon him.* (Mosiah 18:12-13; see also Mosiah 9:8 RE)

He got the authority to baptize. If you're going to use the priesthood—no matter what the Church has told you, and no matter what quorum leaders and respected others, including your own father perhaps, have taught you—before you do so, *ask God* to give you the authority. And if you get it, you get it from Him, and then you're not dependent upon someone else. But get the authority from Him. Power is required. It *must* come from Christ. The pattern must be followed.

John the Baptist, when he restored the authority (in Joseph Smith, verse 69—Joseph Smith History 1:69), said that it,

> *Holds the keys of the ministering of angels, and of the gospel of repentance, and of baptism by immersion for the remission of sins; and this shall never be taken...from the earth until the sons of Levi do offer again an offering unto the Lord in righteousness.* (Joseph Smith History 1:69; see also T&C Joseph Smith History 14:1 RE)

The Gospel of repentance is returning to face God. Baptism by immersion is for the remission of sins. And John's declaration does not say that it will not be taken from the church; it says it will "*be [not] taken...from* ***the earth***." It was restored to remain on the earth. And no matter what happens among those that choose to abuse one another, it needs to be preserved by a faithful few so that it doesn't cease from the earth. It *is* still here—though it has been much neglected and it has been much abused. But with you, renew it. Renew it using Alma's example.

He'd been previously ordained as one of the priests in wicked King Noah's court. And he'd been ordained by him *precisely* because he was wicked. He qualified; he was corrupt. Noah wanted him, and so he got ordained. But before he undertook to use the authority, he *asked God* to give him power. And God, seeing penitence on the earth, respected it and poured out His Spirit upon him, so that Alma could baptize with authority. And the proof of that consisted not merely in what it was that Alma experienced, with the Spirit empowering him to perform the ordinance, but it consisted also in the effect that the ordinance itself had upon *both* Helam and Alma—who himself went into the water at the same time. The Spirit was poured out upon them. Renew it!

Likewise, we need to renew a community—not an organization, but a fellowship; not a hierarchy, but a group of equals. The community needs to be renewed. Men who have been ordained already should renew this in the manner I just described. Continuing then with what Christ said:

> *And he said unto them: On this wise shall ye baptize; and there [should] be no disputations among you. Verily I say unto you, that whoso repenteth of his sins through your words, and desireth to be baptized in my name, on this wise shall ye baptize them—Behold, ye shall go down and stand in the water.* (3 Nephi 11:22-23; see also 3 Nephi 5:8 RE and T&C 175:8 RE)

I would recommend, if it is at all possible, that the water for a living ordinance be living water. I would not perform this— I would get out of the buildings that are built by the hands of men and I would use the things of God. You're trying to connect to God; use the things that He has made. I recognize there may be circumstances where that becomes impossible. I've been baptized twice—once in the Atlantic and once in a stream in the Little Cottonwood Canyon. Both times it was so cold my lips were blue. And I recognize that some of you hardy people may not want to experience a baptism that invigorates you to the point of turning your lips blue, but I would recommend when you go down and stand in the water, that it be living water.

> *And in my name shall ye baptize them...now behold, these are the words...ye shall say, calling them by name, saying: Having authority given me of Jesus Christ, I baptize you in the name of the Father, and of the Son, and of the Holy Ghost. Amen.* (3 Nephi 11:23-25; see also 3 Nephi 5:8 RE and T&C 175:8-9 RE)

When I was baptized into the LDS Church, the baptismal prayer was: "Having been *commissioned* of Jesus Christ, I baptize you in the name of the Father…." When I was re-baptized, I was re-baptized by one who had authority from Christ; therefore, in that baptism the words were: "Having *authority*...of Jesus Christ." If all you're going to do is baptize someone again according to the LDS pattern, with a commission in a Church, don't bother doing it. But if you follow these principles, and if the Spirit empowers you to baptize, then baptize having authority from Christ and follow His words. We've deviated long enough. It's time to return.

> *Then shall ye immerse them in the water, and come forth again out of the water. And after this manner shall ye baptize in my name; for behold, verily I say unto you, that the Father, and the Son, and the Holy Ghost are one; and I am in the Father, and the Father in me, and the Father and I are one. And according as I have commanded you thus shall ye baptize.* (3 Nephi 11:26-28; see also 3 Nephi 5:8 RE and T&C 175:10 RE)

I'm telling you in the name of the Lord, that that commandment is renewed again *by Him* today, to you. This is His command. Do it on this wise.

And then the question is, "Do you lay on hands?" Yes, I would follow everything that has been given to this point. We're 'adding to;' we're not throwing away. We're trying to preserve, and we're trying to return, and we're trying to renew. We are not trying to tread under our feet anything that is useful, laudable, worthy, desirable, or that came down from the Restoration. It is not God's purpose to abandon the Restoration, but it is His purpose to preserve it.

There are changes presently underway that are going to *jar* the LDS community more and more in the coming years. If you are not prepared to preserve what has been given, *everything* will be lost in what will soon happen. It's necessary that there be someone who seeks for some community that tries to preserve, in its purity, what is rapidly becoming at an accelerating pace more and more corrupted. It *has* to be preserved. Every one of you have some issue that you would say to yourself, "*If this*, then I would no longer follow." All of the "*if this's*" are in the wings. Inexorably, they are coming. It has to be preserved, and it has to be preserved in a manner in which it can remain pure.

As to the Sacrament, *only an anti-Christ* would forbid you from partaking of the Sacrament in the way commanded by your Lord. *That* is an abomination. If you get together, even if it's only in your own family, partake of the Sacrament together. Let *no one* forbid you from partaking in remembrance of Christ, because *He* commanded that you do it. Follow the pattern that is given to us. In Doctrine and Covenants section 20, verse 76, one of the things that used to be practiced—that has since been abandoned and ought to be renewed among you—is that when the Sacrament is blessed, kneel. Kneel. "*Kneel with the church*" (D&C 20:76; see also T&C Joseph Smith History 16:24 RE). Remember it. Keep it. Do the things that have been instructed, in the pattern that He commanded that they be observed.

If you partake of wine— And for some reason you either are opposed to alcohol or, alternatively, you have some medical condition, use grape juice. Use red grape juice. Use the symbol of the blood of our Lord. I can tell you that, generally, red wine is *bitter* for a reason. And partaking of that *bitter* wine in remembrance of the blood that was shed is apt.

Here is the doctrine that is required for us *to be gathered.* Doctrine and Covenants section 10, beginning at verse 57:

> *Behold, I am Jesus Christ, the Son of God. I came unto mine own, and mine own received me not. I am the light which shineth in darkness, and the darkness comprehendeth it not.* (D&C 10:57-58; see also T&C Joseph Smith History 10:18 and 13:10 RE)

Even today, He is the light that shines in the darkness, not comprehended because there's just too much darkness. We *forbid* His presence by quenching the Spirit and not allowing utterance in our meetings. *That's* where we should be hearing from the Spirit and edifying one another.

The foregoing excerpts are taken from:

- Denver's talk titled "Christ's Discourse on the Road to Emmaus," given in Fairview, Utah, on April 14, 2007,
- Denver's *40 Years in Mormonism Series*, Talk #2, titled "Faith," given in Idaho Falls, Idaho, on September 28th, 2013,
- Denver's *40 Years in Mormonism Series*, Talk #3, titled "Repentance," given in Logan, Utah, on September 29th, 2013,
- Denver's *40 Years in Mormonism Series*, Talk #5, titled "Priesthood," given in Orem, Utah, on November 2nd, 2013, and
- Denver's *40 Years in Mormonism Series*, Talk #10, titled "Preserving the Restoration," given in Mesa, Arizona, on September 9th, 2014.

108. Renewal, Part 2

This is Part 2 of a special series on renewal, where Denver discusses the pattern and concept, how it appears in nature, how it appears in our lives, and how it is evident in the Restoration.

DENVER: In Third Nephi chapter 21, the Lord talked about some things that become exceptionally relevant in light of what we've covered today.

> *And verily I say unto you, I give unto you a sign, that [you] may know the time when these things shall be about to take place—that I shall gather in, from their long dispersion, my people, O house of Israel, and...establish again among them my Zion.* This is addressing all of those various remnants, wherever that they may be found, so long as they are some residue of the house of Israel. (3 Nephi 21:1; see also 3 Nephi 9:11 RE)

> *And behold, this is the [sign] which I will give unto you for a sign—for verily I say unto you that when these things which I declare unto you, and which I shall declare unto you hereafter of myself, and by the power of the Holy Ghost which shall be given unto you of the Father, shall be made known unto the Gentiles* [see, the Gentiles had to first receive some things] *that they* [the Gentiles] *may know concerning this people who are a remnant of the house of Jacob, and concerning this my people who shall be scattered by them* [the Gentiles]. *Verily, verily, I say unto you, when these things shall be made known unto them* [some constituent group of Gentiles] *of the Father, and shall come forth of the Father, from them unto you;* (3 Nephi 21:2-3; see also 3 Nephi 9:11 RE)

It can't come from any source other than from the Father—the Father and Christ being one—the authority to minister and to deliver it coming from Them, the power to baptize being brought forth from some remnant of the Gentiles who care to bear it.

> *For it is wisdom in the Father that they* [the Gentiles] *should be established in this land, and be set up as a free people by the power of the Father, that these things might come forth from them unto a remnant of your seed, that the covenant of the Father may be fulfilled which he hath covenanted with* [this] *people… with his people, O house of Israel.* (3 Nephi 21:4; see also 3 Nephi 9:11 RE)

"O house of Israel" is much more. "O house of Israel" is that same inclusive of all bits and remnants, wherever they may be found. I talked about covenants when we were in Centerville and about the fulfillment of the covenants. *All* of the covenants which apply to people scattered everywhere, all of those included within the previous remnants—they need to be gathered into one constituent group.

> *Therefore, when these works and the works which shall be wrought among you hereafter shall come forth* ***from*** *the Gentiles…* (3 Nephi 21:5; see also 3 Nephi 9:11 RE, emphasis added)

Not their "book"; their *works*. Not their "book"; the works—bringing to pass the Doctrine of Christ, establishing repentance, declaring and baptizing by the authority of Christ, having people visited by fire and the Holy Ghost—these are the works. These are the works.

> *Shall come forth from the Gentiles, unto your seed which shall dwindle in unbelief because of iniquity; For thus it behooveth the Father that it* ***should*** *come forth from the Gentiles, that he may show forth his power unto the Gentiles.* (3 Nephi 21:5-6; see also 3 Nephi 9:11 RE, emphasis added)

That's what He needs now to do. That's what He intends *to* do—if you will receive it.

> *For this cause that the Gentiles, if they will not harden their hearts, that* ***they*** *may repent and come unto me and be baptized in my name and know of the true points of my doctrine, that* ***they*** *may be numbered among my people, O house of Israel.* (3 Nephi 21:6; see also 3 Nephi 9:11 RE, emphasis added)

You can't get there except through the power of the doctrine and the power of the ordinance that God has given, in the way that it has been given, performed with the exactness, fidelity, and language that has been given to us by Christ Himself.

> *When these things come to pass that thy seed shall begin to know these things —it shall be a sign unto them, that they may know that the work of the Father hath already commenced unto the fulfilling of the covenant which he...made unto the people who are of the house of Israel.* (3 Nephi 21:7; see also 3 Nephi 9:11 RE)

All of them. It's a witness that His work has commenced.

And when that day shall come, it shall come to pass that kings shall shut their mouths; for that which had not been told them shall they see; and that which they had not heard shall they consider. For in that day, for my sake shall the Father work a work, which shall be a great and...marvelous work among them; and there shall be among them those who will not believe it, although a man shall declare it unto them. But behold, the life of my servant shall be in my hand; therefore they shall not hurt him, although he shall be marred because of them. Yet I will heal him, for I will show unto them that my wisdom is greater than the cunning of the devil. Therefore it shall come to pass that whosoever will not believe in my words, who am Jesus Christ, which the Father shall cause him to bring forth unto the Gentiles, and shall give unto him power that he shall bring [it] forth unto the Gentiles, (it shall be done even as Moses said) they shall be cut off from among my people who are of the covenant. ...[whoever] will not believe in my words, who am Jesus Christ. (3 Nephi 21:8-11; see also 3 Nephi 9:11-12 RE)

These are Christ's words. We touched on these words all the way back in Boise. It was quoted by the angel Moroni, referring to Joseph Smith. Acts 3, verses 22 to 23:

For Moses truly said unto the fathers, A prophet shall the Lord your God raise up unto you of your brethren, like unto me; him shall ye hear in all things whatsoever he shall say unto you. And it shall come to pass, that every soul, which will not hear that prophet, shall be destroyed from among the people. (see also Acts 2:3 RE)

That prophet is Christ. It doesn't say Christ is going to come and deliver His words; it says, His "words." Those who *will not believe in my words, who am Jesus Christ, ...they shall be cut off* (3 Nephi 21:11; see also 3 Nephi 9:12 RE). And the angel Moroni said to Joseph, in verse 40 of the Joseph Smith History, *The day had not yet come when 'they who would not hear his voice should be cut off from among the people,' but soon would come* (see also Joseph Smith History part 3:4 RE).

That prophet is Christ. His words are what I've spoken to you today.

And my people who are a remnant of Jacob shall be among the Gentiles, yea, in the midst of them as a lion among the beasts of the forest, as a young lion among the flocks of sheep, who, if he go through both treadeth down and teareth in pieces, and none can deliver. Their hand shall be lifted up upon their adversaries, and all their enemies shall be cut off. Yea, wo be unto the Gentiles except they repent; for it shall come to pass in that day, saith the

> *Father, that I will cut off thy horses out of the midst of thee, and I will destroy thy chariots; And I will cut off the cities of thy [lands], and throw down all thy strongholds; And I will cut off witchcrafts out of [the] land, and thou shalt have no more soothsayers; Thy graven images will I also cut off.* (3 Nephi 21:12-17; see also 3 Nephi 9:12 RE)

Graven images are people you worship. Graven images include men to whom you submit as objects or idols of authority in whom you trust, thinking that they can deliver you by some magic, using some key that they purport to hold, whether Catholic or Mormon or Fundamentalist. Graven images—they're going to be cut off.

> *Thou shalt no more worship the works of thy hands; And I will pluck up thy groves out of the midst of thee; so will I destroy thy cities. And it shall come to pass that all lyings, and deceivings, and envyings, and strifes, and priestcrafts, and whoredoms, shall be done away. For it shall come to pass, saith the Father, that at that day whosoever will not repent and come unto my Beloved Son, them will I cut off from among my people, O house of Israel* [that's all remnants gathered together]*; And I will execute vengeance and fury upon them, even as upon the heathen, such as they have not heard. But if they...* [speaking of the Gentiles] *if they will repent and hearken unto my words, and harden not their hearts, I will establish my church among them, and they shall come in unto the covenant and be numbered among this the remnant of Jacob, unto whom I have given this land for their inheritance.* (3 Nephi 21:17-22; see also 3 Nephi 9:12, 10:1 RE)

Because every time there's a covenant, there is always a land. And this is the land that God covenants He will give. And the people to whom He will give it are those that come back and receive the covenant, including the Gentiles *in whose ears* this first shall sound...if they will come. And coming unto the covenant—that is not yet possible. It requires more than has at present been given. It is possible to come in and become part of His church. It is possible, if you follow as you've been instructed today, to become part of the church He recognizes and will preserve. But coming fully into the covenant... That will require more than has at present been given. It will require a covenant. It will require adoption. It will require sealing. It was what Joseph looked forward to have happen at some point in the future during the days of his prophecy.

> *And they shall assist my people, the remnant of Jacob, and also as many of the house of Israel as shall come, that they may build a city, which shall be called the New Jerusalem. And then shall they assist my people that they may be*

> *gathered in, who are scattered upon all the face of the land, in unto the New Jerusalem. And then shall the power of heaven...* [In this case, it is the singular—it's not the "powers"—because when you have Him present with you, you have all the authority.] *then shall the power of heaven come down among them; and I also will be in the midst. And then shall the work of the Father commence at that day...* (3 Nephi 21:23-26; see also 3 Nephi 10:1 RE)

Christ will come. Once the covenant has been renewed, the city of Zion will follow. The Lord's presence will come, and then the final stage begins.

> *Even when this gospel shall be preached among the remnant of this people. Verily I say unto you, at that day shall the work of the Father commence among...the dispersed of my people, yea, even the tribes which have been lost, which the Father hath led away out of Jerusalem. Yea, the work shall commence among all the dispersed of my people, with the Father to prepare the way whereby they may [be]come [in] unto me, that they may call on the Father in my name. Yea, and then shall the work commence, with the Father among all nations in preparing the way whereby his people may be gathered home to the land of their inheritance. And they shall go out from all nations; ...they shall not go out in haste, nor...by flight, for I will go before them, saith the Father, and I will be their rearward.* (3 Nephi 21:26-29; see also 3 Nephi 10:1 RE)

It's not gonna happen in haste. And the work of the Father that will commence in those nations, to commence the possibility for the gathering, will involve destroying a great deal of political, social, and military obstructions that prevent the gathering—prevent even the preaching to those that would gather if they could hear. But the work of the Father (and it's always masculine when it comes to destruction)... The work of the Father is going to bring this to an end. All the scattered remnants will be brought back again. The original, unified family of God will be restored again. The Fathers will have our hearts turned to them because in that day, once it's permitted to get that far, we will be part of that family again.

Our day is *filled* with darkness and deception. Our day is the day about which Nephi wrote. If you turn to Second Nephi chapter 28, beginning halfway through verse 4; *They shall teach with their learning, and deny the Holy Ghost, which giveth utterance* (see also 2 Nephi 12:1 RE).

This is why the ordinance has to be renewed. This is why the pattern has to be followed. This is why the light has to be turned on. Because the Holy Ghost has not assisted with the kind of robust assistance that it can if you're penitent. God cannot dwell in unclean vessels, and so He remedies that by cleaning the vessel—cleaning it in accordance with the pattern that He's given, thereby making it possible that the Holy Ghost *can* give to *you* utterance.

All, universally all of the various iterations of Mormonism are less and less like the foundation and we need to return. If you go back to what I said about baptism, you will find that on the topic of baptism, there is an example taken from the Book of Mormon in which Alma—who had been ordained in the court of King Noah—he was chosen precisely because he was wicked. Alma, who probably had a line of authority that was compromised by wickedness that had intervened, went out to baptize Helam, and before he did so, he asked heaven to give him the power to baptize. Kay? He got the power to baptize and he baptized Helam.

What I suggest in the talk, is that everyone who has been ordained in the LDS tradition, who fits in the category that President Boyd Packer, in general conference, lamented that we've done a good job of spreading the authority of the priesthood, but we've done a poor job of getting power in the priesthood. Go out and obtain from heaven the connection that gives the power in the priesthood. And let's have… Those who get the power from heaven, let's have them go out and baptize again, so that we know it is done with power; and not done merely with an authoritative tradition lacking in power that cannot be accepted by heaven.

The evidence of Alma's authoritative baptism was the outpouring of the Spirit. There have been those who have been baptized, and spent their life in Mormonism, or some other sect —Mormon related, who say they never felt like they had the confirmation of the Spirit. They have gone out, sought for, obtained power from heaven, baptized, and the ordinances had an effect upon people.

The purpose of renewing baptism is to take what may be a hollow gesture, performed by people who have authority with no power, and turn it into an event with power that connects people to heaven; so that we can renew the restoration like it was renewed in the days of Alma, through Alma, and in the model of the Book of Mormon—which answers so many doctrinal, imponderables for us today. 'Why do we have authority and no power?' as the president of the quorum of the twelve apostles in general conference lamented to the church. It's because we're not doing what we should be doing. It's not necessary to have a revolution that divorces us from the restoration. It's necessary to have a revolution that connects us back to the restoration and its beginnings.

How you get from where you are now, to the point where it would be suitable and appropriate for an event like that to even be considered, is a long, long effort; because we have a restoration to complete. We have prophecies to fulfill, we have things that need to be done, and we have covenants that need to be renewed. And all of that begins again in embryo at the very basic level of faith, repentance, baptism, fellowships, collecting tithing, assisting one another, and acting like we're Christians; and acting like we care about one another. And, in fact, stopping with the notion that climbing up and having authority over someone is a *good thing*, and recognizing it for what it is—it's an evil thing. No power or influence can or ought to be exercised by one man over another. The only way that you should exercise influence is by meekness, and gentleness, and persuasion. If you know more than I do, then enlighten me. Persuade me. Teach me that my heart will resonate with what you have to say. But don't presume that you have the right to call me, and afflict me, and tell me that if I don't bend my knee at this particular moment, then you're going to use some compulsory means in order to get, from me, exactly what you hope to extract from me. No one should be imposing upon anyone else.

When Alma heard the message of Abinadi, he went out and he sought to repent. Then, when he performed the first baptism of Helam, before doing so, he did what you did before blessing the sacrament, and that was to ask God for authority to proceed. And then he proceeded to baptize both Helam and himself and started anew. The Book of Mormon mentions that people ordain according to the gifts and power that is in them, given by God. Kay?

In order for us to accomplish what presently needs to be done, we need to have the ability to spontaneously move this work forward globally. A young man who's a returned LDS missionary, who had been ordained an Elder in the LDS Church, became disaffected, kept his testimony of Joseph, the Book of Mormon, the Restoration; but what he saw in the Church convinced him that the Church itself had little, if anything, to offer him any longer. As a result of his prayerful searching and studying, he became convinced that there was something afoot that God was doing, right now, among us. He contacted people through Request Baptism and the Fellowship Locator and began a series of correspondence. Because of a whole lot of complications, no one was able to go to Africa where this fellow is located in order to minister there. But he had a line of authority from the Church. And so he was walked through the process of going to God, and praying that God ratify what he'd been given, so that he could perform baptisms. And on October… Or, excuse me, on December 29th (I don't know how many days ago that was—a week or so ago), 22 people were baptized in Uganda using authority from heaven; that once God said to him, "You may proceed," is exactly the same as Alma being told to go forward with Helam and, thereafter, with others. We do not need to send people all over the world. We have the ability, because of what has been put in place, to spontaneously have this arise globally, and we just had an example of that occurring.

Now, I've mentioned this before. Largely the purpose of Aaronic priesthood is to curse people, and the purpose of Melchizedek priesthood is to bless people. Aaronic priesthood is a fairly durable kind of priesthood. It was what was involved in all kinds of rites and performances under the Law of Moses, which were pretty easy to run afoul of and wind up in a state of uncleanliness or ceremonial condemnation. And you had to renew... heavens, the High Priest had to renew, and he was the top of the pyramid. And you had to go through the Day of Atonement ceremonies. You had to purge from top to bottom, and then everyone was expected to purge with some regularity. Even a woman's regular monthly cycle resulted in ceremonial uncleanliness requiring renewal. Childbirth was considered something that required a sacrifice and a ceremonial cleansing. Every time you turn around under the Law of Moses you became unclean, and every time you turned around under the Law of Moses you had to fetch another animal, run up to the temple, offer sacrifice, and undo the ceremonial uncleanliness. And so what the purpose of the Aaronic priesthood ministry was, was to bring you under condemnation regularly. Well, it's pretty durable precisely because of its functionality.

When the Aaronic priesthood was restored, a promise was given, or a timeframe for its persistence was described, depending on whether you listen to the Oliver Cowdery account or the Joseph Smith account. It's supposed to endure that the sons of Levi may yet offer an offering in righteousness unto the Lord, or until the sons of Levi do offer an offering unto the Lord in righteousness. Well, that event has not occurred. It's persistent. Offices and positions and organization are not necessarily proof of possession of priestly authority. And someone raised the problem of Heber J Grant's practice of ordaining people to an office but not conferring upon them priesthood—a practice that persisted for about twenty years. I mean John Taylor predicted that there would come a time when members put people in the church, claiming to hold priestly authority, would not know whether or not they actually did.

I guess the proof is in the pudding in whether or not angels minister and other things happen, which if they do, it's probably pretty good evidence. And if it doesn't, maybe raises a question about, well,... "Maybe I ought to be reordained." But, I would use and rely on the LDS lines of authority until they get displaced at some point in the future. But right now, for this incipiant work, we really need as broad a base from which to begin to change the direction of the decay, and renew the direction in the hopes of restoration; so that we get far enough along that God approves of some of the things that we're doing, and gets behind it. I think the last conference up in Boise is evidence that God's somewhat approving even if He's somewhat scolding.

The reason why father Abraham had to go to Melchizedek in order to then rejoice and say, "I have gotten me a priesthood," was because, although, the line may have had fatherly connections from father Shem down to Abraham, the immediate ancestors of father Abraham were idolaters. True enough, his father repented for a short period of time but he didn't persist in that. And therefore, despite the fact that Melchizedek certainly held authority, there were members of the posterity of Melchizedek, between him and father Abraham, who were lost; and then Abraham was required to come and reconnect because of the apostasy.

When you're talking about the greatest blessings that God offers for the salvation of his children—when you're talking about the family of God, if it could simply be put in one time forever, then putting it into father Adam would have solved the problem all the way down to us today. It can and it has been broken. It can and it has been restored. It can and it has been reconnected after a period of apostasy. In fact, once you reconnect Abraham with Melchizedek, you actually have, then, a family of God, beginning with Adam, that runs in one continuous line right down to Ephraim. Then you have Joseph's comment about the prophets of the Old Testament. I'm not sure that he means all of them, but he certainly means... he certainly means a number that are identifiable. All prophets held Melchizedek priesthood and were ordained by God himself. Joseph said that, okay? So I don't think what Joseph is talking about is like, you know, "I confer upon you something." I think he's talking about this very connection where you have an isolated faithful individual, who honors the fathers and is doing everything that he can in his day, but for whom there is no existing possibility for having it occur. God fixes that problem for that individual, not in order to establish a new dispensation in which salvation procedes with the gathering of a people, and a making of a people; but it's a dispensation to that individual for purposes of trying to call others to repentance. And if others were to repent, then God could do something with that.

The reason He lead away Lehi, and the family of Lehi, was to try and establish a righteous branch and a vineyard of the Lord, and the only way to do that was to get them away from the people who were corrupt in Jerusalem; and, maybe, give them the potential for holding onto and becoming a people of promise. And they were on again, off again, and faithful. A number of troubling moments in their history, but in general, they were sufficiently intact by the time that the Lord came, that He visited with them, and He renewed that with them; and that connection was certainly fulsome at that point.

The only purpose behind the last days work, both what was happening at the time of Joseph and what the Lord is offering to us today, is to accomplish that fulsome restoration of the family of God. I mean, Joseph talked about temples, and they were built incrementally, and they never reached the finish line, even on the second one before he was killed. But he laid a fabulous foundation, and pointed in a direction that the restoration necessarily must go to and complete. Because if we don't… If we don't have the tabernacle of God where he comes to dwell with his people, which he does when he has a family on earth, then the prophecies are not going to be fulfilled. Then the promises that were made to Enoch will not be realized. Then the statements of what will happen in the last days, through Moses, will not be vindicated. Then Adam's prophecy concerning his descendants to the end of time will not be realized. All of these things point, so we know it is going to happen. The question is not, "Is it going to happen?" The question is, "Will we rise up or will we not? Because what he's offering is, in fact, a legitimate opportunity for that to indeed happen.

We seem to get so easily distracted that we have a hard time… we have a hard time staying on task. It's one of the gentile afflictions. We're very ambitious people and we're very ego-centric. And a lot of what is going to be required will require sacrifice and selflessness.

This world is a place of trial and testing. Before creation, it was planned that when we came here we would be "proven" by what we experience. That happens now. Prove yourself by listening to God, hearing His voice, and obeying. Sometimes we are like Alma and want to do greater things to help God's work, but the greatest work of all is to respond to God's voice and prove you are willing to listen and obey Him.

I want to show you the depths of truth that spreads through the ocean, distances and directions that are infinite. But I must be content to use only a cup to give what little a man can measure and convey. Only God can show it because it is too great, too far above man's poor ability. *It's not lawful for man, neither is man capable to make it known, for it is only to be seen and understood by those who purify themselves before God; to whom He grants this privilege of seeing and knowing for themselves, while in the flesh* (paraphrased from D&C 76:115-118; see also T&C 69:29 RE).

It was a year ago that a renewed covenant was given to all willing to accept it by God. New covenant people sprang into existence when a few accepted that gift. Until that moment, there were only lost and scattered remnants who, although the object of God's earlier covenants, lived in ignorance of God's renewed labor in His vineyard. Now, in addition to other remnants, there is a new covenant remnant aware of God's renewed labor. A remnant who has been asked to labor alongside the Master of the Vineyard as He sends His final invitation to come to His wedding feast. Christ spoke of this very thing when He taught the Nephites. He foretold that the barren gentiles would eventually produce more children for His Kingdom than the remnants on this land and at Jerusalem. Christ said:

> *And then shall that which is written come to pass: Sing, O barren, thou that didst not bear; break forth into singing and cry aloud, thou that didst not travail with child, for more are the children of the desolate than the children of the married wife, saith the Lord. Enlarge the place of thy tent and let them stretch forth the curtains of thy habitations; spare not, lengthen thy cords and strengthen thy stakes, for thou shalt break forth on the right hand and on the left, and thy seed shall inherit the gentiles and make the desolate cities to be inhabited. Fear not for thou shalt not be ashamed, neither be thou confounded for thou shalt not be put to shame, for thou shalt forget the shame of thy youth and shalt not remember the reproach of thy widowhood any more. For thy maker, thy husband, the Lord of Hosts is his name, and thy Redeemer, the Holy One of Israel: the God of the whole earth shall he be called.* (3 Nephi 10:2 RE).

We can see a new and different meaning in Christ's Book of Mormon prophecy to the Nephites. Before, Christ's words seemed to foretell that the lost and scattered remnants would build the Lord's House and the New Jerusalem. Now it appears that there are covenant receiving gentiles who are included. Gentiles, who repent and hearken to Christ's words and do not harden their hearts, will be brought into the covenant as His people.

Christ mentions three distinct bodies. First, those who have accepted the covenant and are numbered among the remnant of Jacob to whom Christ gave this land for their inheritance. Second, the lost descendants of the remnant of Jacob, on this land, who will repent and return. Third, as many from the House of Israel who will repent and return. These three will build a city that shall be called the New Jerusalem. All three of those will come to know God in gathering and laboring to build the New Jerusalem. Then they will go out to assist all of God's people in their lost and forgotten state to be awakened to the work of God, and gathered as if one body of believers. Then all who have any of the blood of Abraham, who are scattered upon the face of the land, will come to be taught in the New Jerusalem. There the Power of Heaven will come down to be among them. The angels and Enoch, with his ten thousands, will come down. The Ancient of Days, or Adam—our first father, and Christ will also be in the midst of His people.

The foregoing excerpts are taken from:

- Denver's *40 Years in Mormonism Series*, Talk #10 titled "Preserving the Restoration," given in Mesa, AZ on September 9th, 2014
- A Q&A session titled "A Visit with Denver Snuffer," held on May 13, 2015
- A regional conference Q&A session, held at Big Cottonwood Canyon, UT on September 20, 2015
- A fireside talk titled "Cursed, Denied Priesthood," given in Sandy, UT on January 7th, 2018; and
- Denver's remarks titled "Keep the Covenant: Do the Work," given at the Remembering the Covenants Conference in Layton, UT on August 4, 2018

109. Renewal, Part 3

This is Part 3 of a special series on renewal where Denver discusses the pattern and concept, how it appears in nature, how it appears in our lives, and how it is evident in the Restoration.

DENVER: The first and primary question you have to ask is: Take a look around this world and ask yourself if, in this world, it makes sense to you that there is no Creator? Does it make sense to you that everything that's going on here simply is a haphazard accident? That there is no creation; there's no creator; there's no divine plan; there's nothing here that operates on any other basis than random chance? If you reach the conclusion that everything that's going on here could possibly be by random chance, then read Darwin's *Black Box.* There's a little over 200 different things that have to… have to line up perfectly in order for your blood to clot. If any one of those 200 things don't happen simultaneously (it's a little over 200), if any one of those don't happen simultaneously, you will die. For some of those, if you get a cut and they're not present, you'll bleed out. You'll simply die because you'll exsanguinate. For others of those, if you get a cut, your entire blood system will turn solid, and you will die because clotting knows no end. Darwin's *Black Box* makes the argument that it is evolutionarily impossible for trial and error to solve the problem of blood clotting, because every one of the steps that are required, if nature simply experiments with it, kills the organism. And that ends that. You don't know that you're going to succeed until you've lined them all up, and you've made them all work. It's an interesting... It's an interesting book—Darwin's *Black Box.* In essence, it's saying that the evolutionists require more faith really, than do people that believe in God; because the theory upon which they base their notion requires far too many things to occur by trial and error than is conceivably possible.

Well, if there is a creation, then there is a Creator. If there is a Creator, then the question is… I assume all of you have had a father or a grandfather—someone that you respected—a mother or a grandmother, an aunt or an uncle that over the course of a lifetime developed skills and talents and humor and character—someone that you admire—and then they pass on. How profligate a venture is it to create someone that you… a creation that you view as noble, as worthy, as admirable, as interesting, as fascinating—some person that you love; take that and just obliterate it. God, who can make such a creation, surely doesn't waste a creation. He's not burning the library at Alexandria every day by those who pass on. God had to have a purpose behind it all. I don't know how many of you have had a friend, or a loved one, or a family member who passed on who, subsequent to their death, appeared to you, had a conversation with you in a dream, in a thought. I can recall going to my father's funeral; and his casket, with his body, was in the front of the little chapel we were in, but his presence was *not* there. That may have been the hull he occupied while he was living and breathing. I had no sense at all that my father was there. I did have a sense that he was present, but he wasn't in the coffin. He was elsewhere in the room. I couldn't see him, but I could have pointed to him and said, "He's here." In fact, I made a few remarks at my father's funeral, and I largely directed them at him.

Nature testifies over and over again. It doesn't matter when the sun goes down, there's going to be another dawn. It doesn't matter when all the leaves fall off the deciduous trees in the fall, there's going to come a spring. There's going to be a renewal of life. There are all kinds of animals in nature that go through this really loathsome, disgusting, wretched existence, and then they transform. And where they were a pest before, now they're bright, and they're colorful, and they fly, and they pollinate. Butterflies help produce the very kinds of things that their larvae stage destroyed. These are signs. These are... These are testimonies. Just like the transformation of the caterpillar into the butterfly—the pest into the thing of beauty; the thing that ate the vegetables that you were trying to grow, into the thing that helps pollinate the things that you want to grow—that's the plan for all of us. So, when you study the scriptures, the objective should not be: Can I trust the text? Can I evaluate the text? Can I… Can I use a form of criticism against the text in order to weigh, dismiss, belittle, judge? Take all that you know about nature. Take all that you know about this world and the majesty of it all. Take all that you know that informs you that there is hope, there is joy, there is love. Why do you love your children? Why do your children love you? These kinds of things exist. They're real. They're tangible. And they're important. And they're part of what God did when He created this world. Keep *that* in mind when you're studying. And search the scriptures to try and help inform you how you can better appreciate, how you can better enjoy, how you can better love, how you can better have hope. What do *they* have to say that can bring you closer to God? Not: Can I find a way to dismiss something that Joseph said or did? As soon as Joseph was gone off the scene, people that envied the position that he occupied took over custody of everything, including the documents. And what we got as a consequence of that, is a legacy that allowed a trillion dollar empire to be constructed. Religion should require our sacrifice. It should not be here to benefit us. We should have to *give*, not get. And in the giving of ourselves, what we get is in the interior—it's in the heart. It's the things of enduring beauty and value.

The Lord is equal to the challenge. He will establish a new civilization. It will be founded on the fullness of His gospel. Lost truths will be restored; the path of righteousness will be returned.

Society is broken. Everywhere we see corrupt cultures based on corrupt laws, corrupt religions, corrupt values, and ultimately, corrupt thought. Beginning again requires re- civilizing people. To be free from corruption requires a change in thinking. If the Lord's to accomplish this, there will need to be a new temple at the center of that new civilization.

The Lord talked with Enoch regarding His return and started with a description of His temple. *For* ***there*** *shall be my tabernacle, and it shall be called Zion, a New Jerusalem* (Moses 7:62; see also Genesis 4:22 RE, emphasis added). It can only become Zion and a New Jerusalem if the Lord's tabernacle is there. His temple will be where He teaches all that must be understood to please God. Then, when people rise up to become what the Lord expects, His risen Tabernacle of glory, and the Lord Himself, will come to dwell there.

There's a great deal of work to be done to establish a foundation. And an even greater work thereafter. When God has His people, they are always commanded to build a temple. Joseph Smith explained:

> What was the object of gathering the...people of God in any age of the world?...The main object was to build unto the Lord a house whereby He could reveal unto His people the ordinances of His house and the glories of His kingdom, and teach the people the way of salvation; for there are certain ordinances and principles that when they are taught and practiced, must be done in a place or house built for that purpose. (*DHC* 5:423)

Joseph Smith taught the Relief Society that "the church is not now organized into its proper order, and cannot be until the temple is completed" (*Joseph Smith Papers,* Relief Society Minute Book, p. 36). Some believe that meant temple rites would fit inside the existing church organization. However, it is possible, if the temple had been completed, the people might have been organized in a new and different order, resembling the order in the age of the patriarchs. Joseph never had the opportunity to participate in that advancement. Before the temple was finished, Joseph was dead, and those who were leading had no intention or ability to reorganize the church into the "proper order."

The need for covenant people to cooperate in building a temple has been the same in any age. Temple builders founded the earliest civilizations. They did this to imitate the antediluvians. The Book of Abraham account suggests there was something *in* Egypt, below the floodwaters, worth waiting for the waters to recede. Some observers claim there is physical evidence that the earliest temple-complex structures in Egypt were built prior to the flood. They use archeological evidence at the Giza site to conclude the place was once under water, consistent with the description in the Book of Abraham.

When the first temples were built—or inherited by ancient civilizations—the center of life, government, education, culture, and art was at the temple. This was handed down from the first generations. The temple was founded before and will be needed to be the foundation again. When there has been an apostasy, temple building has been part of restoring. A *new* civilization will only become possible through teachings learned in the future House of God. The necessary ordinances can only be restored *in that setting*. There you will receive an uncorrupted restoration of the original faith taught to Adam and the patriarchs.

Joseph Smith was told that God intended to restore what was lost—meaning the fullness of the priesthood—but it was only to be accomplished through a temple. These were the Lord's words to Joseph:

> *For, for this cause I commanded Moses that he should build a tabernacle, that they should bear it with them in the wilderness, and to build a house in the land of promise, that those ordinances might be revealed which had been hid from before [the foundation of] the world... Therefore, verily I say unto you, that your anointings, and your washings, and your baptisms for the dead, and your solemn assemblies, and your memorials for your sacrifices by the sons of Levi, and for your oracles in your most holy places wherein you receive conversations, and your statutes and judgments, for the beginning of the revelations and foundation of Zion, and for the glory, [and] honor, and endowment of all her municipals, are ordained by the ordinance of my holy house, which my people are always commanded to build unto my holy name.* (D&C 124:38-39; see also T&C 141:12)

Joseph was martyred before there was a place where God could come to restore what had been lost. Joseph began to roll out a portion of temple ceremonial worship, but it was never completed. Uninspired men, who have changed, deleted, and added to what remained from Joseph, have corrupted those incomplete ceremonies.

The gospel is for redemption. Redemption from the fall returns man to God's presence. Ascending the heavenly mount is always taught in a properly-organized temple ceremonies. Ascending to heaven, redemption, and becoming part of the Family of God are all part of the ancient temple rites and must also be part of future temple rites.

The concept of "adoption" is widely recognized as part of Christianity. The term is employed loosely to mean that a person believes in Christ and recognizes Him as their Savior. The language of Paul is often cited and understood to claim believers are adopted into God's family.

> *For [you] have not received the spirit of bondage again to fear; but [you] have received the spirit of adoption, whereby we cry, Abba, Father. The Spirit itself [bears] witness with our spirit, that we are the children of God: And if children, then heirs; heirs of God, and joint-heirs with Christ; if [it] so be that we suffer with him, that we may be also glorified together.* (Romans 8:15-17; see also Romans 1:34 RE)

Language in the Book of Mormon has also been used to support a loose understanding of the term "adoption."

> *Marvel not that all mankind, yea, men and women, all nations, kindreds, tongue[s] and people, must be born again; yea, born of God, changed from their carnal and fallen state, to a state of righteousness, being redeemed of God, becoming his sons and daughters.* (Mosiah 27:25; see also Mosiah 11:28 RE)

The loose understanding of "adoption" was considerably tightened around October 1843 when Joseph Smith expanded his use of sealing authority. It grew from establishing marriages to include, also, man-to-man sealing through adoption. The last eight months of his life, Joseph sealed or "adopted" other men to himself. There was no settled, formal ordinance that has been preserved; and the proof of Joseph's practice is mostly post-mortem, as those who were exposed to the practice only vaguely recalled what he had done.

Nearly a decade after Joseph died, when temple ceremonial work resumed in the Endowment House in Salt Lake, Brigham Young declared that adoption was the crowning ordinance. It was *more* important than any other temple rites, including washing, anointing, endowment, and marriage sealing.

> This Chain must not [be] broken for mankind Cannot be saved any other way. This Priesthood must be linked together so that all the Children may be linked to Father Adam. ...we will seal men to men by the keys of the

> Holy Priesthood. This is the highest ordinance. It is the last ordinance of the kingdom of God on the earth and above all the endowments that can be given [to] you. It is a final sealing an Eternal Principle and when once made cannot be broken by the Devil. (*The Complete Discourses of Brigham Young*, Vol. 5, 13 January 1856, Vol. 2, p. 1033-1034)

In that talk, Brigham Young taught that the "turning of hearts to the fathers" foretold by Malachi was only to be fulfilled through adoption. He also taught the fulfillment of God's promise to Abraham regarding "his seed" would only be fulfilled through the temple ordinance of adoption. LDS Church leaders unsuccessfully tried to sort out how to practice adoption.

In a meeting of the reorganized School of Prophets, in Salt Lake City, on January 20, 1868, attended by the church presidency (Brigham Young, Heber C. Kimball, and Daniel Wells, along with Elders John Taylor, Orson Hyde, George A. Smith, Erastus Snow, George Q. Cannon, Phineas Young, and Joseph Young) the topic of adoption was discussed. President Wells conjectured: "On Adoption he supposed it had reference to the linking together of the Priesthood...that it might reach back to the link that had long since been broken, that it might present one unbroken chain" (*Salt Lake School of the Prophets: 1867-1883*, pp. 11-12; entry of 20 January 1868). In response Orson Hyde said: "The Doctrine of Adoption he knew but little about and should decline touching it until the line is chalked out" (ibid, p. 12). Scholars struggle to make sense of what Joseph was doing. And the attempts to reconstruct Joseph's later adoption innovation are insufficient to give any firm understanding of what took place, how, or why.

Thirty years before he would become church president, Wilford Woodruff concluded that adoptions would be something a resurrected Joseph Smith would return to sort out during the millennium: "Man also will have to be sealed to man until the chain is united from Father Adam down to the last Saint. This will be the work of the Millenium and Joseph Smith will be the man to attend...it or dictate it" (*Salt Lake School of the Prophets: 1867-1883*, p. 42; December 11, 1869).

A half-century after Joseph's death, the apostles struggled to know how it ought to work or who should be sealed to whom—how and what effect it would have in the afterlife. In a meeting on June one, 1893, attended by Lorenzo Snow, Franklin D. Richards, Francis M. Lyman, John Taylor, Marriner Merrill, Abraham Cannon, George F. Gibbs, John D. McAllister, Nephi Cannon..., and James Jack, they "had some talk about the ordinance of adoption in the temple. Joseph F. Smith said Pres. [Brigham] Young had told him to follow in ordinance work for the dead the rules which [would] ordinarily govern similar work for the living" (*Candid Insights of a Mormon Apostle: The Diaries of Abraham H. Cannon*, 1889-1895, p. 388). The practice was to seal faithful children to parents, and faithful parents to Joseph Smith. Woodruff explained: "I was sealed to my father, and then had him sealed to the Prophet Joseph" (ibid, p.488).

The concept of adoption affected how people understood the afterlife. This led some people to view adoption as a chance to pursue their self-interests. People began to aspire to improve their post-mortality by recruiting and acquiring descendants using adoption. The Logan Temple president was told to end his practice of recruiting adoptees. Eventually president Wilford Woodruff announced a final adoption practice on April 8, 1894: "Pres. Woodruff announced the doctrine of the sealing of children to parents as far back as...possible to trace the genealogy, and then seal the last member to the Prophet Joseph [Smith]" (ibid, p. 496).

Family relationships were reckoned by sealing, not biology. For example, Heber J. Grant was the biological son of Jedediah Grant, but because his mother was sealed to Joseph Smith, he was regarded as Joseph Smith's son.

What Joseph Smith understood about adoption did not get passed to subsequent church leaders clearly enough to preserve the practice intact. In September 1887, two months after John Taylor died, his son-in-law, John Whitaker, wrote in his diary:

> I went back to the office where I found [Apostle] Brother Lorenzo Snow and [First Council of the Seventy member] Jacob Gates. They were conversed... They conversed a long time. He finally entered into a deep subject on "The Law of Adoption." Brother Gates said he didn't believe in it as did also Brother Snow. He [?] referenced back to the time that Brigham Young was in Kirtland[;] he had a person [ask] him about it and he said, "I know nothing about it." President Taylor on one different occasion had a letter written to him for the following reason: it was [two undecipherable words followed by] of ... J[oseph] Smith or rather Sister Eliza R. Snow Smith (Brother Gates didn't know which)...about 70 persons were adopted into President J[oseph] Smith's [family;] Sister Snow Smith said "she didn't understand the law" but had no objections to them being sealed to her husband. And this led Brother Gates to write to President Taylor asking him if he knew anything about it. He never answered the letter. But on another occasion Brother Gates saw him and asked him plainly. President Taylor said he knew nothing about it. And

> also just lately when asked by Brother Snow, President...Woodruff knew nothing about it. ["]It hadn't been revealed to him." I know this at this time to say [or show] a prevailing feeling among the Twelve that they don't understand it. George...Cannon also said he didn't understand it. ("Adoptive Sealing Ritual in Mormonism," *Journal of Mormon History,* Vol. 37, No. 3, Summer 2011, p. 3; pp. 101-102)

As John Taylor's health was declining in the last month of his life, Wilford Woodruff recorded in his journal on June 8, 1887: "I wrote 4 Letters to Jaques Emma Clara & Roskelly. I did not rest well. Too much deep thinking to Sleep" (*Wilford Woodruff's Journals*, Vol. 8: 1 January 1881 to 31 December 1888, p. 441). Roskelly was employed as the recorder in the Logan Utah temple. That letter included the following mention of adoption:

> I have adopted this rule in Sealing and Adoptions: to take such as the Lord has given me, and leave the result[s] in His hands....Paul talked a good deal about Adoptions, but we did not understand much about it, until the Lord revealed it to Joseph Smith, and we may not, perhaps, understand it now as fully as we should. Still the Sealings and Adoptions are true principles, or our Prophets have been badly deceived. ("Adoptive Sealing Ritual in Mormonism," *Journal of Mormon History,* Vol. 37, No. 3, Summer 2011, p. 3; p. 103)

Adoption became progressively more controversial as time passed. Since the idea was not well understood by church leaders, they could provide no answers to questions on the subject. While bishop, Edward Bunker denounced the idea altogether, resulting in an 1892 church court that the church president and one of his counselors attended. The former bishop was charged with teaching false doctrine, and in his defense, he wrote a letter to the high council stating:

> The adoption of one man to another out of the lineage, I do not understand and for that reason I would not enter into it. And adopting the dead to the living is as adopting the father to the son. I don't believe there is a man on earth that thoroughly understands the principle. If there is, I have never heard it taught as I could understand it. I believe it is permmited [sic] more to satisfy the minds of the people for the present until the Lord reveals more fully the principle. (Edward Bunker, Letter to the Bunkerville High Council, April 25, 1891, *Edward Bunker Autobiography* (1894) 37, microfilm of holograph, MS 1581, LDS Church History Library)

In his summary of the court proceeding, Wilford Woodruff relegated the subject of adoption to one of the "mysteries" which church members ought to avoid discussing because they cause difficulties. He wrote: "June 11, 1892 We Met in the Tabernacle at 10 oclock on the trial of Bishop Bunker on Doctrin [sic]. We talked to them Plainly of the impropriety of indulging in Misteries [sic] to Create difficulties among the Saints. They professed to be Satisfied" (*Wilford Woodruff's Journal*, supra, 9:203).

Although John Taylor perpetuated the practice, over time it diminished and then disappeared beginning with Wilford Woodruff's presidency. Woodruff changed the policy in April 1894 to seal within biological families as far back as were known, and then to seal and adopt the last parents to Joseph Smith. This made adoption less of an issue and the genealogical search for ancestors of greater concern. But by 1922 the de-emphasis on adoption allowed it to be ignored altogether. The practice Woodruff announced in 1894 was *deleted* in the published account by the Utah Genealogical Society *and* from Clark's *Messages of The First Presidency*. Today adoption has *vanished* from the LDS church and was never practiced by the RLDS church or other branches of the Restoration.

Joseph Smith did not leave the Christian practice of "adoption" a loose idea, with believers becoming sons of God by conversion, belief, or baptism. He tied it to both authority to seal and an authoritative ordinance. Both of those were lost when Joseph and Hyrum were killed.

If adoption is (as Brigham Young thought in 1856) the highest ordinance above all the endowments that can be given, if it is needed for the gospel (as taught to Abraham) to be restored, then the loss of adoption rites is indeed a sign of apostasy. Brigham Young taught adoption would bind a person beyond the devil's power to break. But adoption was abandoned before the end of the 1800s. Adoption will need to be restored as a rite—with an accompanying authoritative ordinance and sealing—in order for the things Joseph Smith alone understood and taught, to be renewed.

As Mormon completed the record of Christ's visit to the Nephites, he provided this description of the Book of Mormon's purpose:

> *When the Lord shall see fit, in his wisdom, that these sayings shall come unto the Gentiles according to his word, then ye may know that the covenant which the Father hath made with the children of Israel, concerning their restoration to the* ***lands*** *of their inheritance, is already beginning to be fulfilled. And ye may know that the words of the Lord, which have been*

> *spoken by the holy prophets,* ***shall all be fulfilled;****... The Lord will remember his covenant which he hath made unto his people of the house of Israel* (3 Nephi 29:1-3; see also 3 Nephi 13:7 RE, emphasis added).

And as Moroni concluded the record, *he* inserted some final words of instruction for the people who would receive the Book of Mormon in the last days. These words were taught to him by his father. He says:

> *Hath miracles ceased?...I say unto you, nay; neither have angels ceased to minister unto the children of men. For...they are subject unto him, to minister according to the word of his command, [showing] themselves unto them of strong faith and a firm mind in every form of godliness. And the office of their ministry is to call men unto repentance, and to fulfill and to do the work of the* ***covenants*** *of the Father, which he hath made unto the children of men, ...declaring the word of Christ unto the chosen vessels of the Lord, that they may bear testimony of him. And by so doing, the Lord God prepareth the way that the residue of men may have faith in Christ, that the Holy Ghost may have place in their hearts, according to the power thereof; and [this after] the manner... and [this] after this manner bringeth to pass the Father, the* ***covenants*** *which he hath made unto the children of men.* (Moroni 7:6 RE, emphasis added)

There are numerous other passages in the Book of Mormon that speak to the same thing. The Book of Mormon is a forerunner—a harbinger—that was intended to say to the people who receive it: There are covenants that go back to the very beginning, to the original Fathers. Those covenants got renewed, they got restored, they got continued in the form of Abraham (who received all that had been there originally) coming out of apostasy and being adopted back into that line of Patriarchs. That original covenant material provoked the creation of the Book of Mormon, and it is one of the major testimonies that is given to us by the Book of Mormon about the work that God intends to do in the last days. You can believe in the Bible; you can accept Jesus as your Savior; you can be (in the words of the Evangelical community) "born again." You can be (in the words of Latter-day Saints) someone whose calling and election is made sure. But the work of God, at this point, is not about merely individual salvation; it is the work of fulfilling the covenants that were made with the Fathers. It is the work of restoring again that original gospel, of which the law given to Moses pointed forward to, but did not comprehend.

We tend to view priesthood in institutional ways. And it's hard to be terribly critical of misunderstandings because, quite frankly, priestly authority (following the success of the Petrine branch of original Christianity and its triumph, with emphasis on authority and priesthood and keys) predisposed the entire Christian world. Even the Christian world, after the Protestant Reformation, succeeded in finally breaking off areas in which a different form of protest Christianity could be practiced that was not subservient to the Roman "See" and papal decree. They still had this misapprehension about priesthood. So, when Joseph Smith began to talk about priesthood and to begin the process of restoring it, he gave a new kind of vocabulary, but possession of a vocabulary does not mean possession of the thing.

When Abraham talks about becoming a rightful heir and becoming a high priest, it would be best if you threw out everything that you have heard, or learned, or understood about the concept of priesthood. Priesthood includes the prerogative, the right, the obligation, or the duty to go out and perform ordinances that are effective, that God will recognize to be sure—and that's part of it, and it's a true principle.

However, priesthood in the original sense, was something far more vast. It included an understanding of things that relate back all the way to the beginning—or before the world was—and goes forward through all periods of time until the end. It includes a basis of knowledge. So, when you read Abraham's description of what it was he looked for, and he mentions priesthood, you have to merge that into the entirety of what he's talking about: knowledge, understanding, commandments, instructions; having the capacity to see things in their correctly-ordered fashion similarly to how God originally intended that it be ordered—so that you are no longer out-of-sync with this creation and doing your best to "reign with blood and horror" by subduing nature with the iron plow, and gunpowder, and lead—but instead you find yourself situated in a place that Eden itself can be renewed, and harmony can be achieved between man and the earth.

The Book of Mormon is talking about something vast, but it continually points back to Abraham. And I do not care what arguments can be made, or what a pitiful effort has been put together to defend the Book of Abraham that Joseph Smith provided us. It was essential to the Restoration that the Book of Abraham be given to us, because without it, we would not understand a great deal about the Restoration and what the final objective of the Restoration was to achieve.

If you're going to please God, you don't please Him by having your "born again" experience (or having your "calling and election made sure" experience) if the result of that is to make you proud, conceited, self-assured, and arrogant, and to disconnect you from the restoration process that was begun through Joseph Smith and has yet a greater work to be done than was achieved at the time of Joseph Smith. Go off and be saved, but you will not fulfill the work of the covenants that God intends to achieve. He has committed himself to that end.

Those who will labor alongside Him—whether they be Gentile, or Lamanite or Jew, it does not matter—if they will repent and accept the process of the Restoration, as it began through Joseph Smith, not only to say it correctly but to do what it tells us needs to be done, then you will be numbered among those people that God has covenanted to gather against the coming harvest.

But if you want to be the lone guru, whose commentaries fill pages of blogging and hours of pontification, but you're going to labor at odds, I read you the warning: All that fight against Zion are going to perish. So, you can shout your hallelujahs in the spirit world, and you can proclaim your calling and election guarantees you something, but quite frankly, practically everyone's calling and election can be made sure. You get to continue progress. You get to continue to repent. God's not gonna terminate you at the end of this cycle of creation, but you're gonna be allowed to go on, and upward, if you'll continue to repent.

You will always be free to choose, but the work of the covenants that the Book of Mormon foretell are to be accomplished through the reclaiming (by repentance and returning to Him) of Gentiles that will, ultimately, reach out to (and include) restoring the Lamanites/ restoring the Jews to a knowledge of the works of the Father, that... *that* is what is on the mind of God today. *That* is the purpose of the covenant that was given unto us in Boise, just a few years ago—two years ago. *That* is what fulfilling the covenant ultimately requires that *we* labor to achieve.

That effort began in earnest with the reclaiming of the scriptures and the presenting of those to the Lord for His acceptance; and the marvelous news, that God accepted them as adequate for His purpose for us, and the commitment that He would labor with us to go forward.

Anyone can join the party. Anyone can come into this work. Anyone can remain a Catholic or a Presbyterian, a Catholic or a Latter-day Saint. It doesn't matter. Those things are more like civic clubs. I don't care if you're a Rotarian or a Kiwanis Club member—means about the same thing as belonging to any of those organizations. Associate with whoever you like to associate with, but you *must* accept baptism. You *must* accept the Book of

Mormon. It *is* a *covenant*. The covenant *must* be accepted, and you *must* help labor alongside those who seek to return Zion.

The foregoing excerpts are taken from:

- Denver's remarks titled "Book of Mormon as Covenant," given at the Book of Mormon Covenant Conference in Columbia, SC on January 13, 2019

- Denver's conference talk titled "Civilization," given in Grand Junction, CO on April 21, 2019; and

- Denver's conference talk titled "The Book of Mormon Holds the Covenant Pattern for the Full Restoration," given in Boise, ID on September 22, 2019

110. Whipsaw

The following podcast was recorded by Denver on April 4, 2020.

DENVER: We have something going on called the Wuhan Virus (or the COVID-19 virus or the Chinese virus or the "Kung Flu"). I'm not sure which name to call it by, so I'll just use Wuhan even though, apparently, there are those that take offense at referring to it as anything that may imply it originated in China.

There's a… There's a series of dominos that have fallen over that begin with the fear that this particular strain is toxic enough to kill in a number that is significantly greater than the common flu but, apparently, less than the SARS epidemic. But the problem with evaluating how serious a threat this is to health is a mathematical problem.

If you know for certain that ten people have this condition, and you know for certain that one person has died (and those are the only numbers that you have), then you know that one out of every ten people that have had this died (or ten percent of the people who have had it will die from it or have died from it). The problem is, then, extending it to the next stage, which is predictive. If ten percent that **have** had it died, then projecting it forward, you **assume** that ten percent of the people that **will** have it are going to die. And then that's a serious, serious concern, because it's communicable, and it can spread like wildfire, and you're gonna lose a big number of people.

But so far, we've got unknown numbers. The number of people who get actually diagnosed usually include only those that have been either alarmed enough by their physical symptoms to go in and have a test done, or they've taken up the offer of public testing, and they've shown up to be tested—but that has amounted to a very small portion of the population.

In other words, we do not know what the denominator is in the equation. We're trying to come up with a statistical number for how great a threat this thing is, but we don't know how many have had it. **And** it's further complicated by the fact that many people **could** have had it, but they weren't symptomatic. They didn't get tested. They experienced it; it was mild enough that they dismissed it; they never went in and got tested; they haven't been diagnosed; and there's no way, therefore, to know that we ought to be including **them** in the denominator equation. But as this has been further tested, we've wound up with a bigger denominator. So, where—at first—the prediction was that the death rate could be above 4%, that number has been dropping as the denominator has grown. If ten people have had it and one has died, that's 10%. But if you test a bunch of others and you find out that a hundred people have had it and only one person has died, then you know that the death rate that has occurred is 1%. But what if the number of people who've had it but dismissed it (and that number is significantly greater than anyone anticipated) turns the denominator into a thousand, and only one person has died? Well, then the death rate drops all the way down to .01%, and it's no worse than typical seasonal flu.

Right now there's an abundance of ignorance about what the denominator ought to be. Furthermore, we have no assurance that whatever the denominator turns out to be that the history of what **has** happened is reliable as a **predictor** for what **will** happen.

So, right now, I think, listening to the news and listening to the advocates who are trying to sell you your attention to their broadcast, your attention to their news cast, your attention to their media material online... They have every incentive, because they want you to tune in; they want you to listen. And the way to get you to do that is to alarm you. They really would like to turn this into something that is so historic, so threatening, so troubling that you'll go back time and time again to find out what the very latest word is about this.

Right now what we've got is a whole bunch of ignorance. We don't know the denominator. We don't know whether the denominator—when it finally is known—can serve as a predictor for what **will** happen. And it may be that there are many multiples of people who have been contracting this and have been asymptomatic. We will never know how to include them in the overall number.

So, the amount of alarm that you feel about this (as a personal threat, right now) is extraordinarily speculative, and (based on the latest numbers) the predicted death rate appears to be dropping down into the area of normal seasonal flu. And the victims appear to be like the common victim of normal seasonal flu—that is, people who already have lung issues, heart issues, diabetes, compromised immune symptoms, or other pre-existing conditions. The people who have been dying (with extraordinarily rare exceptions) appear to have co-morbidity issues; they have a pre-existing serious medical condition (or more than one serious pre-existing medical condition). And people who fall into that category should be taking precautions against the flu and should be taking care of—as best they can—staying away from environments where they may catch the flu, like this one.

But that just sets the stage. That's the current **cause** of hysteria. It's the **response** to the hysteria that is particularly both unprecedented and very troubling.

The way in which state and national government has responded in the United States (and national governments have responded in other countries) is more alarming to me than the condition that they're responding to. To deny people the freedom of movement, to interfere with the ability to assemble, to compromise on rights that are spelled out in the Constitution and in the Bill of Rights is particularly alarming as a coercive step by government. We're reacting to what has been called a "pandemic" as if it were a sufficient cause for suspending civil rights and constitutional rights.

Right now the United States divides largely into two political camps. Both of them are highly charged, but they're two political camps: the progressive or liberal or Democratic side (which is a hodgepodge of different sorts of people), on the one hand, and the conservative or the Republican or the traditionalist group of people, on the other hand (although, again, that's a really difficult generalization to refer to—and I'd include Libertarians within that second group), are largely opposed to one another on a whole bunch of philosophical and other issues. The liberal wing, in particular, is willing to curtail the scope of the Second Amendment and what's called "gun rights." The conservative side advocates fiercely protecting the Second Amendment right to get a firearm, in part because they are serious about viewing the government as a potential threat, and therefore, you know, "You can have my gun when you pry it from my cold, dead fingers" is one of the bumper stickers that that second group uses.

Well, going back in history, when President Nixon went to China and met with the Chinese leaders and opened up the dialogue between the United States and China, one of the recognitions that political commentators made at the time was that only Nixon could have gotten away with opening up relations with China—because the Chinese were viewed as conspiratorial, an enemy, a threat. They had, after all, supplied a great deal of the weaponry (if not the outright personnel) that had fought against American forces in Southeast Asia, beginning in Vietnam and then spreading out to Laos and Cambodia. The belief was that they were an active, on-the-field participant in the Vietnam War against the United States. But Nixon went over and met with them, and the conservative/the gun-rights folks/the traditionalists were not alarmed at the conservative Richard Nixon opening the door to relations with China, because they trusted him. He was one of them, they thought—so, he had the credibility, the standing and the correct political suit on in order for that second conservative group to acknowledge and accept the step that he took in opening up the relations.

Right now, the abrogation of civil rights and the tolerance of the interference with freedom of movement, freedom of assembly, commerce itself, the suspension of business activities is something that Donald Trump is tolerated—because the group that believes in the Second Amendment, is traditionalist, and is interested in protecting their constitutional rights are satisfied that Trump is one of them—that he's for small government; he's for draining the swamp in Washington, D.C.—and he's one of them. And as a result of him being one of them, their guard is down, and they tolerate these things in a way that if President Obama had attempted to do anything like this, the human cry that would have come out would probably have made the measures-that-are-currently-being-undertaken absolutely impractical to adopt. In fact, the effort to shut down gun stores in various states would have probably been greeted with outright violence had the person doing it been both Barack Obama (as President) and a Democratic governor (as someone seconding the choice to shut down access to purchase of firearms).

So, in the present circumstances, it should not matter to anyone that you trust a President. It shouldn't matter that you think the activities are being done by someone you regard as benign. Everything that's happening at the moment is precedential, not presidential. It is a **precedent**. It establishes a mark in history in which later Presidents can refer back to the earlier President's adoption of measures and can say, "I'm doing no different than the earlier President did, and therefore, what I'm doing is accepted, traditional, historic, and constitutional." The problem is that what's going on right now is none of those things. And it's our reaction to this ill-defined, unproven, unknown viral threat that has interfered with commerce, shut down businesses, confined people to homes, resulted in police going about telling groups of people that they have to break up. The idea of social distancing and crowd- control isolates people and puts everyone in an extraordinary, vulnerable, and disadvantageous position because of the inability to assemble freely and the inability to move and exercise your liberties that are guaranteed by the Constitution.

So, whatever it is that you think you are submitting to for exigent circumstances right now, **if** this proves to be no more threatening than the common flu in any given flu season, we're establishing the precedent that public health and welfare can be guarded by the abrogation of constitutional and civil rights, in order to protect people against what may be a relatively small threat in the end. We simply don't know what that end will be, but we're **acting as if** the presence of the mere threat (with its ill-defined contours) is enough to justify all of the extraordinary measures that are currently being taken.

Because this is "popular"—that the approval of President Trump's handling of this is greater than 50%—what that means is the majority of the American people, at present, are willing to allow totalitarian steps to be taken in order to guard against an ill-defined and currently unknown natural threat that exists. That ought to alarm you more than anything else that's currently going on. Democracy and freedom is a very delicate flower. It can be destroyed by conspiring men that we have been warned about in revelation (that addresses, specifically, the government of the United States). It may be that, in all of this, President Trump has the best of intentions. It may be that he **can** be trusted. **However**, trusting one man with the ability to do it (simply because his political views align with your political views) sets a precedent which a later President (that you **do not** trust and whose political views are greatly at variance with your own) can rely upon and point back to and pose the question, "Why, if it's wrong, did you submit before? Why, if you didn't expect this to be the role for the government to occupy in circumstances that require dramatic steps to be taken in order to guard public health, why did you not raise a protest?"

Well, that's the second leg of this problem. Here's the third leg of the problem. Right now, we have shut down commerce. They have passed a $2.2 trillion bill to compensate for the interference with commerce on this national scope. This has never been done before. It is a violation of the Bill of Rights' "Constitutional Takings" clause that requires the government to give "just compensation" whenever they take anything from you. "Takings" by the Federal Government include interference with your ability to conduct business. So, if the government comes in and says, "We have good reason to justify shutting your business down temporarily," and they do so, they owe you under the "Takings" clause for the amount of the loss that you sustain in consequence of being shut down. The Relief Bill that has been passed is—at least in part—motivated by a Federal Government desire to stop 500 million lawsuits from being filed by those that have been adversely affected. If, for example, 500,000 lawsuits are filed and **one** of them succeeds under the "Takings" clause to get compensation, then that precedent could be used in every other case against the Federal Government—and you would have all these advertisements on your television stations for joining in the class-action lawsuit against the Federal Government (much like you see them going against Big Pharma right now with class actions).

On average, the Gross Domestic Product of the United States generates $2 trillion in business activity every month—so $2.2 trillion is an attempt to compensate the public for about what happens with the loss of one month's activity in the marketplace. But there is an enormous difference between getting paid by the government for **not** doing business and generating that level of business activity **on your own**. We have never had a circumstance in which the Federal Government has shut down the economy in the way that they have done it at present. Therefore, **there is no economic model** that can predict what the effect is going to be of this extraordinary draconian step that the Federal Government has taken in response to a threat whose contours are presently unknown and unproven. So, we shut down the economy. We try to make up for that by printing (through the Federal Reserve) $2.2 trillion dollars, and then we dump that back into the economy as a compensatory measure for the ill-effects of shutting things down.

But economists aren't just concerned with pluses and minuses or numbers on a balance sheet. There's an extraordinary effect in the marketplace that happens as a result of what people **think**, of whether they are calm or whether they are upset, whether they're fearful. Buying and selling in commerce is based upon the confidence that people have in their ability, then, to go forward and to meet the obligation. If you're talking about the obligation of purchasing some expensive commercial product for the home—a refrigerator or a stove—then you need to know that you're gonna be able to either pay cash to purchase the thing or the ability to make payments on it maybe for 3 months, maybe for 5 months, maybe for 6 months. You have to have even **more** confidence in what is going on in the economy and in your life in order to commit to and purchase a **car** that may require you to make payments over a period of 5 years and have the confidence you're gonna be able to do that. But if you're gonna buy a **house**, then you need to have the confidence that you're gonna be able to go out and to incur a loan, buy the home, and meet the payments for a minimum of 15 years but perhaps as much as 30 years.

Donald Trump is a developer, and he **knows** that the economy is largely driven by home sales. When people buy a home, everything that goes into the home requires a great deal of manufacturing activity. But after the house itself is built, then people have to buy—in order to furnish the home—washers and dryers, dishwashers, couches, beds, chests of drawers, all kinds of goods and services that are required in order to furnish the home. If you want to stimulate the economy, you **need** to stimulate house-building. If you can get houses built, it will pull along enough related economic activity that the overall economy is benefited. So, new home sales, new home starts, new home construction—these are pillars upon which vast amounts of the overall economy are built.

We don't know, as a result of shutting the economy down and the number of people that have lost their jobs right now, numbering in the millions... We don't know what the effect is going to be upon the attitudes of those people if economic activity resumes. Even if it resumes today, it's gonna take a little while for it to get back up to normal. But "normal" on the other side of the trauma of what has happened with the Federal Government shutting things down may not at all be the normal—because of the minds, the hearts, the fears, the apprehensions, the trauma that has been introduced by this—may not at all be the same as it was before. We have no economic model that we can use. In short, this is an entirely elaborate economic venture that is **also** unprecedented. And that on the other side of this, we don't know how long it will take for the economy to get back to where it was or whether the results of this are gonna create a lot of apprehension that's gonna be hard to shed.

So, the reason for this particular podcast is to say, "Let's take one step back, and let's think about all this"—because we are culturally, economically, and governmentally right now being whipsawed by a whole lot of apprehension based on unproven, unknown data that has resulted in massive market shutdown that is **probably** precedential and **likely** to be repeated at some point in the future.

So, if you want to be independent of every other thing under heaven (as Zion has been described to achieve), then you ought to ask yourself, "Upon what basis, then, is that kind of security **able** to be created? What is it that allows some people, somewhere, to exist without the whipsaw effect of public hysteria and governmental interference in the marketplace and economic collapse because of unemployment?"

Well, there are two things that comprise enduring security and wealth. Those two things are **land** and **water**. If you have access to land, you can grow food, you can cultivate what you need to eat, you can raise animals, you can have chickens that lay eggs, and you have the ability to sustain yourself. No matter what else happens, if you've got land on which you can have food production, you have some security that's independent of everything else under heaven. But that land does **not** create those activities without a lot of husbandry and water. You have to work the land in order to have it yield, and you need water in order to work the land. So, ultimately, there is a need to acquire land and the need to develop water resources on the land in order to be able to sustain life.

I gave a talk down in Hurricane, Utah where I talked about some of these things. Right now, this is a great opportunity for everyone who's interested in this idea of Zion to take a moment and reflect on what it would take in order to have even a small population be able to find itself self-sufficient and able to endure even in the times of extraordinary upheaval. The ability to have land is dependent upon the ability to make the purchase. We're not justified in taking anything. As I spoke in Hurricane, I explained that we can only acquire land by purchase. We can't acquire it in any other way. But the ability to make a purchase and the ability to even develop after the purchase is made is entirely driven by the amount that Babylon is gonna demand be paid in order to acquire it and our ability to have that kind of funding to go forward.

Well, I've spoken about it. I'm not doing anything personally to be the one to collect any funds. I won't do that because, in my view, those who promote an undertaking and ask you to support their venture are almost always looking to do so because they intend to personally profit. I do not intend to personally profit. And to make that **clear**, I'm not even collecting the money. I'm allowing other people to do so. And I'm supporting their effort because **I do not intend to ever profit** from this venture. I plan to sacrifice to support the venture. To that end, I expect to give far more than I expect anyone else to give in order to make this happen—but **the time is passing**. The need exists, and the opportunity for us to take steps today may be **limited** by whatever it is that we're willing to do at the moment to sacrifice.

I understand there are poor who need to be cared for. I understand there are people in need that have crying needs that ought to be addressed. I understand that people of good faith have chosen to do everything they can in that regard and have not contributed otherwise, and I think the Lord is pleased with them. I think that there's every reason to **respect** that choice. But what's going on right now is a great illustration of **why** it would be better to stand independent than it is to remain inside a social and cultural construct that the Lord has **told us** is doomed both to fail and to be destroyed.

We have a season to prepare. Things **will** get better. This lesson will be a passing illustration of panic and I hope an over-re...—later regarded as an over-reaction, later regarded as an inappropriate government response—and that on the other side of this, there'll be a vow to never again allow that kind of nonsense to take place based purely upon fear. I doubt that'll be the case, but **we** should remember, no matter who else forgets. We should point to it as an illustration. Its timing has been designed to drive home, particularly to **us**, the vulnerabilities that exist in the current social/governmental/political/economic construct. We have a Scripture Project that has been affected by at least 21 days as a result of what's going on right now in response to the same fear in the nation of India where our printing is taking place.

The fact is that at the very time that we are getting far more concretely along in the effort to try and bring about the fulfillment of prophecy, this opportunity presents itself, and it interferes with what we're planning, what we're trying to achieve—but it serves as a lesson to us along the way. The adversary's desire to frustrate this process—and the commitment of the opponent to this work is as real and as tangible as anything else that exists in this world. The fact is that the culmination of this effort and the vindication of God's promises made to the Fathers is coincidental with the loss of control by the god of this world. The Lord Himself intends to assert governance over the nations and intends to bring about a full end of all nations in order to initiate His own rule. He plans to take this world over, and to do so will require the shaking of Babylon and its collapse. We have a great illustration of what that might look like at the beginning going on right now.

What we **don't** have is a concerted effort to try and make the necessary preparations— because you **can't** do this stuff in **haste**. It takes… It takes land to know how to engineer the land. It takes perhaps as much as a year and a half in order to engineer it, and then it takes time to be able to install what the engineering has designed, all of which **precedes** the ability to begin to occupy and farm or construct a temple upon the land.

There are extraordinary things that have to take place before we get that far. But right now, let this current uproar serve as a useful illustration to you of how God, with very small means, can shake the nations—and how unreliably steady and unreliably established your rights are and your ability to move and to assemble and to do as you would like to do. If you have your own land, you can go out and work on your land no matter what's going on on Main Street in the rest of the nation.

So, those are the points that I think ought to be taken from the current mess, above all others.

111. Nature, Part 1

This is the first part of a multi-part series on nature where Denver discusses some of the many ways that things in nature point to Christ.

DENVER: So, it did not surprise me at all when Joseph went out to pray in the grove, and as he began that search, he got attacked by the adversary. And then, calling upon God with all his strength, he got delivered. It did not surprise me when I got attacked by a malevolent source before I encountered an angel. And it didn't put me off the trail. In fact, I was, again, stupid enough to say, "Oh! This is kinda like what happened when Joseph was trying to approach God. He encountered opposition."

So, to me, the opposition suggested the presence of God and God's reality and God's bona fide existence and work—because if the enemy is there, there has to be the opposite of the enemy, also. It was sometime later that I encountered an angel. And I haven't talked much about the miraculous things that have gone on because I don't think that it's particularly helpful to put a lot of details out about any of that stuff. But, I want you to know that it does happen. And it happens as much today in people of faith as it happens in the course of the Scriptures.

I do **not** believe for one moment that God carefully limits and cautiously apportions the things that come from Him to a select few. I think that God's abundance is meant for everyone. And the regulator, the inhibitor, the limiter isn't up there. It's within us.

I think that, you know, the farther up you look, the more vast— At a glance, if you look up into heaven, you can see distances that are so great that they are measured in the distance light will travel in a year. In fact, you can see, if you look upward, distances that take billions of years for light to cross them. Those are the distant stars you're seeing up there. Heaven is vast and filled. It's us that limits that. The farther out you go, the more you see up there, the more you should realize that the vastness of God is beyond anything that we can contain. So, let a little of that in. Every one of you has **some direct linkage** to God. It's called a *gift*. Every one of you has some unique gift as a way that God talks to you. Let it in. Be sensitive to it.

I was mentioning at dinner last night— Monarch butterflies migrate. Do you see a monarch butterfly up here? Oh, look, right there. They migrate. That butterfly has probably flown from here to somewhere in Central America, okay? They cover thousands of miles, and they do it annually—those little things—okay?

The last time we had a snowstorm (and it was a lot of snow down where we live in Sandy), my wife and I went hiking the next day. It was cold the day before. Lots of snow came down, and when we went out hiking, a lot of it had melted off because it was so warm the next day. And on that hike, the next day, I saw a monarch butterfly flying along the trail. (A monarch butterfly will be killed by snowfall.) When I saw the monarch butterfly on that hike, I told my wife, "It's not going to snow again. That was the last snow of the season; it's over with," —because the monarch butterfly has a life that is dependent upon arriving when it's safe to arrive.

God talks to us through all kinds of things. When you see the geese moving, flying south, their lives depend upon knowing when to go. There's so many things in nature if you'll just observe it, if you'll just let it in. God is speaking to all of us **more or less** all of the time. And we determine how much of that we're willing to let in.

So, the dispensation of the meridian of time when the Lord is going to come begins right here in this spot. That ought to tell us something, too, about the terrible significance of tying into everything that the Lord does—the temple. So, here we are, standing on this side of the veil with the dispensation launched, with an angel who has emerged, not from just the figurative or symbolic but from the literal presence of the Lord. And we're going to have to, as part of this dispensation at some point, pass through that veil and enter into the Holy of Holies.

When Moses passed through the veil, the presence of the Lord was shielded by a covering of a thick cloud. The cloud operated as a veil to the onlookers of Israel, but Moses was allowed to pass through or enter through the cloud into the very presence of God. We have an account of that in Exodus chapter 24, in verses 15-18.

> *And Moses went up into the mount, and a cloud covered the mount. And the glory of the Lord abode upon mount Sinai, and the cloud covered it six days: and [on] the seventh day he called unto Moses out of the midst of the cloud. And the sight of the glory of the Lord was like devouring fire on the top of the mount in the eyes of the children of Israel. And Moses went into the midst of the cloud, and gat him up into the mount: and Moses was in the mount forty days and forty nights.* (Exodus 24:15-18; see also Exodus 13:26 RE)

See, just like in the mountain of the Lord's house, you have the pinnacle, the spot at the top of the mountain at which, when one stands there, they are no longer of the earth, but they have become a part of the sky. It's one of the reasons why the mountain of the Lord's house is the symbol that gets used in Scripture to describe the phenomenon—because it is no longer connecting you to the earth. The only thing that touches is the soles of your feet. You have become part of the heavens. Moses ascends up, and the ascension that's being talked about here (in the cloud at the top of the mountain of the Lord's house), inside there is where we find the presence of the Lord.

Similarly, as Christ asked, "Ought not these things to have happened?" one of the things that had happened was: In the dispensation of the meridian of time, Christ also passed through the cloud and entered into the presence of the Father. There were three disciples who were able to see Moses, Elias, but they were not permitted to see the Father, though they heard His voice. They heard the voice speaking from inside the cloud. Only Christ passed into the Father's presence. That's recorded in Matthew chapter 17, verses 1-8.

The relevant part:

> *After six days Jesus taketh Peter, James, and John his brother, ...bringeth them...into an high mountain apart, was transfigured before them: and his face did shine as the sun, ...his raiment was white as the light. And behold, there appeared unto them Moses and Elias talking with him. Then answered Peter, and said unto Jesus, Lord, [it's] good for us to be here: if thou wilt, let us make [thee] three tabernacles; one for thee, ...one for Moses, ...one for Elias. While he yet spake, behold, a bright cloud overshadowed them: and behold a voice out of the cloud, which said, This is my beloved Son, in whom I am well pleased; hear ye him, and when the disciples heard it, they fell on their face, and were sore afraid.* [It's intimidating.] *...Jesus came and touched them, and said, Arise, ...be not afraid. ...when they...lifted...their eyes, they saw no man, save Jesus only.* (Matthew 17:1-8; see also Matthew 9:4 RE)

See, Christ tells these disciples to *tell the vision to no man, until the Son of man shall be risen again from the dead* (Matthew 17:9; see also Matthew 9:5 RE). Well, on the road to Emmaus, He was risen again from the dead. There is no reason now to withhold the information about the Lord having passed through the veil on the Mount of Transfiguration into the presence of God the Father. So, this would have been available subject fodder for the discussion on the road as well.

Isaiah described a coming age of peace when righteousness and truth have their opportunity to bear fruit. He spoke of Christ and of the power in Christ's teachings to transform the world itself. That same world that Enoch heard lamenting, pained by the violence on her face, **will** find rest. Isaiah foretells what will happen **just prior** to the Lord's return:

> *And there shall come forth a rod out of the stem of Jesse, and a branch shall grow out of his roots: And the spirit of the Lord shall rest upon him, the spirit of wisdom and understanding, the spirit of counsel and might, the spirit of knowledge and of the fear of the Lord; And shall make him of quick understanding in the fear of the Lord. And he shall not judge after the sight of his eyes, neither reprove after the hearing of his ears: But with righteousness shall he judge the poor, and reprove with equity for the meek of the earth: and he shall smite the earth: with the rod of his mouth, and with the breath of his lips shall he slay the wicked. And righteousness shall be the girdle of his loins, and faithfulness the girdle of his reins. The wolf also shall dwell with the lamb, and the leopard shall lie down with the kid; and the calf and the young lion and the fatling together; and [the] little child shall lead them. And the cow and the bear shall feed; their young ones shall lie down together: and the lion shall eat straw like the ox. And the sucking child shall play on the hole of [an] asp, and the weaned child shall put his hand on the cockatrice'[s] den. They shall not hurt nor destroy in all my holy mountain; for the earth shall be full of the knowledge of the Lord, as the waters cover the sea. And in that day, there shall be a root of Jesse, which shall stand for an ensign of the people; to it shall the Gentiles seek: and his rest shall be glorious.* (Isaiah 11:1-10; see also Isaiah 5:4 RE)

How will Christ smite the earth with the rod of His mouth? By teaching peace to people who are willing to obey and live at peace. What will it take to see the wolf dwell with the lamb? Why does the wolf kill the lamb today? The wolf kills because it's hungry. If the same shepherd who feeds the lamb also fed the wolf, then the wolf would not need to kill.

Wolves can be domesticated. I once owned a mixed Wolf Malamute we named Cicely after the fictitious town in Alaska that was the setting for the TV show *Northern Exposure*. Cicely looked **entirely** like a wolf, and her behavior was lupine. She was **very** gentle with her clan—our immediate family and friends. My children were still young then, and our neighborhood had other young children who came over. Cicely recognized **them** and accepted them as belonging. However, an adult man trying to read an electrical meter once entered our backyard, and Cicely regarded this as a threat to her clan. The man scarcely escaped through the gate. Wolves are intelligent animals and inside their clans are capable of treating young children with gentle, protective care. They are also capable defenders against threats.

Under the peaceful guidance of a kindly shepherd, the wolf and the lamb could learn to lie down together. Lions have been domesticated, as have bears. When Adam was given dominion over the earth, all the animals that came to him for naming dwelt together peacefully. Why do we assume that nature is violent? Why regard it as *red of tooth and claw*?

The Scriptures speak of an idyllic time in the beginning when man and nature were entirely at peace with one another. The Scriptures also foretell of a **coming** idyllic age when that peace is restored again.

Why do we accept these bookends as true without ever considering the role of man in destroying the original peace? Why do we assume we have no obligation imposed upon us to **reform** creation back to the original? The prophecy of Isaiah is not magic imposed by God on a reluctant creation. It will require shepherds to **care** for creation.

Who are *they* in this passage? ***They*** *shall not hurt nor destroy in all my holy mountain* (Isaiah 11:9; see also Isaiah 5:4 RE). And why is the passage, ***They*** *shall not hurt nor destroy in all my holy mountain* followed by the statement: *for the earth shall be full of the knowledge of the Lord as the waters cover the sea* (ibid, vs. 9; ibid, vs. 4 RE)? These are connected thoughts. It should be obvious to you that this can only be fulfilled by a different civilization than the one in which **we** live. **Ours** can **never** produce such results.

Isaiah also describes what it will be like **after** the Lord's return. After He comes to dwell with those prepared to welcome His return, events will unfold in this way:

> *For behold, I create [a] new [heaven] and a new earth, and the former shall not be remembered nor come into mind. But be glad and rejoice for ever in that which I create; for behold, I create Jerusalem a rejoicing, and her people a joy. And I will rejoice in Jerusalem and joy in my people, and the voice of weeping shall be no more heard in her, nor the voice of crying. In those days, there shall be no more from there an infant of days, nor an old man that has not [ful]filled his day; for the child shall not die, but shall live to be a hundred years old. But the sinner living to be a hundred years old shall be accursed. And they shall build houses and inhabit them, and they shall plant vineyards and eat the fruit of them. They shall not build and another inhabit, they shall not plant and another eat; for as the days of a tree are the days of*

> *my people, and [mine] elect shall long enjoy the work of their hands. They shall not labor in vain, nor bring forth for trouble; for they are the seed of the blessed of the Lord, and their offspring with them. And it shall come to pass that before they call, I will answer, and while they are yet speaking, I will hear. The wolf and the lamb shall feed together, and the lion shall eat straw like the bullock, and dust shall be the serpent's food. They shall not hurt nor destroy in all my holy mountain, says the Lord.* (Isaiah 24:9 RE)

The same words are used to describe the prepared people **before** the return of the Lord and those with whom He will dwell **after** His return. Neither of these *shall not hurt nor destroy in all my holy mountain, says the Lord.* What will they be like who do not hurt nor destroy? Can you imagine such a society? Isaiah's description reflects this incident involving Joseph Smith and Zion's Camp:

> In pitching my tent we found three massasaugas or prairie rattlesnakes, which the brethren were about to kill, but I said, "Let them alone—don't hurt them! How will the serpent ever lose his venom, while the servants of God possess the same disposition, and continue to make war upon it? Men must become harmless, before the brute creation; and when men lose their vicious disposition and cease to destroy the animal race, the lion and the lamb can dwell together, and the sucking child can play with the serpent in safety." The brethren took the serpents carefully on sticks and carried them across the creek. I exhorted the brethren not to kill a serpent, [a] bird, or an animal of any kind during our journey unless it became necessary in order to preserve ourselves from hunger. (*Teachings of the Prophet Joseph Smith*, p. 71)

Last year while my wife and I were hiking the Bonneville Shoreline Trail in Draper, Utah, she was in the lead. We were going at a rapid pace. (She always does that! That's why she's in the lead—because she wants to set the pace.) We were going at a rapid pace, and she passed a rattlesnake so quickly that when it began to rattle its warning, she'd already passed. But I heard it before I reached it, lying only inches off the trail. When I stopped to look... (I grew up in Idaho, and rattlesnakes are very common there.) After watching it for a few moments, I started to talk to it in a calm voice and made no menacing movement towards it. As I took the time to talk calmly without advancing toward it, its nervous rattle began to slow and eventually stopped. Then it uncoiled—which only happens when the snake is not defensive. I suppose the calm of my voice and my nonthreatening demeanor relieved the little animal's fear. It began to slowly move away, and I encouraged it to stay off the trail because another passing hiker or bicyclist would probably try to kill it.

I thought of Joseph Smith's words when I encountered that snake: "How will the serpent ever lose his venom...? Men must become harmless…men [must] lose their viscious disposition[s] and cease to destroy... (*History of the Church* 2:71-72; see also *Teachings of the Prophet Joseph Smith*, pp. 71-72)."

I know however well I may treat an animal, another will soon come by and mistreat the same animal. Nature will refuse to be at peace with mankind while mankind continues to slay, abuse, and misuse the animal kingdom.

But the prophecy is about God's *holy mountain*. It raises the question: If there were a place occupied by people who do not hurt or destroy in that holy mountain, could nature reach peace with the people in that place?

Cicely acted to protect the children in my yard from what she regarded as an intruding threat. It was her nature to do so. She wanted her clan to be safe. Toward her clan, she showed affection, played, and gave us all companionship. But to the threat, she was menacing.

In the first Zion, the people were at peace with nature. But **that** place was apparently protected **by** nature. What scripture describes is not magic or fairy dust but a perfectly natural process. This creation has been ordained by God and framed with intelligence to follow certain principles established before the foundation of the world. Any people in any age who follow the same pattern will receive the same result. What is described in this passage about Enoch and his city?

> *And so great was the faith of Enoch that he led the people of God, and their enemies came to battle against them, and he spoke the word of the Lord, and the earth trembled, and the mountains fled—even according to his command —and the rivers of water were turned out of their course, and the roar of…lions [were] heard out of the wilderness. And all nations feared greatly, so powerful was the word of Enoch, and so great was the power of the language which God had given him.* (Genesis 4:13 RE)

Would a lion that had been befriended by Enoch and his people be inclined, by its nature, to protect the people it viewed as part of its clan? Would a bear protect its shepherd and guardian? Would a wolf? Is it possible for a civilization to exist that does not hurt nor destroy in all their land? If they would not hurt nor destroy in all their land, would it be a holy place? We live in a very different civilization from the one described in prophecy. But the one described prophetically will not just one day appear. It will require effort, learning, obedience, and sacrifice to change.

The earth rejoiced at Enoch's people. The earth **protected** those people. Earthquakes, landslides, and floods stopped the wicked—and the animal kingdom, including predators like the lion, rose up to protect the city of Enoch. For those who are prepared to receive the people of Enoch and Melchizedek, and those who will welcome the Lord to dwell among them, that can and will happen.

Everybody will have to make changes. The most important changes have been provided in a blueprint revealed in the Answer to Prayer for Covenant including the terms of the Covenant. We are expected to remember and obey these words:

> *My will is to have you love one another. As people, you lack the ability to respectfully disagree among one another...Wisdom counsels mankind to align their words with their hearts, but mankind refuses to take counsel from Wisdom...[There've] been sharp disputes between you that should have been avoided. I speak these words to* ***reprove*** *you that you may learn, not to* ***upbraid*** *you so that you mourn. I want my people to have understanding.* (T&C 157:3-5 RE)

> *Satan is a title and means* ***accuser****,* ***opponent*** *and* ***adversary****; hence once he fell, Lucifer became, or in other words was called, Satan, because he accuses others and opposes the Father. I rebuked Peter and called him Satan because he was wrong in opposing the Father's will for me, and Peter understood and repented...In the work you have performed there are those who have been Satan, accusing one another, wounding hearts and causing jarring, contention, and strife by their accusations. Rather than loving one another, even among you who desire a good thing, some have dealt unkindly as if they were...opponents, accusers and adversaries. In this they were wrong.* (ibid, vs. 8-9 RE)

> *For you are like a man who seeks for good fruit from a neglected vineyard—unwatered, undunged, unpruned and unattended. How shall it produce good fruit if you fail to tend it? What reward does the unfaithful husbandman obtain from his neglected vineyard? How can saying you are a faithful husbandman ever produce good fruit in the vineyard without doing the work of the husbandman? For you seek my words to recover them even as you forsake to do them. You have heretofore produced wild fruit, bitter and ill formed, because you neglect to do my words.* (ibid, vs. 17 RE)

> *You have not yet become what you must be to live together in peace. If you will hearken to my words I will make you my people and my words will give*

you peace. Even a single soul who stirs up the hearts of others to anger can destroy the peace of all my people. Each of you must equally walk truly in my path, not only to profess, but to do as you profess...The Book of Mormon was given as my covenant for this day and contains my gospel, which came forth to allow people to understand my work and [to] obtain my salvation. Yet many of you are like those who reject the Book of Mormon, because you say, but you do not do. As a people you honor with your lips, but your hearts are corrupt, filled with envy and malice, returning evil for good, sparing none—even those with pure hearts among you—from your unjustified accusations and unkind backbiting. You've not obtained the fullness of my salvation because you do not draw near to me. (ibid, vs. 19-20 RE)

Hear therefore my words: Repent and bring forth fruit showing repentance, and I will establish my covenant with you and claim you as mine (ibid, vs. 23 RE).

It's not enough to receive my covenant, but you must also abide it. And all who abide it, whether on this land or any other land, will be mine, and I will watch over them and protect them in the day of harvest, and gather them...as a hen gathers her chicks under her wings. I will number you among the remnant of Jacob, no longer outcasts, and you will inherit the promises of Israel. You shall be my people and I will be your God, and the sword will not devour you. And unto those who will receive will more be given, until they know the mysteries of God in full. (ibid, vs. 48 RE)

You pray each time you partake of the sacrament to always have my Spirit to be with you. And what is my Spirit? It is to love one another as I've loved you. Do my works and you will know my doctrine; for you will uncover hidden mysteries by obedience to these things that can be uncovered in no other way. This is the way I will restore knowledge to my people. If you return good for evil, you will cleanse yourself and know the joy of your Master. You call me Lord and do well to regard me so, but to know your Lord is to love one another. Flee from the cares and longings that belong to Babylon, obtain a new heart, for you've all been wounded. In me you will find peace, and through me will come Zion, a place of peace and safety. (ibid, vs. 51RE)

Be of one heart, ...regard one another with charity. Measure your words before giving voice to them (ibid, vs. 53 RE).

There remains [a] great work yet to be done. Receive my covenant and abide in it, not as in the former time when jarring, jealousy, contention and backbiting caused anger, broke hearts and hardened the souls of those

> *claiming to be my saints. But receive it in spirit, in meekness and in truth. I have given you a former commandment that I, the Lord, will forgive whom I will forgive, but of you it is required to forgive all men. And again, I have taught [you] that if you forgive men their trespasses, your Heavenly Father will also forgive you; but if you forgive not men their trespasses neither will your Heavenly Father forgive your trespasses. How do I act toward mankind? If men intend no offense, I take no offense, but if they are taught and should've obeyed, then I reprove and correct, and forgive and forget. You cannot be at peace with one another if you take offense when none is intended. But again I say, Judge not others except by the rule you want used to weigh yourself.* (ibid, vs. 58 RE)

One of the questions that someone asked is why we're admonished to pursue judgment. The answer are those words I just read to you: *I say, Judge not others except by the rule you want used to weigh yourself.* Pursue judgment whenever the opportunity presents itself. Use judgment to evaluate based upon the standard you want applied to yourself and pursue judgment.

> *The earth groans under the wickedness of mankind upon her face, and she longs for peace to come. She withholds the abundance of her bounty because of the offenses of men against me, against one another, and against her. But if righteousness returns and my people prove by their actions, words, and thoughts to yield to my Spirit and hearken to my commandments, then will the earth rejoice, for the feet of those who cry peace upon her mountains are beautiful indeed, and I, the Lord, will bring again Zion, and the earth will rejoice...In the world, tares are ripening. And so I ask you, What of the wheat?...Cry peace. Proclaim my words. Invite those who will repent to be baptized and forgiven, and they shall obtain my Spirit to guide them.* (ibid, vs. 63-65 RE)

That excerpt contains nearly 2,000 words of instruction. There is no basis to claim ignorance. Is it possible for people to change their civilization and go from strident, quarrelsome, and pugnaciousness to loving one another?

Now, I want to be clear about what I am **not** saying: Nothing in what has been said implies that people must be vegan. In the age of the first patriarchs, we learn this about the second generation: *And Abel listened unto the voice of the Lord. And Abel was a keeper of sheep...And Abel, he also brought [forth] the firstlings of his flock and of the fat thereof. And the Lord had respect unto Abel and to his offering...* (Genesis 3:6-7 RE).

There are animals whose lives are given them for the benefit of mankind. Abel raised sheep for the benefit their lives offered in food, clothing, and even company.

I am **also not** suggesting we attempt to domesticate wild animals. Until there is a community that has tamed the wild hearts of human residents and has a land to occupy, animals will remain justifiably fearful of man. Nature will not distinguish between the righteous and the wicked, the hostile and the benign, the people of peace and the people at war with the animal kingdom **until** there is a *holy mountain*. That will be the place made holy by the actions of the people who dwell there. When the earth sees **that** righteousness has returned to **her** face, she will yield her abundance for those whose feet walk in the way that is beautiful.

If we obey the commandments that have been given, we can qualify to inherit a land on which to build a temple. The objective of the covenant was to confer the right to live on the land, surviving the judgments coming upon the wicked. **We** need to live up to our end of the covenant. It is clear the Lord is willing to bear with, guide, give commandments to help prepare, and reprove His people when needed. We should not rely on the Lord's patience but should be eager to obey His guiding instruction. His commandments are not to limit us but to increase light and truth. Some intelligence is only gained by obedience to His commandments.

The foregoing excerpts are taken from:

- Denver's remarks at "A Day of Faith and Connection" youth conference in Utah on June 10, 2017;
- His talk titled "Christ's Discourse on the Road to Emmaus" given in Fairview, Utah on April 14, 2007; and
- Denver's conference talk titled "Civilization" given in Grand Junction, Colorado on April 21, 2019.

112. Nature, Part 2

This is the second part of a multi-part series on nature where Denver discusses some of the many ways that things in nature point to Christ.

DENVER: Every one of us— If I say the word *perfection*, every one of us have something that comes to mind. In the course of your life, my guess is that every one of you have had moments that you could point to and say, "That moment was absolutely perfect. There's nothing about it that I would have changed."

When you ride a motorcycle, roads have a design that is, for safety reasons, capable of handling traffic at speeds that are called the *design speed*, which means that a vehicle can operate up to that design speed on that road safely. But the speed limit is **never** the design speed because they build in this margin of safety. So, they tell you to drive five or ten or fifteen miles below the design speed of the road so that there's a margin of safety built into it.

If you're riding a motorcycle on a road, particularly a rural, winding road (like Idaho 5 that goes from the Montana border to the Washington border), and you go the posted speed limit, the motorcycle does not cooperate with you. It doesn't like that speed; it's hard to handle. But if you speed up, where the motorcycle and the road and you are in syncopation with one another, and you're riding at the design speed, everything is easier. In fact, it is almost **thoughtless** as you go—the rhythm of the road, the design of the road, the pace the motorcycle is at—everything about that.

On Idaho 5, there are places where the *banking* (they call it *super elevation*) of the road is 25 or **30** miles an hour **above** the posted speed limit. We were returning from the Black Hills of South Dakota, coming through northern Idaho on Idaho 5, going the design speed. It was a moment of absolute perfection when the joy of the experience, the feel of the humidity, the pace of the road— Everything about that moment was perfect until it was interrupted by an Idaho State patrolman [audience laughter] who, fortunately, was pointed in the opposite direction as we went by at the design speed of the road. Well, he had a lot of recovery to do to reorient himself and to start from zero to get where we were.

And we happened into, fortunately, a little village and went a block off the road, found a gas station, hopped off. And there was a fellow there who owned—he owned a Moto Guzzi, which, in northern Idaho, it's a pretty rare motorcycle to be driving. It's a V-twin, but unlike a Harley Davidson, which is an inline V-twin with a front and a back, this one has V's that go out either side. It's still a V. It's not like a BMW (that's a Boxster, horizontally opposed). And so, we acted like we'd been there all week. And the police came through making their noise, and they went on their (happily) way. And he said, "They looking for you [audience laughter]?" We said, "That's possible [audience laughter], but..."

There are moments where, because you can't be planning next week or regretting last month, you can't be doing anything other than that moment. If you're on the bike, and your mind is elsewhere, and you're going the design speed, and your mind is elsewhere, you can kill yourself, or you can badly injure yourself. You can do extraordinarily stupid, haphazard, dangerous things if you're not absolutely in the moment.

Perfection is one of those things which occurs **absolutely** in the moment. Think back over your lifetime in those moments where you would not change a thing. You were so content. There was nothing else that you could want or you would change about that moment.

There's a character, a samurai, that an American struggled to try and understand in the movie *The Last Samurai*. And although they grew to have this friendship with one another, ~~Kamatsu~~ was always— Katsumoto— was always looking for the perfect cherry blossom. He would study the cherry tree as it blossomed in the Spring at his (outside), his own temple, always looking for the perfect cherry blossom and never finding. There was always a problem with it. Well, as he lay dying on the battlefield at the end of his life (one of his last breaths), he's looking up, and he's seeing in the distance the cherry trees blooming, and he observes, "Perfect. They are **all** perfect." And it didn't matter what flaws they had. The fact is, they were all perfect.

I can remember—sometime. The scene presents itself vividly in my mind. I can't tell you how old I was or what grade I was in, but during recess, playing marbles with friends—and recess may be 15 minutes? But it was timeless! Out playing marbles with a friend in the dirt with your marble, all eternity could come and go in that moment of such profound contentment.

I have dogs. And dogs are **always** content, and we're told that dogs do not have any sense of time. They may live only 10 to 12 years, but as far as they're concerned, they've lived for all eternity because there's a timelessness to the experience of being a dog. They're not in a hurry to get somewhere unless, of course, you've got the leash, and you're gonna take them out, in which event they'll anticipate that moment. But there's a **timelessness** to the idea of perfection.

I can recall an afternoon. I had come out of my house, and I was sitting on the front porch, and I was all alone. The temperature that day must have been **exactly** the same temperature as the temperature of my skin so that I could not tell where outside of me and inside of me began and ended by feeling the breeze. The temperature was exactly the same temperature as I felt. And it was so calm an afternoon, so calm a moment sitting there that I was taken in by the moment itself. A bird flew by, and I could feel the movement of the bird's wings through the vibration of the air because it was **just that calm**. I thought as I sat there, "This **is** Heaven." **This**, this moment, this experience—**this is** Heaven because it, at that moment, was perfect, something that I would not change.

I was out walking, and I came upon this songbird that was just singing the happiest little tune you could ever imagine. I don't know what kind of bird it was, but it was, you know, sparrow-size and small and very happy and singing its tune and doing all that God endowed it to do. And I came upon it abruptly. And because of where it had situated itself and because of where I came upon it from, it was trapped. And it was singing loudly. And when I got there, it was so loud and so startling that I stopped and looked at it, and it **immediately** stopped singing. And it knew (it was like the bird realized) if I wanted to, I could capture it; if I wanted to, I could kill it; if I wanted to, I could exercise whatever control I wanted over the bird. And it **looked** frightened, less than an arm's length away. (Foolish to let a human get that close to you in that vulnerable a spot.) And the stopping of the singing was so abrupt. It's like the last note still hung in the air as this frightened little creature looked at me.

And I thought, "Hey, I'm harmless, but it doesn't know that. So, what's the best way to communicate to this trapped little animal that I'm harmless?" I turned, and I walked away, and I tried to whistle a little like what the bird had been whistling like—miserable imitation. I mean, it was probably *screeching* to that poor thing, but I whistled as I'm walking away. And within a few steps (if there's any way to describe it), I would say that the bird's tune resumed on a happier note than it had been before. That was a moment that was perfect.

I'm sure every one of you have had moments in your life that you can point to and recall and say, "That moment; that incident; that—that was perfect." If we can conceive of perfection, or if we can **experience** it even for just a moment, that means perfection exists. It's real. It's attainable. It can be had even in this place and even with you and even with me. Perfection **is** possible.

In this creation, there are two opposing forces that cause everything there is to be and to exist. Those two opposing forces are not good and evil, although we tend to **call** them good and **call** them evil. The two opposing forces are, in fact, *love* and *fear*. Everything that is *generative* or *creative* comes about as a consequence of love. If you think about **all** the problems that people have with one another and what would solve them, the one thing that could solve **every** problem is love—if we loved one another enough. And **all** of those vices, all of the suffering—the anger, the pride, the envy, the impatience, the greed—have their root in fear: I fear I will not have enough, and therefore, I envy; I fear for my own inability, and therefore, I resent your ability. Everything that produces negativity comes about as a consequence of fear.

When it comes to signs, faith does not get produced by signs. So, you can't do that. That's why Pharaoh never got impressed. Signs are inconsequential. Whatever the sign is, it was like Brother Pratt was explaining: So what? Bad weather happens all the time. The plagues are still going on in Egypt. The remarkable nature of the sign is that it happened on cue, not that a sign happened.

I'm having a conversation with a fellow. It involves a true gospel principle. We're standing in the back parking lot of my office. While we're finishing the conversation, I say, "Do you see the dove sitting atop the pole in the distance?" And when he saw the dove, it took off. It flew clockwise one circle around us, and it landed back on the pole. To him, it was a sign. To **me**, it was a sign. If it was a crow, and it went counterclockwise, I'd probably say, "Hey, there's something wrong with you [audience laughter]! But the Lord told me I'd be okay, but I'm pretty sure [audience laughter]..."

Signs are not controlled [laughs] by men but are God's to give as God determines. And signs are not supposed to be the subject of boasting. Some of the most remarkable signs that've been given to me are silently recorded in my journal but are astonishing. Signs exist. Many of the signs recorded in the lives of believers may be unknown to you, but, nevertheless, there are signs in rich abundance among believers today.

The adulterers are the ones who seek signs, according to our Lord, and He said it twice. We know He said it twice because Matthew's account includes Him saying that to two different audiences on two different occasions. Adulterers are sign-seekers.

I would include within the definition of the adulterous, as did the Lord, those who commit adultery in their heart; hence, the need to reject polygamy by men [audience applause]. It is adultery in your heart to continue to entertain the possibility that you will one day have 72 virgins or whatever the hell it is that you have going in your skull. Just get rid of that crap. It does not belong in the life of a meek and a humble man—doesn't belong there.

People are very different, one from another. Not only are men and women different from one another, women are different from each other, and men are different from each other; and personalities are **always** going to be ill-fitted. Getting people to mesh together?— That's not going to result in, somehow, this universal similarity of personality. It's important that people preserve their differences. It's important that people have the gifts that have been given to them by God preserved intact and not suppressed because someone doesn't like the way that their gift gets expressed.

I've mentioned it before. I just find the artwork that Monet does, with his version of impressionism, the highest and greatest use of the paintbrush. But I think Van Gogh's impressionism is crude and elementary; and quite frankly, I mean, his suicide stopped the outpouring of that stuff. And in some ways, you know, maybe the art world was benefited by that [audience laughter]. When he was a realist in the early stages, some of what Van Gogh did was rather lovely, but his impressionism... I see that, and when my wife substitutes in 4th grade, and she brings presents home from her kids [audience laughter] — But there are people who **love** Van Gogh. "Sunflowers" sold for 44 million last time it sold. Some people really love Van Gogh! I assume that in the resurrection, they'll figure out that they were duped [audience laughter]. But for here and now, in this fallen world with its perverse set of priorities, that's all good and well, and if they've got the money, and they wanna use it that way, that's fine.

Zion is going to have people whose artistic outpouring is going to be **fabulously** different from one another. You look at the totem pole artistry of the Alouettes; and you look at the carved artistry of the Hawaiian Islands; and you look at the sculpture of Michelangelo—and these are radically, radically different one from the other, so much so that you're bridging these enormous cultural divides to look at these different kinds of sculpture. Why would we ever want to have a studied school of artistic discipline that produces nothing more than some uniform product when beauty and artistry can find so many unique forms of expression? Why would we ever want that?

Why would you want to go to a fellowship meeting in Uganda, a fellowship meeting in the Philippines, and a fellowship meeting in Spain and hear the same lesson on the same Sunday everywhere throughout the world? That is managerial overkill designed to destroy the unique spirits of the sons and daughters of God [audience applause].

Facial recognition technology works because no one wears your face but you! Fingerprints distinguish every one of us from one another so much so that if you leave a print, and everyone else leaves a print, we can distinguish yours from everyone else. Every single snowflake crystal is unique. Every leaf of every tree is unique. Nature cries out that God treasures the differences that exist from one soul to the next. And when describing the gifts that are given, the gifts are very different, but how the gifts manifest themselves, even if someone possesses exactly the same gift...

Read the description of the seership of Enoch and the description of the seer Joseph; and the way in which they manifest themselves were **decidedly** different. Even the gifts do not come out the same when put through one person and then put through another. Every one of you are unique, and when we deal with one another, the objective is not to compel you to be me. The objective is not to compel any one of us to be the same as another one of us. The objective is to rejoice and to respect and to hallow the work that God has done in making us so unique from one another.

Even twins are dissimilar. My father was a twin. There's a picture of him and his twin brother in their high school class. (I think there were 12 kids in their class.) The way in which my father was dressed and the way in which his twin brother was dressed in the picture foreshadowed the course that these two men's lives would take.

My father left that area in rural Appalachia, and he went into the military. He fought in World War II. He landed on Omaha Beach on the morning of D-Day. He settled in the West.

He worked his life to support his children, encouraging my sister and I to go to college to receive an education that he did not receive because by the time he had an opportunity to do that, life and family and work prevented it. (My sister holds two Bachelor's degrees, a Master's degree, and I've got an

Associates, Bachelor's, and Juris Doctorate degree.) Because of the priorities that my father had, he was willing to work for the **long** game, the **long** vision —to sacrifice.

His twin brother looks rather dandy. He outdressed his twin. He was somewhat showy. He wanted to get there and get there now and quickly. And so, when he finished school, he immediately went to the best-paying job he could find; and he went to work in the coal mine where the United Mine Workers Union wages paid him a great living. He never left Appalachia, developed black lung as a coal miner—which they often did. But he had gratification early on that my father did not have; but my father had satisfaction that his twin brother never had for himself. Twins are dissimilar. (And they were identical twins; they were not fraternal.)

We're unique, and we're meant to be so. We dishonor God when we disrespect that and when we insist on uniformity. However different we may be from one another, however, we can still be kindly. We can still be patient. We can still try to uplift, to edify, and to **honor** the differences that exist between us.

The Lord, when He lets you know you're wrong, lets you know in a way that's like [pause] our dog Mowgli. She cannot bear to displease her family. She just wears it on her. Everything about her—the ears, the tail—everything about our dog droops when she has familial ire directed her way. That's how you feel when the Lord is letting you know that you've offended Him. And I've offended Him far too many times for me to even recount. Sometimes I wonder why I'm still involved. I assume at some point, He's just gonna get tired, and I'm gonna ignite like a match head, and He's gonna say, "Well, he probably had that coming."

The Lord is real. He is working. The time is short. The evidence of what is going to happen and is presently underway is not just in scripture; it's also in nature. The evidence of this is written everywhere. And if some of you are lucky enough to be able to hang out for a six o'clock fireside with John Pratt, try to keep him here long enough to let the stars come out [illegible]. And then, he'll need a laser pointer; and then, he'll really entertain you.

Oh, I love this question: Share some more of the ways that nature testifies of Christ.

I hope you garden. If you don't, you should garden in order to experience all the plagues of Egypt because that's what happens [audience laughter] whenever I attempt to garden.

There are these loathsome pests that will come along and consume and destroy and invade your garden. They'll eat everything except zucchini, as it turns out [audience laughter]. And zucchini produces in such abundance (and so quickly) and ripens so quickly that all you're left with is a bag of seeds, and they're dreadful.

But there is a pest that invades the garden that will eat everything and destroy and wreak havoc that eventually entombs itself in a chrysalis. And the pest, while it's inside this apparent self-made tomb, has died and gone away. But eventually, it will arise from that cocoon, from that tomb, and it will come out, and it has assumed a wholly different form. Unlike that loathsome creature that crawled around (ugly and haltingly) across your garden, consuming and destroying, once it emerges from the tomb, it now takes flight. It's joined with the sky, with the heavens itself. And it goes about thereafter taking pollen and fertilizing the garden and becoming productive. Where before it had destroyed, now it helps create. Now it becomes an agent that produces fruit, that produces vegetables.

This little insect is a powerful sermon embedded in nature to testify of who Christ was and, more importantly, to testify of what Christ did that will affect **you**, that will turn **you** from what we are now into something glorious, heavenly, and capable of ascending in flight up on high.

The foregoing excerpts are taken from:

- Denver's *Christian Reformation Lecture Series*, Talk #7, given in Boise, Idaho on November 3, 2018;

- His conference talk titled "Things to Keep Us Awake at Night" given in St. George, Utah on March 19, 2017;

- His conference talk titled "Our Divine Parents" given in Gilbert, Arizona on March 25, 2018;

- His comments at the "Unity in Christ" conference in Utah County, Utah on July 30, 2017; and

- The Q&A Session following Denver's conference talk given in Grand Junction, Colorado on April 21, 2019.

113. Nature, Part 3

This is the third part of a multi-part series on Nature, where Denver discusses some of the many ways that things in nature testify of Christ.

DENVER: (Question:) "You addressed this in your lectures. Let's say for argument's sake I believed you. What can or should a university student do? I can't drop out because I would immediately have to pay back student loans. Do I just keep attending school and trust that everything works out? Or, let's say I'm in high school. Would you recommend young people even go to college? Should young people who want to be lawyers just quash their dreams because everything is going to hell? That's my general problem with gloom-and-doom prophecy, it stagnates individual growth and development. People isolate themselves from the rest of the world, spend a bunch of money on guns and emergency supplies, and generally waste their lives living in fear. Is there a balanced approach to watching out for that dastardly thief in the night?"

I would say, finish high school. I would say, go to law school. And, I mean, one of the first things on the agenda that Christ will destroy— It's not the lawyers, it's the *bankers* and the insurance companies; they're all evil. [Audience laughter.] But your student loans won't need to be repaid because there will be nothing left of the institutions who hope to collect on them. You don't live your life in contemplation of the fearful return of the Lord; you live your life in a grateful celebration for everything God has done and given to us.

As I was flying here, we had— I think we were taking off just as the first rays of the sun were creeping up in the east, and there was this *brilliant* scarlet ribbon on the horizon. And my wife pointed it out to me—I was sitting in an aisle and the only thing I got to see was the cart they bring you treats with. As I looked across at the sunrise, it was spectacular.

Where I live in Utah we have this Wasatch Front. These are jagged, granite cliffs that go upward. The top of one of the ski resorts is 11,000 feet, and we live at about 4,000 feet. When the sun sets as you are in the valley, you see the sun go down in the west; but in the east on the mountains, you see the sunlight creep up, and creep up, and creep up the mountain, until finally just the *very top peaks* remain with light. What happens is that the light as it goes up the mountain in its nightly retreat, because of the refraction of the atmosphere, it tends to shift to the blue and to the purple. And every night those mountains— And it's particularly spectacular when there's snow up there because the hues of the sunlight refraction become *very* colorful up there.

Now, I happen to like impressionist art, and my favorite impressionist is Monet. We have a couple of the Monet— Well, I mean, they're forgeries. [Audience laughter.] They were given to me as a fee; we didn't pay for them. But they're actual Monet paintings with right down to the brush strokes being reproduced, and they're beautiful. Every night as the sun sets, God does something on the mountains that is *never* the same, always beautiful, and greater in beauty and splendor than anything Monet ever put on canvas.

We ought to love life, and we ought to love one another, and we ought to pursue our education. And we shouldn't bunker down with guns and ammo, fearfully waiting for a direful end to things. Of all people, Christians should have the most hope, the most optimism, the most vitality, and the greatest amount of joy in life. We ought to celebrate every day.

Oh, here's a good one: "Having studied evolutionary biology in college, I came to appreciate the vast amounts of evidence for this scientific theory. [I'll pause there; read *Darwin's Black Box*.] Recent anthropological data, Gobekli Tepe, is pushing the origins of civilization far beyond 4,000 B.C. It is an increasingly tenuous position to accept [aah... typo there] a strictly literal interpretation of Genesis in regards to creation and chronology, especially among the younger millennial generation I am a part of. Having also had a few mystical experiences that led me to accept Jesus as Lord, I feel somewhat torn. Whatever I do, it seems like I'm rejecting truth. Whether I consider ignoring physical scientific evidence or effectively dismissing parts of the Bible, both are not satisfying solutions to me. Is there a way to make secular data fit into the Christian metaphysics?"

Yes. Yes, there is. I'm gonna go ahead and answer this fellow, for what it's worth. The problem with biblical literalism is not necessarily that what is in the Bible is untrue, but it may be that what is in the Bible is speaking using a vernacular that mankind is unacquainted with. For example, the work of the Creation is referred to generally as "a day." There is no reason to believe that calling it a day, in the language that gets employed in Scripture, has reference to anything other than a discrete event.

It would be more accurate to say that there were labors that were performed during the incremental progression of the Creation, which took however long, and when the *labor* was completed then that labor was called "a day." There is nothing to suggest that the labor of the first day was exactly the same amount of time as the labor of the second day, nor is there anything to suggest that the labor of the third day was equal in time to either the first or the second, and so on.

How many eons of time were required in order for God, through the process that we see in nature, to form the earth was the first day. However long it took, through seismic and volcanic and other activities, to cause the dry land to appear was labor that took however long it took—in the vernacular of Scripture.

The earth is moving in two ways. It is circling the sun on a tilt. Twice a year that tilt aligns so that we have an equinox, which means that there's exactly twelve hours of sunlight and twelve hours of darkness on that one day, twice a year. And then there are solstices when, in the north, the days are the longest because it's leaning towards the sun. And when it gets to the other side, it's leaning away, and at that moment, the nights are very long because in the north you're leaning away from the sun.

As it makes this movement in one direction, it's also wobbling at the poles. The earth is not perfectly stable in how its axis fits; it wobbles. It takes 25,900 years, roughly, for it to complete one wobble at the pole. In the ancient vernacular—because of that wobble we have a pole star. It happens at this moment to be Polaris, but if you go back several thousand years, we have a different pole star. That pole star changes.

We also have around the circumference a group of constellations that *everyone on earth* can see. It doesn't matter if you're in the south; it doesn't matter if you're in the north—south being below the equator (not Atlanta) [audience laughter], or the north (not meaning Canada)—it means everything: the northern hemisphere and the southern. There are a group of constellations *everyone* can see. There are twelve of them. All twelve of them had a story behind them in the beginning. All twelve of them have symbols that represent Christ. That's for another day.

When the pole star changes—which happens about seven times every 25,900 years—when the pole star changes, anciently that change was called "a new heaven." Likewise, there is a different constellation that appears at sunrise on the vernal equinox, and *that* constellation tells you what age you're in. Star fields overlap, and sometimes there are gaps. Right now we are in an overlap between— Christ said, "*I will make you fishers of men*" (Matthew 3:2 RE and

Mark 1:5 RE), and the constellation that that age was identified with is Pisces: two fish. One fish caught in the net is *endlessly* circling the equator, but another fish—and it's much smaller—this other fish is headed to the north where you will find God.

That constellation is going to be replaced by the One who is coming. We call Him "Aquarius." We also call Him "The Waterman"—He is pouring out; a new age will come. If you go back far enough, what He is pouring out is two streams. One stream is water, which gives life, and one stream is fire. He who is coming, in the great day of the Lord, is coming for "*the great* (the water) *and dreadful* (the fire) *day of the Lord,"* to pour something out (Malachi 1:12 RE; Alma 21:2 RE; 3 Nephi 11:5 RE; Joseph Smith History 3:4 RE; and T&C 151:13 RE).

Well, it just so happens that the star fields of these two overlap. If you date the return of the Lord by the star field of Aquarius, at its earliest star, then the first sign of the times of refreshing would have been about in the 1840s, when Joseph Smith was saying that Christ appeared to him and gave him a message to preach. We have not yet fully exited the star field of Pisces.

Now, all of that is to make this comment: When there's a new pole star, that's called "a new heaven." When there's a new constellation on the horizon at the vernal equinox, that's called "a new earth." There will be a new heaven and there will be a new earth when Christ returns (see Luke 10:5 RE; 2 Peter 1:13 RE; Revelation 8:8 RE; Ether 6:3 RE; and T&C 9:7 RE). And all of these are given, as Christ said in Genesis 1 verse 14, "*for signs and for seasons"* (Genesis 2:6 RE), and *everything* testifies of Him.

So, there's a lot of scientific proof, but there's a *lot* of material in the Bible that is simply misunderstood. This earth is pretty old, and how long it existed before it was considered sufficiently complete, for man to occupy it, is not to be measured in days. It's to be measured in epochs of time, referred to generically as "a day"—meaning a period, meaning an agenda.

STEPHANIE: This one came in this morning: "Why doesn't God talk about science in Scriptures? I have learned about symbolic things in my chemistry, microbiology, and astronomy classes that denote there is a God, but I've always wondered why the laws of nature and scientific ideas are never discussed."

So, we're gonna break this one up. First thing I would say is, I don't know, I tend to think that science *is* God. Now I know scien*tists* don't think that, and they're looking for ways to disconnect science and God. But I happen to believe that if there was no God, there would be no science, and they wouldn't have jobs. And so, to me, there is no separate— There is *literally* no separation. So, the fact that this person is *finding* God in microbiology and chemistry and astronomy is no surprise.

The second thing I would say is I am finding science in human growth and development. I am finding sci— Did I say "science" or "God"?

DENVER: You said science, but you meant God.

STEPHANIE: Oh, no, I'm not finding science. Well, I might be finding that too, but that's not what I meant. I am finding God in human growth and development. I am finding God in counseling theories and practices. I am finding God in substance abuse principles. I am finding God in every textbook I am currently engaged in. So, I would say, much like Jeff said earlier, God is everywhere. And the fact that we should never *limit* our search for God, or even our presumption of finding Him, to Scripture—which is a wonderful place to find Him—but if I can find Him in substance abuse practices and principles, you can certainly find Him in astronomy and microbiology. And then you—

DENVER: Yeah. But all things bear testimony of Christ—*all things*. Whether they are on the earth or under the earth or in the earth or above the earth, all things bear testimony of Christ. The Scriptures say so. You think about the caterpillar that's a pest, that's something to wreck your garden, that goes into a cocoon—and then it comes out of the cocoon, and it's now something that helps fertilize and pollinate. And it leaves its grubby, earthly confines to become airborne and colorful, and a contributor to life and to your gardening. It's the same animal. And tell me *that* isn't a testimony of Christ. All things bear testimony of Him, and science simply ratifies that.

The question is, "Do you run any risks by studying, that you can just as easily study your way out of belief as you can study your way into belief?"

The way that I think that works is everyone wants to understand—because of how proximate, how close Joseph Smith is—everyone wants to understand *how* Joseph Smith did it. So, if we think we can figure out how Joseph Smith did it, then presumably that will equip us to understand or put it into context. But most people who are studying to figure out how Joseph Smith did it are only interested in debunking it. "I want to know how he pulled this off because I'm a little skeptical that what he pulled off is actually genuine.

And maybe if I can understand how Joseph Smith pulled that off, then I can understand how Jesus pulled it off; then I can understand how Moses pulled it off; then I can put it all to rest because I needn't worry about it." *Or*, "I wanna understand how Joseph Smith pulled it off so I can pull it off; and when I get that and I figure it out, and I try it and it doesn't work for me, then I can say Joseph made it up because it didn't work for me." I mean, there are a lot of pitfalls along the course of study.

The first and primary question you have to ask is— Take a look around this world and ask yourself if, in this world, it makes sense to you that there is no Creator? Does it make sense to you that everything that's going on here simply is a haphazard accident? That there is no Creation; there's no Creator; there's no divine plan; there's nothing here that operates on any other basis than random chance? If you reach the conclusion that everything that's going on here could possibly be by random chance, then read *Darwin's Black Box*.

There's a little over 200 different things that have to line up perfectly in order for your blood to clot. If any one of those 200 things don't happen simultaneously—it's a little over 200—if any one of those don't happen simultaneously, you will die. For some of those, if you get a cut and they're not present, you'll bleed out. You'll simply die because you'll exsanguinate. For others of those, if you get a cut, your entire blood system will turn solid and you will die because clotting knows no end.

Darwin's Black Box makes the argument that it is evolutionarily impossible for trial and error to solve the problem of blood clotting, because every one of the steps that are required, if nature simply experiments with it, kills the organism —and that ends that. You don't know that you are going to succeed until you've lined them all up and you've made them all work. It is an interesting book: *Darwin's Black Box*. In essence, it's saying that the evolutionists require more faith, really, than do people that believe in God, because the theory upon which they base their notion requires far too many things to occur, by trial and error, than is conceivably possible.

Well, if there is a Creation, then there is a Creator. If there is a Creator, then the question is— I assume all of you have had a father or a grandfather (someone that you respected), a mother or a grandmother, an aunt or an uncle, that over the course of a lifetime developed skills, and talents, and humor, and character (someone that you admire), and then, they pass on. How profligate a venture is it to create someone that *you*...a creation that *you* view as noble, as worthy, as admirable, as interesting, as fascinating—some person that you love—take that and just obliterate it. God, who can make such a creation, surely doesn't *waste* a creation. He's not burning the library at Alexandria every day by those who pass on. God *had* to have a purpose behind it all.

I don't know how many of you have had a friend or a loved one or a family member who passed on, who, subsequent to their death, appeared to you, had a conversation with you—in a dream, in a thought. I can recall going to my father's funeral, and his casket with his body was in the front of the little chapel we were in, but his presence was *not* there. That may have been the hull he occupied while he was living and breathing, but I had no sense at all that my father was there. I did have a sense that he was present, but he wasn't in the coffin; he was elsewhere in the room. I couldn't see him, but I could have pointed to him and said, "He's here." In fact, I made a few remarks at my father's funeral and I largely directed them at him.

Nature testifies over and over again. It doesn't matter when the sun goes down, there's going to be another dawn. It doesn't matter when all the leaves fall off the deciduous trees in the fall, there's going to come a spring. There's going to be a renewal of life. There are all kinds of animals in nature that go through this really loathsome, disgusting, wretched existence, and then they transform. And where they were a pest before, *now* they're bright and they're colorful, and they fly and they pollinate. Butterflies help produce the very kinds of things that their larva stage destroyed. These are signs. These are testimonies.

Just like the transformation of the caterpillar into the butterfly, the pest into the thing of beauty, the thing that ate the vegetables that you were trying to grow into the thing that helps pollinate the things that you want to grow—that's the plan for all of us. So, when you study the Scriptures, the objective should not be, "Can I trust the text? Can I evaluate the text? Can I use a form of criticism against the text in order to weigh, dismiss, belittle, judge?"

Take all that you know about nature; take all that you know about *this* world and the majesty of it all; take all that you know that informs you that there is hope, there is joy, there is love. Why do you love your children? Why do your children love you? These kinds of things exist. They're real; they're tangible; and they're important. And they are part of what God did when He created this world. Keep *that* in mind when you're studying, and search the Scriptures to try and help inform you how you can better appreciate, how you can better enjoy, how you can better love, how you can better have hope.

What do they have to say that can bring you closer to God? *Not,* can I find a way to dismiss something that Joseph said or did? As soon as Joseph was gone off the scene, people that envied the position that he occupied took over custody of everything, including the documents. And what we got, as a consequence of that, is a legacy that allowed a trillion-dollar empire to be constructed.

Religion should require our sacrifice; it should not be here to benefit us. We should have to *give,* not get. And in the giving of ourselves, what we get is in the interior; it's in the heart. It's the things of enduring beauty and value. If your study takes you away from an appreciation of the love, the charity, the things that matter most, reorient your study.

The foregoing excerpts are taken from:

> Denver's *Christian Reformation Lecture Series,* Talk #3, given in Atlanta, Georgia, on November 16, 2017;
>
> Denver & Stephanie's "Youth Q&A Session," at The Heavens are Open Conference in Hurricane, Utah, on March 22, 2020; and
>
> Denver's remarks given at the Book of Mormon Covenant Conference, in Columbia, South Carolina, on January 13, 2019.

114. Zion People

Today, Denver discusses the attributes of people who will be called to Zion, as well as the attributes and behaviors that will clearly disqualify people from being invited to that gathering.

DENVER: Zion will be cooperative, not competitive. They will be *one* in every sense of the word. No one will need to say, *Know ye the Lord*, because everyone will know Him, from the greatest to the least. He will be able to dwell among them because He will already be known by them.

Collectivist efforts are never going to work. First, we must become individually the kind of people whom the Lord can visit. Then, after that, the gathering together of like-minded people will be a gathering of equals. It will not be an hierarchical gathering of *leadership* and *drones*. There won't be a single drone in Zion. Everyone will be equal and no one will mind mowing the grass or taking out the garbage.

I envision this scene from Zion:

A man walks down the street, early in the morning, and notices that the bakery is unmanned. Its door's open because there is no need for locks in Zion. So, on an impulse, he enters, looks about for the instructions left by someone, and begins to prepare bread. As the morning goes on, a few others join him. They make bread. Others come and take the bread for their homes. At the end of the day, the man goes home. This was his first time working in a bakery. He did it because he saw it needed to be done.

He returns to the bakery because he enjoys it. Day after day he works in the bakery for months, perhaps years. One day, on his way, he notices that the grass needs to be cut and the mower has been carefully left beside a tree along the parkway; so he starts to cut the grass. He finds he likes it. And this is, now, what he does—this day and the next. And within a month, he's cut out all the grass needing cutting, in his immediate neighborhood, and starts over again, where he began. He enjoys it.

Eventually, he is asked by someone to help move clothing and journals from one home to another. A couple, whose children have all moved out, no longer need the larger home they occupy, and are moving across town. So he puts the mower carefully beside a tree and begins to help. Homes are occupied based upon need, and these people no longer have need of the larger space they once occupied.

Across town, he notices there is a new neighborhood being built. He decides, after finishing the move for the couple, that he will assist at the site. He returns there for over a year as he provides help with stocking and distributing materials, framing, installing shingles, painting, and clean-up.

He has no job. He's never without work. He asks for no pay, because some labor to feed others. He has no need for housing, because what is available is shared.

In 4th Nephi, verse 2, it tells us that *[all] the people were...converted unto the Lord, upon all the face of the land, both Nephites and Lamanites* [and that's all good and well, but it goes on to say], *and there were no contentions and disputations among them.* (see also 4 Nephi 1:1 RE)

And so, it's not just being converted. See, they're narrowing it down. You get converted, but then you reach, at some point, a unanimity or an agreement upon what the Gospel really means.

So, after they manage, not only to have the same faith and to eliminate from them contentions and disputations, then they go on and *every man did deal justly one with another* (ibid). See, there's a difference between mercy and justice. Justice is a tougher standard. We don't want justice. We want a merciful Redeemer, who will come in and who will make up for our defects. But this is saying, every man (Me, inside me. This is the turf we're talking about.) did deal justly (the higher standard) with one another. You don't have to give me mercy, because I'm going to give *you* justice. I'm going to be tougher on myself. It is *fair* that I do this for you. "Oh no, no, you don't have to do that." No, no, no! The standard by which they are evaluating their conduct, internal to themselves, is the more difficult standard. They're going to deal justly with one another. I will break my heart, I will break my wallet, I will break my life before I will not deal justly with you, and give you everything that you're entitled to. See, it's putting the shoe on the other foot, and it's not the more relaxed and kindly and gentle standard; because when they're dealing with one another, they want to deal justly.

The path back to God is so that you can meet with and be instructed by our Savior. The purpose of our Savior is to prepare us in all things so that we can, at last, become Zion. Because if your heart is right and my heart is right, and if I'm looking to God and God only, and you're looking to God and God only, then the trivial things of having things in common are of so little import that they matter not.

If you're faithful to the Lord, you have no reason to pick a fight with anyone else. Our Lord was a peacemaker. We ought to be peacemakers as well.

And 76 is a transcript that is given to Joseph that was dictated, transcribed, read back, approved; then the dictation continued until he reached the end. But look at... beginning at verse 113:

> *This is the end of the vision which we saw, which we were commanded to write while we were yet in the Spirit. But great and marvelous are the works of the Lord, and the mysteries of his kingdom which he showed unto us, which surpass all understanding in glory, and in might, and in dominion; Which he commanded us we should not write while we were yet in the Spirit, and are not lawful for man to utter; Neither is man capable to make them known, for they are only to be seen and understood by the power of the Holy [Ghost], which God bestows on those who love him, and purify themselves before him; To whom he grants this privilege of seeing and knowing for themselves; That through the power and manifestation of the Spirit,* ***while in the flesh****, they may be able to bear his presence in the world of glory.* (See also T&C 69:28-29, emphasis added)

Is this related to not denying the power of godliness? I mean, to have the ability to *bear his presence in the world of glory,* as we get farther along in our discussion about the topic of Zion, it becomes critical that you become able to bear His presence. For those, who are unable to bear His presence, will be destroyed at His coming. Therefore, whatever this power of godliness is, I think we need to get some.

We are asked to prepare so we can begin to found Zion. But preparing or even beginning is not the same thing as accomplishing. Whether anything can or will be accomplished must be proven—cannot just be claimed. Braggarts do not impress heaven and have no claim to any title or status they have not first lived.

The Lord is offering an opportunity. He's promised to labor alongside to help us reach the prophesied Zion. With His help, Zion is possible; but we can fail. And Zion be left for another people in another time.

The greatest false spirit of all is the one that inspires you to accuse your brethren, condemn your sisters, and judge others unfairly. This is Satan. We cannot be Satan and also be the Lord's.

I believe we will see Zion established. Sadly, I do not think all can be gathered. Those, who find fault now, will surely find fault when people start to sacrifice and hard work is expected. It makes little sense to assemble the discontent, angry, and bitter souls into a community seeking to find peace. Zion *shall be the only people that shall not be at war one with another* (D&C 45:69; see also T&C 31:15 RE). That promise of the Lord's cannot be fulfilled by people fighting a war of words and a tumult of opinions. It was such fighting about religious differences that inspired Joseph Smith to ask God for answers. His inquiry led to the Restoration. But Joseph's Restoration has now lapsed into infighting and dividing into separate sects. Our modest return to restoring is not yet free from a tumult of conflicting opinions.

Because the way in which Zion is going to come about, is going to necessarily be something that is so comfortable, and so familiar, on the earth (as a pattern; reflecting what it is that exists in the heavens), that they who come, not only do not burn them up, but they fall upon them and they kiss their necks. Because, at last, they have a sister and a brother, on the earth, united by belief; united by covenant; united by knowledge; united by light and truth or, in other words, the glory of God, which is intelligence. Because the purpose of the Gospel has always been to inform, to edify, to raise up, to instruct. It was never meant to be reduced to something that is merely repetitious. It was intended to challenge you to your very core. And what you do, and what you think, and how you act—it's intended to make you godlike in your understanding.

This is Moses chapter 7, verse 27. *Enoch beheld* ***angels*** *descending out of heaven, bearing testimony of the Father and Son; and the Holy Ghost fell on many, and they were caught up by* ***the powers of heaven*** *into Zion* (see also Genesis 4:15 RE, emphasis added). There they show up again—the powers of heaven (plural), in the same verse where it's talking about angels descending. This is the kind of thing that is littered throughout the scriptures, if you have the eyes to see it, because there is actually a structure there.

There are, within what we regard as priesthood, two brotherhoods or two fellowships:

- One is between men (or women). It is a fellowship that exists among us here on this side.
- There is a second one—there is a second fellowship *that* exists with us to the other side. And on that other side, there is a fellowship or a priesthood.

- And by and large, when the scriptures speak about priesthood having authority— priesthood having power that is connected by a mortal, with a fellowship that extends into the immortal, to the other side; it's a relationship with the "Powers of Heaven."

It is particularly clear that the prophecies, about the last day's Zion, require a people to belong to God, and to be regarded, by Him, as His.

In Isaiah, foretelling the future Zion we learn:

> *And then shall they say, How beautiful upon the mountains are the feet of him that brings good tidings unto them, that publishes peace, that brings good tidings unto them of good, that publishes salvation, that says [to] Zion, Your God reigns! Your watchmen shall lift up the voice; [and] with the voice together shall they sing, for they shall see eye to eye when the Lord shall bring again Zion. Break forth into joy, sing together [ye] waste places of Jerusalem, for the Lord has comforted his people, he has redeemed Jerusalem. The Lord has made bare his holy arm in the eyes of all the nations, and all the earths... all the ends of the earth shall see the salvation of our God. Depart, depart, go out from there, touch no unclean thing; go out of [the midst of her], be clean, ...that bear the vessels of the Lord. For you shall not go...with haste, nor go by flight; for the Lord will go before you, and the God of Israel will be your rear guard.* (Isaiah 52:7-12; see also Isaiah 18:8 RE)

None of us is spared from mutual failure. We are not Zion. We will never be Zion if we do not repent. All of us must repent, turn to face God with full purpose of heart, acting no hypocrisy, or we will not establish godly peace among us.

The Answer to the Prayer for Covenant and the Covenant are the beginning blueprint. That blueprint teaches the need to be better people. Following it is more challenging than reciting it. No one can learn what is required *without doing*. Working together is the only way a society can grow together. No isolated, spiritual mystic is going to be prepared for Zion through his solitary, personal devotions. Personal devotion is necessary, of course, but the most pious hermit will collide with the next pious hermit when they're required to share and work together, in a society of equals, having all things in common. Do not pretend it will be otherwise. Failing to do the hard work, outlined in the covenant, is failing to prepare for Zion. It's failing to have oil in the lamp. It's failing to put upon you the wedding garment.

If you think you are one of the five virgins, who will be invited in when the bridegroom arrives, and have never attempted to obey the Lord's commandments, you will find yourself left outside when the door is shut. If you come from the highways and byways without a wedding garment, because you failed to keep the covenant, you'll be excluded.

As aggravating and trying as people are on one another, we need to go through this. There's no magic path to loving one another. Some people refuse, and must be left outside. When it comes to loving others, some things must be abandoned, some things must be added, some things must be forgotten, and some things must be ignored. But learning what to abandon, add, forget, or ignore is only through the doing. We chip away at ourselves, and others, by interacting and sharing.

We will learn things about one another that will distress us. And we may well wish we didn't know some things about others. How will the socially offensive become socially acceptable without help from a loving society? And how can a society become loving if people are not broadminded enough to figure out that some things just don't matter. Few things really are important. If a man is honest, just, virtuous and true, should you care if he swears? If a man has a heart of gold, and would give you assistance if he thought it was needed, should you care if he's rough and uncouth?

God knows what He's doing. This is the culmination of a plan to finish the ages and vindicate all the promises made to the fathers. The fact that there are wayward and strident children, among a people, does not mean they will be permitted to either stop the forward movement or to come to the Lord's Zion.

What amazes me is that He has continued to pour out teaching, guidance, and profound truths that have been kept hidden from the knowledge of the world, to a small body of believers. There is more light and truth being poured out now, than has been given to almost any prior generation back to the time of Adam. Few have been privileged to know what we have been allowed to speak of publicly. For some, that has made a great difference. For others, it has not affected their hearts and minds enough to remove their hardness, their strident and discordant voices, nor to remove their froward countenances. But remember, the Heavenly Parents *hate* the froward. That clearly disqualifies those individuals from being invited to the Lord's gathering.

I think the Lord knows what He is about, and everything before Him, to decide what to do, how to do it; and when to separate the chosen and bring them to a land of peace. I'm just hoping to be able to receive that invitation and bring my family there.

The foregoing excerpts are taken from:

- Denver's blog post from May 3, 2010, titled "Is it Your Hope to be a Part of Zion?" subsequently recorded on May 17, 2020
- His talk given at the "Zion Symposium" in Provo, Utah on February 23rd, 2008
- Denver's fireside talk on "The Temple," given in Ogden, UT on October 28th, 2012
- Denver's *40 Years in Mormonism Series*, Talk #1 titled "Be of Good Cheer," given in Boise, ID on September 10th, 2013
- Denver's conference talk titled "The Heavens are Open," given in Hurricane, UT on March 22, 2020
- Denver's *40 Years in Mormonism Series*, Talk #4 titled "Covenants," given in Centerville, UT on October 6th, 2013
- Denver's *40 Years in Mormonism Series*, Talk #5 titled "Priesthood," given in Orem, UT on November 2nd, 2013
- Denver's conference talk titled "Civilization," given in Grand Junction, CO on April 21, 2019; and
- His blog post from April 11, 2018, titled "How can Zion Come from This?" subsequently recorded on May 17, 2020.

115. Sabbath Day

Today, Denver answers the question, "On Mount Horeb, the Lord gave a commandment to '*Remember the Sabbath day, to keep it holy*' (Exodus 12:7 RE). How do we keep a day '*holy*?' What does the Lord expect or desire of us in keeping this commandment? Why do we no longer worship on Saturday?"

First, this from The Old Covenants, Isaiah 20:7 RE:

> *Cry aloud, spare not, lift up your voice like a trumpet, and show my people their transgression and the house of Jacob their sins. Yet they seek me daily and delight to know my ways, as a nation that did righteousness and forsook not the ordinance of their God. They ask of me the ordinances of justice, they take delight in approaching to God. Why have we fasted, say they, and you see not? Why have we afflicted our soul and you take no knowledge? Behold, in the day of your fast you find pleasure, and exact all your labors. Behold, you fast for strife and debate, and to smite with the fist of wickedness. You shall not fast as you do this day to make your voice to be heard on high. Is it such a fast that I have chosen? A day for a man to afflict his soul? Is it to bow down his head as a bulrush, and to spread sackcloth and ashes under him? Will you call this a fast and an acceptable day to the Lord? Is not this the fast that I have chosen: to remove the bands of wickedness, to undo the heavy burdens, and to let the oppressed go free, and that you break every yoke? Is it not to deal your bread to the hungry, and that you bring the poor that are cast out to your house? When you see the naked, that you cover him, and that you hide not yourself from your own flesh? Then shall your light break forth as the morning, and your health shall spring forth speedily, and your righteousness shall go before you; the glory of the Lord shall be your rear guard. Then shall you call and the Lord shall answer, you shall cry and he shall say, Here I am. If you take away from your midst the yoke, the putting forth of the finger, and speaking vanity, and if you draw out your soul to the hungry, and satisfy the afflicted soul, then shall your light rise in obscurity and your darkness be as the noonday. And the Lord shall guide you continually, and satisfy your soul in drought, and make fat your bones; and you shall be like a watered garden, and like a spring of water whose waters fail not. And they that shall be of you shall build the old waste places. You shall raise up the foundations of many generations, and you shall be called the repairer of the breach, the restorer of paths to dwell in. If you turn away your foot from the Sabbath — from doing your pleasure on my holy day — and call the Sabbath a delight, the holy of the Lord honorable, and shall honor him, not doing your own ways, nor finding your own pleasure, nor speaking your own words, then shall you delight yourself in the Lord. And I will cause you to ride upon the high places*

of the earth, and feed you with the heritage of Jacob your father; for the mouth of the Lord has spoken it.

DENVER: Teachings and Commandments 46, paragraphs 2-4 states:

*Wherefore, I give unto them a commandment, saying thus: You shall love the Lord your God with all your heart, with all your might, mind, and strength, and in the name of Jesus Christ you shall serve him. You shall love your neighbor as yourself. You shall not steal, neither commit adultery, nor kill, nor do anything like unto it. You shall thank the Lord your God in **all** things. You shall offer a sacrifice unto the Lord...in righteousness, even that of a broken heart and a contrite spirit.*

*And that you may more fully keep yourself unspotted from the world, you [should] go to the house of prayer and offer up your sacraments upon my holy day. For verily, this is a day appointed unto you to rest from your labors, and to pay your devotions unto the Most High. Nevertheless, your vows shall be offered up in righteousness on **all** days and at **all** times, but remember that on this, **the Lord's day**, you shall offer your oblations and your sacraments unto the Most High, confessing your sins unto your brethren and before the Lord. And on this day, you shall do none other things — only let your food be prepared with singleness of heart, that your fasting may be perfect, or in other words, that your joy may be full. Verily, this is fasting and prayer, or in other words, rejoicing and prayer.*

*And inasmuch as you do these things with thanksgiving, with cheerful hearts and countenances (not with much laughter, for this is sin, but with a glad heart and a cheerful countenance), verily I say that inasmuch as you do this, the fullness of the earth is yours — the beasts of the fields and the fowls of the air, and that which climbs upon trees and walks upon the earth, yea, and the herb, and the good things which come of the earth, whether for food, or for raiment, or for houses, or for barns, or for orchards, or for gardens, or for vineyards. Yea, **all** things which come of the earth, in the season thereof, are made for the benefit and the use of man, both to please the eye, and to gladden the heart, yea for food and for raiment, for taste and for smell, to strengthen the body and to enliven the soul. And it pleases God that he has given all these things unto man, for unto this end were they made, to be used with judgment, not to excess, neither by extortion.* ([Emphasis added.] T&C 46:2-4 RE)

What a happy thought is contained in all of that: commandments that constrain us from evil, blessings and opportunities intended to benefit us, make us cheerful, and provide for our needs—everything. But it begins with the self-discipline to keep the commandments and to no longer be a threat to one another, to no longer introduce elements of disobedience and chaos continuously into this world, because mankind has been continuously off the mark. Therefore, we *aren*'t glad at nature because we threaten one another. We aren't rejoicing at the peace that this world gives to us, with enough and to spare, *because* we hoard, *because* we are not generous and kindly and loving one towards another. We're fearful, and we find this world a threatening place, because *we* make it so. God, on the other hand, never intended that it should be so.

We just finished the Easter celebration last weekend; and as a result of celebrating Easter, I wanted to take some comments from the account of that very first day when the Lord came out of the grave. The fact that Easter is in the springtime, I don't think is any accident. I think it's intended to align with the testimony of nature about the promise of eternal life, the promise of the renewal that comes every spring, and I think the Lord intended that His death and His resurrection should associate with spring. And I think it's appropriate that that be the subject that we look at today.

The incident that I want to look at is recorded only one place in Scripture. And even though it only appears one place in the Scripture, I think it's one of the most thought-provoking and potentially-rewarding discussions about the Lord than appears anywhere else. I'm talking about the incident that Luke records of two disciples who were walking from Jerusalem to Emmaus on the day that the Lord rose from the dead. I'm going to be using the Luke material throughout this as the exclusive source, if Luke talks about it. If someone else talks about it and Luke didn't, then we'll look at that. But the distance that they're going to walk is beyond what was then viewed as a Sabbath day's journey, so they couldn't take this walk on the Sabbath. They had to wait until the first day of the week when the Sabbath was over, which was also the day on which the Lord would be resurrected.

The incident appears in Luke chapter 24. And it begins (in chapter 24): *Now upon the first day of the week, very early in the morning, they came unto the sepulchre, bringing the spices which they had prepared*" (Luke 14:1 RE). He doesn't tell us this, but there's a detail you can find over in John chapter 20: *The first day of the week cometh Mary Magdalene early, when it was yet dark* (John 11:1 RE and Testimony of St. John 12:1 RE). All that Luke says is it was very early in the morning. John lets us know that this was not only very early in the morning, it was still dark out.

If you brought your Scriptures it might be useful to use them as we go along. So, there is a walk that's going to take place in which two disciples (we have the names of only one of the two) are walking back to Emmaus, and this is what the account reads, beginning in verse 13:

> *And, behold, two of them went that same day to a village called Emmaus, which was from Jerusalem about threescore furlongs.* [That's about seven miles which clearly, under their tradition, would have been too far.] *And they talked together of all these things which had happened. And it came to pass, that, while they communed together and reasoned, Jesus himself drew near, and went with them. But their eyes were holden that they should not know him.* (See also Luke 14:2 RE)

Their eyes were holden. The Lord is with them; He's resurrected; He's walking along with them and they don't recognize Him. Christ has the capacity to withhold His identity. As Paul reminded us in Hebrews chapter 13, verse 2: *Be not forgetful to entertain strangers: for thereby some have entertained angels unawares* (Hebrews 1:58 RE). From this incident on this day with the Lord, we learn that the *"strangers"* can include the Lord Himself. And so, when he says to be careful how you treat *"the least of these my brethren"* (Matthew 11:23 RE), you ought not be surprised if, on the day of judgment, one of those *"least"* was the Lord Himself, and your eyes were holden that you should not know Him.

> *And he said unto them, What manner of communications are these that you have one to another, as you walk, and are sad?* (Luke 14:2 RE)

Clearly a rhetorical question. This is the risen Lord joining this fellowship in their walk and He's asking them, "What are you talking about?" That ought to tell you something about Him. The Lord doesn't make any effort to displace their attention from the subject they're discussing. He joins them right where they are, on the subject that they're focused on, as a ready participant in the subject that's already on the table. That tells you something else about us—He really does want to help us where He finds us. *Our* concerns are really His concerns.

When it comes to the Gospel of Jesus Christ, which according to Joseph Smith comprehended all truth, it is our own fear that limits our capacity to gain from what's being offered. And it's a measure of our ingratitude when, declining the invitation that Joseph extended to search deeper and deeper into the mysteries of God, we elect to withdraw fearfully, and conclude that we're just not interested in what might have been had. It's actually a trick of the devil to get people to close their minds and close their hearts, because they fear what they may be learning will do damage to them.

You see, when Adam and Eve partook of the fruit and then Satan called to their attention the fact that they were naked, and that's the beginning of the mischief that gets visited on humanity by the adversary—who seeks to bind and control and to limit the freedom of all mankind, to imprison them—he pointed out to them that they ought to be ashamed. And when, therefore, they heard the voice of God speaking, they withdrew—not because of shame but because the shame triggered within them fear. They were afraid to come into the presence of that Being who they knew to be just and holy, because now they were in a state in which, fearfully, they were naked.

And their "nakedness" came to them as a consequence of understanding the difference between what they were and what they are. And that knowledge came to them by partaking, out of season, of the fruit that they weren't scheduled to receive a command to partake of until after a day of rest had been observed. So now, not only are they naked before God, they're also violating the Sabbath and beginning the labor of the mortal existence—out of time, out of sequence, out of season. And that's the way a great number of errors are made in humanity.

You see, we're commanded not to partake of some things out of season, and then we are commanded *to* partake within season. And when we get the timing wrong, we wind up with difficulties and problems that ought not to have been visited. Well, the other references on that same statement, about the opposite of *love* is *fear,* is 2 Timothy 1:7 and Moroni 8:16 (2 Timothy 1:2 RE and Moroni 8:3-4 RE).

Repentance is a critical thing. It is *the* message of the Book of Mormon. It is the greatest message that's contained within the Book of Isaiah, and it is *the* message of all the true prophets. The thing that stirs you up to repenting is actually two things: The first thing is to awaken to your *awful* situation, and the second thing is to arise—and that is to connect with *the* Source which will cure what is wrong with you because we're not self-curing. We are filled with that same shame that came to us in the beginning as a consequence of doing what we were not supposed to be doing.

But the greatest way in which the adversary keeps us in a state of slumber is to prevent us from looking about and becoming awakened to the awful situation in which we find ourselves. Hugh Nibley commented on more than one occasion that there is nothing quite so terrible as being awakened out of a deep sleep. No one really likes *that*. I mean, when it comes right down to it, unconsciousness is a very good thing, particularly when what you are looking at is what we have here.

QUESTION: So... "In the Elijah talk, you made reference to the fact that Adam and Eve partook of the fruit out of order—that they were to wait until after the Sabbath; that partaking prior to the Sabbath caused work to be done on the Sabbath. Can you explain and expand on this subject, please?"

DENVER: The problem was not that they were never going to be told to partake, to not to ever partake of the fruit of the Tree of Knowledge of Good and Evil, it's that they were forbidden to partake so that there could be a day of rest—a Sabbath. Everything was supposed to stand down. And then after they stood down for the day of rest, on the first day of the next week They were then to introduce the knowledge of good and evil in a way that would've been benign, in a way that would've transitioned from the original, paradisiacal state into a state in which knowledge of good and evil, and mortality itself, could enter the world—much as it will be present during the Millennium among the righteous.

But instead, in an act of defiance that resulted in them being kicked out of the Garden because of transgression, and an act that caused labor then to occur on the Sabbath, they partook out of season—in obedience to the one who seeks to *always* counsel people to rebel against the order of Heaven, to disobey and to set at naught the commandments and instructions of the Father, even when doing so means harm to yourself or to others, because the adversary is only interested in the destruction of people, even those who trust and rely upon him. He has no good end in mind for them. And so, they partook out of the ordinary course. As a consequence, there was a Fall.

The Fall introduced—on the Sabbath day—the mortal experience. And so, the seventh day, the day of rest, would then require six days of labor to precede their next day of rest, which always put the Sabbath out of sync because of the original rebellion. Which is why the Lord was resurrected on what they thought was the *first* day of the week. It was, in fact, the first day of the week according to their reckoning and the seventh day of the week according to the original creation—had everything been honored in the original commandment and instruction. And so, the worshipers moved the

Sabbath day from Saturday to Sunday, to that first day of the week, which was in reality simply restoring back the original, violated time frame. And the early Christians observed, as the seventh day of the week, the correct day of worship—the day that we worship on, which is Sunday and not Saturday. Although the tradition of following, in a number of places, remains to do so on Saturday.

It's more important that you keep a day holy, that you set it aside as a day of worship, than it is to figure out the chronology of everything that's gone on. If it was so important for us to get exactly the right day of the week aligned with everything, then we'd all be John Pratt. [Audience laughter.]

The Book of Mormon's religious structure—and I'm not talking about the era of the judges where there were governmental and church functions that were going on, and you really don't have a distinct separation of the two adequate in the record. What you have— The best description of this was given in Alma about how they functioned. The priests came and would teach them on Sunday. Everyone would drop what they're doing; they'd come; they'd be taught; and then when they were done with their Sabbath observances, everyone would go back and they'd work and they'd labor. There was no professional clergy; there was no hierarchy. They had a high priest, who was apparently an itinerant that traveled around.

The more you consolidate power and authority into an office, the more you tempt the adversary to gain control of the office, because the one thing about salvation is it is entirely other-worldly. If you can get gain in saving the souls of men, you will be unable to save the souls of men, because faith, and the first principle of faith, is obedience to God and sacrifice of *everything*. Without the willingness to sacrifice *everything*, it is impossible to gain the faith that will save your soul.

I got some questions on the internet. There are some of you who are here and were told you could ask questions, and I want to leave a little time for that. I'm only going to answer one of the questions that came in that hasn't already been addressed in the talk, and it's an obvious question from an obvious source.

A Seventh-day Adventist inquired if I keep the Sabbath. So, that cuts right to the rub, doesn't it? The answer is yes, I keep the Sabbath. But let me explain to you why I do keep the Sabbath *as* I do.

In the Creation, God had a plan for six days of labor and one day of rest. And that one day of rest was to be continually observed (would later be memorialized in the Law of Moses), *but* on the day of rest, Adam and Eve managed to get the boot out of the Garden of Eden. And so, instead of a day of rest, they were laboring. The reckoning of the week was disturbed by the fact that we lost the first one, and the calendar resulted in a day's disparity from the Fall of Adam and Eve. When Christ was resurrected, He was resurrected— Instead, it's called the first day of the week because it was the first day of the week reckoned according to the Fall of Adam. But Christ's atonement was intended to fix the Fall of Adam, to put everything back right again, to repair the damage that had been done. And therefore when Christ was resurrected, His resurrection coming (as it was) one day late, was actually *just on time.* And He repaired not only the damage done in the original Fall, He repaired the Sabbath as well; hence, the observance of the day of resurrection as the day of rest—called the first day of the week instead of the seventh because that's how time had been reckoned from the Fall of Adam until the resurrection of Christ.

I observe the Sabbath as the day on which Christ was resurrected—as a symbol of His repair of the premature Fall and the loss of the *original* day of rest, going back to the time of Adam and Eve. But yes, I keep the Sabbath. Now, having said that, the original Christians would let you worship on Saturday and would let me worship on Sunday, because as long as you keep the doctrine of Christ and you accept the law of Christ, we'll figure it out together over time, and eventually one will persuade the other. Not perhaps by argument and debate, but by the quiet example that persuades the heart that there's something more to be preferred in one than in the other.

It is not possible to list all commandments. In one sense there are only two: love God; love your fellow man. All others are extensions of those. If you love God, you will do what He asks of you. Whenever something comes to your attention He would have you do, you do it! For example, Christ was baptized and said to follow Him. So, because of your love of God, you follow Him.

But Christ also showed repeatedly that the second commandment was greater than the rules. Keeping the Sabbath day holy, for example, was subordinate to loving and freeing His fellow man. He freed men from sin on the Sabbath by forgiving sins. He freed them from physical injury or disease by healing them on the Sabbath. Both were considered work at the time, and therefore an offense to the commandment to keep the Sabbath day holy.

Your individual path back to God will begin with following the teachings of The Church of Jesus Christ of Latter-day Saints. At some point, however, you will find that individual service, and obedience to God's will for you, will create disharmony between you and institutions. *It can't be avoided.* If you're following Christ, you will find the same things *He* found. Helping someone in need will take you away from church meetings on occasions. You can't make a list and keep it because as soon as you do, the list will interfere with loving God and loving your fellow man.

So, the whole matter can be reduced to this: Follow Christ, receive the ordinances, accept the Holy Ghost who will teach you all things you must do. Any list beyond that will inevitably result in conflicts and contradictions.

Paul's teachings in Romans chapter 14 (Romans 1:67-72 RE) is the only way we can become "one" as a people. I respect your motivation more than your actions because *they* are pure. But we err when we judge another's actions and attribute to them motive. Pure motive cannot be known by observing actions. If we could judge motive from acts, then we would condemn Nephi for murdering Laban and stealing the brass plates. We would condemn Abraham for lying about the status of his wife Sarah, claiming her to be a sister. We would condemn Jesus for violating a clearly-understood teaching about the Sabbath and not doing any labor upon the Sabbath. *We* would be wrong. Nephi was constrained to implement God's judgment; Abraham was acting on the direction of the Lord; and Jesus was honoring the Sabbath by keeping it holy, even if that came at the expense of performing labor.

Adam and Eve could not have children while they were in the Garden of Eden. They lacked the capacity to bear children in the innocent state in which they then existed (see 2 Nephi 1:10 RE). They had been given the gift of childbearing as an endowment from God. The endowment of the capacity did not mean they had the means or understanding at the time to act upon it. Without the Fall, they would not have been able to act on the endowment. They were like little children, who have been born male and female with the capacity to one day become parents, but who are immature and innocent, and therefore unable to bear children.

The great offense was in Satan's control of the timing. Had they remained in the Garden throughout the Sabbath day of rest, then they would have received the commandment to partake of the fruit in the Lord's timing. At this point they would have moved from their innocent state into a condition not unlike the Millennial day. The Fall would have transitioned to a terrestrial state rather than a telestial state.

Adam and Eve were ordained for a priestly role in the Garden of Eden, and were in God's presence while serving in that capacity. Once cast out, the challenge forever after has been to recreate Eden and have God's presence return to the earth—not just to visit but to take up His abode here. That's the reason for establishing temples by God's people repeatedly in history. But the objective has always been the same: the return of Eden, the return of God, and the redemption of the earth from the Fall.

The problem was not partaking of the knowledge of good and evil—*that* was *always* the destiny of Adam and Eve. The problem was partaking in violation of the Sabbath. We lost the day of rest, mankind made himself—rather than God—the center of creation, and the original Sabbath day did not return until Christ's resurrection.

It is apparent that Christ never intended to re-establish Eden in the Old World. He made some considerable advancement to that end among the Nephites. Who knows what was done among the others He visited in the post-resurrection ministry? But the burden of prophecy is clear: There will be a final Temple of God in which He returns to dwell on earth. That will require priestly men and women to perform the obligations imposed for Divine worship, opening the heavens, and having the Gods, angels, and mankind associate with one another.

God always intended to have mankind gain knowledge of good and evil. But God also intended that the center would be occupied by God, not by man's ambition and self-will. Christ did nothing but what the Father directed be done. He said nothing other than what the Father commanded Him to say. He suffered the will of the Father in all things. Christ performed the priestly service that Adam and Eve neglected to perform.

The foregoing excerpts are taken from:

- Teachings & Commandments Section 46, paragraphs 2-4, with additional comments recorded by Denver on June 6, 2020;
- Denver's talk titled "Christ's Discourse on the Road to Emmaus," given in Fairview, Utah, on April 14, 2007;
- His talk titled "The Mission of Elijah Reconsidered," given in Spanish Fork, Utah, on October 14th, 2011;

- The Q&A Session following Denver's conference talk given in Grand Junction, Colorado, on April 21, 2019;
- Denver's comments during an assembly on "Missionary Work," in Eden, Utah, on July 2, 2016;
- Denver's *Christian Reformation Lecture Series*, Talk #2, given in Dallas, Texas, on October 19th, 2017;
- His Blog Post from March 1, 2010, titled "Keep the Commandments," subsequently recorded by Denver on June 6, 2020;
- His Blog Post from August 5, 2020, titled "Trivial Pursuit," subsequently recorded by Denver on June 6, 2020;
- His Blog Post from March 6, 2010, titled "Adam and Eve," subsequently recorded by Denver on June 6, 2020; and
- His Blog Post from May 3, 2020, titled "Email about Adam and Eve," subsequently recorded by Denver on June 6, 2020.

116. True Vine, Part 1

This is Part 1 of a special series on the "True Vine" where Denver answers the question, "Why is Christ referred to as the 'True Vine' in scripture, and what can we learn from this analogy?"

———

DENVER: Once again, Joseph is called by name—this is verse 33 (see JSH 1:32-33; see also JSH 3:2 RE). He was afraid; the fear soon left him. The reason he was afraid was because he was seeking forgiveness of his sins. A perfectly white, bright, lit individual appears who represents the cleanliness of heaven itself. Joseph, in contrast to that... He's inquiring to know about his sins. Now, a visibly cleansed being stands before him; he's afraid. And why is he afraid?—because, once again, you see the remarkable contrast. I know what lies in my heart. I know what failings I have had, and I know this being can see through me. Therefore, I need **something** that will remove from me my fear. *He called me by name.* It's the same thing. Moroni dispels it by letting him know: We have a brotherhood; we have a relationship. *Fear soon left me. He called me by name* (ibid, vs. 32-33; vs. 2-3 RE; emphasis added).

Well, this is what we want to talk about. He tells him about the stuff, the accoutrements that he's gonna be handed, in verse 34 and 35 (ibid; vs. 3 RE). But then he gets, in verse 36 (vs. 4 RE), and this is where... Ooooh, this is where we've got something now. This is Moroni delivering a message, but his message is not like we find in the King James version of the Bible. He says: *Behold, the day cometh that shall burn as an oven, and all the proud, yea,...all that do wickedly shall burn as stubble; for* ***they [they]*** *that come shall burn them, saith the Lord of Hosts, that it shall leave them neither root nor branch* (ibid, vs. 37; vs. 4 RE; emphasis added).

Root, branch: genealogical words. *They that come*: who are they?

> *Again, he quoted the fifth verse...: Behold, I will reveal unto you the Priesthood, by the hand of Elijah the prophet, before the coming of the great and dreadful day of the Lord. He...quoted the next verse differently* [he said]: *...he shall plant in the hearts of the children the promises made to the fathers, and the hearts of the children shall turn to their fathers. If it were not so, the whole earth would be utterly wasted at his coming.* (JSH 1:38-39; see also JSH 3:4 RE)

Oh, we'll probably get this parsed about Spanish Fork in the coming year. Everything about this is telling you something that is remarkably different from where we find ourselves:

The day is coming that will burn them. When?

- *They that come.* Who?
- *Neither root nor branch.* This is genealogical.
- Elijah and the Priesthood. We'll talk about that on another day.
- Children get planted in their hearts.
- *Promises made to the fathers.*
- Children's hearts turned to their Fathers.

There is so much in that that we need to pick apart; we need to understand. And we're gonna go there because understanding this is understanding the foundation of Zion.

The foundation of Zion consists largely in the reconnecting the children (as a consequence of the promises that were made to the Fathers) back **to** the Fathers so that there might be a wielded link that connects the children who are on the earth with the Fathers who are in heaven—not your kindred dead that are in the spirit world. They are in desperate need of your ministration to save them. Connecting yourself to them is to connect yourself with the, essentially, the damned, the dead, the disembodied. The Fathers who are in heaven are the ones to whom you need to form the link. (And I've written that paper on it which I assume some of you have read. And if you haven't, just send a note to the blog, and I'll email it to you. It's *The Mission of Elijah Reconsidered.*) But see, the whole purpose behind this is to fix this problem because if it were not so, the whole earth would be utterly wasted—utterly wasted at His coming.

Then he says: *He quoted the eleventh chapter of Isaiah, saying that it was about to be fulfilled* (JSH 1:40; see also JSH 3:4 RE).

Okay, let's go back to that 11th chapter of Isaiah because—Man! Have we made a mess of that! Okay, this is *about to be fulfilled.*

There shall come forth [this is chapter 11 of Isaiah]— *There shall come forth a rod out of the stem of Jesse* (Isaiah 11:1; see also Isaiah 5:4 RE)... The *Rod* is a servant who is a descendant of Jesse—who is a Levite—and Ephraim, unto whom is rightly belonging the priesthood. Keep your finger there on that chapter 11 of Isaiah and turn back to Doctrine and Covenants section 113, and you'll see where these words are explained.

> *Who is the Stem...spoken of... Verily thus saith the Lord: It is Christ...* [Verse 3] *What is the Rod spoken of in the fifth verse of the 11th chapter of Isaiah, that should come of the Stem of Jesse? Behold...saith the Lord: It is a servant* [a servant!] *in the hands of Christ, who is partly a descendant of Jesse as well as of Ephraim, or of the house of Joseph, on whom there is laid much power.* (D&C 113:1-4; see also T&C 129:1-2 RE)

Well, look, until you succeed, you fail. I don't care who comes along claiming whatever they want to claim. Until the work is done, you can't take credit for it—period. There's all kinds of nonsense that circulates about "Ooooh, who has the keys? Button, button who's got the button?" Look, someone's going to do a work. When the work is done, you will know. Until the work is done, no one can be identified with the role—period. It is arrogance; it is pretentiousness; it is foolishness for anyone to step forward and say: "I, I, I am that man!" Do the work. Finish the course. Fulfill the covenant. You do that, you can take the name. Until you do the work, it's just noise.

So, there's gonna come forth:

> *A rod out of the stem of Jesse...a Branch shall grow out of his roots: ...the spirit of the LORD shall rest upon him, the spirit of wisdom and understanding, the spirit of counsel and might, the spirit of knowledge and...the fear of the LORD.* [Oh, thank God! Someone will finally fear the Lord more than they fear man. I look forward to that moment.] *And shall make him of quick understanding in the fear of the LORD: and he shall not judge after the sight of his eyes, neither reprove after the hearing of his ears: But with righteousness shall he judge the poor, and reprove with equity for the meek of the earth: ...he shall smite the earth with the rod of his mouth* [in this context, it is the word of God], *and with the breath of his lips [he shall] slay the wicked. And righteousness shall be the girdle of his loins, ...faithfulness the girdle of his reins. The wolf...shall dwell with the lamb, ...the leopard shall lie down with the kid; and the calf and the young lion and the fatling together; and a little child shall lead them.* [These things are shortly to come to pass.] *And the cow and the bear shall feed; their young ones shall lie down together: and the lion shall eat straw like the ox. And the sucking child shall*

> *play on the hole of the asp, and the weaned child shall put his hand on the cockatrice's den. They shall not hurt nor destroy in all my holy mountain: for the earth shall be full of the knowledge of the LORD, as the waters cover the sea.* [You see, it's *knowledge*, full of *knowledge of the Lord*. That's what you have to lay hold on.] *And in that day there shall be a root of Jesse, which shall stand for an ensign of the people; to it shall the Gentiles seek: and his rest shall be glorious. And it shall come to pass in that day, that the Lord shall set his hand again the second time to recover the remnant of his people, which shall be left...* (Isaiah 11:1-11; see also Isaiah 5:4-5 RE)

Well, this shall shortly come to pass—not then, not that day—by and by.

You know, when a branch is spoken of, if you look at John 15:1-6 (see also John 9:10 RE; Testimony of St. John 10:17 RE)... I'm not going to do that because our time is far spent, but Christ gives a sermon about Him being the *true vine*, about how you cannot bear fruit unless you are connected to the true vine. Once again, that is a genealogical term. That is a *family of God* term. That is a *son of God* term. And He intends to make many sons of God.

Joseph is receiving in this first interview with the angel Moroni an announcement about the first indications of the restoration of God's intent to restore a holy family. God is telling us what **He** wants—**He, God**—wants to have upon the earth again: His family. But **we** must respond—**we**. This is your dispensation; this is your time. You came down here with the intent of living and finding the things that will bring you back. This is your opportunity. Don't let some other group claim that it doesn't belong to you. These scriptures are only going to be fulfilled when enough people awake and arise to realize that it is devolving upon you the obligation to find, to heed, to seek, to search, to pray, to obey, and to form what is necessary in order to fulfill all the promises and the covenants that were made to the Fathers.

Well, tonight we're gonna talk about covenants and, in particular, covenants that are being referred to in a verse that we find in the Joseph Smith History, verse 39—Moroni changing the content of the text of Malachi to render it to Joseph Smith (on this fall equinox occasion) to read this way: *And he shall plant in the hearts of the children the promises made to the fathers, and the hearts of the children shall turn to their fathers. If it were not so, the whole earth would be utterly wasted at his coming* (JSH 1:39; see also JSH 3:4 RE).

So, there is some peril if we do not have our hearts turned to these Fathers. That peril is that we will be *utterly wasted at his coming* if we fail. But His coming is not limited merely to the singular *Him*, being the Lord. If you go back to verse 37, it says: ***they*** *that come shall burn them*. And therefore, when He comes, *they* that come with Him shall burn those who are unprepared, those who are scheduled for being *utterly wasted* at His coming. And so, we need to inquire into what, exactly, it is the promises were; who the Fathers were that the promises were made to; and then avoid this peril of those who come burning them—that *it shall leave them neither root nor branch* (terms which, in Boise, I referred to as being genealogical) because it becomes the end of the line at that point.

In looking at the promises that were made, I want to go back to Second Nephi chapter 3 and begin there (which we also referred to earlier) because when we're tracking back the covenants that were made, and we're talking about the promises that were made to the Fathers, and we're trying to identify who the Fathers are, we get a real advantage in making the determination by what we have in Lehi's blessing to his son, Joseph.

Beginning at verse 4 of chapter 3 of Second Nephi, Lehi says, *I am a descendant of Joseph who was carried [away] captive into Egypt. And great were the covenants of the Lord which he made unto Joseph* (2 Nephi 3:4; see also 2 Nephi 2:2 RE).

As soon as you encounter the word *covenants*, an alarm ought to go off because much of what's going to go on in the history of the world is gonna go on as a consequence of these covenants that have been made—one of the possessors of those promises and covenants being Joseph who had been carried away captive into Egypt.

> *Wherefore, Joseph truly saw our day* [meaning Lehi's day—and when Lehi is talking, he's talking about events that he believed that Joseph of Egypt had foreseen about what would happen in his own day]. ...*He obtained a promise of the Lord, that out of the fruit of his loins the Lord God would raise up a righteous branch unto the house of Israel; not the Messiah, but a branch which was to be broken off, nevertheless, to be remembered in the covenants of the Lord that the Messiah should be made manifest unto them in the latter days, in the spirit of power, unto the bringing of them out of darkness....Joseph truly testified,...*[verse 6] *A seer shall the Lord...God raise up, who shall be a choice seer unto the fruit of my loins. Yea, Joseph truly said: Thus saith the Lord unto me: A choice seer will I raise up out of the fruit of thy loins...* [and he goes on to talk about... This choice seer is going to bring...] *them to the knowledge of the covenants which I have made with thy fathers.* (2 Nephi 3:5-7; see also 2 Nephi 2:2-3 RE)

So, the assignment that is given to this choice seer, descendant of Joseph, is that this person is going to bring to the world, to us, to the descendants, to the people in the last days *knowledge [concerning] covenants which [God had] made with thy fathers—thy fathers* in **this** statement being: thy Fathers, Joseph of Egypt. So, the promises that God made to **Fathers** before Joseph of Egypt —a seer is going to restore the knowledge about that. It may be complex wording, but it's dealing with very simple events, and the identities are important.

I will give unto him [that is, this choice seer] *a commandment that he shall do none other work...*(ibid, vs. 8; vs. 3 RE). That is to say, he will not cause Zion to come. That was not the assignment of the choice seer. Joseph Smith was not in charge of and not required to do the work of bringing again Zion.

> *None other work, save the work which I shall command him...I will make him great in mine eyes; for he shall do my work...he shall be great [and] like unto Moses, whom I…said I would [deliver] up* [verse11] *But a seer [I will] raise up out of the fruit of thy loins;...unto him will I give power to bring forth my word unto the seed of thy loins.* (ibid, vs. 9-11; vs. 3 RE)

In verse 12, it talks about how there's gonna be this restoration of *knowledge of their fathers in the latter days...also to the knowledge of my covenants, saith the Lord* (ibid, vs. 12; vs. 4 RE).

And then in 15, it says, *his name shall be called after me...it shall be after the name of his father* [after *me* being Joseph of Egypt—so, the name should be Joseph; that will also be the name of his father]. *He shall be like unto me; for the thing, which the Lord [God] shall bring forth by his hand, by the power of the Lord shall bring my people unto salvation* (2 Nephi 3:15; see also 2 Nephi 2:5 RE).

And then he goes on, and he tells Lehi (he tells his son) in verse 23: *Because of this covenant* [that is, the one that was done with Joseph of Egypt], ***[he]*** [the son of Lehi] *[is] blessed; for* ***[his]*** [the son of Lehi's] *seed shall not be destroyed,...they shall hearken unto the words of the book. And there shall rise up one mighty among them* [I talked about that in Boise] (2 Nephi 3:23-24; ibid, vs. 7 RE).

And so, if Joseph Smith fulfills the prophecy that was delivered to Joseph that is recovered, in part, in the Book of Mormon in this third chapter of Second Nephi, then Joseph Smith should give to us the ability to know something about these covenants that were made with the Fathers.

Well, we do not have to rely upon merely what we have in Second Nephi chapter 3. Nor do we have to have the brass plates, as it turns out, because Joseph Smith restored the prophecy of Joseph of Egypt. And you can read it right now in the Joseph Smith Translation, beginning in Genesis chapter 50 at verse 24. It reads slightly different than Lehi's summation given. And Lehi's choice of what he adds in, and what he selects out, and what Joseph says has some interesting things. It's absolutely worth your time to study out all the differences and to pick apart what it is that Lehi did because it tells you much about Father Lehi, what he chose to include, and what he chose to pass over.

However, for our purposes tonight, I want to look at what was said to Joseph that we find in the Joseph Smith Translation, Genesis chapter 50, beginning at verse 24. Joseph of Egypt says: *The Lord [hath] visited me and I have obtained [a] promise of the Lord* (see also Genesis 12:36 RE). This is what Lehi will refer to in his prophecy to his son Joseph as a *covenant* because when the Lord delivers a promise to someone, He delivers it by way of covenant. God is bound by His word. Therefore, when He delivers a promise, it is a covenant.

> *I have obtained a promise of the Lord, that out of the fruit of my loins* [this is the covenant with Joseph of Egypt—out of **his** loins], *the Lord God will raise up a righteous **branch** out of **my** loins* [so, that is talking about Joseph of Egypt, one of the sons of Israel, one of the twelve tribes]; *and* [now we're changing topics] *and unto **thee**, whom my father Jacob hath named Israel* [so, this is not just the descendants of Joseph; this is **all** of the twelve tribes, raised up unto **all** of the twelve tribes], *a prophet; (not the Messiah who is called Shiloh;) and **this** prophet shall deliver my people out of Egypt in the days of thy bondage.* [That's a covenant about deliverance to be had for **all** the tribes of Israel, not merely the descendants of Joseph.] (JST Genesis 50:24; see also Genesis 12:36 RE; emphasis added)
>
> *And it shall come to pass that they* [that is, all of Israel] *shall be scattered again; and a branch shall be broken off, and shall be carried into a far country; nevertheless they shall be remembered in the covenants of the Lord, when the Messiah cometh; for he shall be made manifest unto them in the latter days* [Now, when is that? Is it when he was resurrected, and He appears in Third Nephi? Or is the latter days some other time?], *in the Spirit of power; and shall bring them out of darkness into light; out of hidden darkness, and out of captivity unto freedom. A **seer** shall the Lord my God raise up, who shall be a choice seer unto the fruit of **my*** [that is, **Joseph's**] *loins* [different topic, different person, different time frame]. *Thus saith the Lord God of my fathers* [this is Joseph speaking; his Fathers would

> include at a minimum, Abraham, Isaac, and Jacob—his *fathers,* in the plural] *unto me* [so, the Lord God of Joseph's Fathers said unto him], *A choice seer will I raise up out of the fruit of thy* [that is, Joseph's] *loins,…he shall be esteemed highly among the fruit of thy* [that is, Joseph's] *loins; and unto him will I give [a] commandment that he shall do a work for the fruit of thy* [that is, Joseph's] *loins,* ***[and] his brethren*** [that is, other members of Israel]. *And he shall bring them to the knowledge of the covenants which I have made* ***with thy fathers***. (ibid, vs. 24-28; vs. 36-38 RE; emphasis added)

Now we're beginning to have laid out in the restoration through Joseph Smith, part of what it is that we need to know in order to avoid being utterly wasted.

> *He* [the seer] *shall do whatsoever work I shall command him. And I will make him great in mine eyes, for he shall do my work; and he* [that is, Joseph of Egypt's descendant-seer] *he shall be great like unto* ***him*** *whom I have said I would raise up unto you, to deliver my people, O house of Israel* [*him* that he's going to raise up is Moses, okay?] *…for a seer will I raise up to deliver my people out of the land of Egypt* [this is Moses];*…he shall be called Moses. And by this name he shall [be known] that he is of thy house* [that is, *O house of Israel*—that's the house, not Joseph's—the house of Israel]; *for he shall be nursed by the king's daughter, and shall be called her son. And again* [so, we're changing topics again] *a seer will I raise up out of the fruit of thy* [that is, Joseph's] *loins, and unto him* [that is, this seer] *will I give power to bring forth my word unto the seed of thy loins* [that's Joseph's seer, and he's to give us God's word]. (JST Genesis 50:28-30; see also Genesis 12:38-39 RE; emphasis added)

And then he goes on to say in verse 31:

> *The fruit of thy loins* [that is, Joseph's loins] *shall write,…the fruit of the loins of Judah shall write;…that which shall be written by the fruit of thy loins,…also that which shall be written by the fruit of the loins of Judah, shall grow together unto the confounding of false [doctrine],…laying down of contentions, and establishing peace among the fruit of thy loins* [a yet-future event], *and bringing them to a knowledge of their* ***fathers*** *in the latter days; and also to the knowledge of my covenants, saith the Lord.* (JST Genesis 50:31; see also Genesis 12:39 RE; emphasis added)

Joseph's seer is to do this. This is what Moroni is telling Joseph in verse 39 of the Joseph Smith History.

> *Out of weakness shall he be made strong, in that day when my work shall go forth among* ***all*** *my people* [*all my people* include all of the various branches of Israel], *which shall restore* ***them****, who are of the house of Israel, in the last days* (ibid, vs. 32; vs. 39 RE; emphasis added).

That's the objective, to fix and reconnect the house of Israel, restoring them in the last days.

> *And that seer will I bless, and they that seek to destroy him shall be confounded; for this promise I give unto you* [Joseph of Egypt]; *for I will remember you* [Joseph of Egypt] *from generation to generation; and his* [that latter-day seer] *[his] name shall be called Joseph* [as if the Lord Himself wanted to be had in remembrance in all generations, Joseph of Egypt—Joseph of Egypt who was sold into slavery; Joseph of Egypt who kept his faith; Joseph of Egypt who was sold into slavery by the jealousy of brothers whom he only sought to declare the truth to]. *His name shall be called Joseph...it shall be after the name of his father* [so, his father shall be that, too]; *and he shall be like unto you* [that is, like unto Joseph of Egypt]; *for the thing which the Lord shall bring forth by his hand shall bring my people unto salvation. And the Lord* ***sware*** *unto Joseph that he would preserve his* [Joseph's] *seed forever, saying, I will raise up Moses, and a rod shall be in his hand, and he shall gather together my people,...he shall lead them as a flock,...he shall smite the waters of the Red Sea with his rod...He shall have judgment, and [he] shall write the word of the Lord...he shall not speak many words, for I will write unto him my law by [my] finger of mine own hand. And I will make a spokesman for him, and his name shall be called Aaron. And it shall be done unto thee in the last days also, even as I have sworn.* (JST Genesis 50:33-36; see also Genesis 12:40-42 RE; emphasis added)

So, the Lord to Joseph is swearing. It is from this text that Father Lehi lifts out what Father Lehi lifts out in order to write what he composes, in Second Nephi chapter 3, in the patriarchal blessing he gives to his son Joseph (the names, Joseph and the son named Joseph, commending to the mind of Lehi attention to this very material that we've just looked at).

And so, if the seer of the last days who was responsible for completing this assignment and fulfilling this foretold opportunity is Joseph Smith, then through Joseph Smith, we should be able to say: We can learn something about knowledge of covenants, covenants that were made with the Fathers.

And the seer will do none other work...

- He will have power to bring forth God's words;
- He will restore knowledge of their Fathers;
- He will restore knowledge of God's covenants;
- He will restore, ultimately, a basis that makes the house of Israel alive again;
- His name will be after Joseph of Egypt;
- It will be the same name as his father—that is, Joseph.

And in every particular, Joseph Smith seems to be the one about whom this is written and, therefore, doesn't seem that we need to look for another.

Chapter 4 of Second Nephi talks about... This is Nephi now, interjecting: *He* [that is, Joseph, verse 2 of chapter 4] *[He]* [Joseph of Egypt] *truly prophesied concerning all his seed* (2 Nephi 4:2; see also 2 Nephi 3:1 RE).

All his seed include not just the folks that were included in the tribe of Manasseh and through others that joined the party—Ephraim, descendants of Joseph in the Book of Mormon—but it includes as well other portions of the tribe of Joseph scattered wherever they were throughout the world, many of whom may be here among us tonight in your bloodlines.

Well, it's not a prophecy about Joseph's seed only. It's talking about the ministry of this latter-day prophet and this latter-day prophet restoring knowledge. Through Joseph, then, we should be able to find knowledge of covenants made to the Fathers and to identify who the Fathers are.

All right, so, I want to skip to the time period that is relevant to our day, in Jacob chapter 5, beginning at verse 48, because all the rest of that stuff is past history, and what we're trying to do now is to figure out from where we are how we get to the spot in which we might not be burned up, root and branch.

Beginning at verse 48: *And it came to pass that the servant said unto his master: Is it not the loftiness of [the] vineyard—have not the branches thereof overcome the roots which are good?* (Jacob 5:48; see also Jacob 3:22 RE).

That is to say, the roots, the original covenant, the original stock from which we reckon—they were good. But we've become lofty in the way in which we approach things, and as a consequence of that, we have done something that has so cumbered the construct of where we find ourselves that we've essentially destroyed the ability of the roots to do us any good.

> *And because the branches have overcome the roots thereof, behold they grew faster than the strength of the roots, taking strength unto themselves* [that is, their pride, their haughtiness; they decided that they were driving this and not the covenants that were originally made in the beginning]. *Behold, I say, is this not the cause that the trees of thy vineyard have [all] become corrupted? And it came to pass that the Lord of the vineyard said unto the servant: Let us go to and hew down the trees of the vineyard and cast them into the fire, that they shall not cumber the ground of my vineyard, for I have done all. What could I have done more for my vineyard? But, behold, the servant said unto the Lord of the vineyard: Spare it a little longer. And the Lord said: Yea, I will spare it a little longer, for it grieveth me that I should lose the trees of my vineyard.* (ibid, vs. 48-51; vs. 22-23 RE)

See, the Lord, despite the fact that He can't think of anything else that He's left undone in all of His preparations—and it is only that; it is only His preparations…

Go to Doctrine and Covenants section 19 and look at what it is that the Lord did for us in the atonement. In describing what He went through in verse 19 of section 19 of the Doctrine and Covenants, the Lord says: *Glory be to the Father,...I partook and finished **my** preparations unto the children of men* (D&C 19:19; see also JSH 17:5 RE; T&C 4:5 RE). [That's what **He** did! And He has finished that. He finished His preparations.] But 20, now, is us: *Wherefore, I command you again to repent, lest I humble you with my almighty power* (ibid, vs. 20; JSH vs. 5 RE; T&C vs. 6 RE). [That's us. He's done His part.]

What more could He do? Well, the only other thing He could do is rob us of our agency, and He's not prepared to do that because our existence then would come to an end—because without the freedom to choose, we don't have existence. Therefore, what more could He have done? But it does grieve Him that He's going to lose the trees of his vineyard.

> *Wherefore* [the Lord says], *let us take of the branches of these which I have planted in the nethermost parts of my vineyard* [that's where we find ourselves], *and let us graft them into the tree from whence they came* [that is, let's restore the covenant or, at least, make it possible for it to be so]; *and let us pluck from the tree those branches whose fruit is most bitter* [that's coming], *and graft in the natural branches of the tree in the stead thereof.*

> *And this will I do that the tree may not perish, that,* ***perhaps*** [**perhaps**, on the off-chance that... *that* without the ability to control the outcome; *that* depending upon what **you** decide to do], *[perhaps, the Lord] may preserve unto [Himself] the roots thereof for mine own purpose* [that is, some of the promises that were made back to the Fathers, that their seed would not be utterly destroyed, might be fulfilled—*perhaps*]. (Jacob 5:52-53; see also Jacob 3:23 RE; emphasis added)

How great a number is required in order for the Lord to vindicate His promise? It's not numerosity. It's never been about a big volume. It's the quality of the salvation—because if you can save but one, what you have saved is infinite and eternal. And therefore, it continues on forever.

> *Behold, the roots of the natural branches of the tree which I planted whithersoever I would are yet alive....* [Those promises remain; they are still in play. What the Father promised, what the covenants that were established did remain in play. It is **yet** possible for the Lord to vindicate everything that has been given.] *Wherefore, that I may preserve them also for mine own purpose, I will take of the branches of this tree, and I will graft them in unto them.* [This is the process by which the house of Israel is restored, not in the way that you mass-produce but in the way in which some rise up and lay hold upon that original religion that belongs to the Fathers, that came down from the beginning, that existed one time. That is to exist again.] *Yea, I will graft [into] them the branches of their mother tree, that I may preserve the roots also unto mine own self* [notice the word *mother* appears in there, too—the mother tree]...*when they [may] be sufficiently strong perhaps they may bring forth good fruit unto me, [that] I may yet have glory in the fruit of my vineyard.* (ibid, vs. 54; vs. 23 RE)

And then they go through things:

Verse 61:

> *Call servants, that we may labor diligently with our might in the vineyard, that we may prepare the way, that I may bring forth again the natural fruit....*(Jacob 5:61; Jacob 3:24 RE)

That's the whole purpose of the endeavor. And when they call servants in order to help them, the labor of the servants is confined to trying to make the vineyard finally produce fruit again.

Verse 62:

> *Let us go to and labor with our might this last time, for behold the end draweth nigh, and this is for the last time that I shall prune my vineyard* (ibid, vs. 62; vs. 25 RE).

He tells them again in verse 64:

> *The last time, for the end draweth nigh. And if it [so be] that these last grafts shall grow, and [shall] bring forth...natural fruit, then [ye shall] prepare the way for them, that they may grow* (ibid, vs. 64; vs. 25 RE).

Again in verse 71:

> *For behold, this is the last time that I shall nourish my vineyard; for the end is nigh...the season speedily cometh;...if ye labor with your might with me ye shall have joy in the fruit which I shall lay up unto myself against the time which will soon come. And it came to pass...the servants did go and labor with their mights; and the Lord of the vineyard labored also with them...* [because the Lord, in the last effort, is not going to leave the servants that He sent unattended to by **His** ministration]. (ibid, vs. 71-72; vs. 26-27 RE)

This is why, in the verses we've been reading and every location we've been at, we find the personal ministry of the Lord Jesus Christ direct, immediate, and involved. He continues to remain personally in charge of what is going to happen. But as it begins to happen, they have to sit back and watch because the question isn't: Is the laborer any less...any ...well-prepared, any less capable, any less complete? The question is: What are the branches going to do?

You can minister all you want to the tree, but the tree has to respond sometimes to what they view as offensive pruning, offensive digging, offensive conduct of cutting and moving and grafting—and saying, "What you have here is error; what you have here is a bundle of false tradition that will damn you."

You can plant the doctrine; you can restore the truth; you can have the Prophet Joseph Smith declare to you that he wants to be held to account for every word of the testimony that he delivers to you in a canonized set of scripture. But if you decide that you're going to throw that away, and you will not allow it to graft in and inform you about the nature of God and the nature of the religion that God is seeking to deliver to you, then the ministration and the pruning and the care does not result in fruit. It simply results in a rather damaged vineyard, continuing to produce precious little other than what is suitable to be gathered in bundles and burned: the *loftiness* of the people.

Grafting is to restore, to reconnect, to return or, in other words, to *plant in the hearts of the children the promises made to the fathers, and the hearts of the children shall turn to [the] fathers.* [That's what Moroni said. That's why Moroni reworked the language of Malachi in verse 39 of the Joseph Smith History.] *He shall plant in the hearts of the children the promises made to the fathers, and the hearts of the children shall turn to their fathers* (JSH 1:39; see also JSH 3:4 RE).

The work has been for one purpose. Joseph Smith began it and laid out all the information necessary for you to be able to identify who the Fathers are. And he laid out all the information necessary for you to be able to identify what the covenants were. And now the question is: Are we able, at this point, to preserve the roots (which is the Lord's purpose) by producing fruit in our day?

Well, I'm hoping, as a consequence of the things that we've looked at tonight, that you conclude that the choice seer in Second Nephi chapter 3, verse 7 and in Genesis chapter 50 was more than answered by the ministry of the Prophet Joseph Smith. And I hope that you conclude that the knowledge that was supposed to be restored through Joseph of the Fathers and the covenants given to the Fathers that will ultimately result in restoring Israel (that's referred to in Second Nephi chapter 3, verse 15) has also been something that Joseph Smith accomplished.

The foregoing excerpts are taken from:

- Denver's *40 Years in Mormonism Series*, Talk #1 titled "Be of Good Cheer" given in Boise, Idaho on September 10, 2013.
- Denver's *40 Years in Mormonism Series*, Talk #4 titled "Covenants" given in Centerville, Utah on October 6, 2013.

117. True Vine, Part 2

This is Part 2 of a special series on the "True Vine" where Denver answers the question, "Why is Christ referred to as the 'True Vine' in scripture, and what can we learn from this analogy?"

———

DENVER: The vineyard that the Lord began the restoration in was cumbered with all sorts of strange fruit.

(I mean, I've spent a lifetime referring to it as the Jacob chapter 5. In the new Book of Mormon layouts, it's one of the very few chapters that I can actually point you to from memory. It's Jacob chapter 3 in the new layout. So, I'm becoming familiar with it.)

Talking about the condition of this vineyard in its cumbered...with all sorts of strange fruit (none of it worth harvesting, none of it work keeping, none of it worth laying up and preserving against the harvest), the allegory says:

> *This is the last time that I shall nourish my vineyard, for the end is nigh at hand and the season speedily cometh. And if ye labor with your mights* ***with*** *me, ye shall have joy in the fruit with which I shall lay up unto myself against the time, which will soon come. And it came to pass that the servants did go and labor with their mights, and the Lord of the vineyard labored also with them. And they did obey the commandments of the Lord of the vineyard in all things.* (Jacob 3:26-27 RE, emphasis added)

Well, **that's** fairly critical! The Lord's gonna labor with you, but He's gonna expect you to obey His commandments in all things. Have you recently read the *Answer to the Prayer for Covenant*? Are you determined to obey the master of the vineyard and His commandments in all things? Maybe we ought to read that twice before we berate one another, belittle one another, argue with one another, dismiss one another. Otherwise, we're really not laboring with the Lord of the vineyard to help for the coming harvest. Instead, we're embracing a false spirit, and we're dividing one another, and we're trying... Our ambition—whether we're willing to acknowledge it or not—our ambition is to set this into the same sort of divisive factions as the Lord condemned to Joseph in 1820: They have *a form of godliness, but they deny the power thereof. They teach for [commandments] the [doctrines] of men* (JSH 2:5 RE). They're **all corrupt**.

> *And there began to be the natural fruit again in the vineyard. And the natural branches began to grow and thrive exceedingly, and the wild branches began to be plucked off and to be cast away* (Jacob 3:27 RE).

Some of the plucking and some of the casting away is voluntarily done by those who submit to false spirits that stir them up to anger against one another, and they depart from fellowship thinking themselves justified before God when in fact, all they're doing is being plucked and cast away.

And they did keep the root and the top thereof equal, according to the strength thereof (ibid, vs. 27). We are seeking to keep it equal. Every one of us is on the same plain. No one's getting supported by tithing money. If they are, that's done by a local fellowship that has voluntarily determined that they have one among them in need—because the tithes are gathered and used to help the poor. There's no general fund being accumulated, and there's no one who does anything that they get compensated for.

This is the only group of people whose religion requires, **incessantly**, *sacrifice.* No one gets paid. No one gets remunerated. Everything that's done is done at a price of sacrifice. If you are a person in need among a fellowship, the tithes are appropriately used because that's what they're for. They're for the poor. They're not for a leader.

You have to keep the root, and you have to keep the top equal. If you allow inequality to creep in at the beginning, the end result is lavish palaces in which some fare sumptuously, and others ask to eat the crumbs that fall from the table because they're treated so unequally. And their despair and their poverty and their need goes ignored.

Among us, it can't go ignored because the money is gathered at a fellowship level. And if there is someone in need among you, and you don't minister to their needs, you're cruel. You're…

> *And thus they labored with all diligence, according to the commandments of the Lord of the vineyard, even until the bad had been cast away...*(ibid, vs. 27).

If you can't tolerate equality; if you can't tolerate the top and the root being equal; if you can't tolerate peace among brethren, then go ahead and be *bad* and *cast* yourself *away.* If you feel moved upon to do that, well, that's the Lord of the vineyard getting rid of you.

*Even until the bad had been cast away out of the vineyard and the Lord had preserved unto himself, that the trees had become again the natural fruit. And they became like unto one body, and the **fruit** were equal* (ibid, vs. 27, emphasis added).

That word *equal* shows up so often in the labor that the Lord of the vineyard is trying to accomplish with the people that you ought to take note.

We ought to probably typeset it **EQUAL** in double-sized font.

We're not going to do that. So, you have to underline the word or circle the word or pay attention to it. The purpose is to go and become equal with one another. As soon as you set out to create rank and position and hierarchy...

Admittedly, within the parable, there is a top, and there is a root—admittedly. But the objective is to achieve equality. If you start out saying the one is greater or better than the other, you're never gonna arrive at the point that is the purpose of the parable, the purpose of the labor of the Lord of the vineyard: *and the fruit were equal.*

The Book of Mormon has had libraries of material written, and almost every single volume in the libraries of Book of Mormon material are filled with debates between polemics and apologists. All the literature basically debates the pro and the con. I spent decades studying the back-and-forth of polemicists and apologists.

One of the fellows that I admire greatly is Hugh Nibley; and Hugh Nibley was one of the very first serious-minded Mormons to take the Book of Mormon seriously. If you read what I wrote about the Book of Mormon history of scholarship in *Eighteen Verses*, you find that literally, it was Hugh Nibley that ultimately persuaded the First Presidency that the Book of Mormon should be studied and taken seriously.

There were stake presidents and bishops in the LDS tradition who never read the book at the time. And when Hugh Nibley mounted a defense of the Book of Mormon, then-President David O. McKay essentially said, "You talk about it like you think it's true," and Hugh Nibley defended it. At the end of the day, however, Hugh Nibley is an apologist. He's defending the faith.

The Book of Mormon itself, on the other hand, has this passage from Alma where he invites you to experiment upon the word. He says you ought to *plant* it. Now think for a moment what it means to plant something. Alma says:

> *But behold, if ye will awake and arouse your faculties, even to an experiment upon my words, and exercise a particle of faith, yea, even if ye can no more than* ***desire to believe****, let this desire work in you, even until ye believe in a manner that ye can give place for a* ***portion*** *of my words.* [Just think for yourself, for a moment, how you would do that.] *Now we will compare the word unto a seed. Now, if ye give place [unto that seed] that a seed may be planted in your heart, behold, if it be a true seed, or a good seed — if ye do not cast it out by your unbelief, that ye will resist the spirit of the Lord — behold, it will begin to swell within your breasts. And when you feel these swelling motions, ye will begin to say within [yourself], It must needs be that this is a good seed, or that the word is good,* ***for it beginneth to enlarge my soul****; yea, it beginneth to* ***enlighten my understanding****; yea,...it beginneth to* ***be delicious [unto] me****. Now behold, would not this increase your faith? I say unto you, yea.* (Alma 16:27-28 RE, emphasis added)

And he goes on to describe what happens after that, and how it converts into knowledge once you've gained experience with the process.

> *For ye know that the word hath swelled your souls,...ye also know that it hath sprouted up, that your* ***understanding doth begin to be enlightened*** *and your* ***mind...begin to expand****. O then, is [this not] real? I say unto you, yea, because* ***it is light****; and whatsoever is light is good, because it is discernible; therefore, ye must know that it is good. And now behold, after ye have tasted this light, is your knowledge perfect? Behold, I say unto you, nay; neither must ye lay aside your faith, for ye have only exercised your faith to plant the seed, that ye might try the experiment to know if the seed was good. And behold, as the tree beginneth to grow, ye will say, Let us nourish it with great care, that it may get root, that it may grow up and bring forth fruit unto us. And now behold,* ***if ye nourish it with [great] care****, it will get root, and grow up, and bring forth fruit. But if ye neglect the tree and take no thought for its nourishment, behold, it will not get any root; and when the heat of the sun cometh and scorcheth it, because it hath no root, it withers away, and ye pluck it up and cast it out. Now this is not because the seed was not good, neither is it because the fruit thereof would not be desirable, but it is because* ***your*** *ground is barren and* ***ye*** *will not nourish the tree; therefore, ye cannot have the fruit thereof. And thus it is: [And] if ye will not nourish the word, looking forward with an eye of faith to the fruit thereof, ye can never pluck of the fruit of the tree of life. But if ye will nourish the word, yea, nourish the tree as it beginneth to grow, by your faith,* ***with great diligence, and with***

> ***patience****, looking forward to the fruit thereof, it shall take root; and behold, it shall be a tree springing up unto everlasting life. And because of your* ***diligence, and your faith, and your patience*** *with the word, in nourishing it that it may take root [ye shall] by and by...pluck the fruit thereof, which is most precious, which is sweet above all that is sweet,...which is white above all that is white, yea,...pure above all that is pure...* (ibid, vs. 29-30, emphasis added)

...and then you thirst not, and you hunger not. Diligence, patience. Diligence, faith, patience.

We want a faith that will respond like Google. We don't want God to prepare a banquet. We want fast food and a short-order cook and someone that will slap something on our plate fast, fast, fast. And the Book of Mormon is saying, "Slow down. Diligence isn't quick. Patience isn't fast."

Planting the seed... It's like the kids in elementary school that plant the pumpkin seed in the styrofoam cup, and every day they go over and look at the styrofoam cup, and nothing seems to be happening. And before long, a third of the class has killed the seed because they've dug it up to see what's going on.

Patience. Patience and diligence—three times. Diligence and patience. Diligence and patience.

I have had spiritual breakthroughs that are so profound and so sacred that when I described them one time, I did so with only nine words. But I can tell you why it happened.

I taught the Book of Mormon in a Gospel Doctrine class for four different years on cycles while I was a Gospel Doctrine teacher—each time pushing the Book of Mormon deeper and deeper, always (for the first couple of decades) being a little reticent, being a little skeptical. I mean, I accepted the arguments of the apologists. I knew, I understood, and I had studied the arguments of the polemicists.

But Alma was asking that I do something different. Alma was saying, "Hey, why don't you just experiment with this thing and plant it **as if** you believed it. Plant it **as if** you had faith in it. So, forget about the pros and cons, accept the Book of Mormon at face value, and let the Book of Mormon define itself. Let the Book of Mormon be the source from which you evaluate whether or not it enlightens you, whether or not it appeals to your heart, to your soul, and to your mind."

And so, I experimented on the word, and I took the Book of Mormon as if it were actually a revelation from God, translated by the gift and power of God and delivered to me through no human instrumentality. Joseph Smith may have dictated it, and Oliver Cowdery may have penned most of it, but it was translated by the gift and power of God. Therefore, the book was translated into English by the Lord.

And so, I took the Book of Mormon seriously. I entertained no doubts. I employed no apologetics. I just accepted the book and tried to understand it. As I did so, going through the text of the Book of Mormon, there were moments when there were glints where something leapt off the page to me as if someone had flashed the reflection of the sun off a windshield passing down the street, and it aligns with the right angle of the sun. The text itself seemed to spark to me.

As I took it seriously, I could breathe the spirit of the writers. I beheld more as I went through that text than the text will yield to the cautious and wary reader. The Book of Mormon—like the spirits I referred to earlier—the Book of Mormon also has a spirit, and that Spirit is Christ. If you want to relate to the Spirit of Christ and not a false spirit, drop all your apprehensions, lower your guard, and see if the Book of Mormon does not yield the Spirit of Christ. It was a better text than any other I had encountered in conveying the Spirit of Christ. It is, in fact, the most correct book, and a man can get closer to God by abiding its precepts than any other book.

Jacob (Nephi's brother) delivered a sermon that Nephi records in his second book. In his second book, after Jacob had read from Isaiah to teach his brethren that were interested in learning about things, he then elaborates or explains the prophecy given by Isaiah:

And now my beloved brethren, I have read these things that ye might know concerning the covenants of the Lord, that he has covenanted with ***all*** *the house of Israel* (2 Nephi 6:1 RE, emphasis added).

That's important because *all the house of Israel* is greater than those that they left behind at Jerusalem. All the house of Israel is greater even than the Nephites plus those left at Jerusalem. The ten tribes had left the northern kingdom. They had migrated away years before Lehi left Jerusalem. Therefore, all the house of Israel (which includes those scattered on the isles of the sea as the Nephites were) were remembered, and Jacob wants his brethren to understand that God's plan is all-inclusive, wherever they are, in whatever scattered condition. Even if they've altogether lost their identity as members of the house of Israel, yet they are remembered in the covenants of the Lord.

> *[He's] spoken unto the Jews by the mouth of his holy [prophet], even from the beginning, down from generation to generation, until the time cometh that they shall be restored to the true church and fold of God, when they shall be gathered home [into] the lands of their inheritance* [lands, plural, not singular] *and shall be established in* ***all their lands*** *of promise.* (ibid, vs. 1 RE, emphasis added)

What Jacob is teaching to his brethren is that there are those who have received (who belong to the house of Israel) covenants that have handed to them—by covenant—**lands**, plural. This land has people upon it today who have entered into a covenant with the Lord today, that has made this land a place of their inheritance. The descendants of the Lamanites likewise descend from Fathers with whom a covenant was made that **they** inherit this land. The Jews in Israel have a promise given them. That land is theirs by divine decree —God gave it to them; it is their land. And there are **other** broken branches from the house of Israel living on lands (their descendants today) that they possess by right.

Jacob continued his sermon over a second day. And in the sermon the second day, this is the second part of Jacob's teaching concerning the covenants:

> *Wherefore, for this cause, that my covenants may be fulfilled which I have made unto the children of men, that I will do unto them while they are* ***in the flesh****, I must needs destroy the secret works of darkness, and of murders, and of abominations. Wherefore, he that fighteth against Zion, both Jew and Gentile, both bond and free, both male and female,* ***shall perish****; for they are they who are the whore of all the earth. For they who are not for me are against me, saith our God. For I will fulfill my promises which I have made unto the children of men that I will do unto them* ***while they are in the flesh****.* (2 Nephi 7:3 RE, emphasis added)

This isn't some dreamy, distant, other-worldly event. He says He is going to establish, in the flesh, a people that will become Zion; and He will defend those people who are His Zion.

As Nephi closes his record, he explains plainly what he wants us, the Gentiles, to understand from his record:

> *Woe...unto him that shall say, We have received the word of God, and we need no more of the word of God, for we have enough....Unto him that*

> *receiveth I will give more; and from them [which] say, We have enough — shall be taken away even that which they have....I will be merciful unto them, saith the Lord God, if they will repent and come unto me....There shall be many at that day when I shall proceed to do a marvelous work among them, that I...remember my covenants which I have made unto the children of men, that I may...remember the promises which I have made unto thee, Nephi, and also unto thy father, that...shall say, A bible, a bible, [we've] got a bible,...there cannot be any more bible. But thus saith the Lord...O fools, [that] shall have a bible....O ye gentiles, have ye remembered the Jews, mine ancient covenant people? Nay, but [you've] cursed them, [you've] hated them, and have not sought to recover them....Thou fool that shall say, A bible, [we've] got a bible and we need no more bible. Have ye obtained a bible, save it were by the Jews? Know ye not that there are more nations than one?....I, the Lord your God, have created all men, and...I remember those [that] are upon the isles of the sea? ...I rule in the heavens above and [I rule] in the earth beneath....Wherefore murmur ye because...ye shall receive more of my word?* (2 Nephi 12:6-9 RE)

That was the very objective that Abraham sought—to get more of God's word. He **wanted** to know more; he **wanted** to receive commandments; he **wanted** to receive instructions.

> *Because that I have spoken one word, ye need not suppose that I cannot speak another....The Jews shall have the words of the Nephites, and the Nephites shall have the words of the Jews, and the Nephites and the Jews shall have the words of the lost tribes of Israel, and the lost tribes of Israel shall have the words of the Nephites and the Jews.... My people which are of the house of Israel shall be gathered home [into] the* ***lands*** *of their [possession], and my word also shall be gathered in one....I am God, and...I covenanted with Abraham that I would remember his seed for ever.* (ibid, vs. 10 RE, emphasis added)

That includes those portions of the family of Abraham that migrated out of the view of the scriptures we presently possess so that when they drop out of the Biblical narrative, or they drop out of the Book of Mormon narrative, God was still with them. He was still doing with them; He was still leading them and teaching them; and ultimately, He visited them. All of them kept records. Those are all to be restored.

> *Ye need not suppose that the gentiles are utterly destroyed. For behold, I say unto you, as many of the gentiles as will repent* ***are*** *the covenant people of the Lord....For the Lord covenanteth with none save it be with them that repent*

and believe in his Son, who is the Holy One of Israel. (ibid, vs. 11 RE, emphasis added)

Therefore, the covenant people of the Lord (according to the Book of Mormon) who will inherit the promises of Abraham necessarily include those gentiles who are willing to covenant with Him to allow Him to labor through them to restore things that will bring the remainder of the house of Israel back to the knowledge of their God.

Mormon interrupts his narrative summary of events by an observation he makes about the work of the Lord (inserted into his account just prior to the final round of apostasy, violence, and the great tempest that destroyed the wicked—and then, Christ's visit to the other sheep that are covered in the Book of Mormon). This is Mormon's insertion into the record:

> *Surely shall he again bring a remnant of the seed of Joseph to the knowledge of the Lord their God. And as surely as the Lord liveth [he will] gather in from the four quarters of the earth all the remnant of the seed of Jacob....He hath covenanted with all the house of Jacob, even so shall the covenant wherewith he hath covenanted with the house of Jacob be fulfilled, in his own due time, unto the restoring all the house of Jacob unto the knowledge of the covenant [which] he hath covenanted with them....Then shall they know their Redeemer, who is Jesus Christ, the Son of God.* (3 Nephi 2:18 RE)

In Christ's teachings to the Nephites **after** He had been resurrected, appeared to them, had them come and be in contact and witness of His death and resurrection, He delivered to them the Sermon on the Mount in a slightly different form, the Sermon at Bountiful. And after He had taught that sermon, He commanded that they write down and preserve these teachings that He's going to give.

Someone wrote in the margin of my book; it looks like my handwriting. So, I wanted to read that: *The remnant of their seed, who [should] be scattered forth upon the face of the earth because of their unbelief, may be brought in...* (3 Nephi 7:4 RE).

Okay, He's now talking to the Nephite believers about the descendants of the Nephite believers, and He's telling them, "You have to write this down." And He tells them what they're to write down is that eventually their descendants are gonna be scattered upon the face of the earth because of their **unbelief**, but those descendants may be brought in. The note I wrote in the margin is that even the Lamanite remnant, who are the target of the covenant, **have to**

be reclaimed, have to be brought in, have to know of their inheritance in order to take advantage of it. If they're not brought in, then they still suffer under the plague of unbelief.

> *Because...their unbelief, may be brought in, or may be brought to a knowledge of me....I [will] gather them in....I [will] fulfill the covenant which the Father hath made unto all the people of the house of Israel....In the latter day shall the truth come unto the gentiles, that the fullness of these things shall be made known unto them.* (ibid, vs. 4)

In other words, He's promising to the Nephites their descendants are going to fall away, but He promises their descendants will be gathered back in. In order to bring the descendants back in, He's promising them that the Gentiles shall receive **this knowledge**.

> *The truth [shall] come unto the...[knowledge] that the fullness of these things shall be made known unto them....I will remember my covenant unto you, O house of Israel, and ye shall come unto the knowledge of the fullness of my gospel. But if the gentiles will repent and return unto me, saith the Father, behold, they shall be numbered among my people, O house of Israel.* (3 Nephi 7:4-5 RE)

When the Gentiles repent, and they return, then they're numbered back—just like the descendants of the Nephites when they are awakened and repent and are taught the truth and return unto God. All become one house, one fold, one people.

Then, after Christ had introduced the sacrament and had commanded that Isaiah's words be searched because they tell of fulfilling of God's covenant, Christ then teaches:

> *This people will I establish in this land unto the fulfilling of the covenant which I made with your father Jacob, and it shall be a New Jerusalem. And the Powers of Heaven shall be in the midst of this people, yea, even I will be in the midst of you.* (3 Nephi 9:8 RE)

Christ is reiterating to this group, in this setting, promises directly to them that He had previously given to Enoch about what would happen in the last days. When He told Enoch about it, He said that there would come a point at which righteousness and truth would spring forth; it would be upon the earth; there would be a tabernacle or a temple there; and that He, along with Enoch's people, would return and fall upon and kiss the necks of those who gather there. This is the same prophecy that was given to Enoch, one of those first Fathers in that first direct descent. This is a covenant that Christ is reiterating, but it goes back to the first Fathers. Indeed, if we had a full restoration of all that had been given, we would know that the gospel in its fullness was understood far better by the first generations, or the original Fathers, than it is understood by us today. He says to the people gathered there (this is Christ, same talk):

> *Ye are of the covenant which the Father made with your fathers, saying unto Abraham, And in thy seed shall all the kindreds of the earth be blessed, the Father having raised me up unto you first, and sent me to bless you in turning away every one of you from his iniquities — and this because ye are the children of the covenant. And after...ye were blessed, then fulfilleth the Father the covenant which he made with Abraham, saying, In thy seed shall all the kindreds of the earth be blessed, unto the pouring out of the holy ghost through me upon the gentiles.* (ibid, vs. 8)

In genealogical research, what you find is that if you start with yourself, and you go backwards generations for about 500 years, your genealogy chart expands and expands and expands. And at about the 500-year-mark, it begins to contract and contract and contract so that the genetic spread of the blood of Abraham throughout the world is so far and so wide that you practically can't find people anywhere on the earth that don't have some of the blood of Abraham, to whom He said,...*all the kindreds of the earth will be blessed [in thy seed]* (3 Nephi 9:8).

> *If they shall harden their hearts against me, I will return their iniquities upon their own heads, saith the Father. And I will remember the covenant which I have made with my people, and I have covenanted with them that I would gather them together in mine own due time, that I would give unto them again the land of their fathers for their inheritance.* (ibid, vs. 8)

So, it should begin to emerge into your view that physical descendancy is one thing to open up an opportunity—but covenanting, remembering, repenting, returning, accepting what God has to offer is the component in the last days that distinguishes whether or not they are **redeemed**, whether or not they are to be **gathered**, whether or not they are to be **recognized** in the own due time of the Lord as **His**, to be protected and to be preserved against the harvest. It's not enough merely to have genealogical connection back to some remnant of Father Abraham.

I can trace my genealogy back to Jewish ancestry, to Native American ancestry. That doesn't mean a thing if I don't repent and return. I remain on the outside; I remain a Gentile; I remain a disbeliever, unworthy to be gathered. I suspect everyone in this room has a direct genealogical connection, probably not only to Abraham but also Joseph—and perhaps eleven out of the twelve tribes of Israel. It's just the way that descendancy works.

Christ continues:

> *Then shall this covenant which the Father hath covenanted with his people be fulfilled;...then shall Jerusalem be inhabited again with my people, and it shall be the land of their inheritance. When these things which I declare unto you — and which I shall declare unto you hereafter of myself and by the power of the holy ghost...shall be made known unto the gentiles, that they may know concerning this people who are a remnant of the house of Jacob...it shall be a sign unto them that they may know that the work of the Father hath already commenced unto the fulfilling of the covenant which he hath made unto the people who are of the house of Israel...the gentiles, if they will not harden their hearts, that they may repent, and come unto me, and be baptized in my name, and know of the true points of my doctrine, that* ***they may be numbered among my people, O house of Israel*** [means that it was always the design that the Gentiles should also be gathered in, or that what is (in all likelihood) an unsavory, bitter-fruit-producing branch of the original tree should be taken and gathered back to the original root and gather nourishment from that original root that they may come in and be numbered among the house of Israel. It's always been the intention of the Lord to restore the Gentiles and to make them the means through which the last days' work would become accomplished]. (3 Nephi 9:10-11 RE, emphasis added)

As Mormon completed the record of Christ's visit to the Nephites, he provided this description of the Book of Mormon's purpose:

> *When the Lord shall see fit in his wisdom that these sayings shall come unto the gentiles according to his word, then ye may know that the covenant which the Father hath made with the children of Israel concerning their restoration to the* ***lands*** *of their inheritance is already beginning to be fulfilled. And ye may know that the words of the Lord which have been spoken by the holy prophets* ***shall all be fulfilled****.... The Lord will remember his covenant which he hath made unto his people of the house of Israel.* (3 Nephi 13:7 RE, emphasis added)

And as Moroni concluded the record, he inserted some final words of instruction for the people who would receive the Book of Mormon in the last days. These words were taught to him by his father. He says:

> *Hath miracles ceased?...I say unto you, nay; neither have angels ceased to minister unto the children of men. For...they are subject unto him, to minister according to the word of his command, shewing themselves unto them of strong faith and a firm mind in every form of godliness. And the office of their ministry is to call men unto repentance, and to fulfill and to do the work of the* ***covenants*** *of the Father which he hath made unto the children of men, ...declaring the word of Christ unto the chosen vessels of the Lord, that they may bear testimony of him; and by so doing, the Lord God prepareth the way that the residue of men may have faith in Christ, that the holy ghost may have place in their hearts, according to the power thereof; and this after this manner bringeth to pass the Father the* ***covenants*** *which he hath made unto the children of men.* (Moroni 7:6 RE, emphasis added)

There are numerous other passages in the Book of Mormon that speak to the same thing. The Book of Mormon is a forerunner—a harbinger—that was intended to say to the people who receive it: There are covenants that go back to the very beginning, to the original Fathers. Those covenants got renewed, they got restored, they got continued in the form of Abraham (who received all that had been there originally) coming out of apostasy and being adopted back into that line of Patriarchs. That original covenant material provoked the creation of the Book of Mormon, and it is one of the major testimonies that is given to us by the Book of Mormon about the work that God intends to do in the last days. You can believe in the Bible; you can accept Jesus as your Savior; you can be (in the words of the Evangelical community) *born again*. You can be (in the words of Latter-day Saints) someone whose *calling and election is made sure*. But the work of God at this point is not about merely individual salvation. **It is the work of fulfilling the covenants that were made with the Fathers. It is the work of restoring again that original gospel of which the law given to Moses pointed forward to but did not comprehend.**

We tend to view priesthood in institutional ways. And it's hard to be terribly critical of misunderstandings because, quite frankly, priestly authority following the success of the Petrine branch of original Christianity and its triumph with emphasis on authority and priesthood and keys, predisposed the entire Christian world. Even the Christian world after the Protestant Reformation succeeded in finally breaking off areas in which a different form of *protest Christianity* could be practiced that was not subservient to *the*

Roman See and papal decree, they still had this misapprehension about priesthood.

So, when Joseph Smith began to talk about priesthood and to begin the process of restoring it, he gave a new kind of vocabulary, but possession of a vocabulary does not mean possession of the thing.

When Abraham talks about becoming a rightful heir and becoming a high priest, it would be best if you threw out everything that you have heard or learned or understood about the concept of priesthood. Priesthood includes the prerogative, the right, the obligation, or the duty to go out and perform ordinances that are effective that God will recognize, to be sure, and that's part of it; and it's a true principle.

However, priesthood in the original sense was something far more vast. It included an understanding of things that relate back all the way to the beginning, or before the world was, and goes forward through all periods of time until the end. It includes a basis of knowledge. So, when you read Abraham's description of what it was he looked for, and he mentions priesthood, you have to merge that into the entirety of what he's talking about: knowledge, understanding, commandments, instructions, having the capacity to see things in their correctly-ordered fashion (similarly to how God originally intended that it be ordered) so that you are no longer out of sync with this creation and doing your best to *reign with blood and horror* by subduing nature with the iron plow and gunpowder and lead. But instead, you find yourself situated in a place that Eden itself can be renewed, and harmony can be achieved between man and the earth.

The Book of Mormon is talking about something vast, but it continually points back to Abraham. And I do not care what arguments can be made or what a pitiful effort has been put together to defend the book of Abraham that Joseph Smith provided us. It was essential to the Restoration that the book of Abraham be given to us because without it, we would not understand a great deal about the Restoration and what the final objective of the Restoration was to achieve.

If you're going to please God, you don't please Him by having your *born again* experience or having your *calling and election made sure* experience if the result of that is to make you proud, conceited, self-assured, and arrogant, and to disconnect you from the Restoration process that was begun through Joseph Smith and has **yet** a greater work to be done than was achieved at the time of Joseph Smith. Go off and be saved, but you will not fulfill the work of the covenants that God intends to achieve. He has committed Himself to that end.

Those who will labor alongside Him, whether they be Gentile or Lamanite or Jew, it does not matter. If they will repent and accept the process of the Restoration as it began through Joseph Smith (not only to **say** it correctly but to **do** what it tells us needs to be done), then you will be numbered among those people that God has covenanted to gather against the coming harvest.

But if you want to be the lone guru whose commentaries fill pages of blogging and hours of pontification, but you're going to labor at odds... I read you the warning: All that fight against Zion are going to perish. So, you can shout your hallelujahs in the spirit world, and you can proclaim your calling and election guarantees you something—but quite frankly, practically everyone's calling and election can be made sure. You get to continue progress; you get to continue to repent. God's not gonna terminate you at the end of this cycle of creation, but you're gonna be allowed to go on and upward if you'll continue to repent.

You will always be free to choose, but the work of the covenants that the Book of Mormon foretell are to be accomplished through the reclaiming by repentance and returning to Him of Gentiles that will ultimately reach out to and include restoring the Lamanites/restoring the Jews to a knowledge of the works of the Father. **That—that** is what is on the mind of God today. **That** is the purpose of the covenant that was given unto us in Boise just a few years ago—two years ago. **That** is what fulfilling the covenant ultimately requires that we labor to achieve.

That effort began in earnest with the reclaiming of the scriptures and the presenting of those to the Lord for His acceptance and the marvelous news that God accepted them as adequate for His purpose for us and the commitment that He would labor with us to go forward.

Anyone can join the party. Anyone can come into this work. Anyone can remain a Catholic or a Presbyterian, a Catholic or a Latter-day Saint. It doesn't matter. Those things are more like civic clubs. I don't care if you're a Rotarian or a Kiwanis Club member—means about the same thing as belonging to any of those organizations. Associate with whoever you like to associate with.

But you **must** accept baptism. You **must** accept the Book of Mormon. It **is** a covenant. The covenant must be accepted, and you **must** help labor alongside those who seek to return Zion.

The foregoing excerpts are taken from:

- Denver's lecture titled "Signs Follow Faith" given in Centerville, Utah on March 3, 2019.
- Denver's conference talk titled "The Book of Mormon Holds the Covenant Pattern for the Full Restoration" given in Boise, Idaho on September 22, 2019.

118. True Vine, Part 3

This is Part 3 of a special series on the "True Vine" where Denver answers the question, "Why is Christ referred to as the 'True Vine' in scripture, and what can we learn from this analogy?"

DENVER: We're enacting ancient events. We're part of a process that began a long time ago and is going on still. You read (what is it, Genesis chapter 49?) the patriarchal blessings of the various Patriarchs. You look at the lives of those men in the flesh. We're just reenacting them on a grander scale and with more of us, to be sure, but the patterns are there.

The records of the prophets are not just history. As the Book of Mormon demonstrates very ably, it's not history. It's highly edited, very limited, highly selected—at one point, they estimate less than one percent of their history even gets alluded to—material that has been selected on account of prophetic foreknowledge of our circumstance. And so, it constitutes not merely a history but a prophetic pattern in which they try to get us to see the process that we ought to be reenacting in our lives to do the things that they did that brought them to know the Lord.

Nephi couldn't have been more plain if he had said, "Here's my guidebook; here's my rule book; here's my pattern-recognition sequence. You go and do likewise." He's trying to get us to get our hands around, as Joseph Smith put it, the fullness of the gospel of Jesus Christ. And the fullness of the gospel of Jesus Christ involves the path to and through the veil into the presence of God, becoming joint heir, becoming a Son of God. *Teachings of the Prophet Joseph Smith*, page 375— He refers to, and I don't have a copy of it with me, but I think I can quote it: "Sons of God who exalt themselves to be God even before they were born, and all can cry Abba, Father." Joseph wanted us to take the religion that he restored to the earth rather seriously and to search into and contemplate both the heavens and the darkest abyss.

In an— I don't want to use the word *evangelical*; I'll use the *evangelistic*... In a proselytizing church, in a church in which, at any given moment, the largest segment of the adult population are *novices* (introductory novices to a faith), you should never expect the church to forfeit the interests of the novices (who rightly need to be fed and nurtured) for the interests of those who are maybe a little more mature and have a little more robust comprehension of what the Savior was trying to teach us all.

And it's probably rightly so that the Church makes no effort to really address that, and rightly so that you're left to your own. We have the scriptures. I mean, when the rich man said to Abraham in Christ's parable, "Well, send Lazarus back so he can warn my brothers," Abraham's response in Christ's parable was: "They have Moses, and they have the prophets, and if they won't believe them, they won't believe Lazarus even *though one...rise from the dead* (See Luke 9:20 RE), which is a very interesting foreshadowing of how people would treat the Lord."

Here's the problem: People do not believe Him even though He rose from the dead—period. Today. Us. You and I—do not believe Him even though He rose from the dead. It was not intended to be a one-off event that occurred in the meridian of time. It was intended to be a gathering. I mean, the little seed grows up into the great mustard plant into which the birds, or as Joseph put it, the angels, were intended to come and watch. It was intended to be a super structure for housing contact between the divine and the mortal. It was intended to be the moment of intersection between all that is in eternity and the life of the mortal. It was intended to be the journey into the Holy of Holies, into the presence of God.

In the ordinances as they have been restored in the temple today, everyone who enters in is expected to come to the veil possessing certain knowledge, capable of identifying themselves as having been true and faithful, and be received in an embrace and then welcomed into the presence of God. It's a normal and expected part of the ordinances as they have been restored.

Those ordinances are supposed to be teaching us something. They are the Lord's way of shouting in a multimedia presentation, "Here is how I did what I did, and what I would like you to do in the process of you becoming like me, a Son of God, a Daughter of God, a member of the household of faith, and part of the church and kingdom of the Firstborn." You have to become the Firstborn. You have to become one with Him. You have to become part of that, not in an organized group-think kind of way—in an individual way in which you connect up with holiness, in which you become a vessel of holiness. You are someone to whom sacred things have been entrusted, and you become, in turn, sacred as the bearer of them.

The Law of Moses prescribed the death penalty for a variety of offenses. One of the ways to avoid the execution of the penalty was to go to one of the *safe harbor* cities. Another way was to go and to come in contact with the altar because if you came in contact with the altar, it was considered most holy. Things that are most holy communicate holiness. You can't profane them. If you come in contact with them, and you are unholy, you don't make it unholy. It makes you holy because it is most sacred.

Part of the rites in the temple are intended to communicate to you things that are most holy. They are intended to make you holy. They are intended to make you a suitable recipient for an audience. They are intended to make you a suitable companion for a walk down a dusty road with the risen Lord who is trying to get you to notice exactly who it is that speaks to you. It's intended to have you understand that He lives and that He's willing to associate with you and that it's not, as Joseph Smith put it, relying on the words of an old book (the people who lived once long ago) that's going to save anyone. It's the dialogue that you engage in with Him now. It's the living, breathing, vital— He uses the figure of the living vine, and you have to connect to the living vine. And He's the vine, and you connect to it, and you get life through that. Words could not be more plain.

He's trying to get— I mean, what does it mean to be connected up with the vine and to derive sustenance from it? Well, you have to be alive, which is not inert or an object that you move from there to there. If it's alive, it's going to grow; it's going to increase; it's going to improve; it's gonna have connection with; it's gonna have...

And Christ was extraordinary in His selection of the things that He wanted to use to communicate to us what He intended the gospel to be. And we read them and say, "*That's cool. I'll pay my tithing. I'm connected. I got a card, and I'm connected.*" Well, it's intended to be more than that. And the way that it becomes more than that is an individual journey in which you receive from Him and become a part of Him. And He does His best to try and use analogies and parables and stories to make it clear to us. And the history of the events that are recorded in scripture are intended to try and make it clear to us. But at the end of the day, it's up to you to have the *aha!* moment and realize He really is talking to and inviting you, **you**, individually—whoever you are, wherever you're at, whatever your confusion, whatever your doubts, whatever your uncertainties. He wants to talk to *you* about them.

I do not like the Gentile reaction to the word or understanding of *not lawful* or the term *forbidden*. I think those words convey an idea that today can be easily misunderstood. I think I would prefer those words to be understood that it's not wise to tell Gentiles because they will abuse it when they learn it; and it's because of that potential for abuse why man is not capable of making it known. But it is only to be understood by the Spirit because when it comes to a person by the power of the Spirit, it comes to them in a way that helps them understand who our Lord is and what He's about.

Likewise, the word *dominion* in the understanding of the Gentile can convey the impression of a prison warden who is exercising control over captives. I think the word *dominion* should be understood, instead, to convey the idea of a gardener who's responsible for making the garden **thrive** and **grow** and **bear fruit**.

To be clear, the three greatest examples of wielding dominion in the correct manner that we should understand it are: first, Christ who is probably without any peer, unquestionably the greatest example of one holding the greatest dominion, and who, also, likewise showed the greatest example of how to wield dominion. He beseeched people to believe. He pled with them for their own good. He knelt to serve them. He denied that He had a kingdom of this world; He tried to prepare people for a better one. But He was more intelligent than they all, and He was the greatest of them all, unquestionably holding the greatest dominion, and He wore it as a light thing. His yoke was easy.

Adam likewise (after Christ in this world) held the greatest dominion. But Adam taught and pled and instructed but did not abridge the agency of his children, even when one of his sons killed another of his sons. Adam did not execute Cain. Cain was sent away. Adam held dominion, but he exercised that like our Lord, pleading for the best interest of others, inviting and enticing them, hoping for their best interests.

And then, there's Moses, who is called in scripture, the meekest of all men (see Numbers 7:22 RE), and Gentiles depict him as a bully and a strongman. And yet, Moses saw no reason to be jealous when others were out prophesying—would that all men would do that (see Numbers 7:19 RE). Moses, like Adam, like Christ, is an example of how the word *dominion* should be understood: all three gardeners—responsible for trying to make their garden thrive, grow, and bear fruit. In reality, those who have held the greatest dominion given by God have all lived lives of meekness and service. They were the opposite of what Gentiles regard as a strongman, the opposite.

Think about what it would take to transplant various populations from various locations (not in haste) with everything having been prepared in advance. And in our currently fragmented society, unless you're willing to experiment with your own effort to live the law of tithing by organizing yourselves and governing yourself... Miscellaneous groups will never make it, but people of God will.

Doctrine and Covenants section 65, verse 5:

> *Call upon the Lord, that his kingdom may go forth upon the earth, that the inhabitants thereof may receive it, and be prepared for the days to come, in the which the Son of Man shall come down in heaven, clothed in the brightness of his glory, to meet the kingdom of God which is set up on the earth. Wherefore, may the kingdom of God go forth, that the kingdom of heaven may come, that thou, O God, mayest be glorified in heaven so on earth, that thine enemies may be subdued; for thine is the honor, power and glory, forever and ever. Amen.* (D&C 65:5-6; see also T&C 53:2-3 RE)

If you read that, and you know that the Lord is going to come to that, you realize that He cannot come unless it exists. If it doesn't exist, He cannot come to it. If He cannot come to it, then He delays the day of His coming. And generation after generation may come and go, never having accomplished what the Lord invites us to **do**, what the Lord invites us to **be**.

Moses chapter 7: This is the Lord speaking to Enoch in a vision recorded subsequently by Moses by revelation. But it is a restoration of the book of Enoch, and the conversation and the speaker is the Lord. Beginning in Moses chapter 7, verse 60:

> *And the Lord said unto Enoch: As I live, even so will I come in the last days, in the days of wickedness and vengeance, to fulfil the oath which I have made unto you concerning the children of Noah.* [This is the Lord's oath to Enoch. He's going to come. He's going to come in the last days.] *And the day shall come that the earth shall rest, but before that day the heavens shall be darkened, and [the] veil of darkness shall cover the earth; and the heavens shall shake, and also the earth; and great tribulations shall be [had] among the children of men, but my people will I preserve; And righteousness will I send down out of heaven; and truth will I send forth out of the earth, to bear testimony of mine Only Begotten; his resurrection from the dead; yea, and also the resurrection of all men; and righteousness and truth will I cause to sweep the earth as with a flood* [a thing that is possible now by you sitting at a keyboard anywhere in the world; you can cause the truth to flood the earth], *to gather out mine elect from the four quarters of the earth, unto a place which I shall prepare, an Holy City, that my people may gird up their loins, and be looking forth for the time of my coming; for there shall be my tabernacle* [In this context, the tabernacle to be built is His house], *and it shall be called Zion, a New Jerusalem. And the Lord said unto Enoch: Then*

> *shalt thou and all thy city meet them there, and we will receive them into our bosom, and they shall see us; and we will fall upon their necks, and they shall fall upon our necks, and we will kiss each other* [this is the second return of Enoch, as well—first, His house, then, Enoch]; *And there shall be mine abode, and it shall be Zion, which shall come forth out of all the creations which I have made; and for the space of a thousand years the earth shall rest. And it came to pass that Enoch saw the day of the coming of the Son of Man, in the last days, to dwell on the earth in righteousness for the space of a thousand years.* (Moses 7:60-65; see also Genesis 4:22-23 RE)

Zion exists before these things can happen. If Zion does not exist, these things will be delayed. They will not be prevented because the Lord has, by a covenant, insured that they will happen. But the fact that the Lord has, by a covenant, insured that it will happen, is no guarantee that **we** will see it. Because **we** will only see it if **we** undertake to abide the conditions by which He can accomplish His work.

This is a Joseph Smith Translation of Genesis chapter 9:

> *And the bow shall be in the cloud; and I will look upon it, that I may remember the everlasting covenant, which I made unto thy father Enoch; [yea] that, when men should keep all my commandments, Zion should again come on the earth, the city of Enoch which I have caught up unto myself. And this is mine everlasting covenant, that when thy posterity shall embrace the truth, and look upward, then shall Zion look downward, and all the heavens shall shake with gladness, and the earth shall tremble with joy; And the general assembly of the church of the firstborn shall come down out of heaven, and possess the earth, and shall have place until the end come. And this is mine everlasting covenant, which I made with thy father Enoch* [the covenant that God made again with Noah; the covenant that He made originally with Adam; the covenant which **some** generation will rise up to receive. Whether that's you or whether you go to the grave without realizing it or not is entirely up to you]. (JST Genesis 9:21-23; see also Genesis 5:22 RE; emphasis added)

Now, I need to read you something. This is Ezekiel, beginning in chapter 33 at verse 25:

> *Wherefore say unto them, Thus saith the Lord GOD; Ye eat with the blood, and [ye] lift up your eyes toward your idols, and shed blood: and shall ye possess the land? Ye stand upon your sword, ye work abomination, and ye defile every one his neighbour's wife: and shall ye possess the land?*

Say thou thus unto them, Thus saith the Lord GOD; As I live, surely they that are in the wastes shall fall by the sword, and him that is in the open field will I give to the beasts to be devoured, and they that be in the forts and in the caves shall die of the pestilence. For I will lay the land most desolate, and the pomp of her strength shall cease; and the [mountain] of Israel shall be desolate, that none shall pass through. Then shall they know that I am the LORD, when I have laid the land most desolate because of all their abominations which they have committed.

Also, thou son of man, the children of thy people still are talking against thee by the walls and in the doors of the houses, and [speaking] one to another, every one to his brother, saying, Come, I pray you, and hear what is the word that cometh forth from the LORD. And they come unto thee as the people cometh, and they sit before thee as my people, and they hear thy words, but they will not do them: for with their mouth they shew much love, but their heart goeth after their covetousness. And, lo, thou art unto them as a very lovely song of one that hath a pleasant voice, and can play well on an instrument: for they hear thy words, but they do them not. And when this cometh to pass, (lo, it will come,) then shall they know that a prophet hath been among them.

AND the word of the LORD came unto me, saying, Son of man, prophesy against the shepherds of Israel, prophesy, ...say unto them, Thus saith the Lord GOD unto the shepherds; Woe be [unto] the shepherds of Israel that do feed themselves! should not the shepherds feed the [flock]? Ye eat the fat, and ye clothe you with the wool, ye kill them that are fed: but ye feed not the flock. The diseased have ye not strengthened, neither have ye healed that which was sick, neither have ye bound up that which was broken, neither have ye brought again that which was driven away, neither have ye sought that which was lost; but with force and with cruelty ye have ruled them. And they were scattered, because there is no shepherd: and they became meat to all the beasts of the field, when they were scattered. My sheep wandered through all the mountains, and upon every high hill: yea, my flock was scattered upon all the face of the earth, and none did search or seek after them.

Therefore, ye shepherds, hear the word of the LORD; As I live, saith the Lord GOD, surely because my flock became a prey, and my flock became meat to every beast of the field, because there was no shepherd, neither did my shepherds search for my flock, but the shepherds fed themselves, and fed not my flock; Therefore, O ye shepherds, hear the word of the LORD;

Thus saith the Lord GOD; Behold, I am against the shepherds; and I will require my flock at their hand, and cause them to cease from feeding the flock; neither shall the shepherds feed themselves anymore; for I will deliver my flock from their mouth, that they may not be meat for them.

For thus saith the Lord GOD; Behold, ***I****,* ***even I****, will both search my sheep, and seek them out. As a shepherd seeketh out his flock in the day that he is among his sheep that are scattered; so will* ***I*** *seek out my sheep, ...where they have been scattered in the cloudy and dark day. And* ***I*** *will bring them out from the people, and gather them from the countries, and will bring them to their own land, and feed them upon the mountains of Israel by the rivers, and...all the inhabited places of the country.* ***I*** *will feed them in a good pasture, and upon the high mountains of Israel shall their fold be: there shall they lie [down] in the good fold, and in a fat pasture [and they shall] feed upon the mountains of Israel.* ***I will feed my flock****, and* ***I will cause them to lie down****, saith the Lord GOD.* ***I*** *will seek that which was lost, and bring again that which was driven away, and will bind up that which was broken, and will strengthen that which was sick: but I will destroy the fat and the strong; I will feed* ***them*** *with judgment.*

And as for [thou], O my flock, thus saith the Lord GOD; Behold, I [will] judge between cattle and cattle, between the rams and the he goats. Seemeth it a small thing unto you to have eaten up the good pasture, but ye must tread down with your feet the residue of your pastures? and to have drunk [from] the deep waters, but ye must foul the residue with your feet? And as for my flock, they eat that which ye have trodden with your feet; ...they drink that which ye have fouled with your feet.

Therefore thus saith the Lord GOD unto them; Behold, I, even I, will judge between the fat cattle and between the lean cattle. Because ye have thrust with [the] side and with [the] shoulder, and pushed all the diseased with your horns, till ye have scattered them abroad; Therefore will I save my flock, and they shall no more be a prey; and I will judge between cattle and cattle. And I will set up one shepherd over them, and he shall feed them, even my servant David; he shall feed them, and he shall be their shepherd. And I the LORD will be their God, and my servant David a prince among them; [for] I the LORD have spoken it.

And I will make with them a covenant of peace, and will cause the evil beasts to cease out of the land: and they shall dwell safely in the wilderness, and sleep in the woods. And I will make them...the places round about my hill a blessing; and I will cause the shower to come down in his season; there shall be showers of [blessings]. And the tree of the field shall yield her fruit, and the

> *earth shall yield her increase, and they shall be safe in their land, and shall know that* ***I am the LORD****, when I have broken the bands of their yoke, and delivered them out of the [hands] of those that served themselves of them. And they shall no more be a prey to the heathen, neither shall the beast of the land devour them; but they shall dwell safely, and none shall make them afraid. And I will raise up for them a plant of renown, and they shall be no more consumed with hunger in the land, neither bear the shame of the heathen any more. Thus shall they know that I [am] the LORD their God am with them, and that they, even the house of Israel, are my people, saith the Lord GOD. And ye my flock, the flock of my pasture, are men, and I am your God, saith the Lord GOD.* (Ezekiel 33:25–34:31; see also Ezekiel 17:2-11 RE; emphasis added)

Today marks a moment when the stirrings that have been underway for years result in God's offering to establish His people on Earth by a covenant He ordains. The few ready to receive the Lord's offer today are scattered to the nethermost parts of His vineyard. It's verse 52 (see Jacob 5:52; see also Jacob 3:23 RE).

Despite this, a live broadcast on the internet allows them to be grafted in at the same moment this is happening in Boise, Idaho. Correspondingly, those who utterly refuse to accept the offered covenant are plucked from the restoration's tree of life because they are bitter fruit, unable to meet the Lord's requirements. The Lord is taking the step to preserve part of humanity, not to destroy it. That's verse 53 (ibid; vs. 23 RE).

A few descendants of the covenant Fathers have the natural gift of faith. That gift belongs to the natural branches. That's verse 54 (ibid; vs. 23 RE).

When grafted, we are connected to the natural roots, or covenant Fathers, as heirs of the promises made to them. Even after the covenant, there will still be those who are bitter and wild who will be unable to produce natural fruit despite the covenant. These will remain for a time despite their bitterness—verses 56 and 57 (ibid; vs. 24 RE). Today, only the most bitter who refuse to be grafted in will be trimmed away.

We look forward to more *nourishing*, or restoring of truths, lights, and commandments which will bless those who receive. But for those who will not, the continuing restoration will prune them away—verse 58 (ibid; vs. 24 RE).

These bitter and wild branches must still be cut off and cast away. These steps are necessary to preserve the opportunity for the natural fruit to fully return. It's verse 59 (ibid; vs. 24 RE).

The **good** must overcome the **evil**. This takes time, and it means that the Lord's patience is extended to give time to develop and further improve. We are not expected and cannot become natural fruit in a single step. But we are expected to accept the initial graft today.

The Lord is taking these steps **so that *perhaps***—that's a deliberate word—**perhaps** we may become natural fruit, worthy to be preserved in the coming harvest. That's verse 60 (ibid; vs. 24 RE). ***Perhaps*** is the right word. Some who are grafted will still be plucked away and burned. But others will bear natural fruit and be preserved.

Accepting the covenant is not the final step. Our choices will determine whether we are bitter or natural fruit. T**hat** will decide our fate.

Just as the ancient allegory foretold, the covenant makes us servants and laborers in the vineyard—verse 61 (ibid; vs. 24 RE). We are required to (this is from the covenant): *Seek to recover the lost sheep remnant of this land and of Israel and no longer forsake them. Bring them unto the Lord and teach them of His ways to walk in them.* If we fail to labor to recover them, we break the covenant.

We must labor for this last time in the Lord's vineyard. There **is** an approaching, final pruning of the vineyard—verse 62 (Jacob 5:62; see also Jacob Jacob 3:25 RE).

The first to be grafted in are Gentiles so that the last may be first, the lost sheep remnant next, and then, Israelites so that the first may be last—verse 63 (ibid; vs. 25 RE).

But grafting is required for all, even the remnants, because God works with His people through covenant-making. There will be more grafting and further pruning. As more is revealed—and therefore, more is required—some will find the digging and dunging too much to bear and will fall away or, in other words, will be pruned despite the covenant. That's verse 64 (ibid; vs. 25 RE).

The covenant makes it possible for natural fruit to return. The bad fruit will still continue, even among the covenant people, until there is enough strength in the healthy branches for further pruning. It requires natural fruit to appear before the final pruning takes place —verse 65 (ibid; vs. 25 RE). The good and bad will coexist. It will damage the tree to remove the bad at once.

Therefore, the Lord's patience will continue for some time yet. The rate of removing the bad is dependent fully upon the rate of the development of the good.

It is the Lord's purpose to create **equality** in his vineyard. In the allegory **equality** in the vineyard appears three times in verses 66, 72, and 74 (ibid; vs. 25, 27 RE). We cannot be greater and lesser nor divide ourselves into a hierarchy to achieve the equality required for Zion. When a group is determined to remain equal (and I am personally determined to be no greater than any other), then it faces challenge that never confront unequal people. A religion of bosses and minions never deals with any of the challenges of being equals.

Critics claim we will never succeed because of our determined desire for equality. **None of our critics** can envision what the Lord has said in verses 66, 72, and 74 about His people. But equality among us is the **only** way **prophesied** for us to **succeed**. That does not mean we won't have a mess as we learn how to establish equality.

Similarly, Zion cannot be established by isolated and solitary figures proclaiming a testimony of Jesus from their home keyboard. The challenge of building a community must be part of a process. Zion is a community, and therefore, God is a God of community. And His people must learn to live together with one heart, one mind, with no poor among us. Isolated keyboardists proclaiming their resentment of community can hardly speak temperately of others. How could they ever live peacefully in a community of equals?

We must become *precious* to each other.

Although the laborers in this final effort are few, you will be the means used by the Lord to complete His work in His vineyard—verse 70 (Jacob 5:70; see also Jacob 3:26 RE). You're required to labor with your might to finish the Lord's work in His vineyard—verse 72 (ibid; vs. 27 RE). **But He will labor alongside you.**

He, not a man or a committee, will call you to do work. When He calls, do not fear, but do not run faster than you have strength. We must find His people in the highways and byways, invite them to join in. Zion will include people from every part of the world. This conference is broadcast worldwide as part of the prophecy to Enoch that God would send:

Righteousness and truth will [He] cause to sweep the earth as with a flood, to

> *gather out mine elect from the four quarters of the earth, unto a place which I shall prepare, an Holy City, that my people may gird up their loins, and be looking forth for the time of my coming; for there shall be my Tabernacle, and it shall be called Zion, a New Jerusalem.* (Moses 7:62; see also Genesis 4:22 RE)

We must proclaim this to the world.

Do not despair when further pruning takes place. It must be done. Only through pruning can the Lord keep His tree of life equal without those who are lofty overcoming the body—verse 73 (Jacob 5:73; see also Jacob 3:27 RE). The lofty branches have always destroyed equality to prevent Zion.

The final result of the Lord's labor in His vineyard is declared by the ancient prophet in unmistakable clarity: *The trees have become again the natural fruit; and they became like unto one body; and the fruits were equal; and the Lord of the vineyard had preserved unto himself the natural fruit, which was most precious unto him from the beginning.* Mark those words. That's verse 74 (ibid; vs. 27 RE).

When the Lord explained this to me, I realized how foolish it was to expect natural fruit, worthy of preservation, in an instant. The Lord works patiently, methodically, and does not require any to run faster than they have strength.

We cannot allow ourselves to be drawn into inequality when the result of this labor is to make us one body, equal with one another. We cannot imitate the failures of the past by establishing a hierarchy, elevating one above another, and forgetting that we must be of one heart, one mind, and no poor among us.

The restoration was never intended to just restore an ancient Christian church. That is only a halfway point. It must go back further. In the words of the ancient prophet, God intends to do according to His will and to preserve the natural fruit, *that it is good, even like as it was in the beginning*—verse 75 (ibid; vs. 28 RE). This means the beginning, as in the days of Adam, with the return of the original religion and original authority. Everything must be returned as it was in the beginning.

Civilization began with the temple as the center of learning, law, and culture. The temple was the original university because it taught of man's place with God in the universe.

God will return the right of dominion once held by Adam to man on earth to make us humble servant gardeners laboring to return the world to a peaceful paradise. The covenant received today restores part of that right.

There is a land inheritance, given to us as part of the covenant, and therefore, if we keep the covenant, we have the right to remain when others will be swept away. Ultimately, all rights given to us must be turned back to the Fathers who went before, who will likewise return them to Adam, who will surrender them to Christ. When Christ returns, He will come with the right to exercise complete dominion over the earth and to exercise judgment over the ungodly. Things set into motion today are part of preparing the way for the Lord's return in glory.

In the name of Jesus Christ. Amen.

The foregoing excerpts are taken from:

- Denver's talk titled "Christ's Discourse on the Road to Emmaus" given in Fairview, Utah on April 14, 2007;
- His conference talk titled "Things to Keep Us Awake at Night" given in St. George, Utah on March 19, 2017;
- Denver's *40 Years in Mormonism Series* Talk #6 titled "Zion" given in Grand Junction, Colorado on April 12, 2014; and
- His Opening Remarks given at the Covenant of Christ Conference in Boise, Idaho on September 3, 2017.

For more information on this topic, please see the following blog posts:

- The "Jacob 5" Series beginning March 23, 2012 and continuing through April 12, 2012: https://denversnuffer.com/2012/03/jacob-chapter-5/
- Themes from Jacob 5, April 12, 2020: https://denversnuffer.com/2012/04/themes-from-jacob-5/

119. God Forgives

In this episode, Denver discusses God's willingness to forgive us—to leave our errors in the past and remember them no more.

DENVER: Isaiah, in the temple, saw God high and lifted up, and his first reaction is, *Woe is me! ... I am undone; ...I am a man of unclean lips, ...I dwell [among] a people of unclean lips* (Isaiah 6:5). And a Seraphim, one of the "fiery ones" (we ought to know more about that), improvises an ordinance where they take a coal with tongs off the altar and touch his lips to purify them. And the Lord says: *[Who] shall I send?* And Isaiah says: *Here am I; send me* (ibid, vs.8; see also Isaiah 2:2 RE). Same man that is cowering, *Woe is me,* is now *Here am I; send me.* And what accounts for the difference? The compassion, the forgiveness, the integrity of the Lord. *I know thou art a God of truth, and [cannot] lie* (Ether 3:12; see also Ether 1:12 RE). When He testifies to you that your sins are forgiven, only a fool will thereafter charge you with sin. The world is stocked with fools, though.

The parable starts with the Lord, who's trying to get people to come to the wedding, telling the servants the wedding's ready but those that I've asked are not worthy:

> *Go...into the highways, and as many as ye shall find, bid [them] to the marriage. So those servants went out into the highways* [always the servants, always angels do this work; they do the gathering], *and gathered together all as many as they found, both bad and good: and the wedding was furnished with guests. ...when the king came in to see the guests, he saw there [was] a man which had not...a wedding garment...saith unto him, Friend, how camest thou...hither not having a wedding garment?...he was speechless...the king [said], Bind him hand and foot...take him away...cast him into outer darkness; there shall be weeping [and wailing] and gnashing of teeth.* (Matthew 22:9-13; see also Matthew 10:18-19 RE)

So, I want to put that on the table, because in this part of this parable, you have anyone who will come being invited, because the people that were targeted for attendance simply aren't worthy to come. So anyone gets to come. And now you have among them someone who doesn't have on a wedding garment. And for that I want to refer you to Luke chapter 15, because in Luke chapter 15 we run into the Lord talking about a robe being supplied. This is the son who found himself, having been in a far-off land, filling *his belly with the husks that the swine did eat; ...no man gave unto him. ... [He comes] to himself, ...[says], How many hired servants of my father's have bread enough and to spare, and I perish with hunger!* So when he goes back to see his father, look at what happens in verse 22 of Luke chapter 15. *But the father said to his servants* [again, it's the angels that do this], *Bring forth the best robe, and put it on him; ...put a ring on his hand, and shoes on his feet* (Luke 15:16,17,22; see also Luke 9:13-14 RE).

You see, this, I think, has to be kept in mind whenever you're looking at someone who has arrived at the feast, bidden from the highway, who arrives and doesn't have on the robe. The Master is the one that wants you to wear it. The Master is the one that will furnish it. Don't think that the purpose of the Lord is to judge. The purpose of the Lord is to redeem; and for that purpose, He is infinitely patient and willing, if you will respond with forgiveness of your sins, as He does consistently throughout the Book of Mormon.

You must look to Christ for forgiveness of your sins, and follow His example of self-sacrifice, patience, obedience, and virtue. I can only urge you to patiently allow the True Shepherd to guide us all into His pastures—showing Him the respect due to a Redeemer. Remember, the Great King, Christ, came not to be served but to serve. He did not "lord it over" others, but He knelt to elevate them. He came as a meek and lowly servant, and went about doing good. He died to save the lives of others. When He arose from the dead, He went to the Father and advocated forgiveness for those who despised and abused Him.

He knew what it was like for men to satisfy their ambition by clothing their hypocrisy in religious garb. He also felt what it was like to be the victim of religious oppression by those who pretend to practice virtue while oppressing others. He knew the hearts of those who would kill Him. Before confronting their condemnation of Him in the flesh, He suffered their torment of mind when they recognized He was the Lord, and then found peace for what they would do by rejecting Him. In this extremity, there was madness itself as He mirrored the evil which would destroy Him, and learned how to come to peace with the Father after killing the Son of God; and to love all those involved—without restraint and without pretense—even before they did these terrible deeds. His suffering, therefore, encompassed all that has happened, all that did happen, and all that would happen in the future.

As a result of what the Lord suffered, there is no condition—physical, spiritual, or mental— that He does not fully understand. He knows how to teach, comfort, succor, and direct any who come to Him seeking forgiveness and peace. This is why the prophet wrote:

> *By his knowledge shall my righteous Servant justify many, for he shall bear their iniquities* (Isa. 19:3). And again: *Surely he hath borne our griefs and carried our sorrows, yet we did esteem him stricken, smitten of God, and afflicted. But he was wounded for our transgressions, he was bruised for our iniquities; the chastisement of our peace was upon him, and with his stripes we are healed.* (Isa. 19:2)

He obtained this knowledge by the things he suffered. He suffered that we might avoid sin by being obedient to His commandments. None of us need harm another, if we will follow Him. He knows fully the consequences of sin. He teaches His followers to avoid sin.

> *But remember that without the fruit of repentance, and a broken heart and a contrite spirit, you cannot keep my covenant; for I, your Lord, am meek and lowly of heart. Be like me. You have all been wounded, your hearts pierced through with sorrows because of how the world has treated you. But you have also scarred one another by your unkind treatment of each other, and you do not notice your misconduct toward others because you think yourself justified in this. You bear the scars on your countenances, from the soles of your feet to the head, and every heart is faint. Your visages have been so marred that your hardness, mistrust, suspicions, resentments, fear, jealousies, and anger toward your fellow man bear outward witness of your inner self; you cannot hide it. When I appear to you, instead of confidence you feel shame. You fear and withdraw from me because you bear the blood and sins of your treatment of brothers and sisters. Come to me and I will make sins as scarlet become white as snow, and I will make you stand boldly before me, confident of my love.*
>
> *I descended below it all, and know the sorrows of you all, and have borne the grief of it all, and I say to you, Forgive one another. Be tender with one another, pursue judgment, bless the oppressed, care for the orphan, and uplift the widow in her need, for I have redeemed you from being orphaned and taken you that you are no longer a widowed people. Rejoice in me, and rejoice with your brethren and sisters who are mine also. Be one.* (T&C 157:49-50)
>
> *There remains a great work yet to be done. Receive my covenant and abide in it, not as in the former time when jarring, jealousy, contention, and backbiting caused anger, broke hearts, and hardened the souls of those claiming to be my saints. But receive it in spirit, in meekness, and in truth. I have given you a former commandment that I, the Lord, will forgive whom I*

> *will forgive, but of you it is required to forgive all men. And again, I have taught that if you forgive men their trespasses your Heavenly Father will also forgive you; but if you forgive not men their trespasses neither will your Heavenly Father forgive your trespasses. How do I act toward mankind? If men intend no offense, I take no offense, but if they are taught and should have obeyed, then I reprove and correct, and forgive and forget. You cannot be at peace with one another if you take offense when none is intended. But again I say, Judge not others except by the rule you want used to weigh yourself.* (ibid. vs. 58)

> *But this shall be the covenant that I will make with the house of Israel; After those days, saith the LORD, I will put my law in their inward parts, and write it in their hearts; and will be their God, and they shall be my people. And they shall teach no more every man his neighbour, and every man his brother, saying, Know the LORD: for they shall all know me.* (Jeremiah 31:33-34; see also Jeremiah 12:9 RE)

This is not, "They shall all know *about* Me." This is, "They shall *know* Me." And it will no longer be necessary for anyone to say, know the Lord, because you shall *know* Him. It's not knowledge concerning Him; It's Him. And those that know Him shall be *from the least of them unto the greatest of them, saith the LORD: for I will forgive their iniquity, and I will remember their sin no more* (Jeremiah 31:34; see also Jeremiah 12:9 RE). That's who He is. That's what He does. He doesn't want to remember your sin. He would rather prefer it if **you** don't remember your sin. Because if you don't remember your sin and you go on in a positive way, having laid down the burden that He so willingly will accept from you, and remove from you that burden of guilt, then you can go on and become healthy again. You needn't be troubled about all of those things that have bogged you down. He wants to remove that. He wants to carry them.

> *I will remember their sin no more. Thus saith the LORD, which giveth the sun for a light by day, and the ordinances of the moon and of the stars for a light by night, which divideth the sea when the waves thereof roar; The LORD of hosts is his name: If those ordinances depart from before me, saith the LORD, then the seed of Israel also shall cease from being a nation before me for ever.* (Jeremiah 31:34-36; see also Jeremiah 12:9-10 RE)

If I can help you envision our Lord a little more, let me describe Him in terms of His characteristics. Our Lord was and is affable, but He is not gregarious. He was approachable, and He is approachable, and He's not aloof. He's patient. He's willing to guide, and He's willing to teach. He's intelligent, but He is not overbearing. He's humble in His demeanor, even though the power that He possessed and possesses is undeniable. He is, therefore, both a Lamb and a Lion.

I want you to entertain three truths about Him in your mind as we begin the subject today. Those three truths are:

- He is quick to forgive sin;
- He allows all to come unto Him; and
- He is no respecter of persons.
- In some respects, our own respect for (or our disrespect for) ourselves is the impediment in coming to Him, because we tend to think that we aren't good enough. Because He is quick to forgive sins, it really doesn't matter if you're not good enough, because one of the first orders of business when you come into His presence is He forgives you. He cannot look upon sin with the least degree of allowance, but He has the capacity and the ability to forgive sin. Therefore, although your sins may be as scarlet, He can, He will, and He does make you white as snow, no longer accountable. Therefore, you needn't fear, but you can approach boldly, our Lord.

You must each decide whether I'm sent by Him and acting as a true witness, or whether I'm just another of the many deceivers who use God's name in vain, having no authority. I claim to testify to the truth and do not deceive you; and I claim that He has sent me to preach deliverance from sin by obedience to Him. It is His Doctrine that all mankind should repent and be baptized, in His name, for the remission of sins. If you do so, He will be faithful and forgive.

Repentance means to turn from whatever else is distracting you and face God. Heed Him, follow Him, and obey His will. Repentance substitutes virtues for sin, trades weakness for strength, and remakes us heart, mind, and spirit into a new creature—a son or daughter of God.

I know I am no better than any other man. My weaknesses and foolishness have provoked the Lord to sternly rebuke me on several occasions. My many shortcomings cause me to mourn, and wish someone else were responsible for the things entrusted into my hands.

But I will not refuse the Lord. He warned me, long ago, that once we begin, we cannot look back. Therefore, I dare not depart from the course, no matter how difficult. Like you, I hope to do what the Lord asks, when He asks it, in the way He requires it to be done; and I leave everything else to the Lord.

It is a terrible thing for anyone to presume that they can proscribe and limit the scope of truth into which any of you can inquire and get an answer for yourselves. It is a terrible responsibility. I would suggest that anyone who tries to keep you from inquiring of your Father, to know the truth of all things, is like Satan, trying to use fear in order to eliminate your approach to that Being who loves you more than life itself.

God is no respecter of persons. All are alike to Him. Qualifications are based upon the behavior and faith of the person, not on their status or past mistakes.

You probably think your errors are more serious an impediment to God accepting you than He ever has. He doesn't want to judge you, He wants to heal you. He wants to give you what you lack, teach you to be better, and to bless you. He doesn't want to belittle, demean, or punish you. Ask Him to forgive and He forgives—even very serious sins. He does not want you burdened with them. He wants you to leave them behind.

His willingness to leave those errors in the past, and remember them no more, is greater than you can imagine. It is a guiding principle for the Atonement. Asking for forgiveness is almost always all that is required to be forgiven.

What alienates us from Him is not our sins. He will forgive them. What we lack is the confidence to ask in faith, nothing doubting, for His help. He can and will help when you do so.

The sins that offend Him are not the errors, weaknesses, and foolishness of the past. He is offended when we are forgiven by Him, and then return to the same sin. That shows a lack of gratitude for His forgiveness. Even then, however, there are addictions, compulsions, and weaknesses that we sometimes struggle with for years, even decades. When the sin is due to some difficulty based on biology, physiology, or an inherent weakness that we fight for years to overcome, then His patience with us is far greater than our own. He will help in the fight. He will walk along side you as you fight. He does not expect you to run faster than you have strength. When, at last, because of age or infirmity, a troubling weakness is at last overcome, He will readily accept your repentance and let you move forward—clean, whole, and forgiven. That is His ministry—to forgive and make whole.

The foregoing excerpts are taken from:

- Denver's *40 Years in Mormonism Series,* Talk #1 titled "Be of Good Cheer," given in Boise, ID on September 10th, 2013;
- Denver's *40 Years in Mormonism Series,* Talk #2 titled "Faith," given in Idaho Falls, ID on September 28th, 2013;
- His conference talk titled "The Doctrine of Christ," given in Boise, ID on September 11th, 2016;
- Denver's *Christian Reformation Lecture Series,* Talk #3 given in Atlanta, Georgia on November 16, 2017;
- The presentation of "Answer and Covenant," given at the Covenant of Christ Conference in Boise, ID on September 3rd, 2017;
- Denver's *40 Years in Mormonism Series,* Talk #7 titled "Christ: Prototype of the Saved Man," given in Ephraim, UT on June 28, 2014;
- His talk titled "The Mission of Elijah Reconsidered," given in Spanish Fork, UT on October 14th, 2011; and
- Denver's blog post titled "God is No Respecter of Persons," posted April 27, 2010.

120. One Heart First

In this episode, Denver discusses the process that groups of people have followed in the past and need to follow today to achieve unity when working together on a project.

———

DENVER: Several years ago there were a number of people who were independently interested in trying to do something to reclaim the Scriptures in a more accurate and authentic way. I heard rumors about the existence of this project—people had talked about it—and the existence of the project came to my attention by rumors, for some time. But it was late in December of that year (and I right now don't recollect what year it was… No, it was—this was when the very thing began)... It was late in December, and it was almost within a two-week time period that one group finished what they believed to be a completed project on the Scriptures, getting them back into shape. And they turned that product over to me.

When they turned it over to me, I was surprised to learn the identity of the people that I had heard the rumors about, and I was interested in looking at what they had completed and what they turned over. But within a two-week time period, a second group stepped up who had likewise completed a Scripture project and turned that project over to me for me to look at. And neither of these groups who'd been working on it had been working together or were even aware that they had independently started on and were working toward the same end.

So, I wind up now in possession of two different sets of the same objective, which is to get a better set of Scriptures put together. And it… The thing that occurred to me was that it really should not be something that I go through and read and compare the two with one another, but it made a whole lot more sense to get the two groups together. And so, the projects that were now done resulted in a meeting (in the same room that we're in right now) of representatives from both groups. Some of the people that were involved in it chose to be anonymous and remain behind the scenes. But both groups were well represented by getting together to talk about "the projects."

They were identical in the objective, and they were very different in the content. Because as you go through and you have to reconcile problems that you find with the version of the Scriptures that are in existence, what you find is that one group discovered some set of problems and resolved those, while another group found a different set of problems and resolved those—but neither group had identical problem-recognition or problem-solving. There were many places where they were identical, but there were also many places in which there was a dissimilarity between the two. And in the meeting that began (in the early discussions), what we learned was that sometimes the same problem had been identified and grappled with by both groups, but for different reasons they had reached a different method to resolve the scriptural problem. And so, the discussion became detailed and lively and interesting. And both sides were willing to take a look at the whys and wherefores of the manner in which the dilemmas had been reconciled. And both sides were very interested in seeing what they had not had come to their attention that the other group had done. And so, a project these two groups had worked on (literally for more than a year, a couple of years)—and both of whom thought their project was now done—in coming together realized that nothing had yet been accomplished, and it all had to start over again.

And so, the work of both groups (that was originally envisioned as having been 100% completed) now turns into the starting point for a combined effort to try and work this problem through. So, the Scripture project had now three beginnings, and it started over again.

There were **numerous** issues that came up. Both groups had strong personalities. Some of those strong personalities were also eccentric people whose strong feelings and eccentricities lent themselves to not merely lively debate, but also conflict and disagreement. One of the things that we confronted, time and time again, were strongly held opinions in conflict with one another that required people to come together and reason with one another.

Now, not everyone was involved in every single part of problem identification. Instead, someone would be trusted to go do and resolve something. (I say "someone"… It was usually a group—two, three, four people working on something.) And then, what was not agreed to with unanimity, the problem was then presented to everyone. And we get together with everyone in the same room (or in the same room with a number of people joining by Zoom or online), and we'd hash it through. The way in which a problem was resolved was by **unanimous** agreement. If there was not unanimous agreement, then the issue was discussed, the opinions were laid on the table, the disagreement was exposed, and then it was tabled. And we would come back at a later point, and we would approach it again—but it required unanimity in coming to a resolution for the problem in order for that issue to be put to bed and things to move on.

Well, the project advanced far enough and the attention to the project had been spoken about widely enough that we began to talk about it publicly and openly and inviting other people to participate. Any number of volunteers… I think at one point we had as many as 200 people that were trying to help out on the project, but any number of volunteers looked, worked, cross-checked, double-checked, worked with manuscripts.

We learned a hard lesson in that process—because the entire objective of the Scripture project was not to innovate. It was to do the hard research work in order to identify (as accurately and completely as it is possible to do so) what it was that Joseph Smith did with the translation of the Book of Mormon/ with the revelations as they tumbled out when they were originally given and originally recorded and what Joseph Smith had done with his revision to the Bible (the Old and the New Testament). So, it was a research project; it was not a drafting, or it wasn't an "innovating" project. It was a reclamation project that was trying to strictly get back what it was that Joseph had originally given to us.

Joseph referred to his effort to recover the Bible in its original form as "the fullness of the Scriptures." So, the Bible—the Old and the New Testament—was what was referred to as the fullness of the Scriptures. The Book of Mormon was the "Book of Mormon," and the revelations given to Joseph was referred to generically (very often) as just the "commandments." And so, when the term "the fullness of the Scriptures" got used by Joseph, he was referring to the work that he was doing in recovering the Joseph Smith translation.

So, we move along happily to the point that we think we've got this project in a robust enough state of completion that it went into print, and it was circulated (as a result of the conference that was held down in St George), and hard copies of these things became available (print-on-demand through Amazon), and people bought them.

One of the folks in whose hands a copy of those Scriptures wound up is in here in the room today. (I'm not naming names today because I don't wanna embarrass anyone.) But one of the people that's sitting in the room happened to have spent years of work on the Joseph Smith translation of the Bible, in which he learned things about the JST version that no one on the committee had had brought to their attention. And so, after they were in print and available in print-on-demand and the JST (that everyone on the committee was so proud of) came to the attention of someone that knew more, he (fortunately) was willing to volunteer; he joined the committee. And so, the project that was complete enough to call it done and "Now we can put it out in print," we find out is not only not complete enough, but it needed to start all over again from scratch. And so, the project—which had been done now another time in its fourth state of completion—began anew because attention had been paid to details that had not yet come to the attention of the committee.

Then we find out that not only was the JST version incomplete and the version we were working with had been modified before its publication by the RLDS Church (who felt at liberty to eliminate some of the changes that Joseph Smith made and also to add some additions to it that the publication's committee at Herald House—the RLDS Church—felt at liberty to make), and so the text had become something other than the Joseph Smith translation. Fortunately, there was resources available and someone who had spent the time invested in those resources to guide through that.

But we also found that the original publication of the Book of Commandments, which was done in Missouri by Oliver Cowdery and W.W. Phelps… That's the version that got destroyed by the mob, and copies (unbound copies) of those got smuggled out by women in their skirts. The Book of Commandments (that was assembled from that printing) later was bound—at a later time, in another place—and the do-over of the Book of Commandments was accomplished in 1835 back in Kirtland where they had a press.

And so, the original expectation was that the Book of Commandments had a better version than did the 1835 Doctrine and Covenants. (They changed the name from Book of Commandments to Doctrine and Covenants for the first time in 1835.) However, what we learned upon further research ('cause this is a research project) is that Oliver Cowdery—who had been given permission in a revelation to write (but not by way of commandment) for the Church—felt at liberty to take the revelations of Joseph when he put it into the Book of Commandments and make changes there. That Book of Commandments version was what the 1835 Doctrine and Covenants teed off of. So, they began with an altered document.

And then the committee that worked on the publications also felt at liberty… 'Cause now you had (in addition to Oliver Cowdery's changes) Sidney Rigdon making changes, and Sidney felt very much at liberty to interject his views into things. And so, the 1835 Doctrine and Covenants included substantially-yet-more revisions to the revelations that have been made. We—after publishing it the first time—discovered that there were fundamental problems with how the revelations or commandments had been incorporated into the Scriptures. And so, that project had to start all over again and ferret out how that would happen.

A couple of brothers, both of whom had strong opinions, were leading up that portion of the effort, and they would come back to the committee with frequent disagreements, in which they felt at liberty (because they're family members, after all) to—you know—verbally spar with one another in a robust and uninhibited fashion, and then we were called upon to referee that. But it was… It was a bunch of strong personalities.

Nevertheless, coming out of all that was a consensus about how we resolve things. And the Doctrine and Covenants project—which has now turned into the Teachings and Commandments (we've retitled it 'cause it's very different from a Doctrine and Covenants)—that project restarted, and then it ran into a few hiccups and restarted yet again. So, now what are we? Five or six times into the thing?

There were times when it was almost impossible to referee and peaceably resolve what was going on among brethren working side-by-side to get the project done. So, I sent an email (and I didn't realize this was gonna show up in the foreword to the Teachings and Commandments), but I sent an email out at one point—when we needed group therapy because we were at impasse and hadn't gotten to unanimous agreement—and this shows up now in the forepart of the Teachings and Commandments as just some background noise. But it was written in the heat of battle, trying to get consensus among people. This is the email:

> I would rather submit to the decision of the group than insist that my view be followed. For me, harmony between brethren is more important than getting what I think [the] best to be followed. I believe harmony can lead to much greater things than can merely enforcement of even a correct view. I know how difficult it is to have a correct view, because of how often [I've] been corrected by the Lord. Sometimes I am humiliated by my foolishness when the Lord reproves me. Humiliation can lead to humility, but my experience is that...humiliation is accompanied by shame, whereas humility can proceed with a clean conscience.
>
> My experience with others leads me to conclude that if we can have one heart first, eventually we can likewise come to have one mind. But if we insist on having one mind at the outset, we may never obtain one heart together.

That was written to try and persuade the Scripture committee to come together at a difficult point when we were high-centered. And apparently, folks valued it enough—that email mattered enough—that it wound up in the forepart of the Teachings and Commandments.

Well, as people had been invited to help proofread, one of the proofreaders apparently misunderstood what the project was. They were entrusted to work on the Book of Isaiah, 'cause that was a hobby horse sort of thing with them. And what we got back from the proofreader was a complete rewrite of the Book of Isaiah—not tacking from the Joseph Smith translation of the Bible, but adopting Avraham Gileadi's explanation of what ought to go into the content of the Book of Isaiah.

Well, Avraham Gileadi is not a dispensation head (however much he may contribute to someone's understanding). He's not Joseph Smith. He was not given the commandment by God to accomplish a specific work, and Joseph Smith was. Therefore, our now boogered-up version of Isaiah comes back from the proofreader, and there's some degree of dismay—I mean, depending upon which member of the committee you talk to, it could be shock and horror. And there's a scramble to find out: Did we keep an electronic version of where we started? Because that was a whole lot closer than what we've got now in the return from our ostensible proofreader.

There's an example of an Isaiah passage that Avraham Gileadi made that I **really** like, 'k? I think Avraham's statement is worth taking the time to illustrate. In the JST version, the passage talking about… In the time period after there has been a period of turmoil—a period of destruction and judgment—and now on the other side of this awful ordeal, Isaiah is looking forward, and he's prophesying what you'll see on the other side of that. In the Joseph Smith translation of the passage, he says (God's speaking says), *I will make a man more precious than fine gold* (Isaiah 6:2 RE). So, the reasonable conclusion that you would reach from that is that those people who go through the ordeal will have gained so much character and so much value from the experience that they will be refined; they will be appreciative, humble, good, good people. That same passage is rendered by Avraham Gileadi quite differently. He says, *I will make man scarcer than fine gold, men more rare than gold of Ophir* (Isaiah 13:12, Isaiah Institute Translation), meaning (in this view of that same language) men will be dead. There will be so few men left occupying this post-apocalyptic society that you'll have to search the earth to find a man in the same way that you now have to search the earth in order to find gold as a precious metal. Two fundamentally different views.

Well, because Joseph Smith reviewed and Joseph Smith corrected the Bible, the version that we ought to have in our standard text is the one that the dispensation head operating under a commandment from God rendered the passage. And so, *I will make a man more precious than fine gold, even a man than the golden wedge of Ophir* (Isaiah 6:2 RE) is the way it appears in the JST, and it's the way it appears now in what is rendered as the Old Covenants.

Well, Joseph Smith got the original commandment to work on this (the revision to the Scriptures) in a revelation that was given in December of 1830. This is almost at the very beginning of Joseph Smith's acquaintance with Sidney Rigdon (Sidney Rigdon being an experienced biblical preacher from a Campbellite tradition, coming to Joseph Smith and meeting him, and converting after he'd been proselytized by the first set of missionaries—including Parley Pratt, himself a Campbellite). So, he traveled to meet Joseph, and a commandment is given on the seventh of December of 1830 which says: *And a commandment I give unto you….* (This is directed at Sidney Rigdon.)

> *…a commandment I give unto you that you shall write for him, and the scriptures shall be given, even as they are in [mine] own bosom, to the salvation of [mine] own elect, for they will hear my voice, and shall see me, and shall not be asleep, and shall abide the day of my coming.* (T&C 18:6)

So, Sidney Rigdon meets Joseph Smith, and a commandment comes: "Sidney Rigdon, you write for Joseph. I'm giving a commandment: you're gonna work on the Scriptures. The Scriptures shall be given."

Well, the Scriptures that are to be given are not the commandments. It's this new revision of the Bible, which they began in this time period in the way that the LDS Church brought the book of Moses into print—originally in England and then later adopted as Scripture—but it was printed in the same format it had been in England. The book of Moses in the Pearl of Great Price tells you the date on which various chapters of the book of Moses were recorded. This is the text that includes the Enoch passages. This is the text that includes, *This is my work and my glory: to bring to pass the immortality and eternal life of man* (Genesis 1:7 RE). This is the text that Enoch is caught up to heaven, and he's weeping, and he's saying, "I refuse to be comforted." And then the Lord shows him the day of the coming of the Son of Man, and he wants to know when will the Son of Man be lifted up, and when will we be relieved of the burden of our sin, in effect? And he rejoices and is overjoyed at seeing the crucifixion of the Lord—which, to us, it sounds like he's celebrating the wrong thing. But in the heavenly condition that Enoch was when he observes this, he's overjoyed because of what it means, because of salvation coming. This is the text that includes the earth being pained, "Woe is me because of the wickedness of man that is upon my face. When shall I rest from this wickedness?" (see Genesis 4:20 RE). This text is what comes out in the Pearl of Great Price in December of 1830, as the **beginning** of the Joseph Smith translation of the Scriptures that he was commanded to do.

Now, I've gone through and read the Teachings and Commandments. Everywhere the "fullness of the Scriptures" or the revision to the Bible appears, I've put a little yellow tag on it. I haven't counted them, but there's probably 19 or 20 of them—those of you who are here can see all the tags. But they go from the command to begin to a... Section 20 of the Teachings and Commandments (also in December of 1830) that it says (to again, Joseph and Sidney Rigdon): *Behold, I say unto you...it is not expedient in me that you should translate anymore until you shall go to the Ohio, and this because of the enemy and for your sakes* (T&C 20:1) So, the work was interrupted later in December, but they were very productive. Much of what we have—in fact, I think all of what we have in the book of Moses of the Pearl of Great Price—existed between the starting point when the commandment was given in December and the ending point when the command was said to them, "Okay, stop for now, and we'll pick this up again in Ohio—that was given on the 30th of December 1830. The first commandment to commence the work was given on the 7th of December. So, in 23 days, they managed to produce what we've got in the book of Moses.

Then the next commandment to deal with it is given on the 9th of February of 1831. *You shall be directed by the spirit, which shall be given you by the prayer of faith, and if you receive not the spirit, you shall not teach. And all this you shall observe to do as I have commanded concerning your teaching,* ***until*** *the fullness of my scriptures are given* (T&C 26:5, emphasis added). Now, we read that first part (in the Latter-day Saint community) as referring to something about how you teach a gospel doctrine or a Sunday school class. But it's all based upon: When you teach, you need to know something, and you teach by the Spirit until I get the fullness of the Scriptures out there—because then you can base what you have to say upon something that is more accurate and more complete. And so, the fullness of the Scriptures gets mentioned again in February.

And then the next reference is made that same month of February. Oh, no. This one is in March. This one is in March. This one says, *Now behold, I say unto you, it shall not be given unto you to know any further than this until the New Testament be translated, and in it all these things shall be made known.*

Wherefore, I give unto you that you may now translate it (T&C 31:13). So, by the time you get to the March 1831 time-period, the effort that had been devoted to getting the Old Testament completed gets shifted—they'll return to the Old Testament—but it gets shifted to the New Testament, and they're told to proceed with the translation of the New Testament.

In all of these revelations that deal with the Scriptures/the fullness of the Scriptures/the revision of the Bible by inspiration through Joseph Smith under the direction of the Lord to give us the Scriptures as they are in the bosom of the Lord, the word that gets used continually to describe that effort is "translate." So, the word "translate" has a highly particularized meaning. It does not mean taking an ancient text and working it through with Hebrew (or working it through—in the case of the New Testament—with New Testament-era Greek language) and making it more accurate as moving it from one language into another. The word "translate" means "operate under the power of the Spirit through revelation to restore that which has been lost and to clarify that which is in the Lord's own bosom." So, when the word "translate" gets used in the context of this project, it's likely that that very same use of the word "translate" (in the vocabulary of Joseph Smith) means exactly the same thing when it comes to the book of Abraham. It would really help sharpen the focus if people were willing to concede that what Joseph Smith was doing was to operate under the spirit of inspiration in order to render what was lost **back** [into] something that is now in view and in a language that we can comprehend.

Well, the commandments about the Scripture translation process continue apace until—and I'm gonna skip all the intermediate ones—until we get to a commandment that was given in January of 1841 that approved Joseph Smith's offer of sacrifice—his prayer on behalf of the Saints—and allow the Saints to go forward with one more opportunity. If they would build a temple and complete it on time, then they would be not moved out of their place. But if they didn't do what was commanded, then they were warned that they would be rejected as a Church and as a people (along with their kindred dead), and they **would** be moved out of their place. And instead of the blessings and the prosperity of remaining anchored in what had been changed to the cornerstone of Zion in Nauvoo, they were warned that they would be cast out, they would be sent off in a place where they will experience plagues and difficulties and challenges, and that very same revelation in January of 1841—a lot of people are very familiar with—the revelation includes: If you will do it, *let him from henceforth hearken [unto] the counsel of my servant Joseph, and with his interest support the cause of the poor, and* ***publish the new translation of my holy word unto the inhabitants of the earth****. And if he* *will do this, I will bless him with a multiplicity of blessings…* (T&C 141:31, emphasis added) and so on. This is a statement to *my servant William* (ibid).

The effort to publish the new translation of the Scriptures (as it was directed in January of 1841) did not happen. There had been earlier commandments given (you can see them in the Teachings and Commandments) where this work was supposed to come out. And Joseph Smith said that if this publication of the revised translation of the Bible did not occur, then the Church would go into apostasy. It was essential for the salvation of the Church that it be given access to the fullness of the Scriptures.

Okay, so the New Testament translation that began in that March of 1831 time-frame apparently influenced how Joseph Smith revised the New Testament. We know that what was Doctrine and Covenants section 76 came as a result of the work having progressed to the book of John and him looking at (you know) the resurrection of the just and the resurrection of the unjust and how there had to be more than one condition in the afterlife. And so, D&C section 76 about the three degrees of glory in the afterlife come as a consequence of the translation of the book of John. So, you can fix exactly where they were in the New Testament effort by the date that D&C section 76 was given.

But before that, they were going through the book of Luke. In the book of Luke, Joseph Smith revised the warning that the Lord gives to the scribes and Pharisees that were confronting Him and questioning Him, and he changes the language of condemnation to read this way: *Woe unto you lawyers, for you have taken away the key of knowledge, the fullness of the scriptures. You enter not in yourselves into the kingdom, and those who were entering in, you hindered* (Luke 8:17 RE). So, He's talking to the scribes and Pharisees and condemning them. And in the original condemnation that was in the bosom of the Lord— telling you what He was upset about when He confronted them in this passage of condemnation—what He was upset about was they had taken away a key of knowledge, as it had once appeared in the Scriptures, before they were corrupted.

So, the revision work that Joseph did—the research necessary to recover it all —got completed, and the Scripture project has now gotten to the point that it has been completed. Everyone on the committee had unanimously agreed that it was completed. The proposal was that we present it to the Lord. Because the presentation of this issue for acceptance to the Lord was a milestone event, it was my conclusion that you don't just get together and spontaneously pray about something like that. It rather requires the same kind of respect and formality that you would have, for example, in the prayer for the dedication of the Lord accepting the Kirtland temple (which appears in the Doctrine and Covenants as section 109). And so, in response to the committee's desire to have prayer, I sat down one evening to compose a prayer that I had thought, "I could write something good to that end." And instead, when I sat down, the "Prayer for the Covenant" was given by revelation. The content of the prayer for acceptance of the project was given as what the Lord wanted to be said in connection with the presentation.

So, it's not—much like the Kirtland temple dedicatory prayer, which was given by revelation—it's not the work of a man or men. It's a revelation of what the Lord expected for the prayer to be. I've written hundreds of thousands of words trying to describe accurately the history of the Restoration and what went awry. The prayer that asks for acceptance in the covenant is far more succinct and far more accurate and far more impressive a statement than all of the words that I've written. And they tell you... I tried to re-create the history based upon what men had furnished and preserved and what could be uncovered in the record, and much of what I wrote was my best conclusion from study of what I think is a likely scenario to have happened. The "Prayer for the Covenant" is an actual statement by revelation of what in fact did happen. So, if you wanna know the history of the Restoration, read that revelatory prayer.

Well, as soon as the prayer was composed, the answer tumbled out. And so, when we got together as a committee, the prayer was approved by everyone unanimously. And then I read the "Answer to the Prayer" to everyone, and everyone unanimously approved it. There was one missing fellow from the committee who wasn't present when that got done. And so, after it had been approved unanimously with one missing vote, he happened to become available and to call in. And so, I took the call, left the meeting, read him everything, and he approved it as well. So, it was unanimously approved by everyone that was involved in the project. And so, it was a happy day for those that are involved.

Time and time again throughout the process, because we learned something that we didn't know before, greater intelligence necessitated starting over. We wound up restarting this project at least a half a dozen times. When people thought they had reached a conclusion, it restarted because greater light and understanding necessitates that you start again. The objective was never to produce a book. The objective was always to try and find—as best as humanly possible, through the most sincere and humble efforts of those involved—the most accurate retelling of what was originally intended.

Well, the truth is that despite all of our best efforts, we all knew that there were areas in which it was no longer possible to recover what might have been recovered when the original condemnation was made and the warning was given that the Church was under condemnation, 18 months after it had been organized. If they had acted on that **then**, they could have recovered all of it.

The original translation manuscript was put into the cornerstone; water damage made it rot. The printer's manuscript was copied; it was still available. But the copying of the printer's manuscript from the original translation manuscript can only be done in a comparison of about 22% of the text, because the original rotted. And so, when the two could be compared, we find that there were copying errors made at a rate of about 1 1/2 errors per page from trying to copy the original revelation into the translation. Joseph Smith made an effort to revise and bring it back more into conformity to the original revelation and was working on that in the 1842 timeframe, but he never finished his revisionary work to try and get the Book of Mormon back into print.

Well, we know there are things that we can't fix. So, when the prayer to the Lord was offered, we did not expect anything other than approving it. We didn't expect an "Attaboy." We didn't expect a "You've delighted Me." And we certainly didn't expect Him to say, "Perfect." And He didn't say that. What He said was that what has been done is adequate for the purposes that He has in mind to finish this up.

Long, arduous trek—everything got approved, not only by committee but by vote of people. Everyone accepted it. The Covenant was presented. The people voted on it, and the Scripture committee (as it turns out) and the effort that they produced led in turn to a Covenantal Restoration that the Lord apparently had intended all along when He inspired people to begin the process (a couple of years before the two groups got together, and we started on the Scripture project).

So, that's a background for what I want to talk about. So, having given the background, there are a couple of other projects that the covenant itself obligates those people who enter into the covenant are supposed to undertake. Those two projects that have been languishing since the time of the Restoration are taking the Book of Mormon—The Stick of Joseph in the Hands of Ephraim—to the remnant of the Jews, "mine ancient covenant people," and to take the Book of Mormon to the remnant of His covenant people that were in the Americas. So, we have a Scripture project that has been brought successfully to a conclusion, as concerns the Gentiles, and it has been made available in covenantal agreement between the Lord and the people to reclaim Gentiles and alter their status. But now the Gentiles who are in possession of this material have an obligation that the Lord imposes, by covenant, to take this same material to His ancient covenant people of the Jews and to take it to the Native American people.

Well, the work on the Hebrew version has taken two steps. One step is essentially an English-language version—because the majority of the Jewish people in the world can read and speak English. That work has been completed and is in publication, and people are aware of that—that's The Stick of Joseph. But a second effort is being undertaken to translate it into a biblical Hebrew version. Because that requires such extraordinarily particularized competency and familiarity with biblical Hebrew, we do not have the competency to accomplish that work through volunteer work. We have to hire that work to be done. We've found wonderfully capable people, and there are those who are donating to have professional people spend their time accomplishing a competent work into ancient Hebrew.

That doesn't mean that questions haven't arisen, because questions necessarily do arise. Some of the language that has been rendered into English (that have been provided in, for example, the Allegory of Zenos) present translation questions because of Hebrew options. And so, the work is being shepherded along as the translation process is undertaken—the objective being to have it be as accurate as possible to achieve a restatement of what the message was that's intended to go to that audience. But it's required from time to time in consultation, prayer, and revelation, and guidance from above, in order to get instructions to the translators correct so that the output reflects accurately what's needed. And that work is ongoing. And there are people who are supporting that financially, and it will continue apace. And when done, both the English version and the Hebrew version are going to be made available to the remnant of the Jews as something we can vouch for and, presumably, something that the Lord will accept before we take it to them, so that **it** operates to achieve covenantal status, again, for the ancient people.

There is also now an effort that has been put together to try and get a project done in order to take a version to the Native American people. And that's really what I wanna talk about. And all of this is just background for the moment we find ourselves there.

Unlike the effort that the Scripture project underwent (where we started with divergent groups, and then we brought it together to form a singular group—and to have, by unanimous agreement, a completed project), the work on a product for reaching out to the Native Americans **began** as a single group, and it has now fractured into multiple groups with, apparently…

I've tried to get the people together, in order to sit down and discuss—in an amicable and open exchange—a free flow of ideas to try and reach a unanimous agreement. And what I've been told is that while one of the fractions is willing to come in and sit down and talk, others are unwilling to do so; and so, the project is at an utter impasse. And apparently, right now the expectation is **multiple** versions of something is going to be put into print, and I can guarantee you that that will not be acceptable. In fact, I wouldn't even… I wouldn't even dream of presenting that to the Lord. That's the kind of thing that runs absolutely contrary to the Answer to the Prayer for Covenant. It runs absolutely contrary to the revelation about building the Master a house. It shows disunion; it shows disunity.

I believe, as I reflect back upon the original Scripture project, that the reason why it was acceptable to the Lord is because very strong personalities were able to come together and become one, that it was more important to the Lord that unity and oneness be achieved through that remarkable process than it was that the final product be absolutely better than it is. I think it was the learning experience of taking strong personalities approaching a difficult assignment and reaching agreement and unanimity by subordinating (as that email I wrote and read to you a minute ago helped facilitate, in the process of going from disunity to unity to enlightened output). In short, the book is evidence of an achievement of oneness, and therefore, the book stands as a symbol of acceptance of the Lord, acceptance of His way. Subordinating our disunity to come to agreement—it is a milestone achievement that represents exactly what the Lord is trying to achieve.

Now, there's a revelation in the Teachings and Commandments that says (this is T&C 138; it's the letter from Liberty Jail—this is the relevant part of that letter):

> *How much more dignified and noble are the thoughts of God than the vain imagination of the human heart? None but fools will trifle with the souls of men. How vain and trifling have been our spirits, our conferences, our councils, our meetings, our private as well as public conversations: too low, too mean, too vulgar, too condescending for the dignified characters of the called and chosen of God, according to the purposes of his will from before the foundation of the world.* (T&C 138:18-19)

We should never view our ambition to achieve a work as more important than submitting to the will of God. When we do that, no matter how well-intentioned we may be, we are trifling with the souls of men.

This whole thing is critically important because of what we learn about last-days' covenantal status of different groups which God is intending to bring back aboard. Now, I'll tell you the punchline before going through the Scriptures. The punchline is this:

The Jews, in their present ignorance, are the covenant people of God. And they are heirs of that covenant and will remain so until they are presented with ~~the Book of Joseph~~ The Stick of Joseph in the hands of Ephraim. At that moment, they must make a decision. If they choose to accept that, their covenant status is not only affirmed but also renewed. But if they reject that, they walk away and cease to be numbered with His Covenant People.

The exact same thing happens to the Native American people. They are currently under covenantal status. If you take the Book of Mormon to the Native Americans in the form that we have it (that has been accepted by covenant) and you present it to them and they accept that, then their covenant status is renewed and affirmed, and they are among the Covenant People of God. But if they reject it, then they are no longer numbered among the Covenant People.

We are trifling with the souls of men when we do a half-assed job to hurry into print a product that is going to cut one way or the other in the salvation of a group of people— remnant people—that the Lord Himself intends to redeem. None but fools would be trifling with this stuff. It is extraordinarily serious.

Gentiles become numbered with the House of Israel based upon their willingness to accept the covenant Book of Mormon that has been sustained and approved by God that was adopted by the people in the conference up in Boise and that is now available for people to look at. But you can't trifle with these things.

So, here's a passage from Second Nephi, the Lord speaking (this is a "Thus saith our God" passage):

> *I will soften the hearts of the gentiles, that they shall be like unto a father to them. Wherefore, the gentiles shall be blessed* ***and numbered*** *among the house of Israel. Wherefore, I will consecrate this land unto thy seed,* ***and they who shall be numbered among thy seed,*** *for ever, for the land of their*

> *inheritance; for it is a choice land, saith God unto me, above all other lands. Wherefore, I will have all men that dwell thereon that they shall worship me, saith God.* (2 Nephi 7:4 RE, emphasis added)

So, if the Gentiles are willing to accept the Book of Mormon because their hearts are soft, they get numbered among Israel, and they inherit the land. That's the status that people achieved when they accepted the Book of Mormon as a covenant.

The book of Alma… It talks about a group of people—these were particularly odious Lamanite people who had engaged in what they themselves viewed as a whole lot of bloodshed, a whole lot of murder. They were convicted in their hearts about all the blood that they had shed. But they repented. They buried their weapons. They would refuse then to fight further. (They would parent children who would fight further. They just themselves thought that there was too much blood that had been lost as a consequence of their own behavior to ever again risk going contrary to the will of God by shedding blood yet again.) So, this group of Lamanites (who were particularly bloody) converted, and then they came over after their conversion, and this is what the Book of Mormon records:

> *They were called by the Nephites, the people of Ammon; therefore, they were distinguished by that name ever after. And* ***they*** [these Lamanites who converted—***they***] *were numbered among the people of Nephi, and also numbered among the people who were of the church of God. And they were...distinguished [by] their zeal.* (Alma 15:9 RE, emphasis added)

So, when they converted and when they accepted it, they ceased to be numbered with the Lamanites, and they became numbered with the Nephites.

Then, in a passage later in Alma… This is Alma the Younger who is recording a visionary experience that he has had, talking about what he sees happening among his people many, many generations later and how that will eventually turn out. He's talking about the people that will be left after the ultimate collapse and slaughter of the Nephite people:

> *Yea, and then shall they see wars and [pestilence], yea, famine and bloodshed, even until the people of Nephi shall become extinct. Yea, and this because they shall dwindle in unbelief and fall into the works of darkness, and lasciviousness, and all manner of iniquities. Yea, I say unto you that because they shall sin against so great light and knowledge, ...I say unto you that from*

> *that day, even [unto] the fourth generation shall not all pass away before this great iniquity shall come. And when that great day cometh, behold, the time very soon cometh that those who are now, or the seed of those who are now numbered among the people of Nephi, shall no more be numbered among the people of Nephi. But whosoever remaineth and is not destroyed in that great and dreadful day shall be numbered among the ~~Nephites~~ [Lamanites].* (Alma 21:2 RE)

They are genealogically descended from Nephites. They lose their status. They cease to be numbered among Nephites; they become numbered among the Lamanites. Genealogically they are Nephite. They are no longer numbered among them in the eyes of God. They lose that status.

And then in the Third Nephi:

> *It came to pass...before this thirteenth year had passed away, the Nephites were threatened with utter destruction because of this war which had become exceeding[ly] sore. And it came to pass that those Lamanites who had united with the Nephites were numbered among the Nephites, and their curse was taken from them.* (3 Nephi 1:11 RE)

So, status changes based upon what one does with a covenantal offering presented to you under the direction and approval of God.

Perhaps you think that the Lamanite remnant aren't ready. And so, maybe fracturing the effort to present something to them that might offer them the hope of being renewed and restored to covenantal status is not going to succeed. So, let's present a fractured, divided, unapproved version that may as well be offered by an LDS missionary, and it won't matter anyway 'cause we're not gonna succeed. But if you figure that's the way to approach this project, then you're setting at naught, and you're defying the opportunity that has been presented through the covenant and the command that has been given to seek after and seek to reclaim these people.

We have a divinely inspired obligation. You can't rush that, and it doesn't matter if you have to start your project over a half a dozen times—or more. The output has to mirror the nobility of the objective that we have in mind. I think there are words to that effect (or I'm paraphrasing; they're better than I just said) in the Answer to the Prayer for Covenant. The cause you seek and the way you go about it both have to be equally noble. If you don't pursue it nobly, then it doesn't matter what your output is. Hastily putting together something that you're expecting to result in "covenantal opportunity" and "restoration" (to be extended to a remnant of people that God particularly had in mind at the time that the Book of Mormon first came out) should never be done in haste, should never be done carelessly, should never be done in a way that represents trifling with the souls of men.

And so, if we cannot come together in agreement to pursue a project as nobly and as unified and in conformity with the expectations the Lord imposed at the time of the Answer to the Prayer for Covenant, then I would say let's leave it for another generation more noble than us to accomplish the work and to do it then. And we'll focus our effort on trying to reach out to the remnant of the Jews. Because that work is proceeding apace, in a unified way (that represents the best efforts we can make with the financial help and support of those that are undertaking the direct work), and with the counsel, and with the inspiration, guidance, and revelation necessary to see that through to a successful completion. It's being pursued without trifling with the souls of men.

But if we can't do it for the Native peoples, then we can't do it. And some other people in some other day can undertake to accomplish a work that reflects the nobility of the purpose and what is in the heart of God. 'Cause if we can't do it the right way, then we ought not attempt it at all. We oughta just confess our sins, our shortness, and our inadequacy, and say, "Yea, so be it."

But if we want to achieve something, then the manner in which you go about attempting to achieve it must be as noble as the attempt to accomplish the work. The work has to be mirrored by the effort in the output and in the process. You can't go about accusing one another like Satan and say, "...And God bless this work, because by damn, we're gonna get you a book. And it's gonna be the best book I can do!" When under the inspiration of God (everyone that worked on the Scriptures knows), there were times when the output was far greater because of the inspiration, guidance, and light from heaven than anything we on our own could ever have achieved. If you expect the inspiration, guidance, and help/assistance from heaven, then you have to approach heaven in a meaningful way.

The foregoing was recorded on August 15th, 2020 in Sandy, Utah in front of a live audience.

121. Precious, Part 1

This is Part 1 of a special series exploring the commandment and need for us to become precious to each other.

DENVER: I'm sorry—I laugh at myself. I'm not a very good student. I'm embarrassingly oblivious to the obvious. I could tell you stories about that, but you would wonder at the Lord's patience. But, I wanted to know about Joseph and the Restoration, and details about what went on in Nauvoo and what has been going since Nauvoo, where and what and who, and I couldn't get enough questions out on the table. I was *obnoxious*—obnoxiously inquisitive. Nothing about the future, I want to know about the past up until now.

I saw what we were doing, and how apparently important that was, and how the Lord's watching over this.

And then the view expanded, and God's working with people that we won't encounter for some time still, to get them ready for what is coming. And He's surprisingly just as involved in caring for them as He is in attending to us.

Then the view increased another order of magnitude, and I could see *every* people, *everywhere*. And it doesn't matter who they are, where they are, or what their culture is—it doesn't matter where they are in this world—He is working to bring about, ultimately, their salvation as well.

And then it got ridiculous, because He has concerns about creations that are without number. But in trying to put it into words, this is the analogy that I've come up with:

Let's liken Zion to a bus station. And someone needs to build the bus station, and that might be us. And if we build a bus station, and we have a place that can receive people and that is a place of safety where they can pass through, when we finish with that, the bus station won't amount to much if someone doesn't build a bus. And *we're* not building that bus. And the buses that get built are not going to go anywhere if they don't have fuel, and someone's got to do *that*—and that's going to involve miners, and explorers, and manufacturers, and refiners—and transport people; and delivery mechanisms that God is working with. And when they finally *fill* the buses, that will be someone over whom God is responsible.

When they finally get to our bus station, we're not going to be the ones who stand there and say, "Yeah, we built the bus station! We rock!"

Zion is an absolutely critical component in the last days' plan of God and indispensable in the salvation of the souls of men, living and dead, but it's *just* a bus station. And through it will pass concourses of people with whom we've had *very* little responsibility.

When He says that there's going to come a time when the prophets are going to awaken and will no longer stay themselves, and they're going to come from the lands of the north, and they're going to come to the bus station to receive something at the hands of His servants Ephraim, in the boundaries of the everlasting hills, He's working on that. And He's working with people *on* that.

And *we* need to be about what He's asked us to do. And it's important; it's indispensable. But it's absolutely no more indispensable than what He's doing among people in Asia and Europe and Africa, and *everywhere else* in the world. And He promises— You read along in the scriptures, He tells you: After the voice of warning then He's going to preach a sermon, and His sermon is going to *shake* and *cause fear*. And it's not because He's an angry God; it's because He's a loving God who knows what it takes to stir people up, to get attention, to consider the things of eternity.

But that's essentially— It's hard to put into words what— That's the analogy, and I think it conveys the meaning because He is the God of the whole world and *every soul* is precious to Him. And Christ's atonement was intended to yield the absolute greatest benefit that can be obtained through the suffering of the Lord, and for some people *their reluctance* is *no deterrent* to the Lord's desire to save them then. I think Zion needs to be people that receive the word with gladness, and not people we'd contend with to bring the word. I am *really* interested to see what will happen up in Boise; I think that is going to be an interesting moment.

Today marks a moment when the stirrings that have been underway *for years* result in God's offering to establish *His* people, on earth, by a covenant He ordains. The few ready to receive the Lord's offer today are scattered to the nethermost parts of His vineyard (that's verse 52). (See Jacob 5; see also Jacob 3:23-28 RE.)

Despite this, a live broadcast on the Internet allows *them* to be grafted in at the same moment this is happening in Boise, Idaho. Correspondingly, those who utterly refused to accept the offered covenant are *plucked* from the

Restoration's tree of life because they are bitter fruit, unable to meet the Lord's requirements.

The Lord is taking this step to preserve part of humanity, not to destroy it (that's verse 53). A few descendants of the covenant Fathers have the natural gift of faith; that gift belongs to the natural branches (that's verse 54). When grafted, we are connected to the natural roots, or covenant Fathers, as heirs of the promises made to them. Even after the covenant there will still be those who are bitter and wild, who will be unable to produce natural fruit, despite the covenant. These will remain for a time, despite their bitterness (verses 56 and 57). Today only the most bitter, who refuse to be grafted in, will be trimmed away.

We look forward to more *nourishing*, or restoring of truths, lights, and commandments, which will bless those who receive. But for those who will not, the continuing Restoration will prune them away (verse 58). These bitter and wild branches must still be cut off and cast away. These steps are necessary to preserve the opportunity for the natural fruit to fully return (that's verse 59). The *good* must overcome the *evil.* This takes time, and it means that the Lord's patience is extended to *give* time to develop and further improve.

We are not expected and cannot become natural fruit in a single step. But we are expected to accept the initial graft today. The Lord is taking these steps so that *perhaps* (and that's a deliberate word), *perhaps* we may become natural fruit worthy to be preserved in the coming harvest (that's verse 60). "Perhaps" is the right word. Some who are grafted will still be plucked away and burned, but others will bear natural fruit and be preserved.

Accepting the covenant is not the final step. Our choices will determine whether we are bitter or natural fruit—*that* will decide our fate. Just as the ancient allegory foretold, the covenant makes us servants and laborers in the vineyard (verse 61). We are required to (this is from the covenant), *"Seek to recover the lost sheep remnant of this land and of Israel, and no longer forsake them. Bring them unto [the Lord] and teach them of [His] ways, to walk in them."* (T&C 158:11 RE.) If we fail to labor to recover them, we break the covenant. We must labor for this last time in the Lord's vineyard.

There *is* an approaching, final pruning of the vineyard (verse 62). The first to be grafted in are Gentiles, so that the last may be first. The lost sheep remnant next, and then Israelites, so that the first may be last (verse 63). But grafting is required for all, even the remnants, because God works with His people through covenant-making.

There will be more grafting and further pruning. As more is revealed, and therefore more is required, some will find the *digging* and *dunging* too much to bear and will fall away; or in other words, will be pruned despite the covenant (that's verse 64). The covenant makes it possible for natural fruit to return. The bad fruit will still continue, even among the covenant people, until there is enough strength in the healthy branches for further pruning.

It requires natural fruit to appear before the final pruning takes place (verse 65). The good and bad will coexist. It will damage the tree to remove the bad at once. Therefore the Lord's patience will continue for some time yet. The rate of removing the bad is dependent wholly upon the rate of the development of the good.

It is the Lord's purpose to create *equality* in his vineyard. In the allegory, equality in the vineyard appears three times—in verses 66, ~~72~~ [73], and 74. We cannot be greater and lesser, nor divide ourselves into a hierarchy to achieve the equality required for Zion. When a group is determined to remain equal (and I am personally determined to be no greater than any other), then it faces challenges that never confront unequal people. A religion of bosses and minions never deals with *any* of the challenges of being equals.

Critics claim we will never succeed because of our determined desire for equality. *None of our critics* can envision what the Lord has said in verses 66, ~~72~~ [73], and 74 about His people. But equality among us is the *only way* prophesied for us to succeed. That does not mean we won't have a mess as we learn *how* to establish equality.

Similarly, Zion cannot be established by isolated and solitary figures proclaiming a "testimony of Jesus" from their home keyboard. The challenge of building a community must be part of a process. Zion is a community, and therefore God is a God of community, and His people must learn to live together with one heart, one mind, with no poor among us. Isolated keyboardists proclaiming their resentment of community can hardly speak temperately of others. How could *they* ever live peacefully in a community of equals?

We must become precious to each other.

Although the laborers in this final effort are few, *you will* be the means used by the Lord to complete His work in His vineyard (verse 70). You're required to labor with your might to finish the Lord's work in His vineyard (verse 72) —but *He* will labor alongside you. *He*, not a man or a committee, will call *you* to do work. When He calls, do not fear—but do not run faster than you have strength. We must find His people in the highways and byways, and invite them to join in. Zion will include people from every part of the world. This conference is broadcast worldwide as part of the prophecy to Enoch that God would send:

> *Righteousness and truth will [he] cause to sweep the earth as with a flood, to gather out mine elect from the four quarters of the earth, unto a place which I shall prepare, an Holy City, that my people may gird up their loins, and be looking forth for the time of my coming; for there shall be my tabernacle, and it shall be called Zion, a New Jerusalem.* (Moses 7:62; see also Genesis 4:22 RE)

We must proclaim this to the world.

Do not despair when further pruning takes place; it must be done. Only through pruning can the Lord keep His tree of life equal, without those who are lofty overcoming the body (verse 73). The lofty branches have *always* destroyed equality to prevent Zion.

The final result of the Lord's labor in His vineyard is declared by the ancient prophet in unmistakable clarity:

> *The trees have become again the natural fruit; and they became like unto one body; and the fruits were equal; and the Lord of the vineyard had preserved unto himself the natural fruit, which was most precious unto him* ***from the beginning***. ([Emphasis added.] Jacob 5:74; see also Jacob 3:27 RE)

Mark those words. (That's verse 74.)

When the Lord explained this to me, I realized how foolish it was to expect "natural fruit," worthy of preservation, in an instant. The Lord works patiently, methodically, and does not require any to run faster than they have strength. We cannot allow ourselves to be drawn into inequality when the result of this labor is to make us one body, equal with one another. We cannot imitate the failures of the past by establishing a hierarchy, elevating one above another, and forgetting that we must be of one heart, one mind, and no poor among us.

The Restoration was never intended to just restore an ancient Christian church—that is only a halfway point; it must go back further. In the words of the ancient prophet, God intends to do *"according to [His] will; and [to preserve] the natural fruit, that it is good, even like as it was in the beginning"* (verse 75). This means the beginning, as in the days of Adam, with the return of the original religion and original authority. Everything must be returned as it was in the beginning. Civilization began with the temple as the center of learning, law, and culture. The temple was the original "university" because it taught of man's place with God in the universe.

God will return the right of dominion, once held by Adam, to man on earth to make us humble, servant-gardeners laboring to return the world to a peaceful Paradise. The covenant received today restores part of that right. There is a land inheritance given to us as part of the covenant, and therefore if we keep the covenant, we have the right to remain when others will be swept away.

Ultimately, all rights given to us must be turned back to the Fathers who went before, who will likewise return them to Adam, who will surrender them to Christ. When Christ returns, He will come with the right to exercise complete dominion over the earth and exercise judgment over the ungodly.

Things set into motion today are part of preparing the way for the Lord's return in glory.

> [Quoting from the Answer & Covenant:] *I covenanted with Adam at the beginning, which covenant was broken by mankind. Since the days of Adam I have always sought to reestablish people of covenant among the living, and therefore have desired that man should love one another, not begrudgingly, but as brothers and sisters indeed, that I may establish my covenant and provide them with light and truth.*
>
> *For you to unite I must admonish and instruct you, for my will is to have you love one another. As people you lack the ability to respectfully disagree among one another. You are as Paul and Peter whose disagreements resulted in jarring and sharp contentions. Nevertheless they both loved me and I loved them. You must do better.*
>
> *I commend your diligent labor, and your desire to repent and recover the scriptures containing the covenant I offer for the last days. For this purpose I caused the Book of Mormon to come forth. I commend those who have participated, as well as those who have offered words of caution, for I weigh the hearts of men and many have intended well, although they have spoken*

poorly. Wisdom counsels mankind to align their words with their hearts, but mankind refuses to take counsel from Wisdom.

Nevertheless, there have been sharp disputes between you that should have been avoided. I speak these words to reprove you that you may learn, not to upbraid you so that you mourn. I want my people to have understanding.

There is great reason to rejoice because of the work that has been done. There is little reason for any to be angry or to harshly criticize the labor to recover the scriptures, and so my answer to you concerning the scriptures is to guide you in other work to be done hereafter; for recovering the scriptures does not conclude the work to be accomplished by those who will be my people: it is but a beginning.

In your language you use the name Lucifer for an angel who was in authority before God, who rebelled, fought against the work of the Father and was cast down to the earth. His name means holder of light, or light bearer, for he had gathered light by his heed and diligence before he rebelled. He has become a vessel containing only wrath and seeks to destroy all who will hearken to him. He is now enslaved to his own hatred.

Satan is a title, and means accuser, opponent and adversary; hence once he fell, Lucifer became, or in other words was called, Satan, because he accuses others and opposes the Father. I rebuked Peter and called him Satan because he was wrong in opposing the Father's will for me, and Peter understood and repented.

In the work you have performed there are those who have been Satan, accusing one another, wounding hearts and causing jarring, contention, and strife by their accusations. Rather than loving one another, even among you who desire a good thing, some have dealt unkindly as if they were the opponents, accusers, and adversaries. In this they were wrong.

You have sought to recover the scriptures because you hope to obtain the covenant for my protective hand to be over you, but you cannot be Satan and be mine. If you take upon you my covenant, you must abide it as a people to gain what I promise. You think Satan will be bound a thousand years, and it will be so, but do not understand your own duty to bind that spirit within you so that you give no heed to accuse others. It is not enough to say you love God; you must also love your fellow man. Nor is it enough to say you love your fellow man while you, as Satan, divide, contend, and dispute against any person who labors on an errand seeking to do my will. How you proceed must be as noble as the cause you seek. You have become your own adversaries, and you cannot be Satan and also be mine. Repent, therefore, like Peter and end your unkind and untrue accusations against one another, and make peace. How shall there ever come a thousand years of peace if the people who are mine do not love one another? How shall Satan be bound if there are no people of one heart and one mind?

For the sake of the promises to the Fathers [I will] labor with you as a people, and not because of you, for you have not yet become what you must be to live together in peace. If you will hearken to my words, I will make you my people and my words will give you peace. Even a single soul who stirs up the hearts of others to anger can destroy the peace of all my people. Each of you must equally walk truly in my path, not only to profess, but also to do as you profess.

The Book of Mormon was given as my covenant for this day and contains my gospel, which came forth to allow people to understand my work and then obtain my salvation. Yet many of you are like those who reject the Book of Mormon, because you say, but you do not do. As a people you honor with your lips, but your hearts are corrupt, filled with envy and malice, returning evil for good, sparing none, even those with pure hearts among you, from your unjustified accusations and unkind backbiting. You have not obtained the fullness of my salvation because you do not draw near to me.

The Book of Mormon is to convince the gentiles, and a remnant of Lehi, and the Jews, of the truth of the words of my ancient prophets and apostles, with all the records agreeing that I am the Lamb of God, the Son of the Father, and I was sent into the world to do the will of the Father, and I am the Savior of the world. All must come unto me or they cannot be saved. And how do men come unto me? It is by faith, repentance, and baptism, which bring the Holy Ghost to then show you all things you must know.

If the gentiles unto whom the Book of Mormon was given had hearkened unto the Holy Ghost, they would have come unto me in Hyrum and Joseph's day. But they did not hearken, and would not allow me to abide with them in word, and in power, and in very deed.

Hear therefore my words: Repent and bring forth fruit showing repentance, and I will establish my covenant with you and claim you as mine.

It is not enough to receive my covenant, but you must also abide it. And all who abide it, whether on this land or any other land, will be mine and I will watch over them and protect them in the day of harvest, and gather them in as a hen gathers her chicks under her wings. I will number you among the remnant of Jacob, no longer outcasts, and you will inherit the promises of Israel. You shall be my people and I will be your God and the sword will not devour you. And unto those who will receive will more be given until they know the mysteries of God in full.

But remember that without the fruit of repentance, and a broken heart and a contrite spirit, you cannot keep my covenant; for I, your Lord, am meek and lowly of heart. Be like me. You have all been wounded, your hearts pierced through with sorrows because of how the world has treated you. But you have also scarred one another by your unkind treatment of each other, and you do not notice your misconduct toward[s] others because you think yourself justified in this. You bear the scars on your countenances, from the soles of your feet to the head, and every heart is faint. Your visages have been so marred that your hardness, mistrust, suspicions, resentments, fear, jealousies, and anger toward your fellow man bear outward witness of your inner self; you cannot hide it. When I appear to you, instead of confidence you feel shame. You fear and withdraw from me because you bear the blood and sins of your treatment of brothers and sisters. Come to me and I will make sins as scarlet become white as snow, and I will make you stand boldly before me, confident of my love.

I descended below it all, and know the sorrows of you all, and have borne the grief of it all and I say to you, Forgive one another. Be tender with one another, pursue judgment, bless the oppressed, care for the orphan, and uplift the widow in her need for I have redeemed you from being orphaned and taken you that you are no longer a widowed people. Rejoice in me, and rejoice with your brethren and sisters who are mine also. Be one.

There remains [a] great work yet to be done. Receive my covenant and abide in it, not as in the former time when jarring, jealousy, contention, and backbiting caused anger, broke hearts, and hardened the souls of those claiming to be my saints. But receive it in spirit, in meekness, and in truth. I have given you a former commandment that I, the Lord, will forgive whom I will forgive, but of you it is required to forgive all men. And again, I have taught that if you forgive men their trespasses your Heavenly Father will also forgive you; but if you forgive not men their trespasses neither will your Heavenly Father forgive your trespasses. How do I act toward mankind: If men intend no offense I take no offense, but if they are taught and should have obeyed, then I reprove and correct and forgive and forget. You cannot be at peace with one another if you take offense when none is intended. But again I say, Judge not others except by the rule you want used to weigh yourself.

My eyes are over the whole earth and all men everywhere are before me. Men conspire to overthrow and oppress, and use violence to control others through fear. My Spirit restrains the destroyer to allow those who are in the world and willing to give heed to my words time to prepare, but I will not always suffer...the wickedness of man.

The Earth groans under the wickedness of mankind upon her face, and she longs for peace to come. She withholds the abundance of her bounty because of the offenses of men against me, against one another, and against her. But if righteousness returns and my people prove by their actions, words, and thoughts to yield to my Spirit and hearken to my commandments, then will the Earth rejoice, for the feet of those who cry peace upon her mountains are beautiful indeed, and I, the Lord, will bring again Zion, and the earth will rejoice.

In the world tares are ripening...so I ask you, What of the wheat? Let your pride, and your envy, and your fears depart from you. [And] I will come to my tabernacle and dwell with my people in Zion, and none will overtake it.

Cry peace. Proclaim my words. Invite those who will repent to be baptized and forgiven, and they shall obtain my Spirit to guide them. The time is short and I come quickly, therefore open your mouths and warn others to flee the wrath which is to come as men in anger destroy one another. The wicked shall destroy the wicked, and I will hold the peacemakers in the palm of my hand and none can take them from me.

Be comforted, be of good cheer, rejoice, and look up, for I am with you who remember me, and all those who watch for me, always, even unto the end.

The foregoing excerpts are taken from:

- Denver's comments during an assembly on "Missionary Work" in Eden, Utah, on July 2, 2016;
- His "Opening Remarks," given at the Covenant of Christ Conference in Boise, Idaho, on September 3rd, 2017; and

- The presentation of "Answer and Covenant," given at the Covenant of Christ Conference in Boise, Idaho, on September 3rd, 2017.

122. Precious, Part 2

This is Part 2 of a special series exploring the commandment and need for us to become precious to each other.

STEPHANIE: Enos 2 and 3 says:

> *Now it came to pass that when I had heard these words, I began to feel a desire for the welfare of my brethren the Nephites; wherefore, I did pour out my whole soul unto God for them. And while I was...struggling in the spirit, behold, the voice of the Lord came into my mind again, saying, I will visit thy brethren according to their diligence in keeping my commandments. I have given unto them this land, and it is a holy land; and I curse it not, save it be for the cause of iniquity. Wherefore, I will visit thy brethren according as I have said, and their transgressions will I bring down with sorrow upon their own heads. And after I, Enos, had heard these words, my faith began to be unshaken in the Lord. And I prayed unto him with many long strugglings for my brethren the Lamanites.*
>
> *And it came to pass that after I had prayed and labored with all diligence, the Lord said unto me, I will grant unto thee according to thy desires because of thy faith. And now behold, this was the desire which I desired of him: that if it should [be so] that my people the Nephites should fall into transgression, and by any means be destroyed, and the Lamanites should not be destroyed, that the Lord God would preserve a record of my people [that] the Nephites, even if it so be by the power of his holy arm, that it might be brought forth some future day unto the Lamanites, that perhaps* ***they*** *might be brought unto salvation. For at the present, our strugglings were vain in restoring them to the true faith. And they swore in their wrath that if it were possible, they would destroy our records, and us, and also [our] traditions of our fathers.* ([Emphasis added.] Enos 1:3-4 RE)

In Helaman 4:2, it says:

> *And it came to pass that in this year Nephi did cry unto the Lord, saying, O Lord, do not suffer that this people shall be destroyed by the sword, but O Lord, rather let there be a famine in the land to stir them up in remembrance of the Lord their God, and perhaps they will repent and turn unto thee. And so it was done according to the words of Nephi, and there was a great famine upon the land, among all the people of Nephi. And thus in the seventy and*

fourth year the famine did continue, and the work of destruction did cease by the sword, but became sore by famine. And this work of destruction did also continue in the seventy and fifth year. For the earth was smitten, that it was dry and did not yield forth grain in the season of grain; and the whole earth was smitten, even among the Lamanites as well as among the Nephites, so that they were smitten that they did perish by thousands in the more wicked parts of the land. (Helaman 4:2 RE)

And then we move on to Nephi—and just as a side note, I'm pretty sure Nephi did not love his brothers, 'kay? I just don't think he did. They were abusive; they were violent; and they were fratricidal, okay? But, this is what he does—Nephi 2:4:

And it came to pass that when I, Nephi, had spoken these words unto my brethren, they were angry with me. [Yes, so what's new? They were always angry with him.] *...But it came to pass that I prayed unto the Lord, saying, O Lord, according to **my** faith which is in thee, wilt thou deliver me from the hands of my brethren? And it came to pass that when I said these words, behold, the bands were loosed from off my hands and feet, and I stood before my brethren and I spake unto them again. ...And it came to pass that **I did frankly forgive them** all that they had done, and I did exhort them that they would pray unto the Lord their God for forgiveness. ...And after they had done praying unto the Lord, we did again [a] travel on our journey towards the tent of our father.* ([Emphasis added.] 1 Nephi 2:4 RE)

Genesis 11:4-9—again, another story of fratricide, 'kay? Pretty sure Joseph didn't love his brothers, and his brothers certainly didn't love him, because 4-9. *And a cert...* Genesis 11:4-9:

And a certain man found him, and behold, he was wandering in the field. And the man asked him, saying, What do you seek? And he said, I seek my [brothers]; tell me, I pray you, where they feed their flocks? And the man said, They are departed from here, for I heard them say, Let us go to Dothan.

And Joseph went after his brethren and found them... [And when he comes, they see him, and they conspire against to slay him.] *And they said one to another, Behold, this dreamer comes.* [They don't even call him by name, okay? And they have so much contempt for Joseph that they just call him "the dreamer."] *Come now therefore and let us slay him and cast him into [the] pit, and we will say some evil beast has devoured him, and we shall see what will become of his dreams.*

> *And Reuben heard it, and he delivered him out of their hands and said, [Let's] not kill him. And Reuben said...Shed no blood, but cast him into this pit...* [That's great—we'll just cast him in this pit…]
>
> [Verse 7:] *And it came to pass when Joseph had come unto his brethren...they stripped Joseph out of his coat, his coat of many colors that was on him, ...they took him and cast him into a pit. And the pit was empty, [and] there was no water....*
>
> *And they sat down to eat...* [And lo and behold, they see] *a company of Ishmaelites [coming] from Gilead with their camels bearing spicery, and balm, and myrrh, going to carry it down to Egypt. And Judah said...*[Hey,] *What profit [it is] if we slay...and conceal his blood? Come...let us sell him to the Ishmaelites...let not our hand be upon him, for he is our brother and our flesh.* [Well, that's nice. We don't hate him enough to kill him, but we just sell him to this band of Ishmaelites.] *And his brethren were content.*
>
> [So, they sell him for 20 pieces of silver. Reuben went back to the pit; Joseph wasn't in it.] *He rent his clothes. And he returned [to] his brethren and said, The child is not; and I, where shall I go? And they took Joseph's coat, ...killed...the [goat], ...dipped the coat in...blood. And they sent the coat of many colors, and they brought it to their father and [they] said,* [Oh, oh, oh, it's so terrible!] (Genesis 11:4-9 RE)

Okay, so you know the story. Lots of stuff happens, and then this—Genesis 11:39 and 40:

> *Then Joseph could not refrain himself before all them that stood by him, and he cried, Cause every man to go out from me! And there stood no man with him while Joseph made himself known unto his brethren. And he wept aloud, and the Egyptians and the house of Pharaoh heard. And Joseph said unto his brethren, I am Joseph. Does my father yet live? And his brethren could not answer him, for they were troubled at his presence.* [Because, yeah, what happened to you?] *And Joseph said unto his brethren, Come near to me, I pray you. And they came near. And he said, I am Joseph, your brother whom you sold into Egypt. Now therefore be not grieved nor angry with yourselves that you sold me here, for God did send me before you to preserve life. For these two years has the famine been in the land, and yet there are five years in which there shall neither be plowing nor harvest. And God sent me before you to preserve your posterity and the earth and to save your lives by a great deliverance. So now it was not you that sent me here, but God. And he has made me a father to Pharaoh, and [a] lord of all his house, and a ruler*

> *throughout all the land[s] of Egypt.* [And more happens and more happens...]
>
> *And he fell upon his brother Benjamin's neck and wept. And Benjamin wept upon his neck. [And], he kissed all his brethren and [he] wept upon them. And after that, his brethren talked with him.* (Genesis 11:39-40 RE)

Wow! The foregoing scriptures illustrate that forgiveness, intercession, and relationships *do not* have to be based on love, as we culturally define it here.

So, let's get back to who our neighbors are. We're going to start with the most intimate relationships and work out from there. At the top should be my relationship with the Gods, which is not always my focus, but ideally, it should be. And then we go partner/spouse, family/children, extended family (aunts, uncles, in-laws), friends, co-workers, religious community, work community, neighborhood—blah, blah, blah— until we get down to our enemies. The makeup of these relationships might look different for everyone. Some of us may have all of them and some of us may have only a few, but we all have intimate and significant associations or relationships, and we all have enemies.

So, how do we do it? How do we love them? So, as a side note, I would like to make a distinction here—*service is not love.* It can be *motivated* by love, but there's a difference because serving is actually quite easy—dropping off my gently-used clothes, tithing, dollar bills, blankets, granola, water bottles, taking my old-but-I'm-getting-a-new washer or dryer to someone in need, plant a garden, make a casserole, take a salad or a dessert. Don't get me wrong —these are great; we should engage in these. These are really nice things to do. However, they can be done at an arm's length—no conversation, no association, no relationship, no love, no risk.

Relationships are where the real work takes place. Relationships are difficult, and effortless; they are risky, and they are safe; they are uncomfortable, and they are comfortable; they are rich and rewarding; and they ebb, and they flow. They are *the vehicle* wherein we move through and into love, charity, sanctification, and ultimately, salvation. To be a part of the family of God up there requires us to *create* a family of God down here.

When I read an article or hear a news story about some tremendous act of forgiveness, on the part of someone who has given absolution to another person for some grievous offense, I think, "So what?!" The dad who forgives the drunk driver who killed his entire family; the woman who forgives the man who raped her; the elderly man who doesn't hold a grudge against the businessman who conned him and stole all his money—so what?! We treat these instances as though they are great acts of emotional heroism. We heap praise and adulation upon the people who are so *magnanimous* that they forgave the horrible bastard who grieved or assaulted or offended them. It's ridiculous! We *lie* to ourselves when and if we think we are *ever* justified in resentment, grudges, judgments, or accusations. *We are not—ever.*

The Lord's standard is pretty clear, and there's not much wiggle room. You want Heavenly Father to forgive *you*? You forgive each other. That sounds like a really good way of *loving yourself.* Forgiveness is a *requirement*—it is a *condition*—and the Lord has this to say about it—3 Nephi 5:34:

> *And forgive us our debts as we forgive our debtors.... For if ye forgive men their trespasses, your Heavenly Father will also forgive you, but if [you] forgive not men their trespasses, neither will your Father forgive your trespasses.* (3 Nephi 5:34 RE)

Colossians 1:13:

> *Put on therefore as the elect of God, holy and beloved, hearts of mercies, kindness, humility of mind, meekness, long-suffering, bearing with one another and* ***forgiving*** *one another. If any man have a quarrel against any, even as Christ forgave you, so also do you; and above all these things put on charity, which is the bond of perfectness...let the word of Christ dwell in you richly, in all wisdom, teaching and admonishing one another in psalms, and hymns, and spiritual songs, singing with* ***grace*** *in your hearts to the Lord. And whatever you do in word or deed, do* ***all*** *in the name of the Lord Jesus, giving thanks to God and the Father by him.* ([Emphasis added.] Colossians 1:13 RE)

This sounds like loving yourself. Teaching[s] and Commandments section 157:58:

> *I have given you a former commandment that I, the Lord, will forgive whom I will forgive, but of you it is required to forgive all men. And again, I have taught that if you forgive men their trespasses, your Heavenly Father will also forgive you; but if you forgive not men their trespasses, neither will your Heavenly Father forgive your trespasses.... If men intend no offense, I take no offense, but if they are taught and should have obeyed, then I reprove and correct, and forgive and forget.* (T&C 157:58)

God is the *only* one who judges correctly. He is the only one who can decide whether an offense was intended or not, and then *He* reproves, corrects, *forgives and forgets.* We are rarely worthy to judge, and we are *only* able to reprove and correct people we have a relationship with—and we are *always* expected to forgive and forget.

So, the real question comes down to this: Do we believe these words? It's pretty much that simple. Relationships—with spouses, children, co-workers, parents, siblings, friends, enemies—require vulnerability, work, and a *deliberate* effort to see the good and *be* the good. Relationships are emotionally fulfilling. People who have community live longer and healthier lives. Working on those relationships and having them be positive and uplifting, for *your* benefit, sounds like *loving yourself.*

I have a simple formula that works for me, and I'll share it with you. I figure that every single interaction I have with another human being will achieve one of three things:

- The experience will either build our relationship with a positive interaction;
- It will leave it unchanged or 'status quo;'
- Or, it will tear down the relationship with a negative interaction.

Grocery store clerks, gas station attendants, students, teachers, husbands, children—doesn't matter.

The good news about this formula for me is that I get to choose, *every single time* with *every single person.* It's *never* out of my control. There is no love for others, *or yourself,* if your time is spent focusing on flaws, criticizing, imputing intent, or taking offense for no good reason.

Here's what the Lord says about judgment, flaws, criticism, ascribing motive, offense, and intent—and it's time we start taking Him seriously. So, He moves on from the Ten Commandments to the Sermon on the Mount. In Matthew 3:40, He says:

> *Now these are the words which Jesus taught his disciples that they should say unto the people: judge not unrighteously, that you be not judged, but judge righteous judgment; for with what judgment you shall judge, you shall be judged, and with what measure you mete, it shall be measured to you again.* (Matthew 3:40 RE)

(It's like a person-with-a-cold's worst nightmare. [Audience laughter.])

The difference here that I see, between the "no judging" and the "righteous judgment," is likely related to Final Judgment—as opposed to all those in-between judgments that we can do, if we *think* we have the Lord on our side, in terms of righteous judgment.

And then moving from Matthew into 3 Nephi—3 Nephi chapter 6, verse 6:

> *And why beholdest thou the mote that is in thy brother's eye, but considerest not the beam that is in thine own eye? Or how wilt thou say to thy brother, let me pull [that] mote out of thine eye, and behold a beam is in thine own eye? Thou hypocrite, first cast out the beam...of thine own eye, and then shalt thou see clearly to cast out the mote out of thy brother's eye. Give not that which is holy unto the dogs, neither cast ye your pearls before swine, lest they trample them under their feet, and turn again, and rend you.* (3 Nephi 6:6 RE)

And so, I say to that: What the heck does that have to do with anything? So, on the assumption that it is actually *related* to what came before that, I spent a reasonable amount of time contemplating it, and this is my version of pearls and swine and dogs, and whatever—it's a strange ending to this particular thought. So, what if it means that *we* are the dogs and swine, and judging is a holy and precious act—one that we don't have anywhere *near* the godliness to engage in, at least without seriously pursuing God's help. And we will get out of the attempt, and *all* we will get out of the attempt at that kind of judging, is trampling and rending. So, that's my take. And so, let's not do it, okay? Let's just not do it.

In the foregoing scriptures, we are being told to worry about ourselves *first*—and *that* should take a long, long, *long* time. And then, if we need to, we can worry about other people after that. So, in theory, if we're as critical towards ourselves as we are others, we should be doing a lot of repenting, improving, growing in love and charity and empathy, as we make ourselves better. Because it's just about beams and motes, people; that's it! Just don't do it!

When it comes to our interpersonal life, knowing how to make yourself better takes a lot of courage and introspection; you have to be willing to be clear on what's wrong with *you*. It's a lot easier to think about what's wrong with other people. So, asking questions like—

- How did I make that better or worse?
- What did I do or say to make them react that way?

- What did I say or do to cause their defensiveness?

- Or, why did I do or say what I did or said, *and* how and what could I have done differently?

—are absolutely necessary in order to become more Christ-like. However, if focusing on other people is your jam, then do it charitably—impute the highest motive and best motive to other people, assume their best intentions, engage in empathy and perspective-taking. These are godly acts. They make *your* life better. They wash away the bitterness, anger, hurt, and unhappiness *you* feel when you're focused on the negative. *This* sounds like *loving yourself.*

Ephesians 12, and 16:

> *I, therefore, the prisoner of the Lord, implore you that you walk worthy of the vocation with which you are called, [and] with all lowliness and meekness, with long-suffering, bearing with one another in love, endeavoring to keep the unity of the spirit in the bond of peace, in one body [in] one spirit, even as you are called in one hope of your calling — one Lord, one faith, one baptism, one God and Father of all, who is above all, and through all, and in you all.*
>
> *Wherefore, putting away lying, speak every man truth with his neighbor, for we are members one of another. Can you be angry and sin not? Let not the sun go down upon your wrath, neither give place to the Devil. Let him that stole steal no more, but rather let him labor, working with his hands for the things which are good, that he may have to give to him that needs. Let no corrupt communication proceed out of your mouth, but that which is good to use of edifying, that it may minister grace unto the hearers. And grieve not the holy spirit of God whereby you are sealed unto the day of redemption. Let all bitterness...wrath, and anger, and clamor, and evil speaking be put away from you with all malice. And be kind one to another, tender-hearted, forgiving one another, even as God for Christ's sake has forgiven you. Be therefore followers of God, as dear children, and walk in love, as Christ [has also] loved us and has given himself for us, an offering and a sacrifice to God for a sweet-smelling savor.* (Ephesians 1:12,16 RE)

So, it still comes down to one simple question: Do I believe the words of God?

And *then*, He raises the standard again—3 Nephi 5:24 through 26, 30, and 31:

> [24:] *Ye have heard that it hath been said by them of old time, and it is also written before you, that thou shalt not kill, and whosoever shall kill shall be in danger of the judgment of God. But I say unto you that whosoever is angry with his brother shall be in danger of his judgment. And whosoever shall say to his brother, Raca, shall be in danger of the council, and whosoever shall say, Thou fool, shall be in danger of hellfire.*
>
> [25:] *Therefore, if ye shall come unto me, or shall desire to come unto me, and rememberest that thy brother hath aught against thee, go thy way unto thy brother and first be reconciled to thy brother, and then come unto me with full purpose of heart and I will receive you.*
>
> *Agree with thine adversary quickly while thou art in the way with him, lest at any time he shall get thee and thou shalt be cast into prison. Verily I say unto thee, thou shalt by no means come out thence until thou hast paid the uttermost senine. And while ye are in prison, can ye pay even one senine? Verily, verily I say unto you, nay.*
>
> *And behold, it is written, An eye for an eye and a tooth for a tooth; but I say unto you that ye shall not resist evil, but whosoever shall smite thee on thy right cheek, turn to him the other also. And if any man will sue thee at the law and take away thy coat, let him have thy cloak also. And whosoever shall compel thee to go a mile, go with him twain. Give to him that asketh thee, and to him that would borrow of thee, turn thou not away.*
>
> *And behold, it is written also that thou shalt love thy neighbour and hate thine enemy; but behold, I say unto you, love your enemies, bless them that curse you, [and] do good to them that hate you, and pray for them who despitefully use you and persecute you, that ye may be the children of your Father who is in Heaven, for he maketh his sun to rise on the evil and...the good. Therefore, those things which were of old time, which were under the law, in me are all fulfilled. Old things are done away and all things have become new.* (3 Nephi 5:24-26;30-31 RE)

These admonitions are designed to make *your life better*. Much like the other eight commandments, the first two are so that we can, and will, live loving, Christ-like lives, being obedient to God's instructions—which we really need to take seriously.

So, in addition to "start looking for them," start asking the question, "What lack I yet?" And then *listen* to the answer. Start seeing people the way *God sees them*, and then engaging with them in a way that reflects that. Start asking

God to take the scales from *your* eyes, so that you are no longer deceived into thinking whatever is untrue—*for you*. Start wanting to change *you*, and start taking the things God says seriously.

Now, you might think I'm being too absolute or too literal, and that's fine. You might even be right. However, ask yourself this: Was Jesus absolute and literal when He ended verse 31 with this— *Therefore, I would that ye should be perfect, even as I or your Father who is in Heaven is perfect* (3 Nephi 5:31 RE).

DENVER: This world is a place of trial and testing. Before creation it was planned that when we came here we would be "proven" by what we experience. *That happens now*. Prove yourself by listening to God, hearing His voice, and obeying. Sometimes we are like Alma and want to do *greater* things to help God's work, but the greatest work of all is to respond to God's voice and prove you are willing to listen and obey Him.

I want to show you the depths of truth that spreads through the ocean—distances and directions that are infinite. But I must be content to use only a cup to give what little a man can measure and convey. Only God can show it because it is too great, too far above man's poor ability. It's not lawful for man, neither is man capable to make it known, for it is only to be seen and understood by those who purify themselves before God, to whom He grants this privilege of seeing and knowing for themselves, *while in the flesh*.

It was a year ago that a renewed covenant was given, to all willing to accept it, by God. New covenant people sprang into existence when a few accepted that gift. Until that moment, there were only lost and scattered remnants who, although the object of God's earlier covenants, lived in ignorance of God's renewed labor in His vineyard. Now, in addition to other remnants, there is a new covenant remnant aware of God's renewed labor, a remnant who has been asked to labor alongside the Master of the Vineyard as He sends His final invitation to come to His wedding feast. Christ spoke of this very thing when He taught the Nephites. He foretold that the barren Gentiles would eventually produce more children for His Kingdom than the remnants on *this* land and at Jerusalem. Christ said:

> *And then shall that which is written come to pass: Sing, O barren, thou that didst not bear; break forth into singing and cry aloud, thou that didst not travail with child, for more are the children of the desolate than the children of the married wife, saith the Lord. Enlarge the place of thy tent and let them stretch forth the curtains of thy habitations; spare not, lengthen thy cords and strengthen thy stakes, for thou shalt break forth on the right hand and on the*

> *left, and thy seed shall inherit the gentiles and make the desolate cities to be inhabited. Fear not for thou shalt not be ashamed, neither be thou confounded for thou shalt not be put to shame, for thou shalt forget the shame of thy youth and [shall] not remember the reproach of thy widowhood any more. For thy maker, thy husband, the Lord of Hosts is his name, and thy Redeemer, the Holy One of Israel: the God of the whole earth shall he be called.* (3 Nephi 10:2 RE)

We can see a new and different meaning in Christ's Book of Mormon prophecy to the Nephites. Before, Christ's words seemed to foretell that the lost and scattered remnants would build the Lord's House and the New Jerusalem; now, it appears that there are covenant-receiving Gentiles who are included. Gentiles who repent and hearken to Christ's words, and do not harden their hearts, will be brought into covenant as His people.

Christ mentions three distinct bodies: First, those who have accepted the covenant and are numbered among the remnant of Jacob, to whom Christ gave this land for their inheritance. Second, the lost descendants of the remnant of Jacob on this land, who will repent and return. Third, as many from the House of Israel who will repent and return. These three will build a city that shall be called the New Jerusalem. All three of those will come to know God in gathering and laboring to build the New Jerusalem.

Then they will go out to assist all of God's people in their lost and forgotten state, to be awakened to the work of God and gathered as if one body of believers. Then all who have any of the blood of Abraham, who are scattered upon the face of the land, will come to be taught in the New Jerusalem. There the Power of Heaven will come down to be among them: the angels, and Enoch with his ten thousands will come down, the Ancient of Days or Adam, our first father, and Christ also will be in the midst of His people.

The spirit of God is withdrawing from the world. Men are increasingly angry without good cause. The hearts of men are waxing cold. The scriptures describe events now underway and call it the end of the times of the Gentiles. This process of the spirit withdrawing will end on this continent, as it did with two prior civilizations, in fratricidal and genocidal warfare. For the rest of the world, it will be as in the days of Noah in which, as the light of Christ or spirit of truth is eclipsed, men's cold hearts will result in a constant scene of violence and bloodshed. The wicked will destroy the wicked.

The covenant established a year ago, if it is kept, will prevent the loss of light and warmth of heart as the spirit now steadily recedes from the world. Be charitable and be patient, and labor to reach others. Even if they should judge you harshly because of their traditions, you should nevertheless be kind to them. They're going to grow to fear you, but it's only part of how darkness responds to light. Give them no reason to fear you. The time will come for us to gather, but between now and then, be leaven. Preserve the world. Be salt. Preserve the world, even if it hates you. The soul of every person is equally precious to God as is yours. If your kindness and example should awaken another soul, you will rejoice with the angels over them.

There is a need "to set in order the House of God," which can only be accomplished through a temple where that work can be performed. The temple is not the "House of God" needing to be set in order. But a temple is required to accomplish the work for God's House, or family, to be set in order. As once described by God:

> *Organize yourselves, prepare every needful thing, and establish a house, even a house of prayer, a house of fasting, a house of faith, a house of learning, a house of glory, a house of order, a House of God, that your incomings may be in the name of the Lord, that your outgoings may be in the name of the Lord, that all your salutations may be in the name of the Lord with uplifted hands unto the Most High.* (T&C 86:29 RE)

Let me end with a few concluding words of wise counsel:

First, just because you young folks have thought about something, that does not necessarily mean you know enough to form a reasonable opinion about it. Likewise, holding an opinion does not mean you know the truth yet. Always be open to learning more and the possibility that more information may well change your thinking, change your opinion, and bring you closer to the truth.

Second, and I hope you remember this, words only have the control over you that you *allow* them to have. Some people use coarse language because they do not know any better. Coarse language *alone* does not necessarily reveal the worth of the individual or the thought underlying the words. As Joseph Smith once said, "I love that man better who swears a stream as long as my arm & [administers] to the poor— & [divides] his substance than the long smoothed faced hypocrite[s]." (*JSP Journals,* Volume 3, p. 303, May 21, 1843 [Edited to correct spelling.])

Many of my childhood friends and most of their fathers could conjugate obscenities into nouns, pronouns, adjectives, adverbs, and conjunctions. That reflected little on their inner character. An afternoon I spent with my father and a few of his friends, all of whom were veterans of World War II, reminded me of the heroic deeds and selflessness for others matters a greater deal more than coarse language. That afternoon humbled me. I was a law student at the time, and thought myself better educated than all those men, my father included. A few hours in their company, however, brought the sober realization that *they* had done great deeds, laying their lives on the line, and through their valiance I had inherited privileges *they* secured. Do not give a handful of coarse words power they do not deserve to have.

God's great power does not require an earthquake, a fire, or a whirlwind. Sometimes God's mighty power comes in a still small voice, or in a dream warning a family to flee to safety. God uses "small means" and "simple things" to accomplish His greatest influence. If you will allow Him to guide you with small means, He will save you from destruction *here*, and in the hereafter.

Finally, virtue matters; morality matters; chastity matters. One of the greatest sources of joy *and misery* is our ability to produce children. The union of man and woman inside a marriage, where children can be born to parents who want them, and are prepared to love and care for them, is how the power of procreation was intended to be enjoyed. Separate from that, it has produced a great deal of misery in this world. Be moral. Be chaste. Guard your virtue.

I teach these things in the name of Jesus Christ, Amen.

The foregoing excerpts are taken from:

- Stephanie Snuffer's remarks titled "Love Others As Yourself," given at a regional conference in Sandy, Utah, on July 14, 2019; and

- Denver's remarks titled "Keep the Covenant: Do the Work," given at the Remembering the Covenants Conference in Layton, Utah, on August 4, 2018.

123. Numbered Among

In this episode, Denver discusses what it means to be "numbered among the House of Israel," how the Covenant plays a role in changing people from being Gentiles into being numbered among the House of Israel and the literal seed of Jacob (and vice versa), and how this influences the message and meaning of prophecy.

———

DENVER: When the sample Scriptures came in, I made a note in the front of three of the volumes (that I've since held onto) that I received them on June 25th of 2020. I started reading them the next day. And between June 25th and August 31st, I read all three volumes of the new Scriptures (in one read-through from front to back). In the Book of Mormon, I noticed something that I made note of that I hadn't particularly noticed before, and then I followed this theme from the beginning of the Book of Mormon to the end of the Book of Mormon and marked the references as I went through.

This is in the second book of Nephi. He is quoting a revelation that came to him from God. And so, this is God speaking.

> *Wherefore, the gentiles shall be blessed and numbered among the house of Israel. Wherefore, I will consecrate this land unto thy seed, and they who shall* ***be numbered*** *among thy seed, for ever, for the land of their inheritance; for it is a choice land, saith God unto me, above all other lands. Wherefore, I will have all men that dwell thereon that they shall worship me, saith God.* (2 Nephi 7:4 RE, emphasis added)

That struck me when I read it—because it's extending the covenant-status from the descendants of Nephi to the Gentiles (those that are blessed that will be numbered among the house of Israel), which struck me as I read it.

Later, Nephi is explaining the major themes of his ministry in writing on the plates and summarizing why he had quoted from the text of Isaiah. (This becomes important again later, but it's important here also.) In Nephi's explanation of what he was doing in his sermon/in his message on the plates that he'd created and carved on, he says, *I say unto you, as many of the gentiles as will repent* ***are*** *the covenant people of the Lord, and as many of the Jews as will not repent shall be cast off. For the Lord covenanteth with none save it be with them that repent and believe in his Son, who is the Holy One of Israel* (2 Nephi 12:11 RE, emphasis added).

So, what Nephi is summarizing from the Isaiah materials (and the others that he has explained in his two volumes of First and Second Nephi) is that covenant-status and becoming the people of the Lord will include Gentiles (on the assumption that the Gentiles accept the Book of Mormon and repent in order to become numbered among the people). But **if** even the people that are referred to as "my ancient covenant people, the Jews" will not repent, then they're cast off. And so, they cease to be numbered among the covenant people of the Lord.

Later on, in the book of Alma, there were a group of Lamanite people who had repented, had been converted by Ammon, who had buried their swords, who had determined never to take up the violence of warfare ever again or shed another person's blood. They were willing to die rather than to be taking the life of someone else, even in defense of themselves. So, they were brought by Ammon over to the land of Jershon, and there they dwelt among the Nephites. And in the course of explaining this transition, it says they were distinguished by that name ever after (that is, the people of Ammon) and also numbered among the people. *They were distinguished by that name ever after. And they were numbered among the people of Nephi, and also numbered among the people who were of the church of God* (Alma 15:9 RE). So, these people who were clearly—as a matter of blood descent— Lamanites were numbered among the people of Nephi and numbered among the people who were of the church of God. So, their status as a matter of genealogy ceased to matter because of their covenant-status. They changed from being Lamanites to being *numbered among the people of Nephi* (ibid).

Then in Alma, there's a prophecy that Alma gives explaining what he knows is going to happen to the Nephites and his descendants. He says,

> *Then shall they see wars and pestilences, yea, famine and bloodshed, even until the people of Nephi shall become extinct. Yea, and this because they shall dwindle in unbelief and fall into the works of darkness, and lasciviousness, and all manner of iniquities. Yea, I say unto you that because they shall sin against so great light and knowledge, ...I say unto you that from that day, even into the fourth generation shall not all pass away before this great iniquity shall come. ...when that great day cometh, behold, the time very soon cometh that those who are now, or the seed of those who are now numbered among the people of Nephi, shall no more be numbered among the people of Nephi. But whosoever remaineth and is not destroyed in that great and dreadful day shall be numbered among the Lamanites, and shall become like unto them.* (Alma 21:2 RE)

So, the prophecy that Alma gives says that whatever remnant there may have been of Nephi that will exist after the great apostasy following four generations after Christ's visit among the Nephites, whoever's left is no longer a Nephite, but they are numbered among the Lamanites, even if they are descendants of Nephi.

So, we get to Helaman, and in Helaman, the theme picks up again. He's describing where things are going to be headed, and as he says,

> *...from one generation to another by the Nephites, even until they have fallen into transgression and have been murdered, plundered, and hunted, and driven forth, and slain, and scattered upon the face of the earth, and mixed with the Lamanites* ***until they are no more called the Nephites****, becoming wicked, and wild, and ferocious, yea,* ***even becoming Lamanites****.* (Helaman 2:4 RE, emphasis added)

So, you can change your identity. You can change your identity from being a Nephite into becoming a Lamanite. You can change your identity from being a Lamanite to being a Nephite. But more importantly, you can change your identity from being a Gentile into being of the house of Israel.

Then we get to Christ and the events that occur at His visit with the Nephites, immediately preceding that. In the 30th year that they're reckoning time from in Third Nephi, *It came to pass that those Lamanites who had [been] united with the Nephites were numbered among the Nephites, and their curse was taken from them* (3 Nephi 1:11 RE). They were numbered among the Nephites and were called Nephites.

So, by the time you get to Christ's visit, you have people who were descendants of Laman, and they were numbered with the Nephites and included within the group of Nephites who were spared and Nephites who Christ came to visit at the House of the Lord in Bountiful. Christ then visits this very same subject when He appears to the Nephites in Third Nephi, but **He** clarifies some things that are even more remarkable than all of this. This is Christ speaking during His visit, *O house of Israel, and ye shall come unto the knowledge of the fullness of my gospel. But if the gentiles will repent and return unto me, saith the Father, behold, they shall be numbered among my people, O house of Israel* (3 Nephi 7:5 RE).

So, Christ speaking to the Nephites, quoting His Father, says that it is the Father's determination that the Gentiles who repent and return unto Christ are gonna be numbered among the people of the house of Israel.

Then Christ, still talking to the Nephites in Third Nephi says, *...that the gentiles, if they will not harden their hearts, that they may repent, and come unto me, and be baptized in my name, and know of the true points of my doctrine, that they may be numbered among my people, O house of Israel* (3 Nephi 9:11 RE).

Then in Third Nephi, Christ goes on to say,

> *But if they* [meaning the Gentiles] *will repent, and hearken unto my words, and harden not their hearts, I will establish my church among them, and they shall come in unto the covenant and be numbered among this the remnant of Jacob, unto whom I have given this land for their inheritance. And they shall assist my people, the remnant of Jacob, and also...many of the house of Israel as [will] come, that they may build a city which shall be called the New Jerusalem. And...they [shall] assist my people, that they may be gathered in, who are scattered upon all the face of the land, in unto the New Jerusalem. And then shall the Powers of Heaven come down among them, and I also will be in their midst.* (3 Nephi 10:1 RE)

So, this building of the new Jerusalem by the Gentiles is actually going to be done by the remnant of Jacob, which includes the Gentiles who come unto Him and repent and are numbered among the house of Jacob.

Then Christ quotes Isaiah, as Nephi had done earlier. It's at this point that the loop closes, and it becomes clear that—first Christ quotes Isaiah, then He interprets Isaiah—that one of the primary messages of the Book of Mormon is the restoration of the covenant-status and the reclaiming into the house of Israel of those who are called Gentiles—in a lost and forsaken condition—who know nothing concerning a covenant with God reclaiming them, converting them, and after they repent, turning them into the house of Israel. Christ quoting Isaiah says:

> *And then shall that which is written come to pass: Sing, O barren, thou that didst not bear; break forth into singing and cry aloud, thou that didst not travail with child; for more are the children of the desolate than the children of the married wife* (3 Nephi 10:2 RE).

So, Isaiah is analogizing what will happen at the very end to a barren woman who has never given birth and saying that woman—who is desolate, without children—is going to have more children than the married woman who conceives and bears her own children.

He goes on to elaborate (this is Christ interpreting Isaiah), *Thy seed shall inherit the gentiles and make the desolate cities to be inhabited* (ibid). "Thy seed shall inherit the gentiles," meaning that the line that had ended because of apostasy that did not preserve itself following four generations—that line of people who became desolate and ~~un~~barren, they—that line is going to inherit as their posterity (to be numbered as thy children) the Gentiles so that the covenant people that are to inherit the land are the repentant Gentiles who were accepted and adopted into the house of Israel in the last days.

Then in the Book of Ether, Moroni also picks up the theme.

> *And they shall be like unto the old, save the old have passed away and all things have become new. And then cometh the New Jerusalem; and blessed are they who dwell therein, for it is they whose garments are white through the blood of the Lamb; and they are they who are* ***numbered among*** *the remnant of the seed of Joseph, who were of the house of Israel.* (Ether 6:3 RE, emphasis added)

So, Moroni adds his own testimony at the end.

This theme of converting Gentiles, through their repentance, from their status as "Gentiles" into a new status of being part of the "house of Israel" is one of the major themes of the Book of Mormon—because the Book of Mormon was intended to come forth in the last days as a text to cry repentance out of the dust, and those who respond change from being "Gentile" into being "numbered among the house of Israel" and to be "numbered among the people of Jacob." The distinction between Israel and Jacob is the difference between Jacob, the birth name of the man who, through covenant-status, altered from the old name of Jacob into the new name of Israel. The use of the name Jacob and the use of the name Israel signifies not only that the Gentiles are gonna become covenant-status as Israel, but also reckoned as if they were directly from the blood of Jacob and (in that last quote) numbered among Joseph, the descendants of Joseph—so that in the last days when the Gentiles come aboard, they come aboard under the "house of Joseph" in order to bring the message of salvation to the rest of the house of Israel, **among whom they are numbered**. Though they may have come last in being numbered among Israel, in the last days they are turned into the first, and from their status as the first of the restored covenant of Israel people, they then are charged with taking the message to reclaim the **other** covenant people and bringing the message to them.

But if the Jews reject the message, or if the remnant of Nephi—the remnant on this land—reject the message, then they're cast off, meaning they lose their covenant status. And so, the obligation of those last days' Gentiles who repent and accept the covenant and come in unto the Lord is to (#1) recognize their status and to (#2) take the message out.

But all of this changes somewhat the way in which the prophecy should be read. Because the Gentiles who come aboard become numbered among Israel/ become numbered among Jacob/become numbered among Joseph—all of whom are Father Jacob (renamed Israel) or his son Joseph. Those individuals are the ones that are prophesied to build the New Jerusalem. If Gentiles are gonna assist in that work, it will be Gentiles who are not yet numbered among the house of Israel. And if "my people Jacob" are to build the New Jerusalem, any Gentile who is numbered among the house of Jacob is going to be the people who build the New Jerusalem, and Gentiles will assist them.

It changes the interpretation as soon as a Gentile becomes numbered among the house of Israel/numbered among the people of Jacob. The prophecy about the people of Jacob and the descendants of Jacob building the New Jerusalem means that the interpretation— correctly—is that it's covenant Gentiles numbered among that house who will do so. And if Gentiles are going to assist them, then the Gentiles are those that have yet to enter into the covenant.

It changes the meaning of these verses—but it is a theme that appears early and often and one that the Lord Himself (when He visits with the Nephites) elaborates upon and (at the end) Moroni returns to. It's a major theme of the Book of Mormon, and it's one of those that ought not be missed.

The foregoing was recorded on September 6, 2020 in Challis, Idaho.

124. The Foolish and the Wise

The following message was delivered by Denver Snuffer on September 27, 2020, in Sandy, Utah.

DENVER: I'm pretty thick-skinned when it comes to myself. I take a lot of criticism, and I don't… It doesn't bother me to have people say things that I know to be untrue. But there's a little different standard when it comes to the reputation of Joseph Smith—because there's a warning that is given about Joseph:

> *The ends of the earth shall inquire after your* [that is Joseph's] *name, and fools shall have you in derision, and hell shall rage against you, while the pure in heart, and the wise, and the noble, and the virtuous shall seek counsel, and authority, and blessings constantly from under your hand.* (T&C 139:7)

That was a statement made by the Lord to Joseph to console him while he was in Liberty Jail. And the statement that "people that hold Joseph in derision are fools" rather changes the game in my view about how one should deal with Joseph Smith.

I put up with a lot as I read the *Joseph Smith Papers*—without comment, except in passing. But this particular podcast is intended to be a warning to the people that are involved with the *Joseph Smith Papers*, as well as Hales, who (in my view) have acted both foolishly and gone over the line. As I will explain in this current podcast, Joseph Smith has consigned you to hell/to damnation, as has also the Book of Mormon. So, I'm hoping that word of this will eventually trickle down to the people that are directly involved in the mischief that I'm gonna discuss today.

Volume 9 of the *Joseph Smith Papers* is attempting to set up a more bold approach in dealing with the subject of the Nauvoo adultery that was going on and to justify (as a religious proposition) that there is something legitimate to the idea of a man having more than one wife, and that that is not damnable, and it originated with Joseph Smith. A fair reading of the history (if you're trying to defend the reputation of Joseph Smith and if you regard the defense of Joseph Smith as something that is "wise" and "virtuous" and "noble," as the Lord said to Joseph in Liberty Jail) suggests that you err on the side of caution when it comes to dealing with a dispensation head.

One of the first documents that I noted is a transcript of a discourse that Joseph Smith gave at the founding of the Relief Society on the 17th of March 1842 (on page 276), where the discussion begins with the "Historical Introduction." And then the actual transcript of Joseph's comments begin on page 279.

See, the Relief Society was founded in part because of sexual improprieties (that had come to the attention of Joseph Smith) that was going on in Nauvoo. And so, the Relief Society was organized as a bulwark and a defense for the women in Nauvoo so that they could stand on their own two feet. In fact, the document that represents the summary of Joseph's comments on that occasion suggests that Joseph turned the key on their behalf so that they had —independent of the men—authority to act in defense of their own righteousness and of their own virtue. The Relief Society was intended to be a bulwark to solidify and empower and liberate the women in order to have their own voice/their own right to stand up and defend the virtue of the members of their society and to protect them against the encroachment.

What I find interesting, and I'll just mention in passing: he says that it's "to assist; by correcting the morals and strengthening the virtues of the female community, and save the Elders the trouble of rebuking" (*Joseph Smith Papers: Documents*, Volume 9, December 1841 to April 1842, pg. 280). So, in this discourse, once Joseph finished with what he was doing to aid the women, when that part of the meeting ended, then the president spoke up. This is Emma Smith. "The Pres^t. [Emma] then suggested that she would like an argument with Elder Taylor on the words Relief and Benevolence" (*Ibid*, pg. 282). John Taylor had been in the meeting, and he had suggested that the name be the Nauvoo Female Benevolent Society, and Emma Smith wanted to argue that point. In other words, she (upon getting the men to shut up) stood up and said immediately, 'The first thing I want to deal with is this **name**.' She was going to reject the name. "Pres^t. Emma Smith, said the popularity of the word benevolent is one great **objection**— no person can think of the word as associated with public Institutions, without thinking of the Washingtonian Benevolent Society which was one of the most corrupt Institutions of the day—do not wish to have it call'd after other societies in the world—" (*Ibid*, emphasis added). And so, Emma Smith demonstrates, when she's put in this position, she's absolutely no shrinking violet. She is not gonna take even the suggestion of the name for granted. She's gonna stand up, she's gonna defend the society, and she's gonna point out that if it associates it by word identification with something that is corrupt, then she's not in on it.

I've said this before: Of the two personalities, Emma Smith's was a stronger personality than Joseph Smith's was. Emma Smith was not likely to be cowed —as she is portrayed in Joseph taking other women and victimizing her and breaking her heart over these other women. There is no way that Emma Smith is the caricature that has been turned into that foolish nonsense.

"Counsellor Whitney mov'd, that..."—after some discussion... And Eliza Snow, she also contributed, and said "she felt to concur with the President, with regard to the word Benevolent, that many Societies with which it had been associated, were corrupt,—" (*Ibid*, pg. 283). And so then, after some discussion, "Whitney mov'd that [the] Society be call'd The Nauvoo Female Relief Society— [it was] secon[d.] by Counsellor Cleveland—" (*Ibid*). And so, the name of the Relief Society was not what **the men** proposed that it be, but the name was what Emma Smith and Eliza Snow and Whitney and Cleveland wanted it—and so, the name, The Nauvoo Female Relief Society. Right there at the beginning of this process, it ought to be noted that not only did it have the desired effect of making the women have the power to stand up in their own right, but they **immediately** began to exercise that. They **immediately** begin to exercise it.

So then, things begin to progress, and on the 31st of March 1842 (the Relief Society having been organized on the 17th, as I recall—yeah, March 17th)... By the time you get a couple of weeks later, 31 March 1842, Joseph Smith wrote a letter to Emma Smith because the actions of John C. Bennett were beginning to tumble out into public discussion.

And so, the letter to Emma Smith of the Relief Society is "explained," but the folks who are in charge of the *Joseph Smith Papers* produce and commend to the people that are reading the history a **version** of this letter that is **not** the same as the version that is committed into the record of the Female Relief Society. Instead, they take **another** copy that includes some language that is not in the Relief Society version, and they introduce the same sort of lie as the *Joseph Smith Papers* evidence/alteration of an introduction of lies elsewhere dealing with the subject of plural marriage. So, as their discussion of the Historical Introduction begins on page 304, they finally get (after a picture of Emma on page 307), "The letter to Emma Smith and the Relief Society appears to be an early response to the actions of Bennett and others who were seducing women in Nauvoo by misrepresenting the [and this is where they introduce their view, the] not yet publicly announced doctrine of plural marriage" (*Ibid*, pg. 307).

So, Joseph Smith is writing a letter to Emma Smith in order to guard against the misconduct of Bennett—and the commentary and the Historical Introduction by the people in charge of the *Joseph Smith Papers* cannot be left alone by saying, 'This is what Joseph did early in response to John Bennett.' They go on to say, "the not yet publicly [introduced]." If you're being **fair** and you want to say **when** it was publicly introduced, I can tell you when it was: It was done in a General Conference of the LDS Church in Salt Lake Valley, some eight years after the **death** of Joseph Smith and **not** when Joseph was alive. Why isn't that footnoted? Why aren't you telling the truth about that? There is no evidence that Joseph intended for this practice to **ever** be made public, **even if** you think it originated with him. It's a damned lie to attribute this as though it were something Joseph intended to be made public.

Then (on that same page 307), they say, "The featured text is the earliest extant version of the letter and **may have**…" (*Ibid*). No, it's not the earliest extant. The earliest extant copy was what was put into the Relief Society minutes, hand-copied by Eliza R. Snow, who was the secretary for the Relief Society. But they say this version of the letter "...may have been either an early draft of the letter **or** the actual correspondence delivered to Emma Smith and the Relief Society. Sometime after September 1842, Relief Society secretary Eliza R. Snow copied the letter into the organization's minute book, including...**one significant omission**" (*Ibid*, pgs. 307-308, emphasis added). One significant omission. You can read the letter and the version that was hand-copied by Eliza R. Snow into the Relief Society minutes, and you will conclude that Joseph Smith utterly rejects plural wifery/spiritual wifery/polygamy and condemns anyone who could advocate it.

The only **exception** to that is the **insertion** into this letter of something that is **omitted** from the version of the letter that Eliza R. Snow copied into the minutes of the Relief Society. I'll read you starting a little bit before that:

> ...we therefore warn you & forewarn you in the name of the Lord to check and destroy any faith that any innocent person may have in any such character for we don't want any body to believe any thing as coming from us contrary to the old established morals & virtues & scriptural laws regulating the habits customs & conduct of Society **unless** it be by message del[iv]ered to you by our own mouth, by actual revelation & commandment. (*Ibid*, pg. 309, emphasis added)

The words I just concluded with, "unless it be by message del[iv]ered to you by our own mouth, by actual revelation & commandment," **is not in** the

Relief Society minutes recording the version of the letter that Joseph Smith sent to Emma Smith. But what is in the letter:

> Can the "Female Releif [sic] Society of Nauvoo" be Trusted with some important matter that ought actually...belong to them to see to which men have been under the necessity of seeing to to their chagrin and Mortification in order to prevent iniquitous characters from carrying their iniquity into effect such as, for instance a man who may be aspiring after power & authority and yet without principle; regardles[s] of god, man or the Devil or the interest or welfare of men, or the virtue o[f] innocence of women? Shall the credulity, good faith, & steadfast feelings of our Sisters for the cause of God or truth be imposed upon by believing such men because they say they have authority from Joseph or [from] the first Presidency or any other Presidency of the church and thus with a lie in their mouth deceive & debauch the innocent under the assumption that they are authorized from these sources! May God forbid!
>
> ...no such authority ever has, ever can, or ever will be given to any man & if any man has been guilty of any such thing let him be treated with utter contempt & let the curse of God fall on his head, & let him be turned out of Society as unworthy of a place among men, ...denounced as the blackest & most unprincipled wretch & finally let him be damned. (*Ibid*, pg. 308)

Those are the words that precede.

> ...we therefore warn you & forewarn you in the name of the Lord to check and destroy any faith that any innocent person may have in any such character for we don't want any body to believe any thing as coming from us contrary to the old established morals & virtues & scriptural laws regulating the [habits and conduct] habits customs & conduct of Society. ...all persons pretending to be authorized by us or having any permit or sanction from us...will be liars and base imposters. ...you are authorized on the very first intimation of the kind to denounce them as such...<shun> them as the fiery flying serpents, whether they are prophets, seers, or Revelators, patriarchs, Twelve apostles, Elders, Priests...Mayors, Generals...city council alderman, Marshall, Police, Lord Mayor or the Devil, are alike culpable. & shall be damned for such evil practices.
>
> ...we want to put a stop to them, & we want you to do your part & we will do ours.

> May [the Lord] God add his blessings upon your head & lead you in all the paths of virtue piety and peace.... (*Ibid*, pg. 309)

This is what Joseph Smith wrote as his initial reaction to the misconduct that he was hearing about John C. Bennett, damning them to hell.

Joseph Smith gave another discourse on the 8th of April 1842 at a conference. It would... The minutes were published in the *Times and Seasons*. In this, while he's talking generally about the subject of the temple baptism for the dead and that they were discontinuing baptisms until the temple was finished, in this same talk, reading from the minutes on page 344:

> He then spoke in contradiction of a report in circulation about Elder Kimball, B. Young [Brigham Young], himself, and others of the Twelve, alleging that a sister had been shut in a room for several days, and that they had endeavored to induce her to believe in having two wives. Also cautioned the sisters against going to the steam boats.
>
> Pres't. [Joseph Smith] J. Smith spoke upon the subject of the stories respecting Elder Kimball and others, showing the folly and inconsistency of spending any time in conversing about such stories or hearkening to them, for there is no person that is acquainted with our principles [who] would believe such lies, except [Thomas] Sharp the editor of the "Warsaw Signal." (*Ibid*, pg. 344)

And so, Joseph Smith, in a **public** discourse—because this problem is growing in its magnitude, and Joseph Smith is denouncing the practice, not just in letters to the Relief Society but now going forward to denounce them publicly in a conference.

Then on the 10th of April 1842, Joseph Smith gives a discourse that I'm gonna read from:

> If you wish to go whare God is you must be like God or possess the principles which God possesses for if we are not drawing towards God in principle we are going from him & drawing towards the devil...I am standing in the midst of all kinds of people search your hearts & see if **you** are like God, [I've] searched mine & feel to repent of all my sins, We have thieves among us Adulterers, liars, hypocritts, if God could speak from heaven he would command ~~us~~...not to steal, not to commit Adultery, nor to covet, nor **deceive** but be faithful over a few things As far as we degenerate from God we desend to the devil & [lose] knowledge '& without Knowledge we cannot be saved...while our hearts are filled with

> evil...we are studying evil their is no room in our hearts for good or studying good...the Church must be cleansed & I proclaim against all iniquity. A man is saved no faster than he gets knowledge for if he does not get knowledge he will be brought into Captivity by some evil power in the other world as evil spirits will have more knowled[g]e & consequently more power than many men who are on the earth. hence it needs Revelation to assist us & give us knowledge of the things of God. (*Ibid*, pgs.351-352, emphasis added, spelling as in original)

Revelation from God reveals their wickedness and abominations. We hear the language quoted about how "a man is saved no faster than he gets knowledge" divorced from what he's really talking about **all the time**. What he's talking about is the descent (in Nauvoo) of the people that he's addressing into wickedness, abominations, adultery, covetousness, stealing—and therefore, "drawing [near] the devil," as opposed to practicing virtue and drawing near to God.

Joseph Smith, then addressed again (on the 28th of April of 1842) the Relief Society, again, in which he said that women of faith… This is a remarkable discourse to the Relief Society, saying women of faith can heal, and there's nothing wrong with them laying hands on and healing the sick—because that is an attribute and a gift that comes as a consequence of possessing **faith** and not necessarily **limited to** people who have priesthood.

But on page 404 at the very bottom, the summary from this discourse lists one attribute, gift, or power of women that's tied directly to virtue. And he says this: "...females, if they are pure and innocent can come into the presence of God" (*Ibid*, pg. 404). Females can come into the presence of God; it's a question that I've had to answer a number of times in emails and private conversations. Joseph answers it here, the caveat being 'purity and innocence before God.'

Well, this then brings me to the most contemptible part of the entire Volume 9 of the Documents in the *Joseph Smith Papers*, which has been the subject of countless citations as evidence of Joseph Smith's secret, private, dishonest, culpable practice of the plural wife thing—and he got caught because of **this** evidence. It's a letter that doesn't belong at all in the *Joseph Smith Papers* project. They have the gall to insert it in the *Papers* (as an appendix)—"Appendix: Letter to Nancy Rigdon, Mid-April 1842." It's the Nancy Rigdon letter that is pointed to by **everyone** as proof positive that Joseph Smith engaged in the secret practice of seducing women.

Now, I want you to think about this for a moment in the context of history at the time. The Warsaw newspaper that Thomas Sharp is editing is claiming that Joseph Smith is engaged in this private, secret, licentious, adulterous practice. And Joseph Smith is saying, 'Anyone that propound this doctrine is damned to hell. It's a lie.' Thomas Sharp is saying, 'No, no, it's really going on over there in Nauvoo.' Joseph Smith is doing everything he can to try and locate those that are involved in this practice, and when he finds someone, he hails them before the High Council of Nauvoo.

And in the midst of this, we are supposed to believe that the husband of **Emma Smith** (who has the backbone to stand up to the men and tell John Taylor, 'I've got an argument with you' as soon as she has the opportunity to speak as the Relief Society President) is going to be weeping, oh so delicately in her home, while she knows... (but she'll lie about it later, you see), she knows her husband's out seducing other women. And this nonsense is supposed to be believed when Joseph Smith (publicly and in private correspondence) is doing everything he can to detect this and to put it away and to denounce it and to call it not only a damnable lie but to consign everyone who's involved in this activity—whether they are apostles or prophets or seers or revelators—they are consigned by Joseph Smith to hell (which, because Joseph Smith was a dispensation head, is just as valid and binding today as it was when Joseph penned those words in 1842). And so, if you are someone who, today, are likewise advancing this lie against Joseph Smith, in the words of a dispensation head, you have been consigned to hell (which is perfectly consistent with other statements that are made in Scripture). We'll get to those in a moment.

But here we have the Appendix, in which those people responsible for the *Joseph Smith Papers* insert the letter to Nancy Rigdon in mid-April 1842-ish. (They can't put a date on it. And there's a reason for that. They'll explain it.) So, here's the first sentence. No, no this is the beginning of the second sentence of the Historical Introduction. "Because J[oseph] S[mith]'s authorship of this letter is uncertain, the letter is presented [in] an appendix to this volume rather than a featured document" (*Ibid*, Appendix, pg. 413).

If Joseph Smith's authorship of this letter is uncertain, why the hell is it in this document at all? If someone wrote a contemporaneous letter denouncing, as an adulterer and a liar, someone today, should that find its way into the authorized biography of that man? I have read scandalous accusations involving President Russell M. Nelson. But there's no appendix to the biography that was written of **that** man, in which those scandalous accusations are added to the record—because, well, there's no proof of it. But it's considered part of the record of the history of the Prophet Joseph Smith, the dispensation head?

This is how we're going to treat the man who wrote, 'Anyone who would engage in this is damned to hell'? This is how we're going to deal with his memory? This is how we're gonna deal with his legacy? We're gonna say, 'Although there's no evidence Joseph wrote this, we're gonna include it in the appendix.' Because we certainly don't want to allow Joseph's character to not be besmirched with what he was fighting against—because it will be picked up and championed by Brigham Young! Just because it makes Brigham Young a liar, that is no reason to drag Joseph Smith into the very practice that he denounced as false, adulterous, wicked, and 'damning one to hell.' You don't improve the reputation of Brigham Young by besmirching the character of Joseph Smith! And yet, the people responsible for the *Joseph Smith Papers* are doing exactly that.

So, they then say, "Bennett…" This is John C. Bennett:

> Bennett launched a vitriolic campaign to disparage J[oseph] S[mith], which included sending the series of letters to the *[Sangamo] Journal.* In the second of these communications, dated 2 July, Bennett claimed to have intimate knowledge of J[oseph] S[mith]'s attempts to court Nancy Rigdon as a plural wife—a marital system [which] Bennett referred to as "spiritual wifery"—and described a letter that J[oseph] S[mith] purportedly wrote to Rigdon to explain the doctrine and justify the proposal. (*Ibid*)

The source of this information is John C. Bennett. Period. This letter appears in *Sangamo Journal.* It was produced by Bennett as evidence of what Joseph Smith was doing.

> Bennett further reported that the letter was in the hands of Rigdon's friends, and that both he and Rigdon's father, Sidney, had read it. (*Ibid,* pgs. 413-414)

So, Bennett doesn't have the letter. He's giving you a transcript of the letter. He's saying that the letter is in the hands of friends of Rigdon's, and that Sidney had read the letter too. All of that could be true without the letter having ever originated with Joseph Smith.

> Because contemporaneous evidence discredits other allegations in Bennett's *Sangamo Journal* letters—and in his subsequent book, *History of*

> *the Saints: or, An Exposé of Joe Smith and Mormonism*, which appeared in early 1842—some debate exists among historians about the authenticity of this purported J[oseph] S[mith] letter. As in the cases of most of his verifiable plural marriages…

And there are none; the verification of that came decades following the death of Joseph Smith, during a lawsuit in which evidence needed to be ginned up. There's nothing contemporaneous.

> ...J[oseph] S[mith] was silent about this issue—neither confirming nor denying either his authorship of the letter or the allegation that he approached Nancy Rigdon to be a plural wife.

That statement is belied by the very next sentence:

> J[oseph] S[mith]'s brother William Smith, editor of the Nauvoo newspaper *Wasp*, denied that J[oseph] S[mith] was the letter's author. (*Ibid*)

Are you telling me that Joseph Smith's brother (who's writing the letter and in contact with his brother) saying that Joseph Smith denies that he's the author of the letter, doesn't constitute a denial of the letter? So, let's get this right. If someone says a hundred falsehoods about you and you've categorically denied all of them and you've only taken the trouble to deny eighty of the hundred, can we say because you didn't deny the eighty-first, that therefore, we can impute that you didn't deny it, when you've been categorical about denying in public and in writing? How foolish is it to assume that the same man that would have written (not long before this, in a preceding month) that it's 'a damnable lie for anyone to advance this, whether they be a president, a prophet, a seer, a revelator, an apostle, a patriarch—it's a damned lie; don't believe it, no matter who the damn thing comes from' to then turn around and to write **this** letter at the very time that he's trying to put this mess behind him?

Just ask yourself how credible that seems to you. So, let me reread those last two sentences:

> J[oseph] S[mith] was silent about this issue—neither confirming nor denying either his authorship of the letter or the allegation that he approached Nancy Rigdon to be a plural wife. J[oseph] S[mith]'s brother William Smith, editor of the Nauvoo newspaper *Wasp*, denied that J[oseph] S[mith] was the letter's author. In September the *Wasp* also

> printed a statement above **Sidney Rigdon's** signature claiming that, "Mr. Smith denied to me the authorship of that letter." (*Ibid*, emphasis added)

So, the editors of the *Joseph Smith Papers* say that:

- Joseph Smith did not deny authorship,
- followed by Sidney Rigdon saying he'd spoken with Joseph Smith, and Joseph Smith denied authorship of the letter.
- The circuitous nature of the pretzel the authors of the *Joseph Smith Papers* twist themselves into in order to perpetuate support for Joseph Smith's lying/adultery/hypocrisy should put them all to shame! This stuff is publishing a lie! This stuff is damnable, wrong, immoral, corrupt, offensive—it is holding Joseph Smith in derision! It is something only a fool would do.
- Rigdon cryptically reported that his daughter Nancy declared that "she never said to Gen. Bennett or any other person, that said letter was written by said Mr. Smith, nor in his handwriting, but by another person, and in another person's handwriting." (*Ibid*)

These are the historical background materials that the *Joseph Smith Papers* authors are willing to concede about this nonsense that they're about to publish in the Appendix and attribute to Joseph Smith.

> Although this particular letter's authenticity is contested…. (*Ibid*)

...and then they go on from there. If it's contested… If Rigdon denied it… Sidney Rigdon denied it. Nancy Rigdon denied it. Joseph Smith's brother denied it. Yet, the Nancy Rigdon letter has become one of the **great supporting proofs** of Joseph Smith's culpability in lying/ dissembling/ hypocrisy/dishonesty.

> If the text was derived from an authentic letter or...copy thereof in Bennett's possession, neither the original letter nor an early manuscript copy has been located. (*Ibid*)

Then I ask you: What the hell is it doing in this book? Why? Why rely upon the *Sangamo Journal* and letters published there from John Bennett, when you admit that John Bennett is such a dubious, dishonest source that other of his letters won't be given any credence whatsoever? Then they acknowledge,

> ...none of the 1842 printed versions or later handwritten copies based on them include a signature, address, or date. (*Ibid*)

That's why at the beginning of this, when the Appendix starts out, it says it's mid-April 1842-ish. Because there's no signature; there's no address; and there's no date.

And then, just before beginning a transcript of the document that they put in the *Papers* to honor Joseph Smith's memory, they include this statement:

> Though his letter to the *Sangamo Journal* did not include any provenance information or explicit physical description, when Bennett included the letter in [the] *History of the Saints* he stated that the original was in Willard Richards's handwriting and that he obtained it from church member Francis M. Higbee. (*Ibid*, pg. 416)

(Keep that name in mind because we'll get around to that.) So, we don't have any provenance information. We don't have any physical description. And yet, there we have this nonsense.

Well, not only is John C. Bennett's letters to the *Sangamo Journal* and his subsequent *History of the Saints* unreliable, when he was exposed and he was excommunicated, he was brought before the Nauvoo High Council and the city leaders and the civic leaders in Nauvoo. And Daniel Wells was an Alderman in the city of Nauvoo; he was someone before whom oaths could be made. And John Bennett swore out an affidavit under oath in the presence of Alderman Daniel H. Wells, which was published in the *Times and Seasons* contemporaneous with John Bennett's exposure. Now, John Bennett will **later** write the letter that he wrote to the *Sangamo Journal*, but **before** he did that and near contemporaneous with his excommunication, he swore this affidavit:

> Personally appeared before me, Daniel H. Wells, an Alderman of said city of Nauvoo, John C. Bennett, who being duly sworn according to law, deposeth and saith: that he never was taught any thing in the least cantrary [sic] to the strictest principles of the Gospel, or of virtue, or of the laws of God, or man, under [any circumstances or upon] any occasion either directly or indirectly, in word or deed, by Joseph Smith; and that he never knew the said Smith to countenance any improper conduct what[so]ever, either in public or private; and that he never did teach to me in private that an illegal illicit intercourse with females was, under any circumstances, justifiable, and that I never knew him so to

> teach others. JOHN C. BENNETT. (*Times and Seasons*, 1 August 1842, vol. 3, no.19, p. 871)

Now, his letters to the *Sangamo Journal* are not under oath. But this declaration is under oath with the penalty of perjury. John Bennett testified before the High Council. This is a summary (also printed in the *Times and Seasons*) of what happened as he testified in front of the city council:

> Dr. John C. Bennett, ex-Mayor, was then called upon by the Mayor...

"Mayor" being Joseph Smith because Joseph had been appointed before the next election to serve as the Mayor, in the interim, in order to make sure that they didn't have someone equally immoral/equally scandalous/equally untrustworthy running the city. And so, they relied upon the virtue and the integrity of Joseph Smith to be the replacement Mayor once John Bennett had resigned.

> Bennett...was then called upon by the Mayor to state if he knew aught [anything] against him [Joseph Smith]; when...Bennett replied: I know what I am about, and the heads of the church know what they are about, I expect. I have no difficulty with the heads of the chucrh [sic]. I publicly avow that anyone who has said that I have stated that General Joseph Smith has given me authority to hold illicit intercourse with wome,nis [sic] a liar in the face of God, those who have said it are damned liars; they are infernal liars. He never, either in public or private, gave me any such authority or license, and any person who states it is a scoundrel and a liar. (*Ibid*, p. 872)

Which means that John Bennett is now declaring in front of the city council what he intends to become—because he will later say the opposite of this; he is a liar, a damned liar, an infernal liar, a scoundrel, and a liar.

> I have heard it said that I should become a second Avard by withdrawing from the church, and that I was at variance with the heads and should [see] an influence against them because I resigned the office of Mayor; this is false. (*Ibid*)

During the difficulties in Missouri, Sampson Avard led a group that he called the Danites into a reign of terrorism and retaliation, which (when it later became the subject of public notice) Avard switched sides and said that it was Joseph Smith (who had, by the way, fired and reduced him—changed him from being in command to being, I think, the cook for the group) Joseph Smith denounced/denied. Well, Avard then switched and attributed to Joseph

Smith all of his (Sampson Avard's) misconduct. And they were saying, 'Oh, you're gonna follow that same pattern.'

Now, sure enough, John Bennett will follow that same pattern. But at this point on this date, while he's still trying to redeem his reputation and remain a member in good standing of the community at least (someone that could repent and come back), he says, That attribution that he intends to become another Sampson Avard is false.

> I have no difficulty with the heads of the church, and I intend to continue with you, and hope the time may come when I may be restored to full confidence, and fellowship, and my former standing in the church; and that my conduct may be such as to warrant my restoration—and should the time ever come that I may have the opportunity to test my faith it will then be known whether I am a traitor or a true man.
>
> Joseph Smith [acting Mayor] then [said]: "Will you please state definately [sic] whether you know **anything** against **my character** either in public or private.["] Gen. Bennett answered: "I do not; in all my intercourse with Gen. Smith, in public and in private, he has been strictly virtuous." (*Ibid*, emphasis added)

Well, time moves on. One of the names that I read to you earlier was Higbee. Higbee will also weigh in on this mess. Higbee will then change sides, and he'll be part of the *Nauvoo Expositor*. But earlier in this debacle, in—this is the very end of 1842—Francis Higbee says,

> I received your letter to-day, under the date of Nov. 13th which contained astonishing news to me indeed; and equally as painful as strange, and that [it] is the fact [that] of Bennett's book containing two letters from me. (*Times and Seasons*, vol. 4, "Extract of a Letter from F. M. Higbee, Nauvoo, Dec. 25th 1842")

This is Francis Higbee saying. So, the letter or the book/the exposé (that John Bennett did) included two letters of Francis Higbee. He's saying this is astonishing.

> ...as such a thing has no foundation in truth. He has not got a scratch on earth, no[t] [ever] did he have, with my name subscribed by my own hand, except the affidavit that fell into his hands. ...And if he has published anything over my signature, or name, it is forged. (*Ibid*)

This is Francis Higbee talking about the man. Francis Higbee then says,

> Bennett has been the instigator probably of more real trouble and misery than any other man we have ever met with, or [shall ever] find in this world. (*Ibid*)

Well…

There's a principle; it's a true principle. I don't know how many people are aware of it, but there's a great difference between receiving a revelation and being a prophet. Revelations are most often for the benefit of the individual and his family—and do not make the recipient a prophet. A **prophet** must be given a message from God to deliver to the world. This rarely happens. When it does, the message must be unadulterated and convey God's message and not the messengers.

But it is a far different thing for a man to stand at the head of a dispensation. He's brought into the Heavenly Council and stands as a member of that council, although but a man on Earth. The breadth, depth, and extent of a dispensation head is so much greater than that of a prophet, that any true prophet would show respect and **defer to** the dispensation head, as a child would respect his father. If you can understand that principle and comprehend it, you'll see how it is played out in all of the prior Scriptures.

Moses lamented (and this is in the book of Numbers)…

> *Joshua the son of Nun, [a] servant of Moses, one of his young men, answered and said, My lord Moses, forbid them* [because Eldad and Medad had been prophesying in the camp]. *And Moses said unto him, Do you envy for my sake? Would to God that all the Lord's people were prophets, and that [God] would put his spirit upon them* (Numbers 7:19 RE).

Because Moses knew that if that Spirit had been put upon them, that they would reinforce and testify to the truthfulness of the message that the dispensation head had been delivering. Because prophets support the dispensation head.

The Apostle Paul said that *a dispensation of the gospel is committed unto me* (in First Corinthians, paragraph 36 in the Restoration Scriptures). He would go on to explain: *If any man think himself to be a prophet or spiritual, let him acknowledge that the things that I write unto you are the commandments of the Lord* (1 Corinthians 1:60 RE). In other words, he's saying, 'If you're really a prophet, then you're going to defer to, support, and testify that the dispensation head has given you the Word of God.'

Well, which leads us then to the next problem that we've got with the *Joseph Smith Papers*. Joseph Smith made clear what his position was. He said anyone that advances this nonsense is a liar, is damnable, and is seeking to consign themselves to hell, which is exactly what we read in the Book of Mormon. Nephi writing said, *Woe unto the liar, for he shall be thrust down to hell* (2 Nephi 6:10 RE).

The message of the Book of Mormon **condemns** those who advance a lie about Joseph Smith, particularly when that lie is something that Joseph testified would result in their damnation. And yet, people feel at absolute liberty to consign Joseph to being a hypocrite and a liar. And they describe his wife as though she were someone so weak, so vulnerable, so easily put upon that she, knowing this stuff, would do nothing about it. This is the same Emma Smith who would testify forthrightly and consistently that her husband never had another wife other than her.

In the revelation that was given to Joseph and Sidney Rigdon (that used to be in the Doctrine and Covenants 76, but which is now included within the Teachings and Commandments as 69), this is talking about the people who are damned. *Last of all, these... are they who will not be gathered with the saints, to be caught up unto the church of the Firstborn and received into the cloud. These are they who are liars* (T&C 69:27), and he goes on to describe other attributes.

If you're lying about the Prophet Joseph Smith, if you're turning him into a hypocrite, if you're among the *fools [who hold Joseph] in derision* and you are not among *the pure in heart, ...the wise, and the noble, and the virtuous [who] seek counsel, and authority, and blessings constantly from under [Joseph Smith's] hand* (T&C 139:7), then you are among those who are liars. It says these are they who love and make a lie. ...*Whosoever loveth and maketh a lie. These are they who suffer the wrath of God on the earth. These are they who suffer the vengeance of Eternal fire* (T&C 69:27). I would suggest that a fair reading of the Scriptures and a fair regard for the reputation of Joseph Smith—as someone who is likewise noble and virtuous and someone whose counsel ought to be sought—suggests that we ought to be a whole lot more careful than those people responsible for preparing the *Joseph Smith Papers* are in guarding the virtue, the reputation, the integrity, the honesty of Joseph Smith and **defending him** against the charges of hypocrisy, instead of attempting to put **into** the official record of Joseph Smith—in order to redeem Brigham Young; in order to redeem John Taylor; in order to redeem Wilford Woodruff; in order to redeem every polygamist leader of the Church, through and including Heber J. Grant, who practiced this adulterous relationship as though it were a sacrament—you should not attempt to vindicate them by besmirching the character of Joseph Smith and attributing to him dishonesty, a lack of integrity, hypocrisy, and (by his own words) someone worthy of the damnation of hell.

It comes down to this: Either Joseph Smith is a damnable liar who ought to go to hell (and if so, then such a contemptible man ought not have founded a church in the first place, and the whole of this ought to be abandoned), **or** he was a prophet; he was a dispensation head; he was someone to whom deference is owed; he is someone that ought to be defended; and the things he taught publicly and wrote in letters to the Relief Society (without their alteration) should be respected and adhered to and upheld.

I am of the view that—after having looked at as much of the historical record as is made public—I am of the view that all of those who attribute to Joseph Smith this practice (that he fought against) are all liars (by the definition that Joseph Smith established, by the definition sworn to by John Bennett under oath).

His subsequent letters were not under oath. His book was not under oath. But his testimony defending Joseph Smith was under oath—both the affidavit that he swore to in front of Daniel Wells, as well as the testimony he gave before ~~the Nauvoo High Council~~ the Nauvoo City Council. Both of those statements were made by him under oath.

And Joseph Smith **did** deny the Nancy Rigdon letter. He denied it, and his brother William said he did so in the publication he made in *The Wasp* in Nauvoo. And Sidney Rigdon denied it, after having talked to Joseph. And so, it is a **lie** to say that Joseph never denounced the letter or refuted it.

The people responsible for putting this together are engaged in a most serious undertaking. Their salvation is dependent upon the absence of deliberate lies from the record involving Joseph Smith. And I can tell you in the name of Israel's God, that what Joseph Smith penned as a warning (in the 1842 timeframe) will stand as a witness against all those liars in the Day of Judgment. And they will have to account for how they dealt with the reputation of that man, because he stood at the head of a dispensation. And if you think you are a prophet, then you better stand up and defend—just as Moses had no problem with prophets being in the camp of Israel, knowing that they would support him; just as Paul said, 'If anyone's a prophet, then let them say that what I write comes from God.'

You need to repent. You need to undo the mischief that you have done. And if you fail to do so, you do that at the peril of your own salvation. And the day will come in which you will stand before the bar of God, and you will be among those who *loveth and maketh a lie*. You will be among those who are liars that are *thrust down to hell*. And that is just as true of those who have written biographies about Joseph Smith. If they're still living, they need to undo the mischief. They need to correct the record. They need to defend the reputation of a dispensation head called by God.

And I say this in the name of Jesus Christ, Amen.

125. Marriage, Part 1

This is Part 1 of a special series on Marriage.

———

READING FROM ANSWER AND COVENANT:

Marriage was, in the beginning, between one man and one woman, and was intended to remain so for the sons of Adam and the daughters of Eve, that they may multiply and replenish the Earth. I commanded that there shall not any man have save it be one wife, and concubines he shall have none. I, the Lord your God, delight in the chastity of women, and in the respect of men for their wives.

Marriage was established [in] the beginning as a covenant by the word and authority of God, between the [wo]man and God, the man and [the] woman, and the man and God. It was ordained by my word to endure forever. Mankind fell, but a covenant established by my word cannot fail, and therefore in death they were not to be parted.

It was my will that all marriages would follow the pattern of the beginning, and therefore all other marriages would be ordained as at the first. But fallen men refused my covenant, did not hearken to my word, nor receive my promise, and marriages fell outside my rule, disorganized and without me, therefore unable to endure beyond the promises made between the mortal man and the mortal woman, to end when they are dead.

Covenants, promises, rights, vows, associations, and expectations that are mine will endure, and those that are not cannot endure. Everything in the world, whether it is established by men, or by Thrones, or by Dominions, or by Principalities, or by Powers, that are not by my word and promise, shall be thrown down when men are dead and shall not remain in my Father's Kingdom. Only those things that are by me shall remain in and after the resurrection.

Marriage by me, or by my word, received as a holy covenant between the woman and I, the man and [the] woman, and the man and I, will endure beyond death and into my Father's Kingdom, worlds without end. Those who abide this covenant will pass by the angels who are appointed, and enter into exaltation. Concerning them it shall be said, You shall come forth in the first resurrection, and if they covenant after the first resurrection, then in the next resurrection, and shall inherit in my Kingdom their own thrones, dominions, principalities, powers, all heights and depths, and shall pass by the angels [and] receive exaltation, the glory of which shall be a fullness and a continuation of their posterity forever.

Marriage is necessary for the exaltation of the man and [the] woman, and is ordained by me through the Holy Spirit of Promise, or in other words, by my covenant, my law, and my authority. Like the marriage in Eden, marriage is a sacrament for a sacred place, on holy ground, in my presence, or where the Holy Spirit of Promise can minister. But rebellion has kept mankind from inheriting what I ordained in the beginning, and therefore women and men have been left to marry apart from me. Every marriage established by me requires that I be [a] part of the covenant for it to endure, for Endless is my name and without me the marriage cannot be without end: for so long as I endure it shall also endure, if it is made by my word and covenant.

But know also that I can do my work at any time, for I have sacred space above, and can do my work despite earth and hell. The wickedness of men has not prevented my will but only kept the wicked from what they might have received.

Whenever I have people who are mine, I command them to build a house, a holy habitation, a sacred place where my presence can dwell or where the Holy Spirit of Promise can minister, because it is in such a place...it has been ordained to recover you, establish by my word and my oath your marriages, and endow my people with knowledge from on high that will unfold to you the mysteries of godliness, instruct you in my ways, that you may walk in my path. [And] all the outcasts of Israel will I gather to my house, and the jealousy of Ephraim and Judah will end; Ephraim will not envy Judah and Judah will not provoke Ephraim.

And again I say to you, Abraham and Sarah sit upon a Throne, for he could not be there if not for Sarah's covenant with him; Isaac and Rebecca sit upon a Throne, and Isaac likewise could not be there if not for Rebecca's covenant with him; and Jacob and Rachel sit upon a Throne, and Jacob could not be there if not for Rachel's covenant with him; and all these have ascended above Dominions and Principalities and Powers, to abide in my Kingdom.

Therefore the marriage covenant is needed for all those who would likewise seek to obtain from me the right to continue their seed into eternity, for only through marriage can Thrones and Kingdoms be established. (T&C 157:34-43 RE)

DENVER: Can it be said concerning your own marriage that it is *not* good for the man to be alone? Are the two of you, together, better than what each of you are alone? Is your marriage a source of joy, of happiness, of contentment, of companionship? The Lord told them to "*multiply, and replenish the earth*" (Genesis 2:9 RE and T&C Lectures on Faith 2:8 RE). Do you find within your family relationship that there's joy and rejoicing and happiness, as a consequence of the environment that you and your wife put together?

Is your relationship— As a woman, is your relationship in the image of God? Is there godliness about the way in which you and your husband interact? If you had to reckon whether or not someone, looking at the two of you, would see within you the image of God, would they do so?

These aren't just happy notions for the afterlife; these ought to be descriptions of what *your* marriage could and should look like. Can you sense the glory of God in your marriage? Remember, we looked at this in 93:36: *The glory of God is intelligence, or in other words, light and truth* —"glory of God" being light; the "glory of God" being truth (D&C 93:36; see also T&C 93:11 RE). Is that something that is present within the marriage that *you* have? Is your marriage filled with life, with light, with truth, with understanding?

Turn back to D&C section 121. There's a couple verses there that I want to suggest, particularly if you view the man and the woman together as one. Read these verses as if it's descriptive of the "one," which is you and your wife:

> *Many are called, but few are chosen.* [This is beginning at verse 40 of section 121.] *No power or influence can or ought to be maintained by virtue of the priesthood; only by persuasion, by long-suffering, by gentleness and meekness, and by love unfeigned, By kindness and pure knowledge, which shall greatly enlarge the soul; without hypocrisy, and without guile.* (D&C 121:40-42; see also T&C 139:5-6 RE)

Within your family, within your marriage, are you and your wife learning to use persuasion? Within your marriage are you and your husband learning to use gentleness in dealing with one another? Are the two of you, together, facing one another in all of the difficulties that come as a result of being married? Are you facing that together in meekness? Do you find that in all the relationship troubles, turmoils, and challenges, what predominates is kindness? Is there a search for understanding that results in pure knowledge when it comes to a dilemma?

So far as I can tell, Joseph Smith *greatly* respected women—in what he said, and what he taught, and how he taught it. And I know all the arguments: I've read all the histories; I've read what the people say; I've read what the accusations are. The fact of the matter is that they are not accurate. And the histories that they are based upon and much of the information was ginned up—in consequence of litigation in which Joseph F. Smith went around gathering affidavits, in the two affidavit books from which we draw most of the information, to redefine what Joseph Smith was doing in Nauvoo, and earlier, with plural marriage.

Plural marriage was denounced by him as an abomination. And He got up and said before a crowd, "I hear all the time that I have wives; I've got seven wives. I'm looking out in the audience and I can only see one," meaning Emma. (See *History of the Church*, vol 6, pg 411.) If you read the letters that Joseph sent to Emma, and you read the letters that Emma sent back to Joseph (and they are preserved in the correspondence and the documents of the Joseph Smith History), you realize that those two, whatever else was going on around them, those two were in love with one another. And Joseph relied on her, respected her, and she loved him. They had a fabulous relationship between the two of them. And I don't care what *In Sacred Loneliness* (Todd M. Compton, 1997) wants to portray otherwise. A fair reading of Joseph's life was that he was a man who was faithful to his wife.

The account continues and describes the creation of the woman. Here the parable distinguishes between the process of creating the man Adam and creating his spouse, the woman Eve:

> *And I, the Lord God, said unto [mine] Only Begotten that it was not good that the man should be alone; wherefore, **I** will make [an] help meet for him.* ([Emphasis added.] Genesis 2:13 RE)

God the Father said to the Only Begotten that He, God the Father, will be the one to make Adam's help meet. It was not good for Adam to be alone because he was not complete without a suitable companion to help him progress and develop. The Creation Parable continues:

> *And I, the Lord God, caused a deep sleep to fall upon Adam, and he slept. And I took one of his ribs…closed up the flesh in the stead thereof. And the rib, which I, the Lord God, had taken from man, [I made] a woman, and brought her unto the man. And Adam said, This I know now is bone of my bones and flesh of my flesh. She [should] be called woman because she was taken out of man.* (Genesis 2:14 RE)

The parable of the creation of the woman, therefore, differs from the creation of the man. She was not formed from the dust of the ground; she was formed from a *rib,* from an already-existing part of the man. She was born from something equal to him and able to stand beside him in all things.

But the parable about the woman Eve means a great deal more. She was at Adam's side before the creation of this world. They were united as one in a prior estate, when they progressed to become *living souls* with both bodies and spirits. They were sealed before this world by the Holy Spirit of Promise and proved to be true and faithful. They once sat upon a throne in God the Father's Kingdom. In that state, they were equal and eternally joined together. She sat beside him and was a necessary part of his enthronement. Her introduction into this world, to join her companion, was needed to complete Adam; it was not good for him to be alone. They were one, and therefore Adam without Eve was not complete—or in the words of the parable, "*not good"* to *"be alone."*

READING FROM THE TESTIMONY OF ST. JOHN, CHAPTER 12:

> *The first day of the week Mary the Elect Lady went in the early morning while it was still dark to the burial sepulcher. She saw the stone was rolled away from the sepulcher, and two angels sitting on it. Then she ran to Simon Peter, who was with the other disciple Jesus loved, and said to them, They have removed the Lord out of the sepulcher, and we do not know where he is now established. Peter and the other disciple departed for the sepulcher, running together. The other disciple outran Peter and arrived first at the sepulcher. And he bent down, and looked in, and saw the linen burial cloths. But he did not enter the tomb. Then Simon Peter joined him, and he went into the sepulcher and saw the linen burial cloths, and also the shroud that covered his body. It was not lying with the other burial cloths. Instead it was folded and set down alone. Then the other disciple who arrived first, also entered the sepulcher, and he saw the empty tomb and believed. They still did not understand the prophecy that he must rise again from the dead. Then the disciples departed to return home.*
>
> *But Mary stood outside the sepulcher weeping. And as she wept, she bent down and looked into the sepulcher. She saw two angels in white, the one at the head, and the other at the feet where the body of Jesus had lain. They asked her, Woman, why are you mourning? She answered them, Because someone has removed the body of my Lord, and I do not know where he is now. After she said this, she walked away and then saw Jesus standing in the garden area. She failed to recognize that it was Jesus. Jesus asked her, Woman,*

> *why are you mourning? Who are you looking for? She assumed he was tending the garden, and answered, Sir, if you have taken him away, tell me where he is, and I will claim him. Jesus said to her, Mary.*
>
> *She raised her face, recognized him, and addressed him, Greatest of Teachers, which is to say, My Lord. They embraced and Jesus told her, You cannot hold me here. I need to ascend right now to my Father. Go to my followers and say to them, I ascend to my Father and your Father, and to my God and your God.*
>
> *Mary the Elect Lady came and told the disciples that she had seen the Lord, and that He had spoken these things to her.* (T&C 171 Testimony of St. John 12:1-4 RE)

DENVER: John wrote that Mary Magdalene saw, even embraced the risen Lord, and related to the others *her* testimony of having seen Him returned to life, resurrected from the dead.

These accounts differ in details. They have similarities and differences. They are universal in the fact that Christ was seen by the women, or *a woman,* first and not by His Apostles. John's account records that Christ told Mary: *"Touch me not"* (John 20:17). In the Joseph Smith Translation the words are changed to read: *"Hold me not"* (John 11:2 RE). Joseph's change of the text was warranted. I tell you that when Mary realized it was Jesus, she embraced Him joyfully. She did not timidly reach out her hand, but she readily greeted Him with open arms, and He in turn embraced her.

It is difficult to describe what I saw of the incident, apart from saying that the Lord was triumphant, exultant, overjoyed at His return from the grave! *She shared His joy!* I was shown the scene and do not have words to adequately communicate how complete the feelings of joy and gratitude were which were felt by *our* Lord that morning. As dark and terrible as were the sufferings through which He passed, the magnitude of which is impossible for man to put into words, these feelings of triumph were, on the other hand, of equal magnitude in their joy and gratitude. He had attained to the resurrection of the dead! Just as He had seen His Father do, He likewise held the keys of death and hell! I do not think it possible for a mortal to feel a fullness of either. And having felt some of what He shares with His witnesses, I know words are inadequate to capture His feelings on the morning of His resurrection.

He had the deep satisfaction of having accomplished the most difficult assignment to be given by the Father, knowing it was a benefit to all of His Father's children. *And it had been done perfectly.*

Mary and Christ embraced. There was nothing timid about the warm encounter she had with Him. Then He said to her, *"Hold me not,"* because He had to ascend, return and report to His Father. Joseph Smith was correct when he changed the language.

I then saw Him ascend to heaven. I saw the golden heavenly light glowing down upon Mary as she watched His ascent. All this happened while it was yet dark on the morning He rose from the dead. He has shown this to me, and I can testify to it as a witness.

Before this Creation, the Mother in Heaven was *with* the Father. She was beside Him when His work began. She was there when the plan was laid, the boundaries established, and the compass applied to establish order for the Creation. All the Father knows, the Mother knows. All the Father established and ordered, the Mother established and ordered. *They* are one. She is the Father's *delight,* and the potential of Her sons to be like Her Husband brings Her delight.

To be like their Father, Her sons must become one with Her daughters; for it is not good for man to be alone. The Father and Mother are one, and Her sons and daughters must likewise *become* one. Only when the man and woman were together was the Creation *good.* When men rebel, disobey, act cruelly, or mistreat Her daughters, we are anything but a delight to the Heavenly Mother. When we offend *Her*, we also offend Her Husband.

Before any of us will plan, measure, set a compass, and apportion the foundations of another earth, we must grow together and become like *Them.* Their work is glorious. They possess love—the power that creates and organizes. Love is the power behind all that They do. *We* cannot be like Them without a loving relationship that mirrors Theirs.

The foregoing excerpts are taken from:

- The presentation of "Answer and Covenant," given at the Covenant of Christ Conference in Boise, Idaho, on September 3, 2017;

- Denver's *40 Years in Mormonism Series*, Talk #9 titled "Marriage and Family," given in St. George, Utah, on July 26, 2014;
- A regional conference Q&A Session, held at Big Cottonwood Canyon, Utah, on September 20, 2015;
- Denver's conference talk titled "Our Divine Parents," given in Gilbert, Arizona, on March 25th, 2018;
- The Testimony of St. John 12:1-4, in the Restoration Edition of the scriptures; and
- Denver's conference talk titled "The Doctrine of Christ," given in Boise, Idaho, on September 11, 2016.

126. Marriage, Part 2

This is Part 2 of a special series on Marriage.

———

DENVER: I have been thinking a lot about Abraham and Sarah and their relationship. Their story is one of the greatest in history.

Little details in the story are touching. The ten years that Sarah waited, in Genesis 16:3 (Genesis 7:25 RE), before urging Abraham to father a child with Hagar, is based upon a custom at that time. Abraham's willingness to follow the custom was because the Lord promised *him* children. Sarah could not conceive, and *Sarah* urged him to do so. In fact, of the three, Sarah's urging was what seems to persuade Abraham. Her urging is tempered by making it seem she is looking out for her own interests: *"It may be that I* [Sarah] *may obtain children by her."* This softens the request, makes it a blessing for Sarah, and casts it in terms which do not belittle or dismiss Sarah. Then the account reads: *"Abram hearkened to the voice of Sarai."*

Abraham was willing to wait on the Lord's promises of children. He was willing to forego the customs that allowed a man to take another wife. It was *Sarah's* gentle persuasion that convinced Abraham to take Hagar. Sarah was loved by Abraham with his whole heart. It was this great marriage relationship that allowed the Lord to preserve them as the parents of "all righteous"—a new Adam for the Lord's covenant people. And, of course, there cannot be an Adam without an Eve—Sarah becomes the "Mother of All Righteous."

This is more critical than most people recognize. It was because of this important relationship that the tenth parable in *Ten Parables* (Denver C. Snuffer, 2008) begins with the marriage relationship. Without this, there is no reason to save the man.

Marriage is separate from its two parties. It has a life of its own. The husband and the wife may be parties *to* the marriage, but the marriage itself is a separate, living thing. It is distinct from the two partners in the relationship and greater than either of them. It lives; it is real.

The only people whose right to eternal life has been secured, to my knowledge, came as a result of the marriage relationship and its worthiness to be preserved into eternity. "*Neither is the man without the woman nor the woman without the man in the Lord*" (1 Corinthians 1:44 RE). Therefore, if you are interested in eternal life, the very first place to begin is inside *your marriage.*

In Doctrine and Covenants section 130 it says, beginning at verse 18 (we've looked at these verses in several contexts, but we need to look at them again today in this context):

> *Whatever principle of intelligence* [and understand that means light and truth] *we attain unto in this life, it will rise with us in the resurrection. And if a person gains more knowledge and intelligence in this life through his diligence and obedience than another, he'll have so much the advantage in the world to come. [There's] a law, irrevocably decreed in heaven before the foundation of this world, upon which all blessings are predicated—And when we obtain any blessing from God, [it's] by obedience to the law upon which it is predicated.* (D&C 130:18-21)

Think about those verses and that admonition as an invitation to work this out inside your marriage first; to work out—inside the relationship between you and your wife—the principle of intelligence that gives you the opportunity to be diligent, the opportunity to be obedient, the opportunity to gain experience that will make you more like God. Your marriage is a laboratory to prove you up and to let you be intelligent.

> *And in that day, Adam blessed God, and was filled, and began to prophesy concerning all the families of the earth, saying, Blessed be the name of God, for because of my transgression my eyes are opened, and in this life I shall have joy, and again, in the flesh I shall see God.* (Genesis 3:4 RE)

That's Adam prophesying what is going to befall the future generations. That's what Adam is doing; now look at what Eve does:

> *And Eve his wife heard all these things* [The prophecy comes through Adam; Eve hears them. Eve hears all these things] *and was glad, saying, Were it not for our transgression, we never should have had seed, and never should have known good and evil, and the joy of our redemption, and the eternal life which God [giveth] unto all the obedient.* (Ibid.)

There is a *profound* difference between the response of the power of the Spirit unfolding upon these two, with respect to its effect upon Adam, on the one hand, and its effect upon Eve, on the other. These are remarkably different reactions. To the man it is that he prophesies; that is, *he* declares the truth—the 'truth' being a knowledge of things as they are, and as they were, and as they are to come. That definition is given to us in the Doctrine and Covenants. This is the *role* of the man, and this is the role that he fulfills.

But to Eve, on the other hand, she obtains wisdom. The role of the man is knowledge; the role of the woman is wisdom. And you see that on display right here in these verses. It is the role of the woman to have the understanding, to take the prophecy that has been delivered now by Adam and to process it, and to say, "Here is what it means." This is the role of the woman. This is the *gift* of the woman. This is *eternally* the role of the woman.

This is why there is a male and why there is a female. Because in many respects, the gift of wisdom eludes the male, and in many respects, the gift of knowledge eludes the female. And together the two of them— And I'm not talking about 'knowledge' in the sense that a woman can't have a Ph.D. Two of the brightest people I know are daughters of mine. It's not *that* that I'm talking about. I'm talking about knowledge in the godly sense, knowledge in "the gift of God" sense, and I'm talking about wisdom in "the gift of God" sense, and in the scriptural sense.

This is an example: Now, *together*, (look at verse 12):

> *And Adam and Eve blessed the name of God* [And how did they do that? They did that by a ritual; they did that by offering sacrifice. They did that by observing what they understood, but they did it together], *and* ***they*** [it is "they" —*they*] *made all things known unto* ***their*** *sons and daughters.* ([Emphasis added.] Moses 5:12; see also Genesis 3:4 RE)

This isn't Adam preaching repentance; this isn't Eve preaching repentance. This is *they*; this is the two of them. They are equally yoked. This is the two of them joined together to make the declaration—*they* together.

Then in the book of Moses, the children of Adam and Eve married two by two, male and female. One of the clarifications that we now have is that the divine purpose of marriage is to multiply and replenish the earth. That answers the question about relationships between the same sex, because you cannot multiply and replenish the earth in any other form than that.

Marriage was instituted by God in the beginning. It's an ordinance. It involves the man and the woman. And it doesn't matter what other kind of social relationship you want to form; it's not marriage. Because at its heart, marriage is from God and confined to that relationship.

When you define marriage as 'given by God,' keep in mind the definition of an abomination. An abomination is something that you practice that is wrong, done as a religious belief. So, marriage that doesn't conform to the pattern of God is, by definition, an abomination. Its result is not only to defile the definition of marriage, but it absolutely precludes multiplying and replenishing the earth. It renders the marriage bed devoid of progeny, incapable of producing offspring. It is desolate.

An abominable practice that produces desolation is something that we all ought to take note of. It's not a social issue; it's not a civil rights issue. In a secular society, I don't care what people do in the privacy of their own homes. But when you begin to say that that is not merely the right of privacy and the right of association, but is a religious right involving marriage, and it produces nothing but desolation, we ought to stop short of that. We ought to say, "Go and do as you will do."

"Neither is the man without the woman, nor the woman without the man, in the Lord," wrote Paul in First Corinthians (1 Corinthians 1:44 RE). You cannot have an eternal marriage without both. In the relationship, the woman's role in creating a king is central, for it is the woman who will establish *him* on his throne. In turn, it is the man who will then establish her on *her* throne. Her act precedes his, and his act confirms and blesses the new government or family unit, as his first act as king, for king without consort is doomed to end. Together they are infinite because in them the seed continues. They may still be mortal as the events take place, but because they continue and produce seed, they are as infinite as the gods.

Fidelity to your spouse is foundational to righteousness. Immorality is disruptive of marriage, destructive of families, and has no place in a City of Peace.

Group sex, immoral relationships, and free intercourse is offensive to God, a violation of the Ten Commandments, and the means of spreading disease. God does not justify carnal relations except between one man and his wife; they two are the image of God. Anything else degrades and corrupts. Participants in immoral behavior become laden with sin.

Those foolish enough to be misled by this darkness deserve to be taken captive and destroyed, as will *certainly* come to pass.

Jacob chapter 3—this is a remarkable, remarkable passage—3, beginning at verse 5:

> *Behold, the Lamanites, your brethren whom ye hate because of their filthiness and the cursings which hath come upon their skins, are more righteous than you; for they have not forgotten the commandment of the Lord which was given unto our father, that they should have save it were one wife, and concubines they should have none, and there should not be whoredoms committed among them...now this commandment they observe to keep. Wherefore, because of this observance in keeping this commandment, the Lord God will not destroy them, but will be merciful unto them, and one day they shall become a blessed people.* (Jacob 2:11 RE)

It was the fidelity of the Lamanites to one wife. They rejected the prophets. They rejected Nephi. They rejected the Gospel. They turned to their *loathsomeness.* They were a wild and a ferocious people. But *this* preserved them in the eyes of God. *This* was important enough that *they* deserved to continue on—unlike the Nephites who had the Gospel, unlike the Nephites who had the prophets.

> *Behold, their husbands love their wives, and their wives love their husbands, and their husbands and their wives love their children; and their unbelief and hatred towards you is because of the iniquity of their fathers. Wherefore, how much better are you than they in the sight of your great Creator?* (Ibid.)

God doesn't judge righteousness the way *we* do. If you've read the Tenth Parable (*Ten Parables,* Denver C. Snuffer, 2008), what was it that attracted the attention of the angels? They looked at the marriage, and they said, "This! This looks like what *we* come from! *This*! This relationship, this marriage, the man and the woman—*this* is what heaven itself consists of. And look! Look, it's on the earth!" And the angels go, and they bring the Lord, and they say, "Behold the man and the woman!" And the Lord sets in motion everything that was needed.

What more do you need to see from the theme of the Book of Mormon than *this* passage, in order to realize that when it comes to the relationship of marriage, *this* is the image of God. *This* is what God would like to preserve into eternity. It is so much easier to take people who have this kind of a marriage and to preserve them into eternity, than it is to take someone who may know all mysteries, but whose marriage is a tattered ruin, and attempt to preserve *them.*

The foregoing excerpts are taken from:

- Denver's blog post titled "Abraham and Sarah," posted April 29, 2010, and subsequently recorded by Denver on October 4, 2020;
- Denver's *40 Years in Mormonism Series*, Talk #9 titled "Marriage and Family," given in St. George, Utah, on July 26th, 2014;
- His comments at the "Unity in Christ" conference in Utah County, Utah, on July 30, 2017;
- Denver's blog post titled "D&C 132, Part 5," posted April 9, 2010, and subsequently recorded by Denver on September 27, 2020; and
- Denver's blog post titled "Fidelity in Marriage," posted October 31, 2015, and subsequently recorded by Denver on September 27, 2020.

127. Gospel Tangents, Part 1

This is the first part of an interview Denver did this past summer with Rick Bennett for his Gospel Tangents podcast, which is presented here in its entirety in this series.

Rick Bennett: Welcome to Gospel Tangents. I'm really excited to have a wonderful guest here in the Restoration movement. Could you go ahead and tell us who you are?

Denver Snuffer: Denver Snuffer, reluctant interviewee.

Rick: [laughter[

Denver: Been persuaded by the promises that you made of remuneration.

Rick: [laughter] Remuneration...

Denver: Yeah, yeah. No, I don't like doing interviews, but after the request was made, I watched a few of the interviews that you've done, and I communicated with Lindsay Hansen Park. And the style of interview that you have really doesn't seem to have an agenda. You're just interested in letting people talk. I watched her interview; I watched Michael Quinn's. So, yeah, this is one of those rare occasions where I'm willing to talk.

Rick: [laughter] Well, I feel really lucky. I'm excited to have you on, so this is fantastic. So, how would you introduce yourself? I mean, I think some people would call you a prophet. Is that a title you accept? Or how do you…? How does that…?

Denver: There's a whole lot of baggage that has accumulated around the idea of some title, some honorific title. And the trappings that go along with those kinds of things are unwanted, unwelcomed, and I just don't like it. I commented one time that in all of scripture, the use of the term *Beloved* is confined almost exclusively to the Savior. It's a sacred appellation—Beloved—and it gets used by the Lord on rare occasion when He is talking to an individual that is in the presence of the Lord, and He's being acknowledged or promised something by God. So, the appellation Beloved is, to me, inappropriate to use because of it's sacred nature outside of talking about the Lord's Beloved, which is Christ.

Beloved prophet: Now you're also going one step further because my understanding of the role of a prophet— It's like Joseph said: A prophet is only a prophet when a prophet's doing something that fits within that framework. Anyone can have a revelation—anyone. It's not confined to Christians; it's not confined to denominational leaders. Revelations are available, generally, to the entirety of mankind in every culture, every religion everywhere in the world. A prophet is someone whose revelation was not intended for necessarily *that* person but was intended to be a public message.

Almost all revelation is individual, personal, and the property correctly belonging to the recipient of that revelation. A prophet's message really doesn't belong to him. In fact, on some occasions, the message a prophet receives is something that he doesn't even understand himself. He's gonna have to parse it through and try to untangle the content to understand it himself. So, the message to a prophet is not personal; it's not directed to merely him. It's a message to the world.

So, in that context, the term gets misused a lot and—in particular, in this culture, in this geography—implies status, control, deference, authority. And I make no claim to authority. I make no claim to preside over anyone. I make no claim to be anything other than a fellow sojourner here trying our best to follow God.

But you caught me at a fortuitous moment because I now have the culmination of years of work by hundreds of volunteers. And maybe the best way to put a context to me is for me to talk about *this* [holding up his RE Scriptures].

Rick: Okay.

Denver: These are prototypes. It'll go into production. But we now have a print copy of a new set of scriptures. There are three volumes. The Old Covenants volume is the Joseph Smith Translation of the Old Testament. It begins with Genesis that most LDS people would recognize as the Book of Moses in the The Pearl of Great Price.

Rick: Okay.

Denver: So, the Joseph Smith Translation-Genesis text begins with the Book of Moses, and then, it follows the Joseph Smith Translation version of the Old Testament to the end. That's all in the first volume called The Old Covenants.

Rick: So, that's basically the Old Testament plus the Book of Moses, basically? Is that it? And Joseph Smith's translation…

Denver: It's the Old Testament-Joseph Smith Translation version.

Rick: Mm-hmm.

Denver: And it's the most accurate version of what Joseph did that has ever found its way into print. The Reorganized Church, now the Community of Christ, published what they called the Joseph Smith Translation.

Rick: *Inspired Version* I think is what they call it.

Denver: The Inspired Version of the Bible.

Rick: Mm-hmm.

Denver: The problem with that is that it was not entirely complete in that they omitted dozens of things that Joseph had done, but the committee that was responsible for publishing it also inserted things that they thought ought be in there. Therefore, the Inspired Version in the RLDS is not what you'll find in this [tapping the RE volume]. The Inspired Version—we've had people compare with the available material, and all of the changes that were omitted are included. All of the additions that were made by others are deleted. And in addition, during talks Joseph Smith gave in the Nauvoo era, there were times when he was talking about a passage of scripture from the Bible, and he would comment that "a more correct translation..." or "a more correct reading..." And then, he would alter the text that he just read out of the Bible. He didn't always do that in the manuscript of the Joseph Smith Translation, but all of those Nauvoo-era comments that he made were picked up and were also added. So, it's the most complete set.

Rick: Wow.

Denver: Joseph Smith also always intended to publish both the New Testament and the Book of Mormon in a single volume. So, the second— The first volume is called The Old Covenants because those are the covenants (plural) that went with Adam and Enoch and Noah and Abraham and Moses down to the time of Christ.

The second volume is called The New Covenants. It's the New Testament and the Book of Mormon. Again, it has the same Joseph Smith Translation version put into it with all of the corrections—most complete version. But, in addition, we have a different Book of Mormon text. Joseph Smith dictated the translation of the Book of Mormon, and it was written by various scribes beginning with Emma Smith's handwriting and ending with Oliver Cowdery's handwriting. That material was then used by Oliver Cowdery to make the printer's manuscript.

The printer's manuscript was intended to be a faithful copy of the original translation, but we know from a comparison between what has survived of the original and the printer's manuscript, that we have 100% of, that Oliver Cowdery made about one and a half copying mistakes per page of the printer's manuscript. That manuscript was then taken to the E. B. Grandin shop, and it was John Gilbert who got hired by E .B. Grandin to typeset the Book of Mormon. John Gilbert took the printer's manuscript, which has no punctuation on it, and then, he punctuated and typeset the Book of Mormon. John Gilbert did what he did in punctuating based upon his understanding of how the words that were on that page should be understood.

There's been this controversy that has existed in Mormonism (scholarly articles being written) about how Joseph Smith's understanding of God changed from, originally, a trinitarian view into, later, a different view where there's different personages who belong to the Godhead. And as evidence for Joseph Smith's earlier trinitarian understanding of the Godhead, they point to the original Book of Mormon text. Well, the punctuation that was put in by John Gilbert, if you repunctuate it, can change from a trinitarian view to the later doctrinal view that Joseph Smith would teach and preach and advocate. I've referred to John Gilbert's use of punctuation (I've coined the term the *trinitarian comma*) because if you take out some commas, or you move them about, you can actually reach exactly the same doctrinal conclusion that Joseph would later teach simply by repunctuating what John Gilbert did.

So, in the second volume, what we've done is— I think I gave two talks in which I changed the punctuation and showed how you could conform to Joseph's later teachings. I think those got in here. But by and large, as much as possible, punctuation has been removed in order to allow the reader a more independent way of coming to grips with the content of the book and to deciding for yourself how best it ought to be understood.

Rick: Hmm.

Denver: It's also— Joseph made a revision, and he was revising again in the 1844 time period, but he revised the Book of Mormon a couple of times while he was still alive. It appears from comparisons that what Joseph was doing in the revisions he was making was trying to take the printed version that we had and make it conform more closely to the original translation, not the printer's manuscript. Errors crept in there. More errors crept in when John Gilbert worked with it. (The printed copy was after John Gilbert's fingerprints were on it.) He took that back to the original translation, and he tried to correct it to conform back to that.

We— Unfortunately, that original translation got put in the cornerstone of the building. It didn't get pulled out until it had rotted. We only have about 22% of the original left. We have 100% of the printer's copy but only 22% of the original. And so, we don't have the ability to go back and completely conform. But as near as it is possible at this point to recapture that, that's the Book of Mormon version that appears in the second volume.

Rick: Hmm.

Denver: Then, the third volume is something called the Teachings and Commandments. It's a chronological layout of the revelations given to Joseph Smith with the exception of the Joseph Smith History. Joseph Smith rewrote the history after ~~John Gilbert~~ [John Whitmer] left the Church and took the history with him. Joseph rewrote the history of the Church in 1838. Then, he published it in the *Times and Seasons* when he was the editor of the *Times and Seasons* (it being based upon the 1838 material) because the internal content of the *Times and Seasons* material is all referencing the 1838 time frame. We don't have that. We do have a copy that was made in 1839, and it was that copy in 1839 that was the basis for the *Times and Seasons* version.

While Joseph Smith was the editor of the *Times and Seasons*, his history began to roll out. It's significantly longer than what is in the Pearl of Great Price-Joseph Smith History that Latter-day Saints would be familiar with. But the entirety of this history, while it was written and published with him as the editor, appears as the first section of the Teachings and Commandments. Then, it follows a chronological layout through all of the revelations of Joseph Smith. And once again, we have access to the revelation as Joseph Smith dictated it.

The revelations of Joseph went through two iterations that altered the text. A copy was taken by Oliver Cowdery to Independence, Missouri, to be published as the Book of Commandments. Oliver Cowdery, in setting up the

Book of Commandments, felt at liberty because there was a revelation about Oliver having the right to write for the Church but not by way of commandment; yet, he could write. He had the liberty, he thought, to alter some of the texts and to add to them. So, he did that in the Book of Commandments. And the press was overrun, and it was destroyed. Copies of that got salvaged in loose form. They later got gathered up and bound together as the Book of Commandments. But that publishing effort in Independence was abandoned because of the mobs and the destruction of the press. So, in 1835, they published the Doctrine and Covenants in Kirtland.

Well, the Doctrine and Covenants contained, as its very first section, the Lectures on Faith. A committee was appointed to deal with the revelations, the Book of Commandments material. Joseph Smith was part of that committee but apparently didn't contribute. His diaries say that he spent *his* time editing and correcting Lectures on Faith.

There are those who say that Lectures on Faith appear to be the product of Sidney Rigdon and not Joseph Smith because they did word comparisons. Joseph Smith, before the publication of Doctrine and Covenants, spent *his* time editing and correcting Lectures on Faith. When he finished with that, and that is apparently the only thing he worked on getting ready for the Doctrine and Covenants to be printed, he said he would vouch for the correctness of the doctrine that is contained in what he had done, that he would stand by every word of it. *That* portion in the front of the D&C is the *doctrine*. The *covenants* are the *revelations*.

Well, the committee that was working on the revelations included Sidney Rigdon, and he took even more liberties than had Oliver Cowdery with revelations that had come to Joseph. And so, what you have in the LDS version of the Doctrine and Covenants are two steps removed from the original revelation to Joseph. And what is in the Teachings and Commandments is a chronological layout that includes Lectures on Faith that, insofar as we are able to accurately do so, recaptures exactly what the original revelation was and states it, as near as we can get at present, comprehensively, chronologically, and accurately in the form that it came as a revelation to Joseph Smith.

Rick: So, you're telling me that you've recanonized Lectures on Faith because that was actually taken out?

Denver: Yes.

Rick: Yeah, so you recanonized it, huh?

Denver: Yeah, it's in here. Lectures on Faith is Section—the Teachings and Commandments Section 110. Yes, recanonized it. It was actually never— See, here's two interesting factoids: first is, Lectures on Faith were canonized by a vote of the Church. They were not removed. They remained, by vote of the Church in General Conference, canonized scripture. They were deleted without a vote by a committee in 1921 that simply took the step of dropping it and saying, "We're not sure it's good material. We're not gonna to keep it in the scriptures." So, it was decanonized.

The second interesting fact is that no conference, until these scriptures, ever accepted and canonized the Book of Mormon. The Book of Mormon was simply accepted, but it was never accepted and canonized by a vote of conference until it was done so for these scriptures.

Rick: You mean in one of your conferences?

Denver: Yeah, it happened in Boise in 2017 as I recall.

So, let me tell you the whole reason behind all of this effort—because hundreds of volunteers, donating thousands of hours of effort, worked tirelessly for a long period of time to put this material together in a correct form.

There was a revelation that was given in September of 1832. The Church got organized in April of 1830. By the time you get to September of 1832, this is the sad news that the Church is getting:

> *Your minds in times past have been darkened because of unbelief, and because you have treated lightly the things you have received, which vanity and unbelief have brought the whole church under condemnation. And this condemnation rests upon the children of Zion, even all, and they shall remain under this condemnation until they repent and remember the new covenant, even the Book of Mormon, and the former commandments which I have given them, not only to say but to do according to that which I have written, that they may bring forth fruit meet for their Father's kingdom. Otherwise, there remains a scourge and a judgment to be poured out upon the children of Zion....* (T&C 82:20)

So, condemnation was brought, and the focus that most people have on those words is to *do.* But what became apparent is that the problem is not merely *doing*. It is also in the *saying*, meaning that the revelations were entrusted to them, but they weren't accurately preserving or accurately saying, "What it was that I..." And the *I* in that statement is God— God saying, "I gave this to you, and you're not saying what I said, and you're not doing what I've required of you; and therefore, you're condemned." And this happens within what? eighteen months of the founding of the Church? The condemnation's there?

Well, if they'd taken that seriously in September of 1832, you still had available to you the original translation manuscript that we don't have. They would still have the original revelations to Joseph that we still don't have (or we have not been able to preserve entirely intact), and the recovery effort could have been done by the time you got to the conference in 1835 where they adopt the Doctrine and Covenants with Lectures on Faith and the others. But they didn't do it.

And so, today, when you say, "You're under condemnation because you failed both to say and to do what the Lord had done and said and required that you do," if you're going to set about, at this late date, to try and make that right and to put it all back together again, what you find is that it is—it's an impossible undertaking. You can get close. You can get a whole lot closer than what you do in a traditional Latter-day Saint set of scriptures or a Community of Christ set of scriptures. You can get a whole lot closer, but you really would have needed to undertake this work while Joseph Smith was *alive* in order to actually accomplish what brought the Church under condemnation in September 1832 to emerge *out* from under that condemnation.

But this effort was undertaken as the best efforts that can be made with the available source material. And it was a labor of love intending to show, at least to the Lord, that although we may not be able to get all the way there, there is a group of people still left on the earth who take seriously the condemnation and would labor as hard and long as they can to try and bring it back into a restored, accurate state. And that was the scripture project which got presented to the Lord for His approval.

The Teachings and Commandments Section 156 is a *prayer* that was offered to try and get the scriptures accepted and acknowledged. That Section 156 then received an *answer*, and that's Section 157.

All of these scriptures are now being produced in a leather-bound set with a 100% cotton paper, leather-bound, gilded edging, finest leather, finest binding, finest printing, and finest materials that we can make. Unfortunately, we had to pay in advance to get them made, so…

Rick: Did you ask Martin Harris to mortgage the farm?

Denver: There were actually a couple people who stepped forward to help with that, individuals who contributed in order to get the minimum order made to satisfy the requirements. I think there— It's more than 2500 but less than 3000 copies of the leather-bound material that's gonna be put out. But they were pre-purchased. So, I think that Benchmark is gonna— I think they ordered 15 sets of the three volumes. I think they'll have 15 sets available for sale. But it will require another pre-order at some point in the future before there's ever a second printing. But they're really quite nice and quite accurate.

Rick: Well, it sounds interesting. When are these gonna be available? Can the public purchase these, then?

Denver: No, they would have had to have ordered at the time that the order went in.

Rick: Oh. So, you have to go to Benchmark to get them, huh?

Denver: Well, there will be 15 lucky souls that are able to get them through Benchmark. But all the copies that were printed were paid for in advance. I think I personally placed the largest single order because I bought them for myself, my wife, all of my children, and if my children are married, for their spouse, also. So I bought a number of copies.

Rick: Wow. How much do they run?

Denver: This is what's interesting. The printer that we got for this wanted to get into the Bible-publishing business because the Bible is the largest-selling book in the world still, today. And he'd never printed a Bible. So, he competed with multiple printers around the world that we got bids for. The best Bible printers are not in the United States.

Rick: Hmm.

Denver: The very best is in the Netherlands: Royal Jongbloed. Well, we passed around a copy of the Royal Jongbloed among the committee, and everyone oohed and aahed, but to get them to put these together, it would've been about $500 for this set. Okay? But we loved it.

It just so happens that a fellow was on the committee who builds books as a living. He restores books; he makes them, handmade. But he'll take a rare book— He's restored the majority of the existing prints of the original E. B. Grandin Book of Mormon that had been restored. He *did* it. He was on the committee. He went through, and he prepared the specs for the printer who wanted to get into the Bible-publishing business. And this set that I'm holding is based upon the Royal Jongbloed workmanship and specifications, and it was done at a fraction of the cost. I think each of these books is about $34 apiece. The whole set is less than $100.

Rick: Hmm.

Denver: And, I mean, they'll obviously all be sold out because you have to pay in advance. But I'm hoping that someday there'll be a second printing, maybe a third. Who knows?

Rick: I'll have to put my order in to Curt Bench.

Denver: Yeah, call Curt.

Rick: [laughter]

Denver: There's another effort that we've undertaken.

Rick: Oh.

Denver: The original purpose of the Book of Mormon was to try to recover two groups of people. One was a remnant in the Americas. Another was a remnant that is referred to as the Jews. There is— There was one Hebrew Book of Mormon that was made (I think it was in the 1940's), but it was taken out of print, taken off the shelf. And the LDS Church has signed a treaty with the nation of Israel that they won't do anything to proselytise. So, one of the very target audiences that the Book of Mormon was intended for, the LDS Church has abandoned, by their commitment, in order to get the BYU Jerusalem Center on the north of the Mount of Olives. They agreed that they won't do anything to proselytise.

Well, we're under no such constraint. So, there are two things that are underway. The first is a separate, bound copy of the Book of Mormon which has been rendered into a Jewish-friendly version using Jewish spellings. The names in the Book of Mormon have been altered to Jewish spellings. The language has been— This is in English. I mean, the closest thing I can get in order for you to understand what we're talking about is: This is a Yiddish version of the Book of Mormon. It's been published and titled The Stick of Joseph in the Hands of Ephraim, and it has a Hebrew subtitle. That has been printed as part of this printing effort, also, and it will be given away. Several hundred copies of that book will be given away to Jewish people for them to consider the Book of Mormon in a more Jewish context.

And then, secondly, the Book of Mormon itself is currently being translated into Hebrew and will be published as a Hebrew text. The LDS Church, after they took the Hebrew Book of Mormon out of print, donated that translation to the Genealogical Society of Utah. The Genealogical Society of Utah microfilmed it, and we got a copy of it on microfilm. But as it turns out, it's not a particularly good Hebrew translation; so, it's being redone. A volunteer…

Rick: So, this is in Hebrew, then?

Denver: [holding the book] This is not. This is in English.

Rick: That's in English.

Denver: But it's in English with Hebrew spellings and Hebrew usages in it. But it's an English version.

Rick: So, instead of using *Jesus*, it's going to use *Yeshua*?

Denver: Yeah, it's—yes, exactly. And *Moshiyah* instead of *Mosiah*. I mean, it'll be Jewish- friendly.

The Hebrew-language version, which will be in Hebrew, is a work that's underway. Volunteers and then, some professionals are being compensated, and then, a PhD who— His specialty for his doctoral thesis was rendering into Hebrew, English material, taking English material and converting it into Old Testament Hebrew language. That was his PhD thesis. He's on the faculty of a major university. He's doing the final edit on the work that is being done to bring it into a Hebrew language. And when that's done and is published, it should withstand scrutiny from the most scrupulous rabbi of anywhere in the world—New York, Jerusalem, Amsterdam—doesn't matter. It will withstand scrutiny as a…

Rick: Are you sure? I've heard the saying, "Take two Jewish rabbis, and you get three opinions." [laughter]

Denver: Well, they may differ on what they do with the text, but they won't differ on the language that got used in order to bring it about. But we're doing an equally serious effort with Native Americans and the remnant there.

We don't necessarily want a lot of attention for the effort that's being made. In fact, there's a lot of disappointment, even bitterness, among Native American people because of what happened historically with the Indian placement program with that Indian School that's now abandoned. Much of it's been dismantled up in Brigham City.

Rick: The Intermountain High School.

Denver: Yeah, the Intermountain High School. There are children who were run through that program, who are now adults, who felt that they had been put upon, abused, belittled, discriminated against, mistreated at the hands of an institution. So, to say, "Hey, we're Mormons, kind of," or "We aren't Mormons, but we're bringing you the Book of Mormon," it's off-putting. You're gonna have an uphill battle to even get a fair hearing because the LDS effort has been disastrously off-putting. So, we're trying to deal with, cope with the trauma that has been inflicted by others in hoping to get a fair hearing for what the Restoration *could* mean to Native American peoples and getting them to respect what Joseph meant and what Joseph was attempting to do and what the Book of Mormon was really intended to accomplish. But we're not doing it with a lot of fanfare because the more fanfare that gets called to something, the more people will draw comparisons and analogies that just aren't true.

I mean, my personal view is that the LDS Church institutionally has pursued an institutional self-interest. A *byproduct* of their self-interest, fortunately, has been the preservation of the Book of Mormon, for which I'm grateful, the preservation of the Doctrine and Covenants, for which I'm grateful. I don't think that they were as interested in accuracy of the material or even in obedience to the material or trying to understand the material. But it served a self- interest, and that self-interest has been a blessing to me—because they may have profited; they may have built themselves a trillion dollar empire off of the back of these things. That doesn't matter to me. What matters to me is that they have gifted to me, generations later, the Book of Mormon text, and now, through *The Joseph Smith Papers*, enough material I can do something to recover it; and through the work of Royal Skousen, enough so that I can compare every edition in one volume side by side.

Rick: Royal Skousen was a big part of this. It sounds like he was.

Denver: His work product was. His work product was a phenomenal help. But he personally didn't participate in anything.

Rick: Right.

Denver: But *The Joseph Smith Papers*, which is also the product of the LDS Church, has been a marvelous aid. I buy *The Joseph Smith Papers* as they come off the press. I've got every volume. But I mark them up. Mine have interlineations, handwriting, cross-references.

The editors will introduce material. In their introduction, they will absolutely contradict the document you're about to read. It's glaringly stupid how they've approached some of this material. They will footnote stuff to say, "There is more to this story, and this is the 'more to the story'" because they sincerely, devoutly believe that it stayed on the rails after Joseph died and that what they inherited (and the traditions require that they take this position)—what they inherited is, in fact, a preservation of the Restoration through Joseph Smith. But *The Joseph Smith Papers* demonstrate that it's anything *but* that. The editorial contributions, the footnotes, the headnotes, the descriptions that they give, and the arguments that they make— It just wouldn't withstand scrutiny if you were subjecting it to, for example, the rules of evidence to get a document admitted in a courtroom. But that's a whole nother story. Anyway, we're trying to fix that in *this*.

Rick: I understand that historians and lawyers have different rules.

Denver: Sure.

Rick: And I have to mention, you are a lawyer, right?

Denver: Yeah, yeah. Yeah.

Rick: I probably should've introduced that earlier.

Denver: Right.

The foregoing was recorded on June 28, 2020 and is presented here with permission from Rick Bennett, who conducted the interview.

128. Gospel Tangents, Part 2

This is the second part of an interview Denver did this past summer with Rick Bennett for his Gospel Tangents podcast, which is presented here in its entirety in this series.

Rick Bennett: All right. So, I've got a bunch of questions that I want to ask. So, since you mentioned the Book of Mormon translation that you've done, you said that if you take out the punctuation, then it becomes less trinitarian.

Denver Snuffer: Yes.

Rick: Also, you mentioned—cuz I've read Lectures on Faith, and one of my understandings is Lectures on Faith is very trinitarian, and I feel like that's kind of why the LDS Church put that away. And so, I'm curious cuz you've recanonized that. To me, the Lectures on Faith sounds very trinitarian. And the Book of Mormon, as we have it, does sound very trinitarian. So, it's interesting to me to hear you say, "Well, if you take out the punctuation…" I guess it would support more of a Nauvoo-style theology. Is that…

Denver: Oh, yeah, yeah, yeah. Yeah. *I* think so.

Rick: So, how would you respond to that, I guess?

Denver: Well [flipping pages], let me see if I can find the language. The lecture that talks about who God is— See, one of my problems is that I just got this on the 25th, and this is the 28th.

Rick: Oh, so you haven't gotten…

Denver: I haven't gotten to Lectures on Faith to look at it just yet [looking up a scripture].

There's a definition given of who God is in Lectures on Faith. And it says that there is God the Father who is a personage of spirit, power, glory. And then, there's God the Son, and He's a personage. And then, there's the Holy Ghost, and the Holy Ghost is the *mind* of the Father and the Son. And that is very Nauvoo-era, doctrinally correct. And that definition of God is one that he returns to. The Holy Ghost in the Lectures on Faith makes the personage of God two individuals. And then, in addition to the two individuals, the Holy Ghost is the mind of the two of them. Well, this is also in your Pearl of Great

Price definition because it's in the Book of Moses; but it's in Genesis chapter 4 in these.

> *Therefore, it is given to abide in you: the Record of Heaven, the Comforter, the keys of the kingdom of Heaven, the truth of all things, that which quickens all things — which makes alive all things, that which knows all things, and* [that which]*has all power according to Wisdom, mercy, truth, justice, and judgment.* [Genesis 4:9 RE]

That's in the Book of Moses in the Pearl of Great Price, Genesis 4 in The Old Covenants. That's the definition of the Holy Ghost, the Comforter that God, or that Christ says He will send (in the Book of John) to the disciples after He ascends. That Comforter is the Record of Heaven, the Comforter, the keys of the kingdom, the truth of all things, and so on—which is exactly what is the lecture-on-faith description of the Holy Ghost, which is the mind of the Father and the mind of the Son, the Record of Heaven, the truth of all things, that which quickeneth all things.

And so, you have two personages in Lectures on Faith. You have the Holy Ghost that is really a manifestation of *their* minds. You have in the Book of Moses the Joseph Smith Translation of Genesis chapter 4, the Holy Ghost being the Record of Heaven, the truth of all things, the Comforter. You have the Holy Ghost *not* as a *personage.* You have the Holy Ghost as a kind of *vibrant force of truth* that is bestowed upon mankind generally. Then, we have from the Willard Richards pocket book that statement by Joseph that "The Father has a body of flesh and bones, the Son also, but the Holy Ghost has not a body of flesh and bones but is a spirit; were it not so, it could not dwell within us."

And there's an interesting article written about how that came about. That didn't stabilize. It went through multiple iterations and multiple expanding and contracting versions of what it was that is attributed to Joseph Smith before Brigham Young finally settled the dispute and reduced it to what is now in the LDS Doctrine and Covenants. That may or may not be a reliable definition of the Holy Ghost. Certainly, what we have in Lectures on Faith that Joseph vouched for the accuracy of, and what we have in the Genesis chapter 4, or Pearl of Great Price-Moses (there! I think it's Moses chapter 6) is a kind of different definition.

So, I don't think Joseph started out trinitarian, although when he reports what he learned from the First Vision (in his story that he wrote in 1838) is that he went home and, essentially, said, "I learned for myself that

Presbyterianism isn't true." And that was his response to his mother when she thought he looked rather haggard from what the encounter was. "Never mind. I'm well enough off. I've learned for myself that Presbyterianism isn't true." And I think that was probably what Joseph got out of the First Vision on the day after the First Vision.

Anyway…

Rick: Okay. So, you're saying that Lectures on Faith is *not* trinitarian, essentially. Is that…

Denver: No, I don't think so.

Rick: You don't think it is.

Denver: Yeah. Yeah.

Rick: Okay. And so, you're saying that the Book of Mormon, if you take out that punctuation as Joseph originally wrote it, is not trinitarian, either.

Denver: Right. I'm saying you can repunctuate. The Book of Mormon in the LDS version is still John Gilbert's punctuation. Today. The LDS Church is living with John Gilbert's punctuation. We're not. And it's easy to repunctuate and to reach a different result.

I've given a talk on this, and there's stuff out there that will demonstrate what I'm talking about if you're interested or if someone listening's interested.

Rick: Yeah. Well, so, a couple other things I want to talk about since we're talking about your scriptures— And I guess I should mention I've read your book, *Passing the Heavenly Gift.* One of the things…

Denver: And you're willing to admit that? Do you still have a temple recommend?

Rick: [laughing] I do, actually.

But, yeah. So, we should probably talk about that one because that was a bit of a controversial book. And I do want to talk about the history of that. But the reason why I bring it up in the context of your scriptures is when I read it, one of the interesting things to me was your take on Section 132 of the Doctrine and Covenants. And from what I understand, you had said—and I've heard various things, so, maybe you can clear up this— but when you wrote in *Passing the Heavenly Gift*, you had mentioned it was really four revelations. And I like that interpretation. I don't know that I necessarily agree that that's historically accurate, but— So, I'm curious if you still stand behind what you've written, cuz I understand you've kind of evolved on your beliefs about polygamy. So, will you talk about that?

Denver: Like any interested and attentive Latter-day Saint, my understanding of the history of what happened in the early Church began using the B. H. Roberts material, the Joseph Smith History as gathered by B. H. Roberts.

I got baptized September 10th of 1973. There was a lady in our ward that ran a Seventies Mission Bookstore. I don't know if anyone in your audience is old enough to remember Seventies Mission bookstores...

Rick: So, Anne Wilde—I interviewed her, and she mentioned it.

Denver: Yeah, yeah. Anyway, it was on her porch. I bought and I read, you know, the *Autobiography of Parley Pratt*. I read all the biographies of Heber C. Kimball, John Taylor. I read the (what's it?) seven-volume set by B. H. Roberts. I read the multiple-volume set that was attributed to Joseph Smith that is the forerunner of *The Joseph Smith Papers* project. I read everything I could get my hands on in order to try and understand. I mean, if this is really the work of God—if God restored something, He's speaking again; and He hasn't done that since we close out the New Testament record. Now, He's speaking, and stuff is rolling forth that tells us the mind of God. Then, we ought to pay particular attention.

So, in the era that I came in, that 1973 time frame, you're really looking at leadership that consists of Joseph Fielding Smith's son-in-law, Bruce R. McConkie, who's the doctrinal go-to guy. You've got, you know, Marion Romney; he can stand his own. You've got Mark Peterson who thinks he's *all that* on doctrine. And, you know, you had— Well, N. Eldon Tanner was a money guy. But you've got men up there— Boyd K. Packer who ran CES at the time. You got men who have *really* strong opinions and, essentially, a consensus about what was and what was not history. And then, you wind up with Arrington, and Arrington winds up hiring D. Michael Quinn. And then, Arrington appears to go a little off the reservation, and D. Michael Quinn appears to go *way* off the reservation. And my initial reaction to what D. Michael Quinn did was to think, "What an awful turn of events that a man would ~~apostasy~~ [apostatize] and then turn around and trash the history of the Restoration in this wretched fashion." But it was Michael Quinn's work that got me looking for and trying to find original source material.

Michael Quinn donated a bunch of the material that he had to Yale University, and then, Signature Books had someone go back to Yale University; or maybe they went back on their own, and Signature was just the ones that would print it. And so, these diaries and these journals begin to roll out that is the source material from which Michael Quinn drew his conclusions cuz he had access to and made copies from the Church archives that weren't particularly open. Arrington made them open somewhat, but they weren't particularly open. So, Church history was written from a closed point of view, a controlled point of view. And Michael Quinn actually represents sort of opening the door and seeing behind the orthodox interpretation.

So, the materials that Michael Quinn made available became available. And this orthodox, traditional view of history which I understood well— I mean, I had studied it. I was a Fielding Smith-McConkie-Packer disciple; and to me, Michael Quinn's view was heretical. But as you begin to examine the source material from which Michael Quinn drew his conclusions, you begin to see that in some respects, he's not at all unfair. And in some ways, he's not just fair, but he's kindly. He's being sympathetic in his viewpoint. He got in a lot of trouble because what he wrote had a far different look and feel than the look and feel that you get from this other narrative.

So, *Passing the Heavenly Gift* was an attempt to take a whole nother bundle of source material that existed and was available, and I'd gone to the trouble of buying these small print— You know, 300 copies were all that were ever put in print. But Curt Bench over at Benchmark is one of the outlets that sells this stuff. So, I was able to access these diaries, these journals, and to look at it myself. And my attitude towards Michael Quinn changed considerably, and my view of what the Church was doing with their history changed considerably.

But of all the subjects that are out there, probably the most controversial, internationally known, dramatic topic of all is the plural marriage subject. I mean, I don't want to get really granular about it, but to me, it required over 40 years of research to reach a conclusion.

It wasn't a single view. I mean, if you're gonna read everything that is said by the advocates and the defenders of the plural marriage establishment through Joseph Smith, you have a library of material that you're gonna have to plow through. And if you're gonna to say, "Okay, what are the arguments, then, on the other side of the coin about the issue of plural marriage?"—because you've got Emma denying that Joseph ever practiced that. But you also have incidents in which Emma Smith was present in something that happened that William McClellan tries to sensationalize in his account, talking about his discussion with Emma about the very incident that you're talking about. And then, you've got Joseph's view of that, and you've got Oliver Cowdery's accusation, and the minutes of the High Council in Far West when Oliver Cowdery was disciplined for what he was saying about that same incident.

Rick: You're talking about Fanny Alger.

Denver: The Fanny Alger stuff. And you've got all of these points to triangulate from, you know. What are you to make of it? I can tell you that story and make Joseph Smith an adulterer and a plural marriage practitioner; or I can tell you that story, and I can make Joseph Smith absolutely chaste and that what happened there was not by any stretch a sexual liaison.

Fanny Alger would have nine children from a husband. Joseph Smith fathered eight children through Emma Smith. They were both at the peak of their fertility when the two of them had something going on, and yet there was no progeny; there was no child. In fact, there's no child born that was fathered by Joseph Smith other than the children that came through Emma Smith. So, if you're gonna turn Joseph Smith into something that is akin to the narrative tour by the LDS Church, one of the questions that ought to enter into your balancing of what happened is the absence of any progeny when you've got a fertile man, and you've got fertile women who bore children to other men but never bore a child for Joseph Smith. What effect ought that have on your thinking and interpretation of the historical events? You got Emma Smith's denial that anything had gone on.

So, it's a long, arduous process to get through enough of the source material in order to form a fair opinion. And even after you form a fair opinion— And the one I had initially (in *Passing the Heavenly Gift*) reached was that if people are reliable— And one of the stories of the angel with the drawn sword comes from Eliza Snow; and Eliza Snow is someone for whom I had some respect. So, I'm gonna give credence to that because of her. And the story that she tells suggested that something happened in order to provoke Joseph to initially begin implementation of something that Joseph Smith was reluctant to implement.

Well, you go to the High Council minutes in Far West, and Joseph is acquitted, and Oliver Cowdery is convicted of slandering him. And everyone heard it. You go to the incident in Nauvoo when Joseph dictated a revelation in July of 1843. It was written down by William Clayton. Hyrum Smith took the revelation; it was read to the High Council of Nauvoo. The High Council minutes in Nauvoo talk about what was read to them, and they say it's an explanation of an ancient order of things, and it has nothing to do with some practice today.

How do you reconcile all of the different triangulation points?—because this, now, is a contemporary statement both in the High Council in Far West and the High Council in Nauvoo. These are contemporaneous things that suggest there's a problem with the narrative that Joseph is out there bedding women including, in the most outrageous form, bedding young teenagers. Well, to his credit, when he wrote *Rough Stone Rolling,* Bushman grapples with this issue. He comes down on the side of the historical storytelling, but he says that—and I'm paraphrasing, but this is pretty close—he says that Joseph Smith was not a nefario and that he didn't father children with other women, that his desire for sealing appears to be related to plentitude in the afterlife, plentitude in the afterlife.

Well, somewhere along the line, the idea of sealing and the idea of marriage become one and the same. And they overlap into "Well, if someone's sealed, then someone's married." And it's not at all clear. If you go back— It's really hard for people to accept this idea.

Well, I had dinner with Michael Quinn, and I posed this…

Rick: Oh, that's interesting.

Denver: Yeah, I posed this to him over dinner. I said, "Okay, let's take June 27th, 1844, and let's say, 'Right there—that's the *end* of the historical record.'"

Rick: That's the death of Joseph Smith.

Denver: Yes, that's the day Joseph is killed, and Hyrum.

"That's the end. You consider *nothing* that got written down or got introduced after June 27, 1844; and you are limited, *absolutely,* to the material that got its existence (put pen to paper) before that date. 'Kay? What do you have? What do you have to support Joseph Smith practicing plural marriage with sexual relations with other women than Emma?"

It was an interesting dinner. It was an interesting evening. We had an...

Rick: What did Quinn say?

Denver: ...interesting conversation.

Well, I don't know if I oughta quote him. I don't know if your listeners are going to be offended. But we got on that topic because he said that his reaction to my position on the plural marriage subject was bullshit. And I said, "Well, okay then, let's start with the proposition that we're gonna take June 27th, and we're only gonna go before." And we went back and forth for a few minutes, and he said, "I see where you're coming from," —because if you consider the source material that only was extant on that date...

Rick: So, you throw out all the Temple Lot case and everything cuz it's after June 27th.

Denver: Yeah, all of that stuff. All the affidavits got gathered. Look, the idea that you get to practice *plural wivery* is not made public until 1852 in a general conference talk in which Orson Pratt was assigned to introduce the topic by Brigham Young; and then, Brigham gets up. And then, you've got the assistant historian that had worked in Nauvoo (and who was working in Salt Lake under the leadership of Kimball) running the historian's office. And he says, in one of his diary entries, that the records that they brought with them from Nauvoo— The records were being altered to conform to the new regime.

Rick: You're talking about Heber Kimball?

Denver: No, he worked under Heber Kimball.

Rick: Oh.

Denver: His name will occur to me in a minute. But he wrote in his diary (who he's working under) that the records were now being altered in order to fit the new system of things, the new regimen. And so, you have to question if they're willing to go so far as to interlineate and alter original source material including William Clayton's own diary being altered.

One entry that you can see in *The Joseph Smith Papers* has this incredibly innocent statement that is about fidelity and monogamy, and it's turned into a statement about how only one man at a time has the authority to introduce the plural wife system, and that he, Joseph, was that guy—from interlineations. I've written about all this.

Anyway, the fact is that if you confine yourself to what existed at the time that Joseph was alive, you have a *very*, *very* difficult time saying that there is evidence Joseph did anything other than practice something called *sealing* that was designed to create plentitude in the afterlife. Joseph Smith, as Bushman described it, wanted large families to go into the eternities. In John Taylor's book, *The Government of God*, he asserts that the government of God in eternity is the family. So, if Joseph Smith is trying to restore on earth the family of God, the way in which you restore the family of God is to bind people together into some sealed family connection—doesn't matter that they're married to one another. If you seal them together, you seal people into a family relationship that can exist on into eternity.

So, Joseph doesn't use the word *adoption* in the context of *sealing* until October of 1843. In *The Joseph Smith Papers*, that's the earliest date I can find that—in his diaries—that the word adoption gets used.

Rick: Like as in the Law of Adoption.

Denver: Yeah, a very misunderstood concept, but Joseph practiced something that was adoption. But apparently, the introduction of that occurs in about the October 1843 time frame.

Until then, if you're talking sealing without defining what *sealing* meant, you weren't using the word *adoption*. You were using the word *marriage*, in people's projection of what the word meant, backward. If the sealing that took place was some form of familial tie that was designed to bind together as a family to Joseph, who had a connection that had been made to heaven, then what was being sealed was a family and not a sexual partner.

But beginning in that October 1843 time frame, there comes out something that results in adoption. Joseph will be dead within six months. Between the October mention and the time of his death six months later, there really isn't enough time in order to develop even an adequate historical record of what Joseph was doing with the idea of adoption in that time period. It gets mentioned. And then, what happens is that following his death, by the time you get to the 1845-November-to-February-1846 time period, there is *adoption practice* going on.

The language that we get in the word and the will of the Lord about captains of 50 and captains of 100— It's actually kind of *code* for public consumption. That was *adoption practice* going on in the Nauvoo era—so, set that aside for just a moment—*adoption* being the organization of the companies that were assigned and organized through temple ceremonies and adoption process, preliminary to the migration, the abandonment of the Nauvoo temple, the companies migrating out into the Salt Lake Valley. And they *practiced* something called *adoption*.

Then, as they migrate across, there are these conversations that enter into journals. One of the funniest to me is John D. Lee's journal where he's talking about someone asking John D. Lee to be sealed to him (adopted to him) because it's going to increase his kingdom, and John D. Lee saying, "Why would I be adopted to you? Why don't you be adopted to me so *I* get to be the boss in the afterlife in the government of God?"

Rick: It's all a great pyramid scheme, right?

Denver: Yeah, it's all just fabulously stupid because they're *aspiring*— If this stuff be truthful, holy, and sacred, they're *aspiring* to manipulate the afterlife by having introduced to them a concept that Joseph only had a six-month time period between introduction and death, and it doesn't get fleshed out. Then, you have to go to many, many years later when you have journal entries by Cannon and by Taylor and by Pratt, Hyde, and their conversations and the notes of meetings that they held where they say things like, "I never understood what Joseph Smith was doing with adoption." Cannon goes so far as to say, "I didn't believe it when he introduced it, and I don't believe it now." And so, the concept of adoption just drips into wreckage. And adoption as a concept related to sealing turns into mush, and it gets abandoned. It wound up being a fight.

But the idea of adoption had a profound effect on the history of the Church. Because Brigham Young led the first company. They come in; *this is the place*; they settle down; he has himself anointed a king and a priest in the log cabin that was built; and then, the king returns across the plains back to Winter Quarters. On his way back, he runs into the company that had John Taylor and Parley Pratt in it. John Taylor and Parley Pratt had some kind of sealing-adoption organization put together for the companies they led in the migration. And when Brigham Young met them, they had reorganized the companies that they were in contrary to the way that Brigham Young had adopted folks together in the ceremonies in Nauvoo. So now, they were in *defiance* of the *priesthood* by what they'd done. Well, they were members of the Quorum of the Twelve. I mean, the vote that was taken on what? August 8th of 1844? was that the Quorum of the Twelve would take care of the Church, not Brigham Young. It was the Quorum! So, John Taylor and Parley Pratt didn't regard Brigham Young as having any right to rule and reign or dictate over them. They were doing what they thought best. After they saw how the company functioned, they realigned the adoptions as they were going west.

Well, Brigham Young fumed from there all the way back to Winter Quarters. And while we didn't have them before, the collected *Complete Discourses of Brigham Young,* which I think were put in print for the first time in 2011—you can look. I mean…

Rick: Yeah, that's a really expensive set.

Denver: Yeah, yeah. I bought one of those. They were meant for libraries, but I bought one. They are expensive, but they're comprehensive. You can read what happened.

When Sidney Rigdon was campaigning to be elected after the death of Joseph Smith, his speechifying in Nauvoo to try and solicit votes for him was bizarre. I mean, he seems deranged. Brigham Young spent several days trying to persuade Wilford Woodruff that he, Brigham Young, needed to be elected president. They *needed* a president. And Woodruff wouldn't relent. His position was it required a revelation to reorganize the First Presidency. And Brigham Young's position was it didn't require revelation. It just required a vote, that Joseph Smith got made president by a vote of the group; he did not get made president by a revelation.

Rick: Common consent.

Denver: Yeah, it was *just* an election; it was *just*— And that he could be elected the same way, and it would have exactly the same effect. No revelation required. And eventually, he wore down Wilford Woodruff. Woodruff got on board with that, and they assembled. They called a general conference, and they held a vote. In the process of holding the vote, Brigham Young did some speechifying. And I tell you, it reminds me of Sidney Rigdon in the August campaign in Nauvoo for the election. He's practically incoherent.

Now, to give him the benefit of the doubt, he'd kept Wilford Woodruff awake haranguing him, and he couldn't sleep if he was doing that. So, he's sleep-deprived at the time he's giving the talk. But one of the things that he says in the aftermath of being elected is that he could hardly wait to get back to Salt Lake to have Parley Pratt and John Taylor confess that they are not Brigham Young, meaning that now *he's* in authority, and he *alone* has the right to dictate what goes on. And that it is an act of apostasy against the priesthood to rebel against what the chief says cuz they apparently were not willing to relent when they came across the plains. So, having been elected as president in Winter Quarters, he goes back to Salt Lake. And the rest of the Quorum of the Twelve, who were back in Salt Lake, have to choose between a fight, again, after relocating from Nauvoo over leadership or submitting to what Brigham was saying. And rather than split things up again, they relented. Brigham was elected, and he says he has the right to dictate.

Well, he still had not yet clarified that he intended to assert that he, and he alone, could seal —because Parley Pratt, even after that, sealed other women to him, including Lenore whose husband would ultimately murder Parley. And Brigham Young would later say that those women that Parley Pratt sealed to himself after Brigham was elected president, was adultery. And he went so far as to say that the murder of Parley Pratt was justified because it was adultery, and he essentially had it coming to him. Because once he was elected president, Brigham Young said, "I, and I alone, am the only guy who gets to do a sealing."

Rick: So, he consolidated the sealing power because it was kind of distributed before that.

Denver: It was far and wide.

All of that history needs to be taken and put into the hopper if you're trying to figure out what Joseph Smith was trying to do with sealing between the Fanny Alger moment and the moment at which Joseph is slain—because if he had absolutely no intention of creating sexual access to women by sealing, but he had, instead, the intention to put together in a form that would be recognized into eternity as a familial connection (as Bushman puts it, *familial plentitude*) then, we really have to put on a whole different lens if we're gonna try and interpret what went on.

So, I was grappling still in *Passing the Heavenly Gift* with the whole subject. I was trying to show appropriate deference to whatever the historical narrative was. I mean, I wrote that book as a member of the Church. I mean, I pulled every punch that I could pull in order *not* to be someone that's just a hostile critic. I believe if the LDS Church had adopted *Passing the Heavenly Gift* like they adopted *Rough Stone Rolling*, and they said, "Look, this is a very different way to look at the history of the Restoration. But you can look at it this way. And if you do, you can still be, you know, happy and associate with us." I believe if they had done that, they would be facing today far less of a religious crisis than they are currently facing with the members of the Church.

I never left Mormonism. I never even left the LDS Church; the LDS Church gave *me* the boot. But, I mean, I was 100% home teacher, I was a tithe payer, I was a temple recommend holder.

Rick: You were on the High Council as I understand?

Denver: I was a…

Rick: You taught Missionary Prep, I think it was?

Denver: I did. I taught Gospel Doctrine. While all this nonsense was going on—the flap about the book—I was helping, at the request of the stake president, a returned missionary who had lost his testimony and was a student at BYU. And so, he said the only one he knew in the stake that could help the young man was me. And so, I had him come over to my house. In fact, I would go to interviews with the stake president preliminary to the issue of whether I'm going to be excommunicated or not, and on my way home from that, I would stop by and get this returned missionary in a faith crisis. He'd come to my house, and we'd spend time talking about what his issues were. The first issue, and the most troubling to him, was polygamy. So, we started with polygamy. And we spent weeks talking about that topic. Then, the next topic— I forget what it was, but we didn't— He had a list of concerns. By the time we got through the first two, he said, "Really, I don't think I've got any other concerns because what you said satisfies me that I'm looking in the wrong place for answers. There's more substantive material out there that answers."

Rick: Could it be— cuz in your book, you basically said— This is really attractive to me. I'm going to tell you about it.

Denver: Yeah, yeah.

Rick: You separated the sealing from the polygamy.

Denver: Yeah.

Rick: And from what I understand with your new version of— I know you don't call it the Doctrine and Covenants.

Denver: Teachings and Commandments.

Rick: Teachings and Commandments.

Denver: Yeah.

Rick: You kind of excise the polygamy parts out of 132. Is that right?

Denver: I tried to fix 132. I actually went through it and tried to make it a consistent document. I said to myself, "Okay, knowing everything that I know about what went on in the Restoration, if I start with this document, can I fix it?" And I made a concerted effort. The dramatically contradictory stuff— I threw out the contradictions. And I tried to edit it.

Rick: You probably threw out the condemnation to Emma. Right?

Denver: Yeah, yeah.

Rick: I'm actually really glad to hear that...

Denver: Yeah.

Rick: ...because that bothers me.

Denver: I tried to fix it. And when I got all done with that, I thought, "Well, maybe *that* is— If they were interlineating— I mean, D&C 132 was hidden until…

Rick: 1852.

Denver: Yeah, when it was first announced in a general conference talk by Orson Pratt. Until then, it was hidden. What do they do with it in the interim?—because the only copy that we've got is in the handwriting of Joseph Kingsbury.

Rick: Well, Emma burned the one, right?

Denver: Yeah, well, Emma was allowed to burn the one. Everyone agreed to it.

Rick: So, well, going back to here, because…

Denver: But think about what the source is—Joseph Kingsbury. *Joseph Kingsbury*. It's not a clerk of Joseph Smith's in the historian's office; it's not a scribe of Joseph Smith. It's a *guy*...

Rick: So, you're saying it's a myth that Emma threw it in the fire.

Denver: No, I'm saying that the copy we have, the only extant copy we have, is in the handwriting of Joseph Kingsbury.

Rick: Mm-hmm.

Denver: Whatever it was that existed before that that he says he copied from what William Clayton wrote (and we've got Kingsbury's word for it), Kingsbury did not work as a scribe or someone that helped write history for Joseph Smith. When Kingsbury was called to testify in the Temple Lot case, he refused to swear to tell the truth about 132.

Rick: Hmm.

Denver: He would not swear that his testimony could be charged with perjury if it wasn't true. He just refused to take that oath.

Rick: So, he did not testify?

Denver: He testified.

Rick: But he refused to take that oath.

Denver: He refused to take the oath, but he testified, anyway. He said, "I'll affirm, but I will not swear to it." And they want to know what the difference was. He says, "*Affirm* is just me telling you what I understand. But if I swear to it, I can be charged with perjury." And he didn't want to do that.

Rick: And they let him testify, anyway?

Denver: Let him testify, anyway.

Rick: Well, I've never heard of that before. That's interesting.

Denver: Yeah, yeah.

Rick: Okay, so with *Passing the Heavenly Gift*, you are under the…

Denver: I was still under the effort to explore and try to understand.

Rick: And so, you believed that Joseph Smith did…

Denver: ...tried to make the Church's story work.

Rick: With polygamy.

Denver: Yes, tried…

Rick: That Joseph practiced polygamy.

Denver: Yeah, trying my best to make *that* story work.

Rick: But, you don't stand by that anymore.

Denver: Well, I finally reached a conclusion. Part of the reason I was able to reach a conclusion is *The Joseph Smith Papers* coming out and source material that didn't exist then existing now, and research that was done by a number of others that has also rolled out. I mean, I thought at the time *Passing the Heavenly Gift* was printed, I thought the evidence was really equivocal. It's *clear...*

Rick: Well, Michael Quinn still thinks it's pretty clear, right?

Denver: What's that?

Rick: Michael Quinn still thinks it's…

Denver: Well, Michael Quinn gives credence to the 1860 affidavits. I mean, he has a hard time envisioning the idea that a whole bunch of people would sign affidavits in Joseph F. Smith's affidavit book to support the lawsuit if they were swearing falsely. And those affidavits were used as evidence in the Temple Lot case. So, they were gathered with a specific purpose in mind.

Well, think about it now. In the 1860's, they're, for the first time, creating a record about what had happened two decades or more earlier. And Joseph is dead. But they've made public, and they have taught you. They've reassured you. They've testified from the pulpit to you since the 1852 time frame that *this* is a revelation that came through Joseph Smith. And you *know* your Church is true. And you *know* that that temple in Kirtland belongs to your group. And you *know*, because he's said it—you *know* Emma's apostate. Brigham Young called her a "wicked, wicked, wicked woman." "If Joseph Smith wants to be with Emma Smith, he's gonna have to go to hell to be with her because that's where that wicked, wicked, wicked woman is." They *know* all that because they've been told that in isolation here for a couple of decades. And Joseph's not around, and you've got a burning testimony of the Restoration. Are you going to sign an affidavit when you *know* it's true? When you *know*? I mean, the Church *leaders* are asking that you sign— a member of the Quorum of the Twelve! A future president of the Church, a member of the First Presidency is asking you to sign an affidavit. Are you going to sign the affidavit?

Rick: An affidavit that makes you look like an unvirtuous woman? Who in their right mind would do that?

Denver: It's not unvirtuous in the state of Deseret in 1860.

Rick: But the entire government is trying to take down the entire Church over this.

Denver: Doesn't matter. They won't succeed in doing that until 1890. In fact, it's those promiscuous *Romans* [speaking sarcastically] that introduced and enforced *monogamy* so they could get a supply of prostitutes. The virtuous, lovely, Christian community, including, according to Brigham Young, Jesus Christ Himself— *They* were all polygamists so that you didn't have to *have* prostitutes. But the wicked Romans— The Romans wanted monogamy because they needed an ample supply of prostitutes to keep themselves happy in their public baths and such. So, the *virtuous* women were the polygamous *wives* that bore children and lived in a familial relationship, not those monogamous fools that pretend to piety and produce prostitutes.

It's like Mark Twain commented in *Roughing It.* He said when he first thought of plural wives, he thought it was an exercise in licentiousness. But when he got a look at the poor, ungainly creatures that were being married, he said he felt inclined to take his hat off in reverence cuz he's standing in the presence of pure Christian charity. The man that would marry *one* of them was a Christian soul. But the man that would marry *ten* of them [laughing] has committed an act of Christian charity and virtue that's unthinkable in the modern world. But that's Mark Twain, and he's always tongue in cheek.

Rick: He's pretty funny.

Denver: But I gotta tell you. Have you seen the picture of Sarah Pratt in Volume 10 of *The Joseph Smith Papers*?

Rick: I have not.

Denver: It's worth the trouble. It's worth the trouble of looking at the picture of Sarah Pratt in Volume 10 of *The Joseph Smith Papers.*

I have a friend I went to law [laughing]— I'll leave his name out. I have a friend I went to law school with who's a descendant of the Pratts. His last name isn't Pratt; he's a descendant of the Pratts. Sarah Pratt looks like my law school buddy with long hair.

Rick: [chuckling]

Denver: Twain was right. It was an act of Christian charity.

Rick: [chuckling]

Denver: Boy, now we're way off.

Rick: All right, yeah.

Denver: We're way off base, and [chuckling]…

Rick: Yeah, let's— All right, so…

Denver: I do know some Pratts. They're probably all gonna be offended at this.

Rick: [chuckling]

Denver: Okay, you go look at the photo, and you decide for yourself.

The foregoing was recorded on June 28, 2020, and is presented here with permission from Rick Bennett who conducted the interview.

129. Gospel Tangents, Part 3

This is the final part of an interview Denver did this past summer with Rick Bennett for his Gospel Tangents podcast, which is presented here in its entirety in this series.

Rick Bennett: Okay. So, I do want to kind of go back to— We'll talk a little bit more about the Remnant Movement. Not to be confused, I should add I previously had an interview with a guy named Jim Vun Cannon. He was a—

Denver Snuffer: Yeah.

Rick: He was in the First Presidency of the Remnant Church of Jesus Christ.

Denver: Right.

Rick: He's no longer part of that church.

Denver: Oh!

Rick: Interesting thing—they've actually split, and it was just kind of like Brigham and Sidney. And he ended up more like Sidney and started his own church: Everlasting Church of Jesus Christ of the Latter Days.

Denver: Ooh, wow!

Rick: Yeah, so—

Denver: How about "The True and Living, Real Authentic, Mostest Correctest Version of the Church of Jesus Christ of Latter-day Saints?" And I'm sure there's an acronym you can put together out of that, that would spell something obscene probably. [*laughter*]

Rick: But anyways, so your movement is kind of named—

Denver: Look, I— Yeah.

Rick: Do you have an official name for your church?

Denver: No, no. There isn't a church. There isn't a church except in the sense that the church was defined in the revelation given to Joseph Smith. The church that existed were people that repented, came unto the Lord, and were baptized. That's it; that's the definition of a 'church' (see T&C JSH 10:19 RE), and that definition preceded the organization in April of 1830.

There were at least three different congregations or fellowships of people that existed before the incorporation took place in April of 1830, and all of them are considered members of Christ's church because the definition was just repent, come unto me, be baptized in my name for a remission of your sins. And that— If you're going to say there's a church, that's it.

We don't require— I don't require— I don't know of anyone that says you have to leave the LDS Church to accept the work that God has got underway today. I have said a Catholic priest could come and be baptized for the remission of his sins, accept the Restoration, and go on his way and retain his status as a Catholic and a priest if he chose to do so. Methodists can join. Latter-day Saints can join. There's nothing to be done except have someone that has authority to baptize, baptize you.

And then the name of the person, because we're required to keep track of the names, has to be submitted to another volunteer who's keeping what's called a Recorder's Clearinghouse; those names get given to him. At the end of a year, all of the names are alphabetized and they're put in for that calendar year, and they're entered by hand into a book. There's no electronic version; no one can hack it; no one can go online and get into it. There's only one, hand-written copy.

If you want to give it to him by mailing it in to him, the mailed-in copy will be recorded. The mailed document will be destroyed. At the end of the year, all the records are destroyed after having been entered into the book. And the only thing that that is done for is because the Lord *requires* that that book be maintained, in order to present it at the Second Coming as one of the things that we're accountable for keeping. We're accountable for keeping very few things, but that *is* one of them.

And so, repent, be baptized for the remission of sins, get your name recorded with the Recorder's Clearinghouse; that's it. Then you're part of it. And you can be a Mormon Latter-day Saint; you can be a Jew. You can be whatever you want to be, but you have to accept the terms that the Lord has outlined in order to come aboard.

And if you want to fellowship with others, there are informal gatherings of people that fellowship together. We're expected to pay tithes from *surplus*, not what's required to support you and your family but of your excess. Of your surplus, one-tenth is paid into the fellowship, and then the fellowship determines who among them has a need. And if someone among them has a need, then the tithe is used to help those who have health problems, medical bills, education problems, food, housing, transportation issues. They get spent inside the group to help and benefit those within the fellowship. It doesn't get gathered— There's no big slush fund. It gets used to help the poor.

If there's an excess that ever accumulates in a fellowship, then ultimately we expect to build a temple and the funds can be donated for *that* purpose. But tithes are not used to support a hierarchy—your religion should require that you sacrifice. If you are going to practice it, you should practice it as a person of faith, sacrificing to do the will of the Lord. No one gets remunerated for anything they do.

I gave a series of lectures. I had to personally pay to rent the facilities that I used in order to give a series of lectures. People organize conferences now voluntarily: *They* rent the venue, and *they* publicize the thing, and *they* do all the work with volunteer efforts. And if there are any costs to be advanced, they advance them. If they ask me to help defray costs, I help. But no one's— I spent a lot of money of my own doing the things that I've done; no one's paid me anything for what it is I do.

Rick: So somebody can join your movement and continue to go to the LDS Church?

Denver: Absolutely. Yeah, a number of them have. In fact, some interestingly-situated people have.

Rick: That's interesting.

Denver: I wanted to clarify that, as it turns out, the website scriptures.info (i-n-f-o) was available. All of the scriptures are available, for free, online at scriptures.info. You can either read them all there *or* you can connect to the website and it will read them to you —in a variety of voices. You can have the scriptures read to you, all of these [*tapping the new scriptures*]; you don't need to buy a leather-bound set. But they're also available, exactly the same document, through Amazon in a soft-bound, not leather-bound copy, available online. So, they're very accessible *for free* online. They're available from Amazon in a paperback form, but the leather-bound copies—there was a limited print of those and they're virtually all spoken for, but Benchmark will have a handful.

(*Note: The most up-to-date, print-on-demand version of the Restoration Edition of the scriptures is available for purchase at scriptures.shop.)

Rick: Wow.

Denver: And so—

Rick: Well, that's good to know. So, yeah, I'm just curious if there's anything else about— So, you're going to try to build a temple? Do you have a location for that?

Denver: Not yet. Not yet, but…

Rick: Here in Salt Lake Valley, I assume?

Denver: I assume not.

Rick: No?

Denver: Yeah, I assume not. I think there would be— The likelihood is there would be active interference, active opposition.

In my view, the adversary cares about *very* little, but the one thing he intensely cares about is the establishment of something that reconnects Heaven and Earth, in a way that fulfills prophecy and opens up the return of the Lord. Because the Lord's promises all have to be vindicated, and right now, there isn't *any possibility* in all of the existing efforts. But, we're hoping to make the effort to accomplish just that. At which point the adversary will feel threatened, and so, I expect there will be some trouble and opposition in getting it done.

And in this place, in particular— I mean, why am I an excommunicated Mormon? I'm an excommunicated Mormon because they don't want people *reading* what I write. They don't want people *listening* to what I have to say. I'm *not* hostile; I'm *just trying* to get to the bottom of the correct story. I'm *not* picking a fight with anyone. If I'm threatening, it's not because I'm trying to overthrow *anything*; it's because I'm trying to understand *correctly* the sequence of events and the content of the Restoration and the effort of the Lord to achieve an end goal that, right now, appears to have been compromised and hijacked into real estate development and hierarchical servitude.

It doesn't make any sense to me. I was happy to pay tithing—give them my money! I was happy to go to their meetings. They didn't want me there because they didn't want people to read what I have to write. And they certainly, I'm sure, don't want this material [*tapping the new scriptures*] becoming generally available because it— In the original iteration in Joseph Smith's day, it was markedly different than what we've got downtown in Salt Lake—or in Independence, Missouri, or in Monongahela, Pennsylvania, or in wherever that group that left Boulder City, Colorado, is now headquartered. They're *all* off the beaten track.

Rick: Would you consider yourself kind of a unification movement, where you're trying to unify Mormon groups?

Denver: We just had a conference in Boise. We invited everyone to come from all the various— A Latter-day Saint spoke; Church of Christ's representative spoke; Church of Christ Temple Lot…

Rick: Community of Christ—is that what you meant?

Denver: Community of Christ. ...Church of Christ Temple Lot; the group of Latter-day Saints out of Monongahela sent a representative.

Rick: That's nice.

Denver: Yeah. We've had Restoration Church of Jesus Christ of Latter-day Saint group— They split off from Community of Christ. They split off because of their desire to emphasize the Book of Mormon, while the Community of Christ is de-emphasizing the Book of Mormon.

I mean, anyone's welcome to come to the conferences. And unifying is unlikely because people don't really want to try and understand and *live* the Restoration as it was promulgated in the revelations to Joseph in the Book of Mormon. They really just want a kind of social-club atmosphere where they can come and be reassured that they belong to the *one and only,* authentic, *real* church that will get you into Heaven with a pass.

And the superficiality of the Latter-day Saint curriculum right now is so *vacuous* that I wouldn't waste my time sitting through two hours of their meetings. I mean, they spare you that third hour now, but it's still vacuous, insubstantial. You can't sustain life with the content that they provide at this point. It's been a series of subtractions. It's the opposite of restoration, which is additive; it's deductive—continually deductive.

And so, no, I don't view anything that I've done as being or holding the potential to be popular, to be unifying. I figure every single group gets offended when you talk about what the straight and narrow path may really look like and what it may really require of you. So, no, I don't expect to unify. I expect to be denounced by just about everyone. The more they learn, the less they like what they're learning. [*laughter*]

Rick: So do you— Is it a big movement in Boise, then? 'Cause it seems like you go there a lot. I know there was a 'Boise Rescue' a while ago.

Denver: There's a lot of activity that's taken place in Boise, but the majority of people are far and wide. I mean, I had a fireside, week-before last Sunday, with a group in Europe that— We did it online. But there were people from Scotland, and England, and Holland, and Slovakia, and various places around Europe. There are people all over. I'm corresponding actively with folks in Japan. We were supposed to have a conference in Japan, when Japan shut down because of the Chinese flu problem that they had going on, and we couldn't. We couldn't get into the country for that conference, but it's now rescheduled to take place in October.

There are people in South America; there are people in Canada; there are people in Alaska, Hawaii. There's a group in Africa. Some of these groups stay under the radar, in part because they don't want to be disciplined or excommunicated or rescued. But they only need to submit their names to the Recorder's Clearinghouse; they don't need to stand up and say, "Hey, please notice me. You'll want to kick me out of your Church too." Because if they find that fellowshipping in an existing congregation of Methodists or Latter-day Saints or Catholics is gratifying or satisfying to them, there's no reason for them—other than being baptized and submitting their name to the Recorder's Clearinghouse—there's no reason for them to become a renegade among another people they want to associate with. If asked, they're probably going to teach something that will be markedly different than what other congregations believe, but I doubt they'll be running around saying, "You're all screwed up and you're practicing priestcraft and you're going to hell." I doubt— Although maybe there's one or two people like that. [*laughter*] But I wouldn't think…

Rick: Are you aware— Are there any efforts to root out— I'm not— You probably don't like the term "Snufferites," but I know that's what you're called.

Denver: Yeah.

Rick: But people in active LDS congregations, who've been rooted out, that say, "Hey we like what Denver's doing"—

Denver: Yeah, yeah. Sure.

Rick: There is kind of an underground movement.

Denver: Oh, yeah.

Rick: Kind of like the polygamists—we go after the polygamists; we go after the Snufferites.

Denver: Yeah, yeah. Pretty much. Two former bishops were—I met with them last night —who were chased off precisely because they were reading and talking about material that I had written. So, yeah. Yeah, it's silly, really.

But if you're not going to teach anything, if you're not going to try and understand what went on in the Restoration, and someone says, "I would like to try and comprehend exactly what went on in the Restoration; I'm willing to explore that"—*but*, you're willing to still stay a member of this institution —why would you care? I mean, you've got to be awfully thin-skinned. You have to be extraordinarily insecure to say, "If you think *that* way, you're *so scary* that I want you kicked out of our organization." Why does that scare you? Why does that alarm you? Why are you so thin-skinned?

I mean, I take all kinds of *foolish*, practically obscene, mischaracterizations made of me on the Internet, and I don't react to any of 'em. Why do I care? I'm not what you think I am if you've envisioned this heretical monster gobbling up, you know, the souls of men. If that's what you think, yeah, go ahead and think that, but it doesn't change the reality. Your foolishness never defines me. So, if they think I'm foolish, why would *my* foolishness define *them*? Why aren't they live-and-let-live?

Rick: So, what would you say is the attraction to people who are attracted to your movement?

Denver: Most people have awakened to the realization that what they're hearing institutionally—either in polygamist groups or Community of Christ or Latter-day Saint— they've awakened to the realization that what they're getting fed from institutional sources is decidedly limited, misrepresentative, lacking depth. It's not soul-satisfying. And these people are— You would call them the best that there are. They're the Seminary teachers; they're the

Bishops; they're the Gospel Doctrine teachers; they're the serious folks that have been on High Councils.

You'd be surprised at the substantial, thoughtful, reflective character of the people that wind up saying, "Oh, I'd like to go there." Because you have essentially two choices: You either stay with something that you realize is not fulfilling and is insubstantial, and in many cases it's compromised and it's not doing its job, *or* you say, "I've lost my faith in the institution, and therefore maybe the whole of it; the Restoration itself is just a sham." Many people are saved from going to "the whole of it is a sham" by discovering that there is great depth, profound insight, transcendentally important material to be culled from the Restoration; and if welcomed into your life, fundamentally change the way you view your existence here, the way you relate to other people here, and how meaningful your life becomes. Marriages have improved. People that were in conflict, who come in a search for the truth, reach a level of harmony between one another that is soul-satisfying.

These aren't people that I've converted. I've been out here trying to piece together as much of the truth as I can piece together, and I've been joined by people who have helped in that process. The work of the volunteers that put this together— I'm 1 - 2% of the effort that got made to do this, but I'm the beneficiary of it. The hard work, some of the hardest work, was done by a fellow who's sitting here on the Joseph Smith Translation material. These are people, on their own, who have discovered that there are others like them — myself being one of them. And that has coalesced into, now, groups of people fellowshipping around the world together, donating tithing and helping one another with their financial needs, and meeting in conferences from time to time. And now, we have leather-bound scriptures to rejoice in.

Rick: Well, from what I understand— I'm trying to remember your other book, *The Second Comforter.*

Denver: Yeah, *The Second Comforter.*

Rick: Because in that book, that's the one where you talk about how—and please tell me if I'm saying it wrong—but how to have angels visit you. Is that right?

Denver: Essentially, yes. *The Second Comforter: Conversing with the Lord Through the Veil* is a book that was written while I was an extraordinarily orthodox, Gospel Doctrine teaching, active Latter-day Saint. And its curriculum, its agenda, its teaching is trying to get a faithful, active Latter-day

Saint to rise up to a higher level of practice of the religion, so that you can stir the Heavens and have some connection be made between you and the Heavens themselves.

It was absolutely correct, orthodox doctrine of the Church when that book was written. The manuscript was submitted to Deseret Book. They spent seven months troubling over whether to print it or not; ultimately decided not to print it but encouraged me to get it into print. It got into print, and it's an orthodox statement of the highest aspirations of the Church at that time.

That teaching has since been renounced. You mentioned the Boise Rescue. One of the things they renounced up in Boise was the teaching of the Second Comforter, and they recently revised the footnoting in the Gospel of John (John 14:16; also John 9:8 RE and T&C Testimony of St. John 10:11 RE) to eliminate the previous footnote that confirms the doctrine you find in *The Second Comforter: Conversing with the Lord Through the Veil*, so that that footnote, that connection, has now been abandoned.

I've been encouraged to do a 3rd edition of the book and to rewrite it from my current perspective, but I believe it is more important as an artifact to show what the orthodox teaching of the LDS Church was in 2006 when that book was printed, in contrast to where they are today in 2020, abandoning what was once welcomed, accepted orthodoxy. It's now heretical and denounced.

Rick: Well, to me it would seem to be bigger— *The Second Comforter* would be a bigger problem than *Passing the Heavenly Gift*.

Denver: Yeah.

Rick: Because the Church doesn't— It would be concerned that angels— And I guess the question…

Denver: But if you read the book and you look at the footnotes, it's hard to say, "Well, someone should be in trouble for writing *that*." It's impossible; it's orthodoxy.

Rick: Well, I'm just trying to understand why *Passing the Heavenly Gift* was the bigger problem, 'cause to me, your first book would be the bigger problem and I don't understand why.

Denver: I believe that *Passing the Heavenly Gift* takes so much varnish off the institution's history that it makes it look like they've failed to perpetuate what was once here, and that they've fallen into disarray. But the end of that book —and I advise readers if they read it to go all the way to the end—the end of that book gives you reason to have continuing faith in the Restoration and to remain affiliated and believing. But I think their view was Brigham Young looks bad; territorially, Utah looks bad.

Rick: Heber J. Grant looks bad.

Denver: Heber J. Grant looks awful. But I'm quoting Heber J. Grant's journals—that's Heber talking about himself. It's actually Heber recording in *his journal* what his mother said to him about himself, and then Heber writing about, you know, what his own limits were.

Rick: Because that was one of the issues—it was denigrating Church leaders, right? That's why you were excommunicated?

Denver: Yeah. Supposedly I denigrated Church leaders, but how is it denigrating Church leaders to quote the Church leader about himself? If he's being candid in his journal and he's telling you, "I've never had an inspired dreaming in my life," if he says that his mother thinks he's more concerned with money than he is with anything spiritual— I mean, if he's writing these things in absolute candor about himself in his diary, how is it denigrating him to quote him? It's understanding him. It's grasping the concept that there's a man who is absolutely, religiously insecure about his status before God, unsure about where he's going in the next life, standing as the President of the Church.

He was probably scared out of his mind every time he got up in a General Conference to address people because he was hollow inside. He *knew* he was an empty suit. But he knew what he cared about, and he cared about managing '*the kingdom*' and making the kingdom function financially and like a business, and he did his best to do that. Whatever his skill set was, that's what he put on the altar, and that's what he had *to* altar. But religiously, there wasn't much there.

And there are a lot of leaders, I think, sitting down in red chairs in Salt Lake *today* that would look at the comments about Heber J. Grant in *Passing the Heavenly Gift* and would identify with that; would say, "That's *me*. That's the awful position in which I find *myself*. I got nothing to offer." I mean, go listen to General Conference and tell me if you think that's vacuous or edifying. If it's enlightening— Joseph Smith, when he gathered a group together to give a talk in a conference, *startled* them with an abundant outpouring of new light and knowledge; talked about how it was his role to always turn up some new thing in order to help edify and move the process along. (From a discourse given May 12, 1844; see *Teachings of the Prophet Joseph Smith*, pg. 364.)

Well, what we're moving along, in a process if there be one, is real estate development, and community development, and condominium development, and land development, and investments in multi-billion-dollar funds. And in that, since the kingdom is in magnificent shape, the kingdom is prospering at the hands of businessmen.

Joseph Smith had a pending petition for bankruptcy at the time he died because he didn't know how to manage money. Joseph Smith was largely responsible for raising the hopes for the Kirtland Safety Society that was an abysmal business failure. Joseph Smith was not a good businessman; he was an awful businessman. In his store, when the poor and needy came in, he gave away the inventory instead of collecting for it. The store was going bankrupt. Everything he touched he failed at in business, as a businessman.

And Brigham Young figured out how to monetize Mormonism and how to turn it into something that would pay off. And the leaders ever since then, they learned some bad lessons; they learned some hard lessons. Heber J. Grant had to go to the bankers in New York to try and get money to make payroll to keep the employees of the Church paid, including the compensated General Authorities. And those were *hard* lessons in *hard* times.

So, then you have Boyd Packer calling the clerk, the financial clerk of the stake before he arrives, and he says to the financial clerk he wants to know the names of the top ten tithe payers in the stake for him to interview when he comes out to call a new Stake President. And the financial clerk gets upset about that, and picks up the phone and calls and tells me what an obscenity *this* is. But *they don't understand* the history. The history is that you put...you *ingratiate* people with money *to the kingdom*, because the kingdom has on occasion run into *huge* deficits. They were afraid of financial collapse on *multiple* occasions and were only rescued by bankers back East.

Well, now that they've turned things around in the post World War II era, and they've got billionaires and multi-millionaires who are out there, you ingratiate them and you get their loyalty to the kingdom by having them called into positions of authority. They become your Stake Presidents; they become your Bishops; they become your Patriarchs; they become your Seventies. They become your leaders because you never know when you're going to have another hiccup.

The joke about the Jesse Knight building down at BYU, when I was there, was that Jesse Knight was a drinking, smoking, swearing Mormon, but he made a fortune in the mining business, and when he finally returned to activity in the Church, his tithing that year cleared all of the debts that the Church had. And so, they have the Jesse Knight building down at Brigham Young University in honor of the tithe that the man paid.

There are pragmatic reasons why choices are made; they are based upon historical precedent. They have very good reasons behind them if you're trying to manage a trillion-dollar empire as the Church leaders are. But you think about what they have— They've undertaken a project in Florida on 133,000 acres of ground, approximately. The development costs will be about a trillion dollars by the time the project is finished. Five-hundred-thousand people will live and work and buy groceries and go to school, and do everything in life, there in that community.

They started that project just a few years ago. There will be members of the Quorum of the Twelve who are not yet added to the quorum, who will come aboard while that project is underway. They will live their entire tenure in the Quorum of the Twelve and die, and that project will not be finished. They will inherit it as a project. They will babysit through the completion, and they have no say in whether or not that's what is going to occupy an extraordinary amount of time. That's the way the Church has wound up today.

They've called good businessmen. N. Eldon Tanner helped straighten out a whole host of problems, and they've gone to school on that. Some of the members of the Quorum of the Twelve were called specifically because of skill sets that they have in the business community—skill sets they have in banking; skill sets they have in law. To his credit, the current Church President didn't come aboard with a background as an accomplished businessman, lawyer, or banker; he came as a surgeon, and that's an oddity among the group that's up there. But I understand and I empathize with the plight. They really don't have elbow room. They've got an empire, and the empire *demands* attention. They *have* to give attention to it, and they're doing a marvelous job in paying attention to it.

That was not what Joseph Smith set out to accomplish. It's not what the Restoration was intended— And if Joseph Smith were here, my guess is he *would* bankrupt the Church— probably go out and find great causes, poor people, needs, fund whole hospitals, don't charge anyone anything, help the benighted, run into the inner cities and see if you can bring peace and an end to the murdering and the violence that goes on there, improve schools, give away schools—do everything you can to fund an effort to try and rehabilitate an entire nation first and then the world second. I think Joseph would wreck the Church; the kingdom would be in disarray. You would have, you know, the hat being passed to see if we can pay the utility bill for the ward building. It wouldn't be the empire that we see if Joseph were here because his priorities were contrariwise.

Rick: Well, I do want to hear your final thoughts on their— Just one more question before we talk about Joseph Smith. As far as— 'Cause I know there was a lot of early gifts. I think my opinion's—in looking at your movement—you know, this idea that angels visiting you is very attractive to some people. Also, I was just curious about speaking in tongues. That was an early gift. Is that something that you've had in your movement?

Denver: The way that Joseph had encouraged the 'tongue thing' was to be able to communicate with other people. Yes, the answer's yes, but the way in which it's manifest itself is not something that we've done a lot to publicize, advertise, or speak about. Signs generally attract the wrong sort of folk. So, while there are abundant things that have and do take place, they're not spoken openly too much because the wrong kind of people get attracted to that sort of stuff. And we're interested more in substantive, reflective, serious-minded people who are genuinely interested in trying to find and do the will of God.

We lost a light.

Rick: I know. [*chuckles*] That's alright; we'll finish up.

But so, anyway, just wanted to hear your final thoughts on Joseph Smith.

Denver: Yeah, I think Joseph *is* a very misunderstood character. Obviously, he felt confident in his role and in addressing the truth and in testifying about the things that he had experienced, but he was *not* the character that people make him out to be. Of the two of them, I think Emma was the stronger personality, and I think Joseph was deferential *to* Emma. I think Joseph had a number of vulnerabilities, including the fact that he didn't regard himself as well-enough educated or erudite to compete with a Sidney Rigdon. And so, he gave Sidney Rigdon a lot of deference and a lot of opportunity to demonstrate leadership because Joseph respected that he was better educated than him. He also respected that Emma was better educated than him.

He was shy around women. I mean, the idea that Joseph was some sexual aggressor around women—he was not *that.* He and Emma were close. You read the correspondence insofar as it's preserved between the two of them: He was devoted to her, and she was defensive of him and devoted to him. And of their two personalities, she was the stronger of the two. The idea that Joseph would, you know, hold her in defiance and get away with it doesn't match up with what you see—to the extent that we've got material to look at to examine their lives.

Emma was a force to be reckoned with. And Brigham Young wanted her as a prize, to be able to say, you know, he's got *her* onboard too. And she would not allow herself to be used in that fashion—to her credit. She went to the grave defending Joseph.

And Joseph, I think, was bold as a lion in defense of the things that came from God, and oftentimes frustrated at people around him, but he kept interpreting their intent to be exactly like his own intent. So, when he uncovers the character flaws of John Bennett, and John Bennett cries and says, "Don't, you know, let it out; I'll be a ruined man," and he betrays sincerity and he makes an attempt at suicide, Joseph Smith is convinced he's repented; he's got a good heart. He assumed a *lot* of people had a good heart who turned out not to have, 'cause he thought they were like he was. That was a flaw; he misread people.

He was insufficiently cynical about the foibles of other humans, and ultimately it wound up costing him his life. But he died with a conscience void of offense towards others because he committed very few offenses towards others—particularly offenses towards women that he's currently charged with. People ought to be ashamed of the way they speak of him. God foretold that fools would hold him in derision, but the noble, and the pure in heart, and the wise, and the prudent would constantly seek blessings under his hand.

And part of his hand under which we seek blessings are in the books that we've put in print. Because I would rather be regarded by the Lord as someone who is wise and noble and pure in heart, than a fool to be held by God in derision as most people regarding Joseph Smith do. They haven't spent the time; they haven't taken the effort; they haven't done the work to figure it out. But Joseph was who Joseph said he was, and if anything he understated *all* that he was—to his credit.

Anyway, thank you! It's been obnoxious, really, to be sitting here. Let's not do this again! [*laughter*]

Rick: [*laughter*] Alright. So, well thank you, Denver Snuffer. I really appreciate you sitting down with us here on Gospel Tangents.

Denver: You bet.

The foregoing was recorded on June 28, 2020, and is presented here with permission from Rick Bennett who conducted the interview.

130. Being Harmless, Part 1

This is Part 1 of a special series on Being Harmless. In the Restoration Edition of the scriptures, we find these references to being harmless:

Matthew 5:3: *Be therefore wise servants and as harmless as doves.*

Philippians 1:8: *Do all things without murmurings and disputings, that you may be blameless and harmless, the sons of God, without rebuke in the midst of a crooked and perverse nation — among whom you shine as lights in the world, holding forth the word of life.*

Alma 12:14: *Now Ammon being wise yet harmless, he said unto Lamoni, Wilt thou hearken unto my words if I tell thee by what power I do these things?*

Today Denver discusses what it means to be harmless and how that is manifested; how being harmless is related to being gentle, kind, meek, forgiving, wise, and easy to be entreated, and how, when, and where that matters the most; how all of this is a reflection of a condition of the heart; and how one who is harmless approaches others, and approaches God, especially when it may be most difficult to do.

DENVER: There's an incident that I think— One word…one word in this incident really explains a great deal of what I have been talking about in this last installment. This is an event that occurs within the Book of Mormon that may seem otherwise quite puzzling. But now that we've looked at the Ether chapter 3 material, and we go back and we look at this incident, it suddenly begins to have a connection to it.

This is in Alma chapter 22. It involves Lamoni's father, the king. I want you to look at the father, beginning in verse 17 of Alma chapter 22:

> *And it came to pass that when Aaron had said these words, the king did bow down before the Lord, upon his knees; yea, even [did he] prostrate himself upon the earth,* ***and cried,*** **[and cried]** *mightily, saying….* (Alma 13:10 RE, emphasis added)

It's *not* the words of the prayer that provoked or gathered the attention of heaven—though the prayer is in fact needed, relevant, and exactly what the Lord answered. It's what came before.

This is the *king*. This is the king that can have people killed if he chooses to do so. This is the one who—*like God* among his people—exercises the power of life and death. This is the one who can exact from them taxes. This is the one who has absolutely no reason to do what he's doing here. But look what he does: He prostrates himself upon the ground, and he *"cries out mightily."* He doesn't *pray*. He mirrors exactly what the brother of Jared did when *he* approached God, in the depths of humility and in the sincerity of his heart, showing absolutely his appreciation for the difference between himself, on the one hand, and God, on the other.

Don't mistake me; I do not think it is necessary to physically engage in this kind of display. When the display is an extension of what is in the heart, that is absolutely fine. But when what is in the heart is right, it doesn't matter how it's displayed because God 'looketh on the inner man' (see 1 Samuel 7:16 RE and Alma 12:15 RE). This king was so overtaken by what he had heard that he was not ashamed to prostrate himself in front of the missionaries. He was not ashamed to cry out in the depths of humility. He didn't care who saw it. He didn't do this 'for to be seen' (see Matthew 3:28 RE; Alma 18:4 RE; 3 Nephi 5:33 RE). He didn't care that he was being seen. He did this because, at that moment, that was what he was: he was seeking grace, from the Throne of Grace.

> *O God, Aaron hath told me that there* ***is*** *a God, and* ***if*** *there is a God, and* ***if*** *thou art God….* (Alma 13:10 RE, emphasis added)

Do you see this? This isn't someone who's certain. This is someone who is convicted of his own inadequacy.

It may not be that you don't know enough; it may actually be that you know too much that's wrong. It may be that what you lack… It's all going to be erased and started over anyway. If you could gaze into heaven for five minutes, you'd realize that people that have been writing about this stuff since the beginning of time, who haven't gazed into heaven, don't know what they're talking about. The suppositions and the connections and the ideas that get floated around are not only false, many of them are offensive to God. They're not right. The board's going to be erased. God's going to re-order it. You're going to see things in a completely different light when it happens. It's not that you're brilliant and a shining light of knowledge; it's what's in your heart, and how has your heart been prepared, and if your heart is open to receive.

> *I will give away all my sins to know thee...that I may be raised from the dead and be saved at the last day. And now when the king had said these words, he was struck as if he were dead.* (Ibid.)

And then, look what happens when he recovers—because as he was struck as if he were dead, he's converted—the Lord ministers to him!

And in verse 23:

> *The king stood forth and began to minister unto* ***them****. And he did minister unto them insomuch that his whole household were converted unto the Lord.* (Alma 13:12 RE, emphasis added)

This is what happens when converted to the Lord! You can't *stand* to look about you and see other people who are left in the dark. You want to invite *them*, rather as Nathaniel was invited, "Come and see for yourself" (see John 1:7 RE and Testimony of St. John 1:14). *You* come to the Lord; *you* come and see for yourself. This little bit of *skeptical* praying, "*if [there's] a God...if thou art God, will [you] make [your]self known to me"—that worked*—not because this is a magic incantation.

Those folks who go through ceremonies think that ceremonies have some powerful mojo, some compelling voodoo, but the purpose of the ceremony is to teach you a *precept.* The precept is what you ought to find within your heart. Rites and ordinances are intended to testify to a greater truth. It was anciently among the Jews—it is an 'Aaronic priesthood function' to turn around and look at the ordinances as if it were an end in itself. It is *not* an end in itself; it is intended to be a *symbol* reminding you of some great truth concerning our God.

[The] capstone of the ceremonies that were restored through Joseph, involving a dialogue between you and the Lord in which you're brought back into His presence, and then following that, you're taken away and you're sealed for eternity—those are *lofty* concepts. They are powerfully portrayed in the ordinances and the rites. They are intended to convey to you the reality that all of this is possible, because God does, in fact, intend to preserve *you* and all of those associations that you prize, so long as they're worthy.

Don't think that you lack the faith! If *this* king, with *this* prayer, can go to God and can ask and get an answer—*that's not* the impediment. The impediment is the pride of your heart, the hardness of your heart, the self-reliance that you think that you own, the traditions that bind you down, the arrogance of your heart, the unwillingness to cry out mightily to God and then to be open to receiving an answer. This was enough, and *you too* can do enough.

The Lord tells a story in Mark. This is Mark chapter 9, beginning at verse 17. There's this fellow who comes to Christ and says,

> *Master, I have brought...thee my son, which hath a dumb spirit;* [the spirit overtakes him and he foams at the mouth, he] *gnash[es]...his teeth....I spake to thy disciples that they should cast him out;...they could not.* [And Christ says], *O faithless generation, how long shall I be with you? How long shall I suffer you?* [They brought the boy] *unto him: and...he saw him, straightway the spirit [tore] him; and he fell on the ground, ...wallowed foaming. ...he asked [the] father, How long [has it been] since this came unto him? And he said, Of a child. And ofttimes it...[casteth] him into the fire, and into the waters, to destroy him: but if thou canst do anything, have compassion on [him], and help us. Jesus said unto him, If thou canst believe, all things are possible to him that believeth. ...straightway the father of the child* ***cried out,*** [**cried out**] *and said with tears, Lord, I believe; help thou mine unbelief.* (Mark 9:17-24; see also Mark 5:8-9 RE, emphasis added)

"Help thou mine unbelief."

You don't need *more* of what you already have. Why are you here? Well, most of you. Some have come only to criticize and gather information. Some of you—in the hardness of your heart—are going to come to the point where, in the day of judgment, you will look back on this moment and realize, "*I damned myself* by the hardness of my heart and the bitterness of my soul, because I came to judge a man whose heart was right before God, and mine was not." Your heart will be broken in *that* day.

But look at this man whose heart was broken on this day. He cried out: "*Lord, I believe; help thou mine unbelief*"— "I have a desire; I have a willingness, but it is so *fragile*; it is so frail. I don't think it's enough."

That's not the problem. Cry out! Ask Him! Remember His disciples who'd been following Him, His disciples who were His faithful followers—His disciples *couldn't fix* this boy. And they'd given up everything to come and follow Him.

Jesus healed him. After the incident the disciples came to Him and said,

> *Why could [we not] cast him out?* [Christ answered to] ***them****, This kind can come forth by nothing, but...prayer and fasting.* (Mark 9:28-29; see also Mark 5:11 RE, emphasis added)

Why do you have to be afflicted by prayer and fasting, if you're a follower of the Lord, in order to get to the point that you can accomplish this? Because *you* don't fall prostrate, crying out with tears. If this man, in this condition, can say, "*I believe; help thou mine unbelief,*" if this man can do this and have the Lord on his behalf work a miracle, *you too* can believe enough; *you too* can accomplish what you desire; *you too* can come to Him.

Matthew covers the same incident, but in Matthew he picks up… This is Matthew chapter 17, beginning at verse 19:

> *Then came the disciples to Jesus apart, and said, Why could not we cast him out? And Jesus said unto them, Because of your unbelief: for verily I say unto you, If ye have faith as a grain of mustard seed, ye shall say unto this mountain, Remove hence to yonder place; and it shall remove; and nothing shall be impossible unto you. Howbeit this kind [come] not out but by prayer and fasting.* (Matthew 17:19-21; see also Matthew 9:7 RE)

"Faith as a grain of mustard seed" was what the Lord said they needed. The *defect* does not consist in the absence of faith in the Lord. The defect consists in the arrogance and hardness of the heart that prevents you from crying out, in the realistic and anguish of your heart, looking to God who is trying to bring you to Him. That depth of humility, that status of being someone who is utterly harmless, that condition in which you present no threat to the righteous—you are harmless as a dove; you seek only the betterment of others—that is who God is and what you must become in order for God to be able to redeem you to be like Him.

That's you voluntarily changing to be that person by your submission *to Him*—because there is no reason to give to the proud, the vain, and the warlike the ability to torment and to afflict others. There is every reason to give to someone—who would ultimately be willing to 'give the rain to fall on the righteous and the wicked, and make the sun to shine on both the righteous and the wicked' (see Mathew 3:26 RE)—the power of God, because the power of godliness consists in this kind of a heart, and in this kind of a heart, God can accomplish anything.

As Nephi paraphrased Isaiah—in the concluding chapter of Nephi's use of Isaiah and his material—he left out a phrase that appears in Isaiah 29, and I believe he did it very wittingly. I believe he did it so that as you look at the material, you'll ask yourself, "Why did he leave *that* out?" And you'll think about the omission. *And the vision of all is become unto you as the words of a book that is sealed* (Isaiah 29:11; see also Isaiah 9:1-3 RE). He left out *"the vision of all"* (see 2 Nephi 27:7; see also 2 Nephi 11:19 RE).

Well, you're talking about Zion here (yesterday and today), and as is usual any time you get to a substantive topic that's worth paying a lot of attention to, the Book of Mormon has something to say. In fact, while it doesn't comment at extraordinary length, the substance of what it has to say on this subject is really quite startling, and that is described for us in the 4th chapter of Nephi.

But before the 4th chapter of Nephi picks up, the last verse of chapter 30 of 3rd Nephi is a precaution to us that are going to inherit this book, which Mormon made sure was inserted at this point in the narrative. What's remarkable as you look at that verse is how it then ties in to the description of what we're going to receive of the practice of Zion among those in the Book of Mormon:

> *Turn, all ye Gentiles, from your wicked ways; and repent of your evil doings, of your lyings and deceivings, and of your whoredoms, and of your secret abominations, and your idolatries, and...your murders, and your priestcrafts, and your envyings, and your strifes, and from all your wickedness and abominations, and come unto me, and be baptized in my name, that ye may receive a remission of your sins, and be filled with the Holy Ghost, that ye may be numbered with my people who are of the house of Israel.* (3 Nephi 30:2; see also 3 Nephi 14:1 RE)

Keep in mind that list of *defects* as we look into the things that are right and proper in the Zion that we find in 4th Nephi. In 4th Nephi, verse 2, it tells us that,

> *[All] the people were...converted unto the Lord, upon all the face of the land, both Nephites and Lamanites* [and that's all good and well, but it goes on to say], *and there were no contentions and disputations among them.* (4 Nephi 1:2; see also 4 Nephi 1:1 RE)

Which you have to add because if you've been to any Gospel Doctrine class, or any High Priest group meeting, or any Elders Quorum or Relief Society, there's always that, you know, fellow or gal or group who have an incapacity to depart from contention. So, it's not just being converted; see, they're narrowing it down. You get converted, but then you reach at some point a unanimity or an agreement upon what the Gospel really means. And, well, take a look around: O ye Gentiles, "turn...from your wicked ways," and ask yourself—okay, confine it to your own ward, to your own quorum, to your own Relief Society group, to your own stake; confine it to whatever you want it to be confined to—are there "no contentions or disputations" among them?

It's a serious defect. It's a serious challenge, and it's one that we aren't meeting very well. And it's one of the reasons why we tend to neglect the Book of Mormon because the Book of Mormon is always stepping on our toes. The relentless message of the Book of Mormon is "Hey, hey, repent. You suck; you're just...you're a mess—*YOU*, not *them*." I mean, it's not a matter of "I got religion; I'm safe; I've got a recommend. I'm on the 'in' club; I can get 'in' those buildings that other people [can't]"—that doesn't matter. You still...you've got to repent. You're a defective item, incapable of resonating at the right frequency and receiving the spirit of the Lord, and finding...not contention but love in bringing people together and coming to become one. You can be absolutely in disagreement over a doctrine, and *lovingly* and *gently* and *patiently* persuade them to come unto Christ. *Or*, you can hold a council and kick 'em out.

So, after they manage not only to have the same faith and to eliminate from them contentions and disputations, then they go on *...and every man did deal **justly** one with another* (4 Nephi 1:2; see also 4 Nephi 1:1 RE, emphasis added).

See, there's a difference between mercy and justice. Justice is a tougher standard. We don't want justice; we want a merciful Redeemer, who will come in and who will make up for our defects. But this is saying, "*Every man* [me—inside *me*; this is the turf we're talking about] *did deal **justly*** [the higher standard] *with one another*."

"You don't have to give me mercy because I'm going to give *you* justice. I'm going to be *tougher* on myself. It is fair that I do this for you. Oh, no, no, you don't have to do that. No, no, no." The standard by which they are evaluating their conduct, internal to themselves, is the more difficult standard. They're going to deal justly with one another. "I will break my heart; I will break my wallet; I will break my life before I will not deal justly with you and give you everything that you're entitled to."

See, it's putting the shoe on the other foot, and it's not the more relaxed and kindly and gentle standard because when they're dealing with one another, they want to deal justly (a real problem for all those car dealers among us).

So, after we've fixed the religious diversity, and we've fixed the contentions and the disputations, and we've grown enough now that we're willing to treat ourselves as the one upon whom justice has reign, *then* they get to the point that *...they had all things common among them* (Ibid.).

Anytime in the Book of Mormon they're ticking off a list (and they do it everywhere in the Book of Mormon—*this,* and *this,* and *this*, and *this*), generally what the writer is doing—because they've had a lot of time to reflect upon it, and they're etching on metal plates which is a difficult thing to do—they are being extraordinarily *careful* with the material that they're committing to you. So, when you encounter a list, you ought to look at it and say to yourself, "Is this a progression? Is what they're doing, is telling you, Here is how you get from one point to another?" And we've encountered that already in 4th Nephi. You encounter it throughout—the Book of Mormon is a manual on how to return to God. And we read it like, well, like we do in Gospel Doctrine where we're going to cover eight chapters in 50 minutes.

So, now that we've gotten to the point that we're able to do these things, then and only then did they have,

> *...all things common among them; Therefore* [and this is as a logical result of what happened before, as an inevitability] *there were [no] rich and [there were no] poor, [and there were no] bond and [there were no] free, but they were all made free, and partakers of the heavenly gift.* (4 Nephi 1:3; see also 4 Nephi 1:1 RE)

This is *not* a description of a socio-economic order alone. The foundation of Zion shows up here yet again—it's the heavenly gift; it's the presence and the abundance of the things of the Spirit. It's *not* that we have now solved the social-welfare state because the social-welfare state is a...really, it's the arm-of-flesh effort to try and imitate something that we all, in our gut, think is probably a fair thing to do—to have everyone be on an equal plane and have every one deal with one another so that there are no rich and poor, or bond or free—but it doesn't work.

And it doesn't work because to get where you need to get, in order for the things to work, it has to be *"the heavenly gift."* It has to be people in harmony with each other because they are in harmony with the Lord. By getting in harmony with the Lord, you find that, well, *you* are a lot more tolerable to others, and others are suddenly more tolerable to you. Even defective others are more tolerable to you—if you're in harmony with the Lord. Because if you can see them as the Lord sees them, they are beautiful; they are wonderful! Everyone you have ever met is a child of your Heavenly Father. And if you can get *"the heavenly gift,"* then you stop seeing things through the lens of this world and you start seeing things as they really are.

Right now, the hearts of this nation, the hearts of this people are harder, are more strident, are more resistant to— I mean, look, what's the tool? Gentleness and meekness and persuasion—that's the tool. That's what you get to use. (See T&C 139:6 RE.) Why do you think the Savior took a beating and forgave them? I mean, He *shows* you the tool. He revolutionized the world, ultimately, simply because He was unwilling to return *to* brutality anything other than the kindness and the forgiveness that broke the hearts of *anyone* who hears the story of who this Man was.

When He appears, you need to be like Him (see Moroni 7:9 RE and Lectures on Faith 7:9 RE). Lay down the burden of guilt; lay down the burden of sin. Stop focusing on *that stuff* and become like Him. And you become like Him by doing His works. And you do His works by serving others, by ministering to the needs of others. And when you do that, it is a *natural* by-product of that process—ordained by laws established before the foundation of the world —that *light* and *truth* will grow within you. You will *have* compassion when you minister *with* compassion to the needs of others. Your heart will open to, and receive within it, light and truth when your conduct reflects the same conduct as a *merciful* and *holy* and *just* God, whom you claim to worship. Worship Him by imitating Him. Worship Him by doing His works. Worship Him by making a living sacrifice.

Set aside the junk that occupies you and go do something that is holy for someone else. However mundane and trivial it may seem to you, when you relieve the suffering of other people, something changes in *you*. You become different. You become better. You become more like our Lord—because when you give whatever it is you give away, you get more in return. But make sure that what you give goes to relieve the suffering of others. *Relieve the suffering of others.*

You're going to have to finish that path. You're going to have to rise up. If you expect to be in His presence when He returns—and He is coming in judgment—then you're going to have to be like Him, because if you are not like Him, you will not be able to endure His presence. Take it seriously. Study it through. Seek to be like Him whom you worship. It *is* possible—not while you're carrying a load of sins that trouble you and worry you and distract you, but that's what the Lord will remove from you; He can take all of that away. But it is entirely up to you to choose, *then* to do something to draw nearer to Him. He can't do *that* because that would violate your free will. *You* have to choose to be like Him. Although He may remove all of the stains upon you, you have to go forward and not stain yourself again—because He can't stop you from doing that; you're free to choose. Therefore, choose the better part.

The atonement isn't like Tinkerbell spreading some magic dust that will make you rise up. The atonement will erase your sins and mistakes, but *you* must rise up. *You* must acquire those virtues. The glory of God *is* intelligence. And repentance requires you to acquire that intelligence, that glory of God, and you acquire it by the things that you do in His name and for His sake.

And those that are here with you in need, they represent Him. And when you do it to even the least of them, He will credit that as having been done for Him (see Matthew 11:23 RE). And no good deed will be gone unnoticed with Him. He even notices when the sparrows fall (see Matthew 5:6 RE). So, is He not going to notice when your knee bends with compassion, praying for His mercy for someone that has offended you? And when you pray for those who have offended you, do you think for one moment that that doesn't change your own heart?

The reason to rejoice and be exceedingly glad when they *...say all manner of evil against you falsely...* (Matthew 3:14 RE and 3 Nephi 5:19 RE) is because it affords *you* the opportunity, with compassion like our Lord, who forgave even those who were in the act of killing Him—not their brutality but their ignorance— Because when the day arrives that they see things aright, finally, and they realize what offense they gave out, they had *no intention* of offending their Redeemer. They were carrying out the execution of a criminal. And so, He had compassion on them for their ignorance.

You have compassion for all those around you who are ignorant. If you think you know a little more than them, then use gentleness and meekness to persuade them. Sometimes what you try to persuade them of is going to offend them. Couple it with your own testimony of the truth; don't let them simply go away offended. Let them know that when you give offense—and you surely will give offense—let them know that you did it because of your love for them, your love of God, and your faith in the things that God is doing. When you offend, do it kindly and while bearing testimony of the truth, and with the compassion that should hail from a possession of greater light and truth, or intelligence. They don't know what they're doing. They don't understand it yet, so help them.

The Lord is going to take care of the abominations that are out there. Our responsibility is to invite people to see a better way, to conceive of a higher and more noble way to live life. Our job isn't to rebuke and condemn and to belittle.

There are really two forces at work in all of creation. One force is generative, creative, and positive. It fabricates new things. It is ongoingly surprising and life-filled and wonderful. And what's opposed to that are the forces of degeneration, decay, negativity, entropy, destruction. There isn't enough being done in order to bring that positivity, that creativity, that newness into this world. Even though children are born every day, and life starts over all new again with the birth of every new child, our minds are preoccupied by the forces of negativity and what opposes us. I could spend all day, every day, responding to negative arguments and negative comments, and if I were to do that, I wouldn't get anything new done, covered, accomplished, or out there.

When we take a message out to people about the Restoration of the Gospel, the work of Joseph Smith, the Book of Mormon, the offering of the Covenant, the expected coming Zion, there is no reason to deal with the criticism. It's going to collapse on its own. Here's a great bit of advice: If the criticism level would condemn Jesus Christ, then the criticism is the problem, not the object of the criticism.

Now, understand this is secondhand because I don't go there and do this, but my wife informed me that in some Facebook group there was complaining about the Prayer for the Covenant (see T&C 156) because that was "praying for to be seen of men;" it's public (see Matthew 3:28 RE and 3 Nephi 5:33 RE). *Okay...* When Jesus taught us to pray, "*Our Father who art in heaven,*" he did it publicly (see Matthew 3:29 RE and 3 Nephi 5:34 RE). It got reduced to writing. It's the most widely read prayer in all of Western society. So, if you are going to condemn on that basis the Prayer for the Covenant, you are going to have to condemn the Lord's Prayer, and in turn, condemn the Lord.

If you can resolve criticism leveled at you by applying the test and saying, "Jesus would have failed that test too," then you don't even need to respond to the criticism. But if they level criticism at you, and you look at it and say, "Well, Jesus would have passed that, and I would fail," then it's time to start saying, "Well, okay, then I need to clean up something in my own life"—

because all of us deserve some level, we merit some level of criticism and condemnation. We're just not perfect.

It's really hard to sit inside your own life and to be realistic about your own personal failings. We always tend to apply tests that are given in scripture outwardly, and to say, "As long as I use this persuasion and pure knowledge, then I can beat you into submission and *never* yield the argument because I'm doing what was said is the criteria." Gentleness? "Okay, I won't yell at you." Meekness? "Okay, I'll be polite enough to let you say what you have to say before I... I won't interrupt." Love unfeigned? "Okay, I *love* ya brother." And persuasion? "Okay, when I get my opportunity to present mine, I'm going for the brass ring. I'm gonna...."

Wait a minute! What if that's God trying to get through to *you*? What if the way in which God is trying to persuade *you* is by the meekness of a humble Lord who speaks to us in plain humility—who comes to us, not to try and overawe us, but comes to us saying: "*You* are *me* in embryo. I know what it took for me to become *The Son of God*, and I know you can do it too." What if the Lord is your greatest cheerleader, and He wants nothing more than to try and get you to *be* more like Him. You can't be more like Him when the center of everything is yourself, and you never self-examine. We all deserve criticism.

D&C section 1, verse 31: *For I the Lord cannot look upon sin with the least degree of allowance* (see also T&C 54:5). So, contrast that with "I cannot look at myself without the *enormous* latitude of allowance because I'm very forgiving of myself." You would be better off saying, "I will recognize, I will admit, and I will hold myself to *every failing* that I am prone to make. But as for all the rest of you, I don't see anything wrong with any of you. I can't detect a flaw in the least because I'm going to judge you with the standard by which I would like to be measured, which is 'I take no offense; I freely forgive.'"

The foregoing excerpts are taken from:

- Denver's *40 Years in Mormonism Series*, Talk #8, titled "A Broken Heart," given in Las Vegas, Nevada, on July 25th, 2014;
- His talk given at the "Zion Symposium" in Provo, Utah, on February 23rd, 2008;

- Denver's fireside talk, titled "Constitutional Apostasy," given in Highland, Utah, on June 7th, 2013;
- Denver's *40 Years in Mormonism Series*, Talk #3, titled "Repentance," given in Logan, Utah, on September 29th, 2013;
- His comments at the "Unity in Christ" conference, in Utah County, Utah, on July 30, 2017; and
- Denver's *40 Years in Mormonism Series*, Talk #6, titled "Zion," given in Grand Junction, Colorado, on April 12th, 2014.

131. Being Harmless, Part 2

This is Part 2 of a special series on Being Harmless. In the Restoration Edition of the scriptures, we find these references to being harmless:

Matthew 5:3: *Be therefore wise servants and as harmless as doves.*

Philippians 1:8: *Do all things without murmurings and disputings, that you may be blameless and harmless, the sons of God, without rebuke in the midst of a crooked and perverse nation — among whom you shine as lights in the world, holding forth the word of life.*

Alma 12:14: *Now Ammon being wise yet harmless, he said unto Lamoni, Wilt thou hearken unto my words if I tell thee by what power I do these things?*

Today Denver discusses what it means to be harmless and how that is manifested; how being harmless is related to being gentle, kind, meek, forgiving, wise, and easy to be entreated, and how, when, and where that matters the most; how all of this is a reflection of a condition of the heart; and how one who is harmless approaches others, and approaches God, especially when it may be most difficult to do.

DENVER: We have, time and time again, focused on 'The Doctrine of Christ.' We have the doctrine of Christ on numerous websites, enshrined in numerous talks, and as a theme that has been adopted for conferences. *Just before* 'The Doctrine of Christ,' He tells you what His doctrine is *not*. This is what Christ says immediately preceding His doctrine:

> *Neither shall there be disputations among you concerning the points of my doctrine, as there have hitherto been. For verily, verily I say unto you, he that hath the spirit of contention is not of me, but is of the devil, who is the father of contention; and he stirreth up the hearts of men to contend with anger, one with another. Behold, this is not my doctrine, to stir up the hearts of men with anger, one against another, but this is my doctrine, that such things should be done away.* (3 Nephi 11:28-30; see also 3 Nephi 5:8 RE).

And then, He proceeds to declare His Doctrine of Christ.

The more we contend and dispute with one another, the better we become at contention; we polish the rhetorical skills to oppose others. That spirit of contention can take possession of us, and when it does, we are hard-pressed to be a peacemaker with others. Christ said, *Blessed are the merciful: for they shall obtain mercy. Blessed are the pure in heart: for they shall see God. Blessed are the peacemakers: for they shall be called the children of God* (Matthew 3:10-12 RE).

But peace should not be made at the cost of truth; truth must be the only goal. Truth, however, belongs to God. Our desires, appetites, and passions are prone to make us stray well beyond the bounds set by God. Therefore:

- When our pride is gratified, we should question if what we are advancing is truth.
- When our ambition is served, we should question if we are in the Lord's employ or our own.
- When we insist upon control, we should question if we are like our Lord, or instead, like His adversary.
- When we use any means for compelling others, we should wonder if we are mocking the God who makes the sun to shine and rain to fall on *all* His fallen children without compulsion.
- When we display unrighteous dominion, we should question whether we are worthy of any dominion at all.
- Our tools must be limited to persuasion, gentleness, meekness, love unfeigned, pure knowledge—all of them mustered without compulsory means—to persuade others to accept the truth (see T&C 139:6; 175:31). And if we fail to make the persuasive case, then the problem is not others. The problem is that we've yet to figure out how to be sufficiently knowledgeable so as to bring them aboard.

I believe every person we encounter down here, no matter who they are, wants to follow Christ. *That's* why we're here. The only reason they *got* here was because they want to follow Christ. Therefore, since they are predisposed to following Christ, the reason they are not doing so at present is because no one has taken the time, no one has taken the trouble of giving sufficient cause to them to change, to turn, to repent, and to follow Christ.

And by the way, at this point none of us know enough in order to be able to truly follow Christ because we are all riddled with half truths, part understanding, and the need for constant repentance—all of us. But if you're further along and you accept Christ, and you understand His will better than your brother or sister, then you have the obligation to present persuasively to them the same reasons that touched their heart before they ever entered this world when they elected to follow Christ into this dark abyss in the first place. They're here trying to find Him.

If you can point to it and give them reason to believe, my view is that *every single individual* on earth has a native, free disposition to turn and face Christ. We just have to figure out how to present that sufficiently persuasively, so that it touches their heart and it resonates with that truth, that light that they came down here in the first instance possessing.

The light of Christ illuminates every single being that is in this world; therefore, Christ is in them already. You just have to animate that so that they realize the truth that you express, the testimony that you bear, the One whom you worship is God indeed and worthy of their worship, worthy of their acceptance as well.

To reflect the image of God, there are two sexes: male and female. Man was organized in this way to help us to understand who and what the Gods are. The importance of this is illustrated in a passage from Lectures on Faith:

> *Let us here observe, that three things are necessary in order that any rational and intelligent being may exercise faith in God unto life and salvation. First, the idea that he actually exists. Secondly, a* ***correct*** *idea of his* ***character, perfections, and attributes****. Thirdly, an actual knowledge that the course of life which he is pursuing is according to his will.* (Lectures on Faith 3:2-5 RE, emphasis added)

Eventually, every man—and I use that word in the Hebrew sense, meaning every male and female—will be brought to stand before the Throne of God. Then all questions about the image of the Gods will be answered by what is apparent to anyone standing in Their presence.

These truths are in the scriptures accepted by every Christian denomination. They are in the scriptures believed by the Jews. Yet, the Heavenly Mother's existence is not acknowledged.

While a great deal more could be said to demonstrate that God the Father necessarily includes God the Mother, we want to know more than merely She exists. We want to understand Her character, perfections, and attributes also.

The Father and the Son are masculine, and therefore personified by the word 'knowledge.' The Mother, as well as the Son's companion, are feminine and personified by the word 'wisdom.' These personifications reflect an eternal truth about these two parts of the One True God.

Knowledge (masculine) initiates; Wisdom (feminine) receives, guides, and tempers. Knowledge can be dangerous unless it is informed by wisdom. Wisdom provides guidance and counsel to channel what comes from knowledge. These are eternal attributes, part of what it means to be a male or a female. Creation begins with the active initiative of knowledge, but *order* and *harmony* for the creation requires wisdom. Balance between them is required for an orderly creation to exist.

A great deal can be learned about Heavenly Mother by searching for the word 'wisdom' in scripture. Very often the reference to 'wisdom' is to Her *distinctly*, and not merely an abstract attribute. If we are blind to Her existence, we cannot see the reference to Her in those passages. Although many scriptures have the Divine Mother's words, Her presence is veiled by our ignorance and refusal to acknowledge Her. There is one extensive passage in scripture *in Her voice* that we will look at today. It teaches us a great deal about Her.

This was once a temple text and has become somewhat corrupted. I'll not make any corrections or clarifications. This is from Proverbs 8 in the King James Version. The version we have has additional passages about the foolish woman at the beginning and again at the end. I am going to discard those words attributed, so that the words that are attributed to the Heavenly Mother alone can be isolated and looked at to be considered. She states:

> *Hear, for I will speak of excellent things and the opening of my lips shall be right things. For my mouth shall speak truth and wickedness is an abomination to my lips. All the words of my mouth are in righteousness, there is nothing froward or perverse in them.* (See Proverbs 1:35 RE)

She proclaims Herself as the reliable source of truth, righteousness, and plain (meaning *clear*) understanding. She is opposed to wickedness, frowardness (meaning *stubbornness* or *contrariness*), and perversity. If *we* are *"froward,"* we are stubborn or contrary with one another. We dispute. We find it difficult to agree. How much debate and anger are produced by frowardness!

Jacob (called James in the King James Bible) mentioned *"wisdom"* in his letter. In contemplating Her, Jacob suggested we should be *"easy to be entreated:"*

> *Who is a wise man, and endowed with knowledge, among you? Let him show out of good conduct his works with meekness of wisdom.* ***But*** *if you have bitter envying and strife in your hearts, glory not and lie not against the*

> *truth.* ***This wisdom*** *descends not from above, but is earthly, sensual, devilish; for where envying and strife are, there is confusion and every evil work. But the* ***wisdom*** *that is from above is* ***first pure, then peaceable, gentle, and easy to be entreated, full of mercy and good fruits, without partiality, and without hypocrisy.*** *And* ***the fruit of righteousness is sown in peace, of them that make peace.*** (Epistle of Jacob 1:14 RE, emphasis added)

"Wisdom...from above" can endow us with the kindly demeanor of brothers and sisters who seek what is good for one another. How often are the words of our mouths *"froward"* and *"perverse?"* The Divine Mother refuses to speak wickedness and abominations, and Her influence brings others to depart from such failures.

Continuing:

> *They are all plain to him that understandeth and right to them that find knowledge. Receive my instruction and not silver, and knowledge rather than choice gold. For wisdom is better than rubies and all the things that may be desired are not to be compared to it.* (See Proverbs 1:35 RE)

Proclaiming *"wisdom is better than rubies,"* she asks us to receive Her instruction rather than seek silver and gold. Nothing else is to be compared with Her wisdom. She instructs in virtues that would make *any* person better, but Her instruction will also make living in peace with others *possible.* Nothing in this world is more desirable than acquiring wisdom—understanding and putting knowledge to wise use. Zion will *require* the wisdom to use pure knowledge in meekness, humility and charity. Zion will require *Her* influence.

Continuing:

> *I, wisdom, dwell with prudence and find out knowledge of witty inventions. The fear of the Lord is to hate evil, pride, and arrogancy, and the evil way and the froward mouth do I hate.* (See Proverbs 1:36 RE)

Wisdom and prudence go together as companions. *"Prudence"* means good judgment or common sense. It is the quality of assessing things *correctly* and making a sound decision in light of the circumstances and persons involved. Prudent judgment is not hasty or unfair. Arrogance is destroyed and pride overtaken by *"fear of the Lord"*—meaning that we do not want to disappoint our Lord by our low, vulgar, and mean conduct.

She mentions a second time Her opposition to the froward. This time, She declares She *hates* the *"froward mouth."* We *repel* Her by being argumentative and contrary with one another.

Continuing:

> *Counsel is mine and sound wisdom. I am understanding, I have strength.* (Ibid.)

The Mother must possess great *"strength"* because She hates the froward—the contentious. She does not welcome that spirit in Herself or any of Her offspring. But yet, She loves us.

Christ taught this idea to the Nephites, which seems to be clearly taken from the Mother's wisdom:

> *And there shall be no disputations among you, as there hath hitherto been, neither shall there be disputations among you concerning the points of my* ***doctrine****, as there hath hitherto been. For verily, verily I say unto you, He that hath the spirit of contention is not of me, but is of the Devil, who is the father of contention; and he stirreth up the hearts of men to contend with anger, one with another. Behold, this is not my doctrine, to stir up the hearts of men with anger, [against one] another, but this is my doctrine,* ***that such things should be done away***. (3 Nephi 5:8 RE, emphasis added)

It requires strength to refrain from contention and disputes with froward and arrogant people. When we feel strongly that we are right, or are firmly convinced someone else is wrong, it's difficult to bridle our tongue and meekly persuade without contention. But the Heavenly Mother possesses the "*strength*" required to look with compassion on our failings. She deals with Her offspring using good judgment and common sense. She is opposed to arrogance, and when we are arrogant, we offend Her.

How many religious arguments, even religious wars, have been caused because mankind is *too weak* to patiently reason together? The history of this world is a bold testimony of what weak and deceived men do when they reject wisdom.

Mankind cannot have Zion without wisdom to guide us. Zion must be a community. Developing wisdom requires us to patiently interact with one another.

Can it be said concerning your own marriage that it is not good for the man to be alone? Are the two of you, together, better than what each of you are alone? Is your marriage a source of joy, of happiness, of contentment, of companionship? The Lord told them to multiply and replenish the earth. Do you find within your family relationship that there's joy and rejoicing and happiness, as a consequence of the environment that you and your wife put together?

Is your relationship… As a woman, is your relationship in the image of God? Is there godliness about the way in which you and your husband interact? If you had to reckon whether or not someone, looking at the two of you, would see within you the image of God, would they do so?

These aren't just happy notions for the afterlife. These ought to be descriptions of what *your* marriage could and should look like. Can you sense the glory of God in your marriage? Remember, we looked at this in [D&C] 93:36: *The glory of God is intelligence, or in other words, light and truth* (see also T&C 93:11)—*"glory of God"* being *"light;"* the *"glory of God"* being *"truth."* Is that something that is present within the marriage that *you* have? Is your marriage filled with life, with light, with truth, with understanding?

Turn back to D&C section 121. There's a couple verses there that I want to suggest, *particularly if* you view the man and the woman together as one. Read these verses as if it's descriptive of *the one*, which is you and your wife:

> *Many are called, but few are chosen.* [This is beginning at verse 40 of section 121.] *No power or influence can or ought to be maintained by virtue of the priesthood; only by persuasion, by long-suffering, by gentleness and meekness, and by love unfeigned, by kindness and pure knowledge, which shall greatly enlarge the soul; without hypocrisy and without guile.* (See also T&C 139:5-6)

Within your family, within your marriage, are you and your wife learning to use persuasion? Within your marriage, are you and your husband learning to use gentleness in dealing with one another? Are the two of you, together, facing one another in all of the difficulties that come as a result of being married? Are you facing that together in meekness? Do you find that in all the relationship troubles, turmoils, and challenges, what predominates is kindness? Is there a search for understanding that results in pure knowledge when it comes to a dilemma?

Look at verse 37:

> *That they may be conferred upon us, it is true; but when we undertake to cover our sins, or to gratify our pride, our vain ambition, or to exercise control, or dominion, or compulsion, upon the souls of the children of men in any degree of unrighteousness, behold, the heavens withdraw themselves, the Spirit of the Lord is grieved, and when it is withdrawn, Amen to the priesthood or the authority of that man.* (See also T&C 139:5)

It's been my observation that so soon as the Spirit of the Lord withdraws, *that quickly* will another spirit step in to assure you that you're right, you should be vindicated, that you ought to proceed on in the arrogance of your heart to feel yourself justified and vindicated.

There are false spirits that go about. But there are no better an audience to receive the whisperings *of* those false spirits than it is the abusers who, having grieved the Spirit and caused it to withdraw, accept then counsel from yet another spirit that says, "You're right; press on! Well done! You're good! You're right; you'll be vindicated. This is *all* God's work, and you're a great man because you're engaged in God's work! Do not back down. Do not relent. Forget about persuasion. You should never be long-suffering. You should make those under *your rule* suffer. They *should* yield to your rule. There is no place for meekness. We believe in a God of strength, a God of power, a God whose work can be done despite the frailties of man; there is no need for men to be meek. And it's kind in the end, after all, to punish and to force and to coerce because we have a good *objective* in mind."

All of the lies and all of the deceit that led in turn to Catholicism falling, into the abyss that it fell into, are presently in play with spirits that worked this out long ago—taking the Restoration of the Gospel as yet another opportunity in which to whisper in, once the Spirit is withdrawn.

So, does your marriage help *you* avoid covering your sins? Does your marriage —because you're never going to solve this problem in the community until you first begin to solve it within the walls of your own home; you're never going to have Zion that exists somewhere among a community until *first* that community is composed of those who have a marriage that is in the image of God—does your marriage help you avoid *"gratify*ing *your pride?"* Does it help hold down your *"vain ambition?"* Is your ambition to exalt the two of you, rather than the one of you? Does it bring you, time and time again, to *not "exercise control"* but to respect the freedom to choose?

Your kids are going to make mistakes. It's *not* your job to force them to *not* make the mistake. It's your job to counsel them and to let them have the experience by which your counsel makes sense and is vindicated. You *hope* the mistakes that they make are not too serious, but even if they're *serious* and they involve lifelong struggles, it's *their* right to choose. And it's your obligation to teach and to persuade, and then to *rejoice* when they return after they're tired of filling their bellies with the husks that the pigs are fed. It's your job to go and greet them, and put a robe on their shoulder, and put a ring on their hand, and to kill the fatted calf (see Luke 9:13-15 RE). It's not your job to beat them and to chain them to the farm, so they can't go away and behave foolishly. They need to know that your bonds of love towards them are stronger than death itself. They need to know that they will endure in your heart into eternity.

And not only your children but one another—because we *all* make mistakes. Do not exercise dominion; do not exercise compulsion. Exercise long-suffering, gentleness, meekness, and kindness. Some of the biggest disasters come when you do not give people the right to choose freely and you attempt to coerce them. Be wise; be prudent; be someone that they would respect and they would listen to.

The Apostle Paul is credited with being the father of the Protestant Reformation. His words about *grace* were used to re-conceive man's salvation. Martin Luther saw in Paul's words the possibility of salvation by grace, separate from institutional authority and control.

At the time when Jesus Christ had living officials administering rites of the Gospel, Paul was able to wrestle from heaven a dispensation. Using that dispensation, Paul became a dispensation head who did more, worked harder, and labored more abundantly in ministering to Christ's sheep and spreading the Gospel than any other man we know of. Paul was not jealous of the others who knew Christ and had been called by Him to the ministry, but there is some evidence of fear and jealousy towards Paul for his success in obtaining an independent dispensation of the Gospel.

Paul explained his diligence in spreading the Gospel:

> *...in labors more abundant, in stripes above measure, in prisons more frequent, in deaths oft. Of the Jews, five times received I forty...save one; three times [I was] beaten with rods; once [I was] stoned; three times I suffered shipwreck; a night and a day I have been in the deep;...journeyings often,...perils of waters,...perils of robbers,...perils by countrymen,...perils by the heathen,...perils in the city,...perils in the wilderness, ...perils in the sea,...perils among false brethren; in weariness and labor, in sleeplessness*

> *often, in hunger and thirst, in fastings often, in cold and nakedness; beside[s] those things that are outside, that which comes upon me daily — the care of all the churches.* (2 Corinthians 1:39 RE)

Despite the opposition Paul experienced among believers and non-believers alike, he remained of a cheery disposition: *I have learned, in whatever state I am, to be content* (Philippians 1:16 RE).

It is *this* kind of contentment we should see among people today. When God's people are stirred to anger with each other, then even God is against them. After the spot for a temple in Missouri was revealed, the people who went there polluted it by their jealousies and fighting. The unbelieving Missourians were used by God to expel them from the place they had hoped to build a temple. They were surprised the holy spot could be taken from them. After it was taken, God explained *why*:

> *Verily I say unto you concerning your brethren who have been afflicted, and persecuted, and* ***cast out*** *from the land of their [inheritance], I, the Lord, have suffered the affliction[s] to come upon them wherewith they have been afflicted, in consequence of their transgressions, yet I will own them, and they shall be mine in that day when I shall come to make up my jewels. Therefore, they must needs be chastened and tried even as Abraham, who was commanded to offer up his only son, for all those who will not endure chastening, but deny me, cannot be sanctified. Behold, I say unto you, There were jarrings, and contentions, and envyings, and strifes, and lustful and covetous desires among them; therefore, by these things they polluted their inheritances. They were slow to hearken unto the voice of the Lord their God, therefore the Lord their God is slow to hearken unto their prayers, to answer* ***them*** *in the day of their trouble. In the day of their peace they esteemed lightly my counsel, but in the day of their trouble, of necessity they feel after me.* (T&C 101:1-2, emphasis added)

If the covenant with God is kept, then He will allow His house to be built. The covenant *cannot be kept* if there is jarring, contention, envy, strife, lustful and covetous desires. If we do the same as those who went before, we would pollute the ground again. I am thankful we do not yet have a place to pollute. It would be better to never gain a promised place for God's house than to take possession and pollute it.

The content Apostle Paul taught the believers of his day:

> *Let your consecrations be without covetousness, and be content with giving such things as you have; for he has said, I will never leave you nor forsake you, so that we may boldly say, The Lord is my helper and I will not fear what man shall do unto me.* (Hebrews 1:58 RE)

Alma taught a lesson that *we* accepted by covenant as a statement of *our* faith:

> *And now, my beloved brethren, I have said these things unto you that I might awaken you to a sense of your duty to God, that ye may walk blameless before him, that ye may walk after the Holy Order of God after which ye have been received. And now I would that ye should be* ***humble****, and be* ***submissive*** *and* ***gentle****,* ***easy to be entreated****, full of patience and long-suffering, being temperate in all things, being diligent in keeping the commandments of God at all times, asking for whatsoever things ye stand in need, both spiritual and temporal, always returning thanks unto God for whatsoever things ye do receive.* (Alma 5:6 RE, emphasis added)

The greatness of a soul is defined by how *easily* they are *"entreated"* to follow the truth. The greatest of those who have ever lived have been *"submissive and gentle"* souls. In a day when Satan accuses and rages in the hearts of men, it requires *extraordinary will* and *steely determination* to remain easily entreated by truth.

> *...I answer you on behalf of all the people, and not as to any individual. For there are those who are humble, patient, and easily persuaded. Nevertheless people who are quarrelsome and proud are also among you, and since you seek to unite to become one people, I answer you as one.*
>
> *I covenanted with Adam at the beginning, which covenant was broken by mankind. Since the days of Adam I have always sought to reestablish people of covenant among the living, and therefore have desired that man should love one another, not begrudgingly, but as brothers and sisters indeed, that I may establish my covenant and provide them with light and truth.*
>
> *For you to unite I must admonish and instruct you, for my will is to have you love one another. As people, you lack the ability to respectfully disagree among one another. You Are as Paul and Peter, whose disagreements resulted in jarring and sharp contentions. Nevertheless they both loved me and I loved them. You must do better.*
>
> *...In your language you use the name Lucifer for an angel who was in authority before God, who rebelled, fought against the work of the Father and was cast down to the earth. His name means holder of light, or light bearer,*

for he...gathered light by his heed and diligence before he rebelled. He has become a vessel containing only wrath and seeks to destroy all who will hearken to him. He is now enslaved to his own hatred.

Satan is a title, and means accuser, opponent, and adversary; hence once he fell, Lucifer became, or in other words was called, Satan, because he accuses others and opposes the Father. I rebuked Peter and called him Satan because he was wrong in opposing the Father's will for me, and Peter understood and repented.

In the work you have performed there are those who have been Satan, accusing one another, wounding hearts and causing jarring, contention, and strife by their accusations. Rather than loving one another, even among you who desire good thing, some have dealt unkindly as if they were...opponents, accusers and adversaries. In this they were wrong.

...[But] you cannot be Satan and be mine. If you take upon you my covenant, you must abide it as a people to gain what I promise. You think Satan will be bound a thousand years, and it will be so, but do not understand your own duty to bind that spirit within you so that you give no heed to accuse others. It is not enough to say you love God; you must also love your fellow man. Nor is it enough to say love your fellow man while you, as Satan, divide, contend and dispute against any person who labors on an errand seeking to do my will. How you proceed must be as noble as the cause you seek. You have become your own adversaries, and you cannot be Satan and also be mine. Repent, therefore, like Peter and end your unkind and untrue accusations against one another, and make peace. How shall there ever come a thousand years of peace if the people who are mine do not love one another? How shall Satan be bound if there are no people of one heart and one mind?

...I desire to heal you from an awful state of blindness so that you may see clearly my will, to do it. I promised to bring unto you much of my gospel through the Book of Mormon and to provide you with the means to obtain a fullness of my gospel, and I have done this; yet you refuse to receive the truth, even when it is given unto you in plainness. How can you who pursue the truth, yet remain unable to behold your own weakness before me?

Unto what can I liken it, that you may understand? For you are like a man who seeks for good fruit from a neglected vineyard — unwatered, undunged, unpruned and unattended. How shall it produce good fruit if you fail to tend it? What reward does the unfaithful husbandman obtain from his neglected vineyard? How can saying you are a faithful husbandman ever produce good fruit in the vineyard without doing the work of the husbandman? For you seek my words to recover them even as you forsake to do them. You have heretofore produced wild fruit, bitter and ill-formed, because you neglect to do my words.

I speak of you who have hindered my work, that claim to see plainly the beams in others' eyes. You have claimed to see plainly the error of those who abuse my words, and neglect the poor, and who have cast you out — to discern their errors, and you say you seek a better way. Yet among you are those who continue to scheme, backbite, contend, accuse and forsake my words to do them, even while you seek to recover them. Can you not see that your works fall short of the beliefs you profess?

For the sake of the promises to the Fathers [I will] labor with you as a people, and not because of you, for you have not yet become what you must be to live together in peace. If you will hearken to my words, I will make you my people and my words will give you peace. Even a single soul who stirs up the hearts of others to anger can destroy the peace of all my people. Each of you must equally walk truly in my path, not only to profess, but to do as you profess.

The Book of Mormon was given as my covenant for this day and contains my gospel, which came forth to allow people to understand my work and then obtain my salvation. Yet many of you are like those who reject the Book of Mormon, because you say, but you do not do. As a people you honor with your lips, but your hearts are corrupt, filled with envy and malice, returning evil for good, sparing none — even those with pure hearts among you — from your unjustified accusations and unkind backbiting. You have not obtained the fullness of my salvation because you do not draw near to me.

...It is not enough to receive my covenant, but you must also abide it. And all who abide it, whether on this land or any other land, will be mine, and I will watch over them and protect them in the day of harvest, and gather them in as a hen gathers her chicks under her wings. I will number you among the remnant of Jacob, no longer outcasts, and you will inherit the promises of Israel. You shall be my people and I will be your God, and the sword will not devour you. And unto those who will receive will more be given, until they know the mysteries of God in full.

But remember that without the fruit of repentance, and a broken heart and a contrite spirit, you cannot keep my covenant; for I, your Lord, am meek and lowly of heart. Be like me. You have all been wounded, your hearts pierced through with sorrows because of how the world has treated you. But you have also scarred one another by your unkind treatment of each other, and you do not notice your misconduct toward[s] others because you think yourself justified in this. You bear the scars on your countenances, from the soles of your feet to the head, and every heart is faint. Your visages have been so marred that your hardness, mistrust, suspicions, resentments, fear, jealousies and anger toward your fellow man bear outward witness of your inner self; you cannot hide it. When I appear to you, instead of confidence, you feel shame. You fear and withdraw from me because you bear the blood and sins of your treatment of brothers and sisters. Come to me and I will make sins as scarlet become white as snow, and I will make you stand boldly before me, confident of my love.

I descended below it all, and know the sorrows of you all, and have borne the grief of it all, and I say to you, Forgive one another. Be tender with one another, pursue judgment, bless the oppressed, care for the orphan, and uplift the widow in her need, for I have redeemed you from being orphaned and taken you that you are no longer a widowed people. Rejoice in me, and rejoice with your brethren and sisters who are mine also. Be one.

You pray each time you partake of the sacrament to always have my Spirit to be with you. And what is my Spirit? It is to love one another as I have loved you. Do my works and you will know my doctrine; for you will uncover hidden mysteries by obedience to these things that can be uncovered in no other way. This is the way I will restore knowledge to my people. If you return good for evil, you will cleanse yourself and know the joy of your Master. You call me Lord, and do well to regard me so, but to know your Lord is to love one another. Flee from the cares and longings that belong to Babylon, obtain a new heart, for you have all been wounded. In me you will find peace, and through me will come Zion, a place of peace and safety.

There are only two ways: the way I lead, [which] goes upward in light and truth unto Eternal lives — and if you turn from it, you follow the way of darkness and the deaths. Those who want to come where I am must be able to abide the conditions established for my Father's Kingdom. I have given to you the means to understand the conditions you must abide. I came and lived in the world to be the light of the world. I have sent others who have testified of me and taught you. I have sent my light into the world. Let not your hearts remain divided from one another and divided from me.

Be of one heart, and regard one another with charity. Measure your words before giving voice to them, and consider the hearts of others. Although a man may err in understanding concerning many things, yet he can view his brother with charity and come unto me, and through me he can with patience overcome the world. I can bring him to understanding and knowledge. Therefore, if you regard one another with charity, then your brother's error in understanding will not divide you. I lead to all truth. I will lead all who come to me to the truth of all things. The fullness is to receive the truth of all things, and this too from me, in power, by my word and in very deed. For I will come unto you if you will come unto me.

Study to learn how to respect your brothers and sisters and to come together by precept, reason and persuasion rather than sharply disputing and wrongly condemning each other, causing anger. Take care how you invoke my name. Mankind has been controlled by the adversary through anger and jealousy, which has led to bloodshed and the misery of many souls. Even strong disagreements should not provoke anger, nor to invoke my name in vain as if I had part in your every dispute. Pray together in humility and together meekly present your dispute to me, and if you are contrite before me I will tell you my part.

...There remains great work yet to be done. Receive my covenant and abide in it, not as in the former time[s] when jarring, jealousy, contention and backbiting caused anger, broke hearts and hardened the souls of those claiming to be my saints. But receive it in spirit, in meekness and in truth. I have given you a former commandment that I, the Lord, will forgive whom I will forgive, but of you it is required to forgive all men. And again, I have taught that if you forgive men their trespasses, your Heavenly Father will also forgive you; but if you forgive not men their trespasses neither will your Heavenly Father forgive your trespasses. How do I act toward mankind? If men intend no offense, I take no offense, but if they are taught and should have obeyed, then I reprove and correct, and forgive and forget. You cannot be at peace with one another if you take offense when none is intended. But again I say, Judge not others except by the rule you want used to weigh yourself. (*Answer to Prayer for Covenant,* T&C 157:1-3, 7-10, 16-20, 48-54, 58)

The foregoing excerpts are taken from:

- A fireside talk, titled "That We Might Become One," given in Clinton, Utah, on January 14, 2018;

- Denver's conference talk, titled "Our Divine Parents," given in Gilbert, Arizona, on March 25, 2018;
- Denver's *40 Years in Mormonism Series*, Talk #9, titled "Marriage and Family," given in St. George, Utah, on July 26, 2014;
- Denver's remarks, titled "Keep the Covenant: Do the Work," given at the Remembering the Covenants Conference in Layton, Utah, on August 4, 2018; and
- The presentation of "Answer and Covenant," given at the Covenant of Christ Conference in Boise, Idaho, on September 3, 2017.

132. Adoption, Part 1

This is the first part of a special series on adoption, where Denver discusses one of the lost ordinances that must be restored as part of the Religion of the Fathers.

DENVER: In the immediate aftermath of Joseph's death and the completion of the Nauvoo Temple, there was a lot of questions that could not then be answered because they simply no longer had the keys with which to get the answers to the questions that were pressing upon them. If they didn't have the ability to ask and get an answer, then they couldn't get direction. And they couldn't. Therefore, what Joseph was doing was left without a culmination.

You can go out, and there's physical proof in the restored Nauvoo Temple. You can see this on the website where the photograph was taken and put up, Bare Record [barerecord.blogspot.com], where there's a place where the brick size changes in the construction of the Nauvoo Temple. They were making small bricks, and you can see how far up the small bricks run on the outside of the temple. When Joseph was killed, in order to complete the temple in greater haste, the size of the bricks increase, and so, there's a point [~~in~~] which the size of the bricks go from small to larger when they're hastening the work in which they're trying to get the building done. The level at which the temple had been completed at the time of the martyrdom essentially was a repetition of what had been built in the Kirtland Temple. It is the Solemn Assembly Room. Okay?

Joseph never lived to tell anyone how to build the top of the Nauvoo Temple. So, when they got to the point that they were finishing the Nauvoo Temple, they didn't have any plans for what happened in the attic area other than the rooms around the perimeter in which the priesthood was supposed to meet. And so, to create the ceremonial setting in which the Nauvoo Temple endowment companies were taken through, they took canvas that Joseph had ordered for a bowery so they could get it out of the weather. And they took the canvas, and they made partitions in the attic area to divide the rooms up in which to present the endowment in the attic of the Nauvoo Temple. Had Joseph lived, he would have been able to finish out that space. He didn't live, and so, they did it with canvas. They did it as a temporary thing, and they administered the endowments in that setting.

In the process of administering those things, there was something that went on that they were trying to imitate what Joseph had been talking about. Brigham Young makes an explanation shortly after they abandoned. I mean, the same month that they abandoned Nauvoo and they're heading west, he gives a talk in Winter Quarters in February 1847. This is the 16th of February. They walked out of town on the 9th. So, this is a week later. He's talking about a subject that really defines what the entirety of this topic is really involved with:

> The Lord introduced the law of adoption for the benefit of the children of men as a schoolmaster to bring them back to the covenant of the priesthood, not as some have supposed to add anything to his glory. This principle I answer is not clearly understood by many of the Elders in this church at the present time as it will hereafter, and I confess that I have only had a smattering of these things; but when it is necessary I will attain to the more knowledge on the subject and consequently will be entitled to teach and practice more and will in the meantime glorify God, the bountiful giver.

The rest of that talk's interesting, and I would comment on it, but we don't have time.

So, this is on the 16th of February. On the 23rd, another week later, Brigham Young gives another talk, and this talk is pointed to for one purpose. I want to read you a more fulsome account and suggest to you the more-important purpose, 'k? This is that great occasion on which Brigham Young went to sleep and had a dream in which Joseph Smith appeared to him, and Joseph Smith… Well, let me read you the account. I'm into the part where he's already introduced that he's dreaming, that he's seen Joseph, and that Joseph is now talking to him:

> I then discovered there was a hand rail between us, Joseph stood by a window, and to the southwest of him it was very light. I was in the twilight and to the north of me it was very dark; [Joseph's in the light; Brigham's in the dark.] I said, "Brother Joseph, the brethren you know well, better than I do; you raised them up, and brought the Priesthood to us. The brethren have a great anxiety to understand the law of adoption or sealing principles; and if you have a word of counsel for me, I should be glad to receive it.

So, now of all the things about which Brigham Young could be talking to the Prophet Joseph Smith, on this occasion the thing that comes thundering to the foreground that he would like to know about is the law of adoption. He wants to know that, standing as he is in the dark:

> Joseph stepped toward me, and looking very earnestly, yet pleasantly said, 'Tell the people to be humble and faithful, be sure to keep the spirit of the Lord and it will lead them right. Be careful and not turn away the small voice; it will teach you what to do and where to go; it will yield the fruits of the kingdom. Tell the brethren to keep their hearts open to conviction, so that when the Holy Ghost comes to them, their hearts will be ready to receive it. They can tell the Spirit of the Lord from all other spirits; it will whisper peace and joy to their souls; it will take malice, hatred, strife and all evil from their hearts; and their whole desire will be to do good, bring forth righteousness and build up the kingdom of God. Tell the brethren if they will follow the spirit of Lord they will go right. Be sure to tell the people to keep the Spirit of the Lord; and if they will, they will find themselves just as they were organized by our Father in Heaven before they came into the world. Our Father in Heaven organized the human family, but they are all disorganized and in great confusion.

And so, Joseph's answer to the pressing question of how do we go about getting these sealings right? is to say, "Oh, go get the Holy Ghost, and let the Holy Ghost guide you. God will get you organized." In other words, Joseph punted on the answer. It would do no good for the answer to be given if the authority with which to administer the answer was something that wasn't there. Therefore, rather than to tell him so that some solemn mockery continued, it was time to bring it to an end. And although they made an effort to continue in that vein for a short while, as I pointed out in *Passing the Heavenly Gift*, everyone talked about.... They didn't understand it. And in fact, some of the leading brethren said, "I didn't believe it when I first heard it and I don't believe it now," and the practice of adoption came to an end. 'K?

I want to go back for a moment to what we **do** know from Doctrine and Covenants section 132 that comes from the Prophet Joseph Smith because **that's it**. That's the entirety of what we have from him. In verse 7 of this section 132, it says:

> *I have appointed on the earth to hold this power and I have appointed unto my servant, Joseph, to hold this power in the last days, (and there is never but one on the earth at a time on whom this power and the keys of this priesthood are conferred).* (D&C 132:7)

And so on. **There is only one**. Only one.

So, when we go to Doctrine and Covenants section 107, it talks about:

> *The order of this priesthood* [I'm reading from verse 40] *was confirmed to be handed down from father to son, and rightly belongs to the literal descendants of the chosen seed, to whom the promises were made. This order was instituted in the days of Adam, and [it] came down by lineage in the following manner: From Adam to Seth, who was ordained by Adam at the age of sixty–nine years, and...blessed by him three years previous to his (Adam's) death, and received the promise of God by his father, that his posterity should be the chosen of the Lord, and that they should be preserved unto the end of the earth; Because he (Seth) was a perfect man, and his likeness was the express likeness of his father, insomuch that he seemed to be like unto his father in all things, and could be distinguished from him only by his age. Enos was ordained at the age of one hundred and thirty–four years and four months, by the hand of Adam. God called upon Cainan in the wilderness in the fortieth year of his age; and he met Adam in [his] journeying to the place Shedolamak. He was eighty–seven years old when he received his ordination. Mahalaleel was four hundred and ninety–six years and seven days...when he was ordained by the hand of Adam.... Jared was two hundred years old when he was ordained under the hand of Adam.... Enoch was twenty–five years old when he was ordained...of Adam...Methuselah was one hundred years old when he was ordained.... Lamech was thirty–two...[and] Noah was ten years old when he was ordained under the hand of Methuselah. Three years previous to the death of Adam, he called Seth, Enos, Cainan, Mahalaleel, Jared, Enoch, and Methuselah, who were all high priests, with the residue of his posterity who were righteous, [in] the valley of Adam-ondi-Ahman, and there bestowed upon them his last blessing.* (D&C 107:40-48, 50-53; see also T&C 154:9-19 RE)

When you go to the story in Moses chapter 5 and you read about Adam and Eve and their posterity, Adam and Eve have children; and the children are seduced by Satan and persuaded to be led astray. Then, they have a son to whom the birthright was going to be granted because he appeared to be interested in the things of God, so much so that he was willing to offer sacrifice. That son, the older one, was named Cain, and the next son born was Abel. But Abel was more attentive to the things of God. Both Cain and Abel offered sacrifices to the Lord. However, the Lord approved the sacrifice of Abel.

At this point in the history of man, if that right of priesthood passed from Adam to Abel, it would have displaced Cain. Cain sought for the right whereunto he would be the one to hold that priesthood. He was the one who wanted it. **P**

The first murder that was committed was committed against the one who would inherit the birthright—done precisely for the purpose of eliminating the posterity of Abel so that Abel, having no posterity, could not be the one through whom the birthright would be perpetuated. When Cain sought to take what God had, instead, appointed his younger brother to receive, Cain was deprived of the right of priesthood; and it passed over him and his descendants so that Cain did not obtain the birthright.

And Eve conceived and she bore a replacement son, and that son, Seth, became the one through whom the promises would be given. And Cain was driven out from the people. Now you have to understand that… This is in Moses chapter 6:

> *Adam lived one hundred and thirty years, and begat a son in his own likeness, after his own image, and called his name Seth. And the days of Adam, after he had begotten Seth, were eight hundred years, and he begat many sons and daughters* (Moses 6:10-11; see also Genesis 3:15 RE).

Adam begat **many** sons and daughters, but the son named Seth was the one to whom this priesthood went—because there is only one appointed.

> *Seth lived one hundred and five years, and [he] begat Enos, and prophesied in all his days, and taught his son Enos in the ways of God; wherefore Enos prophesied also. And Seth lived, after he begat Enos, eight hundred and seven years, and begat many sons and daughters.* (Moses 6:13-14; see also Genesis 3:16 RE)

So, Seth begat Enos and **many** sons and daughters. But the right of the lineage and the priesthood went from Adam to Seth to Enos.

This is a description of that priesthood which was briefly restored in one person, Joseph, to be given to Hyrum because it goes to the oldest righteous descendant. And when it was first restored through Joseph Smith, Hyrum was not yet qualified. But when Hyrum became qualified by January of 1841, in the revelation given then, Hyrum is the one to whom the birthright went (being the eldest and being the one who was qualified). This is why it was necessary for Hyrum to die before Joseph—so that in this dispensation, Joseph and Hyrum can stand at the head because if Hyrum had not died first, but Joseph had died first, Joseph would have died without having had the passing. Well…

Notice that Seth had many sons and daughters. And then, you get to the next, Enos, who lived and begat Canaan. Enos also has many sons and daughters, but Canaan was the one upon whom the birthright… And this follows all the way down—**all the way down**. You can read it in Moses chapter 6, how it descends through the line. This pattern repeats over and over again.

As I'm talking about this, I'm making reference to a diagram that appeared first in the *Millennial Star* on January the 15th of 1847. But what you can see in the *Joseph Smith Papers* on page 298 where they reproduce the same diagram of the kingdom of God (the only difference being that I have filled in the names on this chart so that you can see where the names go)...

Now, we get to the point in the history of the world in which, after the days of Shem, who was renamed Melchizedek, people fell into iniquity. They fell into iniquity, and they lost the birthright. There was no continuation of this. It was broken by an apostasy, and it had to be restored again, which ought to give all of us great hope because Abraham sought for this. He sought for a restoration of the kingdom of God. He sought for a restoration of this, which only one man on the earth can hold at a time. Abraham chapter 1, verse 2:

> *And, finding there was greater happiness and peace and rest for me, I sought for the blessings of the fathers, and the right whereunto I should be ordained to administer the same; having been myself a follower of righteousness, desiring also to be one who possessed great knowledge, and to be a greater follower of righteousness, and ...possess a greater knowledge, and to be a father of many nations, a prince of peace, ...desiring to receive instructions, and...keep the commandments of God, I became a rightful heir, a High Priest, holding the right belonging to the fathers.* (See also Abraham 1:1 RE)

When you are in possession of that, you have no problem asking God and getting an answer. It is the right belonging to the Fathers. After a period of apostasy and the break of this line, Abraham received it by adoption. Therefore, this power has the ability to cure the break. This covenant-making through God has the ability to restore the family of God, even when wicked men kill in order to destroy it; even when a substitute needs to be made; even when the fathers turn from their righteousness. Yet God is able to cause it to persist. And Joseph Smith was doing something which no one else either understood or had the right to perpetuate.

In 1836, sacred rites were introduced in the Kirtland Temple. In 1843, different rites were contemplated, even partially celebrated. The new and improved temple rites were to be completed and housed in a new temple then under construction. A partial endowment was added to the already existing washings and anointings. The expanded rites also contemplated sealing marriages and adoption, or man-to-man sealings, all of which remained ill-defined at the time of Joseph's death.

Joseph's original instruction about sealing dealt with connecting the living faithful to the Fathers in heaven, Abraham, Isaac, and Jacob. The connection was to be accomplished through adoption sealings, not genealogy. Joseph was connected to the Fathers through his priesthood. He and his brother Hyrum were to become Fathers of all who would live after them. (Just read Abraham chapter 1, verse 2.) Families were originally organized under Joseph as the Father of the righteous in this dispensation. Accordingly, men were sealed to Joseph Smith as their Father and they as his sons. This was referred to as *adoption* because the family organization was not *biological* but *priestly*, according to the law of God.

As soon as Joseph died, the doctrine began to erode, ultimately replaced by the substitute practice of sealing genealogical lines together. In between the original adoptive sealing to Joseph and the current practice of tracking genealogical or biological lines, there was an intermediate step when families were tracked back as far as research permitted. Then, the line was sealed to Joseph Smith. (That practice is now forgotten and is certainly no longer practiced by any denomination within Mormonism.) When Joseph died, any understanding of the practice of adoption was quickly lost.

Joseph died with a clear conscience. Few Mormons since him have done likewise.

Somehow Mormonism has tolerated marital misconduct, adultery, concealing criminal misconduct by *lying for the Lord* to evade Federal investigations, aggregating wealth while neglecting the poor, exercising control to abrogate followers' consciences under the claim it is the right of church leaders to do so. It has abandoned adoptions, denounced eternal progression, decanonized Lectures on Faith (without a vote of its members), and concealed church finances. It recently has stretched LDS *sustaining?* into an oath-like obligation binding on us. LDS Mormonism has determined that truth can sometimes be *unhelpful* to it. These deviations have happened as modern Mormonism yet claims Joseph as its founder. Modern Mormonism isn't. It is something far deviant from the original, and as this Sunstone Conference shows, its deviations are metastasizing.

I understand why people of good faith believe all of the propaganda that began upon Joseph's death and are confident that there's truth there. And in fact, the D&C 132— We know something got read to the Nauvoo High Council, and that something that got read dealt with the topic that the current iteration of D&C 132 contains. I'm not denying any of that.

Here's the problem: If you start with the beginning, and I take the position that whatever was revealed was first revealed in 1829… I think that it came during the translation of Jacob chapter 2. (Just like reading about baptism in the Book of Mormon—they pray about baptism, and John the Baptist appeared.) I believe it was Jacob chapter 2 and not the Old Testament translation. In fact, there's plenty of reason to suspect that, but... So, start with 1829 and look at everything that exists up until June the 27th of 1844 and end your inquiry there. Just stop it at that moment and ask yourself, "Is there **any** proof? Is there **any** proof that Joseph was involved in the way that people characterize his involvement?"

Look, if you have **an** ordinance identified—and D&C 132 identifies **an** ordinance—**it's only one**, 'k? It's the old cliché: To a man with a hammer, the whole world looks like a nail. If the **only** ordinance you have is marriage, 'k? and that's the mechanism by which you are going to preserve families into eternity, and you want to preserve another family into eternity, how are you going to accomplish that? The only way in which it is possible to do so is through marriage.

Sometime—and understand, it was **so** late; we're talking a period of a few months— ~~it's~~ sometime very late in the process, Joseph Smith began to do adoptions. We don't even have language for what it was that Joseph was doing.

Brigham Young attempted to mimic that. In fact, that section that Brigham Young wrote in the D&C about captains of tens and captains of fifties and captain... Substitute the word *father* because he organized the companies according to adoption principles.

When Brigham Young got through in the valley, and he was migrating back, and he was going to Winter Quarters, and he encountered John Taylor and Parley Pratt and their company, the reason he blew a gasket, the reason why he went back (and he wanted to become the president) was because he had organized that company according to the priesthood. And he went back and was ranting and raving. When you read that, it makes no sense at all unless you substitute in there the fact that he had organized them in an adopted family; and he viewed what Parley Pratt and John Taylor had done as an offence against the priesthood itself. And that's why he wanted to be elected president. And he got himself elected president, and one of the first things he said was, he can hardly wait to get back to the Salt Lake Valley and have Parley Pratt and John Taylor confess that they aren't Brigham Young because he's the big dog now, and no one can seal anyone to anything without him and his word alone because he substituted.

Almost everyone I know who's a Mormon thinks Joseph Smith was a liar, an adulterer, a dishonest man. I don't. I think Joseph Smith sealed women to him. I think that from the time that the first realization of what sealing power could be used for rolled out until the earliest reference I can find; it is in October of 1843, which was eight months before his death. There appears to have been one and only one ordinance associated with sealing, and that one and only one ordinance was the marriage covenant. And so, using that one and only one ordinance, marriage, didn't mean that what you were trying to achieve was sexual access to other women. It meant you were trying to bring....

One of the things that I liked about Bushman's book (with all the flaws that it has), *Rough Stone Rolling*, was his acknowledgement that Joseph Smith seemed to be very sexually modest and very respectful of women and anything but a *lothario* (and he uses that word), anything but a lustful man. And that what Joseph Smith seemed to want, according to Bushman, and I agree with him on this, was plentitude of family, meaning he wanted to bring everyone into a family together. And so, the sealing mechanism was the means by which you bring family together, **not to commit adultery**—but to bind people together through an ordinance that was authoritative that allowed them to pass out of this life into the next life as part and member of a family of God.

Question: Is that to covenant and be committed to one another?

Comment: Well, he said, "I will carry you on my back."

Denver: Yes. And then you have all of those statements about how Joseph would manipulate people, promising them and their family salvation in the afterlife if this marriage covenant were entered into. Sounds a whole lot like what you are trying to achieve is sealing people together into a family that will endure into eternity so that they can lay claim on one another.

Question: Didn't those later come to be known as adoption?

Denver: No, that's what he set up until eight months before his death. Beginning in October of 1843, there's a mention made of a new ordinance that never gets mentioned by Joseph until then. And beginning in October, he, for the first time, mentions a different ordinance that might be used. And that different ordinance is adoption.

Question: Different than sealing, you're saying?

Denver: He's saying that adoption would accomplish the same thing. P

This is a passing mention. If you're picking up on the fact that Joseph Smith was trying to put together the family of God, and you saw that chart that comes out in the—it was the *Millennial Star*—where you have God, and then you have the tree of the family....

[Inaudible comment]

Denver: Yes, Orson Hyde prepared it, but he did it based upon something that Joseph had been teaching, okay? Now, this is 1839, mind you. There's still only one ordinance associated with sealing at this point. It's gonna be four more years before the word *adoption* ever appears in anything that Joseph writes. P

But listen to this. Thinking in terms of the role Joseph Smith may have occupied (although it was not generally understood at that time) and of what was happening with adoption later on, think about this in terms of covenantal relationships and of what is being assembled as a family of God in order to endure into eternity:

> Time and experience, however, is the only safe remedy against such evils. [Let me back up.] It opens such...dreadful field for the avaricious and indolent and corrupt-hearted to pray upon the innocent and virtuous and honest. We have reason to believe that many things were introduced among the saints before God had signified the times, and not withstanding the principles and plans may have been good; yet aspiring men, in other words, men who had not the substance of godliness about them, perhaps undertook to handle edged tools. Children, you know, are fond of tools while they

> are not yet able to use them. Time and experience, however, is the only safe remedy against such evils. There are many teachers but perhaps not many Fathers. There are times coming when God will signify many things which are expedient for the well-being of the saints, but the times have not yet come but will come as fast as there can be found place and receptions for them. (*Documents Volume Six* of the *Joseph Smith Papers,* pps. 396-397*)*

I hesitated on *receptions* because it's spelled r e s e p t i o n s. Mark Twain said he didn't have any respect for a man that could only spell a word one way.

Question: Can you tell us where you've been reading from?

Denver: Page 396 and 397 of the *Documents Volume Six* of the *Joseph Smith Papers.*

Yeah! So, there are many teachers, but there aren't many Fathers. And the challenge is to put people into position in which you have this family of God reconstituted on earth. And Joseph was aimed in that direction, and it was 1839. But you have one tool, and only one tool.

The foregoing excerpts are taken from:

- Denver's fireside talk on "Plural Marriage" given in Sandy, Utah on March 22, 2015;
- The presentation of Denver's paper titled "Was There an Original" given at the Sunstone Symposium on July 29, 2016; and
- His fireside talk titled "Cursed, Denied Priesthood" given in Sandy, Utah on January 7, 2018.

133. Adoption, Part 2

This is the second part of a special series on adoption where Denver discusses one of the lost ordinances that must be restored as part of the Religion of the Fathers.

DENVER: When the first temples were built or inherited by ancient civilizations, the center of life, government, education, culture, and art was at the temple. This was handed down from the first generations. The temple was founded before and will be needed to be the foundation again. When there has been an apostasy, temple building has been part of restoring. A new civilization will only become possible through teachings learned in the future house of God. The necessary ordinances can only be restored in that setting. There you will receive an uncorrupted restoration of the original faith taught to Adam and the patriarchs.

Joseph Smith was told that God intended to restore what was lost (meaning the fullness of the priesthood), but it was only to be accomplished through a temple. These were the Lord's words to Joseph:

> *For, for this cause I commanded Moses that he should build a tabernacle, that they should bear it with them in the wilderness, and to build a house in the land of promise that those ordinances might be revealed which had been hid from before [the foundation of] the world... Therefore, verily I say unto you that your anointings, and your washings, and your baptisms for the dead, and your solemn assemblies, and your memorials for your sacrifices by the sons of Levi, and for your oracles in your most holy places, wherein you receive conversations, and your statutes and judgments for the beginning of the revelations and foundation of Zion, and for the glory, and honor, and endowment of all her municipals, are ordained by the ordinance of my holy house, which my people are always commanded to build unto my holy name.* (T&C 141:12)

Joseph was martyred before there was a place where God could come to restore what had been lost. Joseph began to roll out a portion of temple ceremonial worship, but it was never completed. Uninspired men who have changed, deleted, and added to what remained from Joseph have corrupted those incomplete ceremonies.

The gospel is for redemption. Redemption from the fall returns man to God's presence. Ascending the heavenly mount is always taught in a properly organized temple's ceremonies. Ascending to heaven, redemption, and becoming part of the family of God are all part of the ancient temple rites and must also be part of future temple rites.

The concept of adoption is widely recognized as part of Christianity. The term is employed loosely to mean that a person believes in Christ and recognizes Him as their Savior. The language of Paul is often cited and understood to claim believers are adopted into God's family.

> *For you have not received the spirit of bondage again to fear, but you have received the spirit of adoption, whereby we cry, Abba, Father. The Spirit itself bears witness with our spirit that we are the children of God. And if children, then heirs: heirs of God and joint-heirs with Christ, if [it] so be that we suffer with him, that we may be also glorified together.* (Romans 1:34 RE)

Language in the Book of Mormon has also been used to support a loose understanding of the term *adoption.*

> *Marvel not that all mankind, yea, men and women — all nations, kindreds, tongues and people — must be born again; yea, born of God, changed from their carnal and fallen state, to a state of righteousness, being redeemed of God, becoming his sons and daughters* (Mosiah 11:28 RE).

The loose understanding of adoption was considerably tightened around October 1843 when Joseph Smith expanded his use of sealing authority. It grew from establishing marriages to include, also, man-to-man sealing through adoption. The last eight months of his life, Joseph sealed or adopted other men to himself. There was no settled, formal ordinance that has been preserved; and the proof of Joseph's practice is mostly post-mortem, as those who were exposed to the practice only vaguely recalled what he had done.

Nearly a decade after Joseph died, when temple ceremonial work resumed in the Endowment House in Salt Lake, Brigham Young declared that adoption was the crowning ordinance. It was **more** important than any other temple rites, including washing, anointing, endowment, and marriage sealing:

> This Chain must not [be] broken for mankind Cannot be saved in any other way. This Priesthood must be linked together so that all the Children may be linked to Father Adam. ...we will seal men to men by the keys of the Holy Priesthood. This is the highest ordinance. It is the last ordinance of the kingdom of God on the earth and above all the endowments that can be given [to] you. It is a final sealing an Eternal

> Principle and when once made cannot be broken by the Devil. (*The Complete Discourses of Brigham Young*, Vol. 5, 13 January 1856, Vol. 2, p. 1033-1034)

In that talk, Brigham Young taught that the *turning of hearts to the fathers* foretold by Malachi was only to be fulfilled through adoption. He also taught the fulfillment of God's promise to Abraham regarding *his seed* would only be fulfilled through the temple ordinance of adoption. LDS Church leaders unsuccessfully tried to sort out how to practice adoption.

In a meeting of the reorganized School of Prophets in Salt Lake City on January 20, 1868, attended by the church presidency, Brigham Young, Heber C. Kimball, and Daniel Wells, along with Elders John Taylor, Orson Hyde, George A. Smith, Erastus Snow, George Q. Cannon, Phineas Young, and Joseph Young, the topic of adoption was discussed. President Wells conjectured: "On Adoption he supposed it had reference to the linking together of the Priesthood...that it might reach back to the link that had long since been broken, that it might present one unbroken chain (*Salt Lake School of the Prophets: 1867-1883*, pp. 11-12; entry of 20 January 1868)." In response Orson Hyde said: "The Doctrine of Adoption he knew but little about and should decline touching it until the line is chalked out (ibid, p. 12)"

Scholars struggle to make sense of what Joseph was doing. And the attempts to reconstruct Joseph's later adoption innovation are insufficient to give any firm understanding of what took place, how, or why.

Thirty years before he would become church president, Wilford Woodruff concluded that adoptions would be something a resurrected Joseph Smith would return to sort out during the millennium: "Man also will have to be sealed to man until the chain is united from Father Adam down to the last Saint. This will be the work of the Millenium and Joseph Smith will be the man to attend...it or dictate it (*Salt Lake School of the Prophets: 1867-1883*, p. 42; December 11, 1869)."

A half-century after Joseph's death, the apostles struggled to know how it ought to work or who should be sealed to whom—how and what effect it would have in the afterlife. In a meeting on June 1, 1893, attended by Lorenzo Snow, Franklin D. Richards, Francis M. Lyman, John Taylor, Marriner Merrill, Abraham Cannon, George F. Gibbs, John D. McAllister, Nephi Cannon and James Jack, they "had some talk about the ordinance of adoption in the temple. Joseph F. Smith said Pres. [Brigham] Young had told him to follow in ordinance work for the dead the rules which [would] ordinarily govern similar work for the living (*Candid Insights of a Mormon Apostle: The Diaries of Abraham H. Cannon*, 1889-1895, p. 388)." The practice was to seal faithful children to parents, and faithful parents to Joseph Smith. Woodruff explained: "I was sealed to my father, and then had him sealed to the Prophet Joseph" (ibid, p.488).

The concept of adoption affected how people understood the afterlife. This led some people to view adoption as a chance to pursue their self-interests. People began to aspire to improve their post-mortality by recruiting and acquiring descendants using adoption. The Logan temple president was told to end his practice of recruiting adoptees. Eventually, President Wilford Woodruff announced a final adoption practice on April 8, 1894: "Pres. Woodruff announced the doctrine of the sealing of children to parents as far back as...possible to trace the genealogy, and then seal the last member to the Prophet Joseph [Smith]" (ibid, p. 496).

Family relationships were reckoned by sealing, not biology. For example, Heber J. Grant was the biological son of ~~Jebediah~~ [Jedediah] Grant, but because his mother was sealed to Joseph Smith, he was regarded as Joseph Smith's son.

What Joseph Smith understood about adoption did not get passed to subsequent church leaders clearly enough to preserve the practice intact. In September 1887, two months after John Taylor died, his son-in-law, John Whitaker, wrote in his diary:

> I went back to the office where I found [Apostle] Brother Lorenzo Snow and [First Council of the Seventy member] Jacob Gates. They conversed a long time. He finally entered into a deep subject on 'The Law of Adoption.' Brother Gates said he didn't believe in it as did also Brother Snow. He [?] referenced back to the time that Brigham Young was in Kirtland[;] he had a person asked him about it and he said 'I know nothing about it.' President Taylor on one different occasion had a letter written to him for the following reason: it was [two undecipherable words followed by] of ... J[oseph] Smith or rather Sister Eliza R. Snow Smith (Brother Gates didn't know which)...about 70 persons were adopted into President J[oseph] Smith's [family;] Sister Snow Smith said 'she didn't understand the law' but had no objections to them being sealed to her husband. And this led Brother Gates to write to President Taylor asking him if he knew anything about it. He never answered the letter. But on another occasion Brother Gates saw him and asked him plainly. President

> Taylor said he knew nothing about it. And also just lately when asked by Brother Snow, President...Woodruff knew nothing about it. [']It hadn't been revealed to him.' I know this at this time to say [or show] a prevailing feeling among the Twelve that they don't understand it. George Cannon also said he didn't understand it. ("Adoptive Sealing Ritual in Mormonism," *Journal of Mormon History*, Vol. 37, No. 3, Summer 2011, p. 3; pp. 101-102)

As John Taylor's health was declining in the last month of his life, Wilford Woodruff recorded in his journal on June 8, 1887: "I wrote 4 Letters to Jaques Emma Clara & Roskelly. I did not rest well. To much deep thinking to Sleep (*Wilford Woodruff's Journals*, Vol. 8: 1 January 1881 to 31 December 1888, p. 441)." Roskelly was employed as the recorder in the Logan Utah Temple. That letter included the following mention of adoption:

> I have adopted this rule in Sealing and Adoptions: to take such as the Lord has given me, and leave the result[s] in His hands....Paul talked a good deal about Adoptions, but we did not understand much about it, until the Lord revealed it to Joseph Smith, and we may not, perhaps, understand it now as fully as we should. Still the Sealings and Adoptions are true principles, or our Prophets have been badly deceived. ("Adoptive Sealing Ritual in Mormonism," *Journal of Mormon History*, Vol. 37, No. 3, Summer 2011, p. 3; p. 103)

Adoption became progressively more controversial as time passed. Since the idea was not well understood by church leaders, they could provide no answers to questions on the subject. While bishop, Edward Bunker denounced the idea altogether, resulting in an 1892 church court that the church president and one of his counselors attended. The former bishop was charged with teaching false doctrine, and in his defense, he wrote a letter to the high council stating:

> The adoption of one man to another out of the lineage, I do not understand and for that reason I would not enter into it. And adopting the dead to the living is as adopting the father to the son. I don't believe there is a man on earth that thoroughly understands the principle. If there is, I have never heard it taught as I could understand it. I believe it is permmited [sic] more to satisfy the minds of the people for the present until the Lord reveals more fully the principle. (Edward Bunker, Letter to the Bunkerville High Council, April 25, 1891, *Edward Bunker Autobiography* (1894) 37, microfilm of holograph, MS 1581, LDS Church History Library)

In his summary of the court proceeding, Wilford Woodruff relegated the subject of adoption to one of the *mysteries* which church members ought to avoid discussing because they cause difficulties. He wrote: "June 11, 1892 We Met in the Tabernacle at 10 oclock on the trial of Bishop Bunker on Doctrin [sic]. We talked to them Plainly of the impropriety of indulging in Misteries [sic] to Create difficulties among the Saints. They professed to be Satisfied" (*Wilford Woodruff's Journal*, supra, 9:203).

Although John Taylor perpetuated the practice, over time it diminished and then disappeared beginning with Wilford Woodruff's presidency. Woodruff changed the policy in April 1894 to seal within biological families as far back as were known and then to seal and adopt the last parents to Joseph Smith. This made adoption less of an issue and the genealogical search for ancestors of greater concern. But by 1922, the de-emphasis on adoption allowed it to be ignored altogether. The practice Woodruff announced in 1894 was **deleted** in the published account by the Utah Genealogical Society **and** from Clark's *Messages of The First Presidency*. Today, adoption has vanished from the LDS Church and was never practiced by the RLDS Church or other branches of the Restoration.

Joseph Smith did not leave the Christian practice of adoption a loose idea with believers becoming sons of God by conversion, belief, or baptism. He tied it to both authority to seal and an authoritative ordinance. Both of those were lost when Joseph and Hyrum were killed.

If adoption is (as Brigham Young thought in 1856) the highest ordinance above all the endowments that can be given; if it is needed for the gospel (as taught to Abraham) to be restored, then the loss of adoption rites is indeed a sign of apostasy. Brigham Young taught adoption would bind a person beyond the devil's power to break. But adoption was abandoned before the end of the 1800s. Adoption will need to be restored as a rite (with an accompanying authoritative ordinance and sealing) in order for the things Joseph Smith alone understood and taught to be renewed.

The LDS Church has attempted to preserve other ordinances Joseph Smith began. Unfortunately, those ordinances have also been poorly preserved, changed, and compromised.

Joseph did not live to see the complete Nauvoo temple, and he never finished the temple ceremonies.

There is work to be done. Almost all of it is internal to us. The five prepared virgins and the strangers who brought a wedding garment will be those who keep the covenant. It is designed to give birth to a new society, new culture, and permit a new civilization to be founded.

The Lord's civilization will require His tabernacle at the center. Through it, a recovered religion will be fully developed. God's house will include a higher law—an education about the universe—and a divine university will be established. It will be an ensign in the mountains, and people from all over the earth will say: "Come, let us go up to the house of the God of Jacob. He will teach us; we will learn of his paths, to walk in them" (see Isaiah 1:5; 2 Nephi 8:4 RE). That place will house a new civilization. There will be no hermit gurus proud of their enlightenment.

No one will offer himself or herself up as some great idol to follow. It will be a place of equality where people are meek and lowly, serving one another without any attempt to compete for "chief seats."

Christ's apostles competed to be greater than one another. In the New Covenants, Luke 13:6, Christ's reaction is recorded:

> *There was also a strife among them: who of them should be accounted the greatest. And he said unto them, The kings of the gentiles exercise lordship over them, and they who exercise authority upon them are called benefactors, but it ought not...be so with you. But he who is greatest among you, let him be as the younger, and he who is chief, as he who does serve. For [whether] is [he] greater...who sits at [the] meal, or he who serves? I am not as he who sits at a meal, but I am among you as he who serves.*

Christ is the great example. Christ would have fit into Enoch's city, would have been welcomed among Melchizedek's people, and could have dwelt in peace with the Nephites of 4 Nephi. Has He, as once before between Jerusalem and Emmaus, walked among them unnoticed to enjoy their peaceful company?

I cannot keep the covenant. You cannot keep the covenant. Only **we** can keep the covenant.

But if we do, God's work will continue and will include the fullness previously offered to the gentiles and rejected by them. P

It is impossible to understand the promises that Elijah will *turn the hearts of the children to the Fathers* (T&C 169:4) unless the fullness is recovered. Joseph Smith cannot fix or finish the Restoration by returning as a resurrected being in the millennium, as conjectured by Wilford Woodruff. If the necessary rites are not returned **before** the Lord's return, *the whole earth would be utterly wasted at his coming* (JSH 3:4 RE). There will be a new civilization built around God's tabernacle where He will dwell. We know the purpose of that house will be for the God of Jacob to teach those people to walk in His ways. We know Joseph Smith began adoption sealing as the highest ordinance and has now been lost.

We have been given a new revelation that explains resurrection and adoption to the Fathers

in heaven are linked together:

> *I was shown that the spirits that rose were limited to a direct line back to Adam, requiring the hearts of the fathers and the hearts of the children to be bound together by sealing, confirmed by covenant and [by] the Holy Spirit of Promise. This is the reason that Abraham, Isaac, and Jacob have entered into their exaltation according to the promises and sit upon thrones and are not angels but are gods (see T&C 157:42-43).* (T&C 169:3 RE)

That's [the information about Abraham, Isaac, and Jacob sitting on thrones] in the Teachings and Commandments section 157, paragraphs 42 and 43.

The fullness can only be returned through a temple accepted by God as His house. He must return to restore that which has been lost. But ungodly people cannot build an acceptable house for God. There is no commandment to build a temple because people are not yet qualified to do so. So far, we have been spared the experience in Nauvoo where an abortive attempt to build a temple in which the fullness could be restored resulted in the Lord not performing His oath. Nor did the Lord fulfill the promise they expected to receive. Instead of blessings, the people in Nauvoo brought upon themselves cursings, wrath, indignation, and judgments by their follies and abominations. If we are going to receive that same condemnation, it would be better to not begin to build a house of God.

Only **we** can keep the covenant. Only those who keep the covenant **together** can establish a new civilization with God's holy house at its center.

Every time there's a covenant, there is always a land. And this is the land that God covenants He will give. And the people to whom He will give it are those that come back and receive the covenant, including the Gentiles **in whose ears** this first shall sound...if they will come. And coming unto the covenant—that is not yet possible. It requires more than has at present been given. It is possible to come in and become part of His church. It is possible if you follow as you've been instructed today to become part of the church He recognizes and will preserve. But coming fully into the covenant—that will require more than has, at present, been given. It will require a covenant. It will require adoption. It will require sealing. It was what Joseph looked forward to have happen at some point in the future during the days of his prophecy.

> *And they shall assist my people, the remnant of Jacob, and also as many of the house of Israel as shall come, that they may build a city, which shall be called the New Jerusalem. And then shall they assist my people that they may be gathered in, who are scattered upon all the face of the land, in unto the New Jerusalem. And then shall the [Power] of heaven* [in this case, it is the singular—it's not the *powers*—because when you have Him present with you, you have all the authority]—*then shall the power of heaven come down among them; and I also will be in the midst. And then shall the work of the Father commence at that day.* (3 Nephi 21:23-26; see also 3 Nephi 10:1 RE)

Christ will come. Once the covenant has been renewed, the city of Zion will follow. The Lord's presence will come, and then the final stage begins.

> *Even when this gospel shall be preached among the remnant of this people. Verily I say unto you, at that day shall the work of the Father commence among...the dispersed of my people, yea, even the tribes which have been lost, which the Father hath led away out of Jerusalem. Yea, the work shall commence among all the dispersed of my people, with the Father to prepare the way whereby they may [be]come [in] unto me, that they may call on the Father in my name. ...Then shall the work commence, with the Father among all nations in preparing the way whereby his people may be gathered home to the land of their inheritance. And they shall go out from all nations; ...they shall not go out in haste, nor...by flight, for I will go before them, saith the Father, and I will be their rearward.* (Ibid, vs. 26-29; Ibid, vs. 1 RE)

It's not gonna happen in haste. And the work of the Father that will commence in those nations—to commence the possibility for the gathering—will involve destroying a great deal of political, social, and military obstructions that prevent the gathering, prevent even the preaching to those that would gather if they could hear. But the work of the Father (and it's always masculine when it comes to destruction)... The work of the Father is going to bring this to an end. All the scattered remnants will be brought back again. The original, unified family of God will be restored again. The Fathers will have our hearts turned to them because in that day, once it's permitted to get that far, we will be part of that family again.

Why is it not your ambition to join the **Fathers** of whom Malachi spoke who were the first Fathers, who are the Fathers now in heaven, having returned back in a resurrected and glorified form to dwell in the heavens? **Those** are the ones about whom the promise is made. You're one motorcycle accident away from your dead kindred. You're one bout of some nasty, infectious disease from joining them. There's no great accomplishment to be spoken of by dying and going into the world of the spirits. The promises are more glorious, but they are also about something **far more ancient**.

> *Behold, I will send you Elijah the prophet before the coming of the great and dreadful day of the Lord. And he shall seal the heart of the Fathers to the children and the heart of the children to their Fathers, lest I come and smite the earth with a curse* (Malachi 1:12 RE).

That is how the prophecy of Malachi is worded in the Old Covenants (in the scriptures that are being published now that include Joseph Smith's interpretation or inspired rendering of the text). *He shall **seal** the heart of the Fathers to the children, and the heart of the children to the Fathers.* That's not there in the typical rendering and not in the King James Version because there it says he'll **turn** the hearts of the children to the Fathers (see Malachi 4:6 LE).

This is referred to, also, in the New Covenants: *And he shall go before the Lord in the spirit and power of Elijah, to turn the hearts of the fathers to the children, and the disobedient to the wisdom of the just, to make ready a people prepared for the Lord* (Luke 1:3 RE). That's how it's rendered in Luke.

In Third Nephi, the Lord quotes Malachi to have this information added to the record in possession of the Nephites. This is how the Lord rendered it:

> *Behold, I will send you Elijah the prophet before the coming of the great and dreadful day of the Lord, and he shall turn the heart of the fathers to the children and the heart of the children to their fathers, lest I come and smite the earth with a curse* (3 Nephi 11:5 RE).

In the Joseph Smith History, when he was visited by the angelic visitor Nephi, **he** quoted the prophecy in these words:

> *And he shall plant in the hearts of the children the promises made to the fathers, and the hearts of the children shall turn to their fathers; if it were not so, the whole earth would be utterly wasted at his coming* (JSH 3:4 RE).

So, now we have in various renderings of this something that is referred to as *sealing hearts*—Fathers to children, children to Fathers—something that is called *turning the hearts*, and something that is called *promises made to the Fathers.*

Promises made to the Fathers are *covenants* that God made with them concerning the last days' work in which there would again be on the earth those who are connected to the Fathers in a way that avoids the earth becoming utterly wasted at His coming. This is something that has to be attended to through the restoration and construction of an authentic temple conforming to the pattern of heaven in which these things can be attended to and the knowledge and understanding imputed in order for people to comprehend what it means to be a *greater follower of righteousness.*

This was a revelation given in March 2015: "Hence, the great need to turn the hearts of the children to the fathers and the fathers to the children—and this, too, by covenant and sealing through the Holy Spirit of Promise" ("Plural Marriage," Denver C. Snuffer, Jr., March 22, 2015).

This is to restore **us**, as God restored Abraham, to the original religion.

Abraham came into this world uniquely different from the Fathers that had gone before. There was an unbroken chain that continued from father to son and father to son from the time of Adam down through the generations until the time of Melchizedek. All of them were participants in an unbroken familial line. Abraham came into an apostate family in which his father worshipped (indeed, *made*) dumb idols as the god to be worshipped. Therefore, Abraham is the first one that will join this line who emerges from apostasy into possession of the original Holy Order. In that sense, Abraham is representative of all who would follow after that seek after righteousness in a world that is constantly overcome by apostasy.

Apostasy exists the **instant** that God ceases to talk; the instant that God ceases to restore; the instant that further light and knowledge by conversing with the Lord through the veil comes to an end. P

Abraham—**because** he came at a time of apostasy and **because** his father had turned to the worshipping of dumb idols—could not inherit that same standing as the first uninterrupted period unless it were possible for that to be accomplished through adoption. Therefore, Abraham represents the revolutionary idea that one can emerge out of a state of apostasy back into, and be adopted into, the line that is in possession of the fullness of the gospel and to be one, equal with them. Abraham represents an astonishing revolutionary moment in the history of God's dealing with mankind; and he also represents the opportunity for redemption for others at remote times in remote places who dwell among people who are apostate.

It represents hope for us. And so, when the hearts of the children are turned to the Fathers, that hope is verified and confirmed **primarily** through God's covenant with Abraham. Abraham inherited the promises that had been given to the first Fathers, to be sure, but Abraham represents hope for us. He represents our opportunity to, likewise, obtain that same hope which was given to Abraham 430 years before the law was added through Moses.

Now, at the time of the founding of Egypt, the original Pharaoh of Egypt was a righteous man who sought earnestly to imitate the order that began with the first Fathers. The government of Egypt was an attempt to imitate Adam and imitate a family order that came down from the beginning. That founding occurred at a period that is referred to as Predynastic; and the Early Dynastic Period also is plagued with some lack of records, some destruction of material. The Old Kingdom really begins with the Fourth Dynasty, and it's **after** the Eighth Dynasty that what is referred to in Egyptian history as the First Intermediate Period took place.

The First Intermediate Period represented a radical period of apostasy from what had gone on before. While there had been an effort to preserve the order that came down from the beginning in Egypt, the First Intermediate Period represented something very much akin to what would take place in the Jewish Kingdom at the time of the bickering and the fighting and the strife of the Deuteronomists when the Southern Kingdom was taken captive into Babylon. And then, a remnant of the Southern Kingdom returned back to rebuild the temple, at which point the religion had been remarkably revised and the content changed to reflect the kind of strife that was taking place just a few years before the "migration out" of Lehi and his family that we read in the first chapters of the Book of Mormon where the idea of the Messiah was trying to be suppressed, trying to be altered. (One of the reasons why Zenos was dropped out of the record of the Old Testament is because it's filled with Christological content that they intended to suppress.)

Well, the kingdom of Egypt was going through something similar, and in the First Intermediate Period, they were forsaking things that had come down from the beginning. What is remarkable is that **Abraham entered Egypt to teach the Pharaoh** immediately following the First Intermediate Period. Now, the right that Pharaoh claimed was not his; indeed, when Abraham went into Egypt, Abraham entered possessing that right. (I don't know that he claimed that in the presence of Pharaoh; that might have been fatal.) But he came to teach, and he came to restore, and he came to reinvigorate the understanding of the Egyptians concerning that first order that came down from the beginning. Therefore, when Abraham came, he came not merely as evidence that you can emerge from apostasy and inherit the rights that belonged to the first Fathers by adoption. He also came as a messenger and a restorer to provide such light and knowledge as those who were his contemporaries were willing to receive.

In many respects, **you** are now in possession of a great body of knowledge—much of it originally established through Joseph Smith but neglected or misunderstood or misapplied or currently being opposed—that the people among whom you live would benefit by having that knowledge restored to them.

The foregoing excerpts are taken from:

- Denver's conference talk titled "Civilization" given in Grand Junction, Colorado on April 21, 2019;
- Denver's *40 Years in Mormonism Series*, Talk #10 titled "Preserving the Restoration" given in Mesa, Arizona on September 9, 2014; and
- Denver's conference talk titled "The Book of Mormon Holds the Covenant Pattern for the Full Restoration" given in Boise, Idaho on September 22, 2019.

134. Equality, Part 1

This is the first part of a special series on Equality, where Denver addresses the question, "What is equality in the eyes of heaven, how can we become equal, and what are the sources of inequality and barriers to equality that we currently struggle with?"

DENVER: The spirit of God is withdrawing from the world. Men are increasingly angry without good cause. The hearts of men are waxing cold. The scriptures describe events now underway, and call it the end of the times of the gentiles. This process of the spirit withdrawing will end on this continent, as it did with two prior civilizations, in fratricidal and genocidal warfare. For the rest of the world, it will be as in the days of Noah in which, as the light of Christ or spirit of truth is eclipsed, men's cold hearts will result in a constant scene of violence and bloodshed. The wicked will destroy the wicked. The covenant established a year ago, if it is kept, will prevent the loss of light and warmth of heart as the spirit now steadily recedes from the world. Be charitable and be patient and labor to reach others. Even if they should judge you harshly because of their traditions, you should, nevertheless, be kind to them. They're going to grow to fear you, but it's only part of how darkness responds to light. Give them no reason to fear you. The time will come for us to gather, but now... between now and then, be leaven. Preserve the world. Be salt. Preserve the world even if it hates you. The soul of every person is equally precious to God as is yours. If your kindness and example should awaken another soul, you will rejoice with the angels over them.

The Book of Mormon is filled with ascension lessons and examples. There is one verse that captures Joseph Smith's ascent theology. That verse compresses into a single sentence. It explains why the Book of Mormon contains the "fullness of the gospel." And it's perhaps Joseph's most inspired declaration:

> *Verily thus says the Lord: It shall come to pass that every soul who forsakes their sins, and comes unto me, and calls on my name, and obeys my voice, and keeps...my commandments, shall see my face and know that I am, and that I am the true light that lights every man who comes into the world.* (D&C 93:1; T&C 93:1 RE)

"Every soul" includes you and me. Every one of us has equal access to the Lord. The conditions are the same for all—forsake sins; come to Christ; call on His name; obey His voice; keep his commandments. This is far more challenging than obedience to a handful of "thou shalt nots" because so much is required to be *done*, so much required to be *known*. A great deal of study and prayer is required to stand in the presence of the Lord. Once done, we shall see His face and know that He is the true light that enlightens every one. He is the God of the whole world.

Long before the Sermon on the Mount taught us to bless those who curse us, and do good for those who hate us, The Dhammapada taught, "Let us live in joy, never hating those who hate us." And when Christ said, in that same Sermon on the Mount, *And why beholdest thou the mote that is in thy brother's eye, but considerest not the beam that is in thine own eye?* (3 Nephi 14:3-6; 3 Nephi 6:6 RE), several centuries earlier the writings of Buddha put it this way: "Do not give your attention to what others do or fail to do; give it to what you do or fail to do." What higher light illuminated Buddha when he spoke those words? Was it the same light that illuminated our Lord? Well, our Mormon scripture puts all light and truth into one, singular source for this world. That source is the Son of God.

Consider the very ecumenical nature of the following revelation given to Joseph Smith:

> *For you shall live by every word that proceedeth forth from the mouth of God. For the word of the Lord is truth, and whatsoever is truth is light, and whatsoever is light is Spirit, even the Spirit of Jesus Christ. And the Spirit giveth light to every man that cometh into the world; and the Spirit enlighteneth every man through the world, that hearkeneth to the voice of the Spirit.* (D&C 84:44-46; T&C 82:18 RE)

Notice this is without any restriction on who can receive the light of the Spirit. *Every man that cometh into the world* receives equally. There is no individual, in any corner of the world, who does not have equal access to obtain *truth* and *light* from the same source, who is Jesus Christ. If any soul, in any age, hearkens, or listens, and follows the "voice of the Spirit," they are in communication with Jesus Christ. To them He bestows light.

Compare the following sample of Biblical Proverbs with corresponding quotes from Buddha:

- Proverbs 23:7; Proverbs 3:11 RE – *For as a man thinketh in his heart, so is he.*
- Buddha – "We become what we think."

- Proverbs 15:1; Proverbs 2:152 RE – *A soft answer turneth away wrath.*

- Buddha – "Speak quietly to everyone, and they too will be gentle in their speech."

- Proverbs 16:32; Proverbs 2:216 – *He that is slow to anger is better than the mighty; and he that ruleth his spirit than he that taketh a city.*

- Buddha – "One who conquers himself is greater than another who conquers a thousand times a thousand men on the battlefield."

The Gods of Mormonism literally mean it when they proclaim:

> *He doeth nothing save it be plain unto the children of men; and he inviteth them all to come unto him and partake of his goodness; and he denieth none that come unto him, black and white, bond and free, male and female; and he remembereth the heathen; and all are alike unto God, both Jew and Gentile.* (2 Nephi 26:33; see also 2 Nephi 11:17 RE)

Now, I'm going to deviate from the paper and just add this thought: I think he's giving a descending order. I think when you get into scripture there are always orders when you get lists. I think he's giving a descending order in which he clarifies what seems superficially to be the most justified, and as he goes on in the list, what becomes truly petty. So let me read the list again:

- Black and white. Easy, divisive.

- Bond and free. Of course, you look down on those that are bond, if you happen to be free.

- Male and female. Now we're descending into the petty.

- Well... All, even those swarthy heathens, are included within the ambit of the Mormon Gods' concern. They speak through the Spirit the same truths to all mankind, and have done so since the beginning of creation. To Mormons, the Gods declare: *I am no respecter of persons* (Acts 10:34; Acts 6:7 RE). To the Hindus, the Gods declare: "None are less dear to me and none are more dear." Both the Mormon and Hindu Gods respect all mankind equally.

At one time the account in Genesis read: *This is my work, to my glory, to bring to pass the immortality and eternal life of man. The Gods of Mormonism take seriously their commitment to the eternal advancement of mankind.* That means ALL mankind, including the heathen, and none are above others.

This raises the question of "chosenness" of the Gods' special people. Israel, after all, was at one point "chosen" by the Gods as *Their* special people. But that does not mean what we think it means. Being "chosen" means we are put on display as either the faithful servant, elevating others; or the unwise steward who is condemned, beaten with a rod, and made the display of Divine ire.

Consider that for a moment. Have we gentile Mormons been told of Gods' other sheep for some important reason? If so, is it to alert us that we are no more special, nor in any greater possession of Gods' words, than many others who have been scattered around the world, and are known to the Gods, but unidentified to us? Is it to make us more careful about how we regard strangers? Ought it to suggest that there are other religious equals in the world? May it suggest there are, perhaps, religious superiors in the world? In other words, have we received news of other sheep to help keep Mormons humble?

If these words from Christ are not enough to make us cautious about dismissing others, in the Book of Alma there's another reminder of how the Gods deal equally with all mankind. Alma 29:8 (see also Alma 15:13 RE) states, *For behold, the Lord doth grant unto all nations, of their own nation and tongue, to teach his word, yea, in wisdom, all that he seeth fit that they should have.* The Lord is concerned about *all nations* and not merely Israelites in their scattered condition. Each nation, in its own tongue, has been given a portion of His teachings. It is measured according to what He *seeth fit that they should have.* I do not believe this means that "while God gives everyone something, we have the most." I think it means, instead; "Everyone is remembered by God, and when you close down revelation, you get less—humble people get more." This more probable meaning is suggested by Alma 12:10 (see also Alma 9:3 RE) which explains; *He that will harden his heart, the same receiveth the lesser portion of the word; and he that will not harden his heart, to him is given the greater portion of the word, until it is given unto him to know the mysteries of God, until he know them in full.* It is abundantly clear that Mormons do not know the mysteries of God in full. The farther back we look in human history, the more appears to have been lost. Earlier stages, including the patriarchal era, knew God and, therefore, understood His path better. How else would Enoch and Melchizedek have achieved their heavenly breakthroughs? Like mankind, institutional Mormonism continually atrophies, knowing less and less, year by year. However significantly this may impact the truth-claims and arrogance of Mormonism, we must at least allow for the possibility that there are "other sheep" who are much better informed than are any of us Mormons.

The Alma 12 material helps clarify the remaining statement in Alma 29:8 (see also Alma 15:13 RE). *Therefore we see that the Lord doth counsel in wisdom, according to that which is just and true.* The Gods' wise counsel does not regulate dispensing truth on things external to us, but on what is internal to us. We determine whether we have hard hearts or open hearts. One of the ways to determine if our hearts are open and not hard is the degree to which we regard those who are "other"—not only with respect and charity, but also curiosity.

Wo be unto the Gentiles except they repent… At that day, whosoever will not repent and come unto my beloved Son, them will I cut off from among my people, Oh House of Israel (3 Nephi 21:14, 20; see also 3 Nephi 9:12 RE). It has been a gift that the people before have failed, because the clock hasn't been ticking, but if a people adopt a covenant and receive what has been restored, the clock will begin to tick.

If they will repent and hearken unto my words and harden not their hearts, I will establish my church among them (Ibid. vs. 22; see also 3 Nephi 10:1 RE). "Church" (not as sister Adolfo explained "institution"), "Church" as she explained, meaning a spiritual body of believers. "Church" as defined by the Lord in the revelations; not "church" as defined by filings with the corporate Secretary of State identifying an institution that owns property. If you want one of those, go choose. There's an infinite variety. We want that group of believers—that assembly who accept covenants from God and who are spiritually connected—not institutionally connected.

Many of us suffer from post-traumatic religious stress. We don't need to go there. We don't need to repeat their mistakes. We should learn from them. I don't care who it is among us. I don't care how soft your heart is, or how inclined you are to follow God. The institutions are such a perfect mouse trap that if I were to call any one of you to be the newest member of the Quorum of the Twelve or the new president of the Relief Society, you couldn't fix it. It cannot be done. The only way is to begin anew, and to learn the sad lessons of where it takes you if you go down one route. No matter who it is you trust at the beginning, *everything* is susceptible of corruption and abuse. Therefore, we need to be equal; we need to be on the same footing.

If [we'll] repent and hearken unto my words, and harden not [our] hearts, I will establish my church among them, and they shall come in unto the covenant and be numbered among THIS...remnant... this the remnant of Jacob, unto whom I have given this land for [an] inheritance (Ibid.).

It's talking about the gentiles, but it's talking about establishing His word, which is a prerequisite to establishing His people.

Numbered among this the remnant of Jacob unto whom I have given his land for their inheritance. And they shall assist my people, the remnant of Jacob, and also many of the house of Israel as shall come, that they may build a city, which shall be called the New Jerusalem. ...then shall they assist my people that they may be gathered in, who are scattered upon all the face of the land, ...unto the New Jerusalem. And ...the power of heaven [shall] come down among them; and I also will be in their midst. ...at that day shall the work of the Father commence among all the dispersed of my people, yea, even the tribes which have been lost, which the Father hath led away out of Jerusalem. (ibid, vs. 22-26; ibid, RE)

Take another look, on your own, at 3rd Nephi chapter 21, and, in particular, pay attention to how the words in the covenant play into the fulfillment of the prophecies, and the reclaiming of the gentiles to become part of His covenant; and then, those who likewise inherit, as their possession, this land.

And recognize that if you want a sign that the work of the Father has commenced, I can think of no more tangible, physical sign to hold up; than that the work has commenced and is now available for your review: and, if you will receive it, can become a covenant that the Lord intends to vindicate.

I desire to heal you from an awful state of blindness so that you may see clearly my will, to do it. I promised to bring unto you much of my gospel through the Book of Mormon and to provide you with the means to obtain a fullness of my gospel, and I have done this; yet you refuse to receive the truth even when it is given unto you in plainness. How can you who pursue the truth yet remain unable to behold your own weakness before me?

Unto what can I liken it, that you may understand? For you are like a man who seeks for good fruit from a neglected vineyard—unwatered, undunged, unpruned and unattended. How shall it produce good fruit if you fail to tend it? What reward does the unfaithful husbandman obtain from his neglected vineyard? How can saying you are a faithful husbandman ever produce good fruit in the vineyard without doing the work of the husbandman? For you

> *seek my words to recover them even as you forsake to do them. You have heretofore produced wild fruit, bitter and ill formed, because you neglect to do my words.*
>
> *I speak of you who have hindered my work, that claim to see plainly the beams in others' eyes. You have claimed to see plainly the error of those who abuse my words, and neglect the poor, and who have cast you out, to discern their errors, and you say you seek a better way. Yet among you are those who continue to scheme, backbite, contend, accuse and forsake my words to do them, even while you seek to recover them. Can you not see that your works fall short of the beliefs you profess?*
>
> *For the sake of the promises to the Fathers will I labor with you as a people, and not because of you, for you have not yet become what you must be to live together in peace. If you will hearken to my words I will make you my people and my words will give you peace. Even a single soul who stirs up the hearts of others to anger can destroy the peace of all my people. Each of you must equally walk truly in my path, not only to profess, but to do as you profess.* (T&C 157:16-19)

We are not like those who organize into hierarchical structures. Every one of us is considered equal. I'm an invited guest here. The people that organized this, asked me to come, and I did the work to prepare to come at their invitation. I don't have any right, other than the same right as all of you, to preach, and teach, and expound. And if what I say persuades or brings light, then you're welcome, as a gift, to receive it. But no one holds authority over me, or over you, or over any of us. We associate freely because we like focusing upon the restoration of the gospel that came through the prophet Joseph Smith, and recognize *that* work was never completed. We also recognize the ease with which having a hierarchy can be compromised. You see, as soon as you create a seat of power and authority, all that's required to overthrow the entirety of the organization is to gain control of that seat of authority. But among a group of equals, so long as anyone remains true and steadfast to the gospel, no one can tell them that they *must* do something other than retain that steadfast conviction, and belief, and practice of the gospel in its fullness.

Zion won't be composed of people who are presided over by anyone other than Christ Himself. As between one another, they're brothers and they're sisters, and they're equals, having one heart, having one mind, and having all things in common; because there's no one that can exert control or authority over one another. That's what we seek, that's what we're working for. However clumsy, however awkward, however difficult it may be for siblings to get along as they grow up through their childhood and adolescence, that's exactly how the people that will form Zion are going to begin. You can't stand back and say, "Oh, I prize the orderly thing I see in the uniformity of lessons, uniformity of dress, uniformity of conduct that I can see in structured and organized congregations; and what I see, among these people, is clamoring disorder." That's because we're alive. That's because we're equal. That's because we respect one another and we want to hear the differences. We want to see the differences. We want to consider an idea that isn't correlated out into the darkness and excluded from our attention. We want to know what others have to say, because we might miss something, if we don't allow them the equality of standing and saying, to us, something about which we may disagree. That's what we call healthy. That's what we call normal. That's how humans relate to one another. In a hierarchy it's possible to suppress all of that, but we're not interested in forming a Kremlin, we're interested in forming Zion.

There is a great deal left to be done. And there is no one seriously entertaining the possibility of constructing a city of holiness, a city of peace, a people that are fruit worthy to be laid up against the harvest. No one has made the effort until now. And while you may look at us and say, "You've done a crude job. You've done a rudimentary job. It needs improvement." Then help us improve it! Stop sitting back and throwing rocks! This is a time to gather, not to disperse. The same garbage that existed at the beginning (when Joseph looked around and saw confusion and disharmony) wants to creep in among us. Recognize that's a false spirit.

If you'll cast it out of yourself, and if you'll look at the words of the covenant that was offered in September of 2017, what you'll find is that Christ wants us—like the Book of Mormon explains—to be meek, to be humble, and to be easily entreated. And therefore, entreat one another to honor God, and recognize that all of us aspire to be equal, whether you're at the top or at the root. The aspiration is the same: to be equal.

I have a real problem—as I hope many of you likewise have a real problem—with the concept that some man or men can vouch for something and say, "Trust me, it's gonna be GOOD for you to go ahead and take the pill we're asking you to swallow." The view that replaces that is the view that no one of us is greater than another. No one has the right to dictate. No one has the right to tell you, "trust me." Instead, everything is being made available, in advance, for everyone to view; so that no one need stand, as was done in the ceremony on the 17th of August, when the Doctrine and Covenants was first sustained; when the audience only heard, second-hand, people telling them, this is a good thing, go ahead and adopt it, without ever having had the opportunity to review it. We ask no such thing. And none of us should expect to be treated that way. We're all equal, we're all accountable, and we all should be shown the respect of being allowed the opportunity to review, and that review critically, and to comment, and to make suggestions, and to advance criticisms, and to deliberate; so that when the end of this is reached, and people raise their hand to accept it as the basis for governing a body of believers—a body of equal believers, a body of believers who respect one another—they do so knowingly, and they do so with the full light of understanding; and not trusting some group to tell them, *"Trust us—we're not going to let you read it, but we're telling you—it's good stuff."* You're going to be able to read, to pray, to examine, to criticize, and to determine that for yourself.

QUESTION: How does equality work when we're all given different gifts, abilities, and levels of understanding, some of which may be more outwardly manifest? Should we encourage one another to use our gifts to benefit all, even though this makes us appear unequal?

DENVER: Equal means that you do what you can do, to the best of your ability to do, for the benefit of all that can receive. Not everyone can do what someone with a gift or a talent can accomplish, but all can appreciate the benefits of that gift or talent. We're supposed to find joy, worship God, and bless our fellow man through the gifts that are given. In fact, I don't know what section it is now (I know what the old number was) but the gifts that are given, the Lord says, specifically, are given as a benefit for the church—the definition of the church being all those who repent and are baptized—not some institution. So the blessing that is given to one has been given in order to bless and benefit the lives of all others. And as a consequence of that, you're depriving the community of faith—of the gifts—when you don't do the best you can with the gifts you've been given. They are intended by you, to be a sacrifice by you, for the benefit of others. And if others look on and say, "Gee, I wish I could do that, but I'm not double-jointed, and I'm not interested in riding on one of those things;" then, you know, you can admire the X-Games, but you don't have to join 'em.

In Alma, the Nehor incident included priests… Nehor advocated priests should not labor with their own hands, that they should get supported with the believers' money, and this was something the Book of Mormon condemned of being guilty of priestcraft. Alma, on the other hand, ordained priests in Mosiah 18:18 and he instructed them that they must labor with their own hands for their own support. In Mosiah 18:24 (see also Mosiah 9:10 RE):

> *And he... commanded them that the priests whom he had ordained should labor with their own hands for their support.*

King Mosiah adopted this standard as the law. In Mosiah 27:4-5 (see also Mosiah 11:24 RE):

> *That they should let no pride nor haughtiness disturb their peace; that every man should esteem his neighbor as himself, laboring with their own hands for their support. Yea, and all their priests and teachers should labor with their own hands for their support, in all cases save it were in sickness, or in much want; and doing these things, they did abound in the grace of God.*

See, I could raise money if I wanted to. I could raise a lot of money if I wanted to. And if I raised money off the religion I preach, I could get a lot more done. Instead I labor with my own hands and I work nights, evenings, weekends. The amount of work that is going into the book that will come out next—that includes not just me, but my wife, and practically every spare moment that we have—involves enormous sacrifice. But it has exactly the effect, "we should esteem our neighbor as ourself laboring with our own hands." We should not think that we are better than anyone.

If you take money from someone in order to advance your religious purpose, the mere act of doing that creates an inequality. It creates an arrogance. It creates... It removes the burden of sacrifice. It removes the humiliation of having to lose sleep, and to fret, and to worry about things, and to face an uphill battle; and everything that you do in order to please God. But you can't please God by taking advantage of your fellowman.

I'm going to talk about Zion, and Zion is going to be gathered. But the gathering of that group will not necessarily come exclusively from any party, group, denomination, or lineage. Priestcraft damages the practitioner, I think more so than those on whom he practices. I don't see how you can destroy equality, and injure and grieve the Spirit by holding yourself up as a light, and interfering with the work of the Lord in bringing about Zion, and not suffer the greater loss.

The foregoing excerpts are taken from:

- Denver's remarks titled "Keep the Covenant: Do the Work," given at the Remembering the Covenants Conference in Layton, UT on September 30, 2018
- The presentation of Denver's paper titled "The Restoration's Shattered Promises and Great Hope," given at the Sunstone Symposium in Salt Lake City, UT on July 28, 2018
- His talk titled "Other Sheep Indeed," given at the Sunstone Symposium in Salt Lake City, UT on July 29th, 2017
- Denver's conference talk titled "Things to Keep Us Awake at Night," given in St. George, UT on March 19th, 2017
- The presentation of "Answer and Covenant," given at the Covenant of Christ Conference in Boise, ID on September 3rd, 2017
- Denver's conference talk titled "Our Divine Parents," given in Gilbert, AZ on March 25th, 2018
- Denver's lecture titled "Signs Follow Faith," given in Centerville, UT on March 3, 2019
- The Q&A Session following Denver's conference talk given in Grand Junction, CO on April 21, 2019
- A Q&A session titled "A Visit with Denver Snuffer," held on May 13, 2015; and
- His talk titled "Zion Will Come," given near Moab, UT on April 10th, 2016.

135. Equality, Part 2

This is the second part of a special series on Equality, where Denver addresses the questions, "What is the transformation process we need to undergo in order to establish and practice equality? What lack we yet, to become equal?"

———

DENVER: Original Christians had no professional clergy. They operated in a way akin to a method described in the Book of Mormon:

> *And when the priests left their labor to impart the word of God unto the people, the people also left their labors to hear the word of God. And when the priest had imparted unto them the word of God they all returned again diligently unto their labors; and the priest, not esteeming himself above his hearers, for the preacher was no better than the hearer, neither was the teacher any better than the learner; and thus they were all equal, and they did all labor, every man according to his strength. And they did impart of their substance, every man according to that which he had, to the poor, and the needy, and the sick, and the afflicted.* (Alma 1:26-27; see also Alma 1:5 RE).

This is how I believe Christianity ought to be practiced today—without a professional clergy, diverting tithes and offerings that ought to be used to help the poor, needy, sick, and afflicted. We need to, and can return, to those early days of Christianity.

Justin Martyr lived from 110-165 A.D., and he wrote in the "sub-apostolic" age. His writings give us a glimpse into how Christianity functioned in its earliest days. In his *First Apology* he describes Christian worship. They met in homes, having no church buildings.

Before being considered a Christian, a candidate was baptized "in the name of God, the Father and Lord of the universe, and our Savior Jesus Christ, and of the Holy Spirit." (*First Apology*, Chapter LXI-Christian Baptism.)

Meetings began with a prayer and "saluting one another with a kiss." Then sacrament was prepared and administered using a "cup of wine mixed with water," and bread which is blessed by "giving praise and glory to the Father of the universe, through the name of the Son and of the Holy Ghost, and offers thanks at considerable length for our being counted worthy to receive these things at His hands." (Id., Chapter LXV-Administration of the Sacraments.)

The early Christians recognized there was an obligation for "the wealthy among us [to] help the needy." Therefore, after reading scripture and "the memoirs of the apostles or the writings of the prophets" donations were collected. (*Id.,* Chapter LXVII-*Weekly Worship of the Christians.*) Then the donations were distributed to help those who were poor or needy among that group of Christians.

These simple observances were resilient enough to preserve Christianity after the death of the apostles and before any great hierarchical magisterium arose. It was the power of baptism, the sacrament, scripture study, and financial aid among believers that gave Christianity its power.

We cannot bear one another's burdens without fellowshipping with one another. And bearing one another's burdens presumes that you know what the burdens are that someone else carries; which means that I have been patient enough, I have been attentive enough, I have been friendly enough, and I have been trusted enough that I can find out what the burden is that they bear.

I have a very good friend (went to elementary, junior high, high school with him, and I've kept in touch with him for many years) and he has recently contracted a terminal form of cancer. He called me to talk about that, without telling his family, without telling his neighbors, without telling his friends; because he and I have a friendship that is built upon the kind of trust that allows me to share that burden with him because of the relationship.

We're supposed to help one another get through this ordeal of mortality. And it is an ordeal. It is not easy. Even the people that you think you… you envy, if you were living inside their world, you'd find out that they have burdens they are carrying as well.

Fellowshipping allows us to bear one another's burdens, and bearing one another's burdens implies a whole universe of connectivity, trust, confidence, friendship, and affection between one another before you get to the point that you even know what their burdens are. But that is supposed to be a blessing and part of what it means to worship together. Worshipping together, by assisting one another, allows all of us to feel a great part of what it is that Christ is and does. It allows us to know *who* we worship, and it allows us to know *how* to worship Him, and it allows us to know *what* makes us one with one another. Now, it's really hard to accomplish that across state lines, but it still can be done.

The example I use of that friend... He and I have spent a lot of time on the phone since I learned of the illness about a month ago. And that's because I care, and that's because he needs to talk to someone, and because he finds it a relief to be able to do that with me. It can be done. It can be done across any barriers.

All of us are victims of institutional abuse. Many of us can sense it when the slightest hint of abuse appears. One recent writer on your blog has identified it as paternalism, and that's not an inappropriate designation for it. We should learn how to be loving and equal with one another. The idea of equality is resisted by a lot of skeptics, who accuse me of wanting authority and control, when I despise control; but I absolutely welcome fellowship, equality, and worship with one another. This isn't easy, but it is godly to pursue. And… and we're going to make mistakes. And there are going to be a lot of institutional habits that we walk in and we want to… we want to "whip this into shape." And the idea of a whip… When Christ resorted to the scourge to drive them out, he didn't drive them out to organize them. He drove them out to cleanse the place. If we're going to whip anything, we're going to drive them out. We would be better off practicing the kind of patience and kindness; and to realize that in terms of Mormonism, almost everyone is a refugee suffering post religious trauma syndrome; and they're going to think you're abusive. They're going to think you want to... they want to be used as a tool for someone else's power base—someone wants to use you. The idea that there's someone who doesn't want to use them, or abuse them, but wants to fellowship with them, and help them bear a burden (that's the idea of Christianity at its core), and that's what's really alien in this world. We need to bring that back again.

And so, the restoration has been in a pause for four and five generations waiting for God to begin it anew. Today marks a moment when the stirrings, that have been underway for years, result in God's offering to establish His people, on earth, by a covenant He ordains.

The few ready to receive the Lord's offer today are scattered to the nethermost parts of His vineyard. It's verse 52 (see also Jacob 3 RE). Despite this, a live broadcast on the Internet allows them to be grafted in at the same moment this is happening in Boise, Idaho. Correspondingly, those who utterly refused to accept the offered covenant are plucked from the restoration's tree of life because they are bitter fruit, unable to meet the Lord's requirements.

The Lord is taking this step to preserve part of humanity, not to destroy it (it's verse 53). A few descendants of the covenant fathers have the natural gift of faith. That gift belongs to the natural branches (that's verse 54). When grafted, we are connected to the natural roots or covenant Fathers as heirs of the promises made to them.

Even after the covenant, there will still be those who are bitter and wild, who will be unable to produce natural fruit,, despite the covenant. These will remain for a time despite their bitterness (verses 56 and 57). Today only the most bitter, who refuse to be grafted in, will be trimmed away.

We look forward to more nourishing or restoring of truths, lights, and commandments which will bless those who receive; but for those who will not, the continuing restoration will prune them away (verse 58). These bitter and wild branches must still be cut off and cast away. These steps are necessary to preserve the opportunity for the natural fruit to fully return (it's verse 59). The good must overcome the evil. This takes time, and it means that the Lord's patience is extended to give time to develop and further improve.

We are not expected and cannot become natural fruit in a single step. But we are expected to accept the initial graft today.

The Lord is taking these steps so that "Perhaps," and that's a deliberate word, *perhaps* we may become natural fruit worthy to be preserved in the coming harvest (that's verse 60). *Perhaps* is the right word. Some, who are grafted, will still be plucked away and burned, but others will bear natural fruit and be preserved.

Accepting the covenant is not the final step. Our choices will determine whether we are bitter or natural fruit. *That* will decide our fate.

Just as the ancient allegory foretold, the covenant makes us servants and laborers in the vineyard (verse 61). We are required to (this is from the covenant): *Seek to recover the lost sheep remnant of this land and of Israel and no longer forsake them. Bring them unto [the Lord] and teach them of [His] ways, to walk in them* (T&C 158:11). If we fail to labor to recover them, we break the covenant.

We must labor for this last time in the Lord's vineyard. There is an approaching, final pruning of the vineyard (verse 62).

The first step to be... The first to be grafted in are Gentiles so that the last may be first. The lost sheep remnant next, and then Israelites, so that the first may be last (verse 63). But grafting is required for all, even the remnants, because God works with his people through covenant making.

There will be more grafting and further pruning. As more is revealed and, therefore, more is required, some will find the digging and dunging too much to bear and will fall away; or in other words, will be pruned despite the covenant (that's verse 64). The covenant makes it possible for natural fruit to return. The bad fruit will still continue, even among the covenant people, until there is enough strength in the healthy branches for further pruning.

It requires natural fruit to appear before the final pruning takes place (verse 65). The good and bad will coexist. It will damage the tree to remove the bad at once. Therefore, the Lord's patience will continue for some time yet. The rate of removing the bad is dependent wholly upon the rate of the development of the good.

It is the Lord's purpose to create equality in his vineyard. In the allegory, equality in the vineyard appears three times in verses 66, 72 and 74. We cannot be greater and lesser, nor divide ourselves into an hierarchy to achieve the equality required for Zion. When a group is determined to remain equal, and I am personally determined to be no greater than any other, then it faces challenge that never confront unequal people. A religion of bosses and minions never deals with any of the challenges of being equals. Critics claim we will never succeed because of our determined desire for equality. None of our critics can envision what the Lord has said in verses 66, 72 and 74 about his people. But equality among us is the only way prophesied for us to succeed. That does not mean we won't have a mess as we learn how to establish equality.

Similarly, Zion cannot be established by isolated and solitary figures proclaiming a testimony of Jesus from their home keyboard. The challenge of building a community must be part of a process. Zion is a community and, therefore, God is a god of community; and his people must learn to live together with one heart, one mind, with no poor among us. Isolated keyboardists, proclaiming their resentment of community, can hardly speak temperately of others. How could they ever live peacefully in a community of equals?

We must become precious to each other.

Although the laborers in this final effort are few, you will be the means, used by the Lord, to complete his work in His vineyard (verse 70). You're required to labor with your might to finish the Lord's work in his vineyard (verse 72). But He will labor alongside you.

He, not a man or a committee, will call you to do work. When He calls, do not fear, but do not run faster than you have strength. We must find His people in the highways and byways and invite them to join in (Luke 14:23; see also Luke 9:7 RE). Zion will include people from every part of the world. This conference is broadcast worldwide as part of the prophecy to Enoch that God would send...

> *Righteousness and truth will [He] cause to sweep the earth as with a flood, to gather out mine elect from the four quarters of the earth, unto a place which I shall prepare, an Holy City, that my people may gird up their loins, and be looking forth for the time of my coming; for there shall be my tabernacle, and it shall be called Zion, a New Jerusalem.* (Moses 7:62; see also Genesis 4:22 RE)

We must proclaim this to the world.

Do not despair when further pruning takes place. It must be done. Only through pruning can the Lord keep his tree of life equal without those who are lofty overcoming the body (verse 73). The lofty branches have always destroyed equality to prevent Zion.

The final result of the Lord's labor in His vineyard is declared by the ancient prophet in unmistakable clarity. *The trees [have] become again the natural fruit; and they became like unto one body; and the fruits were equal; and the Lord of the vineyard had preserved unto himself the natural fruit, which was most precious unto him from the beginning.* Mark those words (that's verse 74).

When the Lord explained this to me, I realized how foolish it was to expect natural fruit, worthy of preservation, in an instant. The Lord works patiently, methodically, and does not require any to *run faster than [they] have strength* (Mosiah 4:27; see also Mosiah 2:6 RE).

We cannot allow ourselves to be drawn into inequality, when the result of this labor is to make us one body, equal with one another. We cannot imitate the failures of the past by establishing a hierarchy, elevating one above another, and forgetting that we must be of one heart, one mind, and no poor among us.

The restoration was never intended to just restore an ancient Christian church. That is only a halfway point. It must go back further. In the words of the ancient prophet, God intends to do *according to [His] will; and [to preserve] the natural fruit, that it is good, even like as it was in the beginning* (verse 75). This means the beginning, as in the days of Adam, with the return of the original religion and original authority. Everything must be returned as it was in the beginning. Civilization began with the temple as the center of learning, law, and culture. The temple was the original "university" because it taught of man's place with God in the universe.

God will return the right of dominion, once held by Adam, to man on earth to make us humble, servant-gardeners laboring to return the world to a peaceful paradise. The covenant received today restores part of that right. There is a land inheritance given to us as part of the covenant, and therefore, if we keep the covenant, we have the right to remain when others will be swept away.

Ultimately, all rights given to us must be turned back to the Fathers, who went before, who will likewise return them to Adam, who will surrender them to Christ. When Christ returns, He will come with the right to exercise complete dominion over the earth, and exercise judgment over the ungodly.

Things set into motion today are part of preparing the way for the Lord's return in glory.

And there began to be the natural fruit again in the vineyard. And the natural branches began to grow and thrive exceedingly, and the ***wild branches began to be plucked off and to be cast away*** (Jacob 3:27 RE; emphasis added).

Some of the plucking and some of the casting away is voluntarily done by those who submit to false spirits that stir them up to anger against one another, and they depart from fellowship thinking themselves justified before God, when in fact, all they're doing is being plucked and cast away.

And they did keep the root and the top thereof equal, according to the strength thereof (ibid). We are seeking to keep it equal. Everyone of us is on the same plain. No one's getting supported by tithing money. If they are, that's done by a local fellowship that has voluntarily determined that they have one among them in need, because the tithes are gathered and used to help the poor. There's no general fund being accumulated, and there's no one who does anything that they get compensated for.

This is the only group of people whose religion requires, incessantly, sacrifice. No one gets paid. No one gets remunerated. Everything that's done is done at a price of sacrifice. If you're a person in need among a fellowship, the tithes are appropriately used because that's what they're for. They're for the poor. They're not for a leader.

You have to keep the root and you have to keep the top equal. If you allow inequality to creep in at the beginning, the end result is lavish palaces in which some fare sumptuously; and others ask to eat the crumbs that fall from the table, because they're treated so unequally, and their despair and their poverty and their need goes ignored.

Among us, it can't go ignored, because the money is gathered at a fellowship level. And if there is someone in need among you, and you don't minister to their needs, you're cruel. You're…

And thus ***they labored with all diligence, according to the commandments of the Lord*** *of the vineyard, even* ***until the bad had been cast away*** (ibid; emphasis added). If you can't tolerate equality; if you can't tolerate the top and the root being equal; if you can't tolerate peace among brethren, then go ahead and be bad, and cast yourself away. If you feel moved upon to do that, well, that's the Lord of the vineyard getting rid of you.

Even until the bad had been cast away out of the vineyard and the Lord had preserved unto himself, that the trees had become again the natural fruit. And they became like unto one body, and ***the fruit were equal*** (ibid; emphasis added).

That word "equal" shows up so often, in the labor that the Lord of the vineyard is trying to accomplish with the people, that you ought to take note. We ought to probably typeset it:

EQUAL

in double-sized font. We're not going to do that, so you have to underline the word, or circle the word, or pay attention to it. The purpose is to go and become equal with one another. As soon as you set out to create rank and position and hierarchy...

Admittedly, within the parable there is a top, and there is a root, admittedly; but the objective is to achieve equality. If you start out saying the one is greater or better than the other, you're never going to arrive at the point that is the purpose of the parable, the purpose of the labor of the Lord of the vineyard: *and the fruit were equal.*

Christ taught parables that included invited guests being barred from attending the wedding feast. In one, the guests are called "virgins" to suggest that they possess moral purity and would be welcomed to the event. In another, there are strangers on the highway invited because others refused to come. Both parables, however, have some who are ultimately excluded from the wedding—a symbol of Christ's return. These parables raise an important issue about the Lord's return. There is a reason why five of the ten virgins could not enter into the wedding celebration. Likewise, those invited to attend the wedding feast, that arrive without a wedding garment, will be excluded. In both cases, those excluded were not welcome as they were unprepared.

There have been only two societies in recorded history that became Zion. Because of the age of the world at the time, both were taken up into heaven. We have very little to help us understand why these two succeeded. Apart from describing them as of "one heart, one mind, and no poor among them," we know little else. But perhaps that is one of the most important things we can know about them. Maybe the point is that *nothing* and *no one* stood out as remarkable or different within the community. There were no heroes and no villains; no rich and no poor; no Shakespearian plot lines of betrayal, intrigue, ambition, conflict, and envy. There was no adultery, theft, robbery, murder, immorality, and drunkenness; in other words, nothing to entertain us. Because all our stories, movies, music, novels, television plots, and social media are based upon and captivated by everything that is missing from these societies.

The centuries-long period of peace described in the Book of Mormon occupies only a few short pages in 4 Nephi. Their society was marked by the presence of peace, the absence of conflict, and abiding stability. This is what they attained:

> *There were no contentions and disputations among them, and every man did deal justly one with another. And they had all things common among them; therefore, there were not rich and poor, bond and free, but they were all made free and partakers of the Heavenly gift.* (4 Nephi 1:1 RE)

Because there was no future ministry for them to perform, their Zion society was not taken up to heaven. Because the world was not yet ready for the Lord to return in judgment, neither Enoch nor Melchizedek returned with their people to fall on their necks and kiss them.

These people were most remarkable for what they lacked. How they grew to lack these divisions, contentions, and disputes is described in very few, simple words:

> *They did walk after the commandments which they had received from [the] Lord...their God, continuing in fasting and prayer, and in meeting together oft, both to pray and to hear the word of the Lord. And it came to pass...there was no contention among all the people in all the land.* (4 Nephi 1:2 RE)

What were the names of their leaders? We don't know because, apparently, there were none. Who were the great teachers? Again, we don't know because they were not identified. Who governed? Apparently no one. They had things in common, obeyed God's commandments, and spent time praying and hearing the word of the Lord. They were so very unlike us.

To make the point clear for us, the record of these people explains: *There was no contention in the land because of the love of God which did dwell in the hearts of the people; and there were no envyings, nor strifes, nor tumults, nor whoredoms, nor lyings, nor murders, nor any manner of lasciviousness* (4 Nephi 1:3 RE). All the negatives were missing because the love of God dwelt in their hearts.

Something else describes them: *And surely there could not be a happier people among all the people who had been created by the hand of God* (ibid). Consider those words carefully. You cannot be happier than by allowing the love of God to dwell in you. The happiest people who have ever lived did so by the profound peace they displayed, equality they shared, fairness they showed one another, and love of God in their hearts.

This is a description of our social opposites. Reviewing the Answer to the Prayer for Covenant, the Covenant, and the recent parable of the Master's House shows that the Lord is pleading for *us* to become *this*. It's not easy; it will require civilizing the uncivilized. However, it is necessary to become the wise virgins and the invited guests wearing the wedding garment.

Five of the virtuous virgins, who were expecting the wedding party to arrive, were, nevertheless, excluded. They were virgins like the others, but the others were allowed to enter, and they were not. They did not lack virginity. They did not lack notice. They were not surprised by an unexpected wedding party arriving. But they lacked "oil" which is a symbol of the Holy Ghost. They failed to acquire the necessary spirit with which to avoid conflict, envy, strife, tumult, and contention. To grow into the kind of people God will want us to welcome into His dwelling requires practice, experience, and effort. People have not done it. Devout religious people are not prepared to live in peace, with all things in common, with no poor among them. God is trying to create a civilization that does not yet exist.

It is a privilege for God to give guidance to help prepare His people. There has always been a promise from the Lord that those who inherit Zion will be given commandments from Him to follow. He declared:

> *Yea, blessed are they whose feet stand upon the land of Zion, who have observed... who have obeyed my gospel, for they shall receive for their reward the good things of the earth, and it shall bring forth [it's] strength. And they...shall [also] be crowned with blessings from above, yea...with commandments not a few, and with revelations in their time, [that] they...are faithful and diligent[ly] before me.* (T&C 46:1)

Those who mock or criticize efforts to complete the Restoration are defining themselves as unworthy by their own words. No matter how good they may otherwise be, when they embrace conflict, envy, strife, tumult, and contention, they cannot be invited to the wedding of the Lamb.

We need more commandments from God to prepare for what is coming. The example in 4 Nephi commends those people who walk after the commandments received from our Lord and God. There should be fasting and prayer. People should meet together, pray, and review the words of the Lord. Every step taken will make us more like those virgins who have oil in their lamps and less like the foolish virgins who took no effort to make the required preparation.

It's not enough to avoid outright evil. We have to be good. Being "good" means to be separate from the world, united in charity towards each other, and to have united hearts. If we are ready when the wedding party arrives, we must follow the Lord's commandments to *us*. They are for our good. He wants us to awaken and arise from an awful slumber.

The third such society will not be taken into heaven. Instead, it will welcome the return of the first two to the earth. Why would ancient, righteous societies caught up to heaven want to leave there to come and meet with a city of people on earth? Why would they fall on their necks and kiss that gathered body of believers? And above all else, why would Christ want to occupy a tabernacle and dwell with such a community? Obviously, because there will be people living on earth whose civilization is like the society in heaven.

The Ten Commandments outline basic social norms needed for peace and stability. Christ's Sermon on the Mount was His exposition on the Ten Commandments. He expounded on the need to align the intent of the heart with God's standard to love your fellow man, do good to those who abuse you, and hold no anger. He took us deeper. Where the Ten Commandments allowed reluctant, resentful, and hard-hearted conformity, the Sermon on the Mount requires a willing readiness to obey. Christ wants us to act with alacrity to follow Him. He taught us to treat others as you would want to be treated.

The answer to these questions is easy to conceptualize and easy to verbalize. But living the answer is beyond mankind's ability to endure. We do not want to lay down our pride, ambition, jealousy, envy, strife, and lusts to become that community.

We're not going to arrive where we need to arrive if we perceive ourselves as unequal, if we think of ourselves as greater and lesser, if we don't think of ourselves as simply common servants—inadequate as we may be, to a Lord who loved and sacrificed Himself for our redemption. He is worthy. We can do our best and we can make a lot of mistakes along the way.

The Answer to the Prayer for Covenant and the Covenant are the beginning blueprint. That blueprint teaches the need to be better people. Following it is more challenging than reciting it. No one can learn what is required *without doing*. Working together is the only way a society can grow together. No isolated spiritual mystic is going to be prepared for Zion through his solitary personal devotions. Personal devotion is necessary, of course, but the most pious hermit will collide with the next pious hermit when they're required to share and work together in a society of equals having all things in common. Do not pretend it will be otherwise. Failing to do the hard work outlined in the covenant is failing to prepare for Zion. It's failing to have oil in the lamp. It's failing to put upon you the wedding garment.

If you think you are one of the five virgins, who will be invited in when the bridegroom arrives, and have never attempted to obey the Lord's commandments, you will find yourself left outside when the door is shut. If you come from the highways and byways without a wedding garment because you failed to keep the covenant, you'll be excluded.

As aggravating and trying as people are on one another, we need to go through this. There's no magic path to loving one another. Some people refuse and must be left outside. When it comes to loving others, some things must be abandoned, some things must be added, some things must be forgotten, and some things must be ignored. But learning what to abandon, add, forget, or ignore is only through the doing. We chip away at ourselves and others by interacting and sharing.

We will learn things about one another that will distress us. And we may well wish we didn't know some things about others. How will the socially-offensive become socially- acceptable without help from a loving society? And how can a society become loving if people are not broad-minded enough to figure out that some things just don't matter? Few things really are important. If a man is honest, just, virtuous, and true, should you care if he swears? If a man has a heart of gold and would give you assistance if he... if he thought it was needed, should you care if he's rough and uncouth?

The adulterous and predatory will rarely reform and must often be excluded. They will victimize and destroy. We are commanded to cast out those who steal, love and make a lie, commit adultery, and refuse to repent. The instructions we have been given state:

> *You shall not kill; he that kills shall die. You shall not steal, ...he that steals and will not repent* ***shall be cast out.*** *You shall not lie; he that lies and will not repent* ***shall be cast out****. You shall love your wife with all your heart, and shall cleave unto her and none else, ...he that looks upon a woman to lust after her shall deny the faith, and shall not have the spirit, and if he repent not...****shall be cast out****. You shall not commit adultery, and he that commits adultery and repents not* ***shall be cast out****; and he that commits adultery and repents with all his heart, and forsakes [it] and does it no more, you shall forgive him; but if he does it again, he* ***shall not be forgiven****, [and]* ***shall be cast out****. You shall not speak evil of your neighbor [nor] do him any harm. You know my laws, they are given in my scriptures.* ***He that sins and repents not shall be cast out****. If you love me, you shall serve me and* ***keep all my commandments****.* (T&C 26:6, emphasis added)

This teaching is still binding. If your fellowship includes those who ought to be "cast out," you have the obligation to do so rather than encouraging evil. Be patient, but be firm. If a person refuses to repent and forsake sins, you may end fellowship with them and include those who are interested in practicing obedience and love.

There is work to be done. Almost all of it is internal to us. The five prepared virgins and the strangers who brought a wedding garment will be those who keep the covenant. It is designed to give birth to a new society, new culture, and permit a new civilization to be founded.

The Lord's civilization will require His tabernacle at the center. Through it, a recovered religion will be fully developed. God's house will include a higher law, an education about the universe, and a divine university will be established. It will be an ensign in the mountains, and people from all over the earth will say: *Come, let us go up to the house of the God of Jacob. He will teach us; we will learn of his paths, to walk in them* (see Isaiah 1:5; see also 2 Nephi 8:4 RE).

That place will house a new civilization. There will be no hermit gurus proud of their enlightenment. No one will offer himself or herself up as some great idol to follow. It will be a place of equality, where people are meek and lowly, serving one another without any attempt to compete for "chief seats."

Christ's apostles competed to be greater than one another. In the New Covenants, Luke 13:6, Christ's reaction is recorded:

> *There was also a strife among them: who of them should be accounted the greatest. And he said unto them, The kings of the gentiles exercise lordship over them, and they who exercise authority upon them are called benefactors; but it ought not...be so with you. But he who is greatest among you, let him be as the younger, and he who is chief, as he who does serve. For [whether] is [he] greater? ...who sits at [the] meal, or he who serves? I am not as he who sits at a meal, but I am among you as he who serves.*

Christ is the great example. Christ would have fit into Enoch's city, would have been welcomed among Melchizedek's people, and could have dwelt in peace with the Nephites of 4 Nephi. Has He, as once before between Jerusalem and Emmaus, walked among them, unnoticed, to enjoy their peaceful company?

I cannot keep the covenant. You cannot keep the covenant. Only *we* can keep the covenant.

But if we do, God's work will continue and will include the fullness previously offered to the gentiles and rejected by them. It is impossible to understand the promises that Elijah will *turn the hearts of the children to the Fathers* unless the fullness is recovered. Joseph Smith cannot fix or finish the Restoration by returning as a resurrected being in the Millennium, as conjectured by Wilford Woodruff. If the necessary rites are not returned before the Lord's return, *the whole earth would be utterly wasted at his coming* (JSH 3:4 RE). There will be a new civilization built around God's tabernacle where He will dwell. We know the purpose of that house will be for the God of Jacob to teach those people to walk in His ways. We know Joseph Smith began adoption sealing as the highest ordinance and is now been lost.

We have been given a new revelation that explains resurrection, and adoption to the Fathers in heaven, are linked together:

> *I was shown that the spirits that rose were limited to a direct line back to Adam, requiring the hearts of the fathers and the hearts of the children to be bound together by sealing, confirmed by covenant and [by] the Holy Spirit of Promise. This is the reason that Abraham, Isaac and Jacob have entered into their exaltation according to the promises and sit upon thrones and are not angels but are gods.* [That's in the Teachings and Commandments section 157, paragraphs 42 and 43.] (T&C 169:3)

The fullness can only be returned through a temple accepted by God as His House. He must

return to restore that which has been lost. But ungodly people *cannot* build an acceptable house for God. There is no commandment to build a temple because people are not yet qualified to do so. So far, we've been spared the experience in Nauvoo, where an abortive attempt to build a temple, in which the fullness could be restored, resulted in the Lord not performing His oath. Nor did the Lord fulfill the promise they expected to receive. Instead of blessings, the people in Nauvoo brought upon themselves cursings, wrath, indignation, and judgments by their follies and abominations. If we are going to receive that same condemnation, it would be better to not begin to build a House of God.

The foregoing excerpts are taken from:

- Denver's *Christian Reformation Lecture Series*, Talk #2 given in Dallas, TX on October 19th, 2017
- A Q&A session titled "A Visit with Denver Snuffer" held on May 13, 2015

- His Opening Remarks given at the Covenant of Christ Conference in Boise, Idaho on September 3rd, 2017
- Denver's lecture titled "Signs Follow Faith" given in Centerville, UT on March 3, 2019
- His conference talk titled "Civilization", given in Grand Junction, CO on April 21, 2019; and
- Denver's remarks titled "Remembering the Covenants" given at the Remembering the Covenants Conference in Layton, UT on August 4, 2018.

136. Commune with Christ, Part 1

This is the first part of a special series where Denver addresses the question, "How can I commune with Christ?"

DENVER: I got an inquiry asking: "I am interested in any thought you would be willing to share about why we were willing to sacrifice to come to *this* earth. I don't think that this earth is the only place in all of creation where one can learn to return to the presence of the Lord, so what is the purpose of the righteous in the pre-existence coming *here*? Why not take an *easier route* and go to a different terrestrial mortal state?"

Because we saw a great benefit in coming. In fact, the opportunity was greeted with shouts of joy (see Job 12:2 RE). Perspective from here is not the same as perspective from above. There is a required *...opposition in all things* (2 Nephi 1:7 RE). To ascend, you must first descend. The path to the highest state runs through the lowest (see, e.g., Genesis 1:3-4 RE and JSH 2:4 RE). You will not see the Father and Son (see, e.g., T&C 69:4) without also seeing the fallen angel cast out for rebellion (T&C 69:6). Nor will you behold the Celestial Kingdom without also seeing the horror of outer darkness (T&C 69:9-13).

To comprehend one you must become acquainted with both glory and darkness. You cannot receive the one without also the other. Joseph put it this way:

> Thy mind, O man! if thou wilt lead a soul unto salvation, must stretch as high as the utmost heavens, **and** search into and contemplate the darkest abyss, and the broad expanse of eternity—thou must commune with God. (TPJS, p. 137; see also T&C 138:18, emphasis added)

You do not get to behold the glory without also beholding the darkest abyss. There is a parallel to comprehension, a symmetry to understanding.

You came here to increase your understanding of truth and to broaden your capacity to appreciate what is good. For that, you wanted and now are receiving exposure to the brackets which allow you to comprehend and to expand. You will eventually leave here, but you will depart with an expanded capacity which could come in no other way.

Read the perils through which Abraham passed and know that this was necessary for him to become the Father of the Righteous. There is no path back to heaven apart from walking through the valley of the shadow of death. Your understanding of eternal life will come from suffering death. Your appreciation of eternal glory will come from having been first composed of decaying dust of this earth. You wanted this. You shouted for joy when it was offered.

I read this before, and it belongs again right here. This is Joseph Smith writing from confinement in Liberty Jail. This is after Joseph has been confined in the Liberty Jail and had months of opportunity to reflect upon what it was that had gone on among the saints while he was still free and living among them:

> *The things of God are of deep import; and time, and experience, and careful and ponderous and solemn thoughts can only find them out. Thy mind, O man! if thou wilt lead a soul unto salvation, must stretch as high as the utmost heavens, and search into and contemplate the darkest abyss, and the broad expanse of eternity—thou must commune with God. How much more dignified and noble are the thoughts of God, than the vain imaginations of the human heart! None but fools will trifle with the souls of men.*
>
> *How vain and trifling have been our spirits, our conferences, our councils, our meetings, our private as well as public conversations—too low, too mean, too vulgar, too condescending for the dignified characters of the called and chosen of God.* (TPJS, p. 137; see also T&C 138:18-19)

Don't waste your time when you're with one another! Learn, study, testify, search the scriptures. *Worship God.*

> *That which is of God is light; and he that receiveth light, and continueth in God, receiveth more light; and that light groweth brighter and brighter until the perfect day. And again, verily I say unto you, and I say it that you may know the truth, that you may chase darkness from among you; He that is ordained of God and sent forth, the same is appointed to be the greatest, notwithstanding he is the least and the servant of all.* (D&C 50:24-26; see also T&C 36:4-5)

This is what we should be. This is how we should teach. This is how we should edify one another. This is how we should be preparing our children. This is what we should lay hold upon: truth, light, understanding, edifying, growing in knowledge of the principles of truth. You should not waste another three-hour block of time fiddling around with nonsense because you don't have permission from God to do that. Preach the principles. And if you don't think you know enough to do anything else, get together and read the scriptures out loud.

In the early church, when they… In this dispensation when they got together, one of the things that they regularly did was they got together, and everyone prayed in turn. Everyone prayed, and the meeting would last until all had prayed. They called it a Prayer Meeting, oddly enough. One of the early brethren didn't like that; he didn't feel like he could pray vocally around other people (see JSH 19:1-3 RE). There's a section in the Doctrine and Covenants admonishing him in a revelation that he needs to pray (see JSH 18:14 RE). If you don't have any wisdom to impart to one another, get together and pray; get together and read the scriptures.

The work of salvation is not achieved by your ignorance and indifference. And the Gospel of Christ is not limited to making you feel better about yourself. Quite frankly, my wife and I marvel all the time at how unprepared and unworthy she and I feel in everything that has gone on. *But*—I know God. And therefore, because I know God, I am confident that you can know Him too—absolutely confident that you can know Him too—and that He will speak to any one of you, just as He spoke to Joseph Smith, and that He will answer any earnest seeker. No one is sent away disappointed.

Do you think the Lord, who would not turn away the blind and the halt, the crippled and the leprous... Do you think the Lord, who seeing the widow whose only son was being carried away dead and was moved with compassion to restore the life of that young man, so that she—in that circumstance, in that culture, in that environment—she now had future security because she had a son to look out for her... Do you think that *that* Lord doesn't intend to answer the prayers of the earnest seeker?

My suspicion is that God has answered, and you've turned a deaf ear to much of what you've looked for because you want something other than the answers He's already given in the material that sits in front of you, unexamined. My suspicion is that if you would spend time looking into the revelations, given us by the Prophet Joseph Smith, and studying the history—however perilous that may prove to be to you—that you will conclude that God's already had an answer to the inquiry that you've made, and that with a little effort you can find it. And when you find it, you'll hear the voice of God saying, "There it is. Now was that so hard? [audience laughter] Why don't you keep going and see what else is in there for you." Because this stuff was given to us at the price of the life of a 38 1/2-year-old young man and his older brother, whose blood was shed in order to restore what we now have in our possession; and we take it lightly, and we look away.

I could write my own Gospel. I could bear my own testimony. I could invent a new narrative about our Lord if it were necessary to do so. But I'll tell you the only thing that is necessary is to open the scriptures and read them, and to tell you the things that we've looked at tonight are true—like Jacob. In fact, if you go all the way back to Jacob chapter 6:

> *And now, behold, my brethren, as I said unto you that I would prophesy, behold, this is my prophecy—that the things which this prophet Zenos spake, concerning the house of Israel, in the which he likened them unto a tame olive-tree, must surely come to pass.* (Jacob 6:1; see also Jacob 4:1 RE)

So, here's the words of my prophecy: That the things that we have looked at this evening, restored through the Prophet Joseph Smith—the seer named Joseph, the son of a father named Joseph—fulfilled the promise of Joseph of Egypt, and they are all true. And I know them to be true. And you can know them to be true too, but the price you have to pay in order to gain that knowledge is to pay some attention to what it was that was restored through the Prophet Joseph Smith. Otherwise, they're just something gathering dust on a shelf.

Don't read them as if you're trying to vindicate the religion that you think you already understand. Don't read them as if you're trying to defend your current group of preferred doctrines. Read them as if you are as ignorant of the will of God as the convert is that you hope to make, living somewhere in Florida or New Guinea or Guatemala. Because the truth of the matter is that we have been devolving in our understanding, from the day of Joseph Smith until today, at an ever accelerating rate. And what we have left, Enoch called "gross darkness" (see Isaiah 22:1 RE).

I bear testimony that Joseph was a prophet. I bear testimony that our Lord lived and lives. I'm one of those who can say that I'm a witness of that. I have seen His suffering. I have heard His voice. He doesn't intend that I be a solitary witness of Him, or Joseph be one. He intends for every one of you to rise up and do as James bids you to do: If you lack wisdom, ask God. He gives to you—He gives to all of us—liberally (see Epistle of Jacob 1:2 RE).

He's real. It is *His* work to bring this stuff to pass. The only thing that we can do is to offer to be a servant. And I am confident that I'm a poor one of those, but I am His servant, and I serve Him—however poorly, however offensively, however inadequately. He intends to call (in the plural) 'servants' to fulfill what needs to be done in the last days. He does intend to bring again Zion. That will be His, and not a man's, work.

There is a great work left undone. The field has been abandoned, and there is no harvesting taking place. We're all required to repent *first*, then to learn something before we attempt to teach others.

In doing the work I've been asked to do, I'm relaying what I have been instructed needs to be taught to this generation, at this time, for the Lord's promises to be fulfilled. That requires *"time, and experience, and careful and ponderous and solemn thought"* to be given to the Lord's design. Although I do *not* consider myself equal to the task, I am nevertheless doing what little I am able to do as part of the Lord's work. To the best of my ability, I seek only to lay out what should be noted about our present challenges. I do my best to avoid a "*fanciful*, or *flowery*, or *heated imagination*" in discussing salvation. While others may do so, I do not intend to "*trifle with the souls of men.*" Joseph Smith's counsel is appropriate and guides my thought on these things:

> *A fanciful and flowery and heated imagination beware of; because the things of God are of deep import; and time, and experience, and careful and ponderous and solemn thoughts can only find them out. Thy mind, O man! if thou wilt lead a soul unto salvation, must stretch as high as the utmost heavens, and search into and contemplate the darkest abyss, and the broad expanse of eternity—thou must commune with God. How much more dignified and noble are the thoughts of God, than the vain imaginations of the human heart! None but fools will trifle with the souls of men.* (TPJS p. 137; see also T&C 138:18)

I have never trifled with men's souls.

I have never given *anyone* permission to speak *for* me, use my name to support their cause, or to advocate using me as their source to make their ideas or teachings credible. If someone has a good idea, it should stand on its own. It should be reasonable. If an idea is so weak and fanciful, then associating my name, Joseph Smith's name, or some general authority's name with it should not overcome the weakness of the idea.

I do not believe in citing any authority other than scripture and Joseph Smith. Check the books I've written and talks I've given. Check my blog. There you can find what is true, taken from the authority of scripture. It is self-evident and capable of standing on its own. The truth I advocate is so self-supporting that I need to make *no* claim to authority. Yes, doubt everything other than truth taken from scriptures. They are the standard by which I teach.

Because this generation does not understand their precarious situation, they are *unable* to repent—but it is only repentance which can save some few souls. People are so quickly and easily drawn away from the challenge to repent before God into some other vain and foolish track. That is necessary, however—because in Joseph's day we failed in Kirtland, failed again in Missouri, failed in Nauvoo, and then lost Joseph. In Brigham's day, we failed in Salt Lake City.

The effort to save great numbers has not and will not work. There have always been comparatively few who have the patience and devotion to allow the Lord to do His work. Men and women charge into the upward pass and are slain by the beast who guards the way, generation after generation, while God works patiently to save some few. In the meantime, if great numbers can be persuaded to wander off or charge impatiently, then so be it. Had they remained, they would have spoiled what lies at the top of the mountain. It is better, therefore, that they be taken in, in their vanity, than to bring it with them into a society where such things would be ruinous.

King Benjamin is a more important topic for today than ever. But I get a flood of emails and comments asking about other ridiculously-extraneous things, propounded by others using my name for credibility. You should already know enough to determine on your own the significance or insignificance of these side-show issues. If you do not, then you deserve your confusion. You are on trial here. You must grow to stand on your own. Do not be dependent on me or *any* man for your knowledge of the truth. You must be able, by the power of the light given to you, to decide between truth and error, between what comes from God and what is of men and devils. If you are unable to determine that for yourself, then relying on others will never qualify you to enter into the Lord's rest.

The reaction to King Benjamin's sermon was for the people to repent. We have not yet taken a look at the overall setting where King Benjamin taught. Nephi established a line of prophet-priests to whom was given the charge to teach the people. That line's work is recorded in the Small Plates of Nephi. At about the same distance in time from Nephi as we find ourselves from Joseph Smith, we read in the Small Plates of Nephi: *I know of no other revelation, save that which has been written, neither prophecy* (Omni 1: 5 RE).

I've discussed this in *Eighteen Verses*. The prophetic line ended in *silence*. Whole generations recorded only one verse, admitting their failure; then the Book of Mormon re-ignites with King Benjamin. After generations of dissipating the light and falling into darkness, he represents the return of the prophetic. He is a symbol of restoration, a type of how God reclaims His people when they err. By his day, the people were overcome again and needed to return to the faith that could save them.

But King Benjamin did not operate on his own. He taught only what had been given to him to teach by an angel (see Mosiah 1:13-4:1 RE). Because God renewed His covenant with King Benjamin, it was through King Benjamin that the people could once again make an acceptable covenant with God. The purpose of sending the angel to King Benjamin was not to offer him *alone* salvation, but to offer once again a valid covenant through which others could repent (see Mosiah 3:1-2 RE).

This is how the Gospel works. Even the chosen people of Lehi and his son Nephi, brought to the promised land, *failed* to abide the conditions of the covenant, but God did not abandon them. When enough generations had passed to allow the Lord's hand to be revealed, then the Lord acted. The heavens were opened, the covenant was offered, and souls were saved.

This is a great type. The Book of Mormon is far more relevant for our day than we imagine. It is a blueprint for how our own history is unfolding. It is a sobering lesson in how to fail and how to wait for the Lord to reclaim and redeem us. We ignore or misunderstand the content of the Book of Mormon at the peril of our own salvation. When we do, then no one can be saved.

Increasing light inside our spirits lets us understand this Creation. The search for truth is the search for light.

In a dark room, many things are hidden from our sight by the darkness. Eyes cannot help you in the darkness. You can feel carefully, and slowly with patience and effort you can discover chairs, and bookcases, and other things in the darkness. Yet, you will not understand any colors nor fully comprehend what is hidden in the darkness. But in the same room with the help of light, you can see everything. Even the colors of the objects are easily understood.

There are many reasons why we do not see this Creation clearly. There are many forms of darkness. The standard of truth today is the 1,000-year record of the people who migrated to the Americas. That record was revealed and translated in 1830. All truth from *every* part of the world should be measured by that record.

Having a record does not mean you understand it. Like Lance who saw only what he expected to see in the forest, and like James who also saw only what he expected, we also read the Book of Mormon to see what we want to see.

You have different minds, a different culture, and different ideas in you. When *you* read our sacred books, you see, understand, and interpret them from your vantage point; you can see what we do not. In the search for truth, we can help one another to see more of what is really there and to notice what is hidden from *one* point of view.

The most accurate book of truth is still not fully understood. We must all be willing to accept light when the Gods offer it to us. The Book of Mormon tells us:

> *He that will harden his heart, the same receiveth the lesser portion of the word. And he that will not harden his heart, to him is given the greater portion of the word, until it is given unto him to know the mysteries of God, until they know them in full. And they that will harden their hearts, to them is given the lesser portion of the word until they know nothing concerning his mysteries.* (Alma 9:3 RE)

In verse 11 of the Seventh Lecture, in the middle there:

> *And the glory which thou gavest me I have given them, that they may be one even as we are one — I in them and thou in me — that they may be made perfect in one.* (Lectures on Faith 7:11)

This is long before Nauvoo. Joseph is declaring the possibility of unification between God and man—the oneness of God and man. This is foreshadowing teachings that he will give in the King Follett Discourse, and it's right there in the Lectures on Faith. The same is true in paragraph 13:

> *He wanted his disciples, even all of them, to be as himself and [as] the Father: for as he and the Father were one, so they might be one with them.* (Lectures on Faith 7:13)

This is marvelous language. It's in the 1835 scriptures—that have been eliminated as a result of a committee in 1921, and it was removed without a vote of the saints, and therefore, I would suggest it belongs in your scriptures still. Paragraph 15:

> *The glory which the Father and the Son have is because they are just and holy beings, and that if they were lacking in one attribute or perfection which they have, the glory which they have never could be enjoyed by them, for it requires them to be **precisely** what they are in order to enjoy it.* [There's that word again—"precisely."]
>
> 16: *These teachings of the Saviour most clearly show unto us the **nature** of salvation, and what he proposed unto the human family when he proposed to save **them**: that he proposed to make them like unto himself, and **he** was like the Father, the **great** prototype of all saved beings. And for any portion of the human family to be assimilated into their **likeness** is to be saved, and to be unlike them is to be destroyed. And on this hinge turns the door of salvation.* (Lectures on Faith 7:15-16, emphasis added)

No human can be saved until that human *is like God.*

There is so much you can do in this world that affords you the opportunity to be *like God.* There are mothers over here with little children. There's a child crying in the distance that has a mother with him. Every infant comes into this world in a condition of profound need. There isn't a mother alive who hasn't held a needy infant and not experienced the love of God—because that child's existence is dependent upon her. Keep in mind that these opportunities exist *everywhere*. Everywhere.

Still... (this is a long paragraph. This is paragraph 17, about—I don't know—a third of the way down):

> *It was a system of faith—it begins with faith and continues by faith. And every blessing which is obtained in relation to it is the effect of faith, whether it pertains to this life or that which is to come. To this all the revelations of God bear witness. If there were children of promise, they were the effects of faith, not even the Saviour of the world excepted:* [The Savior was produced as an act of faith.] *...And through the whole history of the scheme of life and salvation, it is a matter of faith: every man received according to his faith — according as his faith was, so were his blessings and privileges, and nothing was withheld from him when his faith was sufficient to receive it.* (Lectures on Faith 7:17)

This is the way in which God is no respecter of persons. *This* is the way in which you—if you will lay down your ignorance, if you will repent and turn to God—this is the way in which you can find yourself, *also,* the inheritor of blessings and privileges which God will not withhold from *anyone* who understands and gathers to themself the light and the truth that comes through obedience to the Gospel of Jesus Christ.

> *By their faith they could obtain Heavenly visions, the ministering of angels, have knowledge of the spirits of just men made perfect, of the general assembly and church of the firstborn (whose names are written in Heaven), of God, the judge of all, of Jesus, the Mediator of the new covenant, and become familiar with the third Heavens, see and hear things which were not only unutterable, but were unlawful to utter.* (Ibid.)

Later, Joseph Smith made a comment about, "Paul [John the Revelator] said he knew a man who was caught up to the third heaven, but I know a man who was caught up to the seventh heaven [and saw and heard things not lawful for me to utter]." (I'll give you the cite on that in the transcript: Rollins Lightner, Mary Elizabeth. *Autobiography of Mary E. Lightner (1818-1913).* Web. Also Carter, Kate B. Our Pioneer Heritage. Salt Lake City: Daughters of Utah Pioneers, 1958. 5:307.) It is sufficient, however, if you commune with *those* beings. Paragraph 18:

> *How were* ***they*** *to obtain the knowledge of God? (for there is a great difference between believing* ***in*** *God and* ***knowing*** *him — knowledge implies more than faith; and notice that all things that pertain to life and godliness were given through the knowledge of God) — the answer is given: Through faith they were to obtain this knowledge; and having power by faith to obtain the knowledge of God, they could...obtain all other things which pertain to life and godliness.* (Lectures on Faith 7:18, emphasis added)

It is knowledge that saves. Consequently, it is knowledge that you need to repent, and obtain. "Knowledge saves a man," said Joseph Smith. "A man is saved no faster than he gets knowledge," said Joseph Smith (TPJS, p. 217).

Knowledge and salvation; knowledge and repentance—they are all related. But knowledge is not given so that you can take prideful advantage of the fact that you possess something. If you have it, it is given to make you a minister, a servant—someone the Lord might be able to employ in order to raise up others. Because if you can't elevate others, then you've failed in your effort to be *like* Him. He came to serve; you serve too. [Paragraph] 20: *To obtain the faith—* [and this is a ways into that paragraph]:

> B*ecause, to obtain the faith by which he could enjoy the knowledge of Christ Jesus the Lord, he had to suffer the loss of all things. This is the reason that the Former Day Saints knew more and understood more of heaven*

> *and...Heavenly things than all others beside, because this information is the effect of faith—to be obtained by no other means. ...where faith is, there will the knowledge of God...also, with all things which pertain thereto — revelations, visions, and dreams, as well as every...necessary thing, in order that the possessors of faith may be perfected and obtain salvation. For God must change, otherwise faith will prevail with him. And he who possesses it will, through it, obtain all necessary knowledge and wisdom until he shall know God and the Lord Jesus Christ whom he has sent, whom to know is eternal life.* (Lectures on Faith 7:20)

That's the purpose of the Gospel—to give you knowledge. Therefore, the way to get knowledge is to repent. It's to search into, lay hold upon, and obtain for yourself knowledge that saves—not mere theory; not mere recitations of "These symbols in the temple endowment stand for these eight items, and that stands for this, and this stands for that." Trivia is not light and truth. Light and truth will exalt you; trivia can make you prideful.

The foregoing excerpts are taken from:

- Denver's blog post titled "Why Here," originally posted January 11, 2012, and subsequently recorded on February 13, 2021;
- Denver's *40 Years in Mormonism Series,* Talk #10 titled "Preserving the Restoration," given in Mesa, Arizona, on September 9, 2014;
- Denver's *40 Years in Mormonism Series,* Talk #4 titled "Covenants," given in Centerville, Utah, on October 6th, 2013;
- Denver's blog post titled "Themes, Truth and Scripture," originally posted March 12, 2014, and subsequently recorded on February 16, 2021;
- Denver's talk titled "The Search for Truth," presented October 4, 2020, during the Search for Truth online event, originating from Kurayoshi, Japan; and
- Denver's *40 Years in Mormonism Series,* Talk #3 titled "Repentance," given in Logan, Utah, on September 29th, 2013.

137. Commune with Christ, Part 2

This is the second part of a special series where Denver addresses the question, "How can I commune with Christ?"

DENVER: There are some brilliant comments from some of you—profound comments, even—but you must be careful about overthinking things. Doctrine is not to be understood as an academic or scholarly undertaking. Remember the chapter in *Eighteen Verses* on Moroni 10:5 (see Moroni 10:2 RE). It is supposed to be understood in the *doing* (see John 9:20 RE and TSJ 10:31 RE).

When you have done it, as Nephi has, then you will be able to explain the doctrine. To attempt to have a command of the doctrine without having done the will of the Father is to always be left without understanding. It is also not necessary to be able to fully expound the doctrine before *doing* it. It is necessary to take action consistent with the invitation offered to you.

Your mind can work at cross purposes. Remember the chapter on "Becoming as a Child" in *The Second Comforter*. In order to go forward, you must go back. Simplicity is at the heart of God's offer to commune with you.

Angelic ministrants come to people of *...a firm mind in every form of godliness*; calls repentance in order to fulfil and in order to do the work of the covenants, *...to fulfil and to do the work of the covenants of the Father*; and that requires that people *...bear testimony of Him* (Moroni 7:6 RE).

These *are* the essential things that are needed. It doesn't require a fanciful or a flowery imagination (see T&C 138:18). It does not require that we bear testimony of ourselves. It doesn't require us to do something other than to fulfil and do the work of the *covenants*. Therefore, I would suggest this is a pretty good guide to consider when you're evaluating all of the competing claims that are now being made by people to having inspiration or revelation or the word of God to *them*.

We are vulnerable to being misled, even as we claim to be inspired. Now, I'm going to read from a recent study from the National Academy of Science, and I read from it because it's a really interesting study result:

> Religion appears to serve as a moral compass for the vast majority of people around the world. It informs whether same-sex marriage is love or

> sin, whether war is an act of security or of terror, ...whether abortion rights represent[s] personal liberty or permission to murder. Many religions are centered on a god (or gods) that has beliefs and intentions, with adherents encouraged to follow "God's will" on everything from martyrdom to career planning to voting. Within these religious systems, how do people know what their god wills?
>
> When people try to infer other people's attitudes and beliefs, they often do so egocentrically by using their own beliefs as an inductive guide. This research examines the extent to which people might also reason egocentrically about God's beliefs. We predicted that people would be consistently more egocentric when reasoning about God's beliefs than when reasoning about other people's beliefs. Intuiting God's beliefs on important issues may not produce an independent guide, but may instead serve as an echo chamber that reverberates one's own beliefs.
>
> The Jewish and Christian traditions state explicitly that God created man in his own image, but believers and nonbelievers alike have long argued that people seem to create God in their own image as well. (*Proceedings of the National Academy of Sciences,* Vol. 106, No. 51, Dec. 22, 2009)

That's a problem that you find everywhere. God wills this to be so—well, because God agrees with me that it ought to be so, and therefore, I'm comfortably in tune with God.

The greatest help given to us to solve the contradiction between praying to God and the answer being *exactly* what we wanted, *exactly* what we expected, and *exactly* what makes us right and everyone else wrong—the greatest guide is the scriptures. They provide us a lifeline for measuring any inspiration we think we obtain from God. But that's not enough if it's not coupled together with prayerful, ponderous thought and time and experience.

I want to compare these statements from Joseph Smith about this topic:

> *A person may profit by noticing the first intimation of the spirit of revelation; for instance, when you feel pure intelligence flowing into you, it may give you sudden strokes of ideas, so that by noticing it, you may find it fulfilled the same day or soon; (i.e.) those things that were presented unto your minds by the Spirit of God, will come to pass; and thus by learning the Spirit of God and understanding it, you may grow into the principle of revelation, until you become perfect in Christ Jesus.* (TPJS, p. 151)

That seems to suggest that answers can come suddenly, quickly, perhaps even easily. But Joseph also said this:

> *A fanciful and flowery and heated imagination beware of; because the things of God are of deep import; and time, and experience, and careful and ponderous and solemn thoughts can only find them out. Thy mind, O man! if thou wilt lead a soul unto salvation, must stretch as high as the utmost heavens, and search into and contemplate the darkest abyss, and the broad expanse of eternity—thou must commune with God.* (TPJS, p. 137; see also T&C 138:18)

That second quote is taken from a letter that Joseph Smith composed while he was in Liberty Jail, in which he had plenty of time to fashion the language. The first quote, sadly, is taken from a source which may not be reliable or accurate. The source for that first quote is Willard Richards' *Pocket Companion* in which he quoted something which, if Joseph Smith said it, Joseph said it while Willard Richards was in England on a mission, and he could not possibly have heard it. He doesn't even attribute it to Joseph Smith.

But when the *Documentary History* was being compiled, they used the Willard Richards' *Companion* to take that language and attribute it to a talk given by Joseph in 1839 because most of the stuff in the *Pocket Companion* can be tracked to Joseph, and therefore, they conclude this one likewise fits that same category. The second one is clearly, unambiguously, from Joseph Smith and describes the process.

Now, while Joseph was in the Liberty Jail, on occasion he would have a friendly face show up or he would have a letter arrive. And on one of the occasions, he got letters from other people and his wife Emma. Joseph, who had been brooding at the time and longing for the companionship of some friends, describes what his mind was going through at the time of the letter and his response to it. He says his mind was frenzied, and any man's mind can be when contemplating the many difficult issues we are called upon to confront.

Just like Joseph, we have perpetual conundrums and contradictions. We all face them. Some are of our own making, but others are just inherent in living in this existence. When we thoughtfully consider the challenges, just like Joseph it seizes the mind, and like Joseph in Liberty Jail makes us reflect upon so many things with the "avidity [vivacity] of lightning." That was Joseph's word. The mind is in this frenzied state, and with the avidity [vivacity] of lightning, he's jumping from subject to subject, a fence to a fence, from things that console to things that outrage you, from things you know to be true to things that offend you—back and forth, and back and forth until, as Joseph puts it,

> *Finally all enmity, malice, and hatred, and past differences, misunderstandings, and mismanagements are slain victorious at the feet of hope. And when the heart is sufficiently contrite, then the voice of inspiration steals along and whispers...* (T&C 138:11)

It's almost poetry the way Joseph describes what he went through there, but it is poetry describing the actual bona fides of Joseph receiving answers from God.

God's most important inspiration for the most challenging subjects is often not hasty, quick, and without effort at our end. Consider the advice to Oliver Cowdery that he must *...study it out in [his] own mind* first, before asking God to tell him the answer (see JSH 13:26 RE). Many people want a quick, perfunctory response from God with no forethought. What they receive in turn is a quick, perfunctory answer. God is almost always, for the most difficult challenges, *not* a short-order cook, although there are certainly false spirits who are willing to be just that.

I asked God in October what the term "mutual agreement" as used in The Answer meant. Before I asked, I hesitated and pondered the issue for two months. I discussed it with my wife and several others, and then discussed again the views of others with my wife. I read emails from people involved in an active discussion about the meaning of the term.

It requires humility to approach God and ask Him for His answer, and yet *more* humility to know it is from Him and not my own ego, presumptions, hopes, desires, wants, and conceit. It is for me, as it was for Joseph, only *...when the heart is sufficiently contrite, then the voice of inspiration steals along and whispers* the truth (T&C 138:11). *That* comes from a purer source, higher than myself and more filled with light than any man—certainly greater light than I have.

When the definition was given, it was accompanied by the realization the Lord could have disputed every day of His life with someone. He *deliberately* chose to not contend. He was *not* an argumentative personality.

The more we contend with others, the more we are taken captive by the spirit of contention. We become subject to the spirit we submit to follow. Those who are prone to contention become more contentious as they listen to that spirit. Eventually they are overcome by that spirit, and it's a great work involving great effort to subdue and dismiss that spirit from the heart and mind of the victim.

Let me give you a description of the Prayer *for* the Covenant: It took months of pondering, testing, questioning beforehand before I even dared to ask. The idea that presented itself to my mind was that Joseph's prayer at the dedication of the Kirtland Temple was a pattern to be followed when some great event involving God was to take place. The House of the Lord was one such event in Kirtland, but having a new volume of scripture was at least equally important to that. Therefore, a prayer to God asking for His acceptance was an idea that continued to press upon my mind.

But it concerned me that the idea of my offering that prayer may be based on my own will, *and not heaven's*. Before proceeding, I questioned my motive, my desire, and why *I* would even ask. I was haunted by the continuing impression that it needed to be done and was required of me. Finally, when the idea could not be shaken from my mind, I determined it was not my own thought but God's beckoning voice telling me this was an obligation I needed to act upon and not suppress. I want you to think of Joseph's description that says:

> *Never did any passage of scripture come with more power to the heart of man than this did at this time to mine. It seemed to enter with great force into every feeling of …heart. I reflected on it again and again.* (Joseph Smith History 2:3 RE)

Joseph did not act hastily when the impression came to him! He couldn't shake it! It persisted. He reflected upon it *again and again*. I don't know whether that's days, weeks, or months, but I can tell you before the Prayer for the Covenant was offered, for me it was months—because if it isn't of God, I have no right to step forward and do something. I ought not be volunteering for things of that nature.

At length, I determined that I should act on the impulse, and therefore, I ought to offer a prayer for the acceptance of the scripture. When I began to compose the prayer, the content was provided by inspiration from heaven and not my own words. It took me nearly 200,000 words to write a history of the Restoration, from the time of Joseph to the present, in a book that's fairly lengthy. The Prayer for the Covenant, coming by inspiration, only took a few pages and stated in more concise terms, more correctly, the history of the Restoration from the beginning until now. The Prayer for the Covenant, the prayer for the scriptures, is not me being clever and insightful and succinct. The words were given, and the words are God's view of what has happened.

There are those who have claimed inspiration on very important matters who make decisions quickly. Almost as soon as they finish a prayer asking for something, they assume the first thing that pops into their mind is God's infallible answer. I do not doubt that *may* happen; it has happened to me. But for the most important things, I have found that careful, ponderous and solemn thought and meditation over time produces God's will and word, with clarity, that *does not* happen in haste.

Let's make some assumptions for purposes of what's going to be said. Let's assume that we are like ancient Israel. Let's assume that we too were left outside of God's presence when He offered to come and dwell generally among the saints back in Nauvoo.

Let's assume that this was not what God wanted for us. Let's assume that these things *have*, just like they did anciently, kindled God's anger like we read in D&C 84:24 (see T&C 82:13). Let's assume that we have now, as a body generally, been left with something lesser, which is like what was described in D&C 84, verse 26 (see T&C 82:14)—that is, only the lesser priesthood, which includes within it the ministering of angels.

Well, assuming all of that, what shall we do? Well, turn to Alma chapter 12—a great chapter, by the way. And since this is already taking longer than I had hoped, I'm going to insert in the transcript the verses in Alma chapter 12, between 9 and 11, that talks about "if you harden your hearts, you get less; but if your heart is soft and open, you get more" (Alma 12:9-11; see also Alma 9:3 RE).

You're the regulator that determines whether, on the one hand, you get more, or whether, on the other, you get less. And some of those who have come today with a hard heart are going to find themselves being condemned in the day of judgment, because you were given an opportunity to have a soft heart, and you elected knowingly not to do so.

Can you imagine your shame when you, in a council that includes those who are present today, come back from *this* experience and say, "Yes, I was there, but I didn't believe. Yes, I was there, but I wouldn't accept it." None of us would vote to sustain you—in the coming years, in the coming eons, in the coming experience—to be a minister to bring salvation to pass to others. None of us will have confidence in you. Soften your heart *now*. Today is the day of salvation. This is the moment you came down here to face. The test is on; the challenge is in front of you. You better have ears to hear. God will judge you; but more importantly, you will judge yourself.

Well, skipping then over verses 9 to 11, I'm going to go to… Beginning at verse 28:

> *And after God had appointed that these things should come unto man, behold, then he saw that it was expedient that man should* ***know*** *concerning the things whereof he had appointed unto* ***them***. (Alma 12:28; see also Alma 9:7 RE, emphasis added)

He *wants* us to know! The glory of God is intelligence, or in other words, light and truth, which is knowledge of things. He wants us to know these things.

> *Therefore* [because this is God's desire], *he sent angels to converse with them, who* [this is the angels] *caused men to behold...his* [God's] *glory.* (Ibid.)

So, the office of the angels is to educate and to prepare, and then to cause man who receive and entertain the angels to then behold the glory of God—the glory of God being intelligence, or in other words, light and truth.

Ultimately, the greatest truth *is* God Himself. And if you entertain angels and if the angels instruct you and if you have been in their presence, you acquire from them the strength, the fortification, the knowledge—or in other words, the ordination—by which you're able to go on and pass by them, because they surely are sentinels, and enter into the glory of the Lord.

And so, if you will give heed to the process, it really should not matter that you are left in a dispensation in which the only authority gives you the ministering of angels. Because the ministering of angels is sufficient to bring you into the glory of God—if you will receive them, if you will give heed to them. That's the office of *their* ministry; that's what *they're* responsible to do.

> *And they began from that time forth to call on his name; therefore* ***God conversed with them***. (Ibid., emphasis added)

It's part of the title to the first book I wrote: *Conversing with the Lord Through the Veil.* That's the object; that's what the 'lesser priesthood' *can* equip you to accomplish—left behind with nothing but a relic.

And what did Joseph say about all the prophets of the Old Testament? He said they *all* held Melchizedek Priesthood, and they were *all* ordained by God Himself—because they functioned inside a society that was defective, limited, excluded from the presence of God. But *not those who received and entertained angels*; they were brought up to where they need to be, and *God Himself* ordained them.

Should you not have hope? Should you not rise up above the level of those who are content to have less? Should you not be willing to mount up on that fiery mountain—*despite* the thunderings and lightnings, *despite* the earthquakes, *despite* the fact you do not believe yourself to be worthy? You're still capable of coming aboard.

Look at Moroni chapter 7, beginning at verse 29:

> *Because he hath done this, my beloved brethren, have miracles ceased? Behold I say unto you, Nay;* ***neither have angels ceased to minister unto the children of men****. For behold, they* [the angels] *are subject unto him, to minister according to the word of* ***his*** *command, showing themselves unto them of strong faith and a firm mind in every form of godliness. And the office of their ministry is to call men [to] repentance* [repentance], *...to fulfill and to do the work of the* ***covenants*** *of the Father... (*Moroni 7:29-31; see also Moroni 7:6 RE, emphasis added)

Because when you move *from* repentance, you move *into* covenants. Which is why we needed to speak about that in Centerville; which is why this process has been undergoing for the last year, unfolding *how you get back into the presence of God*—because it surely is necessary for there to be a rescue mission, and the rescue mission is designed to raise *you,* to elevate *you*, to redeem *you.*

> *...the work of the covenants of the Father, which he hath made unto the children of men, to prepare the way among the children of men, by declaring the word of Christ unto the chosen vessels of the Lord, that they may bear testimony of him. And by so doing, the Lord God prepareth the way that the residue of men may have faith in Christ, that the Holy Ghost may have place in* ***their*** *hearts, according to the power thereof; and after this manner bringeth to pass the Father, the* ***covenants*** *which he hath made unto the children of men.* (Moroni 7:31-32; see also Moroni 7:6 RE, emphasis added)

In a word, those who receive and entertain angels have an obligation then to declare the words—so that others might likewise have faith in Him. That word, having been declared unto you, gives you the hope, the faith, the confidence that you likewise can do so—so that the covenants that are made by the Father can be brought to pass.

Fortunately, fortunately, Aaronic Priesthood is *exceptionally* durable, fortunately—unlike Melchizedek Priesthood which can only be exercised with extraordinary care and delicacy. The purpose of Melchizedek Priesthood being (as I talked about in Orem) to bless; the purpose of Aaronic Priesthood being to condemn and to judge and to set a law by which men can condemn themselves. Having the authority to do *that* to yourself is remarkably durable and used with great regularity. And those that have it generally abide by so lesser a law that they wind up judging and condemning one another, and parading before God as a…as a march of fools yelling and yammering, pointing and blaming, complaining and bitching about what everyone else's inadequacies are.

The purpose of Melchizedek Priesthood is to sound the signal: *Know ye the Lord*. And eventually, *that* sermon will be heard by enough that there will be none left who need to be told, "Know ye the Lord," for they shall *all* know Him. And *everyone* will take up with *Him* their concerns, and not with one another (see T&C 158:15).

Go to Doctrine and Covenants section 93 and look at verse 1. I've treated this at some length in what I've written, but I just want to read it because it outlines what's required:

> *VERILY, thus saith the Lord: It shall come to pass that every soul who forsaketh his sins and cometh unto me, and calleth on my name, and obeyeth my voice, and keepeth my commandments, **shall** see my face and know* [**know**] *that I am.* (See also T&C 93:1, emphasis added)

Knowing the Lord!

> *This is life eternal to **know** thee, the only wise and true God and...Christ, whom thou hast sent.* (John 17:3; see also John 9:19 RE and TSJ 10:30 RE, emphasis added)

Knowledge—knowledge of the things of God—and in this context, this knowledge *is* salvation; this knowledge *is* the fullness of the Gospel.

Forsake your sins; come to Christ; call on His name; obey His voice; keep His commandments. "Obey His voice" in *your* instance may be very different than "obeying His voice" in my life, because your circumstances are entirely peculiar to you. You're living your life, and I'm living mine. You're asked to minister in *your* family, to minister in *your* neighborhood, to function among *your* friends, to deal with people that *you* know. And I, on the other hand, am required not only to do *that*, but also to come and talk to you good people which, whether you believe me sincere or not, I would much rather not have been asked to do—but apparently, in the economy of God, no one else is willing to do it.

Go to Ether chapter 3. I want to define what the promise of "knowing that I am…" And by the way, those are the words that He uses in section 93: *"know that **I am**."* You need to know "the I am." Verse 13 of Ether chapter 3:

> *And when he had said these words, behold, the Lord showed himself unto him, and said: Because thou **knowest** these things ye are **redeemed** from the fall* [there's the definition; that's what redemption is]*; therefore ye are brought back into my presence; therefore I show myself unto you. Behold, **I am** he who was prepared from the foundation of the world to redeem my people. Behold, **I am** Jesus Christ. **I am** the Father and the Son. In me shall all mankind have life, and that eternally, even they who shall believe on my name; and they shall become my sons and my daughters.* (Ether 3:13-14; see also Ether 1:13 RE, emphasis added)

This is the definition; this is what the promise means. And then, look what happens in verse 18:

> *And he ministered unto him even as he ministered unto the Nephites; and all this, that this man might **know** that he was God, because of the many great works which the Lord...showed unto him.* (Ether 3:18; see also Ether 1:14 RE, emphasis added)

This is the definition of the glory of God. This is the definition of light and truth: to know these things, to know these things about God.

> *And because of the knowledge of this man he could not be kept from beholding within the veil; and he saw the finger of Jesus, which, when he saw, he fell with fear; for he knew that it was the finger of the Lord; and he had **faith no longer**, for he knew, nothing doubting.* (Ether 3:19; see also Ether 1:14 RE, emphasis added)

He had faith yet in things he was commanded to do because they had not yet happened, but he no longer had faith in the existence of Christ—that had been replaced by knowledge of Him. Knowledge supplants faith.

We looked at John's testimony in Doctrine and Covenants section 93, and we need to look at that again just to remind you because this is an important reminder before we get to the next point. Between section 93, verse 7 and verse 20, he describes the process by which Christ was called to be the Son of God. I want to skip to verse 12:

> *I, John, saw that he received not...the fulness at the first, but received **grace for grace**; And he received not...the fulness at first, but continued from **grace to grace**, until he received a fulness; And thus he was **called** the Son of God, because he received not...the fulness at...first.*
>
> *And I, John, bear record, and lo, the heavens were opened, and the Holy Ghost descended upon him in the form of a dove, ...sat upon him, and there came a voice out of heaven saying: This is my beloved Son.*
>
> *And I, John, bear record that he received a fulness of the glory of the Father; ...he received all power, both in heaven and on earth, and the glory of the Father was with him, for he **dwelt** in him.*
>
> *And it shall come to pass, that if you are faithful you shall receive the fulness of the record of John. I give unto you these sayings that you may understand and know **how** to worship, and [to] know **what** you worship, that you may come unto the Father in my name, and in due time receive of his fulness. For if you keep my commandments you shall receive of his fulness, and be glorified in me as I am in the Father; therefore, I say unto you, [that] you shall receive grace for grace.* (D&C 93:12-20; see also T&C 93:4-7, emphasis added)

That's what *you do to worship!* That is *how* you are to worship! We grow in grace as we exhibit the grace that has been given unto us. And we do so in order for *us* to obtain, likewise, the fullness.

Everything I have said so far bears only upon the temple, and that's the purpose of getting here—is to discuss about what the temple's purpose is, what it means, and what it's trying to convey to us.

Is the temple an end or is the temple a means? If the temple is an end, *then* everyone who goes through the temple obtains everything the temple has to offer by virtue of going in and participating in the ceremony. Even more so, those who have conspired to break their temple covenants, and gone in and recorded the temple ceremonies and then transcribed those ceremonies and put them on the internet, have made it possible for everyone who goes to the trouble of finding and reading the temple ceremony that's now available on the internet. If the temple ceremony is an end, then all of those people are the beneficiaries of it as well.

But if the temple ceremony is instead a means, a means of trying to take you somewhere, then it doesn't matter *who* sees the ordinance. You can't steal the ends. You can't come in by some unauthorized way and attain the end because that is a matter that exists between you and God.

If it is a means, then what is it a means to? Because one possible meaning that you should come away with is that it is a means to inform you that there is a veil, and not a wall, to permit you to talk through and to touch through and to feel your way through to the symbolic presence of God. And then, that veil is not a wall but something that can be, with merely the brush of the hand of our Lord, drawn aside so that you may enter into His presence.

And the way you get there is by being prepared in all things, having been true and faithful in all things, coming to learn something from Him—not coming to tell Him something, not coming to impose upon Him, but coming to learn from Him. Our Savior was and is, first and foremost, a teacher. By *His* knowledge... Isaiah and Nephi wrote, He shall justify many by His knowledge (see Isaiah 19:3 RE, Mosiah 8:5 RE, T&C 161:24). He possesses things which we do not yet comprehend. He possesses things which He would like us *to* comprehend. How then are we to comprehend the things which *only* He can teach? By permitting Him to do so by coming to Him.

In the ceremony, there is an account given of the man Adam. And I have a question for you: *Who* in the ceremony is Adam? Is this a history lesson about the first man who lived on the earth, or is this instead a symbolic rendering of the lives of every man, or is it instead *your* life? Are *you* being told that in the beginning you came here in an innocent, even a paradisiacal state? And in that state, everything was possible to the innocent mind. I mean, *we* impose as adults upon the credulity of our children by teaching them about the Easter bunny, and then to pull off the fraud, we have to go the trouble every Easter of acting the role of the Easter bunny, always out of sight. And we impose upon them Santa Clause, and they believe in these things.

That faith and that trust that those children have comes as a consequence of where every one of you began: in a state of innocence, in a state of purity, in a state in which it is possible for *that* mind to comprehend and to accept the things of God. But there comes a point when you become accountable; there comes a point when you grow out of that and you are expelled from that innocence. And then, in order to return there, you have to make certain sacrifices, and you have to be willing to obey, and you have to be willing to pursue the Gospel.

And at length—because there is a difference between the age of 8 (when you begin to become accountable) and puberty—at length, the range of temptation that will confront you will require you then to engage and obey the law of chastity. And then as you grow into adulthood, when you realize that this world really has very little to offer, you learn that the way to happiness does not consist in popularity or wealth or acclaim. It lies exclusively in consecrating yourself to the things of God—and when you have developed through that course and you have come to the recognition that consecrating yourself is the only thing of value.

In the ceremony, it only takes some two hours before you are called "true and faithful in all things." Well, if that's an end and not a means, then in 2½ hours in sitting and occasionally standing and agreeing to some things, you have become "true and faithful in all things."

I would suggest that the temple rite as an end makes *that* notion preposterous because you're the same person walking out of the temple as you were walking into it two hours earlier. You're no more faithful in the temptations that you face on the street; you're no more lovely in the way that you deal with your family; you're no more honest in your business dealings with your fellow man than you were two hours earlier when you walked in, but the ceremony is saying that you've been "true and faithful in all things."

I would suggest that's a means, and it's an admonition, and it's an invitation —even begging you—to recognize that the challenge you face in your life requires you, invariably, to lay aside those things that pull you away and that you always turn and face the Lord. *That's what repentance means.* It means to turn and face the Lord. And you know, when you face Him the first time, you're just not going to be that good or that different than you were the moment before. But if you'll face Him, *He'll work with you.*

It does not matter how badly damaged you are; that's irrelevant. He fixed the Apostle Paul. If you don't think the Apostle Paul suffered from pride, then you don't understand the malignancy of pride. He fixed Alma the Younger and the sons of Mosiah, whose *deliberate* purpose was to overthrow the things of God. I don't care what you've done—the malignancies of those men are highlighted in scripture in order to assure that you can all be reclaimed.

Turn and face Him, and then walk with Him. He does all the guiding and most of the heavy lifting. Well, when it comes to the idea of being true and faithful.... By the way, I don't care if you buy a quad, your scriptures aren't complete until you get the Lectures on Faith. They were voted in and sustained as scripture, and then they were removed without a vote. In the Lectures on Faith—this is 7th lecture; this is 16th verse—talking about the Savior:

> *These teachings of the Savior most clearly show unto us the nature of salvation; and what he proposed unto the human family when he proposed to save them -- That he proposed to make them **like unto himself;** and he was **like the Father**, the **great prototype** of all saved beings: And for any portion of the human family to be assimilated into their likeness is to be saved; and to be unlike them is to be destroyed: and on this hinge turns the door of salvation.* (Lectures on Faith 7:16, emphasis added.)

Jesus Christ *is* the prototype of all saved beings. So, *what was* our Savior—if He's the prototype? He was a blasphemer! He was a sinner! He worked on the Sabbath, and He encouraged his disciples to do so! He associated with the tax collectors and with the publicans and sinners and the harlots, and He let harlots tooooouuuuch Him! This is the prototype of the *Saved* Man. This is the One who was rejected by His people. This is the One who was called *unclean.* This is the One who was rejected, persecuted, and ultimately killed by those who held religious rank and authority in His day. This is the prototype of the Saved Man. This is the example of Joseph Smith; this is Isaiah and Jeremiah.

Was Christ true and faithful in all things? If so, to what, to whom was He true and faithful? Was it the law? I mean, He never spoke ill against the law. The Sermon on the Mount is simply taking the law and showing what it really meant; He took it to another level. If he took it to the level in which *He* took it, Caiaphas would not have been sitting there in the robes of the priesthood —which by that time had been elevated to the status of wealth itself. If you had merely the attire that Caiaphas had on during the trial of Christ, just his attire, you would have been a wealthy man.

The Lectures on Faith; this is Lecture 6:

> *A religion that does not require the sacrifice of all things, never has power sufficient to produce the faith necessary unto life and salvation; for from the first existence of man, the faith necessary unto the enjoyment of life and salvation never could be obtained without the sacrifice of **all*** **[all]** *earthly things.* (Lectures on Faith 6:7, emphasis added)

It's through the medium of the sacrifice of *all* earthly things that men do actually know that they are doing things that are well-pleasing in the sight of God. And then we get to this, verse 8:

> *It is...vain for persons to fancy to themselves that they are heirs with those, or can be heirs with them, who* ***have*** *offered their all in sacrifice, and by this means obtained faith in God and favor with him so as to obtain eternal life, unless* ***they,*** *in like manner, offer unto him the same sacrifice, and through that offering obtain the* ***knowledge*** *that they are accepted of him.* (Lectures on Faith 6:8, emphasis added)

What did the prototype of the Saved Man offer in sacrifice? I mean, we jump to the end of the story, and we point to Gethsemane, and we point to the cross, and we say, "There it is—His life." But He was a living sacrifice for many more years than the week that was spent coming in, confronting them in the temple, celebrating and implementing the sacrament, going into Gethsemane and suffering, being tried and crucified, being laid in a grave, and three days and three nights later arising from the grave. He spent some 30+ years prior to that as the prototype of the Saved Man.

In the ceremony, you come asking for "further light and knowledge from the Lord." And when you enter into the Lord's presence in the ceremony, it hints at something which the scriptures themselves make plain. In John chapter 14, verse 18, the Savior said, *I will not leave you comfortless,* ***I*** *will come to you.* And in verse 23: *If a man love me, he will keep my words: and my Father will love him, and* ***we*** *will come unto him and make* ***our abode*** *with him* (see also John 9:8 RE and TSJ 10:11,13 RE, emphasis added).

Well, that promise in the 23rd verse suggests something beyond the Lord simply coming and visiting with someone. The notion that the Father *and* the Son will take up their abode... I mean, we have that hymn, and that hymn creates a picture: "Abide with Me; 'Tis Eventide." So, abiding means you come and you spend the evening, and there we have taken care of the abode. But the suggestion here is that there is a greater kind of familiarity that attaches to the relationship that is more enduring.

In Revelation chapter 3, verses 20 and 21, there is a promise that John records. Well, [verse] 20 is where He stands at the door and knocks:

> *Behold, I stand at the door and knock...*

You see, in this description it's almost a flip. It's not *you* knocking to get in; it's the Lord knocking to come to *you.* It's the Lord who is the eager One—the

One who would like to have this relationship take up. He's the One knocking. He's the One trying to get into your life. And so, in this account the Lord is speaking:

> *I stand at the door and knock. If any man hear my voice...*

See, His sheep hear his voice. Do you hear His voice?

> *If any man hear my voice and open the door...*

Because you're the one that shut it. You're the one that's saying, "Uh, no thanks; I'll pass. I mean, I've got a skeptical mind now. I've been to college and have received training to practice law. I'm an engineer, and I understand formulas and equations. I'm a mathematician, and I know some things add up and some things don't. And I also know that I've been leading a reasonably decent life, and I've never had Jesus in *my* car."

Our minds are skeptical. *We* have to open the door, because almost invariably the door that *we configure to keep Him out*, from *our* construct, is something that has come about as a consequence of what has happened in *your* life—from the time you left that state of innocence as a child in the Garden until today—every painful experience you've been through, every humiliation you've suffered, everything that has gone on in your life that has led to where you *now* construct a door—some of oak, some of iron. Whatever it is that has happened to you, you use *that* to keep Him out. "Well, if He really cared, He would...."

You know, the *notion* that He doesn't care is the greatest lie of all. If you knew what He suffered, you would *never* say, "If He cared...." But if you will open the door, He says,

> *I will come in to him and will* ***sup*** *with him, and he with me.* (Revelation 3:20; see also Revelation 1:20 RE, emphasis added)

The foregoing excerpts are taken from:

- Denver's blog post titled "Don't Overthink Things," originally posted August 29, 2010, and subsequently recorded on February 16, 2021;
- A fireside talk titled "That We Might Become One," given in Clinton, Utah, on January 14th, 2018;

- Denver's *40 Years in Mormonism Series,* Talk #8 titled "A Broken Heart," given in Las Vegas, Nevada, on July 25th, 2014; and
- Denver's fireside talk on "The Temple," given in Ogden, Utah, on October 28th, 2012.

138. Government of God, Part 1

This is the first part of a special series where Denver discusses what it is that makes God who and what God is, what that has to do with godliness, and the power thereof, and how God governs on Earth as it is in Heaven.

———

DENVER: The first lecture on faith is essentially asserting the primacy of faith as an operative principle of power that exists with God and with all of us. 'K, you've left home, and you've come here. While you're here, your home exists only as a matter of faith to you. You believe it exists; you intend to drive back there. And your family that's there and your dog that's there and that infernal parrot that now can mimic the low battery signal on the fire alarm—she's there, too. And so, it's a matter of faith that, despite the fact that I am here and out of her presence, my bird is waiting for me when I get home.

You act as if these things that you no longer see… See, in the development of a child, what you find in really young children is that they don't have the capacity to entertain the fact that it still exists. When it's gone, it's gone forever. And the child… It takes a while before the child has confidence that what gets removed from their sight continues to exist outside of the presence of their actual observation. It's one of those childhood development things.

Well, God's beyond that. Everything that exists... *Faith, and faith only* (and I'm using a compilation that was published—I don't know; it's from the Brigham Young University archive. I just printed it out. In mine it's verse 11. Excuse me, it's verse 10 of Lecture 1)...

> *It is faith, and faith only, which is the moving cause of all action in them* [that is, in all men, but it's also the principle by which everything is moved into action. Verse 12]: *Faith is the moving cause of all action in temporal concerns, so it is in spiritual; for the Saviour has said, that truly, that He that believeth and is baptized shall be saved. Through faith* [in verse 14]— *Through faith we understand that the worlds were framed by the word of God, so that things which are seen were not made of things which do appear. All things in heaven* [in verse 15] *[or] earth, or under...earth, exist by reason of faith as it existed in Him* [*Him* being God—17]: *Who cannot see, that if God framed the worlds by faith, that it is by faith that he exercises power over them, and that faith is the principle of power? And if the principle of power, it must be so in man as well as in the Deity? This is the testimony of*

> *all the sacred writers and the [lessons] which they have…[endeavored] to teach to man.* (Lectures on Faith 1:10, 12, 14-15, 17 RE)

Your acting, everything that you're doing, the education that you got, the employment that you have, the plans that you undertake, the things that you design to do are all a product of your faith. You are a being filled with, animated by, and continually upholding everything in your life by your faith. And yet, you don't have the faith to see it. You are a creature of faith. All of you are. And you always have been, and you always will be. Do not be doubtful, but be believing. You are here by reason of God's faith. And you have faith to do the things that you do continually. Every movement you undertake, every plan you make is based upon the faith that you have.

Well, we don't have time to pause on the first one because I'm hoping to get far enough along in this process... But I'd like you to value the Lectures on Faith. I'd like you to study the Lectures on Faith. I'd like you to take a lot more time with them than we're gonna to have the time to take tonight.

Let's skip to the second lecture. This is the second verse:

> *We here observe that God is the only supreme governor and independent being in whom all fullness and perfection dwell; who is omnipotent, omnipresent, ...omniscient; without beginning of days or end of life; and that in him every good gift and every good principle dwell; ...that he is the Father of lights; in him the principle of faith dwells independently, ...he is the object in whom the faith of all other rational and accountable beings center for life and salvation.* (Lectures on Faith 2:2 RE)

Did you get that?! It's not me; it's not your bishop; it's not Hugh Nibley; it's not your stake president; it's not the Catholic priest down the street, the pope in Rome, or the president of the Church in Salt Lake. It's no man! The principle of faith must be grounded in God, the Supreme Governor—because if your faith is grounded in anyone or anything else, you cannot have the faith necessary to attain to salvation. All of these lectures are concerned with your salvation.

Look at verse 12. And it's been a discussion of what went on at the beginning —man in the Garden of Eden, God talking to him. Verse 12:

> *From the foregoing we learn man's situation at his first creation, the knowledge [of] which he was endowed, and the high and exalted station in which he was placed—lord, or governor, of all things on [the] earth, and at*

> *the same time enjoying communion and intercourse with his Maker, without a veil to separate between.* (Ibid. vs. 12 RE)

That's where man began. And that's why knowledge of God existed in the first place—because in the beginning, God talked to man. And if you think, Well, yeah, that was then. What about now? We'll get to now. Verse 18, about halfway down:

> *God conversed with him face to face. In his presence he was permitted to stand, and from his own mouth he was permitted to receive instruction. He heard his voice, walked before him...gazed upon his glory, while intelligence burst upon his understanding, and enabled him to give names to the vast assemblage of his Maker's works.* (Ibid. vs. 18 RE)

This was man's original condition, a condition to which the gospel is designed to return man. And, in fact, at the Second Coming, all who remain will be in that condition once again. The earth is going to be renewed and receive its paradisiacal glory, and it's gonna to do so because God will come and dwell here again. And man will be able to converse...Him.

The plan of salvation is the plan of education, the plan of knowledge about God and the principles of godliness and the basis upon which all of you can live together and be of one heart and one mind.

Joseph was sentenced to die on November 1st of 1838. The general who was supposed to carry out the execution rebelled, wouldn't do that. Joseph ultimately wound up being kept in prison in Liberty Jail. While he's in Liberty Jail, he writes a letter. We've taken out three excerpts from the letter, and we've canonized them; and section 121 is one of those three sections. I want you to look at verse 45. Ask yourself whether this has something to do, also, with the power of godliness:

> *Let thy bowels also be full of charity towards all men, and to the household of faith, and let virtue garnish thy thoughts unceasingly; then shall thy confidence wax strong in the presence of God; and the doctrine of the priesthood shall distil upon thy soul as the dews from heaven. The Holy Ghost shall be thy constant companion, and thy scepter an unchanging scepter of righteousness and truth; and thy dominion shall be an everlasting dominion, and without compulsory means it shall flow unto thee forever and ever.* (D&C 121:45-46; see also T&C 139:6 RE)

Oh, that I had the ability to declare it. This is in the middle of one of the three great principles by which God governs and shapes the universe itself. It is not through compulsory means. The only way in which God works is by inviting and enticing.

Joseph Smith said: "I advise all to go on to perfection and search deeper and deeper into the mysteries of godliness." (*TPJS*, p. 364)

Turn to Doctrine and Covenants section 8. *Ask that you may know the mysteries of God* (D&C 8:11; see also T&C 3:3 RE). That's a commandment. I declare to you in the words of Scripture: *Ask that* ***you*** *may know the mysteries of God!* That's a commandment given to us by revelation, enshrined in the Scriptures that you folks claim to believe in.

The mysteries of God largely consist in developing the attributes of godliness in us. The things that matter the most are the things that make us more like Him—better people, more kindly. You want to know more of the mysteries of God, serve your fellow man and be of more value to them. In the process of blessing the lives of others, you find out that you know more of the character of God as a consequence of that.

I would suggest that if law governs all blessings, and it does, the statement isn't just *some*; the statement is *all*. We probably ought to read it. *There is a law, irrevocably decreed in heaven before the foundations of [the] world, upon which all blessings are predicated— And when we obtain any blessing from God, it is by obedience to that law upon which it is predicated* (D&C 130:20-21).

Don't be cowards. Stand and be valiant no matter what it is. In the day of judgment, you will find yourself wanting. And in this life, you will find you lack the power of godliness unless you obey the law upon which all blessings are predicated.

"Which should I join?" Verse 19:

> *I was answered that I must join none of them, for they were all wrong; and the Personage who addressed me said that all their creeds were an abomination in his sight; that those professors were all corrupt; that: "They draw near to me with their lips, but their hearts are far from me, they teach for doctrines the commandments of men, having a form of godliness, but they deny the power thereof."* (JSH 1:19; see also JSH 2:5 RE)

What do you suppose it means, having a *form* of godliness, *denying* the power? How do you deny the power of godliness? How do you obtain the power of godliness? What does it mean to have possession of the power of godliness?

Let's go back to that section 76 again. It's got some nice stuff in it. I want to go to the very end because we're gonna run into this same notion in the First Vision and in section 76. And 76 is a transcript that is given to Joseph that was dictated, transcribed, read back, approved. Then, the dictation continued until they reached the end. But look at beginning at verse 113:

> *This is the end of the vision which we saw, which we were commanded to write while we were yet in the Spirit. But great and marvelous are the works of the Lord, and the mysteries of his kingdom which he showed unto us, which surpass all understanding in glory, and in might, and in dominion; Which he commanded us we should not write while we were yet in the Spirit, and are not lawful for man to utter; Neither is man capable to make them known, for they are only to be seen and understood by the power of the Holy Ghost, which God bestows on those who love him, and purify themselves before him; To whom he grants this privilege of seeing and knowing for themselves; That through the power and manifestation of the Spirit,* ***while in the flesh****, they may be able to bear his presence in the world of glory.* (D&C 76:113-118; see also T&C 69:28-29 RE, emphasis added)

Is this related to not denying the power of godliness? I mean, to have the ability to bear His presence in the world of glory (as we get farther along in our discussion about the topic of Zion), it becomes critical that you become able to bear His presence. For those who are unable to bear His presence will be destroyed at His coming. Therefore, whatever this power of godliness is, I think we need to get some.

No matter who you are, you are only doing one thing at a time your entire life. You are either focusing on one thing or on something else. And whatever it is upon which you dwell, that's what you've chosen; hence, the saying: *Let virtue garnish thy thoughts unceasingly; then shall thy confidence wax strong in the presence of God* (D&C 121:45; see also T&C 139:6 RE). Is the power of godliness related to that? Is the power of godliness related to the presence of God? Well, the Book of Mormon continually declares that to be the case.

In order for you to exercise faith, you must have a correct idea of God's character, perfections, and attributes. You've got to have that. And if you don't have that, then you are missing something that prevents you from having the right kind of faith. Okay, so Lecture Fifth, verse 1:

> *We shall, in this lecture, speak of the Godhead—we mean the Father, Son, and Holy Spirit. There are two personages who constitute the great, matchless, governing, and supreme power over all things—by whom all things were*

> *created and made, [and] that are created and made, whether visible or invisible, whether in heaven, on earth, or in the earth, under the earth, or throughout the immensity of space—They are the Father and the Son: the Father being a personage of spirit, glory, and power, possessing all perfection and fullness. The Son, who was in the bosom of the Father, a personage of tabernacle, made or fashioned like unto man…* (Lectures on Faith 5:1-2 RE)

And then, you go down to the bottom of that verse:

> *He being the Only Begotten of the Father, full of grace and truth, ...having overcome, received a fullness of...glory of the Father—possessing the same mind with the Father, which mind is the Holy Spirit, that bears record of the Father and the Son; and, these three are one; or, in other words, these three constitute the great, matchless, governing and supreme power over all things; by whom all things were created and made that were created and made; and, these three constitute the Godhead and are one; the Father and the Son possessing the same mind, the same wisdom, glory, power, and fullness, filling all in all; the Son being filled with the fullness of the mind, glory, and power; or, in other words, the spirit, glory, and power of the Father—possessing all knowledge and glory and the same kingdom, sitting [on] the right hand of power, in the express image and likeness of the Father…* (Ibid. vs. 2 RE)

And it goes on to say: *The Spirit of the Father, which Spirit is shed forth upon all who believe [in] his name...keep his commandments....all those who keep his commandments shall grow...from grace to grace…[possess] the same mind…* (Ibid. RE) and so on.

The keystone of our religion gives examples of how faith in God does not require any comprehension of the corporeal existence or physical dimensions of God. The understanding of the brother of Jared before he saw God was decidedly limited. Despite this, he was redeemed from the fall by returning to God's presence where he gained greater knowledge of God. Beforehand, he did not understand Christ had a finger, nor did he understand he would one day take upon Himself a mortal body:

> *And the veil was taken from off the eyes of the brother of Jared, and he saw the finger of the Lord; and it was…the finger of a man, like unto flesh and blood. And the brother of Jared fell down before the Lord, for he was struck with fear. And the Lord saw that the brother of Jared had fallen to the earth, and the Lord said unto him, Arise. Why hast thou fallen?* [It's hard to talk to people when they're laying on their face. It's annoying.] *And he [said to]*

> *the Lord, I saw the finger of the Lord, and I feared lest he should smite me, for I knew not that the Lord had flesh and blood.* [See, if I see someone who is big and powerful, and I get a look at his hand, the usual thing that the big man does is slap me with that same damn hand because that's what big, big chiefs do.] *I feared lest he should smite me, for I knew not...the Lord had flesh and blood.* (Ether 3:6-8; see also Ether 1:12 RE)

I knew not. I knew not. This is the guy that has faith sufficient to get through the veil to be in the presence of Christ. I knew not this. But he understood the character, attributes, and perfections. He could have faith.

And the Lord said unto him, Because of thy faith, thou hast seen that I shall take upon me flesh and blood (Ibid. vs. 9; Ibid. RE).

When Ammon was teaching King Lamoni, the instruction began by only acknowledging that God was a *Great Spirit.*

> *Believest thou that there is a God? And he answered unto him, I do not know what that meaneth.... then Ammon said, Believest thou... there is a Great Spirit? And he said, Yea. And Ammon said, This is God. And Ammon said unto him again, Believest thou that this Great Spirit, who is God, created all things which are in Heaven and in... earth? And he said, Yea, I believe... he created all things which are in the earth, but I do not know the Heavens. And Ammon said unto him, The Heavens are a place where God dwells and all his holy angels.* (Alma 18:24-30; see also Alma 12:15 RE)

This man would have the veil taken, and he would be caught up into a heavenly vision with that foundation because that was enough of the character, attributes, and perfections of God to allow him to pass through the veil.

When Aaron taught King Lamoni's father, he likewise described God vaguely as that Great Spirit:

> *Behold, assuredly as thou livest, O king, there is a God. And the king said, Is God that Great Spirit that brought our fathers out of the land of Jerusalem? And Aaron said unto him, Yea, he is that great Spirit,... he created all things both in Heaven and in... earth. Believest thou this? And he said, Yea, I believe that... Great Spirit created all things, and I desire that ye should tell me concerning all these things, and I will believe thy words.* (Alma 22:8-11; see also Alma 13:8 RE)

That's it.

These examples demonstrate that understanding there is both a Father and a Mother who jointly comprise a single Heavenly Father is not essential for mankind to be able to have saving faith in God. Knowing the character, perfections, and attributes does not extend to these particulars. To be like Them is to be patient, faithful, obedient, loving, charitable, and pure. These are the important characters, perfections, and attributes of godliness.

Their character, perfections, and attributes are: mercy, righteousness, love, compassion, and truthfulness. They are without partiality, no respecter of persons, regarding all alike. They make the sun to shine and the rain to fall on both the righteous and the wicked. They regard wickedness as an abomination. They prize truth, meekness, and peacemakers. They abhor the froward, prideful, evil, and arrogant. They are full of grace and truth and are more intelligent than us all. They are the Creators and will be the final judges of this cycle of existence, and no one will be permitted to progress further without Their permission. There is nothing vile or perverse about Them. They are repelled by contention and seek for us all to associate with one another equally as brothers and sisters. They are *perfect* in the sense of having completed the journey to the end of the path and entered into eternal lives and exaltation. They now seek to guide Their children along the same path.

The defect does not consist in the absence of faith in the Lord. The defect consists in the arrogance and hardness of the heart that prevents you from crying out in the realistic and anguish of your heart, looking to God who is trying to bring you to Him. That *depths of humility*, that status of being someone who is utterly harmless, that condition in which you present no threat to the righteous—you are harmless as a dove; you seek only the betterment of others— That is who God is and what you must become in order for God to be able to redeem you to be like Him. That's you voluntarily changing to be that person by your submission to Him—because there is no reason to give to the proud, the vain, and the warlike the ability to torment and to afflict others. There is every reason to give to someone who would ultimately be willing to give the rain to fall on the righteous and the wicked and make the sun to shine on both the righteous and the wicked the power of God because the power of godliness consists in this kind of a heart. And in this kind of a heart, God can accomplish anything.

The foregoing excerpts are taken from:

- Denver's *40 Years in Mormonism Series*, Talk #2 titled "Faith" given in Idaho Falls, Idaho on September 28, 2013;
- Denver's *40 Years in Mormonism Series*, Talk #1 titled "Be of Good Cheer" given in Boise, Idaho on September 10, 2013;
- Denver's remarks titled "Book of Mormon as Covenant" given at the Book of Mormon Covenant Conference in Columbia, South Carolina on January 13, 2019;
- Denver's talk titled "Christ's Discourse on the Road to Emmaus," given in Fairview, Utah on April 14, 2007;
- Denver's conference talk titled "Our Divine Parents" given in Gilbert, Arizona on March 25, 2018; and
- Denver's *40 Years in Mormonism Series*, Talk #8 titled "A Broken Heart" given in Las Vegas, Nevada on July 25, 2014.

139. Government of God, Part 2

This is the second part of a special series where Denver discusses what it is that makes God who and what God is, what that has to do with godliness, and the power thereof, and how God governs on Earth as it is in Heaven.

———

DENVER: It is our relationship to and our connection with God that matters. And you form that not through me or through some other man and not through the groups to which you belong. The groups to which you belong are a place to render service. They are a place where you can sacrifice to help others. And I don't care if that group is Methodist, Presbyterian, Latter-day Saint, or one of the fellowships that have been organized. That is of little consequence. You can be a Christian soul wherever you are, serving whoever you happen to be in contact with.

I'm going to talk about Zion, and Zion is going to be gathered. But the gathering of that group will not necessarily come exclusively from any party, group, denomination, or lineage.

Zion will be God's work, and in the end, it will be His and His alone. He will own it; He will bring it; He will be the author of it; and He is the one who says that He will take credit for it. When it happens, however, it will conform to a pattern.

This is a verse that gets attributed to Enoch who is, in turn, quoting a prophecy that was given by Adam. And so, this is the original prophecy given at the beginning of the world through Father Adam who established, in the beginning, the covenant that God Himself intends to vindicate:

Now this same priesthood, which was in the beginning, shall...in the end of the world [be] also—shall be in the end of the world also [I moved the *be*]. (Moses 6:7; see also Genesis 3:14 RE)

Well, that authority gets explained a little more fully when Abraham sought for the blessing that began in the beginning. He describes what it was that he wanted:

> *I sought for the blessings of the fathers, and the right whereunto I should be ordained to administer the same; having been myself a follower of righteousness, desiring also to be one who possessed great knowledge, and to be a greater follower of righteousness, and to possess a greater knowledge, and to*

> *be a father of many nations, a prince of peace, and desiring to receive instructions, and to keep...commandments of God, I became a rightful heir, a High Priest, holding the right belonging to the fathers. It was conferred upon me from the fathers; it came down from the fathers, from the beginning of time, yea, even from the beginning, or before the foundation of the earth, down to the present time, even the right of the firstborn, or the first man, who is Adam, or [the] first father, through the fathers unto me.* (Abraham. 1:2-3; see also Abraham 1:1 RE)

There are some very bright, well-studied Latter-day Saints who think they know what the gospel and priesthood of Abraham was.

I'm here today to declare to you the truth whether you accept it or not, whether you understand it or not, whether you think you can parse the Scriptures otherwise or not. I'm telling you what the truth is today. Abraham sought for the right that came down through the Fathers from Adam which was the right of the firstborn, which is that priesthood that must be restored in order to bring about the purposes of God in the last days. Abraham chapter 2, verse 11, the Lord says that through him:

> *I will bless them that bless thee, and curse them that curse thee; and in thee (that is, in thy Priesthood) and in thy seed (that is, thy Priesthood), for I give unto thee a promise that this right shall continue in thee, and in thy seed after thee (that is to say, the literal seed, or the seed of the body) shall all the families of the earth be blessed, even with the blessings of the Gospel.* (Abraham 2:11; see also Abraham 3:1 RE)

Abraham's Fatherhood reckons from priesthood. Although the right will continue through the literal seed, it reckons through priesthood. He sought for the right to be one of the Fathers.

We're talking about a time in the last days prophesied and repeated by Jacob as his testimony in the Book of Mormon when the natural fruit is going to reappear upon the Earth. Natural fruit is always genealogical; it is always familial.

There is going to come a time in the last days when the Family of God will return again to the Earth. That *same priesthood* includes a function that is not well understood. Abraham knew what this was when he said he desired to be a *father of many nations*. He's identifying one of the attributes and one of the roles that necessarily must return.

If you go to Moses chapter 5, there is an incident that takes place in which Mother Eve celebrated because after the apostasy of son after son after son, she rejoiced because... Well, I'll read it to you. This is Moses 5:16:

> *And Adam and Eve, his wife, ceased not to call upon God. And Adam knew Eve his wife, and she conceived and bare Cain, and said* [Now, this is her; she conceived, she bare Cain, and she said concerning this son]: *I have gotten a man from the Lord; wherefore he may not reject his words. But behold, Cain hearkened not, saying: Who is the Lord that I should know him?* (Moses 5:16; see also Genesis 3:5-6 RE)

That is to say, Mother Eve looked at Cain in contrast to those that had rejected the gospel message that had been born by her previously. And Cain, apparently an answer to her supplication to the Lord, came as what she anticipated would be the son upon whom the birthright would be conferred, the one through whom the lineage would continue, the one through whom the government of God would continue upon the Earth, the replacement for Adam. But Cain, when he arrived at the age of accountability and beyond,

> *...hearkened not, saying: Who is the Lord that I should know him?*
>
> *And she again conceived and bare his brother Abel. And Abel hearkened unto the voice of the Lord. And Abel was a keeper of [the] sheep, but Cain was a tiller of the ground.* (Moses 5:17; see also Genesis 3:6 RE)

Now mind you, there is no attempt to set out the chronology here other than by milestones. But Cain had determined to reject the Lord and not hearken to Him by the time the replacement, Abel, was born. And when Cain (who thought it his birthright) found that he could be displaced by his younger brother, as an act of overthrowing the government of God, Cain slew Abel in order to prevent the birthright, in order to prevent the promised Messiah, in order to prevent the work of God progressing through any lineage other than his own. This was an act of treason. This was an act of overthrowing the government of God. This was an attempt to force God to place the Messiah that should redeem all mankind into a position inferior to Cain, his father.

But God replaced the slain Abel with Seth. And Seth was the one through whom, then, the promise would be realized.

As you go through the account in Moses chapter 6 at 10 and 11— *Adam lived one hundred and thirty years, and begat a son in his own likeness, after his own image, and called his name Seth* (Moses 6:10: see also Genesis 3:15 RE).

So, *in his own likeness, after his own image* (when Adam was created in God's own likeness after God's own image) makes Seth, like Adam, a godly man.

> *And the days of Adam, after he had begotten Seth, were eight hundred years, and he* (that is, Seth) *begat many sons and daughters.* (Ibid. vs. 11; Ibid. RE)

And there's no indication that any of them were as rebellious as were the descendants of Cain. He begat many sons and daughters. And yet, in the next verses there is only one son who is identified.

> *Seth lived one hundred and five years, and begat Enos, and prophesied in all his days, and taught his son Enos in the ways of God; wherefore Enos prophesied also* (Moses 6:13; see also Genesis 3:16 RE).

So, although there are many sons and many daughters, there is only one name. And you can follow it through. Seth, *many sons,* all of whom are unnamed other than one—and that one that is named is Enos. Enos has *many sons,* all of whom are unnamed other than one, Cainan. And Cainan has *many sons,* all of whom are unnamed other than one. The one that's named is Mahalaleel. And although all of his predecessors had had *many sons,* Mahalaleel had *sons.* (So, the fertility rate is collapsing as we get closer to the flood.) There is only one named son of Mahalaleel, and that is Jared. And there is only one named son out of all the sons of Jared, and that is Enoch. And there is only one named son out of all of the sons of Enoch, and that's Methuselah.

This is not a genealogy. This is a description of the government of God as it descended down through each generation so that upon the death of one, you then knew who stood next in line in order to be *the father of all, the father of many nations,* the role that is occupied by the head of the human family. Okay? It is a priesthood line in which only one in each generation stands at the head as the Father.

This one stands as the Father of all and hence, Abraham's desire to become *a father of many nations*—because if he stepped into the line, he necessarily stepped into the role of providing the government of God.

Christ is the one to whom all generations belong. He is the Redeemer of all mankind, and as the Savior of mankind, He becomes the Father of all. In Isaiah chapter 9, there is a verse that is dealing squarely with this issue. This is chapter 9, verse 6 of Isaiah:

> *For unto us a child is born, unto us a son is given: and the government shall be upon his [shoulders]: and his name shall be called Wonderful, Counsellor, The mighty God, The everlasting Father, The Prince of Peace. Of the increase of his government and peace there shall be no end.* (Isaiah 9:6; see also Isaiah 4:1 RE)

This is a prophecy about Christ coming to restore, in the meridian of time, the government of God in which He, Christ, represented the Father of all as the Redeemer of all, as the bringer again of the holy covenant.

He is prophesied to return with the description provided in the Book of Revelation[s] chapter 19, verse 16, as the *King of Kings*, as the *Lord of Lords*.

In D&C section 76, He explains what His intention is with respect to mankind; and He intends to make men...

They are they who are priests and kings, who have received of his fullness and glory, and are priests of the Most High after the order of Melchizedek, which was after the order of Enoch, which was after the order of the Only Begotten Son (D&C 76:56-57; see also T&C 69:13 RE).

That's the intention that He has for all men—that men should become, like Him, *kings and priests.*

The government of God is the family. The government of God is not stakes and wards and districts and missions and areas and all that. It's family; the government of God is family. Therefore, the sealing is to put together a family.

Now, one of the requests that the mother of John and his brother came and made of Christ was that when Christ got into His kingdom, the mother was asking if her boys could sit on His left and on His right. 'K? And Christ said that "when I get my kingdom, they can be there with me, but I don't have the right to assign who's going to sit on my right and who's going to sit on my left. That's left up to the Father."

The purpose of organizing a family on Earth through the sealing process is to make sure you get into the kingdom. But it's kind of foolish to say I have an ambition to be way up high in the organization of the Family of God because Christ told parables about people that are capable of ruling over a city will be put in that position. People that aren't (I mean, his parable of the talents, his parable of the laborer in the vineyard)— But what you really want is to get into the kingdom. Once you get into the kingdom, then how the kingdom gets organized is going to be entirely up to the Father.

How that will unfold will be the permanent resolution of all issues involving salvation pertaining to this planet at the very end and all those who have lived or come through here. And that organization at the end is more relevant for what will come thereafter.

Zion is a mortal responsibility. Men must cooperate with God for God to be able to bring it. It is not something that Heaven is going to provide for us.

When Enoch and his city were established, it was not until after it was established and people had gathered together that the Lord came and dwelt with them. They prepared the place, they extended the invitation, and the Lord came.

Likewise, in the city that was established by Melchizedek, it wasn't the angels who built his city. He preached repentance; men repented; and as a consequence of having repented, Zion was taken up into Heaven. Enoch's Zion fled. Melchizedek's Zion fled.

The last days' Zion will be built not to flee. It will be built as an established beachhead to which the Powers of Heaven will return in order for He whose right it is to govern the Earth can assume the responsibility of governing the Earth. He intends to overthrow every other government there is and to establish, as the King and as the Prince of Peace and as the Father of Righteousness, His rule and His reign over the Earth once again at His coming.

So, Joseph Smith described the priesthood that will function in Zion preliminary to the Lord's return. And this is a quote from one of his teachings: "That priesthood is a perfect law of theocracy and stands as God to give laws to the people." That's from *The Teachings of the Prophet Joseph Smith* on page 322. In that same talk, there's a better elaboration made in one of the notetakers... You can find this in *The Words of Joseph Smith*, page 246. Joseph said:

> It is understood by many by reading this chapter [referring to Hebrews chapter 7] understood by many by reading this chapter that Melchizedek was a king of some country or nation on Earth. But it was not so. In the original it reads "king of shalom," which signifies 'king of peace or righteousness' and not of any country or nation.

What Melchizedek established was a community of peace, and as the one who preached the peace to which the people came, he was acknowledged as the prince of peace or the king of righteousness.

At the beginning of the Restoration while Joseph was still alive, there was an abortive attempt to get founded what would necessarily need to be reestablished in order for there to be Zion. In a sermon that he delivered in August of 1843, he said that the fullness did not exist in the Church. If it did, he wasn't aware of it because the fullness required a man to become a king and a priest. Joseph Smith was made a king by anointing the following month on September the 28th of 1843. The month before his anointing, he explained, "no one in the Church held the fullness of the priesthood [quote]; for any person to have the fullness of that priesthood must be a king and a priest. A person may be anointed king and priest before they receive their kingdom." (Wilford Woodruff recorded that in his journal on August the 6th of 1843.) The following month, then 28th of September 1843, Joseph was anointed a king and a priest, and the month after that, on October the 8th of 1843, Hyrum Smith was likewise ordained to be a king unto God.

Now, I want to clarify a point because Joseph Smith actually knew what he was doing, and had he been around long enough, would have accomplished a work that was still at its very incipient stage at the time that he was slain. In the Council of Fifty, which he called the Kingdom of God (which was nondenominational because members of other religious beliefs were invited into the Kingdom of God)...

The Kingdom of God was not the Church. The Church was simply a mechanism for promulgating the gospel, disseminating the Book of Mormon, and accomplishing a certain work. But the Kingdom of God was something different. Inside that Kingdom of God, Joseph Smith had himself anointed a king, and Emma, a queen.

So, hold that thought for a moment while we turn to Second Nephi chapter 10, beginning at verse 11:

> *And this land shall be a land of liberty unto the Gentiles, and there shall be no kings upon the land, who shall [rise] up unto the Gentiles. And I will fortify this land against all other nations. And he that fighteth against Zion shall perish, saith God. For he that raiseth up a king against me shall perish, for I, the Lord, the king of heaven, will be their king, and I will be a light unto them forever, that hear my words.* (2 Nephi 10:11-14; see also 2 Nephi 7:2 RE)

So, now we have a paradox. There must be a return of the *same priesthood that was in the beginning* in which there is a theocratic father or king, but God commands there shall not be one; and if you raised one up, then God will destroy him.

Well, in solving the paradox, I would suggest we go to the Book of Mormon first in order to find out exactly how was it that at the time of the Nephites we had successful kings? One of whom is most notable is King Benjamin. We don't even call him Benjamin. We call him King Benjamin because his identity with his role is so linked together that we can't talk about the man without talking about his status. This is King Benjamin in Mosiah chapter 2 explaining himself and explaining the greatness of the kingship which he held.

> *But I am like as yourselves, subject to all manner of infirmities in body and mind; yet I have been chosen by this people, and consecrated by my father, and...suffered by the hand of the Lord that I should be a ruler and a king over this people; and have been kept and preserved by his matchless power, to serve you with all the might, [in] mind and strength which the Lord hath granted unto me. I say unto you that as I have been suffered to spend my days in your service, even up to this time, and have not sought gold nor silver nor any manner of riches of you; Neither have I suffered that ye should be confined in dungeons, nor that ye should make slaves one of another, nor that ye should murder, or plunder, or steal, or commit adultery; nor...have I suffered that ye should commit any manner of wickedness, and have taught you that ye should keep the commandments of the Lord, in all things which he hath commanded you— And...I, myself, have labored with mine own hands that I might serve you, ...that ye should not be laden with taxes, and that there should nothing come upon you which was grievous to be borne—and...all these things which I have spoken, ye yourselves are witnesses this day. Yet, my brethren, I have not done these things that I might boast, neither do I tell [you] these things that thereby I might accuse you; but I tell you these things that ye [might] know that I can answer a clear conscience before God this day. Behold, I say unto you that because I said unto you...I had spent my days in your service, I do not desire to boast, for I have only been in the service of God. And behold, I tell you these things that ye may learn wisdom; that ye may learn that when ye are in the service of your fellow beings ye are only in the service of your God.* (Mosiah 2:11-17; see also Mosiah 1:7-8 RE)

This is King Benjamin explaining kingship, one that God recognized and ratified; one that was approved by Him; one that brought about peace in his day.

> *For he that raiseth up a king against me shall perish. For I the Lord, the King of Heaven, will be their king, and I will be a light unto them for ever that hear my words.* (2 Nephi 10:14; see also 2 Nephi 7:2 RE)

Joseph Smith knew exactly what he was doing. He intended to be a king subordinate to the King of Heaven. He intended to create other kings subordinate to him, **all** of them subordinate to God—because the God of this land and the King that will rule over this land is Christ. *He that raiseth up a king against me shall perish.* Joseph Smith was not seeking to establish a kingdom against God. He was seeking to establish a kingdom subordinate to and obedient to the overall King of Heaven—as a subordinate to Him. Joseph Smith intended to establish the Kingdom of God and to be a king because that is what the Kingdom of God consists of.

The foregoing excerpts are taken from:

- Denver's talk titled "Zion Will Come" given near Moab, Utah on April 10, 2016;
- A fireside talk titled "Cursed, Denied Priesthood," given in Sandy, Utah on January 7, 2018; and
- Denver's talk titled "Authority, Keys and Kingdom" given at a regional conference in Sandy, Utah on July 14, 2019.

140. Government of God, Part 3

This is the third part of a special series where Denver discusses what it is that makes God who and what God is, what that has to do with godliness and the power thereof, and how God governs on Earth as it is in Heaven.

———

DENVER: Christ was born a King. In fact, wise men from the East came inquiring saying, *Where is he that [was] born King of the Jews?*" (Matthew 2:2; see also Matthew 1:6 RE)—because that was His status; that was what the prophecies said of Him; that was the role He occupied. And the person they approached to find out where they might identify the newborn king was the king of the land who knew nothing about the matter and had to go to the scriptorians to ask them who, after some fumbling, came up with Bethlehem. *Bethlehem...of [Judea], [thou] art not the least...* (Ibid. vs. 6; Ibid. RE). Well...

Christ was born as a King, but He explained how He discharged His Kingship. In John chapter 18 beginning at verse 36:

> *Jesus answered* [this is when He's on trial for His life]— *Jesus answered, My kingdom is not of this world: if my kingdom were of this world, then would my servants fight, that I should not be delivered to the Jews: but now is my kingdom not from hence. Pilate [said therefore] unto him, Art thou a king then? Jesus answered, Thou sayest...I am a king. To this end was I born, and for this cause came I into the world, that I should bear witness unto the truth. Every one that is of the truth heareth my voice.* (John 18:36-37; see also John 10:7 RE; Testimony of St. John 11:10 RE)

That's the King. And He suffered Himself to be surrendered into the hands of wicked men who despitefully used, abused, beat, and humiliated Him and then killed Him publicly on a thoroughfare where the notoriety of His death would be on public display; and no one entering or leaving on that day (the city of Jerusalem) could do so without noticing the humiliation of our Lord. That's our King.

He explained Himself further in contrasting who He, the King, the Almighty Father, the Wonderful Counselor—of the end of His government, there shall not be a failure of increase (see Isaiah 9:6-7; see also Isaiah 4:1 RE)... He explained Himself and how He rules to His disciples.

> *And he [saith] unto them* [this is in Luke chapter 22 beginning at verse 25] — *And he [saith] unto them, The kings of the Gentiles exercise lordship over*

> *them; and they that exercise authority upon them are called benefactors. But ye shall not be so: but he that is greatest among you, let him be as the younger; and he that is chief, as he that [doeth service].* (Luke 22:25-26; see also Luke 13:6 RE)

The great King came, above all else, to serve.

Zion will come. It will come, not because of the worthiness of any of us. It will come because of the repentance of us and the worthiness of those with whom God covenanted to bring it to pass including Adam and Enoch and Abraham and Melchizedek. It will come as a consequence of the righteousness of those that went before and with whom God, who cannot lie in a covenant, made a covenant to cause it to happen in the last days. It will surely come.

Mormon wrote his book and had us in mind as his audience. After Mormon finished his book, there was one reader, and that was his son Moroni who buried it. Everything Mormon did, he did for this audience today, the last days, the Gentiles. As he's finishing up his record (this is in Mormon 8:31), he talks about us and says:

There shall be many who will say, Do this, or do that, and it mattereth not, for the Lord will uphold such at the last day. But wo unto such, for they are in the gall of bitterness and in the bonds of iniquity (Mormon 8:31; see also Mormon 4:4 RE).

There is a right way, and it will be done according to the Lord's will. And the Lord is actively working to bring that about right now in our day. The potential for Zion and the covenants being fulfilled in our day is as great as it has been in any generation from the days of Adam until now. And yet, in all those generations, there have only been two successes that the Scriptures have captured.

Well, the original priesthood and the original pattern will have to return in order for the last days' Zion to exist. The first Zion, in Moses chapter 7, verse 13:

> *So great was the faith of Enoch that he led the people of God, and their enemies came to battle against them; and he spake the word of the Lord, and the earth trembled, and the mountains fled, even according to his command; and the rivers of [waters] were turned out of their course; and the roar of...lions was heard out of the wilderness; and all nations feared greatly, ...so great was the power of the language which God had given him.* (Moses 7:13; see also Genesis 4:13 RE)

When the government of God is upon the earth in the form of Zion as it was established by Enoch in his day, then God protects and defends it. God will be the force with which the nations of the earth must contend if they intend to do harm to Zion—because it is His government; it is His handiwork; and it is an affront to Him to challenge His authority in attacking Zion—hence, Enoch's ability to speak the word of God and to have those that would bring harm upon Zion vanquished; hence, further, the reason why, before the flood, it was necessary to remove Zion because God cannot destroy the ~~wicked~~ [righteous]. The wicked can destroy the wicked; the wicked can destroy the righteous. But when Zion is here, the wicked cannot destroy Zion because God is asserting His government. And because the wicked cannot destroy Zion, and God will not do so, Zion necessarily was taken up into Heaven. The same thing happened with Melchizedek's city.

The Lord lamented: *How oft would I have gathered you as a hen gathereth her chicks under her wings, and ye would not!* (3 Nephi 10:5; see also 3 Nephi 4:9 RE). There have been occasions on which it would have been possible to have established Zion, but men would not. And when that happens, and men will not, the same rules apply as applied at the beginning—hence, the necessity for removing Moses out of the midst of Israel because through Moses, we could have had Zion. But the children of Israel were not interested—hence, the reason why Elijah was taken up into Heaven—because Elijah was an opportunity in which it would have been possible for Zion to have been established.

Well, that same priesthood which was in the beginning that allowed ~~Moses~~ [Melchizedek] to establish the city of peace, the city of righteousness, the city that God Himself would defend, necessarily must return. If you look at D&C section 133 beginning at verse 26:

> *And they who are in the north countries shall come in remembrance before the Lord; and their prophets shall hear his voice, and shall no longer stay themselves; and they shall smite the rocks, and the ice shall flow down at their presence. And [a] highway shall be cast up in the midst of the great deep. Their enemies shall become a prey unto them, And in the barren deserts there shall come forth pools of living water; and the parched ground shall no longer be a thirsty land. And they shall bring forth their rich treasures unto the children of Ephraim, my servants. And the boundaries of the everlasting hills shall tremble at their presence. And there shall they fall down and be crowned with glory, even in Zion, by the hands of the servants of the Lord, even the children of Ephraim. And they shall be filled with songs of everlasting joy. Behold, this is the blessing of the everlasting God upon the tribes of Israel, and*

> *the richer blessing upon the head of Ephraim and his fellows.* (D&C 133:26-34; see also T&C 58:3 RE)

Heaven will protect the last days' Zion. It will belong to Him, and therefore, God will not allow it to be overtaken or overcome. D&C section 45 has another prophecy about the last days' Zion. Beginning at verse 66:

> *And it shall be called the New Jerusalem, a land of peace, a city of refuge, a place of safety for the saints of the Most High God; And the glory of the Lord shall be there, and the terror of the Lord...shall be there, insomuch that the wicked will not come unto it, and it shall be called Zion. And it shall come to pass among the wicked, that every man that will not take his sword against his neighbor must needs flee unto Zion for safety. And there shall be gathered unto it out of every nation under heaven; and it shall be the only people that shall not be at war one with another. And it shall be said among the wicked: Let us not go up to battle against Zion, for the inhabitants of Zion are terrible; wherefore we cannot stand.* (D&C 45:66-70; see also T&C 31:14-15 RE)

When they came to arrest the Lord in the Garden of Gethsemane after His suffering—even though He intended to submit Himself and to be abused and ultimately killed—when they entered, the Apostle John records that Christ, despite the ordeal He had just concluded, stood up, confronted them in their arms and said, *Whom seek ye?* (John 18:4; see also John 10:1 RE; Testimony of St. John 11:2 RE). And they said, *Jesus of Nazareth* (Ibid. vs. 5; Ibid. RE; Ibid. vs. 2-3 RE) And He said, *I am he* (ibid, vs. 8; ibid. RE; Ibid. RE). And they stumbled backwards, tripped over one another's feet, and they fell down.

An armed group bearing swords and weapons were intimidated by the Lord identifying Himself. He made no attempt to defend Himself, but had He elected to do so, they could not have taken Him. He went as a lamb to the slaughter because he intended, though the Lion of Judah, to submit Himself to become the sacrificial lamb.

Heaven protected Zion in its first iteration, and Heaven is going to protect the last days' Zion. As a consequence of that, the time is going to come when it will not be the deliverance of Israel out of Egypt that people cite as evidence of the power of God. You see, Egypt had to be subdued. Moses was sent to subdue them because Egypt was, at the time, the greatest kingdom, the greatest nation on the earth. And Moses was sent to them to establish the government of God. When you confront the government of God against the most powerful nation on the earth, it's the most powerful nation that must yield the field and not the Lord.

Well, in the last days, Jeremiah prophesied the time is going to come when the talk about the power of God is no longer making reference to what the Lord did anciently with Egypt. It's going to be what the Lord intends to do with the last days' Zion. This is Jeremiah chapter 16 beginning at verse 14:

> *Therefore, behold, the days come, saith the Lord, that it shall no more be said, The Lord liveth, that brought up the children of Israel out of the land of Egypt; But, The Lord liveth, that brought up the children of Israel from the land of the north, and from all the lands whither he [hath] driven them: and I will bring them again into their [own] land that I gave unto their fathers.* (Jeremiah 16:14-15; see also Jeremiah 6:10 RE)

That will be the reference point to which people will point as evidence of God's intention to establish His rule, His reign upon the earth, His authority over the nations of the earth.

Well… It is going to come to pass. In your enthusiasm, it would be better to demonstrate the virtue of patience as the Lord brings His work about than to exhibit the character flaw of impatience and enthusiasm in trying to bring about what the Lord intends Himself to cause to happen—because you cannot give birth prematurely to a living Zion or it will choke, and it will die because it is unable to be viable outside of the hands of the Lord. We have to wait on Him.

Just a few random concluding thoughts:

One bit of advice: If you're going to have a school of the prophets, you are going to need a prophet.

God's ways are higher than man's ways. He said this to Isaiah: *For as the heavens are higher than the earth, so are my ways higher than your ways, and my thoughts than your thoughts* (Isaiah 55:9; see also Isaiah 20:2 RE).

Jacob, a prophet who stood in the presence of God, expounded on the meaning of God's mysteries to an audience that include now us. Jacob (this is in Jacob chapter 4, verse 8):

> *Behold, great and marvelous are the works of the Lord. How unsearchable are the depths of the mysteries of him; and it is impossible that man should find out all his ways. And no man knoweth of his ways save it be revealed unto*

> *him; wherefore, brethren, despise not the revelations of God.* (Jacob 4:8; see also Jacob 3:3 RE)

In other words, I don't care if you have a PhD in theological studies, and you are the most adept scriptorian of our age. The meaning belongs to God. It does not belong to me; it does not belong to you. It is not found out by our clever or witty parsing of what it is.

In large measure, the prophecies have as their purpose to hide from men what God intends to do until God has done it. And then having accomplished what He intended to do, the Scriptures confirm that He knew the end from the beginning. But if you could know the end from the beginning, you could interfere with the plan of God by going where the prophecies say, when the prophecies say, and interfering with the hand of God in fulfilling it. Even worse still, if your inclination were to priestcraft, if you knew what the prophecies meant beforehand, you could profit from them. And the things of Heaven were never intended to be given into the hands of men so that they might profit from them.

We are expected to sacrifice for God. A religion that does not require sacrifice is a religion that will not produce faith. And if there is one thing that is going to be necessary for the establishment of Zion, it is going to necessarily be faith. You obtain it through sacrifice. You do not obtain it through adoration; you do not obtain it through the praise of men; you do not obtain it by sitting in chief seats; you don't obtain it by faring sumptuously and administering the wealth that is surrendered to you as if you were God. It belongs to God. It is His. You should go get a job to support yourself if you're going to administer the tithes and leave the tithes alone.

I know there are verses that suggest that the laborer is worthy of his hire—I know that. I'm telling you it's toxic. I'm telling you that there are… In the history of mankind, I can think of maybe five men who have lived that would be worthy and beyond corruption in occupying that role. And one of those five was the Lord Himself.

Don't look upon a passing verse as a basis upon which to revoke and to cast aside all of the other many verses and warnings and cautions and prophecies about the abuse of the last days' Gentiles which largely emanate from the corruption of our religion because of priestcraft.

Priestcraft is toxic, not just to the listeners but to the practitioners. If what you're saying, if what you're preaching is greeted with wild enthusiasm, and it doesn't get you shunned, then you're probably not saying anything that God would agree with.

God's purpose is to bring us to repentance. I mean, the Lord is exceptionally positive, but He is positive in stating affirmatively the standard that is acceptable to Him. *Blessed are ye when men shall revile you, and persecute [you], and say all manner of evil against you falsely for my [name's] sake* (3 Nephi 12:11; see also 3 Nephi 5:19 RE). He expected us to be misunderstood, misapprehended, assessed very narrowly just as He was, cast out—not to be handed money and to be given a chief seat, to be adored and to be respected.

Our challenge among ourselves, however diminutive we may seem to be—Priestcraft can invade our little fellowships every bit as much as it can invade multi-billion-dollar institutions. There's no limit on where you can run amiss.

Rest assured that God intends to establish in the last days a Zion in which we will see the return of exactly what was here at the beginning. There will be a return. I mean, the reason why they're coming to the children of Ephraim in the everlasting mountains is because there will be a New Jerusalem. They will bring rich treasures when they come because they have records that they themselves are going to need to have translated. And they're going to be crowned because the family of God consists of people who are, in fact, kings and priests.

All of that infrastructure has to be put in place by the Lord before His return. And therefore, He intends to accomplish this work. And when He accomplishes this work, you're not going to find at the top of it a king like the Gentiles expect. You're going to find something or someone or some group who are meek and lowly, who are rather more like our Savior than the kings who ruled during our Savior's day. You won't find a Caesar, and you won't find a local potentate. You'll find a servant.

Well, there's a parable; it's just one verse. It's a very short parable. It moves along, but it's a response that Christ gave to the question that was put to Him by His disciples asking Him: Tell us what the signs of your return is going to be. And He goes through a list of things, but He ends with a little parable at the end. (And our translation makes it seem kind of morbid; so, I'm gonna substitute *body* for *carcass* because it sounds like what you're dealing with in the current King James version is morbid, not a living body.) But He says one of the signs that is going to be of His return is: "Where the *body* is, that's where the *eagles* will gather." (See Matthew 24:28; see also Matthew 11:7 RE).

The *body* is the New Jerusalem. The *eagles* are going to be angelic ministrants who are going to come.

There has to be an opening that occurs in order to prepare the way. The opening at this end is going to be handled by someone who has remained behind, and the opening at the far end is going to be the one to whom the assignment was given to open the way for His return—Elijah, the one who was promised.

Now, I want to be really clear. I don't expect either of those individuals to have any public ministry again. They have a role in Zion, and those who dwell in Zion are going to have some contact with them. The three Nephites are a great example. They, like John, were given a similar ministry to remain around and administer until the end of the earth. And they did minister. Two of the people to whom they ministered were Mormon and Moroni. They, like ministering angels, ministered to Mormon who, in turn, ministered to the public. They ministered to Moroni and kept his hope up in the waning days of that dispensation. But they did not minister publicly. John will have a role, but the work of Zion is the work of flesh and blood.

Men have to extend the invitation for God to return so that men who extend that invitation are worthy of His return, and the Lord can safely come without utterly destroying all who are upon the earth. Therefore, you need Zion, among other reasons, in order for there to be a place and a people to whom the Lord can safely return without utterly destroying the earth at His coming. However small, however diminutive it may be, there needs to be a Zion that extends the invitation for the Lord to return.

Now the good news is that Zion will be preserved. And the even better news is that all those good people of the earth who live in ignorance but who would've accepted the truth if it were brought to them—they will be preserved, also. There will be a mission field into the millennium.

But the really, really bad news is in the laundry list of those whom the Lord intends to destroy at His coming. That is the description of those who are Telestial and therefore, cannot endure His presence when He shall come—all of the liars; all of the whoremongers; all of the people who have taken our Lord's name in vain, having not authority; all of those who have preached for hire and practiced priestcraft. One of the reasons it needs to be eradicated before you get to Zion is so you're not ignited like a torch head to the amusement of everyone else that is in Zion. There has to be an end of all that nonsense.

Our Lord was and is meek. When He said, *I am more intelligent than [them] all* (Abraham 3:19; see also Abraham 5:4 RE; JSH 17:5 RE); when He said, I am *the greatest of all* (D&C 19:18; see also T&C 4:5 RE; JSH 17:5 RE), there wasn't one whit of arrogance in His announcement of that. What He was saying is: "Please! Have confidence in me. Please! Trust what I say to be true. Please! Recognize I've paid a price in order to be able to minister."

You needn't respect the messenger, but you must respect the message because salvation is limited in every generation to those who are authorized to preach repentance and to baptize. And if they're not authorized, then it is powerlessness. However good it may make you feel, it is powerlessness.

Well, I've covered the things that I was needing to cover. Let me end by saying that I don't talk a great deal about any of the experiences, visitations, revelations. I don't talk a great deal about any of that because the concern I always have is that in the days of Joseph, we made some foolishly laughable mistakes—because when we had a man like Joseph walking among us, it was so easy to take our eyes off of the Lord and put them upon the man; that when Joseph got up to talk to the Relief Society in 1842, he said, "Your minds are darkened because you are neglecting the duty that's devolving upon yourselves. You are depending too much upon the prophet." (*TPJS*, p. 237).

If we don't learn anything from that past example in failure, then we can expect the exact same outcome. We may get Kirtland, we may get Nauvoo, we may get Salt Lake City, but we will not get the New Jerusalem. We have to learn from the past errors. We have to determine not to repeat at least those. We may make new and inventive mistakes of our own, but at least, they will belong to us and not be caused by our arrogance and stupidity in simply repeating what we have seen gone on before.

I don't care how cleverly you parse the Scriptures. God and God alone is responsible for causing them to be written in the first place, and He has a meaning in mind behind them. And He has a work that He intends to do that they will vindicate when the work is done.

If you think that you can outthink the Lord, and you can arrive at the right place at the right time, then go ahead and buy some farmland in or around Independence, Missouri and wait for the burning because you're not going to be at the right place. If Independence, Missouri was where the Lord intended Zion to be, He wouldn't have told them in January of 1841 that He was gonna make Nauvoo the corner of Zion. It is portable until it is fixed by Him.

And Adam-ondi-Ahman is not simply a location that you can find on a map in Missouri. It is a description of an event. The event is Adam in the presence of Son Ahman, Christ. Wherever that happens, that is and will be Adam-ondi-Ahman. So, buy all the land you want, build all the bleachers you expect to build. But the fact of the matter is that when Adam, the Ancient of Days, returns, there is going to be an orderly process in which a king, a mortal king (it necessarily begins there) surrenders the jurisdiction of the earth back to those who once presided over it—in turn, ultimately back to the Ancient of Days. That's why he's gonna be here. And he, in turn, will surrender it to the Father, the Wonderful Counselor, the mighty God, the everlasting Father; of the end of whose government, or the increase of whose government, there shall be no end.

Christ, when He returns, will have the lawful, the legal right, to possess this earth, to rule it and to govern it. And He will come to govern it. But before that day, groundwork has to be laid. There's a process.

The foregoing excerpts are taken from Denver's talk titled "Zion Will Come" given near Moab, Utah on April 10, 2016.

141. Forgiving Others, Continued

In an earlier podcast [#106 – Forgiving Others], Denver and Stephanie discussed the mandatory condition that we forgive others in order to obtain forgiveness ourselves.

In this podcast, Denver and Stephanie discuss more about the mechanics of how we forgive others. Forgiving is a necessary step in the ascension process; without it, we are not qualified to receive the Second Comforter. Denver and Stephanie discuss how we can look upon and handle offenses, and how forgiving others relates to seeking judgment. Forgiving offenses helps us obtain salvation by providing a means for receiving our own forgiveness.

STEPHANIE: The Lord's standard is pretty clear, and there's not much wiggle room. You want Heavenly Father to forgive **you**? You forgive each other. That sounds like a really good way of **loving yourself**. Forgiveness is a **requirement**—it is a condition—and the Lord has this to say about it. Third Nephi 5:34:

> *And forgive us our debts as we forgive our debtors.... For if ye forgive men their trespasses, your Heavenly Father will also forgive you, but if [you] forgive not men their trespasses, neither will your Father forgive your trespasses* (3 Nephi 5:34 RE).

> *And behold, it is written also that thou shalt love thy neighbour and hate thine enemy; but behold, I say unto you, love your enemies, bless them that curse you, [and] do good to them that hate you, and pray for them who despitefully use you and persecute you, that ye may be the children of your Father who is in Heaven, for he maketh his sun to rise on the evil and...the good. Therefore, those things which were of old time, which were under the law, in me are all fulfilled. Old things are done away and all things have become new... (3 Nephi 5:24-26;30-31 RE)*

> *I have given you a former commandment that I, the Lord, will forgive whom I will forgive, but of you it is required to forgive all men. And again, I have taught that if you forgive men their trespasses, your Heavenly Father will also forgive you; but if you forgive not men their trespasses, neither will your Heavenly Father forgive your trespasses... If men intend no offense, I take no offense, but if they are taught and should have obeyed, then I reprove and correct, and forgive and forget.* (T&C 157:58)

God is the only one who judges correctly. He is the only one who can decide whether an offense was intended or not, and then He reproves, corrects, forgives , and forgets . We are rarely worthy to judge, and we are only able to reprove and correct people we have a relationship with—and we are always expected to forgive and forget.

DENVER: Everybody will have to make changes. The most important changes have been provided in a blueprint revealed in the Answer to Prayer for Covenant, including the terms of the Covenant. We are expected to remember and obey these words:

> *My will is to have you love one another. As people, you lack the ability to respectfully disagree among one another....*
>
> *Wisdom counsels mankind to align their words with their hearts, but mankind refuses to take counsel from Wisdom....*
>
> *There have been sharp disputes between you that should have been avoided. I speak these words to reprove you that you may learn, not to upbraid you so that you mourn. I want my people to have understanding....*
>
> *Satan is a title and means accuser, opponent and adversary; hence once he fell, Lucifer became, or in other words was called, Satan, because he accuses others and opposes the Father. I rebuked Peter and called him Satan because he was wrong in opposing the Father's will for me, and Peter understood and repented.*
>
> *In the work you have performed there are those who have been Satan, accusing one another, wounding hearts and causing jarring, contention, and strife by their accusations. Rather than loving one another, even among you who desire a good thing, some have dealt unkindly as if they were...opponents, accusers and adversaries. In this they were wrong...*

In the chapter on the Atonement in Come, Let Us Adore Him there is an explanation given of what Christ suffered and what obligations are devolving on us as a result. We must do as He did, suffer in like manner, and forgive all offenses. His infinite suffering cannot be replicated in one sense, but in our own sphere and time we do suffer offenses and abuses. We are required to forgive as He forgave. It is our own forgiveness of others that qualifies us to receive forgiveness from Him. When we harbor grudges and resentments, we cut ourselves off from His Atonement. IF we are to be forgiven we must in turn FORGIVE others. In The Second Comforter it is shown how we must make intercession on behalf of others, even our enemies, if we are to have a hope in Christ. We must lay down the burden of sin to enter into His presence. Much of that "sin" in each of our lives has been the offenses against us, and the resentment and anger we hold from these abuses. There are people who have done you wrong. There are some who did so intentionally. When you forgive them, and plead on their behalf for the Lord to also forgive them in sincerity and love, you are not far from the Kingdom of Heaven. Your Lord did this. You must do as He did to be like Him. It is the only way to understand your Lord. In this, you must suffer as He did, choosing to forgive offenses rather than to seek justice. When you show mercy, you merit mercy. The beginning of repentance is found in forgiving others.

Your just claims for retribution must be surrendered. Your worthy desire to have vindication must be abandoned. Your right to have judgment against the ones who abused you must be forfeited. And you must go on to pray for their forgiveness.

It does not end, of course, with service and kindness to your fellow Saint. You must also learn to serve the "Samaritan," and to heal and care for them. If it ends with mere Church service, you have not yet overcome xenophobia. It is the "other," the "outsider," and the "stranger and foreigner" through whom sacrifice is perfected. The unlovely and even the persecutor is where Christ's commandments lead us at last. We must develop love for those who persecute us, or despitefully use and abuse us to reach what Christ taught. He really meant it. And He really wants us to get there. When we do, we find ourselves standing on holy ground. For that ground was sanctified by His own blood, shed in His own sacrifice, when He poured out the last full measure of devotion to His Father's will. When you hear His words echoing in your own voice, "forgive them for they know not what they do," then you will begin to see the Master in the mirror. His image will appear to you there first. Your countenance will look more like His: more humble, more contrite, more obedient and filled with more light than you are right now.

The way is strait and narrow, and cannot permit you to pass through while carrying any burden of accusation, desire for revenge or even just complaint about others. When you lay down what you might justly claim against others and seek nothing for their offenses, then you are able to enter in. To be blessed, we must seek peace with those who would make war against us. (Matt. 5: 9.) When we judge all others with mercy, it is with mercy alone we will be judged. (Matt. 7:2.)

This matter does not end there, however. Christ tells us to pray for those who abuse and misuse us. Odd as this may sound, it is what He did. It is one of the things that allows us most to emulate Him. Though it may seem out of character, you should try doing it. You can't sincerely pray for another person without losing your anger toward them. This act of intercession with God for those who have committed offenses is directly related to making sacrifice in the similitude of the great sacrifice of Christ. Lehi did this, as recorded in 1 Ne. 1: 5: "Wherefore it came to pass that my father, Lehi, as he went forth prayed unto the Lord, yea, even with all his heart, in behalf of his people." These people had the judgments of God about to fall upon them. Rather than join in condemning them, Lehi prayed to God about them. He showed mercy to them. 231

Nephi similarly showed mercy and made intercession for his elder brothers. In 1 Ne. 2: 18 it is recorded: "But, behold, Laman and Lemuel would not hearken unto my words; and being grieved because of the hardness of their hearts I cried unto the Lord for them." Nephi's act of showing mercy, refraining from judging, and praying in intercession for brothers who rejected him, made Nephi a "type" of Christ. Meaning that Nephi's example conformed with the later message and ministry of the One who made intercession for all mankind. Christ did it for real. Nephi did it in imitation of Him. We can do it as an imitation as well. That imitation of Him is required to qualify us for the Second Comforter. If we are unwilling to accept these standards and imitate these acts, we are not qualified to receive the Second Comforter. Without resonating at the same frequency as He, we are not going to be moving where we can see Him.

On November 1st Joseph was sentenced to death "at 9 o'clock tomorrow morning in a public square at Far West." Militia leader Doniphan refused to carry out the order, and Joseph's life was spared. In the lead up to his arrest, and then during imprisonment, disaffected Mormons were far more dangerous and threatening to Joseph than the non Mormons. It was Mormon lies about him that caused the peril.

Joseph's original arrest at Far West was arranged by an agreement George Hinkle made with the commander of the Missouri Militia. The church leaders were inside Far West, which at the time was fortified and would be difficult for the militia to take without serious loss of life. Hinkle was sent to negotiate with the militia poised outside Far West as the representative for the community.

Hinkle agreed with militia commander Colonel Lucas to surrender church leaders to the militia, but lied to Joseph and the others. He did not disclose they would be arrested, but led them to believe they were going to meet with Colonel Lucas to negotiate an end to the conflict. Joseph was surprised when Hinkle led him into the camp as a prisoner. George Hinkle was a traitor.

Joseph Smith wrote several documents while imprisoned in Missouri. Specific dissidents are named and their treachery explained in those documents. The individuals and their wrongdoing are set out in what I am about to read:

From jail Joseph Smith petitioned for habeas corpus. In the petition he mentioned George Hinkle. This is an excerpt from that habeas corpus petition:

> Joseph Smith Jr is now unlawfully confined and restrained of his liberty in Liberty jail Clay County (Mo) that he has been restrained of his liberty near five months your petitioners clame that the whole transaction which has been the cause of his confinement was (is) unlawfull from the first to the Last he was taken from his home by a fraude being practised upon him by a man by the name of George M Hinkle… (JSP, Documents Vol. 6, p. 344; as in original.)

Hinkle is mentioned in another letter, along with John Corrill, Reed Peck, David Whitmer and W.W. Phelps. This is Joseph's letter:

> Look at Mr [George M.] Hinkle. A wolf in sheep's clothing. Look at his brother John Corrill Look at the beloved brother Reed Peck who aided him in leading us, as the savior was led, into the camp as a lamb prepared for the slaughter and a sheep dumb before his shearer so we opened not our mouth But these men like Balaam being greedy for a reward sold us into the hands of those who loved them, for the world loves his own. I would remember W[illiam] W. Phelps who comes up before us as one of Job's comforters. God suffered such kind of beings to afflict Job, but it never entered into their hearts that Job would get out of it all. This poor man who professes to be much of a prophet has no other dumb ass to ride but David Whitmer to forbid his madness when he goes up to curse Israel, and this ass not being of the same kind of Balaams therefore the angel notwithstanding appeared unto him yet he could not penetrate his understanding sufficiently so but what he brays out cursings instead of blessings. (JSP, Documents Vol. 6, p. 300-301; as in original.) [That is an allusion to an incident in the Old Testament.]

Sampson Avard led the Danites, a secret Mormon, quasi-military organization that terrorized Missourians and exacted a revenge against them. They burned houses and engaged in assaults to retaliate against the local non-Mormons. Avard was responsible for Joseph, Hyrum and others being held on the charge of treason. Without Avard's testimony it was unlikely for enough evidence to be shown for probable cause to hold them on the charge of treason. Joseph wrote from jail about Avard the following:

> We have learned also since we have been in prison that many false and pernicious things, which were calculated to lead the saints far astray and to do great harm (have been taught by Dr. [Sampson] Avard) as coming from the Presidency and we have reason to fear (that) many (other) designing and corrupt characters like unto himself (have been teaching many things) which the Presidency never knew of being taught in the Church by anybody until after they were made prisoners, which if they had known of, they would have spurned them and their authors from them as they would the gates of hell. Thus we find that there has been frauds and secret abominations and evil works of darkness going on leading the minds of the weak and unwary into confusion and distraction, and palming it all off all the time upon the presidency while mean time the Presidency were ignorant as well as innocent of these things, which were practicing in the Church in their name[.] (JSP, Documents Vol. 6, p. 306)

Joseph wrote about the three witnesses to the Book of Mormon (David Whitmer, Oliver Cowdery and Martin Harris) along with William McLellin, John Whitmer, Thomas Marsh and Orson Hyde. All these were identified in the following condemnation written by Joseph Smith in Liberty Jail:

> Such characters as [William E.] McLellin, John Whitmer, O[liver] Cowdery, Martin Harris, who are too mean to mention and we had liked to have forgotten them. [Thomas B.] Marsh & [Orson] Hyde whose hearts are full of corruption, whose cloak of hypocrisy was not sufficient to shield them or to hold them up in the hour of trouble, who after having escaped the pollutions of the world through the knowledge of God and become again entangled and overcome the latter end is worse than the first. But it has happened unto them according to the words of the savior, the dog has returned to his vomit, and the sow that was washed to her wallowing in the mire. Again if we sin wilfully after we have received the knowledge of the truth, there remaineth no more sacrifice for sin, but a certain fearful looking (for) of judgement and fiery indignation to come which shall devour these adversaries. For he who

> despiseth Moses' law died without mercy under two or three witnesses of how much more severe punishment suppose ye shall he be thought worthy who hath sold his brother and denied the new and everlasting covenant[.] (JSP Documents Vol. 6, pp. 307-308.)

W.W. Phelps was another Mormon dissenter who was removed from leadership and then excommunicated in June 1838. He was one of the witnesses who testified against Joseph Smith in the Missouri treason hearings and accused him of being responsible for violence and treason. Phelps may have been motivated to testify against Joseph Smith to protect himself from criminal charges. He had been seen by Patrick Lynch, the clerk in Stolling's grocery store, as one of the Mormon mob that robbed the store and then burned it. (JSP Documents Vol. 6, pp. 417-419.)

Joseph was not fooled by these men. He recognized they were traitors and liars. But he revealed to his wife his own spirit of forgiveness about them. Writing from jail to his wife, after 5 months and 5 days of imprisonment, Joseph counseled Emma "neither harber [sic] a spirit of revenge." (JSP, Documents Vol. 6, p. 405.) Joseph's advice to his wife contrasts sharply with the revealed word from the Lord to Joseph.

Early in 1839, after nearly a half-year of imprisonment, Joseph Smith wrote a letter from Liberty Jail to the saints. The letter included several revelations. One revelation declared these words:

> [C]ursed are all those that shall lift up the heal against mine anointed saith the Lord and cry they have sin[n]ed when they have not sined before me saith the Lord but have done that which was meat in mine eyes and which I commanded them but those who cry transgresion do it becaus they are the servants of sin and are the children of disobediance themselvs and those who swear false against my servants that they might bring them unto bondage and death. Wo unto them because they have offended my little ones they shall be severed from the ordinances of mine house their basket shall not be full their houses and their barnes shall famish and they themselvs shall be dispised by those that flattered them they shall not have right to the priesthood nor their posterity after them from generation to generation it had been better for them that a millstone had been hanged about their necks and they having drownd in the depth of the see… (JSP, Documents Vol. 6, p. 366; all as in original.)

It was the Lord who said those men who bore false witness against Joseph "shall not have right to the priesthood nor their posterity after them from generation to generation[.]" Even as late as the 1830s it was possible for men to so offend God that He will curse both them and their posterity from any right to the priesthood.

Just as Christ made intercession for all of mankind through the atonement (see 2 Nephi 1:6), so Nephi also makes intercession on behalf of his unbelieving brothers and cried unto the Lord (1 Nephi 1:9) for those who had rejected him. Nephi's conduct makes him a 'type' of Christ. Nephi shows himself to be faithful in the face of adversity. He has been charitable to the critical. As a result of this, he is ready to receive more.2 Christ teaches man to love his enemies, bless those who are trying to do him harm, and pray for his persecutors. This is the only way to become like Him. He is an intercessor. Becoming an intercessor for others is part of one's development, through grace, to become as He is.

STEPHANIE: God is the **only** one who judges correctly. He is the only one who can decide whether an offense was intended or not, and then **He** reproves, corrects, **forgives**, and **forgets**. We are rarely worthy to judge, and we are only able to reprove and correct people we have a relationship with—and we are **always** expected to forgive and forget.

READER: Satan is a title, and means accuser, opponent and adversary; hence once he fell, Lucifer became, or in other words was called, Satan, because he accuses others and opposes the Father. I rebuked Peter and called him Satan because he was wrong in opposing the Father's will for me, and Peter understood and repented.

In the work you have performed there are those who have been Satan, accusing one another, wounding hearts and causing jarring, contention, and strife by their accusations. Rather than loving one another, even among you who desire a good thing, some have dealt unkindly as if they were the opponents, accusers and adversaries. In this they were wrong.

You have sought to recover the scriptures because you hope to obtain the covenant for my protective hand to be over you, but you cannot be Satan and be mine. If you take upon you my covenant, you must abide it as a people to gain what I promise. You think Satan will be bound a thousand years, and it will be so, but do not understand your own duty to bind that spirit within you so that you give no heed to accuse others.

DENVER: The greatest false spirit of all is the one that inspires you to accuse your brethren, condemn your sisters, and judge others unfairly. This is Satan. We cannot be Satan and also be the Lord's.

We are not being asked to lay down our weapons and be killed. *We* are only being asked to lay down our hostility, slander, and abuse of one another to become peaceful and loving. This is a good thing that benefits everybody. Despite this, we keep our pride, ambition, jealousy, envy, strife, and lusts. These destructive desires are preferred over forgiving offenses in meekness, love, and kindness. None of us are asked to die for a covenant, but are only asked to be more like Christ and forgive and love one another. This seems so difficult a challenge that we quarrel and dispute among ourselves. We remain haughty and self-righteous and fail to realize self-righteousness is a lie, a mirage, utterly untrue. We must trade our pride for humility, or we will never be able to keep the covenant.

The context of "judge not that ye be not judged" is framed by the statement that "with what

judgment ye judge, ye shall be judged; and with what measure ye mete, it shall be measured to you again." We do "judge" one another because we must. But the judgment should err on the side of forgiving. It should err in favor of trusting motives to be pure, and intent to be good. We should be generous with our gratitude, evaluations and suppositions. When we know someone is misbehaving, we should make allowances for their shortcomings, forgive them before they ask, and impute no retribution because of their offensive conduct.

This does not make us better than another, it makes us whole. It allows the Lord to forgive us for our own, much greater offenses against Him. For when we are generous, we merit His Divine generosity. It is how we are healed. It is the means for our own salvation. Instead of thinking ourselves better than an offender, we should look upon them with gratitude for they provide the means to obtain salvation-- provided we give them forgiveness from all their offenses. This is why we should rejoice and be exceedingly glad. (3 Nephi 12: 10-12.) They enable us to obtain salvation by despitefully using us, as long as we measure them by the same standard that allows God to forgive us.

What perfect symmetry: You measure to others using instrument that will be used by God to measure back to you. So your ready forgiveness is how God will treat you. All those grudges can be replaced with petitions to God to forgive those who abused you. As you lay aside all those sins against you, committed by others, it will purge from you all your own sins.

Straight and narrow indeed.... But oddly appropriate and altogether within your control.

> *Be of one heart, ...regard one another with charity. Measure your words before giving voice to them...*
>
> *There remains [a] great work yet to be done. Receive my covenant and abide in it, not as in the former time when jarring, jealousy, contention and backbiting caused anger, broke hearts and hardened the souls of those claiming to be my saints. But receive it in spirit, in meekness and in truth. I have given you a former commandment that I, the Lord, will forgive whom I will forgive, but of you it is required to forgive all men. And again, I have taught [you] that if you forgive men their trespasses, your Heavenly Father will also forgive you; but if you forgive not men their trespasses neither will your Heavenly Father forgive your trespasses. How do I act toward mankind? If men intend no offense, I take no offense, but if they are taught and should have obeyed, then I reprove and correct, and forgive and forget. You cannot be at peace with one another if you take offense when none is intended. But again I say, Judge not others except by the rule you want used to weigh yourself....*

(One of the questions that someone asked is, why we are admonished to pursue judgement? The answer are those words I just read to you: *I say, Judge not others except by the rule you want used to weigh yourself.* Pursue judgement whenever the opportunity presents itself. Use judgement to evaluate based upon the standard you want applied to yourself, and pursue judgement).

STEPHANIE: I have a simple formula that works for me, and I'll share it with you. I figure that every single interaction I have with another human being will achieve one of three things:

- The experience will either build our relationship with a positive interaction,
- It will leave it unchanged or status quo, or
- It will tear down the relationship with a negative interaction.
- Grocery store clerks, gas station attendants, students, teachers, husbands, children— doesn't matter. The good news about this

> formula for me is that I get to choose, **every single time** with **every single person**. It's **never** out of my control. There is no love for others **or yourself** if your time's spent focusing on flaws, criticizing, imputing intent, or taking offense for no good reason.

Here's what the Lord says about judgment, flaws, criticism, ascribing motive, offense, and intent—and it's time we start taking Him seriously. So, He moves on from the Ten Commandments to the Sermon on the Mount.

In Matthew 3:40, He says:

> *Now these are the words which Jesus taught his disciples that they should say unto the people: Judge not unrighteously, that you be not judged, but judge righteous judgment; for with what judgment you [shall] judge, you shall be judged, and with what measure you mete, it shall be measured to you again.* (Matthew 3:40 RE)

(It's like a person with a cold's worst nightmare. [Audience laughter.])

The difference ~~it~~ here that I see between the no judging and the righteous judgment is likely related to Final Judgment, as opposed to all those in-between judgments that we can do if we **think** we have the Lord on our side, in terms of righteous judgment.

And then moving from Matthew into Third Nephi—Third Nephi chapter six, verse six:

> *And why beholdest thou the mote that is in thy brother's eye, but considerest not the beam that is in thine own eye? Or how wilt thou say to thy brother, Let me pull ~~that~~ [the] mote out of thine eye, and behold, a beam is in thine own eye? Thou hypocrite, first cast out the beam [out] of thine own eye, and then shalt thou see clearly to cast out the mote out of thy brother's eye. Give not that which is holy unto the dogs, neither cast ye your pearls before swine, lest they trample them under their feet, and turn again, and rend you.* (3 Nephi 6:6 RE)

And so I say to that: What the heck does that have to do with anything? So, on the assumption that it is actually related to what came before that, I spent a reasonable amount of time contemplating it, and this is my version of pearls and swine and dogs and whatever. It's a strange ending to this particular thought; so, what if it means that **we** are the dogs and swine, and judging is a holy and precious act—one that we don't have anywhere near the godliness to engage in, at least without seriously pursuing God's help—and we will get out of the attempt (and **all** we will get out of the attempt) at that kind of judging is trampling and rending. So, that's my take; and so, let's not do it. Okay? Let's just not do it.

In the foregoing scriptures, we are being told to worry about ourselves **first** (and **that** should take a long, long, long time). And then, if we need to, we can worry about other people after that. So, in theory, if we're as critical towards ourselves as we are others, we should be doing a lot of repenting, improving, growing in love and charity and empathy—as we make ourselves better; because it's just about beams and motes, people. That's it—just don't do it.

When it comes to our interpersonal life, knowing how to make yourself better takes a lot of courage and introspection; you have to be willing to be clear on what's wrong with **you**. It's a lot easier to think about what's wrong with other people. So asking questions like:

- How did I make **that** better or worse?
- What did I do or say to make them react that way?
- What did I say or do to cause their defensiveness? or
- Why did I do or say what I did or said, and how and what could I have done differently?

are absolutely necessary in order to become more Christ-like. However, if focusing on other people is your jam, then do it charitably; impute the highest motive and best motive to other people; assume their best intentions; engage in empathy and perspective-taking. **These** are godly acts. They make **your** life better. They wash away the bitterness, anger, hurt, and unhappiness **you** feel when you're focused on the negative. This sounds like loving yourself.

DENVER: We have been a really rancorous group of people who are strongly opinionated. It's like we're refugees from an abusive experience in a hierarchical religion that, as soon as we are set at liberty, everyone wants to pick at the slightest hint that you're aspiring to be the next Relief Society president or the next bishop or—just all of that. There's a decompression, there's a "post-religious trauma syndrome" that was really evident. Everyone was walking around saying, more or less, "I've been abused. Religion has been a source of anxiety and trouble in my life, and you're practicing religion—but by damn, you're not going to practice your religion on me! I mean, I want to have the liberty with which Christ has made me free. I do not want to have that experience repeat itself. I want nothing of that." And that—we were wearing that, and probably every one of us were wearing that chip on all of our shoulders.

I didn't see that over at Grand Junction. I didn't see people worried about the motivations of one another. I didn't see them looking for cause to complain or cause to take offense at what someone else was saying. I thought we turned a corner, and something happened. And maybe we needed a little while to decompress. Maybe we needed a little while to—

And as other people come in, they're probably going to walk in with exactly the same attitude that many of us had for the first several years because of our prior experience. We're just going to have to bear with that. And they need to get over that, because there's a lot of personal intrusiveness and personal abuse that goes on in the name of the Restoration. It's worse among the fundamentalist group. It's worse among the people that have come out from that tradition to say, "Let us—let us join in here." All of them have suffered from religious abuse.

As aggravating and trying as people are on one another, we need to go through this. There is no magic path to loving one another. Some people refuse and must be left outside. When it comes to loving others, some things must be abandoned, some things must be added, some things must be forgotten, and some things must be ignored. But learning what to abandon, add, forget, or ignore is only through the doing. We chip away at ourselves and others by interacting and sharing.

We will learn things about one another that will distress us. And we may well wish we didn't know some things about others. How will the socially-offensive become socially- acceptable without help from a loving society? And how can a society become loving if people are not broad-minded enough to figure out that some things just don't matter? Few things really are important. If a man is honest, just, virtuous, and true, should you care if he swears? If a man has a heart of gold and would give you assistance if he thought it was needed, should you care if he is rough and uncouth?

The adulterous and predatory will rarely reform and must often be excluded. They will victimize and destroy. We are commanded to cast out those who steal, love and make a lie, commit adultery, and refuse to repent. The instructions we have been given state:

> *You shall not kill; he that kills shall die. You shall not steal...he that steals and will not repent* ***shall be cast out.*** *You shall not lie; he that lies and will not repent* ***shall be cast out****. You shall love your wife with all your heart, and shall cleave unto her and none else...he that looks upon a woman to lust after her shall deny the faith, and shall not have the spirit, and if he repent not...****shall be cast out****. You shall not commit adultery, and he that commits adultery and repents not* ***shall be cast out****; and he that commits adultery and repents with all his heart, and forsakes [it] and does it no more, you shall forgive him; but if he does it again, he* ***shall not be forgiven****, [and]* ***shall be cast out****. You shall not speak evil of your neighbor [nor] or do him any harm. You know my laws, they are given in my scriptures.* ***He that sins and repents not shall be cast out****. If you love me, you shall serve me and* ***keep all my commandments****.* (T&C 26:6, emphasis added)

This teaching is still binding. If your fellowship includes those who ought to be "cast out" you have the obligation to do so rather than encouraging evil. Be patient, but be firm. If a person refuses to repent and forsake sins, you may end fellowship with them and include those who are interested in practicing obedience and love.

The Gospel is based upon happiness. Alma writes of this as the "great plan of happiness."_Your affiliation with the Church should bring you happiness. Your faith should be filled with joyfulness. The Gospel is intended to awaken in you security, love, and hopefulness which increase your joy for life.

If you find you are entrenched in fear, anger, and selfishness, then something is wrong. Delightful people should never have their joy curtailed by small-minded and oppressive others. You should not surrender your agency to the opinions of others. It is just fine if you are misunderstood and viewed harshly. It is almost the ideal if people speak about you falsely and misunderstand your true intentions. You are most closely following Him when you suffer under these burdens. He told you: "Blessed are they which are persecuted for righteousness' sake: for theirs is the kingdom of heaven. Blessed are ye, when men shall revile you, and persecute you, and shall say all manner of evil against you falsely, for my sake. Rejoice, and be exceeding glad: for great is your reward in heaven: for so persecuted they the prophets which were before you." (Matt. 5: 10–12.) If you are going to do it right, persecution is part of the package. You get to be understood by Heaven, but misunderstood by your fellowman. There is deep satisfaction in knowing you are more interested in what the Lord thinks of you than in caring about the opinions of men. It is liberating. You will find yourself, as you lose your good name and reputation among men. Unfortunately, you may also be called upon to lose your good name among fellow Saints. We can be pretty hard on each other. We should know better, but we don't. So you need to be tolerant, forgiving and patient even with the Saints. This will free you to find joy. For when you are given offenses, but return good for bad, you grow into something bigger and better. You get to know Him.

The Gospel aims to reunite you with God.

The foregoing excerpts are taken from:

- Stephanie Snuffer's remarks titled "Love Others As Yourself" given at a regional conference in Sandy, UT on July 14, 2019
- Denver's conference talk titled "Civilization", given in Grand Junction, CO on April 21, 2019
- Denver's blog entry titled Come and Be Saved, posted August 9, 2010, and recorded April 17, 2021
- Passages from Denver's book titled The Second Comforter: Conversing with the Lord through the Veil, publishedJune 14, 2006, recorded April 17, 2021;
- Denver's blog entry titled 2 Nephi 30:2, posted August 16, 2010, and recorded April 17, 2021
- A fireside talk titled "Cursed, Denied Priesthood", given in Sandy, UT on January 7th, 2018
- A Glossary of Gospel Terms, "Intercession", recorded April 17, 2021
- The presentation of "Answer and Covenant", given at the Covenant of Christ Conference in Boise, ID on September 3rd, 2017
- Denver's blog entry titled 3 Nephi 14:1-2, posted October 26, 2010, and recorded April 17, 2021
- Denver's conference talk titled "The Heavens are Open", given in Hurricane, UT on March 22, 2020
- Denver's talk titled "Authority, Keys and Kingdom" given at a regional conference in Sandy, UT on July 14, 2019; and

- A passage from Denver's book titled Eighteen Verses, published October 31, 2007, and recorded April 17, 2021

142. Shem, Part 1

This is the first part of a series about Shem, who came to be known as Melchizedek, one of the Patriarchal Fathers, who established a city of peace that ultimately achieved the status of "Zion" and was taken up into heaven.

DENVER: (Moses 7:20-21, 23): "And it came to pass that Enoch talked with the Lord; and he said unto the Lord: Surely Zion shall dwell in safety forever. But the Lord said unto Enoch: Zion have I blessed, but the residue of the people have I cursed. And it came to pass that the Lord showed unto Enoch" and he saw everything. And "...Zion was taken up into heaven, Enoch beheld, and lo, all the nations of the earth were before him;" and so on. So Enoch and his city depart.

Now we have not only the example from Section 107 of the appearance of the Lord, Enoch and his city were taken up. Noah remained behind. Again, here I am offering you my view. I am not offering you something which has been endorsed by anyone, although there are those folk on the fringe who have suggested the same thing that I think. But it is my view that Melchizedek is the new name given to Shem, and that Shem is the son of Noah. When it's talking about the priesthood through the fathers unto Noah as the basis for a doctrinal interpretation, that that means that there were generations separating Noah from Melchizedek; that's not how I read the verse. I read it to say, "Through the fathers, that is, from Adam down to Noah," and the connection between Noah and Melchizedek is immediate, father and son, and Shem is the son, which is why then the next appearance of Zion happens as a connection. These initial appearances of Zion in this world are connected, because the first one in the valley of Adam-ondi-Ahman occurs, and Enoch is present. The second one occurs with Enoch, who was present when the Lord had dwelt with people before. The third one will occur when Melchizedek, who was acquainted with those on the other side of the flood – he's an adult when they enter the Ark. He knew of Enoch, and the option. At that moment in history, here's the dilemma: God is going to destroy the world but a group inside the world had attained the status of Zion. Since they are in the state of being Zion the world cannot destroy them. It is fair game for the wicked to destroy the righteous. The wicked are allowed to destroy the righteous all the time. If you don't believe that then go ask Amulek, whose suggestion to Alma was rejected because Alma was saying, "Oh, no, this is a good deal. Let them burn. The Lord is getting mad right now. Something's going to happen." These people are received up in glory. These people being killed by the wicked, the wicked get to kill them! And they get to kill them because then God will judge the wicked by the taking of the lives. That's the system. The most righteous man who ever lived was allowed to be killed by the wicked. In fact, was indispensable that the wicked get to kill the righteous because otherwise there could not have an Atonement then made. Therefore, Christ was slain at the hands of wicked men. But we have a problem with Zion because when the Lord sets about to destroy, the Lord cannot destroy the righteous, and He's going to obliterate life on the earth except for those who were in the Ark or those in Zion. The wicked can't come against them and all are going to be destroyed.

So what do you do? Well, we've got a new status for humanity. The new status is you take them into heaven. But you don't take people into heaven without an associated calling. There is no reason ever to take a person off the earth, even if they're righteous. Abraham died and was buried. Christ died and He was more righteous than any who ever lived. You don't take them off the earth unless they have a calling to minister, so we have a calling to minister. Enoch and his city could not be destroyed when the Lord was going to destroy. [He] and his city were called and they were given two callings: Their first assignment is as ministering angels, not only here but elsewhere. Their second calling – I don't want to appear irreverent but really they're the crowd – they're the cheering group backing up the Lord at His Coming. They are the ones when He comes in the clouds with the angels. That group is Enoch's people. They are the certifiers, they are the testifiers, they are the chorus, they are the entourage.

There is a reason why our tinhorn dictators and our phony idols have an entourage. It's to mimic the real deal, because when the Lord comes again in His glory he's going to come with an entourage. So they got the job, Enoch and his folk.

Melchizedek, who was acquainted with that condition, in my view had to be offered the option. Going on the Ark and staying down here when there is a group that are going to be leaving and going elsewhere, Noah was qualified to leave. All of them were qualified to leave and they had to be willing to stay. When you are allowed the option, and when you are going to stay but you know that there are those who are taken up, it seems like a reasonable request for Melchizedek to make, that after he finishes his ministry here that he also should be allowed to take a people with him.

In the course of events Melchizedek established a city, a City of Peace, a city of righteousness. He was the king and he was the priest, and he presided over his people in righteousness. Abraham, who was converted to the truth, came to Melchizedek. They had a ceremonial get-together in which, among other things, there is a sacral meal. Melchizedek, who has been waiting for this moment, *'hands the football'* to Abraham and says, "At last! Me and my people are gone!" And so, once again, Zion flees.

When Zion flees again, now we have the people of Melchizedek. Notice, if you will, that the Priesthood after the Order of the Son of God has been renamed the Priesthood of Enoch, and then renamed again the Melchizedek priesthood. That name has become rather more enduring because in each case they came and they established Zion, and when they established Zion they were taken with their people up into heaven.

Now we have...I was going to read this stuff about Melchizedek. You'll find that in the Joseph Smith Translation of Genesis Chapter 14. It's a long enough section that it's back in the back of your bible, beginning with verse 25:

"And Melchizedek lifted up his voice and blessed Abram. Now Melchizedek was a man of faith, who wrought righteousness; and when a child he feared God, and stopped the mouths of lions, and quenched the violence of fire. And thus, having been approved of God, he was ordained an high priest after the order of the covenant which God made with Enoch," (Vs. 25-27.) He's got the same covenant as had been previously made with Enoch. That tells you something if you're paying attention. "It being after the order of the Son of God; which order came, not by man, nor the will of man; neither by father nor mother; neither by beginning of days nor end of years; but of God; And it was delivered unto men by the calling of his own voice, according to his own will, unto as many as (received) his name." (Vs. 28-29.)

Joseph Smith tells us when he got the Melchizedek Priesthood, in my view. And in my view it was not an incident that occurred in which Peter, James and John were present. But it was "the voice of God in the chamber of old Father Whitmer, in Fayette, Seneca county" (D&C 128:21) when Joseph received the Melchizedek priesthood. Peter, James and John, like other angelic ministrants, came to deliver keys but not Melchizedek Priesthood because the priesthood of Melchizedek comes but of God. "It was delivered unto men by the calling of his own voice, according to his own will, unto as many as believed on his name. We can ordain people all day long, but the manner the ordination assumes power is by 'the calling of God's own voice'." That's the description given by the Prophet Joseph Smith in the translation of Genesis

14. He tells us that event took place from the voice of God in the chamber of old Father Whitmer, as referred to in D&C 128:21.

D&C 128 is a letter Joseph Smith wrote in Nauvoo. It's late in his ministry. It's a letter that Joseph wrote while he is in hiding in Nauvoo and he's trying to stay in contact with the saints. I make no reference to this in *Passing the Heavenly Gift* but it is another example, just as it is a glaring omission from the testimony of Oliver Cowdery, that he makes no mention of Elijah's appearance in what we have in D&C Section 110. So also, in the listing of the angelic ministrants who came to Joseph Smith, in a letter that he composed in Nauvoo in 1842, six years after the appearance of Elijah. To our current way of informing one another he does not include Elijah in the letter or the list. And throughout the time period that he's speaking in Nauvoo – you can look at the Nauvoo talks, and we will look at some of them – Joseph speaks of the return of Elijah as a still future event. If the return of Elijah is a still future event in 1842, 1843, and 1844, then the appearance of Elijah in the Kirtland Temple cannot answer to the mission of Elijah.

But now we're ahead of the story. Let's go back to Melchizedek for a moment. In the case of Melchizedek, once again we see a repetition of the pattern in which there is a prophet-ministrant and a people who respond to the message of repentance, and people coming up to the state in which the Lord can come and dwell with them and then they are taken up into heaven. And then the narrative of the appearance of Zion evaporates from the scriptural record. Now, we do have the Nephite experience where the Lord came and He dwelt among them. They were not taken up into heaven. For a moment I want to stay on the idea of Zion's ascent up the heavenly corridor. Just like the first Zion with Adam, all of those, including Adam, died, except Enoch and his city, and they did not die, they were taken up into heaven. Then we have Melchizedek, and his city was taken up into heaven. The subsequent experiences where the Lord visited with people, whether it is in Jerusalem or whether it is in the new world, did not result in Zion going up and ascending into heaven. It didn't happen.

See, everything proceeds according to law. And the government of God is not necessarily limited to an organizational structure, but it hails back to things that were committed, by God—in promises made to the fathers—which have to be fulfilled. And it doesn't matter if we try to capture that. God's purposes are ordained according to a law that was ordained before the world was.

> *I am the Lord thy God; and I give unto you [a] commandment—that no man shall come unto my Father but by me or by my word, which is my law,*

> *saith the Lord.* (ibid, vs. 12)

In other words, if you are going to come—whoever you are—unto the Father, the only way you are going to get there will be through the Son.

> *And everything that is in the world, whether it be ordained of men, by thrones, or principalities, or powers, or things of name, whatsoever they may be, that are not by me or by my word, saith the Lord, shall be thrown down, and shall not remain after men are dead, neither in nor after the resurrection, saith the Lord your God. For whatsoever things remain are by me; ...whatsoever things are not by me shall be shaken and destroyed.* (ibid, vs. 13-14)

This is another way in which we can know that *the keeper of the gate **is** the Holy One of Israel; **and** he employeth no servant there* (2 Nephi 9:41, emphasis added; 2 Nephi 6:11 RE). Because when it comes to this kind of material, involving this kind of salvation—for any of the children of men—God is hands-on. And our Redeemer is the one who not only keeps the gate, protects the way, but greets those along the way whom He is going to introduce to the Father.

And it has to be *by me, or by my word, saith the Lord....* If it is not, *then it shall be thrown down [and it] shall not remain* (D&C 132:13). Only God can, or does, ordain covenants. We do not make covenants. Covenants come as a consequence of God's will, and **only** as a consequence of God's will. We can accept them, or we can reject them—but we cannot create them. He does. Our participation is limited to acceptance of—or rejection of—what He offers.

The way in which we accept the covenants is set out in Doctrine and Covenants section 130: *There is a law, irrevocably decreed in heaven before the foundations of this world, upon which all blessings are predicated—And when we obtain any blessing from God, it is by obedience to that law upon which it is predicated* (D&C 130:20-21). Therefore, what is important for you to understand and to know is whatever it is that law consists of. Because the way in which you accept the covenant that has been offered to you is by learning the principle or the law upon which the blessing you seek is predicated. And then, having learned what law that is upon which it is predicated, obeying it.

We learn all of this through the revelations given to us through Joseph Smith.

Before Joseph of Egypt, one of the fathers that we need to look at is Abraham. And therefore, I want to turn to Abraham chapter 1, beginning at verse 2:

> *And, finding there was greater happiness and peace and rest for me, I sought for the blessings of the fathers...*

Once again, now we have Abraham, and we've gone all the way back to him generations before Joseph of Egypt, and we encounter the same thing—that is, searching for the blessings which belong to the fathers—Abraham looking for the blessings of the fathers, hoping to find, thereby, happiness; hoping to find peace and rest for himself.

> *...and the right whereunto I should be ordained to administer the same; having been myself a follower of righteousness, desiring also to be one who possessed great knowledge...*

You know, when I spoke in Logan, I talked about repentance being related to knowledge and that it's our ignorance that damns us, most of all. Abraham perceived the same thing. And Abraham believed that redemption and possessing great knowledge went hand-in-hand. And if he could obtain that great knowledge, then he wanted to be:

> *a greater follower of righteousness, and* [as a consequence of that] *to possess a greater knowledge...*

Because this is one of those laws upon which blessings are predicated. Knowledge, light, truth, the glory of God—all of those things are obtained by obedience to law. And Abraham sought for and desired to possess more light and truth. And as a result of that, he wanted inevitably to become:

> *...a father of many nations, a prince of peace, and* [he desired most of all] *...to receive instructions, and to keep...commandments of God.* [As a result of all that desire, he] *became a rightful heir, a High Priest, holding the right belonging to the fathers. It was conferred upon me* ***from the fathers;*** *it came down* ***from the fathers****, from the beginning of time, yea, even from the beginning, or before the foundation of the earth, down to the present time, even the right of the firstborn, or the first man, who is Adam, or [the] first father, through the fathers unto me.*

All of this ties back, necessarily, to Adam.

> *I sought for mine appointment unto the Priesthood according to the appointment of God unto the fathers concerning the seed.* (Abraham 1:2-4; see also Abraham 1:1 RE)

Everything about the original form of priesthood, everything about what it is that Abraham was seeking, all of this ties together because there is only one gospel.

In the Lectures on Faith, the Second Lecture paragraphs 37 to 53, there is a chronology given. I'm not gonna go through the chronology, and you needn't have brought it with you tonight. But that chronology is listed in the Lectures on Faith in order to save you the trouble of going through and tracking it yourself. But it was important enough to Joseph Smith to put it into the Lectures on Faith so that you know how to reconstruct the fathers— who they were.

Noah was 502 years old when Shem was born. 98 years later the Flood came. Noah was 600 years old when the Flood came; Shem was 98. (You can see that in paragraph 45 of the Second Lecture.) Shem lived to be 600. Shem was 448 years old when Noah died. Shem was acquainted with both Noah and Abraham. Abraham lived to be 175 years old, and Shem was alive and a contemporary with ~~Shem~~ [Abraham] for 150 of the 175 years of the life of Abraham. Shem knew Noah. And Shem knew those on the other side of the Flood, having lived with them for 98 years before the Flood.

Abraham had the records of the fathers. Look at Abraham chapter 1, verse 31:

> *But the records of the fathers, even the patriarchs, concerning the right of Priesthood, the Lord my God preserved in mine own hands; therefore a knowledge of the beginning of the creation, and also of the planets, and of the stars, as they were made known unto the fathers, have I kept even unto this day, and I shall endeavor to write some of these things upon this record, for the benefit of my posterity that shall come after me* (see also Abraham 2:4 RE).

Since Abraham was acquainted with the priesthood that belonged to the fathers—and since Abraham had a knowledge that was reckoned from priesthood, that goes back to the time of the patriarchs—he, as a consequence of possessing that, knew about the beginning of creation, knew about the planets, knew about the stars as they were made known unto the fathers.

Go back to Doctrine and Covenants section 121; it's talking about our dispensation. I want to look at—beginning at about verse 28:

> *A time to come in the which nothing shall be withheld, whether there be one God or many gods, they shall be manifest* [because that's included within the knowledge that the first fathers had—that's included with what was here at one time]. *All thrones and dominions, principalities and powers,*

> *shall be revealed and set forth upon all who have endured valiantly for the gospel of Jesus Christ. And also, if there be bounds set to the heavens or to the seas, [and] to the dry land, ...to the sun, moon, or stars—All the times of their revolutions, all the appointed days, months, and years, and all the days of their days, months, and years, and all [the] glories, laws, ...set times, shall be revealed in the days of the dispensation of the fulness of times—According to that which was ordained in the midst of the Council of the Eternal God of all other gods before this world was, that should be reserved unto the finishing and the end thereof, when every man shall enter into his eternal presence and into his immortal rest.* (D&C 121:28-32; see also T&C 138:21)

Abraham is not merely talking about something—both in this verse, Abraham 1:31, as well as what we encounter later on in the Book of Abraham about the various stars that were shown to him and the relationship between them and his Facsimile #2, as I recollect—that is, an effort to lay out a relationship in the heavens between certain positions of glory and authority. But Abraham is testifying that it was part of the original gospel that was entrusted to the fathers and that those records were handed down to him. In Doctrine and Covenants section 121, we find out that that's part of what is supposed to have been included within, and is ultimately scheduled for revelation to, those that will receive the restoration of the Gospel, when it is fully upon the earth in the dispensation of the fullness of times.

Abraham received his priesthood ordination through Melchizedek. You can see that in Doctrine and Covenants section 84, verse 14: *Which Abraham received the priesthood from Melchizedek, who received it through the lineage of his fathers, even till Noah* (see also T&C 82:10). Now, Bruce R. McConkie reads that verse, and he disagrees with what the church had previously taught; that is, that Melchizedek was Shem. He takes the position that this 14 means that *Melchizedek, who received it through the lineage of his fathers, even till Noah,* means that there were fathers between Melchizedek, on the one hand, and Noah, on the other—and therefore, Melchizedek could not be Shem. I take the view, instead, that it was received *through the lineage of his fathers even [until] Noah*, meaning from Adam down to the time of Noah, the priesthood was preserved, and that Melchizedek—that is, Shem—received it from Noah. In any event, it's clear in verse 14 that Abraham received it from Melchizedek. But if you go to Abraham chapter 2, in the Book of Abraham, beginning at verse 6:

> *But I, Abraham, and Lot, my brother's son, prayed unto the Lord, and the Lord appeared unto me, and said unto me: Arise, and take Lot with thee; for I have purposed to take thee away out of Haran, and to make of thee a*

> *minister to bear my name in a strange land which [will I] give unto thy seed after thee for an everlasting possession, when they hearken to my voice. For I am the Lord thy God; I dwell in heaven; the earth is my footstool; I stretch my hand over the sea, and it obeys my voice; I cause the wind and the fire to be my chariot; I say to the mountains—Depart hence— ...behold, they are taken away by a whirlwind, in an instant, suddenly. My name is Jehovah, and I know the end from the beginning; therefore my hand shall be over thee. And I will make of thee a great nation, ...I will bless thee above measure, and make thy name great among all nations, and thou shalt be a blessing unto thy seed after thee, that in their hands they shall bear this ministry and Priesthood unto all nations; ...I will bless them through thy name; for as many as receive this Gospel shall be called after thy name, and shall be accounted thy seed, and shall rise up and bless thee, as their father* (see also Abraham 3:1 RE).

"Ordination" and "confirmation by the voice of God" are two separate events. We'll speak more about this in the next talk, which will be on Priesthood. But it's enough to simply take note of that here.

Jehovah, speaking directly to Abraham, tells him that from this moment—from the moment God spoke to Abraham before his departure—Abraham would now become the father of all the righteous. Now you ought to ask yourself: Why would that be the case? Why is it that Abraham becomes the prototype of who will be saved and the father of whomever **is** saved from that point going forward? When you go back to the fathers and you begin with Adam—although there were apostasies (and apostasies began immediately—it was generations before Eve bore Cain and thought she had a son that would, at last, be faithful. They were grandparents when Cain was born. And then Able was born. And Cain slew Able. And Seth came as a replacement to the grandparents, Adam and Eve. And from Seth reckons then the seed of the righteous)—

Father to son to grandson to great-grandson—when you look at the list of those that are gathered together into the valley of Adam-ondi-Ahman, in the first Zion, where the Lord came and dwelt among them—And he rose up and he called Adam, Michael [El being the name of God]—Jehovah appeared in the valley of Adam-ondi-Ahman, and you have— seventh from Adam being Enoch—you have a line of continuity from Adam, directly down all the way until you arrive at Shem.

But when you hit Shem, it interrupts. There is a complete falling away. There are no righteous fathers for Abraham. His fathers had turned to idolatry. Abraham is the prototype of the saved man and the father of all who would be righteous thereafter because Abraham represents coming to the truth in a generation of apostasy. Abraham represents coming back to the light, despite the fact that his fathers taught him idolatry. Abraham represents the challenge that every man who would be saved from that point forward must find themselves within and then overcome: the idolatry of their fathers. Abraham is the prototype.

And so Abraham is acknowledged by that same Jehovah who visited with the fathers in Adam-ondi-Ahman and identified Himself again to Abraham who —after apostasy— becomes, literally, the first—the first to return to the righteousness of the first fathers; the first to return to the religion that belonged in the beginning to mankind; the first to discover *a knowledge of the beginning of the creation, [as] also of the planets, and of the stars, as they were made known unto the fathers* (Abraham 1:31; see also Abraham 2:4 RE).

Abraham was the one who desired to be *a follower of righteousness, ...one who possessed great knowledge, ...to be a greater follower of righteousness and to possess...greater knowledge* still (Abraham 1:2; see also Abraham 1:1 RE). It is this which made him a candidate the Lord could speak to. It's this that made him the prototype in his generation of what it takes to turn away from idolatry, to turn away from the kind of corrupt and degrading religions that were then in play on the earth—the fertility cults and the human sacrifices and the vileness that surrounded him. And then, having done so, to be asked by God to slay his son, as if there was some legitimacy to the rites that were practiced all around him.

Now in the version that we have in the King James Bible, Isaac is not slain. There is an older tradition—that you can find in the book of Hebrews, and you can find it in the Book of Mormon—where Isaac is slain, and he's brought back to life, rather like Lazarus is brought back to life. But it's clear that the Old Testament version that we have in King James: he raises his hand with a knife to commit the act, and then the ram is found in the thicket to deliver him. Sometimes, as it turns out, rams are not found in thickets, and the sacrifice will be required.

The Lord says:

> *I will bless them that bless thee, ...curse them that curse thee; and in thee (that is, in thy Priesthood)* [because fundamentally, what distinguishes Abraham and what distinguishes the covenant is the knowledge that he has—Abraham is in possession of something because Abraham **knows** some things that are true that relate back to the very beginning; and as a

> consequence of that, those who are given the same **knowledge** necessarily have to belong to the same priesthood] *...in thy seed (that is, [in] thy Priesthood)* [because you **become** a son of Abraham if you take upon yourself the requirements for the covenant; you inherit that, just as Abraham inherited it—it comes down from the beginning from the fathers], *for I give unto thee a promise that this right shall continue in thee, and in thy seed after thee (that is to say, the literal seed, or...seed of the body) shall all the families of the earth be blessed, even with the blessings of the Gospel, which are the blessings of salvation, even of life eternal. Now, after the Lord had withdrawn from speaking [un]to me, and withdrawn his face from me, I said in my heart: Thy servant has sought thee earnestly; now I have found thee.* (Abraham 2:11-12; see also Abraham 3:1 RE)

And there again, Abraham stands as the prototype of the saved man, the father of the righteous, the example of all those who, coming out of apostasy, find themselves redeemed—because all the servants that will be acknowledged by Him must seek Him earnestly and will, as the Lectures on Faith promise, assuredly find Him. Everyone who receives the gospel, this gospel (verse 10 of that Abraham chapter 2): *As many as receive this Gospel shall be called after thy name.* You ought to ask yourself: What is *this Gospel?* And are you yet in possession of it? Because it would appear that the promises made to the fathers includes rather more than what we know about, as yet.

But it is, nevertheless, the case that it is through Joseph and Jacob, Isaac and Abraham that the promises remain. You can see that in Doctrine and Covenants section 27. We only need to look at verse 10 of section 27: *[As] also with Joseph and Jacob, and Isaac, and Abraham, your fathers, by whom the promises remain*; that is, promises are still in play, right now, as a consequence of what God did in covenant with Joseph and covenant with Jacob and covenant with Isaac and covenant with Abraham. Those promises are still in play. This is what Moroni was talking to Joseph Smith about. *And* [verse 11] *also with Michael, or Adam, the father of all, the prince of all, the ancient of days.* Promises that are in play today go all the way back to them.

The covenant which we receive will come as consequence of **them**. What **they** got secured for **us** promises which the Lord intends to honor. Therefore, when we are the beneficiaries of those covenants, we are going—like Abraham—to have restored to us a *knowledge of the beginning of creation, ...the planets, ...the stars, as they were made known unto the fathers,* and as Section 121 tells us is going to be the case in the Dispensation of the Fulness of Time.

Go to Joseph Smith Translation of Genesis chapter 14, beginning at verse 25:

> *Melchizedek lifted up his voice and blessed Abram. Now Melchizedek was a man of faith, who wrought righteousness; and when a child he feared God, and stopped the mouths of lions, ...quenched the violence of fire. ...thus, having been approved of God, he was ordained an high priest after the order of the covenant which God made with Enoch, It being after the order of the Son of God.* (JST Genesis 14:25-28; see also Genesis 7:17-18 RE)

There is an order that is after the son of God. But there was a covenant that preceded even the days of Melchizedek; it came down as a consequence of what happened with Enoch.

> *It was delivered unto men by the calling of his own voice, according to his own will, unto as many as believed on his name. For God having sworn unto Enoch and unto his seed with an oath by himself; that every one being ordained after this order and calling should have power, by faith, to break mountains, to divide the seas...dry up [the] waters, ...turn them out of their course; To put at defiance the armies of nations, to divide the earth, ...break every band, to stand in the presence of God; to do all things...according to his command, subdue principalities and powers;* ***and this by the will of the Son of God*** *which was from before the foundation of the world.* (ibid, vs. 29-31, emphasis added; see also Genesis 7:18-19 RE)

See, it's not your will. Even if you're given this ordination, it is by the will of the Son of God. That is to say, nothing gets broken, nothing gets held in defiance, nothing gets done except by the will of the Son.

> *Men having this faith, coming up unto this order of God, were translated and taken up into heaven. ...now, Melchizedek was a priest of this order; therefore he obtained peace in Salem, and was called the Prince of peace...his people* [his **people**] *wrought righteousness, and obtained heaven, and sought for the city of Enoch which God had before taken, separating it from the earth, having reserved* ***it*** *unto the latter days, or the end of the world; And hath said, and sworn with an oath, that the heavens and the earth should come together; and the sons of God should be tried so as by fire.* (ibid, vs. 32-35, emphasis added; see also Genesis 7:19-20 RE)

These are they who are coming, whose glory and brightness will burn them up who are on the earth, who are unprepared to receive them. **These** are they about whom Moroni was speaking to Joseph Smith.

> *And this Melchizedek, having thus established righteousness, was called the king of heaven by his people, or, in other words, the King of peace....he lifted*

> *up his voice, ...he blessed Abram, being the high priest, and the keeper of the storehouse of God; Him [unto] whom God had appointed to receive tithes for the poor. Wherefore, Abram paid unto him tithes of all...he had, of all the riches which he possessed, which God had given him more than that which he had need. And it came to pass, that God blessed Abram, and gave unto him riches, and honor, and lands for an everlasting possession; according to the covenant which he had made, ...according to the blessing[s] wherewith Melchizedek had blessed him.* (ibid, vs. 36-40; see also Genesis 7:20-21 RE)

Joseph Smith restored this information—as he restored the rest of what he gave us—in order for us to understand that when God swears by Himself to the Fathers about what it is He intends to accomplish in the last-days, and we get near enough to that event so that we're over the horizon and inevitably going to fall into that dark day, some few will take it seriously enough to say, like Abraham, "I would like to seek for the blessings of the Fathers. I would like, also, to have from God a covenant. I would like to inherit what it was that was given in the beginning."

The foregoing excerpts are taken from:

- Denver's talk titled "The Mission of Elijah Reconsidered", given in Spanish Fork, UT on October 14th, 2011; and
- Denver's *40 Years in Mormonism Series*, Talk #4 titled "Covenants" given in Centerville, UT on October 6th, 2013.

143. Shem, Part 2

This is the second part of a series about Shem, who came to be known as Melchizedek, one of the Patriarchal Fathers, who established a city of peace that ultimately achieved the status of "Zion" and was taken up into heaven.

DENVER: this is in Moses chapter 6:

> And Adam lived one hundred and thirty years, and begat a son in his own likeness, after his own image, and called his name Seth. And the days of Adam, after he had begotten Seth, were eight hundred years, and he begat many sons and daughters; (Moses 6:10-11.)

Adam begat many sons and daughters, but the son named Seth was the one to whom this priesthood went because there is only one appointed.

> Seth lived one hundred and five years, and begat Enos, and prophesied in all his days, and taught his son Enos in the ways of God; wherefore Enos prophesied also. And Seth lived, after he begat Enos, eight hundred and seven years, and begat many sons and daughters. (Moses 6:13-14.)

Seth begat Enos and many sons and daughters. But the right of the lineage and the priesthood went from Adam, to Seth, to Enos.

This is a description of that priesthood which was briefly restored in one person, Joseph, to be given to Hyrum, because it goes to the oldest righteous descendent. And when it was first restored through Joseph Smith, Hyrum was not yet qualified. But when Hyrum became qualified by January of 1841, in the revelation given then, Hyrum is the one to whom the birthright went, being the eldest and being the one who was qualified. This is why it was necessary for Hyrum to die before Joseph, so that in this dispensation Joseph and Hyrum can stand at the head. Because if Hyrum had not died first but Joseph had died first, Joseph would have died without having had the passing.

Notice that Seth had many sons and daughters. Then you get to the next, Enos. He lived and begat Canaan. Enos also has many sons and daughters but Cannaan was the one upon whom the birthright – this follows all the way down. You can read it in Moses chapter 6 how it descends through the line. This pattern repeats over and over again.

As I'm talking about this I'm making reference to a diagram that appeared first in *The Millennial Star* on January 15, 1847. But what you can see in the *Joseph Smith Papers* on page 298 where they reproduce the same diagram of the "kingdom of God", the only difference being that I have filled in the names on this chart so that you can see where the names go.

We get to the point in the history of the world in which, after the days of Shem, who was renamed "Melchizedek", people fell into iniquity. They fell into iniquity and they lost the birthright. There was no continuation of this. It was broken by an apostasy and it had to be restored again, which ought to give all of us great hope because Abraham sought for this. He sought for a restoration of the kingdom of God. He sought for a restoration of this, which only one man on the earth can hold at a time. Abraham 1:2:

> And, finding there was greater happiness and peace and rest for me, I sought for the blessings of the fathers, and the right whereunto I should be ordained to administer the same; having been myself a follower of righteousness, desiring also to be one who possessed great knowledge, and to be a greater follower of righteousness, and to possess a greater knowledge, and to be a father of many nations, a prince of peace, and desiring to receive instructions, and to keep the commandments of God, I became a rightful heir, a High Priest, holding the right belonging to the fathers.

When you are in possession of that you have no problem asking God and getting an answer. It is the right belonging to the fathers. After a period of apostasy, and the break of this line, Abraham received it by adoption. Therefore, this power has the ability to cure the break. This covenant making through God has the ability to restore the family of God, even when wicked men kill in order to destroy it, even when a substitute needs to be made, even when the fathers turn from their righteousness, yet God is able to cause it to persist. Joseph Smith was doing something which no one else either understood or had the right to perpetuate.

This continued through ten generations from Adam to Melchizedek, but through Abraham it continued five generations. It appeared again once on the earth in a single generation that included Joseph and his brother Hyrum.

Now even the mockery of it has come to an end, because there is no such thing as a perpetuation "in honorable mention" of the descendants of Hyrum Smith in the office of Patriarch in the Church. There have been many signs that have been given by God that He was about to do something new from the time of the death of Joseph Smith till today. All that was left at the end was for a witness to be appointed, to come and to say, "It now has come to an end." In the last talk that I gave in the 10 lecture series I said, a witness has now come, and I am him. It has come to an end. One of the signs of it having come to an end was the passing of Eldred Smith. There are many other signs that have been given if you are looking for them. You can see them all along the line.

In the book of Matthew, chapter 24 is Christ's most extensive prophecy about the future events including the time of His Second Coming. While He gives some details in Matthew chapter 24 there is a statement that He makes: "*As the days of Noah were, so shall also the coming of the Son of man be.*" (Matthew 24:37)

He makes an analogy between the events that occurred during Noah's time and what we will see on the earth at the time of his return. Let me read you a description of the events at the time of Noah—and these are the kinds of events with which we typically associate the days of Noah: "*And God saw that the wickedness of men had become great in the earth; and every man was lifted up in the imagination of the thoughts of his heart, being only evil continually. The earth was corrupt before God, and it was filled with violence. And God looked upon the earth, and behold, it was corrupt, for all flesh had corrupted its way upon the earth. And God said unto Noah: The end of all flesh is come before me, for the earth is filled with violence, and behold I will destroy all flesh from off the earth.*" (See, Genesis 1:5-7; Moses 8:22, 28-30)

Ominous. Terrible. Reason for concern. That is what we generally think of. But there's another side to that. That other side includes obviously Noah. You can't have the days of Noah without having a Noah. Another contemporary who lived at the same time with Noah was Enoch, who built a city of righteousness where people gathered together to worship the only true God, who were then in turn taken up to heaven. That group of people, taken up to heaven, are going to return with the Lord when He comes again in glory. Book of Jude –there is only one chapter in there. "*Enoch also, the seventh from Adam, prophesied of these things saying, Behold, the Lord cometh with ten thousands of his saints.*" (Jude 1:14) There were those that were taken up into the heavens numbering in the tens of thousands who will return with him.

So if there is reason for pessimism when Christ predicts that, "*As it was in the days of Noah, so shall it be at the time of His return,*" (Matthew 24:37) there is also extraordinary reason for optimism because we are going to see things like Noah and his family –that included Shem, who would be renamed Melchizedek, about whom the apostle Paul had a great deal to say in the book of Hebrews comparing that man, a son of Noah, to the Lord Himself –actually we ought to flip that. He compares the Lord Himself to that man. And then there is Enoch. And so while we tend to look at the prophecy Christ gave concerning His coming negatively, about how far degenerate the world is going to go, those are the tares ripening.

Christ said, "*We're not going to uproot the tares, bind them in bundles and burn them, until the wheat also becomes ripe.*" (Matthew 13:30) You are here, you are Christian, and God would like you to be wheat. He would like you to ripen in righteousness while the world ripens in iniquity.

> [The Holy Order] was first given to Adam; he obtained the [first presiding position on the Earth], and held the keys of it from generation to generation. He obtained it in the Creation, before the world was formed. He had dominion given him over every living creature. He's Michael the Archangel, spoken of in the scriptures. Then to Noah, who is Gabriel; he stands next in authority to Adam in the [Holy Order]; He was called of God to this office, and was the Father of all living in this day, and to him was given the dominion. These men held the keys, first on earth, and then in heaven.
>
> The [Holy Order] is an everlasting principle, and existed with God from eternity, and will to eternity, without beginning of days or end of years. The keys have to be brought from heaven, whenever the Gospel is sent. When they are revealed from Heaven it is by Adam's authority.
>
> ...He (Adam) is the father of the human family and presides over the spirits of all men, and all that have had the keys must stand before him in this grand council. This may take place before some of us leave this stage of action. The Son of Man stands before him, and there is given him glory and dominion. Adam delivers up his stewardship to Christ, that which was delivered to him as holding the keys of the universe but retains his standing as the head of the human family. (TPJS, p. 157)

The Holy Order really begins at the point that Adam, the first man, who is called "the son of God" in Luke 3:38. Adam, the first man, obtains the Holy Order in the beginning, and included within it, is the right to preside over all of the human family and then the right to minister to his posterity, and to continue to hold that presiding position until the end of time.

Now Joseph skips from Adam down to Noah because Adam had a position and dominion and a right over all of humanity and Noah occupied the same position. All the descendants were looking to him, genealogically, as a father. The right descended down to Noah, through the Fathers, and these held that same Holy Order. But they had siblings and they had relations who were not their descendants. Therefore, although they were within the Holy Order, unlike Adam and unlike Noah, there were other people living who would descend outside of their genealogical connection. They would not be the father of these people, but the Holy Order was passed down in this fashion. Joseph is looking at this from the perspective of who has it all, and all was combined into Adam and into Noah. There's a shift in the landscape that's going to take place later but we'll get to that in a moment.

Joseph says: "there are two priesthoods spoken of in the Scriptures, viz, Melchizedek and Aaronic or Levitical. Although there are two priesthoods, yet the Melchizedek priesthood comprehends the Aaronic or Levitical and is the grand head, and holds the highest authority which pertains to [I'm going to change the word now to the Holy Order] and the keys of the Kingdom of God in all ages of the world, to the latest posterity on the earth; and is the channel through which all knowledge, doctrine, the plan of salvation, and every important matter is revealed from heaven" comes through the Holy Order. "Its institution was prior to 'the foundation of this [world] where the morning stars sang together or the sons of God shouted for joy' and is the highest and holiest [order] and is after the Order of the Son of God." I'm going to pause there.

We think that the renaming of the Holy Order to the Melchizedek priesthood, in order to avoid the too frequent repetition of the name of the Son of God, was done out of respect for the Messiah, Jesus Christ, and that's true enough. However, the Holy Order, by its very nature, includes the Holy Order after the Order of the Son of God; one of whom was also Adam. When the apostle John wrote his epistle, he described those who had come in by way of conversion through him and received from him what the Lord had given to him, and he says:

> *Behold, what manner of love the Father hath bestowed upon us, that we should be called the sons of God: therefore the world knoweth us not, because it knew him not. Beloved, now are we the sons of God, and it doth not yet appear what we shall be: but we know that, when he shall appear, we shall be like him; for we shall see him as he is. And every man that hath this hope in him purifieth himself, even as he is pure.* (1 John 3:1-3)

I would like to suggest that the Holy Order after the Order of the Son of God includes the fact that those who inherit the Holy Order *are* sons of God. Therefore, in a way, calling it the Holy Order after the Order of the Son of God, is a way of identifying the recipient as someone who has become one of God's sons. I think it's appropriate to regard the primary identifier–that is the subject of who the Son of God is–to be Jesus Christ and Jesus Christ alone. Because quite frankly, He's the only one who attained the resurrection, and it is through the power of the resurrection that we're going to come forth. We do not have the power in ourselves to rise from the dead. The wages of sin are death, we've earned those wages; we all will die. The Savior did not earn those wages, He died, and therefore His death was unjust and the law of justice got broken when He died. Therefore, whenever justice makes a claim on any of us He can point to the fact that justice extracted from Him eternal life, and that is an infinite price for Him to have paid. Therefore He has compensated for all of mankind's shortcomings [and] failures.

Christ is the means by which we lay hold upon the promises but it is His intention to make of us all sons of God. Therefore, the Holy Order after the Son of God is when the name is announced, self-identifying the person holding such a Holy Order as one of God's sons, even though they may be mortal, even though they may be in the flesh. The Holy Order is for that very purpose and is after the Order of the Son of God. "...All other priesthoods are only parts, ramifications, powers and blessings belonging to the same, and are held, controlled and directed by it. It is the channel through which the Almighty commenced revealing His glory at the beginning of the creation of this earth, and through which He has continued to reveal Himself to the children of men to the present time, and through which He will make known His purposes to the end of time."

Therefore, among other things, the purpose of the Holy Order is to put in place a mechanism by which God can reveal from heaven what is necessary for the salvation of man on earth, in every generation, in order to fix what is broken, in order to restore what has been lost, in order to repair, heal, forgive, and reconnect those who are willing to give heed to the message sent from heaven, so that they can rise up to become sons of God.

The Holy Order descended from Adam in turn. We're not going to do it but if you take the time to go through and look at who got ordained, Seth was a replacement for the slain Abel. Cain was an elder brother. Cain would have qualified as the elder brother if he had been righteous for inheriting the Holy Order. He had lived long enough and he had been observed by his parents long enough so that Eve identified Cain as a man who had been gotten from

God. Therefore she knew he would not fail, which means that for at least some prolonged period of time after the sons and daughters of Adam and Eve had drifted into apostasy, Cain exhibited not only an interest but an adherence to what was being taught by the first parents. Eve celebrated that they at last had someone to whom the Holy Order could be passed. Cain was not the oldest son. He was the *oldest righteous son* and as the oldest righteous son it would have passed to him in due course. Abel, his younger brother, was probably in his day righteous because of the positive example of his older brother Cain. If you've got someone in the family who is on the right path, it's so much easier for the sibling to respect the example of someone similarly situated with them than it is to listen to the parents. Abel likewise followed in the path of righteousness.

Satan put it into the heart of Cain to view the inheritance that he was going to receive of the Holy Order as an opportunity to gratify his pride, and to satisfy his ambition, and to exert control and compulsion, because if he were the one in the line then the Messiah would descend through him and he would have a patriarchal position superior to the Messiah himself. This was an important part of the plot of the adversary. If the adversary could gain control over the inheritor under Adam of the Holy Order, then as I just read a moment ago, before the Savior returns, when dominion was given to Adam, it was by God's word and God cannot break His word. The right of dominion had been conferred. It has to be returned to Him. If Cain were the one in the position to exercise control then he could exert whatever conditions Satan put into his heart before he would return the right of dominion back to the Savior. Thus, if a disciple of Satan were to be in possession of that Holy Order in that line holding dominion, all of the conditions that Satan had demanded in the preexistence, which were rejected by the Father and created the war in heaven designed to destroy the agency of man, could become the condition for the redemption of this creation. Therefore, Cain's apostasy represented an enormous threat to the salvation of everyone who would live thereafter. As a consequence of that, the offering by the younger brother was approved and the older brother Cain was told, "You need to stop what you're doing, you need to repent and return, and if you do not, sin lieth at the door. The adversary is ready to enter into your house." This represented a serious frustration or threat to the second great conspiracy to destroy the souls of men and to capture this creation. Therefore, Satan put it into the heart of Cain to murder his brother and Abel was slain so that, the theory was, by controlling the position that necessarily meant that the Messiah would be a descendant of Cain's, the line would come through him, and he would have the authority, the control, the dominion, and the right to change the plan or the conditions for the salvation of the souls of men in this world.

At this point we're at the very beginning, we haven't gotten very far. But it is essential when you begin to talk about the Holy Order that you start here. If you don't start here, if you want to start at the time of Moses and the Aaronic priests, or you want to start at the time of Joseph Smith and talk about ordinations in June 1831, or if you want to talk about the three witnesses identifying the Quorum of the Twelve and then ordaining them, you're not going to comprehend what the Holy Order is all about because the Holy Order has, as part of its implication, the right of dominion over all creation. That was what it was established for and it came down to the beginning. It belonged to God. It is why God is God. In essence the Holy Order is to create of flesh and blood a surrogate for the Father and Mother. That's what the Holy Order was designed to accomplish.

In the beginning, when you're talking about this process, the reason why we have Seth as the next person is because Cain fell, Abel was murdered, and perhaps, because of the example, Adam and Eve in their sorrow were able to inform Seth of things that secured his fidelity to God. It descended in regular course down through these fathers until you get to Shem who was called Melchizedek. Mulek, king; Zedek, priest. It's a new name for the man, Shem, and then it simply falls into disrepair or apostasy and we encounter our first gap in the descent from the days of Adam down, which lasted several generations until we get to Abraham.

Abraham also happened to have a genealogical right but that wasn't what was important. In the case of Abraham "...finding there was greater happiness and peace and rest for me, I sought for the blessings of the fathers..." The "blessings of the fathers" after which he was seeking was the Holy Order. He wanted to become one like those that had been in the beginning.

When God spoke to Cain He called him to repent. So, God speaks to Cain and tells him to repent. He didn't repent; he did forfeit, but he forfeited by becoming the first murderer. So the first time that you do something wrong, would you want God to say, "There you go, you're done, you're cut off, you will never have an opportunity to become what I would like you to become, a son of God," or would you want him to call you to repentance? Because God called Cain to repent and he didn't; he went out and he murdered his brother. He just got more determined to accomplish what he wanted. At that point Cain did not die as a result of the murder of his brother. He was driven out but he wasn't killed, and he did lose the right. So, even though he was living and even though he was alive at the time of his brother Seth, the right went to his brother exactly for that reason. The first instance of error, I mean heavens, [the] Kirtland Safety Society may have been out to get rid of Joseph's position.

> ...I sought for the blessings of the fathers, and the right whereunto I should be ordained to administer the same; having been myself a follower of righteousness, desiring also to be one who possessed great knowledge, and to be a greater follower of righteousness, and to possess a greater knowledge.

When you think of the Holy Order after the Order of the Son of God, don't think of it exclusively as some sort of status. It's implicit that what that includes is possession of *great knowledge and greater knowledge*. "A man cannot be saved in ignorance," as Joseph put it. "A man is saved no sooner than he gets knowledge," but implicit in those statements by Joseph Smith is that the purpose of the knowledge is so that you can be a greater follower of righteousness. It's not so that you can play spiritual Trivial Pursuit and win because the knowledge has to be implemented into practice in order for it to have the desired effect. Without accompanying obedience to the things that are known there is no salvation in that. It has to be as Abraham puts it:

> *To be a greater follower, and to possess a greater knowledge and to be a father of many nations, a prince of peace, and desiring to receive instructions, and to keep the commandments of God, I became a rightful heir.* (Abraham 1:2)

At this point in the creation Adam would have all mankind descend from him and Noah would have all mankind descend from him, and therefore they would be the fathers of nations. Abraham knew that was part of what was involved. It's not merely knowledge for knowledge' sake, it's being put into a position in which there is a posterity involving nations that would look to him as they looked to Noah, [and] as they had looked to Adam, as their father.

Think of fatherhood as an opportunity to nurture, to assist, to provide for, to care for, to bring along, to take what is innocent and malleable, and turn it into something that is God-like, responsible, capable, something or someone who can stand on their own two legs and defend the truth when called upon to do so. Someone that will themselves be a vessel of righteousness. Don't think of a father as a bully with a whip or a belt. What Abraham desired was to be a servant; that was what his ambition to be a father of nations involved. And so he became a rightful heir, holding the right belonging to the fathers.

> *It was conferred upon me from the fathers; it came down from the fathers, from the beginning of time... even from the beginning, or before the foundation of the earth, down to the present time, even the right of the*

> *firstborn, or the first man, who is Adam, or first father, through the fathers unto me.* (Abraham 1:3)

That's where it came from. A son of God descended through those fathers to Abraham, because Melchizedek, after a period of apostasy lasting generations, reconnected father Abraham into the fathers. Which is the issue raised a minute ago about this genealogical thing. This is non-genealogical. This is a righteous man in a world of apostasy, looking to reconnect to heaven. He becomes the father of the righteous because he's the first example of a generation, a man in a world of apostasy coming out of that apostasy and reconnecting to Heaven.

There were generations separating Abraham from Shem. Abraham qualified to receive the rights belonging to the fathers because he sought for his appointment, he possessed knowledge, he lived consistent with the knowledge he had, and he wished to have greater knowledge, so that he could obey more commandments so that he could gain further light and knowledge by the things that he learned through obedience.

When you get to what happens after he's connected up, the Lord talking to him says:

> *My name is Jehovah, and I know the end from the beginning; therefore my hand shall be over thee. And I will make of thee a great nation, and I will bless thee above measure, and make thy name great among all nations, and thou shalt be a blessing unto thy seed after thee, that in their hands they shall bear this ministry and Holy Order unto all the nations; And I will bless them through thy name; for as many as receive this Gospel shall be called after thy name, and shall be accounted thy seed, and shall rise up and bless thee, as their father;* (See Abraham 2:8-10)

That's non-genealogical. That's the same process through which Abraham went to become a descendant of the fathers. It's reconnecting. Whoever does that, in whatever generation, is a descendant and can call Abraham their father.

Abraham 2:9-10, and I am going on to 11, so right in there.

> *...I will bless them that bless thee, and curse them that curse thee; and in thee (that is, in thy Holy Order) and in thy seed (that is, the Holy Order), for I give unto thee a promise that this right shall continue in thee, and in thy seed after thee (that is to say, the literal seed, or the seed of the body) shall all the*

> *families of the earth be blessed, even with the blessings of the Gospel, which are the blessings of salvation, even of eternal life.* (See Abraham 2:11)

Abraham says: "*Now, after the Lord had withdrawn from speaking to me, and withdrawn his face from me, I said in my heart: Thy servant has sought thee earnestly; now I have found thee." (Abraham 2:12).* He's saying, that whenever you receive the Gospel, whenever you receive **this** Gospel, and it's really hard to try and get this Gospel back on the earth. There was still a great deal left to be recovered, restored, and returned when Joseph was killed at 38½ [years old]. But when this Gospel–the one that Abraham had received–was on the earth at any time then whoever receives that is a descendant of Abraham. They are part of the family of Abraham and he is their father, and so he becomes the father of many nations. He instructed and passed along the same birthright to Isaac, and to Jacob, and to Joseph, and to Ephraim, and then it rather turns into the same sort of mess that we had previously until the time of Moses.

The foregoing excerpts are taken from:

- A fireside talk on "Plural Marriage", given in Sandy, UT on March 22, 2015;
- Denver's *Christian Reformation Lecture Series*, Talk #1 given in Cerritos, CA on September 21st, 2017; and
- A fireside talk titled "The Holy Order", given in Bountiful, UT on October 29, 2017.

144. Shem, Part 3

This is the third part of a series about Shem, who came to be known as Melchizedek, one of the Patriarchal Fathers, who established a city of peace that ultimately achieved the status of "Zion" and was taken up into heaven.

DENVER: The reason why father Abraham had to go to Melchizedek in order to then rejoice and say, "I have gotten me a priesthood," was because although the line may have had fatherly connections from father Shem down to Abraham, the immediate ancestors of father Abraham were idolaters. True enough, his father repented for a short period of time but he didn't persist in that. Therefore, despite the fact that Melchizedek certainly held authority, there were members of the posterity of Melchizedek between him and father Abraham who were lost and then Abraham was required to come and reconnect because of the apostasy.

When you're talking about the greatest blessings that God offers for the salvation of his children, when you're talking about the family of God, if it could simply be put in one time forever then putting it into father Adam would have solved the problem all the way down to us today. It can and it has been broken. It can and it has been restored. It can and it has been reconnected after a period of apostasy. In fact, once you reconnect Abraham with Melchizedek, you actually have then a family of God beginning with Adam that runs in one continuous line right down to Ephraim. Then you have Joseph's comment about the prophets of the Old Testament. I'm not sure that he means all of them but he certainly means a number that are identifiable. All prophets held Melchizedek priesthood and were ordained by God himself, Joseph said that. I don't think what Joseph is talking about is, "I confer upon you something." I think he's talking about this very connection where you have an isolated faithful individual who honors the fathers and is doing everything that he can in his day but for whom there is no existing possibility for having it occur. God fixes that problem for that individual, not in order to establish a new dispensation in which salvation procedes with the gathering of a people, and a making of a people. But it's a dispensation to that individual for purposes of trying to call others to repentance, and if others were to repent then God could do something with that.

The reason He lead away Lehi and the family of Lehi was to try and establish a righteous branch and a vineyard unto the Lord, and the only way to do that was to get them away from the people who were corrupt in Jerusalem, and maybe give them the potential for holding onto and becoming a people of promise. They were on again, off again, and faithful. A number of troubling moments in their history, but in general, they were sufficiently intact by the time that the Lord came, that He visited with them and He renewed that with them, and that connection was certainly fulsome at that point.

The only purpose behind the last days work, both what was happening at the time of Joseph and what the Lord is offering to us today, is to accomplish that fulsome restoration of the family of God. Joseph talked about temples and they were built incrementally, and they never reached the finish line even on the second one before he was killed, but he laid a fabulous foundation and pointed in a direction that the restoration necessarily must go to and complete. If we don't have the tabernacle of God where he comes to dwell with his people, which he does when he has a family on earth, then the prophecies are not going to be fulfilled. Then the promises that were made to Enoch will not be realized. Then the statements of what will happen in the last days through Moses will not be vindicated. Then Adam's prophecy concerning his descendants to the end of time will not be realized. All of these things point, so we know it is going to happen. The question is not, is it going to happen, the question is, will we rise up or will we not. Because what he's offering is, in fact, a legitimate opportunity for that to indeed happen.

We seem to get so easily distracted that we have a hard time staying on task. It's one of the gentile afflictions. We're very ambitious people and we're very ego-centric. A lot of what is going to be required will require sacrifice and selflessness.

the purpose of the restoration is to return the hearts of the children to the Fathers because everything that is going to happen in the last days got established at the beginning by a covenant that was made three years previous to the death of Adam, when he gathered together his posterity in the valley of Adam-ondi-Ahman and he prophesied whatsoever should befall them unto the latest generation. And the Lord appeared and administered comfort unto Adam, and the gathering there rose up and called him Michael the Prince (see T&C 154:19-20).

Right there, at that moment, at the beginning of the history of the family of Adam, he prophecies by the power of the Holy Ghost what should befall his descendants unto the latest generation in the presence – Adam-ondi-Ahman – Adam in the presence of Son Ahman. Adam-ondi-Ahman was an event. It's like the Super Bowl. It doesn't matter where you play it. Wherever it is it's the Super Bowl. Adam-ondi-Ahman is an event. When Adam is there in the presence of Son Ahman, that is Adam-ondi-Ahman. Now you can say Springhill, Missouri is Adam-ondi-Ahman but it doesn't matter where it happens. When it happens – and it will happen again, in fulfillment of that original prophecy that was made in the valley of Adam-ondi-Ahman, when Adam was before Son Ahman the first time – when it happens again it doesn't matter if that's in Mesa, Arizona or Springfield... I don't know, where do the Simpsons live? Springfield USA, or Bogus Basin. Wherever it is that that occurs that is Adam-ondi-Ahman and it will certainly happen.

The hearts of the children turning to the Fathers so that the earth is not smitten with a curse means that the purpose of the restoration ultimately is to return us back to something that was here in the beginning, the way in which it once was, the dispensation of Adam, the dispensation of Enoch, the dispensation of Noah, all of which were running simultaneously at the time of the flood. "*As it was in the days of Noah so also shall it be at the time of the coming of the Son of Man*" (Matthew 24:37).

We're gonna have three different kinds of remnants operating at the same time at the coming of the Lord, a dispensation that will reflect somewhat of the Christian era, a dispensation that will reflect somewhat of Joseph Smith's era, and a dispensation that will reflect somewhat of the original, the one in which man stood in the presence of God. Of course we've got a couple of those functioning after a fashion but we lack yet in what necessarily will involve the presence of Son Ahman to achieve, is something that He must bring about. When He said, I will bring again Zion, He literally means that because you can't have it without His presence.

That dispensation, that's the one that needs to occur. Joseph gave a talk where he referred to the spirit of Elias and the spirit of Elijah and the spirit of Messiah, because there are really three great spirits that are involved, with three great stages. Abraham is the father of the righteous because at the time that Abraham lived, the connection back to the government of God that began with Adam, to whom dominion was given over the earth, had been broken. It had been broken for generations. It had existed at one time for ten generations, continuously and uninterrupted from the days of Adam to the days of Shem, but when Abraham lived it had been broken for generations.

Now Shem – who had lived on the other side of the flood and who could have fled with Enoch's people into Zion, because people were taken up into Zion continuously, right up until the flood – and Shem did not need to remain on the earth but he remained on the earth to perpetuate what was there in the beginning. And so Shem, who would be called Melchizedek,

Melek, Zadok, king, priest, the prince of peace, the king of Salem, the king of peace, the teacher of righteousness, he remained through the flood but he held onto the covenant that would allow him to lay hold upon that. And he waited through generations of apostasy.

And Abraham represents every man because Abraham came into the world in a state of apostasy, disconnected from the Fathers, incapable of laying hold upon the promises that go back through Adam, and Seth, and Enos, and Jared, and Mahalaleel and the other descendants, right down until the days of Shem. Abraham was disconnected from that. And he went and he looked and he searched because the records belonging to the Fathers had come down into his possession and he knew there was something to that. He knew there was something more to be obtained, and he longed for his appointment unto that, that which was in the beginning. He obtained a connection for himself into that. That's why he had to connect up with Melchizedek because the bond had to be formed, the covenant had to be established, the connection had to be made. And when it was made, the same right that belonged to Adam in the beginning, that right that belonged to Adam as the one to whom dominion over all the earth had been given, had been passed to Abraham. And Abraham became the rightful heir, the holder of that right belonging to the Fathers, even the first Father, or Adam, that came down from the beginning. **That's** what Joseph Smith sought to have be restored. **That's** something that cannot be done apart from the direct personal involvement of God. **That's** something that when it's restored returns us back to a state in which Eden is again possible.

Our hearts must become one. United hearts seem to be in a distant latitude from where **we** are now. Even then, before any attempt at "sealing" begins, the first question is the identity of the "fathers" to whom our singular heart must be sealed to avoid being "cursed"—or as Christ warned, "utterly wasted at his coming."

There is a **true** religion; it was revealed first to Adam. Adam not only received and practiced that true religion, it is through **him** that **every subsequent** dispensation of the gospel has been revealed. Joseph Smith taught:

> *Commencing with Adam, who was the first man, who is spoken of in Daniel as being the Ancient of Days, or in other words, the first and oldest of all, the great grand progenitor, of whom it is said in another place, He is Michael, because he was the first and father of all, not only by progeny, but he was the first to hold the spiritual blessings, to whom was made known the plan of ordinances for the salvation of his posterity unto the end, and to whom Christ*

> *was first revealed, and through whom Christ* ***has been*** *revealed from Heaven and will continue* ***to be*** *revealed from henceforth.* ***Adam*** *holds the keys of the dispensation of the fullness of times; i.e., the dispensation of all the times have been and will be revealed through him, from the beginning to Christ, and from Christ to the end of all the dispensations that are to be revealed.*
>
> *...that all things pertaining to that dispensation should be conducted precisely in accordance with the* ***preceding*** *dispensations. And again, God purposed in himself that there should not be an Eternal fullness until every dispensation should be fulfilled and gathered together in one, and that all things whatever that should be gathered together in one, in those dispensations, unto the same fullness and Eternal glory, should be in Christ Jesus.*
>
> *Therefore, he set the ordinances to be the same for ever and ever, and set* ***Adam*** *to watch over them, to reveal them from Heaven to man or to send angels to reveal them.* (T&C 140:3,5-6; emphasis added)

God gave to Adam the right of "dominion" over the Earth and everything (correspondingly, **everyone**) on the Earth. That was part of the original true religion. When the true religion was combined with the right to hold dominion or preside as a High Priest, it was called the "Holy Order after the Order of the Son of God." This was shortened to "Holy Order." It has also been called the Melchizedek Priesthood. Because of the too frequent use of the term "Melchizedek Priesthood" by the LDS Church and resulting confusion about the meaning of the term, I've redefined "priesthood" and avoid making use of that term without clarification. In this talk, the term "Holy Order" is used to mean the original priestly position conferred on Adam and thereafter passed on to the one eldest, worthy descendant in each subsequent generation, and the religion then taught by that holder was correct and held salvation.

The Patriarchal Fathers are Adam, Seth, Enos, Cainan, Mahalalel, Jared, Enoch, Methuselah, Lamech, Noah, Shem (or Melchizedek), Abraham, Isaac, Jacob, and Joseph. These 15 generational heads stood, **like Adam**, as God's Patriarchal Father and High Priest at the head of God's family on Earth. There were many others who believed in the religion taught by Adam and the Patriarchal Fathers, but the Holy Order given to Adam was always held in its fullness by the eldest worthy descendant in each subsequent generation until —skipping generations to—Abraham.

Abraham was the first precedent for "**sealing**" into the Order, tying a descendant separated by generations into the position of patriarchal successor to Shem (or Melchizedek). This precedent helps explain Joseph Smith's later practice of sealing others to him. Given the examples of Abraham and Joseph Smith, it becomes clear that the Holy Order does not have to be exclusively dynastic (passing in one family line) but can branch out to include any other worthy member of the line, however distant or separated by generations.

The Patriarchal head of the Holy Order is the shepherd for the faithful, husbandman for the Creation, and teacher responsible for dispensing Divine knowledge. It is more than competent gospel teaching; it is authoritatively dispensing a message from a position established and recognized by God, hence Joseph Smith's observation that *there are many teachers, but perhaps not many fathers* (T&C 139:12). When the Holy Order is active, these obligations attach to the position in every generation.

The first or Patriarchal Fathers learned the true religion from Adam and practiced it under his direction. Adam taught the first eight patriarchs born after him. Their religion was Adam's religion, and their understanding reached back to the Garden of Eden.

Despite nearly universal apostasy and rebellion against God **while Adam lived**, the line of Patriarchal Fathers **preserved** the true religion. Noah had a father who knew and was taught by Adam. Noah's living grandfather, great-grandfather, and ancestors for seven generations knew and were taught by Adam. Learning about God from His messengers and priests was (and still is) necessary to avoid dwindling in unbelief and falling into apostasy. The "angels" who ministered **included mortals** who were given Divine knowledge to teach.

Noah preserved the original religion of God through the cataclysm of the flood. Three of the sons of Noah were taught it, and Noah's most faithful son inherited the right. The fullness of the Holy Order was conferred upon Shem (who received the title "Melchizedek"). A descendant of Ham falsely claimed he held the Holy Order, but he could only institute an imitation of the Order.

After Melchizedek, an apostasy lasted until Abraham. Although he was raised by an idolater and lamented that his fathers offered sacrifices to idols, Abraham searched for the true God of Heaven. Abraham **found** God, and the covenant of the first Fathers was renewed and conferred upon him by Melchizedek. Generations of apostates were excluded from the Holy Order, but Abraham was adopted into the line by Melchizedek, thereby restoring continuity **back** to Adam.

Abraham represents the key Patriarchal Father prophesied of in Malachi. Abraham not only renews the covenant of "the fathers" (**including** Noah and Enoch), but also through the Abrahamic covenant, God established Abraham as the new head of the family of God on Earth. God told Abraham: *As many as receive this gospel shall be called after your name and shall be accounted your seed, and shall rise up and bless you, as unto their Father* (Abraham 3:1 RE). For us, connecting to Abraham is akin to the original Patriarchs' connection to Adam. Turning the heart of the children to the Fathers is a required part of the gospel. And after God's covenant with him, salvation for all subsequent generations is dependent on being accounted Abraham's seed.

In the beginning, Adam kept the Book of Remembrance, which Enoch elaborated upon because Enoch was the great scribe. (His prototype in Egyptian hieroglyphs is Thoth, who is shown ibis-headed with the stylus and writing—that was Enoch.) And Abraham says that the records of the Fathers (that came down from the beginning) came into his hands, and therefore, he (Abraham) had a knowledge of the beginning of the Creation and of the stars and the planets and all the rest of that. And he proceeded to tell us something about the Creation in the book of Abraham, based (apparently) upon the content of the records from the beginning that fell into his hands—followed, in due course, with his full initiation into the Holy Order through the surviving Melchizedek, son of ~~Shem~~ [Noah], who was a pre-diluvian and had a covenant that he could have been translated and taken up to heaven ('cuz that process continued right up into the flood). Even though the city of Enoch had risen before, people were still going through that process right up into the flood, and Melchizedek could lay claim on that promise as an antediluvian, but he tarried until he could hand off (after generations of apostasy) to Abraham. So, Abraham inherits the covenant, and Abraham has possession of the records.

The foregoing excerpts are taken from:

- Denver's fireside talk titled "Cursed, Denied Priesthood", given in Sandy, UT on January 7th, 2018
- Denver's remarks given at the Joseph Smith Restoration Conference in Boise, ID on June 24, 2018
- Denver's general conference talk titled "Religion of the Fathers," presented at Aravada, Nevada on March 27, 2021; and

- Denver's talk titled "Joseph, Joseph, Joseph," given at the 4th Annual Joseph Smith Restoration Conference in Meridian, Idaho on June 26, 2021

145. Shem, Part 4

This is the fourth part of a series about Shem, who came to be known as Melchizedek, one of the Patriarchal Fathers, who established a city of peace that ultimately achieved the status of "Zion" and was taken up into heaven.

———

DENVER: There are two models that you can consider from the scriptures as possibilities for Zion in the last days. The one model is the Book of Mormon model in which Zion gets introduced after destruction and after the return of the Lord and after folks have a season to incorporate the information and the teachings, the ordinances that Christ restores at His coming. Under that model, we will not see Zion until sometime post-Second Coming. There's a second model that we find in the scriptures, however, and that model is the one that Christ suggests, He says "as it was in the days of Noah, so also shall it be at the time of the coming of the Son of Man." And what was it that was going on contemporaneous with Noah? – it was the city of Enoch, in which a people, separated themselves, and they found Zion. Melchizedek was able to do the same thing. The people of the Nephites were able to do the same thing. Whether the model that will actually apply is the model that Christ suggested about the City of Enoch and a righteous people ready to meet the Lord, or the model that the Book of Mormon suggests --a post- holocaust, a post-second coming establishment of Zion, is YOUR choice, and that ought to be the most sobering comment of all.

The statement that's made concerning the Priesthood, Moses 6:7: "Now this same Priesthood, which was in the beginning, shall be in the end of the world also." That statement, "the same Priesthood that was in the beginning, shall be in the end of the world also," when you take that and put it together with the statements that say, "as it was in the days of Noah, so shall also it be at the time of the coming of the Son of man," every time you encounter the existence of Zion, the Zion that we read about, the first one had seven High Priests within it. There was a residue associated with them who were righteous but among them you had the seven High Priests. I have to assume that they each had families, and I have to assume that the families were the ones that were raised by these High Priests in righteousness. I have to assume that that included multiple generations, and so that collection of people was essentially seven families.

The Zion that was established by Enoch thereafter, we don't have any geographic description or numeric description apart from the statement that we get in the book of Jude, which is really quoting from an earlier text of Enoch about the return of Enoch with his ten thousands, "with his ten-thousands" of angels. If that is a representation – and those kinds of things are not particularly reliable, because ten thousands, given the way in which the numeric compilations occurred in those days – the error, if there is one, is an overstatement not an understatement. In other words there would *not* be millions described as ten thousands; but there could be hundreds described as ten thousands.

The area occupied apparently by the people of Melchizedek and his city, in an agrarian setting, could have been located on something that is as small as 20 city blocks of our current type of area.

The significance of Zion is not its numerosity. The significance of Zion is its spiritual endowment. It is the power of heaven, and not the voting block. It's not that you've got big numbers here that intimidate the ungodly. It's that even a handful are sufficient.

So now we should realize, I hope, that that city which Melchizedek, the King of Peace, was able to teach righteousness sufficiently so that it was taken up from the earth, reserved to the last days of the end of the world—

The **next** time we have such an event on the earth, the **next** time there is this kind of gathering and this kind of a population anywhere, it will not be for the purpose of going up. It will be for the purpose of permitting those who have gone up to come back down. It will be for the purpose of having those who can endure the presence of those who come because those who come will burn up all those who are unworthy. And therefore, **some few** need to be gathered so that the earth is not utterly wasted at His coming.

As it was in the days of Noah, so [also shall it be] at the [time of the] coming of the Son of Man (JS-M 1:41; see also Matthew 11:11 RE). How many people were required in order to have the Ark be an acceptable place in which God could preserve all of humanity? It was a portable Ark of the Covenant in which the family was preserved. And so, if it's going to be as it was in the days of Noah—

There is this net that has been cast out to gather together all manner of fish. But as the Lord tells the parable, the angels are going to come, and they're going to pick through all manner of fish, and they're going to keep the good, and the rest are going to be scheduled for burning. And so the question is, how diligent ought the search be into the things of God? How carefully ought we to consider the things that have been restored to us through the Prophet Joseph Smith?

The fact is that this stuff is assigned to our dispensation. And I'm reading from the Book of Mormon, which the world does not have or accept. I'm reading from the Book of Abraham, which the world does not have or accept. I'm reading from the Joseph Smith Translation, which the world does not have and accept. All of you have this information in front of you. All of this material has been restored through someone that we claim we honor and regard as a prophet.

> *Now Melchizedek was a man of faith…* (JST Genesis 14:26)

By the way, Melchizedek is a title; it's a name-title. It's a compound of two words. One is "king," and one is "priest"—and therefore, in one sense, it's a name-title, and in another sense, it's a new name. And it's not the birth name given to someone, rather it is the new name/title which is fashioned after Christ because Christ is the great King and the great Priest who's the King of Kings, and He is the Great High Priest. And so, Melchizedek is really a name-title that belongs to Christ, it being used as a substitute to prevent the frequent repetition when you're talking about the Holy Priesthood—that the correct full name would be the *Holy Priesthood after the Order of the Son of God.* But to prevent the too frequent repetition of that, Melchizedek (which is a name-title for Christ) got used as a substitute.

But Melchizedek—that is, the person who grew up to become the one that got that name-title,

> *was a man of faith, who wrought righteousness; and when a* ***child*** *he feared God, and* ***stopped the mouths of lions,*** *and* ***quenched the violence of fire*** [this is Melchizedek as a child; this is Melchizedek doing something by **faith**]. *And thus having been approved of God, he was ordained* [that is, ordination occurred **after** faith]... (Ibid, vs. 26-27, emphasis added)

Can a man heal **by faith without priesthood**? Of course they can. Can Melchizedek, as a child without priesthood, stop the mouths of lions? Yes, the scriptures say so. Can "by faith" a man (Melchizedek being one who did so) quench the violence of fire without priesthood? Yes. Therefore, is it evidence that…

Oh, what was the guy's name in Oklahoma? The evangelical minister whose ministry was largely based upon healings? Can he heal? Can he do so without priesthood? Yeah, of course. I mean, these are two different things. These are altogether two different things.

So, Melchizedek accomplished these things by faith. And then, having accomplished these things by faith, God ordained him:

> *[a] high priest after the order of the covenant which God made with Enoch. It being after the order of the Son of God; which order came, not by man nor by the will of man…* (Ibid, vs. 27-28)

That is, we can't vote in **that guy**. We can't 'hope and pray and sustain with our prayers and faith and confidence' **that guy**. We can't have our will bundled into **that guy**. **That guy** comes as a consequence, exclusively, not of father, not of mother, not of the will of man, but by the will of God. This is, after all, sons of God that we're talking about.

> *… neither by father nor mother; neither by beginning of days nor end of years; but of God…* (Ibid)

...because God is endless; therefore, His word is endless, and His covenants are endless, and His commitments are endless. And if you lay hold upon it, you lay hold upon something which is itself endless.

And it was delivered, just as we saw in Doctrine and Covenants section 84:

> *And it was delivered unto men by the calling of his own voice, according to his own will, unto as many as believed on his name. For God having sworn unto Enoch and unto his seed with an oath by himself; that every one being ordained after this order and calling should have power, by faith, to break mountains, to divide the seas, to dry up waters, to turn them out of their course; To put at defiance the armies of nations, to divide the earth, to break every band, to stand in the presence of God.* (Ibid, vs.29-31)

Now, take that impressive list of things, and read it in light of this:

> *…to do all things according to **his** will, according to **his** command, subdue principalities and powers; and this **by the will of the Son of God** which was from before the foundation of the world.* (Ibid, vs. 31)

See, such persons holding such power **are not freelancing**. And in fact, evidence of the possession of this power does not come as a consequence of someone displaying **every one** of these things, **but** if they display **any** one of these things… For example, Nephi (when he was bound in the desert and left to die by his brothers) broke every band that bound him, having been strengthened by God (see 1 Nephi 7:16-18; see also 1 Nephi 2:4 RE). And that **same Nephi**, bound to the mast when the storm came that threatened the survival of the ship, not only could not break the band, but when they finally got around to relieving him, he said his hands were much swollen as a consequence of the trauma that he'd suffered (see 1 Nephi 18:15; see also 1 Nephi 5:30 RE). Nephi—who had power given to him by God to break the bands that would've cost him his life—was left subject to the bands because it was not according to the Father's will or the word of the Son when he was bound to the mast. And so, had Nephi called upon that power and not suffered, Nephi would've been offending—and not conforming to—the will of God. And he would have had to suffer some loss.

Moses had power to divide the seas. And he did that by the word of God (see Exodus 14:15-16, 21; see also Exodus 9:3-4 RE). And yet, when Moses used the power to cause the rock to bring forth water (and not at the command of God), he suffered some loss. Possession of the power does not mean you freelance. Because in the very statement about the possession and the capability and the capacity, it says it's according to His will. Therefore, in order to be someone who can be trusted, you have to be someone who will subordinate to His will.

The Lord was not mis-stating the case, when He said, "No man takes my life," because the Lord had the capacity, at His own word, to prevent the entire armies of Rome from doing any harm to him. "Don't you know," he asked Pilate, "if I asked, there'd be twelve legions of angels?" (see Matthew 26:53; see also Matthew 12:11 RE). You know, you don't even need a legion of angels to take on a legion of Rome, much less a little Centurion's cohort in Galilee (or in Judea, rather).

When you have someone who arises to this point **and** can be trusted, they nevertheless can be slain. Because, like our Lord, they don't get to **use**... Well, they are trustworthy enough so as not to **misuse** what has been entrusted to them. Therefore, the fact that they can "hold at defiance the armies of nations" means that they will do so only in accordance with His will —because sometimes it **is** His will to destroy the children of Israel, when they have sinned against Him. And then, they have to detect the error and repent of it before they can go forward. Well,

> *[all] men having this faith, coming up unto this order...were translated and taken up into heaven.* (JST Genesis 14:32)

...that being a statement about not today but the moment of Melchizedek's ordination, his day, and those that had lived before him, in their day. *Translated and taken up into heaven*—we will get to the point later where we'll find out that this same authority that was in the beginning is going to return at the end of the earth, also. But its return at the end of the earth has a different purpose. At the beginning of the earth, **this** was the purpose.

> *And now, Melchizedek was a priest of this order; therefore he obtained peace in Salem, ...was called the Prince of peace* [that is also is one of the titles given to the Lord, the Prince of Peace]. *...his people wrought righteousness, and obtained heaven, and sought for the city of Enoch which God had before taken, separating it from the earth, having reserved it unto the latter days, or the end of the world.* (Ibid, vs. 33-34)

See, and you wonder what they've been doing for lo these many thousands of years; and yet, if you understood the physics of it all, you'd realize that you can go out and back in a hurry, and it's overnight if you travel fast enough and far enough and return. There's really… Ah, well, that's another matter altogether.

> *And [He] hath said, and sworn with an oath, that the heavens and the earth **should** come together…* (Ibid, vs. 35, emphasis added)

See, they… That city of Enoch is reserved until the latter days of the end. It was separated from the earth, but it's going to come again in the latter days. And the Lord swore,

> *…with an oath, that the heavens and the earth should come together; and the sons of God should be tried so as by fire.* (Ibid)

...meaning that when they return again, those sons who remain standing are going to have to be able to endure the fire that is coming. They who come shall burn them up—we talked about that briefly in Boise, and we've been trying to track that down through Idaho Falls, and now we see it again here. Therefore, this priesthood has something to do with all of the talks that I've been giving up to this point and where we go from here.

> *And this Melchizedek, having thus established righteousness, was called the king of heaven by his people, or, in other words, the King of peace* [because he brought peace to them]. *And he lifted up his voice, and he blessed Abram, being the high priest, and the keeper of the storehouse of God; [whom] Him whom God had appointed to receive tithes for the poor. [And] Abraham paid...him...* (Ibid, vs. 36-39; see also Genesis 7:18-21 RE)

...and so on. In any event, Melchizedek established priests/established righteousness; his city was a city of peace.

(And if you don't mind, I'm gonna hold onto this for a minute 'cuz we're gonna go back there, and so... Is your name on it? Oh, good; your name's on it. I'm using Carol's scriptures. And if you see me walking around with a set of scriptures that have Carol's name on it, you **know** I've stolen them.)

Priesthood is **not** a franchise. Priesthood is **not** something that is given in order to control others. Priesthood is an opportunity—afforded you by God, in its highest form—to serve and to bless others. (That's not true of it in other forms, and we'll get to that.) But in its highest form, it is a call to service. It is a call to save; it is a call to redeem; and it is a call to rescue.

> What was the power of Melchizedek? 'Twas not the Priesthood of Aaron which administers...outward ordinances, and the offering of sacrifices. Those holding the fulness of the Melchizedek Priesthood are kings and priests of the Most High God, holding the keys of power and blessings (Ibid)—

...because the Aaronic holds and is given for judgments and destruction. The Melchizedek is given for blessing. And when someone claims to hold Melchizedek priesthood and they use it in order to offer up judgment and condemnation and control and compulsion and authority over the souls of men—and they refuse to constrain themselves, to use persuasion only and gentleness and meekness—then you know you're listening to an Aaronic and not a Melchizedek authority. Because the office and the authority and the keys of the Melchizedek is to bless; it's to enlighten; it's to raise and to bring to you light and truth.

> In fact, that Priesthood is a perfect law of theocracy, and stands as God to give laws to the people, administering endless lives to the sons and daughters of Adam. (Ibid)

Because, once again, it is **always** genealogical. It is **always** familial. It has **always** been "turning the hearts of the children back to the fathers"—the final father in that chain being Adam.

> Abraham says to Melchizedek, I believe all...thou hast taught me concerning the priesthood and the coming of the Son of Man; so Melchizedek ordained Abraham and sent him away. Abraham rejoiced, saying, Now I have a priesthood. Salvation could not come to the world without the mediation of Jesus Christ. How shall God come to

> rescue...this generation? He will send Elijah the prophet. The law revealed to Moses in Horeb never was revealed to the children of Israel as a nation. Elijah shall reveal the covenants to seal the hearts of the fathers to the children, and the children to the fathers. (Ibid)

This talk, on this day by Joseph Smith, is seven years **after** the 1836 Doctrine and Covenants section 110 incident. So,

> Elijah shall reveal the covenants to seal the hearts of the fathers to the children and the children to the fathers. The anointing and sealing is to be called, elected, and made sure. "Without father, without mother, without descent, having neither beginning of days nor end of life, ...made like unto the Son of God, abideth a priest continually." The Melchizedek Priesthood holds the right from the eternal God, and not by descent from father and mother; and that priesthood is as eternal as God Himself, having neither beginning of days nor end of life.

When Adam promises that the priesthood that was in the beginning is going to return at the end of the world also, he is talking about a return at the end of the world of that priesthood which was held by the original patriarchs—a time when, for generations, it was unitary (there was only one) and that the designation (the correct designation) of that priesthood is the "Holy Priesthood" or the "Holy Order after the Order of the Son of God." It's a long name, but it was **that** priesthood that was held by the patriarchs.

> Go to and finish the temple, and **God** will fill it with power, and you will then receive **more knowledge** concerning **this** priesthood.

I'm suggesting to you that something which, by its nature, required the completion of the temple and required the presence of God, which relates to the revelation given in January of 1841 that I read a few minutes ago—*For there['s] not a place found on the earth that he may come to and restore again that which was lost unto you, or which he hath taken away, even the fullness of the priesthood* (D&C 124:28; see also T&C 41:10)… It requires **Him**—God—to come to that place, and for **Him**—God—to restore to you that which has been taken away—**the fullness**. Go to, and God… You finish the temple, "God will fill it with power...you will then receive more knowledge concerning this priesthood."

> The Holy Ghost is God's messenger to administer in **all** those priesthoods. (Ibid)

You see, it was by faith and the power of the Holy Ghost that Melchizedek did all that he did. And if someone gets possession of any or all of these priesthoods, the way in which the priesthood proceeds is in accordance with the power of the Holy Ghost. Joseph just said: it's by the power of the Holy Ghost.

This is a prophecy given by Adam which constituted one of the covenants which I referred to in the talk given at Centerville. Moses… (Oh, excuse me; it's chapter 6, verse 7): "Now this same Priesthood"—this is Adam speaking: *Now this same Priesthood which was in the beginning, shall be in the end of the world, also. Now this prophecy Adam spake, as he was moved upon by the Holy Ghost* (Moses 6:7-8; see also Genesis 3:14 RE). Therefore, it was the power of the priesthood, animated by the Holy Ghost, which established, as a matter of right—and therefore, of covenant—the promise that this thing, this authority, this power, and this relationship which once existed in the beginning of the world is to exist again at the end of the world. And that that, too, arises as a consequence of the covenant given in the beginning.

So, what kind of person receives that ordination? I'm going back to the Joseph Smith Translation of Genesis chapter 14. This is the kind of person: *Melchizedek was a man of faith who wrought righteousness.* You have to have faith. You have to ~~wrought~~ perform righteousness, which is not the same thing as virtue. Virtue… Virtue can be **offended** by righteousness. Virtue is…

Virtue would never kill, okay? It just never would. But it is righteous—in the case of Nephi, at the command of God—to slay Laban. Virtue would never **do** any number of things, **say** any number of things, or **behave** in any number of ways in which John the Baptist behaved. *[You] generation of vipers* (Luke 3:7; see also Luke 3:5 RE). Look, we translate that as if what we're reading is some nicely-phrased King Jamesian version of an insult. If you were trying to put it into modern English… This is John the Baptist (a righteous man with whom the kingdom of God existed) essentially, in the language of their day, saying, "You sons of bitches!" Because in our vernacular, by saying, "...sons of bitches," what you're saying is your mother is a female dog; and therefore, you are a dog; and since you're a dog, you are a cur, and you are unworthy. This is guttural language. We read, "You generations of vipers!" and we say, Oh, isn't that a nice way to parse out that John's thinks he's talking to the bad guys. And yet, we look sometimes at **righteousness**, and we say it can never be so because it is not virtuous. Because we overlay virtue atop righteousness—and it does not work and never has worked that way. Righteousness controls, and virtue surrenders. And virtue yields **every time** to righteousness—else Abraham could never have been commanded to slay his son. Because **that** was not virtuous. Therefore,

> *Melchizedek was a man of righteousness; ...when a child he feared God* [not man], *...stopped the mouths of lions, ...quenched the violence of fire. ...thus, having been approved of God* [not man]… (JST Genesis 14:26-27)

In fact, to be approved of God, in many cases, will make you offensive to man. But the opinions, and the vagaries, and the fashions of men, the opinion-polling and the drifts of what is and what is not popular at one point or another are damnable. They ought not even be considered. Righteousness **does not give** any regard to such things. And yet, it may be virtuous… It may be virtuous to be a limp-wristed, weepy, happy-go-lucky, "have a nice day" kind of chap… But righteousness will kick his ass everyday.

> *…having been approved of God…* (Ibid)

It is God—and God's approval alone—that matters. It is what God regards of you. It is what is in your heart, because God can detect what is in your heart. God knows why you do what you do. God knows why you say what you say. God **knows** what is in your thoughts. Therefore, to be approved of God is to be weighed against the standard of righteousness and not the whims of fashion. Fashion will come and go. Ideas will be popular or unpopular. Righteousness will endure forever. This. This. This is the kind of man upon whom the words get spoken, "My Son."

The **fathers** (about whom I spoke in Centerville) had this association with God. They had this fellowship with God. They had this sonship **with** God. And they had this priesthood **from** God. And the hearts of the children need to turn to the fathers, and that, too, because Elijah is coming to plant in the hearts of the children the promises that were made.

If you go to and you look at Doctrine and Covenants section 76, beginning at verse 50, and you read through the list of things that are descriptors of those that are going to inherit Celestial glory… Beginning at verse 50—and we don't have time to go through all of the things that are there—but in 51 it says that these are people:

> *...who received the testimony of Jesus* [that is, Christ testifying to them that they're saved], *...believed on his name* [these are people who]*...were baptized after the manner of his burial, being buried in...water in his name, ...this according to the commandment which he has given—*

> *That by keeping the commandments they might be washed and cleansed from all their sins, ...receive the Holy [Ghost] by the laying on of the hands of him who is ordained and sealed unto this power* [that sounds a little different than what we do]*; And who overcome by faith, and are sealed by the Holy Spirit of promise, which the Father sheds forth...on all those who are just and true. [These] are they who* ***are*** *the Church of the Firstborn. [These] are they into whose hands the Father has given all things—*
>
> *[These] are they who* ***are*** *priests and kings, who have received of his fulness, and of his glory* [I hope you read those words now with a little different meaning than you did from before 9:30 today]*; And* ***are*** *priests of the Most High, after the order of Melchizedek, which was after the order of Enoch, which was after the order of the Only Begotten Son. Wherefore, as it is written, they are gods...*
>
> *...all things are theirs, whether life or death, or things present, or things to come, all are theirs...they are Christ's, and Christ is God's. ...they* ***shall*** *overcome all things* [that's in the future].
>
> *...let no man glory in man, but rather let him glory in God, who shall subdue all enemies under his feet. These* ***shall*** *dwell in the presence of God and his Christ forever and ever. These are they whom he shall bring with him, when he shall come in the clouds of heaven to reign on the earth over his people. These are they who* ***shall*** *have part in the first resurrection. These are they who* ***shall*** *come forth in the resurrection of the just. These are they who are come unto Mount Zion, and unto the city of the living God, the heavenly place, the holiest of all. These are they who have come to an innumerable company of angels, to the general assembly and Church of Enoch, and of the Firstborn. These are they whose names are written in heaven, where God and Christ are the judge of all. ...just men made perfect through Jesus the mediator of the new covenant...*
>
> ...[bodies] *whose bodies are celestial, ...glory...of the sun* [those who inherit everlasting burnings]... (D&C 76:51-70, emphasis added; see also T&C 69:10-22)

These are those who are referred to as the "El." **These** are those that were referred to when Moroni said that Elijah will come to *plant in the hearts of the children the promises made to the father* (D&C 2:2; see also Joseph Smith History 3:4 RE) and when Joseph spoke in August the 27th of 1843 that Elijah **will** come. He **will** come.

Take a look at Alma chapter 13—because this is where it becomes very important for **us**. Alma chapter 13, beginning at verse 17:

> *Now this Melchizedek was a king over the land of Salem; and his people had waxed strong in iniquity and abomination; yea, they had* ***all*** *gone astray; they were* ***full*** *of all manner of wickedness* [**this is his audience**]. *But Melchizedek having exercised mighty faith, ...received the office of the high priesthood according to the holy order of God, did preach repentance unto his people. And behold, they* ***did*** *repent; and Melchizedek did establish peace in the land in his days; therefore he was called the prince of peace, for he was the king of Salem; and he did reign under his father.* (emphasis added; see also Alma 10:2 RE)

First, he received this priesthood. Second, he preached repentance. But nothing would have happened except for, third, the people who heard him **did** repent. And because of that, people who are described as having *waxed strong in iniquity*, people who are described as being captivated by *abomination[s]*, people who have ***all*** *gone astray* turned out to be the very people among whom this City of Peace got established. But **they** did it. They did it by **repentance**. This isn't something Melchizedek pulled off, this is something that the **people** accomplished, and they accomplished it because of **their repentance**.

I want you to contrast that with another group. This group is in Mosiah chapter 12. Mosiah chapter 12, beginning halfway through verse 12. This is people reacting to the message that Abinadi was delivering to them. They're accusing Abinadi, and they're saying:

> *And he* [Abinadi] *pretendeth the Lord hath spoken it. And he saith all this shall come upon thee except thou repent, and this because of thine iniquities. And now, O king, what great evil hast thou done, or what great sins have thy people committed, that we should be condemned of God or judged [by] this man? ...now, O king, behold, we are guiltless, and thou, O king, hast not sinned; therefore, this man has lied concerning you, and he has prophesied in vain. ...behold, we are strong, we shall not come into bondage, or [being] taken captive by our enemies; yea, and thou hast prospered in the land, and thou shalt also prosper.* (Mosiah 12:12-15; see also Mosiah 7:14-15 RE)

Here is the pride, here is the vanity, here is the very thing which, had the people to whom Melchizedek spoken, had they done this, there would have been no City of Peace, there would have been no Salem, there would have been no second Zion.

You generally hail from a tradition that assures you that you're in the right way. You generally come from a tradition that says you're better than others. You are able to look down your nose at other people who stumble about in the dark because they don't have all the great truths that you have. The fact of the matter is **you** (generally, not specifically, because there are some to whom this absolutely does not apply—your hearts are right before God—but there aren't many)…

You have been handed this tradition, and the wicked one cometh, and he takes away Light and Truth, and he does it because of the false traditions you've been handed. The greatest among us is wholly inadequate. The greatest among us can't be trusted with the power of God, not yet anyway. The greatest among us is still in need of repentance. Every one of us should walk fearfully before God, not because God isn't generous, but because what He offers can turn you into a devil. The only way to be prepared and not fall is to realize the enormous peril that **you** present, potentially, to the universe. Before you get in a position to enjoy the status that God offers to us all, you need to work out your salvation with fear and trembling, exactly like Paul said. You need to purge, remove, reprove.

The foregoing excerpts are taken from:

- Denver's talk given at the "Zion Symposium" in Provo, Utah on February 23rd, 2008
- His talk titled "The Mission of Elijah Reconsidered", given in Spanish Fork, UT on October 14th, 2011
- Denver's *40 Years in Mormonism Series*, Talk #4 titled "Covenants" given in Centerville, UT on October 6th, 2013
- Denver's *40 Years in Mormonism Series*, Talk #5 titled "Priesthood" given in Orem, UT on November 2nd, 2013; and
- Denver's *40 Years in Mormonism Series*, Talk #8 titled "A Broken Heart" given in Las Vegas, NV on July 25th, 2014.

146. Shem, Part 5

This is the fifth part of a series about Shem, who came to be known as Melchizedek, one of the Patriarchal Fathers, who established a city of peace that ultimately achieved the status of "Zion" and was taken up into heaven.

DENVER: These are the kinds of preparations that need to precede Zion. We are not going to get **there** in one step. We're only gonna get **there** incrementally. And there's a great deal of increments yet to be accomplished. It's not gonna happen by fairy dust. There's not gonna be someone who comes along and says to you, "Spiritu Sancto, Ave Maria." You know, get the holy water; get the incense, voodoo—voila, now you're Zion! It's not gonna happen. It doesn't matter if it's a Dominican in a brown robe or a Mormon Elder with a name tag. **You**… **You** must become holy. **You** must receive the guidance, blessing, benefit, and baptism of the Spirit. **You** must become the house of God. You're going to have to be the one that God visits with in order to have the preparations that are necessary take place. This is not something to be accomplished in a single step. Indeed, all of it must precede the gathering.

We looked (a while back, in one of the preceding talks) at how dangerous it would be for an unworthy person to attempt to be in Zion. Because when it finally is acceptable to the Lord—and when His presence does come, finally, to dwell there—it is unsafe for anyone unprepared to face that glory to be in that condition. Therefore, when the gathering takes place and you would like to join in, you do so at your peril if you've not accomplished the things that are expected to be accomplished beforehand.

We read those verses in Alma (yesterday) about Melchizedek's people. Melchizedek's people—Alma chapter 13—about how the people that Melchizedek gathered had waxed strong in iniquity and abomination and had all gone astray. It doesn't matter that you look about and see a tattered ruin of the Restoration. And it doesn't matter that we're filled with all kinds of false notions, inadequate and incomplete teachings. And it doesn't matter that we're a vain and a proud people. It's even worse when, recognizing that we are a vain and a proud people, we tend to gather together and to think of ourselves as even better than they are. Because **we** immediately import that same culture of arrogance. **We** immediately take what is offered, and instead of becoming (as we talked about yesterday) humbled by the greatness of the steps left in front of us, we tend to think that we ought to view this stuff comparatively ("and we **are** slightly better than them, after all") when the standard is absolute! And it doesn't matter if you're kinda, sorta, a little better. It's absolute! It's an on-and-off switch. And if it's on, it's on; and if it's off, it's off. There is no dimmer. It doesn't happen that way. And we aren't better than them. In some respects, we have greater reason to fall into the folly of our own pride. We have greater reason to think ourselves better than the people that think they're better than the rest of the people. And so, we move along incrementally to become yet further **away** from God. If we think we're better than them and they think they're better than the world, then we oughta become a fool for Christ's sake and go and serve among them. We oughta do like the missionary who went out and did everything that the king bid him do and did it with such exactness and such fidelity, because he wasn't trying to serve the king; he was trying to serve the King of Heaven. He was trying to show—in the integrity of his heart and in the integrity of his soul—what was true. Maybe the way to fix some of the problems that exist with your own children is for you to go and ask the Bishop to let you be a Primary teacher. And then you're not only teaching and ministering to your own children, but you're teaching and you're ministering to others as well.

Hearts of people get hard the older they get (although, there is at least one exception, 'cuz I ran into a guy at my office who was like 85 years old, and he's still as young and as nimble and as open and as flexible as a child). That's why we have to become childlike—because we have to be willing to consider these things.

Well, in that Alma chapter 13 material, beginning at 14, it says:

> *Yea, humble yourselves even as the people in the days of Melchizedek, who was also a high priest after this same order which I have spoken, who also took upon him the high priesthood forever. And it was this same Melchizedek to whom Abraham paid tithes; yea, even our father Abraham paid tithes of one–tenth part of all he possessed. Now* ***these ordinances*** *were given after this manner, that thereby the people might look forward on the Son of God, it being a type of his order, or it being his order, and this that they might look forward to him for the remission of their sins, that they might enter into the rest of the Lord.* (Alma 13:14-16, emphasis added; see also Alma 10:1 RE)

And what is *these ordinances* that are being talked about? That's what we looked at in the Orem talk in chapter 13, and we're not gonna repeat it here. That's the material that includes: Everything that God does, He does by an ordinance. Everything that He does and every blessing He confers, He confers by a covenant. One of the good news about the absence of a binding covenant is that you can't damn yourself by taking upon yourself an obligation that you will never honor.

One of the good things about the Restoration is that there are covenantal examples that are given that give you an idea of the kind of behavior that God would want. I wish **everyone** would go to the temple. I wish **everyone** would go to the temple and take on them covenants, learn what they are, and then try to live them. But if you fail (unlike the stuff that comes into play with this Melchizedek character), there is no severe penalty, because it's for your good and for your practice and for your instruction. And if you honor that, there's no reason why God and the angels cannot ratify whatever it is you do if you qualify for it. The Holy Spirit of Promise is embedded within the architecture of the Church's teachings. And it was as recent as—what? General Conference before last?—when President Eyring got up, and he talked about how they had the sealing power, and then he threw in that caveat that everything has to be sealed by the Holy Spirit of Promise. I put that up on my blog; I quoted it, and I said, “That's good doctrine.” And that is good doctrine.

Go to the temple, get your ordinances, and then work to have this Holy Spirit of Promise. Because the Keeper of **that** Gate is the Holy One of Israel, and there's no employee there. It is the Holy One of Israel, and **you** qualify to receive that directly with heaven. There's no other gatekeeper opening and closing doors—there **is** the Holy One of Israel; He employeth **no** servant there.

In Isaiah chapter 9 there is a verse that is dealing squarely with this issue. This is chapter 9 verse 6 of Isaiah:

> *For unto us a child is born, unto us a son is given: and the government shall be upon his shoulder: and his name shall be called Wonderful, Counsellor, The mighty God, The everlasting Father, The Prince of Peace. Of the increase of his government and peace there shall be no end.*

This is a prophecy about Christ coming to restore, in the meridian of time, the government of God in which He, Christ, represented the "Father" of all, as the Redeemer of all, as the bringer again of the holy covenant.

He is prophesied to return with the description provided in the Book of Revelation, chapter 19 verse 16, as "the King of Kings, and the Lord of Lords."

In D&C section 76 He explains what His intention is with respect to mankind. He intends to make men:

> *[T]hey are they who are priests and kings, who have received of his fullness and glory, and are priests of the Most High after the order of Melchizedek, which was after the order of Enoch, which was after the order of the Only Begotten Son.* (D&C 76:56)

That's the intention that He has for all men; that men should become like Him: "kings and priests."

Zion is a mortal responsibility. Men must cooperate with God for God to be able to bring it. It is not something that heaven is going to provide for us.

When Enoch and his city were established, it was not until after it was established and people had gathered together that the Lord came and dwelt with them. They prepared the place, they extended the invitation, and the Lord came.

Likewise, in the city that was established by Melchizedek, it wasn't the angels who built his city. He preached repentance; men repented, and as a consequence of having repented Zion was taken up into heaven. Enoch's Zion fled. Melchizedek's Zion fled.

The last days Zion will be built not to flee. It will be built as an established beachhead to which the Powers of Heaven will return in order for He whose right it is to govern the earth can assume the responsibility of governing the earth. He intends to overthrowing every other government there is and to establish as the King and as the Prince of Peace, and as the Father of Righteousness, His rule and His reign over the earth once again at His coming.

Joseph Smith described the priesthood that will function in Zion preliminary to the Lord's return. This is a quote from one of his teachings: "That priesthood is a perfect law of theocracy and stands as God to give laws to the people." (That's from *The Teachings of the Prophet Joseph Smith* on page 322.) In that same talk there is a better elaboration made [by] one of the note-takers. You can find this in *The Words of Joseph Smith*, page 246. Joseph said: *"It is understood by many by reading this chapter* [referring to Hebrews chapter 7] *that Melchizedek was a king of some country or nation on earth. But it was not so. In the original it reads 'king of shalom,' which signifies 'king of peace or righteousness' and not of any country or nation."*

What Melchizedek established was a community of peace, and as the one who preached the peace to which the people came he was acknowledged as the prince of peace or the King of righteousness.

At the beginning of the restoration, while Joseph was still alive, there was an abortive attempt to get founded what would necessarily need to be reestablished in order for there to be Zion. In a sermon that he delivered in August of 1843, he said that the fullness did not exist in the church; if it did he wasn't aware of it, because the fullness required a man to become a king and a priest. Joseph Smith was made a king by anointing the following month on September 28 of 1843. The month before his anointing he explained, "no one in the Church held the fullness of the priesthood; for any person to have the fullness of that priesthood must be a king and a priest. A person may be anointed a king and priest before they can receive their kingdom." (Wilford Woodruff recorded that in his journal on August 6, 1843.) The following month then, 28th of September 1843, Joseph was anointed a king and a priest, and the month after that, on October [28], 1843, Hyrum Smith was likewise ordained to be a king unto God.

Hold that thought for a moment while we turn to 2 Nephi chapter 10 beginning at verse 11:

> *And this land shall be a land of liberty unto the Gentiles, and there shall be no kings upon the land, who shall raise up unto the Gentiles. And I will fortify this land against all other nations. And he that fighteth against Zion shall perish, saith God. For he that raiseth up a king against me shall perish, for I, the Lord, the king of heaven, will be their king, and I will be a light unto them forever, that hear my words.*

So now we have a paradox. There must be a return of the "same priesthood that was in the beginning," in which there is a theocratic father or king, but God commands there shall not be one, and if you raise one up then God will destroy him.

In solving the paradox I would suggest we go to the Book of Mormon first, in order to find out exactly how was it that at the time of the Nephites we had successful kings. One of whom is most notable is King Benjamin. We don't even call him "Benjamin," we call him "King Benjamin," because his identity with his role is so linked together that we can't talk about the man without talking about his status. This is King Benjamin in Mosiah chapter 2 explaining himself and explaining the greatness of the kingship which he held.

> *But I am like as yourselves, subject to all manner of infirmities in body and mind; yet I have been chosen by this people, and consecrated by my father, and was suffered by the hand of the Lord that I should be a ruler and a king over this people; and have been kept and preserved by his matchless power,* ***to serve you*** *with all the might, mind and strength which the Lord hath granted unto me. I say unto you that as I have been suffered to* ***spend my days in your service****, even up to this time,* ***and have not sought gold nor silver nor any manner of riches of you****; Neither have I suffered that ye should be confined in dungeons, nor that ye should make slaves one of another, nor that ye should murder, or plunder, or steal, or commit adultery; nor even have I suffered that ye should commit any manner of wickedness, and* ***have taught you that ye should keep the commandments of the Lord, in all things which he hath commanded you****— And even* ***I, myself, have labored with mine own hands that I might serve you****, and that ye should not be laden with taxes, and that there should nothing come upon you which was grievous to be borne—and of all these things which I have spoken, ye yourselves are witnesses this day. Yet, my brethren,* ***I have not done these things that I might boast****, neither do I tell these things that thereby I might accuse you; but I tell you these things that ye may know that* ***I can answer a clear conscience before God*** *this day. Behold, I say unto you that because I said unto you that I had spent* ***my days in your service****, I do not desire to boast, for I have only been in the service of God. And behold, I tell you these things that ye may learn wisdom; that ye may learn that* ***when ye are in the service of your fellow beings ye are only in the service of your God.***

This is King Benjamin explaining kingship; one that God recognized and ratified; one that was approved by Him; one that brought about peace in his day.

Christ was born a King. In fact, wise men from the East came inquiring saying: "Where is he that was born King of the Jews?" Because that was His status, that was what the prophecies said of Him. That was the role He occupied. And the person they approached to find out where they might identify the newborn king was the king of the land who knew nothing about the matter, and had to go to the scriptorians to ask them, who after some fumbling came up with "Bethlehem." Bethlehem of Judea, thou art not the least.

Christ was born as a King, but He explained how He discharged His Kingship. In John chapter 18 beginning at verse 36, Jesus answered. This is when he was on trial for His life:

Jesus answered, My kingdom is not of this world: if my kingdom were of this world, then would my servants fight, that I should not be delivered to the Jews: but now is my kingdom not from hence. Pilate therefore said unto him, Art thou a king then? Jesus answered, Thou sayest that I am a king. To this end was I born, and for this cause came I into the world, that I should bear witness unto the truth. Every one that is of the truth heareth my voice.

That's the King. He suffered Himself to be surrendered into the hands of wicked men who despitefully used, abused, beat, and humiliated Him and then killed Him publicly on a thoroughfare where the notoriety of His death would be on public display. No one entering or leaving on that day, the city of Jerusalem, could do so without noticing the humiliation of our Lord. That's our King.

He explained Himself further in contrasting who He, the King, the Almighty Father, the Wonderful, Counselor, of the end of His government there shall not be a failure of increase, He explained Himself and how He rules to his disciples. This is in Luke chapter 22 beginning at verse 25:

And he said unto them, The kings of the Gentiles exercise lordship over them; and they that exercise authority upon them are called benefactors. But ye shall not be so: but he that is greatest among you, let him be as the younger; and he that is chief, as he that doeth service.

The great King came, above all else, to serve. Zion will come. It will come, not because of the worthiness of any of us, it will come because of the repentance of us, and the worthiness of those with whom God covenanted to bring it to pass, including Adam and Enoch and Abraham and Melchizedek. It will come as a consequence of the righteousness of those who went before and with whom God, who cannot lie in a covenant, made a covenant to cause it to happen in the last days. It will surely come.

Mormon wrote his book and had us in mind as his audience. After Mormon finished his book there was one reader, and that was his son Moroni, who buried it. Everything Mormon did he did for this audience today, the last days, the gentiles. As he is finishing up his record – this is in Mormon 8:31 – he talks about us and says:

There shall be many who will say, Do this, or do that, and it mattereth not, for the Lord will uphold such at the last day. But wo unto such, for they are in the gall of bitterness and in the bonds of iniquity.

There is a right way, and it will be done according to the Lord's will. And the Lord is actively working to bring that about right now in our day. The potential for Zion and the covenants being fulfilled in our day is as great as it has been in any generation from the days of Adam until now. And yet in all those generations there have only been two successes that the scriptures have captured.

Well, the original priesthood and the original pattern will have to return in order for the last days Zion to exist. The first Zion, in Moses chapter 7 verse 13:

> *And so great was the faith of Enoch that he led the people of God, and their enemies came to battle against them; and he spake the word of the Lord, and the earth trembled, and the mountains fled, even according to his command; and the rivers of water were turned out of their course; and the roar of the lions was heard out of the wilderness; and all nations feared greatly, ...so great was the power of the language which God had given him.*

When the government of God is upon the earth in the form of Zion, as it was established by Enoch in his day, then God protects and defends it. God will be the force with which the nations of the earth must contend if they intend to do harm to Zion. Because it is His government, it is His handiwork, and it is an affront to Him to challenge His authority in attacking Zion, hence Enoch's ability to speak the word of God and to have those that would bring harm upon Zion vanquished.

Hence, further, the reason why, before the Flood, it was necessary to remove Zion, because God cannot destroy the [righteous]. The wicked can destroy the wicked, and the wicked can destroy the righteous. But when Zion is here, the wicked cannot destroy Zion because God is asserting His government. And because the wicked cannot destroy Zion, and God will not do so, Zion necessarily was taken up into heaven. The same thing happened with Melchizedek's city.

The Lord lamented: "How oft would I have gathered you as a hen gathers her chicks under her wings, and ye would not!" There have been occasions on which it would have been possible to have established Zion, but men would not. When that happens, and men will not, the same rules apply as applied at the beginning. Hence the necessity for removing Moses out of the midst of Israel because through Moses we could have had Zion, but the children of Israel were not interested. Hence the reason why Elijah was taken up into heaven, because Elijah was an opportunity in which it would have been possible for Zion to have been established.

Well, that same priesthood which was in the beginning that allowed [Melchizedek] to establish the city of peace, the city of righteousness, the city that God Himself would defend, necessarily must return. If you look at D&C Section 133 beginning at verse 26:

> *And they who are in the north countries shall come in remembrance before the Lord; and their prophets shall hear his voice, and shall no longer stay themselves; and they shall smite the rocks, and the ice shall flow down at their presence. And an highway shall be cast up in the midst of the great deep. Their enemies shall become a prey unto them, And in the barren deserts there shall come forth pools of living water; and the parched ground shall no longer be a thirsty land. And they shall bring forth their rich treasures unto the children of Ephraim, my servants. And the boundaries of the everlasting hills shall tremble at their presence. And there shall they fall down and be crowned with glory, even in Zion, by the hands of the servants of the Lord, even the children of Ephraim. And they shall be filled with songs of everlasting joy. Behold, this is the blessing of the everlasting God upon the tribes of Israel, and the richer blessing upon the head of Ephraim and his fellows.*

Heaven will protect the last day's Zion. It will belong to Him, and therefore God will not allow it to be overtaken or overcome. D&C Section 45 has another prophecy about the last day's Zion. Beginning at verse 66:

> *And it shall be called the New Jerusalem, a land of peace, a city of refuge, a place of safety for the saints of the Most High God; And the glory of the Lord shall be there, and the terror of the Lord also shall be there, insomuch that the wicked will not come unto it, and it shall be called Zion. And it shall come to pass among the wicked, that every man that will not take his sword against his neighbor must needs flee unto Zion for safety. And there shall be gathered unto it out of every nation under heaven; and it shall be the only people that shall not be at war one with another. And it shall be said among the wicked: Let us not go up to battle against Zion, for the inhabitants of Zion are terrible; wherefore we cannot stand.*

When they came to arrest the Lord in the Garden of Gethsemane after His suffering, even though He intended to submit Himself, and to be abused and ultimately killed. When they entered the Apostle John records that Christ, despite the ordeal he had just concluded, stood up, confronted them in their arms and said: "Whom seek ye?" And they said: "Jesus of Nazareth." And He said: "I am he." And they stumbled backwards, tripped over one another's feet, and they fell down.

An armed group bearing swords and weapons were intimidated by the Lord identifying Himself. He made no attempt to defend Himself, but had He elected to do so, they could not have taken Him. He went as a lamb to the slaughter because he intended, though the Lion of Judah, to become the sacrificial lamb.

Heaven protected Zion in its first iteration and heaven is going to protect the last day's Zion. As a consequence of that, the time is going to come when it will not be the deliverance of Israel out of Egypt that people cite as evidence of the power of God. You see, Egypt had to be subdued. Moses was sent to subdue them because Egypt was, at the time, the greatest kingdom, the greatest nation on the earth. Moses was sent to them to establish the government of God. When you confront the government of God against the most powerful nation on the earth, it's the most powerful nation that must yield the field, and not the Lord.

In the last days Jeremiah prophesied that the time is going to come when the talk about the power of God is no longer making reference to what the Lord did anciently with Egypt. It's going to be what the Lord intends to do with the last days Zion. This is Jeremiah chapter 16 beginning in verse 14:

> *Therefore, behold, the days come, saith the Lord, that it shall no more be said, The Lord liveth, that brought up the children of Israel out of the land of Egypt; But, The Lord liveth, that brought up the children of Israel from the land of the north, and from all the lands whither he had driven them: and I will bring them again into their land that I gave unto their fathers.*

That will be the reference point to which people will point as evidence of God's intention to establish His rule, His reign upon the earth, His authority over the nations of the earth.

It is going to come to pass. In your enthusiasm, it would be better to demonstrate the virtue of patience as the Lord brings His work about, than to exhibit the character flaw of impatience and enthusiasm in trying to bring about what the Lord intends Himself to cause to happen because you cannot give birth prematurely to a living Zion, or it will choke and it will die because it is unable to be viable outside of the hands of the Lord. We have to wait on Him.

Don't be misled by a false model that you look out and you see somewhere else. Look, we admire a man -- we -- believers and followers of the Lord -- admire **a man** so much so that the priesthood was renamed after him, because he was the last one to really accomplish Zion, that is Melchizedek, priesthood was named after him. You go and you look carefully at why Melchizedek qualified to obtain the priesthood, and it was because he, by faith, quenched the violence of fire, he subdued lions, by faith he achieved all these things -- **not by priesthood; By faith**.

If you wanna know what one can accomplish without faith but with an ordination to the priesthood, there's a whole discussion of that in *A Man without Doubt* about the first attempt to distribute the highest order of priesthood in Joseph's day. There's a description of what an utter failure that was. In fact it was so great a failure that what Joseph did was he backed up, and he started over again with trying to solve the problem. And The problem did not consist of priesthood -- it consisted of the lack of faith. The lectures on Faith are an attempt to create faith that will have power which is separate from Priesthood.

Men, women, and children can have faith. There was a time when the Mary Fielding story had her anointing her oxen and healing them. In the world of the correlated LDS model, she's now calling for the equivalent of Home Teachers to come anoint her oxen. Mary Fielding's faith was what healed the oxen.

Would you rather have priesthood without faith, or faith without priesthood? If you have faith, everything else is possible. Faith is what is lacking.

The foregoing excerpts are taken from:

- Denver's *40 Years in Mormonism Series*, Talk #9 titled "Marriage and Family" given in St. George, UT on July 26th, 2014;
- His talk titled "Zion Will Come" given near Moab, UT on April 10th, 2016; and
- His conference talk titled "The Doctrine of Christ", given in Boise, ID on September 11th, 2016.

147. Shem, Part 6

This is the sixth part of a series about Shem, who came to be known as Melchizedek, one of the Patriarchal Fathers, who established a city of peace that ultimately achieved the status of "Zion" and was taken up into heaven.

———

DENVER: There's more about that subject in the Book of Mormon than anyone has ever bothered to talk about. When the people of Jared were brought to the Americas, they were brought to the Americas by an act and direction of God in order for them to inherit a land of promise. When they inherited the land it was theirs, but they wore out their welcome by their rebellion, their forgetfulness, their failure to honor the God of this land. It is within the Book of Ether that we find out that this land comes with a restriction on it that those that possess it have to worship the God of this land or they will be swept away.

Now the sweeping away sometimes takes generations before it happens. But it happens. It happened to the Jaredites and then the Nephites were brought over—the party of Lehi—and they were also given the land to possess as a covenant. Throughout the time, though, that the Nephites inherited this land as their covenant land of promise, there was a constant reference to a future moment, a future time, a time in which the Nephites themselves would be destroyed. And they'd be destroyed by the Lamanites. And then the Lamanites would inherit the land, and they would in turn be displaced because they forgot the God of this land. And a new group would be brought over, and the new group would eventually likewise enter into a covenant and receive the land of promise. Now very often in order for the Lord to achieve his end you have to have three attempts. You have to have two attempts that fail before you finally have one that succeeds.

The purpose behind establishing a covenant with the gentles in the last days is not so that the gentles get to inhabit the land as a place for them to celebrate and rejoice. It's to bring about the Lord's purposes in creating Zion. If the youth enter into the covenant and then keep the covenant it has one and only one purpose and that is to bring about Zion. We've had persistent failures of humanity to create Zion, but it's happened once in the time of Enoch, it happened again in the time of Melchizedek, and it's going to happen a third time at some point on this land. The existence of Zion in this land will precede the redemption in Jerusalem, but Jerusalem will also become one of the places where for a thousand years our Lord is going to have a jurisdiction.

Take courage! Life was meant to be a living sacrifice, to be lost in the service to God, only by losing your life will you find it. Saving faith is so rare precisely because it requires courage to engage the opposition in this world and to cheerfully endure the abuse, lies, threats and fiery darts sent by those who fear your faith above everything. Faith in God will save you through His grace, it can render every weapon of this world and hell powerless, but it takes courage. When friends betray you and fear overtakes your associates and causes the knees to buckle under the weight of the burdens God allows to be imposed upon you, remember the Lord descended below it all and when He cried out asking for the bitter cup to be removed, there was no relief. He is the prototype of the saved man and the Father loved Him for his sacrifice. It was the Lord's sacrifice for us that perfected His love for us. He values us because of the great price He paid for each one of us. If you love God you will be given the opportunity to prove your love. You will be proven by the things you endure for His name's sake. Do not fail. Melchizedek's people in the land of Salem were like this people they had waxed strong in iniquity and abominations, yeah, they had all gone astray, they were full of all manner of wickedness but Melchizedek having exercised mighty faith and received the office of the high priesthood according to the Holy Order of God did preach repentance unto his people and behold they did repent.

The Covenant being offered does not require one to reject it, only voluntary acceptance. It assumes mankind's rejection and therefore to reject one need do nothing. Entering into the Covenant offered by the Lord today does not mean there is a church or organization to be joined, it only means that you affirm that you will accept and abide the terms set by the Lord for being one of His people. You can be one of His covenant people and also hold membership in any church of your choosing.

However, the Covenant imposes the responsibility to **help** others who also accept the Covenant. To regard **them** also as the Lord's, to honor God, seek to recover Israel, teach children to honor God, care for the poor among God's people and to help lighten the burdens of others. None of those responsibilities involve establishing or joining an institution. The words of the Covenant...the words of the Covenant require us to have left behind the destructive and vile practices of the world. It reads in part, "all you who have turned from your wicked ways and repented of your evil doings of **lying** and **deceiving** and of all **whoredoms** and of **secret abominations, idolatries, murders, priestcrafts, envying and strife** and from all wickedness and abominations and have come unto Me and been baptized in My name and received a remission of your sins and received the Holy Ghost are now numbered with My people who are of the House of Israel." Those enumerated vile and destructive things must end among us today. **We** are all equal. We all accept the Book of Mormon as a Covenant for us to be numbered among the Lord's covenant people. This land, in particular, is a land of promise to those who serve the God of this land who is Jesus Christ. The time is coming when those who are not the Lord's people will be swept off the land.

There is so much left to be done. I know that we can't jump hastily from point to point along the way and that we have to carefully proceed with every step. But it's astonishing to me the steps that people decide to get hung up on and to spend a great deal of time, when time could better be spent moving further along on the path. I don't know what it will take to get people to enthusiastically welcome and to move along with alacrity on the pathway that the prophecies foretell someone is going to achieve in the last days. Because it seems like all that murmuring that we read about in the Book of Exodus going on in the camp of Israel, when we scratch our heads and say, why are they complaining about missing the fleshpots of Egypt when God is leading them with a pillar of smoke by day and a pillar of fire by night? One would think that you'd be happy eating manna in the wilderness if you knew God was with you.

I also think that in our current state of technological development it's possible for the discontent to magnify the voice electronically over the Internet and to make any level of discontent seem to be much greater than it really is. But if one person is discontent and 500 people are arguing with the one who is discontent it appears that the argument includes at least half a thousand, maybe more. As between one another, that is every one of us, because every one of us is involved in a relationship with one another; you choose. Mind you, Christ could have disputed, he could have corrected, he could have challenged every one of the ongoing religious and social conventions of his day. *You are doing that wrong. Oh, you should stop doing that. Would you quit it! And by the way, you're so dark in your mind that I don't know where it begins, except for him, he's worse, and then her. Oh!* [cross talk and audience laughter]

How much of the gospel of Christ would not have been possible for Him to preach if He'd gone about contending? He chose not to. In that respect, perhaps His most godly example was the patience with which He dealt with those around him; kindly, patiently, correcting them when they largely came to Him with questions trying to trap Him, but affirmatively stating in the Sermon on the Mount how you could take any group of people and turn them into Zion itself, if we would live the Sermon on the Mount.

I figure that I'm not that good a teacher because it appears to me that there are a lot of mistakes being made that are perfectly avoidable. I don't take King Benjamin's statement that the number of errors that people can make, the number of sins that people can commit are endless, there is no way to possibly number them, as I don't take that as consoling words. I take that as a challenge to say, *Okay, but your people did find peace among one another.* And even Enoch's people found peace among one another. Melchizedek was called the Prince of Peace because he preached but what he preached was repentance. The office of the ministering of angels is to spread the message of repentance. So then all of us have an obligation there, to join in the same thing, repenting, turning to face God. The more we face Him, the more light we take in, the more differently we behave, individually and in connection with each other.

I am certain we will see Zion because it's been promised and it's been prophesied from the beginning of time. When father Adam prophesied, being overcome by the Spirit in the valley of Adam-ondi-Ahman, and foretold what would happen to his posterity down to the latest generations, Zion was pointed to. Therefore, from the days of Adam on, all the holy prophets have looked forward to that as the essential moment in the history of the world, because Christ will come and will redeem the world. It will be the end of the wicked; it will be the beginning of something far better. That's been the hope, that's been the promise, that's been what they've looked forward to. I wonder how many of us share that same longing, that same hope, that same desire that originated in the beginning, because if we don't subdue our desires, appetites, and passions enough to try and deal peaceably one with another, choosing deliberately to not contend, even when we know people are wrong. When Christ was confronted and he corrected the error he corrected only that error, he didn't go on with a list of other weaknesses, failings and challenges, He only addressed the one that was put to him.

We have an opportunity. We have a bona fide, actual offer from God to allow us to be that generation in which the promises get fulfilled. But we have the freedom of choice that allows us to elect to be stubborn, to be contentious, to be agents of disruption, and to discourage and break the hearts of those who would willingly accept the challenge to repent and follow God.

Don't be reading into it what I'm saying that I dislike or condemn the LDS Church. The LDS Church just is. It's like the Community of Christ; it's like the Remnant Church. There are a lot of good people that belong to these various institutions who are very trusting of what the institutions are doing. The leaders of these institutions I'm fairly certain don't intend to do evil but the result is evil, and all of the good intentions not withstanding. Where, where is the fulfilment of the promise? Amassing wealth and waiting is not going to achieve any good end. Repentance, baptism, and finding yourself accountable directly to God, that's where the work of the restoration is going to continue. As far as the scriptures inform us, the only thing that Enoch claimed for himself was the role of being a teacher. Melchizedek was given the praise of being called a King and a Priest, new name given to him, but his role was that of a preacher of righteousness.

Christ taught parables that included invited guests being barred from attending the wedding feast. In one, the guests are called "virgins" to suggest that they possess moral purity and would be welcomed to the event. In another, there are strangers on the highway invited because others refused to come. Both parables, however, have some who are ultimately excluded from the wedding, a symbol of Christ's return. These parables raise an important issue about the Lord's return. There is a reason why five of the ten virgins could not enter into the wedding celebration. Likewise, those invited to attend the wedding feast that arrive without a wedding garment will be excluded. In both cases, those excluded were not welcome as they were unprepared.

There have been only two societies in recorded history that became Zion. Because of the age of the world at the time, both were taken up into heaven. We have very little to help us understand why these two succeeded. Apart from describing them as of "one heart, one mind, and no poor among them," we know little else. But perhaps that is one of the most important things we *can* know about them. Maybe the point is that *nothing* and *no-one* stood out as remarkable or different within the community. There were no heroes and no villains; no rich and no poor; no Shakespearian plot lines of betrayal, intrigue, ambition, conflict, and envy. There was no adultery, theft, robbery, murder, immorality, and drunkenness—in other words, nothing to entertain us. Because all our stories, movies, music, novels, television plots, and social media are based upon and captivated by everything that is missing from these societies.

The centuries-long period of peace described in the Book of Mormon occupies only a few short pages in 4 Nephi. Their society was marked by the presence of peace, the absence of conflict, and abiding stability. This is what they attained: *There were no contentions and disputations among them, and every man did deal justly one with another. And they had all things common among them; therefore, there were not rich and poor, bond and free, but they were all made free and partakers of the Heavenly gift* (4 Nephi 1:1 RE). Because there was no future ministry for them to perform, their Zion society was not taken up to heaven. Because the world was not yet ready for the Lord to return in judgment, neither Enoch nor Melchizedek returned with their people to fall on their necks and kiss them.

These people were most remarkable for what they *lacked*. How they grew to lack these divisions, contentions, and disputes is described in very few, simple words: *They did walk after the commandments which they had received from their Lord and their God, continuing in fasting and prayer, and in meeting together oft, both to pray and to hear the word of the Lord. And it came to pass...there was no contention among all the people in all the land* (4 Nephi 1:2 RE).

What were the names of their leaders? We don't know because, apparently, there were none. Who were their great teachers? Again, we don't know because they were not identified. Who governed? Apparently no one. They had things in common, obeyed God's commandments, and spent time praying and hearing the word of the Lord. They were so very unlike us.

To make the point clear for us, the record of these people explains: *There was no contention in the land because of the love of God which did dwell in the hearts of the people; and there were no envyings, nor strifes, nor tumults, nor whoredoms, nor lyings, nor murders, nor any manner of lasciviousness* (4 Nephi 1:3 RE). All the negatives were missing because the love of God dwelt in their hearts.

Something else describes them: *And surely there could not be a happier people among all the people who had been created by the hand of God* (ibid). Consider those words carefully. You cannot be happier than by allowing the love of God to dwell in you. The happiest people who have ever lived did so by the profound peace they displayed, equality they shared, fairness they showed one another, and love of God in their hearts.

This is a description of our social opposites. Reviewing the Answer to the Prayer for Covenant, the Covenant, and the recent parable of the Master's House shows that the Lord is pleading for *us* to become *this*. It's not easy; it will require civilizing the uncivilized. However, it is necessary to become the wise virgins and the invited guests wearing the wedding garment.

Five of the virtuous virgins who were expecting the wedding party to arrive were, nevertheless, excluded. They were virgins like the others; but the others were allowed to enter, and they were not. They did not lack virginity. They did not lack notice. They were not surprised by an unexpected wedding party arriving. But they lacked "oil," which is a symbol of the Holy Ghost. They failed to acquire the necessary spirit with which to avoid conflict, envy, strife, tumult, and contention. To grow into the kind of people God will want us to welcome into His dwelling requires practice, experience, and effort. People have not done it. Devout religious people are not prepared to live in peace, with all things in common, with no poor among them. God is trying to create a civilization that does not yet exist.

It is a privilege for God to give guidance to help prepare His people. There has always been a promise from the Lord that those who inherit Zion will be given commandments from Him to follow. He declared:

> *Yea, blessed are they whose feet stand upon the land of Zion, who have obeyed my gospel, for they shall receive for their reward the good things of the earth, and it shall bring forth [it's] strength. And they...shall [also] be crowned with blessings from above, yea...with commandments not a few, and with revelations in their time, [that] they...are faithful and diligent[ly] before me.* (T&C 46:1)

Those who mock or criticize efforts to complete the Restoration are defining themselves as unworthy by their own words. No matter how good they may otherwise be, when they embrace conflict, envy, strife, tumult, and contention, they cannot be invited to the wedding of the Lamb.

We need more commandments from God to prepare for what is coming. The example in 4 Nephi commends those people who walk after the commandments received from our Lord and God. There should be fasting and prayer. People should meet together, pray, and review the words of the Lord. Every step taken will make us more like those virgins who have oil in their lamps and less like the foolish virgins who took no effort to make the required preparation.

It's not enough to avoid outright evil. We have to be good. Being "good" means to be separate from the world, united in charity towards each other, and to have united hearts. If we are ready when the wedding party arrives, we must follow the Lord's commandments to *us*. They are for our good. He wants us to awaken and arise from an awful slumber.

The third such society will not be taken into heaven. Instead, it will welcome the return of the first two to the earth. Why would ancient, righteous societies caught up to heaven want to leave there to come and meet with a city of people on earth? Why would they fall on their necks and kiss that gathered body of believers? And above all else, why would Christ want to occupy a tabernacle and dwell with such a community? Obviously, because there will be people living on earth whose civilization is like the society in heaven.

The Ten Commandments outline basic social norms needed for peace and stability. Christ's Sermon on the Mount was His exposition on the Ten Commandments. He expounded on the need to align the intent of the heart with God's standard to love your fellow man, do good to those who abuse you, and hold no anger. He took us deeper. Where the Ten Commandments allowed reluctant, resentful, and hard-hearted conformity, the Sermon on the Mount requires a willing readiness to obey. Christ wants us to act with alacrity to follow Him. He taught us to treat others as you would want to be treated.

The answer to these questions is easy to conceptualize and easy to verbalize. But living the answer is beyond mankind's ability to endure. We do not want to lay down our pride, ambition, jealousy, envy, strife, and lusts to become that community.

Enoch prophesied about the last-days Zion. He saw the earth was pained by the wickedness upon her. He wrote this account:

> *Enoch looked upon the earth and he heard a voice from the bowels thereof, saying, Woe, woe is me, the mother of men. I am pained; I am weary because of the wickedness of my children. When shall I rest and be cleansed from the filthiness which has gone forth out of me? When will my Creator sanctify me, that I may rest, and righteousness for a season abide upon my face? And when Enoch heard the earth mourn, he wept, and cried unto the Lord, saying, O Lord will you not have compassion upon the earth?* (Genesis 4:20 RE)

The answer describes things that have not happened—but may happen in our day, if we choose to follow the Lord. The opportunity has been offered. The Lord's answer to Enoch was in the form of a covenant. That covenant will be vindicated, but only by those who will rise up to obey Him. God's words will not fail, and this will happen:

> *And the Lord said unto Enoch, As I live, even so will I come in the last days, in the days of wickedness and vengeance, to fulfill the oath which I have made unto you concerning the children of Noah. And the day shall come that the earth shall rest. But before that day, the heavens shall be darkened, and a veil of darkness shall cover the earth; and the heavens shall shake, and also the*

> *earth. And great tribulations shall be among the children of men, but* ***my people*** *will I preserve. And righteousness will I send down out of Heaven…[I will] gather out [mine] own elect from the four quarters of the earth, unto a place which I [have] prepare[d], a holy city, that* ***my people*** *may gird up their loins and be looking forth for [a] time of my coming. For there shall be my tabernacle…it shall be called Zion, a New Jerusalem. And the Lord said unto Enoch, Then shall you and…your city meet* ***them*** *there, and we will receive* ***them*** *into our bosom. And they shall see us, and we will fall [on]* ***their*** *necks, and* ***they*** *shall fall [on] our necks, and we will kiss each other, and there shall be my abode.* (Genesis 4:22 RE, emphasis added)

The last-days Zion and her people were planned, foretold, and chosen thousands of years ago to live on earth when righteousness would come down out of heaven. They will be here when truth is sent forth out of the earth to bear testimony of Christ. And, like a flood, righteousness and truth will sweep the earth. Any who have witnessed a flood know floodwaters carry a great deal of debris, dirt, and detritus. Today there is a flood of information, recordings, and teachings sweeping the earth. The Internet has made it possible for an individual sitting at a keyboard to speak to the entire world. Righteousness is sweeping the earth, while floodwaters are disturbing the whole world.

In Joseph Smith's day it was required for an army of messengers to be sent. There was a practical limit on how many people Joseph could personally teach. Outside the direct sound of his voice only printed words could carry the message. He and those who followed him invested in a press to publish newspapers and books to carry the truth. But that still was not enough— It required an organized body of missionaries to take the publications, repeat the message, and convey the new truths came through revelation to Joseph Smith. Even with the enormous investment of time and resources made while Joseph was alive, there were places and people who never heard a thing about the Restoration while Joseph lived.

Today we must still warn others. However, we have much more greater means available to us. We can use a keyboard to reach the whole world. There are people in Africa, Asia, Europe, Australia, and South America, and across North America who participate in our conferences. I want to send greetings to our brothers and sisters in Africa, Asia, Europe, South America, Australia, New Zealand and elsewhere who cannot travel to be with us. The flood of overflowing the world today includes the promised righteousness and truth, but it requires the Lord's elect to distinguish between the filth, folly, and foolishness to find freedom from sin through Christ, who is the foundation of righteousness and truth.

Prophets have described how this will happen. Isaiah described a coming age of peace when righteousness and truth have their opportunity to bear fruit. He spoke of Christ and of the power in Christ's teachings to transform the world itself. That same world that Enoch heard lamenting, pained by the violence on her face, will find rest. Isaiah foretells what will happen just prior to the Lord's return:

> *And there shall come forth a rod out of the stem of Jesse, and a branch shall grow out of his roots. And the spirit of the Lord shall rest upon him—the spirit of wisdom and understanding, the spirit of counsel and might, the spirit of knowledge and of the fear of the Lord—and shall make him of quick understanding in the fear of the Lord. And he shall not judge after the sight of his eyes, neither reprove after the hearing of his ears, but with righteousness shall he judge the poor, and reprove with equity for the meek of the earth. And he shall smite the earth with the rod of his mouth, and with the breath of his lips shall he slay the wicked. And righteousness shall be the girdle of his loins, and faithfulness the girdle of his reins. The wolf also shall dwell with the lamb, and the leopard shall lie down with the kid; and the calf, and the young lion, and the fatling together, and [the] little child shall lead them. And the cow and the bear shall feed, their young ones shall lie down together, and the lion shall eat straw like the ox. And the sucking child shall play on the hole of [an] asp, and the weaned child shall put his hand on the cockatrice's den. They shall not hurt nor destroy in all my holy mountain, for the earth shall be full of the knowledge of the Lord as the waters cover the sea. And in that day, there shall be a root of Jesse [which] shall stand for an ensign of the people; to it shall the gentiles seek, and his rest shall be glorious.* (Isaiah 5:4 RE)

How will Christ smite the earth with the rod of His mouth? By teaching peace to people who are willing to obey and live at peace.

In the first Zion, the people were at peace with nature. But that place was apparently protected *by* nature. What scripture describes is not magic or "fairy dust," but a perfectly natural process. This creation has been ordained by God and framed with intelligence to follow certain principles established before the foundation of the world. Any people in any age who follow the same pattern will receive the same result. What is described in this passage about Enoch and his city?

> *And so great was the faith of Enoch that he led the people of God, and their enemies came to battle against them, and he spoke the word of the Lord, and the earth trembled, and the mountains fled—even according to his command*

> *—and the rivers of water were turned out of their course, and the roar of...lions were heard out of the wilderness. And all nations feared greatly, so powerful was the word of Enoch, and so great was the power of the language which God had given him.* (Genesis 4:13 RE)

Would a lion that had been befriended by Enoch and his people be inclined, by its nature, to protect the people it viewed as part of its clan? Would a bear protect its shepherd and guardian? Would a wolf? Is it possible for a civilization to exist that does not hurt nor destroy in all their land? If they would not hurt nor destroy in all their land, would it be a holy place?

We live in a very different civilization from the one described in prophecy. But the one described prophetically will not just one day appear. It will require effort, learning, obedience, and sacrifice to change.

The earth rejoiced at Enoch's people. The earth protected those people. Earthquakes, landslides, and floods stopped the wicked—and the animal kingdom, including predators like the lion, rose up to protect the City of Enoch. For those who are prepared to receive the people of Enoch and Melchizedek, and those who will welcome the Lord to dwell among them, that can and will happen.

The foregoing excerpts are taken from:

- Denver's remarks at "A Day of Faith and Connection" youth conference in UT on June 10th, 2017
- His Opening Remarks given at the Covenant of Christ Conference in Boise, Idaho on September 3rd, 2017
- A fireside talk titled "That We Might Become One", given in Clinton, UT on January 14th, 2018
- Denver's remarks titled "Keep the Covenant: Do the Work" given at the Remembering the Covenants Conference in Layton, UT on August 4, 2018; and
- Denver's conference talk titled "Civilization", given in Grand Junction, CO on April 21, 2019.

148. Shem, Part 7

This is the seventh and final part of a series about Shem, who came to be known as Melchizedek, one of the Patriarchal Fathers, who established a city of peace that ultimately achieved the status of "Zion" and was taken up into heaven.

DENVER: If we obey the commandments that have been given, we can qualify to inherit a land on which to build a temple. The objective of the covenant was to confer the right to live on the land, surviving the judgments coming upon the wicked. *We* need to live up to our end of the covenant. It is clear the Lord is willing to bear with, guide, give commandments to help prepare, and reprove His people when needed. We should not rely on the Lord's patience, but should be eager to obey His guiding instruction. His commandments are not to limit us, but to increase light and truth. Some intelligence is only gained by obedience to His commandments.

Joseph Smith tried to teach the people. They failed to do as they were commanded. They lost the opportunity to have the fullness of the priesthood restored to them. As a result of their failure, for nearly two centuries, institutions have pretended the fullness was restored and they inherited it. Until now, no people have acknowledged the failure, repented, and asked the Lord to restore the fullness of the priesthood.

Salem was a land filled with abominations. Melchizedek, by faith, obtained the Holy Order, taught repentance, and persuaded them to reform. Nauvoo was a viper's den. It was a place with widespread adultery and conspirators who precipitated the murders of Joseph and Hyrum.

Why, during His mortal ministry, did Jesus Christ not establish a place of peace, a city of Zion? Was not Christ the greatest teacher of all?

Reflect on this and consider whether the people who were taught by Melchizedek lived with and were taught by Joseph Smith, would they have repented, obeyed and obtained the fullness?

If Enoch's people lived in Nauvoo, would they have repented? If Joseph, instead of Enoch, taught the people of Enoch, would there have been Zion? Had Joseph, instead of Melchizedek, taught the people of Salem, would they have forsaken their abominations?

Is Zion the result of the teacher or the people?

The people matter more than the teacher. As long as the gospel is taught, including the need for repentance and obedience, any faithful teacher may be enough. But nobody can bring Zion with people who refuse to repent and obey God's commandments. The teacher is necessary, but only a community of people willing to heed the gospel can fulfill the prophecies.

I have to temper the foregoing by the lesson Alma preserved (I think perhaps quoted from the writings of Zenos) about Melchizedek:

> *Now this Melchizedek was a king over the land of Salem, and his people had waxed strong in iniquity and abominations—yea, they had all gone astray; they were full of all manner of wickedness. But Melchizedek, having exercised mighty faith and received the office of the High Priesthood according to the Holy Order of God, did preach repentance unto his people. And behold, they did repent. And Melchizedek did establish peace in the land in his days; therefore, he was called the Prince of Peace, for he was the King of Salem; and he did reign under his father. Now there were many before him, and...there were [also] many afterwards, but none were greater.* (Alma 10:2 RE)

If people who had all gone astray and were filled with iniquity and abominations were moved by his message of repentance, could Melchizedek have persuaded Nauvoo to abandon their wickedness, strife, ambition, jealousy, and adultery? There is no answer because of Christ's inability to bring Zion. Christ was greater than Melchizedek, and He could not accomplish with His contemporaries what Melchizedek did with his.

None of us is spared from mutual failure. We are not Zion. We will never be Zion if we do not repent. All of us must repent, turn to face God with full purpose of heart, acting no hypocrisy, or we will not establish godly peace among us.

The Answer to the Prayer for Covenant and the Covenant are the beginning blueprint. That blueprint teaches the need to be better people. Following it is more challenging than reciting it. No one can learn what is required *without doing*. Working together is the only way a society can grow together. No isolated spiritual mystic is going to be prepared for Zion through his solitary personal devotions. Personal devotion is necessary, of course, but the most pious hermit will collide with the next pious hermit when they are required to share and work together in a society of equals having all things in common. Do not pretend it will be otherwise. Failing to do the hard work outlined in the covenant is failing to prepare for Zion. It's failing to have oil in the lamp. It's failing to put upon you the wedding garment.

If you think you are one of the five virgins who will be invited in when the bridegroom arrives and have never attempted to obey the Lord's commandments, you will find yourself left outside when the door is shut. If you come from the highways and byways without a wedding garment because you failed to keep the covenant, you'll be excluded.

As aggravating and trying as people are on one another, we need to go through this. There is no magic path to loving one another. Some people refuse and must be left outside. When it comes to loving others, some things must be abandoned, some things must be added, some things must be forgotten, and some things must be ignored. But learning what to abandon, add, forget, or ignore is only through the doing. We chip away at ourselves and others by interacting and sharing.

We will learn things about one another that will distress us. And we may well wish we didn't know some things about others. How will the socially-offensive become socially- acceptable without help from a loving society? And how can a society become loving if people are not broad-minded enough to figure out that some things just don't matter? Few things really are important. If a man is honest, just, virtuous, and true, should you care if he swears? If a man has a heart of gold and would give you assistance if he thought it was needed, should you care if he is rough and uncouth?

The adulterous and predatory will rarely reform and must often be excluded. They will victimize and destroy. We are commanded to cast out those who steal, love and make a lie, commit adultery, and refuse to repent. The instructions we have been given state:

> *You shall not kill; he that kills shall die. You shall not steal...he that steals and will not repent* ***shall be cast out.*** *You shall not lie; he that lies and will not repent* ***shall be cast out****. You shall love your wife with all your heart, and shall cleave unto her and none else...he that looks upon a woman to lust after her shall deny the faith, and shall not have the spirit, and if he repent not...****shall be cast out****. You shall not commit adultery, and he that commits adultery and repents not* ***shall be cast out****; and he that commits adultery and repents with all his heart, and forsakes [it] and does it no more, you shall forgive him; but if he does it again, he* ***shall not be forgiven****, [and] s****hall be cast out****. You shall not speak evil of your neighbor [nor] or do him any harm. You know my laws, they are given in my scriptures.* ***He that sins and***

> ***repents not shall be cast out****. If you love me, you shall serve me and* ***keep all my commandments****.* (T&C 26:6, emphasis added)

This teaching is still binding. If your fellowship includes those who ought to be "cast out" you have the obligation to do so rather than encouraging evil. Be patient, but be firm. If a person refuses to repent and forsake sins, you may end fellowship with them and include those who are interested in practicing obedience and love.

There is work to be done. Almost all of it is internal to us. The five prepared virgins and the strangers who brought a wedding garment will be those who keep the covenant. It is designed to give birth to a new society, new culture, and permit a new civilization to be founded.

The Lord's civilization will require His tabernacle at the center. Through it, a recovered religion will be fully developed. God's house will include a higher law—an education about the universe—and a divine university will be established. It will be an ensign in the mountains, and people from all over the earth will say: Come, let us go up to the house of the God of Jacob. He will teach us; we will learn of his paths, to walk in them (see Isaiah 1:5; 2 Nephi 8:4 RE). That place will house a new civilization. There will be no hermit gurus proud of their enlightenment.

No one will offer himself or herself up as some great idol to follow. It will be a place of equality, where people are meek and lowly, serving one another without any attempt to compete for "chief seats."

Christ's apostles competed to be greater than one another. In the New Covenants, Luke 13:6, Christ's reaction is recorded:

> *There was also a strife among them: who of them should be accounted the greatest. And he said unto them, The kings of the gentiles exercise lordship over them, and they who exercise authority upon them are called benefactors, but it ought not...be so with you. But he who is greatest among you, let him be as the younger, and he who is chief, as he who does serve. For whether is he greater who sits at [the] meal, or he who serves? I am not as he who sits at a meal, but I am among you as he who serves.*

Christ is the great example. Christ would have fit into Enoch's city, would have been welcomed among Melchizedek's people, and could have dwelt in peace with the Nephites of Fourth Nephi. Has He, as once before between Jerusalem and Emmaus, walked among them unnoticed to enjoy their peaceful company?

I cannot keep the covenant. You cannot keep the covenant. Only *we* can keep the covenant.

The path to Zion is so far beyond the reach of mankind that we know of only two successful times in scripture where heaven and earth united in Zion. One was at the time of Enoch; the other, the city of Melchizedek. In Eden, heaven and earth were united—but Eden fell. Following the visit of Christ to the Nephites, there were several hundred years of peace. But Christ's visit was temporary, and they did not reunite with heaven as a people.

We face a challenge to become something very rare, godly—even holy. It's perplexing how people were able to lay aside all envy, strife, ambition, selfishness, and enmity between one another—yet that is exactly what **we** are asked to do.

The saints in Joseph Smith's day failed. The Lord, speaking of that, said:

> *Behold, I say unto you, were it not for the transgressions of my people, speaking concerning the church and not individuals, they might have been redeemed, even now. But behold, they have not learned to be obedient to the things which I require at their hands, but are full of all manner of evil, and do not impart of their substance, as becomes saints, to the poor and afflicted among them, and are not united according to the union required by the law of the Celestial Kingdom. And Zion cannot be built up unless it is by the principles of the law of the Celestial Kingdom, otherwise I cannot receive her unto myself. And my people must needs be chastened until they learn obedience, if it must needs be by the things which they suffer.* (T&C 107:1) (D&C 105:2)

This building up of Zion, according to the principles of the law of the Celestial Kingdom, does not initially involve the law of consecration. Joseph Smith ended that practice. He said, "...that the law of consecration could not be kept here and that it was the will of the Lord that we should desist from trying to keep it, and if persisted in, it would produce a perfect abortion, and that he assumed the whole responsibility of not keeping it until proposed by himself" (*History of the Church*, 4:93; cf. 105:34). And Joseph died, of course, without ever proposing again the keeping of that law, although there were subsequent attempts made which proved to be a perfect abortion.

Consecration will eventually follow, but like everything that is distant and above this fallen world, it is not a single step. It is a stepped-process and cannot be done in haste nor in a single instant. We have to grow, degree by degree, measure by measure, in order to attempt.

This is another revelation:

> *Therefore, in consequence of the transgression of my people, it is expedient in me that my elders should wait for a little season for the redemption of Zion that they themselves may be prepared, and that my people may be taught more perfectly, and have experience, and **know** more perfectly concerning their **duty** and the things which I require at their hands. And this cannot be brought to pass until my elders are endowed with power from on high, for behold, I have prepared a great endowment and [the] blessing to be poured out upon them, inasmuch as they are faithful and continue in humility before me. Therefore, it is expedient in me that my elders should wait a little season for the redemption of Zion.* (T&C 107:3)(D&C 105:9)

It is clear, at least to me, that the temple is where the Lord intends for people to be taught more perfectly and have experience and know more perfectly concerning their duty and the things which He requires at our hands. He calls that an endowment with power. Knowledge is power, but to qualify to receive that endowment, we're required to be like Abraham, who described himself in these words:

> *Having been myself a follower of righteousness, desiring also to be one who possessed great knowledge, and to be a greater follower of righteousness, and to possess a greater knowledge…* (Abraham 1:1 RE)(Abraham 1:2)

All of those things go together. These are not disconnected thoughts. They are also not thoughts that are unrelated to "returning knowledge and understanding that reaches back into the creation itself, and before the creation," and then goes forward to the end of this cycle of creation. So, he desired to possess:

> *…great knowledge…to be a greater follower of righteousness, and to possess a greater knowledge* [those things go together], *…to be a Father of many nations* [he was situated at a time where that was **necessarily** one of the things that followed from obtaining what he sought after], *a prince of peace, and desiring to **receive instructions** and to keep the commandments of God* [We tend to think that instructions and commandments from God can be burdensome. Abraham viewed it as an opportunity to gain greater knowledge, greater understanding, and therefore, with a better perspective and understanding of what God expected of us, to be a

> greater follower of righteousness, to fit into a pattern], "*I became a rightful heir, a high priest, holding the right belonging to the Fathers. It was conferred upon me from the fathers: it came down from the fathers, from the beginning of time, yea, even from the beginning (or before the foundations of the earth) to the present time, even the right of the firstborn (or the first man — who is Adam — or [the] first Father) through the Fathers unto me.* (Abraham 1:1 RE)(Abraham 1:2-3)

This is what God has in mind for the Restoration to be completed. This is what God intended for us to inherit as our endowment, as our greater knowledge, and enabling us to be greater followers of righteousness.

"Promises made to the fathers" are covenants that God made with them concerning the last days' work, in which there would again be on the earth those who are connected to the Fathers in a way that avoids the earth becoming utterly wasted at His coming. This is something that has to be attended to through the restoration and construction of an authentic temple conforming to the pattern of heaven, in which these things can be attended to and the knowledge and understanding imputed, in order for people to comprehend what it means to be a "greater follower of righteousness."

This was a revelation given in March 2015: "Hence, the great need to turn the hearts of the children to the fathers and the fathers to the children—and this too by covenant and sealing through the Holy Spirit of Promise" (*Plural Marriage*, Denver C. Snuffer, Jr. March 22, 2015). This is to restore **us**—as God restored Abraham— to the original religion.

Abraham came into this world uniquely different from the fathers that had gone before. There was an unbroken chain that continued from father to son and father to son, from the time of Adam, down through the generations until the time of Melchizedek. All of them were participants in an unbroken familial line. Abraham came into an apostate family in which his father worshipped—indeed made—dumb idols as the god to be worshipped. Therefore, Abraham is the first one that will join this line, who emerges from apostasy into possession of the original holy order. In that sense, Abraham is representative of **all** who would follow after, that seek after righteousness, in a world that is **constantly** overcome by apostasy.

Before Adam was cast out of the Garden of Eden (into the world in which death would enter, and Adam would be obligated to succumb to that death), there was an anointing oil prepared in Eden itself that was designed to be used in order to help the Descendant of Adam who would come to crush the head of the serpent—that, once He was anointed, would equip Him to come back from the grave and be resurrected. And that was entrusted into Adam's care before he was cast out of the Garden, as something to be preserved and handed down until the time that the Messiah comes. And as circumstances would have it, that got passed from those that had the responsibility, down through the generations— until finally, Melchizedek turned it over to father Abraham, who, in turn, handed it down through his lineage. And subsequently, there was a line—entrusted not only with possession of the anointing oil that came from Eden but also knowledge about the signs that would be given when the moment came for the oil to be delivered.

And so it was that the sign was given. They recognized and interpreted it correctly. They went to the place where it had been stored by their ancestors. They retrieved it, and then they traveled to find Him who was born the King of the Jews. And upon finding the family (with a sign that signified—from above, according to their understanding and interpretation of the signs—that this was the child, this was the family), they delivered the gifts, which were, in turn, used.

But the oil for anointing was kept. And that oil was handed down, until finally, the moment came when the Savior intended to go up and to provoke His crucifixion. And preliminary to that moment, Mary (the mother) instructed Mary (the consort of Christ) in the manner by which this was to be done. And so, He was anointed—in preparation for His death and His burial and His rising again—with what had been set out and kept (originating in Eden), to be used in order to complete the process of qualifying Him to return again, to have strength in the loins and in the sinews, and the power to rise again from the dead and to lay hold upon all of the faculties of the immortal, physical body.

And so, He was anointed—at the end—with the oil that had been entrusted, originally, to Adam and handed down with an obscure and small body of believers (who were dying out and who were older—and the last of their tradition, it seemed). But the Messiah came, and they discharged the obligation; and the blessing was able to be given, and the Savior was able to rise from the dead. And so, He opened the way, then, for the return from the grave of **everyone** who has faith on His name and accepts (on condition of repentance) the terms to have His atonement applied to us.

So, ask yourself:

- Do the Gentiles now qualify?

- Have they met this standard?
- Have the Gentiles repented of their iniquity and become clean before the Lord?
- Do the Gentiles now exercise faith in the Lord even as the brother of Jared did?
- Have the Gentiles now become sanctified in Christ? or
- Do the foolish Gentiles still fall victim to lying spirits that interfere with and compromise the work of preparing to establish Zion?

Economic realities and legal obligations must be dealt with. The path to Zion does not go **through** consecration. Consecration comes **after** there is a Zion. Even Father Abraham did not live the law of consecration. He was sanctified and qualified to receive all the blessings of the Fathers and now sits on a throne, but he paid **tithes** to Melchizedek.

When Joseph Smith restored Enoch's record (now found in Genesis), Joseph learned about the last days' Zion. It revealed, *And the Lord called his people Zion because they were of one heart, and...one mind, and [dwelt] in righteousness, and there [was] no poor among them* (Genesis 4:14 RE).

I do not believe this was their ancient goal, but it was a byproduct. Such a society cannot be organized but can be gathered. Individuals rarely are able to persuade one another through arguing to expose the other man's error.

Even among people who keep their eyes on the Lord and pay no heed to their neighbor's failure still must grow to become:

- People who refuse to judge and belittle others;
- Those who are humbled by the opportunity to build a house of God;
- Those who refuse to become an accuser.

Even among humble people the Lord can use to restore His house, there will be many things on which to disagree. Therefore, we should ask ourselves:

- What if I don't need to always be right?
- What if you don't need to be wrong?

- What if we don't need to debate?
- Can people with different backgrounds be of one heart?
- Can we have different ideas, value one another, and be of one mind?
- Is it possible to disagree with one another about meanings of Scriptures and still dwell in righteousness?
- Can we explore, consider, and respectfully discuss incomplete or inaccurate ideas?
- What if *no poor among us* includes sharing the wealth of diverse and interesting ideas?

This path of sober, thoughtful, open welcoming of differences is the only way first steps can be taken. We cannot jump into Zion. We must crawl there on bended knee, asking the Lord to bring us there.

The foregoing excerpts are taken from:

- Denver's conference talk titled "Civilization", given in Grand Junction, CO on April 21, 2019
- Denver's conference talk titled "The Book of Mormon Holds the Covenant Pattern for the Full Restoration" given in Boise, ID on September 22, 2019
- The Q&A session at the Keeping the Covenant Conference in Boise, ID on September 22, 2019; and
- Denver's conference talk titled "The Heavens are Open", given in Hurricane, UT on March 22, 2020.

149. We've Lost the Argument

In this installment, Denver discusses the pervasive malignment of Joseph Smith throughout the scholarly world, how it stacks up in light of the actual evidence, and how and why it has been perpetuated and promoted ever since Joseph's murder in 1844.

DENVER: My wife, daughters, and daughters-in-law have a book—I don't know what they call it—book gang or something. (I know it's not a book "club"; they wanted to sound more militant than that.) Whatever the group calls themselves—and they read books every month and then talk about them. And as a result, a book came to my wife's attention that (the two of us) we read together (which is not altogether true; we listened to the book on tape as we were driving or sitting in a sauna until we finished the thing). However, we own a copy of the book. So I have looked into the text itself. It was a New York Times bestseller. [The] copyright is 2018, so it's been around for a few years (although I'd not heard of it). [I] mentioned it to some people, and apparently, a lot of people have read this book. It's called *Educated, A Memoir*, written by Tara Westover. It's autobiographical, but a number of things have been changed, as the book **tells** you; names and identifying details got changed because, apparently, some of the people who are living and who are identifiable if you knew her and her family well enough or her experiences well enough, you'd be able to identify them. So in that sense, it's autobiographical—but it's not altogether nonfiction; there is some fictionalized details to it.

She had a dysfunctional family, a father who was a survivalist and a conspiracy theorist. And they lived in Idaho on a farm with a junkyard on it, and he was a junker. And the family included a brother who was both abusive and suffered a number of head injuries that made him even more prone to violence. And she suffered at the hands of that abusive brother. But the family was "Mormon" (after a fashion)—a kind of conspiracy-theorist-based family with a strong patriarch who (the father, you know) ruled with an iron hand. She (in the book) would characterize her father as being bipolar and having some mental deficiencies.

But essentially she grew up uneducated, and then (through self study) managed to get herself through the ACT and got admitted and attended Brigham Young University where she got a bachelor's degree and got the notice of a faculty member who sent her on a program to Cambridge. She wound up on a scholarship to Cambridge, got her Master's of Philosophy (after her Bachelor's at Brigham Young), her Master's from Trinity College in Cambridge, [and] subsequently became a visiting fellow at Harvard University, and then returned to Cambridge where she got her Ph.D. in History in 2014.

Throughout the book… The story is gripping. I mean, it's… Once you get started, it's hard to put the book down. I imagine that if you were to ask for an account of the same events through the eyes of other people, that you may come away with a different conclusion about many of the people, many of the personalities, and many of the events in the book—and she makes no pretensions about it being altogether accurate.

But in her journey to become educated, she has to fight against the limitations of her background and overcome that—in a way that is a heroic story. And the details of the characters as they're being unraveled in the story, it's really quite gripping. And it's remarkable. And she's a remarkable person.

As she gets into her Ph.D. program and along the way, it becomes apparent that her command of historical investigation, different historical philosophies, and different historians are something with which she's acquainted at a doctoral level. And it's an impressive sojourn throughout the whole of it. (And her writing style is really good; she creates a world through the words she employs that pulls you in and really lets you see the scenes unfold as she narrates them through.)

But there was one thing in the book that saddened me considerably, because what it tells me is that—at this point, with the current state of historical analysis—we've altogether lost the argument, and people have reached a conclusion which, in my view, is unsupported by the historical record. But when a Ph.D. historian that writes such a compelling book includes this passage in it, it's just now taken for granted that the thing I will read to you in a moment is an established fact beyond all dispute, and that you needn't even investigate the matter any further. Here's the paragraph:

> I thought of Joseph Smith, who'd had as many as 40 wives. Brigham Young had had 55 wives and 56 children. The church had ended the temporal practice of polygamy in 1890, but it had never recanted the doctrine. As a child, I'd been taught by my father but also in Sunday School that in the fullness of time, God would restore polygamy, and in the afterlife, I would be a plural wife. The number of my sister wives

> would depend on my husband's righteousness. The more nobly he lived, the more wives he would be given.

Well, that might be true enough about where the LDS Church is at present, because they've said as much in their essays that they've put out on their website. But for someone who's investigating the provenance of polygamy in the LDS Church, the picture is considerably more muddled than the paragraph that she's given there. And she allows no room for doubt. She allows nothing for the possibility that perhaps what the church is advocating is not, in fact, supported by the historical record but was rather introduced by Brigham Young after the death of Joseph Smith.

The work that has been done by Rob Fotheringham in the videos that he's put out on YouTube, the book that has been written by Whitney Horning, and efforts by others (myself included) to go back and look at the source material raises considerable doubt about whether or not Joseph Smith ever had what would be called a "wife" other than Emma Smith. He proclaimed to the contrary, that he had that one wife. Joseph Smith certainly did something that was called "sealing." But at the time that the word "sealing" was used during Joseph Smith's lifetime, the word did not necessarily imply marriage, and it certainly didn't imply marital relations in a sexual sense. That changed considerably when the public practice was announced in 1852, and the effort to advocate it by Brigham Young turned sealing into not only marriage, but sexual relations and the production of progeny and so on. I mean, the form that it existed in before the death of Joseph Smith was nothing like the form that sealing took after it was adopted by Brigham Young.

I would hope that historians would be a little more humble about the whole subject. The multi-volume set that Brian Hales put together advocates the party line and makes assumptions based upon the post "public announcement" of it in 1852 and the affidavits that got gathered when they were in the middle of litigation over the authenticity of the church's claim to be the original during the Kirtland Temple lawsuit—and then, subsequently, the constitutional challenge to determine that it was an authentic part of the belief of Mormons that plural wives was in-and-of-itself "salvific."

Brigham Young attributed advice that he got from a U.S. Senator—and the likely candidate for that was Stephen Douglas; he doesn't identify who the senator was—but that the senator had advised Brigham Young that if he could defend plural wives as an "essential part of salvation in the religion of the Mormons" that it would pass scrutiny under the First Amendment before the United States Supreme Court. That resulted in a whole series of sermons that, in fact, tied salvation directly to having plural wives (which, as it turns out following the Manifesto, becomes really clear that that was a convention that was adopted—a teaching that was adopted—for litigation purposes).

They backed off of it, and Wilford Woodruff (and all those subsequent church leaders that followed after him) never once said, "Oh, and by the way, we continue to be damned because we don't have plural wivery going on." It just got eliminated, and salvation was still possible (in the Mormon religion) without the presence of the plural marriage. That epoch between the 1852 time period and the decision of the United States Supreme Court—in Reynolds vs. United States—was a period in which illegal contrivance was used in order to buttress a lawsuit that the church had hoped to win. And nothing more than that.

But those statements—those dogmatic statements involving salvation—produced, in turn, a whole host of offshoot fundamentalist groups that believe that their salvation (using quotes from that era, using the *Journal of Discourses*, using things that were said by presidents of the church, things that were said by members of the Quorum of Twelve to justify winning a lawsuit), they rely on those today to justify the continued practice, with the mistaken belief that their salvation is dependent upon that. The whole of Mormon history has been polluted by the extravagant claims that Brigham Young made and attributed to Joseph Smith—because Brigham didn't think that he had the persuasive authority to get people to adopt the practice if he was the originator. He had to lay it at the feet of the more respected predecessor, Joseph Smith. And so, he and others who wanted access to more women went along with him.

But if you go to the historical record and you limit your inquiry to anything that was in existence on June 27th, 1844 (the day that Joseph Smith was murdered) and before that date, you don't have anything to tie Joseph to the practice other than rumors and innuendos and accusations, many of which are from people that are not credible.

In the *Joseph Smith Papers* (volume 12 of the *Joseph Smith Papers*), there's a letter that Joseph got in the ~~June~~ [May] timeframe of 1843 in which a fellow is complaining to Joseph about the dishonesty and self-serving conduct of Robert D. Foster [and] Wilson and William Law. The letter (that was written by a member of the church who was a convert that had come over from England) was complaining about the way in which people were being exploited by these land speculators. They were borrowing money, they were attributing the credit worthiness of themselves to Joseph Smith's backing them. The fellow who wrote the letter is Thomas Rawcliffe. The letter is in May of 1843. It begins on page 330, and it runs through page 342 of volume 12 of the *Joseph Smith Papers*, in which he complains about the dishonesty and the deceitfulness of Robert Foster and Wilson Law and William Law.

William Law (at the time) was a member of the First Presidency. Robert Foster would be tried for his membership in the December timeframe of 1843, and he would be excommunicated from the church in April of 1844. William Law, as a member of the First Presidency at the time, was bitter and disaffected from Joseph because Joseph refused to seal William Law's marriage (because William Law was an adulterer, and Joseph considered it inappropriate to do the sealing).

Well, the three people that the fellow complains about to Joseph (Thomas Rawcliffe complains about)—Robert D. Foster, Wilson Law, William Law—all three were later involved as publishers and writers in the *Nauvoo Expositor* that made the accusations (the original accusations) against Joseph Smith: that he was practicing some kind of plural wivery in Nauvoo. Now, that becomes one of the bases for historians to say, "Ahah! People in high position blew the lid off Joseph's secret practice, and the *Nauvoo Expositor* is at least a contemporaneous source that you can look to and rely upon to say, 'Yeah, something was going on behind the scenes.' And these guys exposed it!"

The problem is that all three of them had reasons to lie. All three of them had history, if you believe Rawcliffe—all three of them have history of being deceitful, dishonest, self-dealing, and not only that, of **attributing their dishonest behavior to Joseph Smith**. Here's from the letter:

> I cannot imagine that you are aware of the devilish transactions that are going on in this place and the way that your name is used to accomplish them.

He goes on—Rawcliffe goes on—to say:

> See if you will suffer men holding high offices in the church and city to swindle me out of my little money, whether I'd be Mormon or not.

So, his concern (Rawcliffe's concern) is that these guys were doing things—duping people under the cloak of religion to get them to trust them—and then saying that Joseph Smith was really responsible for what they were doing. One of the things that Robert Foster did (and he's quoted by Rawcliffe) is that he promises to repay him: "So help me God, and Joseph will be bound with me." Rawcliffe talks about them "using Brother Joseph's name so much."

The fact that Joseph was accused of doing the very thing that these witnesses were themselves up to was similar to what Sampson Avard had done previously in Missouri, who testified against Joseph Smith when it was, in fact, Sampson Avard that was responsible for the violence and the burning and the thieving that went on. Mormon history is plagued with the insiders with credibility—ostensibly with credibility—who turn on Joseph; people that we later know were themselves violent or adulterous or dishonest turn on Joseph, and then, because they were in a position close to him, they say things about Joseph that Joseph says **is a lie**. But their status is used as evidence that they are telling the truth and that Joseph is lying.

Mormon history is plagued with this kind of a problem, through and through, top to bottom. Mormon history—early Mormon history, in particular—has (without any question) a lot of scoundrels involved in high positions. The thing that has to be asked is: Does the presence of Judas make Christ something less than Lord? Does the presence of "Judases" in the time of Joseph Smith make Joseph Smith something less than a virtuous prophet?

I have a very hard time believing that all of the lofty, lovely, virtuous, profound, deeply insightful things emanated from a man who was corrupt, dishonest, deceitful, treacherous, and unfaithful to his wife. He protested and claimed himself to be loyal to Emma throughout his life. After his death, Emma defended his character and said the same thing about Joseph's virtue as Joseph had said when he was alive. I don't think a corrupt fountain can bring forth good water. And I think Joseph was a good fountain, a pure one that brought forth things lovely, virtuous, and of good report.

LDS history—because they want to claim authority through Joseph Smith, that there was this continuity because Brigham Young succeeded him, and Brigham Young could not have been a corrupt deviator who innovated and adopted an adulterous practice that Joseph Smith had condemned—they have to turn Joseph into a liar in order to rescue authority they want to claim through Brigham Young.

I don't think Brigham Young deserves to have a life raft thrown at him at the expense of the character of Joseph Smith. And I'm disappointed that we've lost the argument, but lost it has been. And when you have someone that has studied history, going back and looking at what she thinks is an adequate basis for making the statement, and she writes, "I thought of Joseph Smith, who'd had as many as 40 wives," I don't think it's possible to win the argument in the popular mind.

The only question is: Can people of deep reflection, can people who are willing yet to consider a matter, can people who reject the idea of whoredoms and adultery and dishonesty and lying and who would never consider it appropriate to be a bald-faced liar in order to protect or preserve your religion, can people who have pure hearts and real intent, can **they** still be taught and persuaded that Joseph Smith was a virtuous man, loyal to his wife, and the glaring fact that he never fathered a child with anyone other than Emma Smith, the one he professed to be his only wife, can that still persuade some few people to practice virtue in their own lives and to accept the truthfulness of the things that were restored through Joseph Smith?

I think rather than abandon the argument altogether, I think it needs to be conceded that in the public mind, the argument's over, and we lost. But the few who are the humble followers of Christ (the people to whom I dedicated the very first book I wrote, *The Second Comforter, Conversing with the Lord Through the Veil*, the few who are the humble followers of Christ) may **still** be rescued from this pile of lies that has taken over this subject.

The foregoing was recorded on November 14, 2021 in Sandy, Utah.

150. The Testimony of Jesus

Today Denver discusses the content of and purpose behind his new book, *The Testimony of Jesus: Past, Present, and Promise*, which is the culmination of five years of outreach to Christians everywhere and now available in hardback as a standalone addition to the *Teachings of Denver Snuffer* series.

DENVER: I have a number of books that are in print that are appropriate for people that understand and accept the idea of the Restoration. I have two books in print that are designed for a Christian audience. One of them is defending Joseph Smith in *A Man Without Doubt*. And the other one is suitable for any Christian, titled *Come, Let Us Adore Him*, but it also would appeal to the Latter-Day Saint audience.

I finally have a new book out that is altogether suitable and addressed to (exclusively) a Christian audience. There's a statement in the King James Version of the Bible that *the testimony of Jesus is the spirit of prophecy* (Revelation 7:10 RE), and that phrase, borrowed from the book of Revelation, is part of the title for the new book. It's titled *The Testimony of Jesus: Past, Present, and Promise*. The book is about the history of Christianity, and the Reformation, and the Counter-Reformation, and the Restoration, and what God is up to presently, working with mankind.

Christianity makes a number of sweeping claims that the history doesn't really support. Catholicism—the word "catholic" means universal—Catholicism is not the same thing as what we read in the New Testament. The New Testament church ended sometime before the beginning of the Roman Catholic Church. And there were so many divergent kinds of Christianity in existence at the time of Constantine adopting Christianity as the state religion for the Roman Empire, that once he adopted it, he was surprised to learn that Christians were actually killing Christians over doctrinal disputes. Constantine assumed that Christianity would unite the kingdom, but Christianity itself at that time wasn't united. And so, he sequestered (in Nicaea) the leading bishop-voices of Christianity to have them agree on a creed that they could accept—to have peace. And after some amount of wrangling between the various parties who were disputing, they essentially reached agreement with all but a handful—and those that did not agree were exiled—so that they got their Christianity.

At the time that the apostles left Christianity by their natural lives coming to an end (with the exception of John who, at the end of that time, converted from being a mortal ministrant to being a flaming sword/an angel who would minister as an angel but remain here on the earth), they left behind different **forms** of Christianity. There was a Pauline church. There was a Petrine church. There was a Matthean church. There was a Johannine church. There were different forms of Christianity. The apostles were commissioned by Christ to take a message out, but the message they took out and the way that it was implemented reflected the individual personalities, strengths, and preferences of the individual apostle who came with the message. The result was a divergent kind of Christianity that did not reflect one single "universal" view of what Christianity meant. That was probably deliberate, and it was probably healthy to allow people to understand and come to different vantage points to view Jesus Christ, His mission, and what He accomplished.

Well, by the time you get to about 324 A.D. and the adoption of Christianity as the state religion of the Roman Empire, having that kind of divergence was unacceptable to an emperor who was trying to unite—under one umbrella—the Roman people to have them come to peace so that they could resist the outside threats and not have internal conflicts tearing them apart. And make no mistake about it: Christianity was tearing itself apart internally, violently, by their different views of what the doctrines/teachings/principles of Christianity involved.

In the second and third century, there were debates about what kind of person or being Jesus Christ was. There was (what ultimately became schismatic) a view that Christ was not born theSon of God; He was just a normal man like any other man, but He got adopted by God at the time of His baptism. And that "adoptionist" theory was in conflict with those that believed He was the actual Son of God and that His Father was, in fact, God the Father, and His mother was Mary, and therefore, He was divine—He was a demigod, and He came into this world as deity itself.

Well, those debates became so hostile and violent that they wound up editing the text of the Gospels to change the wording. There's evidence (and Bart Ehrman did research on this) that shows how, in ancillary texts, the statement that was made at the time of the baptism of Christ was, *Thou art my Son, this day have I begotten thee* (Psalms 2:7-8 KJV), which is a quote from the Old Testament. That statement was changed to a declaration: *This is my beloved Son, in whom I am well pleased* (Matthew 3:17 KJV), and they edited the text in order to support an outcome of the Christological debates in the second and third century. And so, the text of the Bible itself became subject to alteration by the people who are fighting over the meaning of Christianity. You can still find—even in Christian texts of the Bible—the statement, *Thou art my Son, this day have I begotten thee,* in the writings of the apostle Paul in the book of Hebrews. And so, they got rid of it in the Gospels, but they didn't get rid of it in the book of Hebrews of the New Testament.

Well, Christianity fundamentally changed over the course of those first three centuries. And at the 324 [A.D.] mark, when Constantine decided to make it the state religion, it changed even further still. But once Christianity became triumphant in the Roman Empire, the Christian religion became institutionalized. And even when the governance of Rome collapsed over the ensuing millennium, the Catholic church that had been made the state religion triumphed, persisted, and dominated. But when you have a monopoly on religion and you have an idea of authority being given by God to the Pope and the archbishops and the bishops, abuses will inevitably ensue.

The book (*The Testimony of Jesus: Past, Present, and Promise*) goes into discussing some of this material in order to reassure Christians today—who are so dogmatic and opposed to the idea of there being something afoot that God Himself has authorized to reestablish Christianity in a more pure, more vibrant, more clear method—it goes to reassure the Christians that they really need to take a careful look at that, because Christianity became a tattered ruin over the course of the centuries in which Roman Catholicism was the dominant religion, so much so that the common man didn't even have access to the Bible. The common man heard sermons in a language they didn't speak. They learned about Christianity from the tapestries and the icons and the statuary that was around the cathedrals. But understanding and being able to read biblical Christianity just didn't exist.

It was Martin Luther who, as a Catholic priest, understood and had access to the Scriptures and concluded that there were abuses underway. He rebelled over the sale of indulgences, and that began the Protestant Reformation.

The Protestant Reformation, however, began (as its point of origin) with a Catholic priest that was rebelling against the hierarchy. The hierarchy had maintained their stranglehold on Christianity because of the claims to authority. Martin Luther, reading in the book of Romans, concluded that if salvation came by grace and grace alone, that it would be possible to be saved independent of the Catholic priestly hierarchy. That enabled salvation separate from the Catholic priesthood, and it made possible the idea of the priesthood of man.

Well, from the rebellion of Martin Luther sprang a number of other protesters that led to the Protestant Reformation, and those Protestant fathers are discussed in *The Testimony of Jesus: Past, Present, and Promise*. Their names and some of their biographies are provided for people to understand the background. But Evangelical Christianity (which is one of the more self-confident forms of Christianity) is something of very late creation. So late, in fact, and so different from where Christianity was for the first millennium and a half that Evangelical Christians of today would not even be recognized as Christians for the overwhelming majority of Christian history. So, their self-confidence about their salvation is really predicated upon a complete dismissal of Christian history and the fact that if they're right, then they have damned centuries, millennia (more than a millennia) of people that claimed themselves to be Christians.

Well, in the cacophony of Christian religions—estimated today at something more than 40,000 different sects—there is one theme that they all look for and that is the belief that Jesus was, in fact, a Savior, sent into the world to rescue them from sin and from death, and that He was, in fact, a descendant that God sent into the world for our salvation.

But if Jesus organized **something** and that something fell into corruption, the question has to be posed whether you can take corruption and spring out of it something that will, in fact, save you, that reconnects and restores or reforms Christianity back into an original form. Roger Williams said that it couldn't happen without God sending new apostles. And so the "Promise" part of the new book talks about how the purpose of the prophecies of the New Testament and the rescuing of mankind by the Lord is something that necessitated a return of the original authority directly from Heaven. And the book discusses how that's a **crying need** in order for Christianity to reassume an authentic form. And that, in fact, has begun.

Not only that, but in its recommencement, there are a number of prophecies that have to be fulfilled in order for the Lord to keep His promises before His return in glory to judge the world. So, the book walks through what those prophecies and promises are and how they are currently underway.

This book is one of the few books that I think anyone that believes in the Restoration can comfortably hand to a friend or relative who is a Protestant or a Catholic and to invite them to consider whether or not there needs to be something more than a protest, something more than a reform, or something more than an abusive Catholic hierarchy. The question of whether God can and **would** do something before His return in glory is really answered by both the Old Testament and New Testament prophecies. Those are discussed in the book.

If you have someone who is a Christian that you would like to approach in a way that will open their mind to the idea of there being a work by God, promised from Old Testament times on that has begun today, and that the God of Heaven who cared for the ancients cares just as much for the current people living on the earth, and that the God who once spoke from Heaven can—and is—speaking again today, if you want to present those ideas to someone, that's the purpose of this book.

It came out and became available on Thanksgiving Day. It's something that I intend to purchase for and give to members of my own family who are not believers in the Restoration, and I'm hoping that a number of the Christian friends I have will likewise consider the book (when I give it to them) as something that at least explains why we have reason to believe that God can, has, and does speak today in an effort to prepare the world for His return in glory to judge the world.

You **cannot** believe the Bible to be true and rule out the possibility that God is going to do something preliminary to His Second Coming to prepare the world. That message is embedded right into both the Old and the New Testament, and this book is an attempt to show that those promises that God made He not only intends to keep, but He is **in the present act** of keeping those promises.

The book is available on Amazon. After this podcast goes up, I will put a link to it. It's being published only in hardback form because if we're going to give it to someone (even though it costs more for us to be able to publish it as a hardback book), people tend to respect hardback books, and they also tend to wear better than paperback. And so, it's coming out in a form that, I think, we would be pleased to share with someone as a quality product. It's available now, and if anyone has any interest in getting a copy for the purpose it was intended (that is, for a Christian audience), I would encourage you to take a look and consider whether or not you think the book would be suitable.

The foregoing was recorded on November 14, 2021 in Sandy, Utah.

Appendix 1: Episodes Containing New Material

The following episodes include new material that was recorded for the podcast, or material that was previously unreleased to the public, as indicated:

106. Forgiving Others	Contains some new material
110. Whipsaw	All new material
114. Zion People	Contains some new material
115. Sabbath Day	Contains some new material
119. God Forgives	Contains some new material
120. One Heart First	All new material
123. Numbered Among	All new material
124. The Foolish and the Wise	All new material
126. Marriage, Part 2	Contains some new material
127. Gospel Tangents, Part 1	All new material
128. Gospel Tangents, Part 2	All new material
129. Gospel Tangents, Part 3	All new material
136. Commune with Christ, Part 1	Contains some new material
137. Commune with Christ, Part 2	Contains some new material
141. Forgiving Others, Continued	Contains some new material
149. We've Lost the Argument	All new material
150. Testimony of Jesus	All new material

Appendix 2: Index

Index

B

E

G

J

S

T